Adam Nathan

Windows® 8.1
Apps
with XAML and C#

UNLEASHED

SAMS | 800 East 96th Street, Indianapolis, Indiana 46240 USA

Windows® 8.1 Apps with XAML and C# Unleashed

Copyright © 2014 by Pearson Education

ISBN-13: 978-0-672-33708-6

ISBN-10: 0-672-33708-8

Library of Congress Control Number: 2013951289

Printed in the United States on America

First Printing December 2013

Trademarks

Warning and Disclaimer

Special Sales

For information about buying this title in bulk quantities, or for special sales opportunities (which may include electronic versions; custom cover designs; and content particular to your business, training goals, marketing focus, or branding interests), please contact our corporate sales department at corpsales@pearsoned.com or (800) 382-3419.

For government sales inquiries, please contact governmentsales@pearsoned.com.

For questions about sales outside the U.S., please contact international@pearsoned.com.

EDITOR-IN-CHIEF
Greg Wiegand

EXECUTIVE EDITOR
Neil Rowe

DEVELOPMENT EDITOR
Mark Renfrow

MANAGING EDITOR
Kristy Hart

SENIOR PROJECT EDITOR
Betsy Gratner

INDEXER
Tim Wright

PROOFREADER
Kathy Ruiz

TECHNICAL EDITOR
Ashish Shetty

PUBLISHING COORDINATOR
Cindy Teeters

COVER DESIGNER
Mark Shirar

COMPOSITION
Nonie Ratcliff

Contents at a Glance

Table of Contents

About the Author

Adam Nathan is a principal software architect for Microsoft, a best-selling technical author, and arguably the world's most prolific developer for Windows Phone. He introduced XAML to countless developers through his books on a variety of Microsoft technologies. Currently a part of Microsoft's Startup Business Group, Adam has previously worked on Visual Studio and the Common Language Runtime. He was the founding developer and architect of Popfly, Microsoft's first Silverlight-based product, named by *PCWorld* as one of its year's most innovative products. He is also the founder of PINVOKE.NET, the online resource for .NET developers who need to access Win32. His apps have been featured on Lifehacker, Gizmodo, ZDNet, ParentMap, and other enthusiast sites.

Adam's books are considered required reading by many inside Microsoft and throughout the industry. Adam is the author of *Windows 8 Apps with XAML and C# Unleashed* (Sams, 2013), *101 Windows Phone 7 Apps* (Sams, 2011), *Silverlight 1.0 Unleashed* (Sams, 2008), *WPF Unleashed* (Sams, 2006), *WPF 4 Unleashed* (Sams, 2010), *WPF 4.5 Unleashed* (Sams, 2013), and *.NET and COM: The Complete Interoperability Guide* (Sams, 2002); a coauthor of *ASP.NET: Tips, Tutorials, and Code* (Sams, 2001); and a contributor to books including *.NET Framework Standard Library Annotated Reference, Volume 2* (Addison-Wesley, 2005) and *Windows Developer Power Tools* (O'Reilly, 2006). You can find Adam online at www.adamnathan.net or @adamnathan on Twitter.

Dedication

To Mom and Dad.

Acknowledgments

First, I thank Eileen Chan for the encouragement and patience that enabled me to complete this book. I'd also like to give special thanks to Ashish Shetty, Tim Heuer, Mark Rideout, Jonathan Russ, Joe Duffy, Chris Brumme, Eric Rudder, Neil Rowe, Betsy Gratner, Ginny Munroe, Bill Chiles, and Valery Sarkisov. As always, I thank my parents for having the foresight to introduce me to Basic programming on our IBM PCjr when I was in elementary school.

Finally, I thank *you* for picking up a copy of this book! I don't think you'll regret it!

We Want to Hear from You!

As the reader of this book, *you* are our most important critic and commentator. We value your opinion and want to know what we're doing right, what we could do better, what areas you'd like to see us publish in, and any other words of wisdom you're willing to pass our way.

You can email or write us directly to let us know what you did or didn't like about this book—as well as what we can do to make our books stronger.

Please note that we cannot help you with technical problems related to the topic of this book.

When you write, please be sure to include this book's title and author as well as your name and phone or email address. We will carefully review your comments and share them with the author and editors who worked on the book.

E-mail: consumer@samspublishing.com

Mail: Sams Publishing
            ATTN: Reader Feedback
            800 East 96th Street
            Indianapolis, IN 46240 USA

Reader Services

Visit our website and register this book at informit.com/register for convenient access to any updates, downloads, or errata that might be available for this book.

Introduction

If you ask me, it has never been a better time to be a software developer. Not only are programmers in high demand—due in part to an astonishingly low number of computer science graduates each year—but app stores make it easier than ever to broadly distribute your own software and even make money from it.

When I was in junior high school, I released a few shareware games and asked for $5 donations. I earned $15 total. One of the three donations was from my grandmother, who didn't even own a computer! These days, of course, adults and kids alike can make money on simple apps and games without relying on kind and generous individuals going to the trouble of mailing a check.

The Windows Store is an app store like no other, and it keeps getting better. When you consider the number of people who use Windows 8.1 (and Windows RT) compared to the number of people who use any other operating system on the planet, you realize what a unique and enormous opportunity the Windows Store provides. That's one of the reasons that the Windows Store is the fastest-growing app store in history.

When you write a Windows Store app, you have three main choices for programming language and UI framework pairings:

→ JavaScript with an HTML user interface

→ C#, Visual Basic, or C++ with a XAML user interface

→ C++ with a DirectX user interface

You can also leverage a number of features and componentization techniques to mix and match these languages and UI frameworks within the same app.

C# and XAML has been a very popular choice for writing Windows Store apps. It is the choice for apps such as Netflix, Hulu Plus, Fresh Paint, SkyDrive, Evernote Touch, Reader, Alarms, Movie Moments, Maps, OneNote, Lync, and many, many more. It is also the implementation choice for many core experiences in Windows, such as the PC Settings app, the Search app, and new Contact/Calendar functionality in Windows 8.1. The XAML team has stated that their goal is to be the high fidelity, high performance framework for ꞏꞏꞏꞏꞏ ꞏꞏ ꞏ ꞏꞏꞏꞏꞏꞏ

Then why does Microsoft provide so many choices? The idea is to enable you to work with whatever is most comfortable for you, whatever best leverages your existing assets, or whatever most naturally consumes the third-party SDK you must use.

Your choice can have other benefits. HTML tends to be the best choice if you need to support your versions of your app on non-Microsoft platforms or a website. XAML is best at interoperability, as it's easy to mix both HTML and DirectX content in a XAML app. DirectX, the best choice for hardcore games, provides the most potential for getting the highest performance.

Common perceptions of performance differences between the UI frameworks are often wrong, however. It's important to realize that no matter which of the three UI frameworks you use, about 80% of their core implementation is identical, the Windows APIs are the same, and the graphics are hardware accelerated. Although DirectX offers the most *potential* for getting the highest performance, you have to do a lot of work to realize that potential! Often, a C#/XAML implementation can outperform a simple C++/DirectX implementation due to the impressive optimizations that the XAML UI Framework does on your behalf. Not only that, but the XAML UI Framework gives you a number of additional features automatically, such as accessibility and localization.

Although your choice of language is generally dictated by your choice of UI Framework, each language has its strengths. JavaScript benefits from a large community that produces interesting libraries. C# has the best features for writing concise asynchronous code, and doesn't have the same multithreading limitations that plague JavaScript. C++ provides the most potential for getting the highest performance. (Does that line sound familiar?) Of course, you have to earn that performance, and you have to be especially careful with how you mix standard C and C++ code with the C++/CX code that is needed to communicate with Windows.

The key to the multiple language support is the Windows Runtime, or WinRT for short. You can think of it like .NET's Common Language Runtime, except it spans both managed and unmanaged languages. To enable this, WinRT is COM-based. Most of the time, you can't tell when you interact with WinRT. And most of the time, it doesn't matter. This is a modern, friendlier version of COM that is more amenable to *automatic* correct usage from environments such as .NET or JavaScript. (Contrast this to over a decade ago, when I wrote a book about mixing COM with .NET. This topic alone required over 1,600 pages!)

WinRT APIs are automatically *projected* into the programming language you use, so they look natural for that language. Projections are more than just exposing the raw APIs, however. Core WinRT data types such as String, collection types, and a few others are mapped to appropriate data types for the target environment. For C# or other .NET languages, this means exposing them as

> Although WinRT APIs are not .NET APIs, they have metadata in the standardized format used by .NET. Therefore, you can browse them directly with familiar .NET tools, such as the IL Disassembler (ILDASM). You can find these on your computer as .winmd files. Visual Studio's "Object Browser" is also a convenient way to search and browse WinRT APIs.

System.String, System.Collections.Generic.IList<T>, and so on. To match conventions, member names are even morphed to be Camel-cased for JavaScript and Pascal-cased for other languages, which makes the MSDN reference documentation occasionally look goofy.

In the set of APIs exposed by Windows:

→ Everything under the **Windows.UI.Xaml** namespace is XAML-specific

→ Everything under the **Windows.UI.WebUI** namespace is for HTML apps

→ Everything under **System** is .NET-specific

→ Everything else (which is under **Windows**) is general-purpose WinRT functionality

As you dig into the framework, you notice that the XAML-specific and .NET-specific APIs are indeed the most natural to use from C# and XAML. General-purpose WinRT APIs follow slightly different conventions and can sometimes look a little odd to developers familiar with .NET. For example, they tend to be exception-heavy for situations that normally don't warrant an exception (such as the user cancelling an action). Artifacts like this are caused by the projection mechanism mapping HRESULTs (COM error codes) into .NET exceptions.

I wrote this book with the following goals in mind:

→ To provide a solid grounding in the underlying concepts, in a practical and approachable fashion

→ To answer the questions most people have when learning how to write Windows Store apps and to show how commonly desired tasks are accomplished

→ To be an authoritative source, thanks to input from members of the team who designed, implemented, and tested Windows 8.1 and Visual Studio 2013

→ To be clear about where the technology falls short rather than blindly singing its praises

→ To optimize for concise, easy-to-understand code rather than enforcing architectural patterns that can be impractical or increase the number of concepts to understand

→ To be an easily navigated reference that you can constantly come back to

To elaborate on the second-to-last point: You won't find examples of patterns such as Model-View-ViewModel (MVVM) in this book. I *am* a fan of applying such patterns to code, but I don't want to distract from the core lessons in each chapter.

Whether you're new to XAML or a long-time XAML developer, I hope you find this book to exhibit all these attributes.

Who Should Read This Book?

This book is for software developers who are interested in creating apps for the Windows Store, whether they are for tablets, laptops, or desktops. It does not teach you how to program, nor does it teach the basics of the C# language. However, it is designed to be understandable even for folks who are new to .NET, and does not require previous experience with XAML.

If you are already well versed in XAML, I'm confident that this book still has a lot of helpful information for you. And if you are already familiar with writing Windows Store apps for Windows 8 (perhaps thanks to the first edition of this book), you will still benefit from the significant amount of new content that covers new features in Windows 8.1. It also covers features that were already present in Windows 8 in more depth than ever before. At the very least, this book should be an invaluable reference for your bookshelf.

Software Requirements

This book targets Windows 8.1, Windows RT, and the corresponding developer tools. The tools are a free download at the Windows Dev Center: http://dev.windows.com. The download includes the Windows 8.1 SDK, a version of Visual Studio Express specifically for Windows Store apps, and miscellaneous tools. It's worth noting that although this book almost exclusively refers to Windows 8.1, the content applies to Windows RT as well.

Although it's not required, I recommend PAINT.NET, a free download at http://getpaint.net, for creating and editing graphics, such as the set of icons needed by apps.

Code Examples

Source code for examples in this book can be downloaded from www.informit.com/title/9780672337086.

How This Book Is Organized

This book is arranged into seven parts, representing the progression of feature areas that you typically need to understand. But if you want to jump ahead and learn about a topic such animation or live tiles, the book is set up to allow for nonlinear journeys as well. The following sections provide a summary of each part.

Part I: Getting Started

This part includes the following chapters:

→ Chapter 1: "Hello, *Real* World!"

→ Chapter 2: "Mastering XAML"

Part I provides the foundation for the rest of the book. If you have previously created Windows Phone apps or worked with XAML in the context of other Microsoft technologies, a lot of this should be familiar to you. There are still several unique aspects for Windows 8.1 and the Windows Store, however. Chapter 1 helps you understand all the tools available at your disposal, and even dives into topics such as accessibility and localization, so you can be prepared to get the broadest set of customers possible for your app. This last set of topics is new to this edition of the book.

Part II: Building an App

This part includes the following chapters:

→ Chapter 3: "Sizing, Positioning, and Transforming Elements"

→ Chapter 4: "Layout"

→ Chapter 5: "Interactivity"

→ Chapter 6: "Handling Input: Touch, Mouse, Pen, and Keyboard"

Part II equips you with the knowledge of how to place things on the screen, how to make them adjust to the wide variety of screen types, and how to interact with the user. Windows 8.1 introduces a new model for how apps should resize, and this is covered in Chapter 4. In Chapter 6, this edition contains new coverage on supporting pens, including rendering strokes and performing handwriting recognition.

Part III: Working with the App Model

This part includes the following chapters:

→ Chapter 7: "App Lifecycle"

→ Chapter 8: "Threading, Windows, and Pages "

→ Chapter 9: "The Many Ways to Earn Money"

The app model for Windows Store apps is significantly different from the app model for desktop applications in a number of ways. It's important to understand how the app lifecycle works and how you need to interact with it in order to create a well-behaved app. But there are other pieces to what is sometimes called the *app model*: how one app can launch another, how to work with the Windows Store to enable free trials and in-app purchases, and how to deal with multiple windows and pages. This edition greatly expands the coverage on trials and in-app purchases, and covers the new Windows 8.1 in-app purchase features. It also contains new coverage on integrating ads into your apps, the threading model for Windows Store apps, and new support for having multiple windows.

Part IV: Understanding Controls

This part includes the following chapters:

→ Chapter 10: "Content Controls"

→ Chapter 11: "Items Controls"

→ Chapter 12: "Text"

→ Chapter 13: "Images"

→ Chapter 14: "Audio, Video, and Speech"

→ Chapter 15: "Other Controls"

Part IV provides a tour of the controls built into the XAML UI Framework. There are many controls that you expect to have available, plus several that you might not expect. Windows 8.1 adds many new controls and many features to existing controls. Windows 8.1 also introduces speech synthesis features, which are covered in Chapter 14.

Part V: Leveraging the Richness of XAML

This part includes the following chapters:

→ Chapter 16: "Vector Graphics"

→ Chapter 17: "Animation"

→ Chapter 18: "Styles, Templates, and Visual States"

→ Chapter 19: "Data Binding"

The features covered in Part V are areas in which XAML really shines. Although previous parts of the book expose some XAML richness (applying transforms to any elements, the composability of controls, and so on), these features push the richness to the next level.

Part VI: Exploiting Windows 8.1

This part includes the following chapters:

→ Chapter 20: "Working with Data"

→ Chapter 21: "Supporting Charms"

→ Chapter 22: "Leveraging Contracts"

→ Chapter 23: "Reading from Sensors"

→ Chapter 24: "Controlling Devices"

→ Chapter 25: "Thinking Outside the App: Live Tiles, Notifications, and the Lock Screen"

This part of the book could just as easily appear in a book about JavaScript or C++ Windows Store apps, with the exception of its code snippets. It covers unique and powerful Windows features that are not specific to XAML or C#, but they are things that all Windows Store app developers should know. The most notable new support in Windows 8.1 is covered in Chapter 24: supporting custom devices.

Part VII: Advanced Features

This part includes the following chapters:

→ Chapter 26: "Integrating DirectX"

→ Chapter 27: "Custom Controls and Components"

→ Chapter 28: "Layout with Custom Panels"

The advanced features covered in the last part of the book highlight very different scenarios. Integrating DirectX into your XAML app enables you to do things that aren't possible otherwise, whereas the last two chapters are about ways to reuse your code. The coverage of all these features is new to this edition. These features all existed in Windows 8, although the DirectX integration support has been improved for Windows 8.1.

Conventions Used in This Book

Various typefaces in this book identify new terms and other special items. These typefaces include the following:

Typeface	Meaning
Italic	Italic is used for new terms or phrases when they are initially defined and occasionally for emphasis.
Monospace	Monospace is used for screen messages, code listings, and filenames. In code listings, `italic monospace type` is used for placeholder text.
	Code listings are colorized similarly to the way they are colorized in Visual Studio. `Blue monospace type` is used for XML elements and C# keywords, `brown monospace type` is used for XML element names and C# strings, `green monospace type` is used for comments, `red monospace type` is used for XML attributes, and `teal monospace type` is used for type names in C#.
Bold	When appropriate, bold is used for code directly related to the main lesson(s) in a chapter.

Throughout this book, and even in this introduction, you will find a number of sidebar elements:

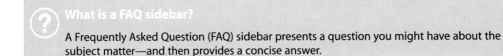

What is a FAQ sidebar?

A Frequently Asked Question (FAQ) sidebar presents a question you might have about the subject matter—and then provides a concise answer.

• • •

Digging Deeper

A Digging Deeper sidebar presents advanced or more detailed information on a subject than is provided in the surrounding text. Think of Digging Deeper material as something you can look into if you're curious but can ignore if you're not.

A tip offers information about design guidelines, shortcuts or alternative approaches to produce better results, or something that makes a task easier.

This is a warning!

A warning alerts you to an action or a condition that can lead to an unexpected or unpredictable result—and then tells you how to avoid it.

Chapter 1

HELLO, *REAL* WORLD!

"Oh, no, not another cliché 'Hello, World' example," you might be thinking as you examine this book. However, the length of this chapter alone should tell you that it is not about creating a typical "Hello, World" app.

Sure, we're going to get started with a simple, contrived app to demonstrate the anatomy of any Windows Store XAML app and the tooling available in Visual Studio. But we'll also see how to make it really say "hello" to the *entire* world; not just English-speaking people with no disabilities. This means understanding how to localize an app into other languages so you can exploit the vast, global scale of the Windows Store. It also means understanding how to make your app accessible to users who require assistive technologies such as screen readers or high contrast themes. No app deserves to be called "Hello, World" without considering these features.

Creating, Deploying, and Profiling an App

In Visual Studio, let's create a new Visual C# **Blank App** (XAML) project called HelloRealWorld. This gives us a project that's ready to compile and run. Although pressing F5 or clicking the **Start Debugging** button in Visual Studio launches the app locally, you've got three slick options to choose from via the button's dropdown menu, shown in Figure 1.1 under Visual Studio's light theme (used throughout this book).

With the **Remote Machine** option, you can deploy and debug to any other Windows 8.x computer reachable on your network (although not over the Internet). This is extremely handy for testing things on a Surface or other tablets. The target device must have the Remote Tools for Visual Studio installed and running, which you can download from the Windows Dev Center.

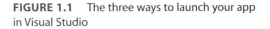

FIGURE 1.1   The three ways to launch your app in Visual Studio

The **Simulator** option is the next best thing to having a real tablet, as it provides mechanisms to simulate touch input, device orientations, network conditions, location services, and more. The simulator is shown in Figure 1.2. In fact, it has one huge advantage over testing on a physical device: It enables you to experience your app in a number of different resolutions and virtual screen sizes, including different aspect ratios. Given the wide variety of shapes and sizes of screens out there that run Windows Store apps, testing your app in this fashion is a must.

FIGURE 1.2   Testing your app on the simulator is like testing it on an army of different-sized devices.

> ! **The simulator is your actual computer!**
>
> Although the simulator simulates several things, what you see on the virtual device is your real "host" computer running with your actual user account, apps, files, and so on. (Running the simulator is like initiating a special kind of remote desktop connection to yourself.) Changes you make inside the simulator affect your computer just as if you made them outside the simulator.

> **How do I run my app outside of Visual Studio?**
>
> Although compiling your app produces an `.exe` file in the `bin\Debug` or `bin\Release` subfolder, you can't simply double-click it from the Windows desktop to run it. If you try, you get an error that explains, "This application can only run in the context of an app container." (An "app container" refers to the sandbox in which all Windows Store apps run.)
>
> Instead, you can launch it from the searchable list of apps underneath the tiles on the Start screen. Visual Studio automatically installs your app the first time you launch it. Like all Windows Store apps in Windows 8.1, however, its tile does not automatically get pinned. Because the Start screen has been enhanced to make it easier to find apps, pinning is now meant to be done selectively by a user, the same as with pinning apps to the desktop taskbar.

When you run the `HelloRealWorld` project without any changes, you'll see why the project type was called "Blank App." The app doesn't actually do anything other than fill the screen with darkness. (If you launch the app in debug mode, you'll also see four numbers on the top edge of the screen. These are frame rate counters described in Chapter 17, "Animation.") It does, however, set up a lot of infrastructure that would be difficult and tedious to create from scratch. The project contains the following items:

→ The package manifest, a temporary certificate used to sign it, and some images

→ The main page (`MainPage.xaml` and `MainPage.xaml.cs`)

→ The application definition: `App.xaml`, `App.xaml.cs`, and `AssemblyInfo.cs`

The next section examines the package manifest and the images used by it. After that, we'll look at the XAML and C# files and make some code changes.

Visual Studio provides some amazing tools for diagnosing performance problems in your app. You can access them by clicking **Performance and Diagnostics** on the **Debug** menu. On this page, select a tool to collect data while your app is launched. You perform the scenario you want to measure, and then stop the data collection. A rich, interactive report is then presented to you. The three tools on the Performance and Diagnostics page are:

→ **XAML UI Responsiveness**—Attributes the time spent to activities such as parsing XAML and layout of your elements. Shows you the performance cost of each UI element. You can also investigate times when you're not achieving the desired 60 frames per second on the UI thread.

→ **CPU Sampling**—Traditional profiling, with interactive graphs, diagrams of hot paths complete with annotated code integration, and much more.

→ **Energy Consumption**—Estimates how power-hungry your app is, based on its usage of the CPU, display, and network.

In addition to the Visual Studio tools, you can download the Windows Performance Toolkit for additional analysis. This includes a Windows Performance Recorder tool for capturing a trace, and a Windows Performance Analyzer tool for analyzing the trace.

Understanding the App Package

The *package manifest* in the Visual Studio project is a file called `Package.appxmanifest`. ("AppX" is a term sometimes used within Microsoft for Windows Store app packages that stuck around in the filename.) This manifest describes your app to Windows as well as the Windows Store—its name, what it looks like, what it's allowed to do, and more. It's an XML file, although you have to tell Visual Studio to "View Source" in order to see the XML. There's usually no need to view and edit the XML directly, however. The default view is a tabbed set of forms to fill out, which is the easiest way to populate all the information. There are six tabs:

→ Application

→ Visual Assets

→ Capabilities

→ Declarations

→ Content URIs

→ Packaging

For our `HelloRealWorld` app, we don't need to change anything in the package manifest. But now is a good time to understand what can be done on each of these tabs.

Application

On the Application tab, you can set the app's name and description, default language, its minimum width, and notification settings (if your app supports them). Notifications are covered in Chapter 25, "Thinking Outside the App: Live Tiles, Notifications, and the Lock Screen." You can even restrict the preferred orientations of your app if you'd rather not have it automatically rotate to all four of them:

→ **Landscape** (horizontal)

→ **Landscape-flipped** (horizontal but upside down)

→ **Portrait** (vertical, with the hardware Start button on the left)

→ **Portrait-flipped** (vertical, with the hardware Start button on the right)

Disabling the *flipped* orientations would be an odd thing to do, but disabling some orientations can make sense for certain types of games that wish to be landscape only. Note that this is just a *preference*, not a guarantee, because not all devices support rotation. For example, a portrait-only app launched on a typical desktop PC must accept the one-and-only landscape orientation. However, if a device that *does* support rotation is currently locked to a landscape orientation, a portrait-only app actually runs in the portrait orientation, ignoring the lock setting.

Visual Assets

On the Visual Assets tab, you set the characteristics of your app's tile and splash screen, as well as artwork used in a number of other contexts.

Customizing the Splash Screen

To ensure that every app's splash screen can be displayed practically instantaneously (before your app even gets loaded), you have little control over it. You specify a 620x300 image (plus two optional larger sizes to support high DPI screens), and a background color for the splash screen. That's it. Visual Studio gives you an appropriately sized place-holder SplashScreen.scale-100.png file in an Assets subfolder, intentionally made ugly to practically guarantee you won't forget to change it before submitting your app to the Windows Store.

When your splash screen is shown, the image is displayed centered on top of your chosen background color. Figure 1.3 shows an example SplashScreen.scale-100.png containing a Pixelwinks logo, and Figure 1.4 shows what this looks like on the simulator. The splash screen is given a yellow background for demonstration purposes. A real app should make the background color match the background of the image or simply make the image's background transparent.

FIGURE 1.3   An example SplashScreen.scale-100.png with a nontransparent background for demonstration purposes

When your app is launched, the splash screen automatically animates in and automatically fades out once your app has loaded and has made a call to Window.Current. Activate. This gives you the flexibility to do arbitrarily complex logic before the splash screen goes away, although you should avoid doing a lot of work here. (Your app is given about fifteen seconds to remain on the splash screen before it gets terminated by Windows.)

Customizing Logo Images

The **Tile Images and Logos** section on the Visual Assets tab can be confusing and over-whelming. Besides the **Store Logo**, which supports up to three different sizes, it lists five different logo sizes, although each one actually accepts 4–8 different sizes of image files! All told, you can assign *twenty seven* different image files representing your logo! Let's start making some sense out of these images. Figure 1.5 shows what each logo *should* have been called to make things less confusing, and the following list explains each one using the terminology found in the package manifest:

→ **Square 70x70 Logo**—This is used for the **small** version of your app's tile on the Start screen. Although assigning an image here is optional, the small tile size is not. If you don't provide an image, the medium tile image is used (and scaled down) when a user changes your tile size to small.

→ **Square 150x150 Logo**—This is used for the **medium** version of your app's tile on the Start screen. The medium tile size is the one required size, so at least a 100% scale image is required.

→ **Wide 310x150 Logo**—This is used for the **wide** version of your app's tile on the Start screen, if you choose to support that tile size. If you assign at least a 100% scale image here, your app automatically supports the wide tile size. Otherwise, it doesn't.

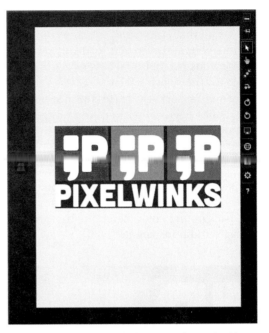

FIGURE 1.4   A live splash screen shown inside the simulator with a garish yellow background to clearly show the bounds of the image

→ **Large 310x310 Logo**—This is used for the **large** version of your app's tile on the Start screen, if you choose to support that tile size. If you assign at least a 100% scale image here *and* for the wide logo, your app automatically supports the large tile size. (Your app can only support a large tile if it also supports a wide tile.) Otherwise, it doesn't.

→ **Square 30x30 Logo**—This is used throughout Windows, including on the desktop. It is used by the apps list, search results, the Share pane, the file picker, an overlay on live tiles, the Alt+Tab user interface, Task Manager, file icons for associated file types, and so on. At least the 100% scale image is required. Although the image is nominally 30x30 pixels, this logo supports four additional sizes to be used for file icons on the desktop (if your app has associated file types): 16x16, 32x32, 48x48, and 256x256.

→ **Store Logo**—A 50x50 image (at 100% scale) used by the Windows Store. At least the 100% scale image is required.

Visual Studio provides placeholder image files for the required logo images only: the square 150x150 logo, the square 30x30 logo, and the store logo.

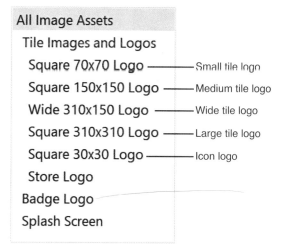

All Image Assets
  Tile Images and Logos
    Square 70x70 Logo ———————— Small tile logo
    Square 150x150 Logo ——————— Medium tile logo
    Wide 310x150 Logo ————————— Wide tile logo
    Square 310x310 Logo ——————— Large tile logo
    Square 30x30 Logo ————————— Icon logo
    Store Logo
    Badge Logo
    Splash Screen

FIGURE 1.5   More understandable names for the different logo images you can provide

To make your tile look good on all devices (and to increase the chances of Microsoft promoting your app in the Windows Store or in advertisements), you should support all scale sizes for each logo you provide. It's perfectly okay to omit large tile and wide tile logos, however. Many of Microsoft's own apps omit them.

Furthermore, it's best *not* to support a large tile and/or wide tile unless you're going to make it a live tile (covered in Chapter 25). Otherwise, your pinned app occupies more space without adding any extra value.

Why does each tile logo support four different image sizes, and how are they used?

Depending on the pixel density of the screen, Windows automatically scales all non-desktop user interfaces to prevent items from being too small to touch or too hard to read. This applies to all Windows Store apps as well as system UI such as the Start screen, file picker, and so on. To prevent your images from looking unsightly by being scaled upward, you can provide multiple versions of any image: one at its normal size, one at 140% of its normal size, and one at 180% of its normal size. The Start screen additionally supports shrinking its content to an 80% scale.

Windows uses a file naming pattern to manage this, and the package manifest designer in Visual Studio automatically names your assigned image files accordingly. By default, the medium tile icon is assigned to Assets\Logo.png. However, at runtime, Windows automatically looks for a file with the following name instead, depending on the current scale being applied:

→ `Assets\Logo.`**`scale-80`**`.png` (for 80% scale)

→ `Assets\Logo.`**`scale-100`**`.png` (for 100% scale)

→ `Assets\Logo.`**`scale-140`**`.png` (for 140% scale)

→ `Assets\Logo.`**`scale-180`**`.png` (for 180% scale)

This is why the file in your project is actually named `Logo.scale-100.png` despite it being referenced as simply `Logo.png`. (It could drop the `.scale-100` part, however, because 100% scale is assumed for a file without that specification.) If an exact match doesn't exist for the current scale, Windows uses the next best match and scales it accordingly.

The store logo and splash screen images don't support the 80% scale size because they are never shown on a tile on the Start screen. The additional four sizes of the square 30x30 logo, assigned to `Assets\SmallLogo.png` by default, use a similar naming scheme:

→ `Assets\SmallLogo.`**`targetsize-16`**`.png` (for 16x16 file icons)

→ `Assets\SmallLogo.`**`targetsize-32`**`.png` (for 32x32 file icons)

→ `Assets\SmallLogo.`**`targetsize-48`**`.png` (for 48x48 file icons)

→ `Assets\SmallLogo.`**`targetsize-256`**`.png` (for 256x256 file icons)

You can use a similar technique for providing different files for high contrast mode, different cultures, and more. This applies not just for the images here, but for images used inside your app as well. See Chapter 13, "Images," for more details.

As with the splash screen, you can specify a background color for your tile. For the best results, this color (as well as the tile images) should match what you use in your splash screen. The desired effect of the splash screen is that your tile springs to life and fills the screen in a larger form. Even if your tile background color is completely covered by opaque tile images, there are still contexts in which the color is seen, such as the zoomed-out Start screen view or the Alt+Tab user interface. Therefore, choose your background color (and determine whether you want your images to use transparency) carefully!

You can choose a "default size," which is the initial size of your tile if the user decides to pin it to the Start screen. This can only be set to the medium tile or the wide tile (if you support a wide tile). If unset, wide is given precedence over medium.

You can also choose a "short name," which is the text that gets overlaid on the bottom of your tile. You can even specify which tile sizes should show the text: medium, wide, and/or large. (Small tiles do not support overlaid text.) Many apps turn off the text because their images already include a logo with the name.

Finally, you can decide whether you want the overlaid text to be "light" (which means white) or "dark" (which means a dark gray). Although most apps use white text, you may need to choose the dark option if you want your tile to have a light background color.

To create a logo that fits in with the built-in apps, it should have a transparent background and the drawing inside should:

→ Be completely white

→ Be composed of simple geometric shapes

→ Use an understandable real-world metaphor

The drawing used in all logo images should look the same, just scaled to different sizes and with different margins.

For example, the drawing for the 150x150 image should generally fit in a 66x66 box centered but nudged a little higher to leave more space for any overlaid text. Typically the drawing has a 42-pixel margin on the left and right, a 37-pixel margin on top, and a 47-pixel margin on the bottom. The drawing for the 30x30 image should generally fit in a 24x24 centered box, leaving just 3 pixels of margin so it's easier to see at the small size. Similarly, the 50x50 store logo drawing should occupy a centered 40x40 square (leaving 5 pixels of margin on each side).

Creating white-on-transparent images requires some practice and patience. You'll want to use tools such as PAINT.NET, mentioned in this book's "Introduction" section. A few of the characters from fonts such as Wingdings, Webdings, and Segoe UI Symbol can even be used to help create a decent icon! Resources like thenounproject.com can also be helpful.

Of course, games or apps with their own strong branding usually do *not* follow these guidelines, as being consistent with their own identity outweighs being consistent with Windows.

Capabilities

On the Capabilities tab, you select each capability required by your app. A *capability* is a special permission for actions that users might not want certain apps to perform, whether for privacy concerns or concerns about data usage charges. In the Windows Store, prospective users are told what capabilities each app requires before they decide whether to download it. To users, they are described as *permissions*, sometimes with more descriptive names, as shown in Figure 1.6.

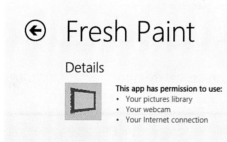

FIGURE 1.6 The Fresh Paint app uses three capabilities: Pictures Library, Webcam, and Internet (Client).

For the most part, user approval of all requested permissions is an implicit part of down-loading an app. However, the use of privacy-related capabilities, such as location services, prompts the user the first time an app invokes a relevant API. Furthermore, some capabilities can be disabled or reenabled at any time by a user. When the Settings charm is invoked while a Windows Store app is running, it contains a "Permissions" link that displays an app's capabilities and toggle switches for any that can be turned on and off. Figure 1.7 shows what this looks like while running `HelloRealWorld`, both with the default capability already chosen in our package manifest—Internet (Client)—and after selecting every listed capability in the package manifest.

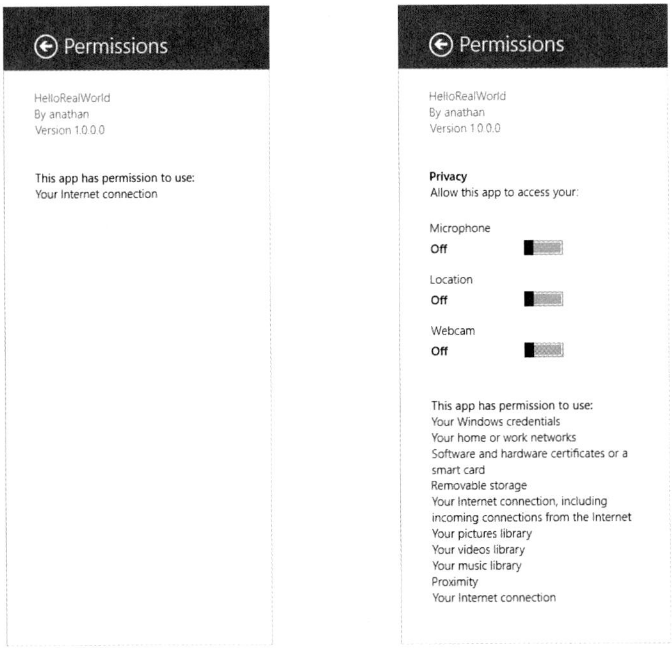

When the app uses the
Internet (Client) capability

When the app uses
every listed capability

FIGURE 1.7   The "Permissions" section of the Settings charm lists the current app's capabilities, and enables turning some of them on or off at runtime.

The long list of available capabilities can be grouped into four different categories:

> You want to restrict the set of capabilities requested by your app as much as possible, because it is a competitive advantage. For example, users might decide not to buy your fun piano app if it wants permission to use the Internet!

→ File capabilities

→ Device capabilities

→ Network capabilities

→ Identity capabilities

Most of them can be used freely, although some of them are restricted. Apps that use restricted capabilities must go through extra processes when uploaded to the Windows Store and are only granted to business developer accounts with written justification. Fortunately, the restricted capabilities (called out in the upcoming lists) are for uncommon scenarios.

File Capabilities

As you'll read in Chapter 20, "Working with Data," apps can read and write their own private files in an isolated spot, and those files can even participate in automatic roaming between a user's devices. In addition, users can give apps explicit permission to read/write other "normal" files and folders via the Windows file picker. This is all that most apps need, and does not require any capabilities.

Beyond these two features, however, programmatic reading and writing of files requires special capabilities. There is one for each of the four built-in libraries (Documents, Music, Pictures, and Videos) plus another for attached storage devices:

→ **Music Library**, **Pictures Library**, and **Videos Library**—Enables enumerating and accessing all music, pictures, and videos, respectively, *without* going through the file picker.

→ **Documents Library**—Enables adding, changing, and deleting files in the Documents library on the local computer *without* going through the file picker. However, this capability is restricted to specific file type associations that must also be declared in the package manifest (on the Declarations tab). This is listed separately from the preceding three capabilities because it is a restricted capability that needs special approval from Microsoft in order to publish the app in the Windows Store. And unlike the capabilities for the Music, Pictures, and Videos libraries, this cannot be used to access Documents libraries on other computers in the same HomeGroup.

→ **Removable Storage**—Enables adding, changing, and deleting files on devices such as external hard drives or thumb drives connected to the local computer, again *without* going through the file picker. As with the preceding capability, this is restricted to file type associations that must also be declared in the package manifest.

Device Capabilities

Apps can access simple sensors such as an accelerometer or devices such as a printer without any capabilities. Accessing other sensors or devices does require specific capabilities, however. The list of device types grows over time (and can be extended by third parties), but the Capabilities tab exposes four choices, listed below. For all of them except proximity, users can disable them at any time, so apps must be prepared to handle this gracefully.

→ **Location**—Reveals the computer's location, either precise coordinates from a GPS sensor (if one exists) or an estimation based on network information.

→ **Microphone**—Enables recording audio from a microphone.

→ **Webcam**—Enables recording video—or capturing still pictures—from a camera. Note that this doesn't include sound. If you want to record audio and video, you need both Webcam and Microphone capabilities.

→ **Proximity**—Enables communication with nearby devices, either via Wi-Fi Direct or near field communication (NFC).

Chapters 14, "Audio, Video, and Speech," and 23, "Reading from Sensors," explain how to write apps that take advantage of these capabilities. Additional device capabilities exist that don't appear on the Capabilities tab. These must be added manually to the package manifest XML. See Chapter 24, "Controlling Devices," for more information.

Network Capabilities

Without any network capabilities, a Windows Store app cannot do any communication over any kind of network except for the automatic roaming of application data described in Chapter 20, the seamless opening/saving of network files enabled by the file picker, or the peer-to-peer connections enabled by the Proximity capability. Four types of network capabilities exist:

→ **Internet (Client)**—This is the only network capability that most apps need. It provides outbound access to the Internet and public networks (going through the firewall).

→ **Internet (Client & Server)**—This is just like the preceding capability except it provides both inbound and outbound access, which is vital for peer-to-peer apps. It's a superset of "Internet (Client)" so if you request this capability in your manifest, then you don't need to request the other one.

→ **Private Networks (Client & Server)**—Provides inbound and outbound access to trusted home and work networks (going through the firewall).

→ **Enterprise Authentication**—Enables intranet access using the current Windows domain credentials. This is a restricted capability.

Identity Capabilities

This is not really a fourth category of capabilities, but rather a single outlier that doesn't fit anywhere else. The Shared User Certificates capability enables access to digital certificates that validate a user's identity. The certificate could be installed on the computer or stored on a smart card. This is mainly for enterprise environments, and it is a restricted capability.

> **Visual Studio project templates enable the "Internet (Client)" capability by default!**
>
> This is done because the Visual Studio team feared that it would be too confusing for developers if simple network-dependent calls failed in their brand new projects. Therefore, be sure to remove the capability if you don't need it. Otherwise, your app's store listing will say that your app "has permission to use your Internet connection."

Declarations

The Declarations tab is the one with the most options. This is where you declare your app's support for one or more *contracts*, if applicable. Contracts enable your app to cooperate with another app, or Windows itself, to complete a well-defined task. Every contract has a *source* that initiates the task and a *target* that completes it.

Your app can be the source for a contract without doing anything in the package manifest. (It just makes various API calls.) To be the target, however, your app must be activated in a special manner. This is what requires the declaration in the package manifest. Therefore, you can think of the list of available *declarations* as the list of available *contract targets*.

Unlike capabilities, contract target declarations are *not* listed in the Windows Store as potentially unwanted features. In fact, you should go out of your way to mention your supported contract scenarios, because they can be very useful! There's nothing about being a contract target that is inherently dangerous for the user. Supporting certain contracts does require relevant capabilities, but many don't require any. See Chapter 22, "Leveraging Contracts," for specific examples.

Content URIs

This tab, new to Windows 8.1, only applies if you are hosting HTML content inside your XAML app. It simply houses a list of HTTPS URLs whose JavaScript is allowed (or disallowed) to raise events that can be handled by your app. For more information, see the discussion of the WebView control in Chapter 15, "Other Controls."

Packaging

The Packaging tab is meant to describe information needed for the app's listing in the Windows Store. However, for apps in the store, this information is managed by the Windows Dev Center dashboard. You therefore don't normally need to change these values in your local package manifest:

→ The **package name** is a unique identifier. Visual Studio automatically fills it in with a globally-unique identifier known as a GUID. That said, for easier debugging and identification of your app's local data store, it's best to replace the GUID with a human-readable name, such as *CompanyName.AppName*. This name doesn't impact real users of your app, as the Windows Store assigns this value in the package that users download.

→ The **package display name** is the name of your app in the store, but this also gets replaced when you follow the procedure to upload an app, so you can leave this item alone.

→ The **version**, set to 1.0.0.0 by default, is a four-part value interpreted as *Major.Minor.Build.Revision*. You can set this value however you like. There are only two requirements enforced by the Windows Store:

1. Each new published version has a higher version number than previous published versions (for the same target version of Windows).

2. If your app simultaneously has a package for Windows 8 and a package for Windows 8.1, the Windows 8 package version number must never exceed the version number of your first published Windows 8.1 package.

→ The bottom of this tab contains publisher information based on the certificate used to authenticate the package. Visual Studio configures this to work with the temporary certificate it generates, and the store upload process reconfigures it to work with your developer account.

For testing certain notification or purchase scenarios that depend on an app's identity in the Windows Store, you can automatically update your local package manifest's packaging values to match the values maintained by the Windows Store. To do this, you can select **Associate App with the Store…**, which can be found on the **Store** menu in Visual Studio Express or on the **Project**, **Store** menu in other editions.

Updating XAML and C# Code

With the tour of the package manifest complete, we are ready to fill our blank app with a little bit of content. Let's look at the remaining files in our project and update them where necessary.

The Main Page User Interface

Every app consists of one or more windows with one or more pages. Our `HelloRealWorld` project, created from the Blank App template, is given a single window with a single page called `MainPage`. It defines what the user sees once your app has loaded and the splash screen has gone away. `MainPage`, like any page that would be used in a XAML app, is implemented across two files: `MainPage.xaml` contains the user interface, and `MainPage.xaml.cs` contains the logic, often called the *code-behind*. Listing 1.1 shows the initial contents of `MainPage.xaml`.

LISTING 1.1   `MainPage.xaml`—The Initial Markup for the Main Page

```
<Page
  x:Class="HelloRealWorld.MainPage"
  xmlns="http://schemas.microsoft.com/winfx/2006/xaml/presentation"
  xmlns:x="http://schemas.microsoft.com/winfx/2006/xaml"
  xmlns:local="using:HelloRealWorld"
  xmlns:d="http://schemas.microsoft.com/expression/blend/2008"
  xmlns:mc="http://schemas.openxmlformats.org/markup-compatibility/2006"
  mc:Ignorable="d">
  <Grid Background="{ThemeResource ApplicationPageBackgroundThemeBrush}">
  </Grid>
</Page>
```

At a quick glance, this file tells us:

→ This is a class called MainPage (in the HelloRealWorld namespace) that derives from a class called Page (the root element in this file).

→ It contains an empty Grid (an element examined in Chapter 4, "Layout") whose background is set to a theme-defined color. From running the app, we know this color is a very dark gray (#1D1D1D).

→ It contains a bunch of XML namespaces to make adding new elements and attributes that aren't in the default namespace more convenient. These XML namespaces are discussed in the next chapter.

Listing 1.2 updates the blank-screen MainPage.xaml with a few elements to produce the result in Figure 1.8.

LISTING 1.2   MainPage.xaml—Updated Markup for the HelloRealWorld App

```
<Page
  x:Class="HelloRealWorld.MainPage"
  xmlns="http://schemas.microsoft.com/winfx/2006/xaml/presentation"
  xmlns:x="http://schemas.microsoft.com/winfx/2006/xaml"
  xmlns:local="using:HelloRealWorld"
  xmlns:d="http://schemas.microsoft.com/expression/blend/2008"
  xmlns:mc="http://schemas.openxmlformats.org/markup-compatibility/2006"
  mc:Ignorable="d">
  <Grid Background="{ThemeResource ApplicationPageBackgroundThemeBrush}">
    <StackPanel Name="stackPanel" Margin="100" Background="Blue">
      <TextBlock FontSize="80" TextWrapping="WrapWholeWords" Margin="12,48">
        Hello, English-speaking world!</TextBlock>
      <TextBlock FontSize="28" Margin="12">Please enter your name:</TextBlock>
      <Grid>
        <Grid.ColumnDefinitions>
          <ColumnDefinition/>
          <ColumnDefinition Width="Auto"/>
        </Grid.ColumnDefinitions>
        <TextBox Name="nameBox" Margin="12"/>
        <Button Grid.Column="1" Click="Button_Click">Go</Button>
      </Grid>
      <TextBlock Name="result" FontSize="28" Margin="12"/>
    </StackPanel>
  </Grid>
</Page>
```

This listing adds a bunch of new content inside the topmost Grid. The Grid and StackPanel elements help to arrange the user-visible elements: TextBlocks (i.e. labels), a TextBox, and a Button. All of these elements are described in depth in upcoming chapters.

FIGURE 1.8   The HelloRealWorld user interface asks the user to type his or her name.

The idea for this app is to display the user's name in the TextBlock named result once
he or she clicks the Go Button. (Granted, this is not a useful app, but it's all we need to
demonstrate the concepts throughout the remainder of this chapter.) To act upon the
Button being clicked, this XAML specifies that a method called Button_Click should be
called when its Click event is raised. This method must be defined in the code-behind
file, which we'll look at next.

The Main Page Logic

Listing 1.3 shows the initial contents of MainPage.xaml.cs, the code-behind file
for MainPage.xaml. Until we add our own logic, it contains only a required call to
InitializeComponent that constructs the page with all the visuals defined in the XAML
file. The class is marked with the partial keyword because its definition is shared with a
hidden C# file that gets generated when the XAML file is compiled.

LISTING 1.3   `MainPage.xaml.cs`—The Initial Code-Behind for the Main Page

```
using System;
using System.Collections.Generic;
using System.IO;
using System.Linq;
using System.Runtime.InteropServices.WindowsRuntime;
using Windows.Foundation;
using Windows.Foundation.Collections;
using Windows.UI.Xaml;
using Windows.UI.Xaml.Controls;
using Windows.UI.Xaml.Controls.Primitives;
using Windows.UI.Xaml.Data;
using Windows.UI.Xaml.Input;
using Windows.UI.Xaml.Media;
using Windows.UI.Xaml.Navigation;

// The Blank Page item template is documented at
// http://go.microsoft.com/fwlink/?LinkId=234238

namespace HelloRealWorld
{
  /// <summary>
  /// An empty page that can be used on its own or navigated to within a Frame.
  /// </summary>
  public sealed partial class MainPage : Page
  {
    public MainPage()
    {
      this.InitializeComponent();
    }
  }
}
```

We need to add an implementation of the `Button_Click` method referenced by the XAML. It can look as follows:

```
void Button_Click(object sender, RoutedEventArgs e)
{
  this.result.Text = this.nameBox.Text;
}
```

The named elements in the XAML correspond to fields in this class, so this code
updates the result TextBlock with the

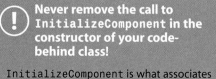

Never remove the call to InitializeComponent in the constructor of your code-behind class!

InitializeComponent is what associates your XAML-defined content with the instance of the class at run-time.

text from the `nameBox` TextBox. Figure 1.9 shows what this looks like, after the user types "Adam" then clicks the `Button`.

FIGURE 1.9   The `result` TextBlock contains the typed text after the user clicks the `Button`.

The Application Definition

The application definition is contained in `App.xaml` and its code-behind file, `App.xaml.cs`. `App.xaml` is a special XAML file that doesn't define any visuals, but rather defines an `App` class that can handle application-level tasks. Usually the only reason to touch this XAML file is to place new application-wide resources, such as custom styles, inside its `Application.Resources` collection. Chapter 18, "Styles, Templates, and Visual States" contains many examples of this. Listing 1.4 shows the contents of `App.xaml` in our `HelloRealWorld` project.

LISTING 1.4   `App.xaml`—The Markup for the App Class

```
<Application
  x:Class="HelloRealWorld.App"
  xmlns="http://schemas.microsoft.com/winfx/2006/xaml/presentation"
  xmlns:x="http://schemas.microsoft.com/winfx/2006/xaml"
  xmlns:local="using:HelloRealWorld">
</Application>
```

Listing 1.5 contains the auto-generated contents of the code-behind file for App.xaml. It contains three vital pieces:

→ A constructor, which is effectively the app's main method. The plumbing that makes it the app's entry point is enabled by an "Entry point" setting in the package manifest (on the Application tab). When you create a project, Visual Studio automatically sets it to the namespace-qualified name of the project's App class (HelloRealWorld.App in this example).

→ Logic inside an OnLaunched method that enables the frame rate counter overlay in debug mode, navigates to the app's first (and in this case only) page, and calls Window.Current.Activate to dismiss the splash screen. If you want to add a new page and make it be the starting point of the app, or if you want to customize the initialization logic, this is where you can do it. See Chapter 7, "App Lifecycle," for more information.

→ An OnSuspending method that is attached to the base class's Suspending event. This gives you an opportunity to save state before your app is suspended, although the generated code does nothing here other than provide a TODO comment. Chapter 7 examines app suspension.

LISTING 1.5   App.xaml.cs—The Code-Behind for the App Class

```
using System;
using System.Collections.Generic;
using System.IO;
using System.Linq;
using System.Runtime.InteropServices.WindowsRuntime;
using Windows.ApplicationModel;
using Windows.ApplicationModel.Activation;
using Windows.Foundation;
using Windows.Foundation.Collections;
using Windows.UI.Xaml;
using Windows.UI.Xaml.Controls;
using Windows.UI.Xaml.Controls.Primitives;
using Windows.UI.Xaml.Data;
using Windows.UI.Xaml.Input;
using Windows.UI.Xaml.Media;
using Windows.UI.Xaml.Navigation;

namespace HelloRealWorld
{
  /// <summary>
  /// Provides application-specific behavior to supplement the base class.
  /// </summary>
  sealed partial class App : Application
```

```csharp
  {
    /// <summary>
    /// Initializes the singleton application object.  This is the first line
    /// of authored code executed; the logical equivalent of main/WinMain.
    /// </summary>
    public App()
    {
      this.InitializeComponent();
      this.Suspending += OnSuspending;
    }

    /// <summary>
    /// Invoked when the application is launched normally by the end user.
    /// Other entry points are used when the application is launched to open
    /// a specific file, to display search results, and so forth.
    /// </summary>
    /// <param name="args">Details about the launch request and process.</param>
    protected override void OnLaunched(LaunchActivatedEventArgs args)
    {
#if DEBUG
      if (System.Diagnostics.Debugger.IsAttached)
      {
        this.DebugSettings.EnableFrameRateCounter = true;
      }
#endif

      Frame rootFrame = Window.Current.Content as Frame;

      // Do not repeat app initialization when the Window already has content,
      // just ensure that the window is active
      if (rootFrame == null)
      {
        // Create a Frame and navigate to the first page
        var rootFrame = new Frame();

        if (args.PreviousExecutionState == ApplicationExecutionState.Terminated)
        {
          //TODO: Load state from previously suspended application
        }

        // Place the frame in the current Window
        Window.Current.Content = rootFrame;
      }
```

```csharp
    if (rootFrame.Content == null)
    {
      // When the navigation stack isn't restored, navigate to the first page
      if (!rootFrame.Navigate(typeof(MainPage), args.Arguments))
      {
        throw new Exception("Failed to create initial page");
      }
    }

    // Ensure the current Window is active
    Window.Current.Activate();
  }

  /// <summary>
  /// Invoked when application execution is being suspended.  Application state
  /// is saved without knowing whether the application will be terminated or
  /// resumed with the contents of memory still intact.
  /// </summary>
  /// <param name="sender">The source of the suspend request.</param>
  /// <param name="e">Details about the suspend request.</param>
  private void OnSuspending(object sender, SuspendingEventArgs e)
  {
    var deferral = e.SuspendingOperation.GetDeferral();
    //TODO: Save application state and stop any background activity
    deferral.Complete();
  }
}
}
```

There's one more file—AssemblyInfo.cs—but it's not worth showing in this book. It contains a bunch of attributes where you *can* put a title, description, company name, copyright, and so on that get compiled into your assembly (the EXE or DLL). But setting these is unnecessary because all of the information used by the Windows Store is separately managed. Still, the AssemblyVersion and AssemblyFileVersion attributes, typically set to the same value, can be useful for you to keep track of distinct versions of your application:

If you want to create a richer splash screen, perhaps with an animated progress graphic, the way to do this is by mimicking the splash screen with a custom page. Inside App.OnLaunched, you can navigate to an initial page that looks just like the real (static) splash screen but with extra UI elements and custom logic. The instance of LaunchActivatedEventArgs passed to OnLaunched even has a SplashScreen property that exposes an ImageLocation rectangle that tells you the coordinates of the real splash screen image. This makes it easy to match the splash screen's appearance no matter what the current screen's resolution is. Such a user interface is often called an "extended splash screen."

```
[assembly: AssemblyVersion("1.0.0.0")]
[assembly: AssemblyFileVersion("1.0.0.0")]
```

By using *-syntax, such as "1.0.*", you can even let the version number auto-increment every time you rebuild your app.

Making the App World-Ready

At this point, our HelloRealWorld app still only says "hello" to the English-speaking parts of the world. The Windows Store serves hundreds of markets and over a hundred different languages, so ignoring them greatly reduces the audience for your app. Making your app world-ready involves two things: *globalization* and *localization*.

Globalization refers to making your app act appropriately for different markets without any changes or customizations. An example of this is formatting the display of currency correctly for the current region without writing special-case logic. The Windows.Globalization namespace contains a lot of functionality for handling dates and times, geographic regions, number formatting, and more. Plus, built-in XAML controls such as DatePicker and TimePicker, discussed in Chapter 15, are globalization-ready. For many apps, these features might not apply.

Localization, which is relevant for practically every app, refers to explicit activity to adapt an app to each new market. The primary example of this is translating text in your user interface to different languages and then displaying the translations when appropriate. Performing this localization activity is the focus of this section.

To make an app ready for localization, you should remove hardcoded English strings that are user-visible, and instead mark such elements with a special identifier unique within the app. Listing 1.6 updates our XAML from Listing 1.2 to do just that.

LISTING 1.6   MainPage.xaml—Markup with User-Visible English Text Removed

```
<Page
  x:Class="HelloRealWorld.MainPage"
  xmlns="http://schemas.microsoft.com/winfx/2006/xaml/presentation"
  xmlns:x="http://schemas.microsoft.com/winfx/2006/xaml"
  xmlns:local="using:HelloRealWorld"
  xmlns:d="http://schemas.microsoft.com/expression/blend/2008"
  xmlns:mc="http://schemas.openxmlformats.org/markup-compatibility/2006"
  mc:Ignorable="d">
  <Grid Background="{ThemeResource ApplicationPageBackgroundThemeBrush}">
    <StackPanel x:Uid="Panel" Name="stackPanel" Margin="100">
      <TextBlock x:Uid="Greeting" FontSize="80" TextWrapping="WrapWholeWords"
                                                 Margin="12,48"/>
      <TextBlock x:Uid="EnterName" FontSize="28" Margin="12"/>
      <Grid>
        <Grid.ColumnDefinitions>
```

```
      <ColumnDefinition/>
      <ColumnDefinition Width="Auto"/>
    </Grid.ColumnDefinitions>
    <TextBox Name="nameBox" Margin="12"/>
    <Button x:Uid="GoButton" Grid.Column="1" Click="Button_Click"/>
  </Grid>
  <TextBlock Name="result" FontSize="28" Margin="12"/>
  </StackPanel>
 </Grid>
</Page>
```

The x:Uid marking is completely independent from an element's Name. The former is specifically for the localization process, and the latter is for the benefit of code-behind. Note that Listing 1.6 not only removes the three hardcoded strings from the two TextBlocks and the Button, but it also removes the explicit "Blue" color from the StackPanel! This way, we can customize the color for different languages in addition to the text.

With the IDs in place and the text and color for English removed, we need to add them back in a way that identifies them as English-only. To do this, add a new folder to the solution called **en**. This is the language code for all variations of English. If you want to target the United Kingdom separately, you could add a folder called **en-GB**. If you want to target Canada separately, you could add a folder called **en-CA**. And so forth.

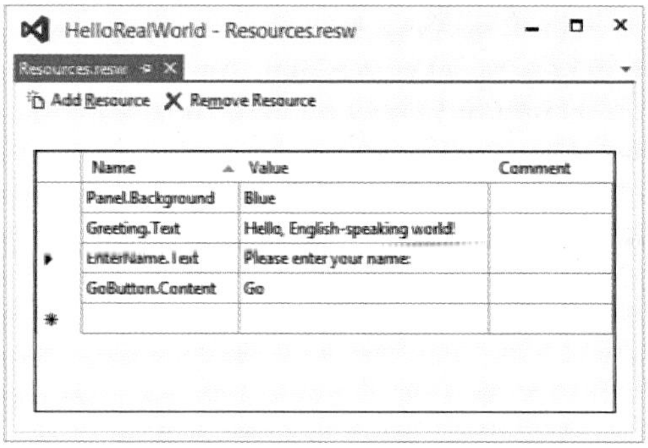

Right-click on the **en** folder and select **Add, New Item**, then pick **Resources file** from the **General** tab. The default name of Resources.resw is fine. This file is a table for all your language-specific strings. Figure 1.10 shows this file populated for English.

FIGURE 1.10   The Resources.resw file in the en folder is populated with English-specific values.

Each value must be given a name of the form *UniqueId.PropertyName*. *UniqueId* must match the x:Uid value for the relevant element, so the Panel.Background entry in Figure 1.10 sets Background to Blue on the StackPanel marked with x:Uid="Panel" in Listing 1.6. From the listing, it's not obvious that GoButton's relevant property is called Content, unlike the TextBlocks' property called Text, but as you learn about the different elements throughout this book, you'll understand which properties to set.

After filling out the `Resources.resw` file, you can run the `HelloRealWorld` app and the result is identical to what we saw earlier in Figures 1.6 and 1.7. However, the app is now ready to be localized for other languages.

We could add additional folders named after language codes and manually populate translated resources with the help of a knowledgeable friend, a professional translator, or translation software. Depending on the current user's

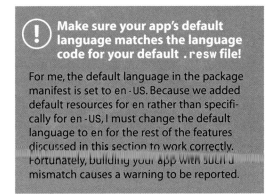

Make sure your app's default language matches the language code for your default `.resw` file!

For me, the default language in the package manifest is set to en-US. Because we added default resources for en rather than specifically for en-US, I must change the default language to en for the rest of the features discussed in this section to work correctly. Fortunately, building your app with such a mismatch causes a warning to be reported.

language settings, the appropriate resources are chosen at runtime, with a fallback to the default language if no such resources exist.

However, a better option exists. To take advantage of it, you must download and install the Multilingual App Toolkit from the Windows Dev Center. Once you do this, you can select **Enable Multilingual App Toolkit** from Visual Studio's **Tools** menu. This automatically adds an `.xlf` file to a new subfolder added to your project called **MultilingualResources** for a test-only language called Pseudo Language.

We'll leverage the Pseudo Language in a moment, but first let's add support for a second *real* language: Traditional Chinese. To do this, right-click on your project in Solution Explorer and select **Add translation languages....** This produces the dialog shown in Figure 1.11.

In this dialog, Pseudo Language and our default English language is already selected, but we can scroll down and select **Chinese (Traditional) [zh-Hant]** from the list. After pressing OK, the **MultilingualResources** folder now has two `.xlf` files: one for Pseudo Language, and one for Traditional Chinese.

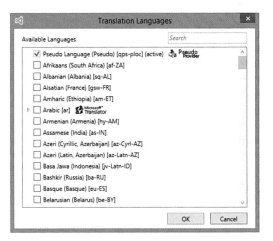

FIGURE 1.11   The Multilingual App Toolkit automates the process for supporting new languages.

> ## ? What is Pseudo Language?
>
> Pseudo Language is designed to test how well your app handles being localized to various (real) languages. When leveraging machine translation to Pseudo Language, you get an English-looking string whose contents are still recognizable, but designed to catch problems.
>
> Pseudo Language strings are longer than the corresponding English strings, to help you catch cases where text might get truncated or cause issues from wrapping when you translate to a *real* language whose text tends to be longer than English. Each string also begins with an ID, to help you track a problematic piece of text to its original resource. For example, a Pseudo Language translation of Hello, English Speaking World! can look like [07223] [!!_Ĥę𝚕ĺó, Éŉ𝑔ļįśĥ-śƥêāᶄįŉ𝑔 ẁòŕ𝐙đ!_!!] Because of the unique appearance of Pseudo Language, it also helps you catch user-visible text in your user interface that you forgot to extract to a resource.

> ## ? What are .xlf files?
>
> These files, which are generated by the Multilingual App Toolkit, are XLIFF files, an industry-standard XML format for localizable data. In addition to listing source and target strings (with optional comments), these files enable a workflow in which resources can be marked as New, Needs Review, Translated, Final, or Signed Off.
>
> The benefit of using XLIFF files to store translations is that you can send them directly to a professional translation vendor, as they should already have a workflow involving this format. Or, if you leverage friends to do your translations, you can have them install the Multilingual App Toolkit and use its Multilingual Editor in a standalone fashion. No Visual Studio installation is necessary.
>
> Visual Studio includes functionality for packaging and sending XLIFF files, as well as importing updated files that merge with your local content. These options can be found by right-clicking an .xlf file in Solution Explorer.

Now rebuild the HelloRealWorld app. This populates each .xlf file with a "translation" for each item from the default language .resw file. Initially, each translation is just the duplicated English text. However, for some languages, such as the two we've chosen, you can generate machine translations based on the Microsoft Translator service! To do this for the entire file, right-click on each .xlf file and select **Generate machine translations**. Voilà! Now we've got initial translations for all of our resources, which you can see by opening each .xlf file and examining the list inside the multilingual editor. This is shown in Figure 1.12.

Your willingness to trust the results from machine translation is a personal decision, but at least machine translation is a good starting point. (Notice that the generated translations are automatically placed in a "Needs Review" state.) That said, we definitely don't want the Blue text translated to 藍色! This isn't a user-visible string, and 藍色 is not a valid value for Background. Instead, let's "translate" it to Red, which will serve as our language-specific background color. Similarly, we don't want Blue's Pseudo Language translation of [D05A0][!!_B𝚓ùè_!!], so let's change that to Green.

Chinese (Traditional)

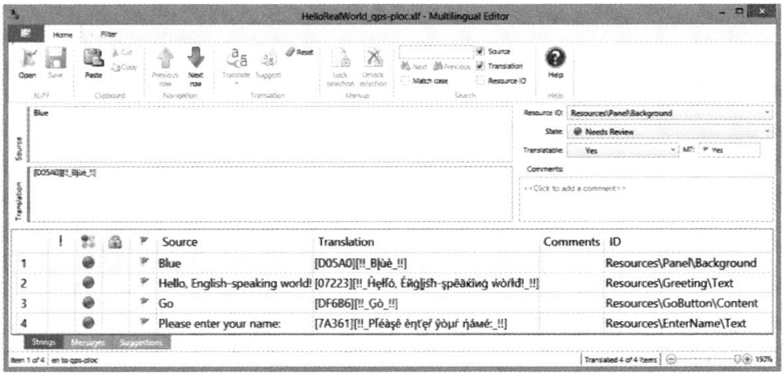

Pseudo Language

FIGURE 1.12   Each `.xlf` file contains machine-generated initial translations, courtesy of Microsoft Translator.

We have one more change to make. We don't want "Hello, English-speaking world!" to be translated to Chinese, but rather "Hello, Chinese-speaking world!" Both Microsoft Translator and a colleague tell me that "你好, 華語世界 !" is a valid translation, so we can paste that into the appropriate spot of the Chinese `.xlf` file.

After rebuilding the project, we are now ready to test the localized versions of `HelloRealWorld`. Just as if we had manually added separate `.resw` files in per-language folders, the translated resources are used automatically based on the current Windows language settings.

To change the default language used by Windows, you can either use the PC Settings app or the desktop Control Panel. In PC Settings, this can be found under **Time & language**; **Region & language**. In Control Panel, it's under **Clock, Language, and Region**; **Language**. Add **Chinese (Traditional)** and make it the default language to test the Traditional Chinese resources.

To add Pseudo Language (and make it the default language), you have to use a hidden trick in Control Panel. After clicking **Add languages**, type **qps-ploc** in the search box for the entry called **English (qps-ploc)** to appear. You must type *the whole thing* for this to work! This language is hidden in this way because no normal user should ever enable it.

Figure 1.13 shows the result of running `HelloRealWorld` when Windows is set to use each of the two non-English languages. These changes are handled completely by the resource-loading mechanism. Other than the switch to marking elements with `x:Uid`, no code changes were needed. This figure also highlights Pseudo Language's knack for using really long strings that can highlight potential weaknesses in your app's layout.

Chinese (Traditional)   Pseudo Language

FIGURE 1.13   `HelloRealWorld` now acts appropriately for Traditional Chinese and for the test-only Pseudo Language.

You can add additional languages to your apps that have already been published in the Windows Store, thanks to *resource pack* support in Windows 8.1. As long as you don't update any code or your version number, your new resources get downloaded only to users with a matching language preference.

The Microsoft Local Language Portal (http://www.microsoft.com/language) is a fantastic resource for getting translations. You can search for terms and get a translation in every language supported by Windows (over 100). These are not machine translations, but rather translations Microsoft has used in their own products. As such, they tend to be geared towards the kind of user-visible labels that are commonly found in software. The portal even shows you which products have made use of the translated terms. Just be sure you agree with the license and terms of use, which can be found on the website.

Making the App Accessible

XAML apps have a number of accessibility features built in, designed to help users with disabilities. You can test this support by enabling various features in the Ease of Access section in the PC Settings app. You can configure Narrator, a screen reader, and witness it convey information about your app with varying degrees of success. (You can quickly toggle Narrator on and off by pressing Windows+Enter.) You can choose a high contrast theme and watch controls used by your app automatically change to match the theme. You can turn off standard animations. And so on.

To make your app usable to the broadest set of customers, including people with disabilities, you should take steps to ensure it works even better with these assistive technologies. In this section, we look at improving the screen reading experience for our `HelloRealWorld` app, and accounting for high contrast themes.

> The Windows SDK includes several tools that help you ensure that your app is accessible. The most important one is **UI Accessibility Checker**, which reports missing accessibility information in your app. Others are **Inspect**, which is a viewer for accessibility data on your elements, and **Accessible Event Watcher**, which focuses on the accessiblity events that should be raised.

Improving Screen Reading

If you turn on Narrator and launch the `HelloRealWorld` app (with English as the Windows default language), you hear the following:

> *"HelloRealWorld window"*

> *"Editing"*

The first utterance is triggered by the app's window getting focus, and the second utterance is triggered by the `TextBox` getting focus (which happens automatically).

This experience isn't good enough, because Narrator doesn't report the purpose of the `TextBox`. To fix this, we need to leverage the UI Automation framework, which is as simple as setting the following automation property on the `TextBox`:

```
<TextBox AutomationProperties.Name="Please enter your name"
         Name="nameBox" Margin="12"/>
```

If you add this property then rerun `HelloRealWorld` with Narrator on, you will hear the following:

> *"HelloRealWorld window"*

> ***"Please enter your name"***

> *"Editing"*

Note that when you give the Go `Button` focus, such as by pressing Tab, Narrator says:

> *"Go button"*

This works automatically, thanks to built-in `Button` behavior that reports its content to the UI Automation framework.

When you click the `Button`, however, Narrator gives no indication that text has been added to the screen. If a message is worth showing, then it's worth hearing as well. To fix this problem, we can add the following automation property to the `result` TextBlock that identifies it as a live region:

```
<TextBlock AutomationProperties.LiveSetting="Polite"
           Name="result" FontSize="28" Margin="12"/>
```

A live region is an area whose content changes. This `AutomationProperties.LiveSetting` property can be set to one of the following values:

→ **Off**—This is the default value.

→ **Polite**—Changes should be communicated, but they should not interrupt the screen reader.

→ **Assertive**—Changes should be communicated immediately, even if the screen reader is in the midst of speaking.

Live region changes are not detected automatically, however. You must trigger them in C#. In our example, we just need to add an extra line of code to the existing `Button_Click` event handler:

```
void Button_Click(object sender, RoutedEventArgs e)
{
  this.result.Text = this.nameBox.Text;
  // Notify a screen reader to report this text
  TextBlockAutomationPeer.FromElement(this.result).RaiseAutomationEvent(
    AutomationEvents.LiveRegionChanged);
}
```

TextBlock, as with other controls, has a peer class in the `Windows.UI.Xaml.Automation.Peers` namespace. These classes are named with the pattern *ElementName*AutomationPeer, and have several members that are designed for accessibility as well as automated testing.

After the work we did to localize the `HelloRealWorld` app, it would be unfortunate to give screen readers a hardcoded English string, as shown earlier:

```
<TextBox AutomationProperties.Name="Please enter your name"
         Name="nameBox" Margin="12"/>
```

Fortunately, automation properties can be localized just like any other property. To do this, remove the explicit setting and give the element an `x:Uid`:

```
<TextBox x:Uid="NameBox" Name="nameBox" Margin="12"/>
```

In this example, you should then add an entry in the `Resources.resw` file named `NameBox.AutomationProperties.Name`, and its value for English should be `"Please enter your name"`.

Handling High Contrast Themes

The built-in controls automatically adjust their appearance when the user enables a high contrast theme. They adjust their colors to match the theme's eight user-customizable colors, and in some cases they change their rendering in other ways. Because of this, your app *can* automatically look correct under a high contrast theme without you doing extra work. However, when you use images or hardcoded colors, which are quite common, problems arise. Images can be a problem when they convey information but do not use enough contrast. Hardcoded colors are a problem for the same reason, but also because they can make things completely unreadable when intermixed with colors that drastically change under a high contrast theme. In general, mixing hardcoded colors with dynamic colors can be a recipe for disaster.

`HelloRealWorld` doesn't use any images, but Chapter 13 explains how you can provide separate versions of your images that can be used for high contrast themes only.

For `HelloRealWorld`, the hardcoded blue (or red or green) background color could be problematic as the colors of the other elements change. (Although none of the high contrast themes use blue, red, or green as a text color by default, the user could always choose it for the color of text.) We can fix this in code-behind by checking whether the app is running under high contrast and simply removing the `StackPanel`'s `Background` in that case:

```
public sealed partial class MainPage : Page
{
  Brush defaultBackground;

  public MainPage()
  {
    InitializeComponent();

    // Save the default background for later
    this.defaultBackground = this.stackPanel.Background;
```

```
    AccessibilitySettings settings = new AccessibilitySettings();

    // Update the background whenever the theme changes
    settings.HighContrastChanged += OnHighContrastChanged;

    // Set the background appropriately on initialization
    OnHighContrastChanged(settings, null);
  }

  void OnHighContrastChanged(AccessibilitySettings sender, object args)
  {
    this.stackPanel.Background =
      sender.HighContrast ? null : this.defaultBackground;
  }

  ...
}
```

Because the user could change the theme while our app is running, we need to handle the HighContrastChanged event to adjust accordingly. The rest of the app's elements already adjust automatically. Figure 1.14 shows the result of adding this code then running the app under two different high contrast themes. Chapter 18 explains how you can define theme-specific colors without needing to write C# code such as this.

High contrast #1 theme   High contrast white theme

FIGURE 1.14   Removing the explicit StackPanel background makes the app look appropriate under any high contrast theme.

By defining and using the defaultBackground member, the code that handles the HighContrastChanged event preserves the language-specific background color that comes from one of the Resources.resw files. It does so without needing to programmatically retrieve the current resource value. However, if you need to do so, you can use code like the following for the Panel.Background value:

```
ResourceCandidate rc = ResourceManager.Current.MainResourceMap.GetValue(
  "Resources/Panel/Background", ResourceContext.GetForCurrentView());
string backgroundString = rc.ValueAsString;
```

If you do the following:

→ check that the Windows SDK accessibility tools have no high-priority complaints about your app

→ verify that your app acts appropriately when using Narrator

→ verify that your app acts approrpiately when running under high contrast

→ verify that your app can be used when navigating using only the keyboard

then you should take credit for your work and check the "My app meets accessibility guidelines" checkbox within your app's listing in your Windows Dev Center dashboard. This fact gets advertised in the Windows Store, and it makes your app shows up for users who search for accessible apps.

Submitting to the Windows Store

Once your app is finished, you can submit it to the Windows Store via items on the **Store** menu in Visual Studio Express, or via the **Project, Store** menu in other editions of Visual Studio. The Visual Studio integration works in concert with pages on the Windows Dev Center website to help you complete your submission. Before doing this, however, you have some tasks to complete:

→ **Set up your developer account** at http://dev.windows.com, get it verified, and fill out your payout and tax information. This can take a couple of days for an individual account, or a couple of weeks for a business account.

→ **Reserve your app name** with the Windows Store, as it requires each app's name to be unique. You can reserve names at any time, and you have up to a year to submit the app before losing each reservation. You can also reserve additional names for other languages.

➔ **Download, install, and run the Windows App Certification Kit** (WACK) from the Windows Dev Center. This tests your app for violations that cause it to fail the Windows Store certification process, so running it in advance can save you a lot of time.

The Windows Store certification process consists of three parts:

➔ **Technical checks.** This is simply running the Windows App Certification Kit on your app. If you pass its tests before submitting your app, you should have nothing to worry about here.

➔ **Security checks.** This ensures that your software isn't infected with a virus, which again should not be a concern for most developers.

➔ **Content checks.** This is the trickiest part of the process and, unlike the other two, is performed manually by human reviewers. Reviewers ensure that the app does what it claims to do and follows all the app certification requirements published in the Windows Dev Center.

The very first certification requirement is that the app "must offer customers unique, creative value or utility," so HelloRealWorld is bound to fail this requirement. This requirement may be obvious, but there are some requirements that often surprise people and cause many apps to fail certification:

➔ If your app requires a network capability, you must write a privacy statement that explains what data you collect, how you store or share it, how users can access the collected data, and so on. Requirement 4.1 in the Windows Dev Center helps you figure out how to write one. Furthermore, a link to the statement must be reachable from the Settings pane for your app, and the same link must be included in your listing in the Windows Store. See Chapter 21, "Supporting Charms," for information about adding content to the Settings pane.

➔ You must select an appropriate age rating, using guidelines from the Windows Dev Center. For example, most apps that share personal information must be rated at least 12+. Regardless of your app's rating, its *listing* for the Windows Store cannot contain content that is considered too mature for a 12+ rating.

➔ You must provide descriptions and screenshots for every language you support. If your app is only partially localized for some languages, you must mention this in your listing.

If you fail certification, you must address the issue(s) and resubmit your app. When you do so, it goes through the entire process again, at the end of the line. Fortunately, at the time of this writing, the average length of certifica tion is only about 2.5 days.

> **(!) Don't forget to remove capabilities you don't need!**
>
> The certification process doesn't warn you about capabilities you don't actually use, so it's up to you to make sure the list is not larger than it needs to be.

> Be sure to fill out the **Notes to testers** section in your Windows Dev Center dashboard to help the reviewers understand how to use any features of your app that might not be obvious. This is also the place to give them test credentials, if your app requires some sort of sign in.

> To increase the chances of Microsoft promoting your app in the Windows Store, put a lot of effort into your listing. Every screenshot should be compelling, and you should feel free to enhance screenshots with explanations or other branding that increases the "wow factor" (as long as it's clear what is part of the app and what isn't). To get a feel for what makes a good description, you should look at the descriptions for apps that are already featured prominently in the Windows Store. In general, you should think of designing your listing like designing a box to sell your software in a retail store.
>
> The optional **promotional images** are not optional at all if you want a chance for your app to be promoted. Again, they don't necessarily have to be screenshots, but they should be compelling and professional. You don't need to provide all possible sizes, but the 414x180 and 414x468 sizes are very important.

Summary

You've now seen the basic structure of a Visual Studio project for a XAML-based Windows Store app and gotten a taste for making an app that is ready to sell across the world. If you've previously done .NET development, much of this should look familiar. If you've previously dabbled in Windows Presentation Foundation (WPF) and/or Silverlight, the role of the XAML files and the C# files should be obvious. And if you've previously done development for Windows Phone, then all of these concepts, including things like capabilities, shouldn't surprise you one bit. If you don't have any such experience, then you should at least be able to appreciate how easy it is to hit the ground running.

Personally, I'm struck by how easy it has become to localize your app and make it accessible. Software development has come a long way over the years, and you'll see evidence of this throughout the book, when it comes to handling heterogeneous screen DPI, making money through the Windows Store, communicating with slick peripherals, and much more. The team behind Windows Store apps has taken the best ideas from .NET, XAML, Windows Phone, the Web, C++, and COM in order to create a compelling platform that's easy for developers to dive into. And now it's time to dive much deeper into the language of XAML.

Chapter 2

MASTERING XAML

You might be thinking, "Isn't Chapter 2 a bit early to become a *master* of XAML?" No, because this chapter focuses on the mechanics of the XAML *language*, which is a bit orthogonal to the multitude of XAML elements and APIs you'll be using when you build Windows Store apps. Learning about the XAML language is kind of like learning the features of C# before delving into .NET or the Windows Runtime. Unlike the preceding chapter, this is a fairly deep dive! However, having this background knowledge before proceeding with the rest of the book will enable you to approach the examples with confidence.

XAML is a dialect of XML that Microsoft introduced in 2006 along with the first version of Windows Presentation Foundation (WPF). XAML is a relatively simple and general-purpose declarative programming language suitable for constructing and initializing objects. XAML is just XML, but with a set of rules about its elements and attributes and their mapping to objects, their properties, and the values of those properties (among other things).

You can think of XAML as a clean, modern (albeit more verbose) reinvention of HTML and CSS. In Windows Store apps, XAML serves essentially the same purpose as HTML: It provides a declarative way to represent user interfaces. That said, XAML is actually a general-purpose language that can be used in ways that have nothing to do with UI. The preceding chapter contained a simple example of this. App.xaml does not define a user interface, but rather some characteristics of an app's entry point class. Note that

almost everything that can be expressed in XAML can be naturally represented in a procedural language like C# as well.

The motivation for XAML is pretty much the same as any declarative markup language:
Make it easy for programmers to work with others—perhaps graphic designers—and
enable a powerful, robust tooling experience on top of it. XAML encourages a nice separation between visuals (and visual behavior such as animations) and the rest of the code,
and enables powerful styling capabilities. XAML pages can be opened in Blend as well as
Visual Studio (and Visual Studio has a convenient "Open in Blend…" item on its View
menu), or entire XAML-based projects can be opened in Blend. This can be helpful for
designing sophisticated artwork, animations, and other graphically rich touches. The idea
is that a team's developers can work in Visual Studio while its designers work in Blend,
and everyone can work on the same codebase. However, because XAML (and XML in
general) is generally human readable, you can accomplish quite a bit with nothing more
than a tool such as Notepad.

Elements and Attributes

The XAML specification defines rules that map object-oriented namespaces, types, properties, and events into XML namespaces, elements, and attributes. You can see this by
examining the following simple XAML snippet that declares a Button control and
comparing it to the equivalent C# code:

XAML:

```
<Button xmlns="http://schemas.microsoft.com/winfx/2006/xaml/presentation"
  Content="Stop"/>
```

C#:

```
Windows.UI.Xaml.Controls.Button b = new Windows.UI.Xaml.Controls.Button();
b.Content = "Stop";
```

Declaring an XML element in XAML (known as an *object element*) is equivalent to instantiating the corresponding object via a default constructor. Setting an attribute on the
object element is equivalent to setting a property of the same name (called a *property
attribute*) or hooking up an event handler of the same name (called an *event attribute*). For
example, here's an update to the Button control that not only sets its Content property
but also attaches an event handler to its Click event:

XAML:

```
<Button xmlns="http://schemas.microsoft.com/winfx/2006/xaml/presentation"
  Content="Stop" Click="Button_Click"/>
```

C#:

```
Windows.UI.Xaml.Controls.Button b = new Windows.UI.Xaml.Controls.Button();
b.Click += new Windows.UI.Xaml.RoutedEventHandler(Button_Click);
b.Content = "Stop";
```

This requires an appropriate method called `Button_Click` to be defined in a code-behind file, as seen in the preceding chapter. Note that XAML, like C#, is a case-sensitive language.

Namespaces

The most mysterious part about comparing the previous XAML examples with the equivalent C# examples is how the XML namespace `http://schemas.microsoft.com/winfx/2006/xaml/presentation` maps to the Windows Runtime namespace `Windows.UI.Xaml.Controls`. It turns out that the mapping to this and other namespaces is hard-coded inside the framework. (In case you're wondering, no web page exists at the `schemas.microsoft.com` URL—it's just an arbitrary string like any namespace.) Because many Windows Runtime namespaces are mapped to the same XML namespace, the framework designers took care not to introduce two classes with the same name, despite the fact that the classes are in separate Windows Runtime namespaces.

> ### Order of Property and Event Processing
>
> At runtime, event handlers are always attached *before* any properties are set for any object declared in XAML (excluding the `Name` property, described later in this chapter, which is set immediately after object construction). This enables appropriate events to be raised in response to properties being set without worrying about the order of attributes used in XAML.
>
> The ordering of multiple property sets and multiple event handler attachments is usually performed in the relative order that property attributes and event attributes are specified on the object element. Fortunately, this ordering shouldn't matter in practice because design guidelines dictate that classes should allow properties to be set in any order, and the same holds true for attaching event handlers.

The root object element in a XAML file must specify at least one XML namespace that is used to qualify itself and any child elements. You can declare additional XML namespaces (on the root or on children), but each one must be given a distinct prefix to be used on any identifiers from that namespace. `MainPage.xaml` in the preceding chapter contains the XML namespaces listed in Table 2.1.

TABLE 2.1   The XML Namespaces in Chapter 1's `MainPage.xaml`

Namespace	Typical Prefix	Description
`http://schemas.microsoft.com/winfx/2006/xaml/presentation`	(none)	The standard UI namespace. Contains elements such as `Grid`, `Button`, and `TextBlock`.
`http://schemas.microsoft.com/winfx/2006/xaml`	x	The XAML language namespace. Contains keywords such as `Class`, `Name`, and `Key`.
`using:HelloRealWorld`	local	This `using:XXX` syntax is the way to use any custom Windows Runtime or .NET namespace in a XAML file. In this case, `HelloRealWorld` is the .NET namespace generated for the project in Chapter 1 because the project itself was named "HelloRealWorld."

TABLE 2.1   Continued

Namespace	Typical Prefix	Description
`http://schemas.microsoft.com/expression/blend/2008`	d	A namespace for design-time information that helps tools like Blend and Visual Studio show a proper preview.
`http://schemas.openxmlformats.org/markup-compatibility/2006`	mc	A markup compatibility namespace that can be used to mark other namespaces/elements as ignorable. Normally used with the design-time namespace, whose attributes should be ignored at runtime.

The first two namespaces are almost always used in any XAML file. The second one (with the x prefix) is the *XAML language namespace*, which defines some special directives for the XAML parser. These directives often appear as attributes to XML elements, so they look like properties of the host element but actually are not. For a list of XAML keywords, see the "XAML Keywords" section later in this chapter.

> Most of the standalone XAML examples in this chapter explicitly specify their namespaces, but in the remainder of the book, most examples assume that the UI XML namespace (`http://schemas.microsoft.com/winfx/2006/xaml/presentation`) is declared as the primary namespace, and the XAML language namespace (`http://schemas.microsoft.com/winfx/2006/xaml`) is declared as a secondary namespace, with the prefix x.

Using the UI XML namespace (`http://schemas.microsoft.com/winfx/2006/xaml/presentation`) as a default namespace and the XAML language namespace (`http://schemas.microsoft.com/winfx/2006/xaml`) as a secondary namespace with the prefix x is just a convention, just like it's a convention to begin a C# file with a `using System;` directive. You could declare a `Button` in XAML as follows, and it would be equivalent to the `Button` defined previously:

```
<UiNamespace:Button
  xmlns:UiNamespace="http://schemas.microsoft.com/winfx/2006/xaml/presentation"
  Content="Stop"/>
```

Of course, for readability it makes sense for your most commonly used namespace (also known as the *primary* XML namespace) to be prefix free and to use short prefixes for any additional namespaces.

The last two namespaces in Table 2.1, which are injected into pages generated by Visual Studio and Blend, are usually not needed.

Markup Compatibility   •••

The markup compatibility XML namespace (http://schemas.openxmlformats.org/markup-compatibility/2006, typically used with an mc prefix) contains an Ignorable attribute that instructs XAML processors to ignore all elements/attributes in specified namespaces if they can't be resolved to their types/members. (The namespace also has a ProcessContent attribute that overrides Ignorable for specific types inside the ignored namespaces.)

Blend and Visual Studio take advantage of this feature to do things like add design-time properties to XAML content that can be ignored at runtime. mc:Ignorable can be given a space-delimited list of namespaces, and mc:ProcessContent can be given a space-delimited list of elements.

If you're frustrated by how long it takes to open XAML files in Visual Studio and you don't care about previewing the visuals, you might consider changing your default editor for XAML files by right-clicking on a XAML file in Solution Explorer then selecting **Open With..., XML (Text) Editor**, clicking **Set as Default**, then clicking **OK**. This has several major drawbacks, however, such as losing IntelliSense support and other editor shortcuts. And in Visual Studio 2013, XAML IntelliSense and editor shortcuts are better than ever!

Property Elements

Rich composition of controls is one of the highlights of XAML. This can be easily demonstrated with a Button, because you can put arbitrary content inside it; you're not limited to just text! To demonstrate this, the following code embeds a simple square to make a Stop button like what might be found in a media player:

```
Windows.UI.Xaml.Controls.Button b = new Windows.UI.Xaml.Controls.Button();
b.Width = 96;
b.Height = 38;
Windows.UI.Xaml.Shapes.Rectangle r = new Windows.UI.Xaml.Shapes.Rectangle();
r.Width = 10;
r.Height = 10;
r.Fill = new Windows.UI.Xaml.Media.SolidColorBrush(Windows.UI.Colors.White);
b.Content = r; // Make the square the content of the Button
```

Button's Content property is of type System.Object, so it can easily be set to the 10x10 Rectangle object. The result (when used with additional code that adds it to a page) is pictured in Figure 2.1.

That's pretty neat, but how can you do the same thing in XAML with property attribute syntax? What kind of string could you possibly set Content to that is

FIGURE 2.1   Placing complex content inside a Button

equivalent to the preceding Rectangle declared in C#? There is no such string, but XAML fortunately provides an alternative (and more verbose) syntax for setting complex property values: *property elements*. It looks like the following:

```
<Button xmlns="http://schemas.microsoft.com/winfx/2006/xaml/presentation"
  Width="96" Height="38">
  <Button.Content>
    <Rectangle Width="10" Height="10" Fill="White"/>
  </Button.Content>
</Button>
```

The Content property is now set with an XML element instead of an XML attribute, making it equivalent to the previous C# code. The period in Button.Content is what distinguishes property elements from object elements. Property elements always take the form *TypeName.PropertyName*, they are always contained inside a *TypeName* object element, and they can never have attributes of their own.

Property element syntax can be used for simple property values as well. The following Button that sets two properties with attributes (Content and Background):

```
<Button xmlns="http://schemas.microsoft.com/winfx/2006/xaml/presentation"
  Content="Stop" Background="Red"/>
```

is equivalent to this Button, which sets the same two properties with elements:

```
<Button xmlns="http://schemas.microsoft.com/winfx/2006/xaml/presentation">
  <Button.Content>
    Stop
  </Button.Content>
  <Button.Background>
    Red
  </Button.Background>
</Button>
```

Of course, using attributes when you can is a nice shortcut when hand-typing XAML.

Type Converters

Let's look at the C# code equivalent to the preceding Button declaration that sets both Content and Background properties:

```
Windows.UI.Xaml.Controls.Button b = new Windows.UI.Xaml.Controls.Button();
b.Content = "Stop";
b.Background = new Windows.UI.Xaml.Media.SolidColorBrush(Windows.UI.Color.Red);
```

Wait a minute. How can "Red" in the previous XAML file be equivalent to the SolidColorBrush instance used in the C# code? Indeed, this example exposes a subtlety with using strings to set properties in XAML that are a different data type than System.String or System.Object. In such cases, the XAML parser must look for a *type converter* that knows how to convert the string representation to the desired data type.

You cannot currently create your own type converters, but type converters already exist for many common data types. Unlike the XAML language, these type converters support case-insensitive strings. Without a type converter for Brush (the base class of SolidColorBrush), you would have to use property element syntax to set the Background in XAML as follows.

```
<Button xmlns="http://schemas.microsoft.com/winfx/2006/xaml/presentation"
  Content="Stop">
  <Button.Background>
    <SolidColorBrush Color="Red"/>
  </Button.Background>
</Button>
```

And even that is only possible because of a type converter for Color that can make sense of the "Red" string. If there were no Color type converter, you would basically be stuck. Type converters don't just enhance the readability of XAML; they also enable values to be expressed that couldn't otherwise be expressed.

Unlike in the previous C# code, in this case, misspelling Red would not cause a compilation error but would cause an exception at runtime. However, Visual Studio does provide compile-time warnings for mistakes in XAML such as this.

Markup Extensions

Markup extensions, like type converters, extend the expressiveness of XAML. Both can evaluate a string attribute value at runtime and produce an appropriate object based on the string. As with type converters, you cannot currently create your own, but several markup extensions are built in.

Unlike type converters, markup extensions are invoked from XAML with explicit and consistent syntax. Whenever an attribute value is enclosed in curly braces ({}), the XAML parser treats it as a markup extension value rather than a literal string or something that needs to be type-converted. The following Button uses two different markup extensions as the values for two different properties:

```
<Button xmlns="http://schemas.microsoft.com/winfx/2006/xaml/presentation"
        xmlns:x="http://schemas.microsoft.com/winfx/2006/xaml"
        Height="50"
        Background="{x:Null}"      ── Markup extension
        Content="{Binding Height, RelativeSource={RelativeSource Self}}"/>
                          │                       │
                   Positional para-          Named
                        meter               parameter
```

The first identifier in each set of curly braces is the name of the markup extension. The `Null` extension lives in the XAML language namespace, so the x prefix must be used. `Binding` (which happens to be a class in the `Windows.UI.Xaml.Data` namespace), can be found in the default XML namespace.

If a markup extension supports them, comma-delimited parameters can be specified. Positional parameters (such as `Height` in the example) are treated as string arguments for the extension class's appropriate constructor. Named parameters (`RelativeSource` in the example) enable you to set properties with matching names on the constructed extension object. The values for these properties can be markup extension values themselves (using nested curly braces, as done with the value for `RelativeSource`) or literal values that can undergo the normal type conversion process. If you're familiar with .NET custom attributes (the .NET Framework's popular extensibility mechanism), you've probably noticed that the design and usage of markup extensions closely mirrors the design and usage of custom attributes. That is intentional.

In the preceding `Button` declaration, `x:Null` enables the `Background` brush to be set to null. This is just done for demonstration purposes, because a `null` `Background` is not very useful. `Binding`, covered in depth in Chapter 19, "Data Binding," enables `Content` to be set to the same value as the `Height` property.

• • •

Escaping the Curly Braces

If you ever want a property attribute value to be set to a literal string beginning with an open curly brace ({), you must escape it so it doesn't get treated as a markup extension. This can be done by preceding it with an empty pair of curly braces, as in the following example:

```
<Button xmlns="http://schemas.microsoft.com/winfx/2006/xaml/presentation"
        Content="{}{This is not a markup extension!}"/>
```

Alternatively, you could use property element syntax without any escaping because the curly braces do not have special meaning in this context. The preceding `Button` could be rewritten as follows:

```
<Button xmlns="http://schemas.microsoft.com/winfx/2006/xaml/presentation">
<Button.Content>
  {This is not a markup extension!}
</Button.Content>
</Button>
```

Markup extensions can also be used with property element syntax. The following `Button` is identical to the preceding one:

```
<Button xmlns="http://schemas.microsoft.com/winfx/2006/xaml/presentation"
        xmlns:x="http://schemas.microsoft.com/winfx/2006/xaml">
  <Button.Height>
```

```
  </Button.Height>
  <Button.Background>
    <x:Null/>
  </Button.Background>
  <Button.Content>
    <Binding Path="Height">
      <Binding.RelativeSource>
        <RelativeSource Mode="Self"/>
      </Binding.RelativeSource>
    </Binding>
  </Button.Content>
</Button>
```

This transformation works because these markup extensions all have properties corresponding to their parameterized constructor arguments (the positional parameters used with property attribute syntax). For example, Binding has a Path property that has the same meaning as the argument that was previously passed to its parameterized constructor, and RelativeSource has a Mode property that corresponds to its constructor argument.

• • •

Markup Extensions and Procedural Code

The actual work done by a markup extension is specific to each extension. For example, the following C# code is equivalent to the XAML-based Button that uses Null and Binding:

```
Windows.UI.Xaml.Controls.Button b = new Windows.UI.Xaml.Controls.Button();
b.Height = 50;
// Set Background:
b.Background = null;
// Set Content:
Windows.UI.Xaml.Data.Binding binding = new Windows.UI.Xaml.Data.Binding();
binding.Path = new Windows.UI.Xaml.PropertyPath("Height");
binding.RelativeSource = Windows.UI.Xaml.Data.RelativeSource.Self;
b.SetBinding(Windows.UI.Xaml.Controls.Button.ContentProperty, binding);
```

Children of Object Elements

A XAML file, like all XML files, must have a single root object element. Therefore, it should come as no surprise that object elements can support child object elements (not just property elements, which aren't children, as far as XAML is concerned). An object element can have three types of children: a value for a content property, collection items, or a value that can be type-converted to the object element.

The Content Property

Many classes designed to be used in XAML designate a property (via a custom attribute) that should be set to whatever content is inside the XML element. This property is called the *content property*, and it is just a convenient shortcut to make the XAML representation more compact.

Button's Content property is (appropriately) given this special designation, so the following Button:

```
<Button xmlns="http://schemas.microsoft.com/winfx/2006/xaml/presentation"
  Content="Stop"/>
```

could be rewritten as follows:

```
<Button xmlns="http://schemas.microsoft.com/winfx/2006/xaml/presentation">
  Stop
</Button>
```

Or, more usefully, this Button with more complex content:

```
<Button xmlns="http://schemas.microsoft.com/winfx/2006/xaml/presentation">
<Button.Content>
  <Rectangle Height="10" Width="10" Fill="White"/>
</Button.Content>
</Button>
```

could be rewritten as follows:

```
<Button xmlns="http://schemas.microsoft.com/winfx/2006/xaml/presentation">
  <Rectangle Height="10" Width="10" Fill="White"/>
</Button>
```

There is no requirement that the content property must be called Content; classes such as ComboBox and ListBox (also in the Windows.UI.Xaml.Controls namespace) use their Items property as the content property.

Collection Items

XAML enables you to add items to the two main types of collections that support indexing: lists and dictionaries.

Lists

A *list* is any collection that implements the IList interface or its generic counterpart. For example, the following XAML adds two items to a ListBox control whose Items property is an ItemCollection that implements IList<object>:

```
<ListBox xmlns="http://schemas.microsoft.com/winfx/2006/xaml/presentation">
<ListBox.Items>
  <ListBoxItem Content="Item 1"/>
  <ListBoxItem Content="Item 2"/>
</ListBox.Items>
</ListBox>
```

This is equivalent to the following C# code:

```
Windows.UI.Xaml.Controls.ListBox listbox =
  new Windows.UI.Xaml.Controls.ListBox();
Windows.UI.Xaml.Controls.ListBoxItem item1 =
  new Windows.UI.Xaml.Controls.ListBoxItem();
Windows.UI.Xaml.Controls.ListBoxItem item2 =
  new Windows.UI.Xaml.Controls.ListBoxItem();
item1.Content = "Item 1";
item2.Content = "Item 2";
listbox.Items.Add(item1);
listbox.Items.Add(item2);
```

Furthermore, because Items is the content property for ListBox, you can shorten the XAML even further, as follows:

```
<ListBox xmlns="http://schemas.microsoft.com/winfx/2006/xaml/presentation">
  <ListBoxItem Content="Item 1"/>
  <ListBoxItem Content="Item 2"/>
</ListBox>
```

In all these cases, the code works because ListBox's Items property is automatically initialized to any empty collection object. If a collection property is initially null instead (and is read/write, unlike ListBox's read-only Items property), you would need to wrap the items in an explicit element that instantiates the collection. The built-in controls do not act this way, so an imaginary OtherListBox element demonstrates what this could look like:

```
<OtherListBox>
<OtherListBox.Items>
  <ItemCollection>
    <ListBoxItem Content="Item 1"/>
    <ListBoxItem Content="Item 2"/>
  </ItemCollection>
</OtherListBox.Items>
</OtherListBox>
```

Dictionaries

A *dictionary* is any collection that implements the IDictionary interface or its generic counterpart. Windows.UI.Xaml.ResourceDictionary is a commonly used collection type that you'll see more of in later chapters. It implements IDictionary<object, object>, so it supports adding, removing, and enumerating key/value pairs in procedural code, as you would do with a typical hash table. In XAML, you can add key/value pairs to any dictionary. For example, the following XAML adds two Colors to a ResourceDictionary:

```
<ResourceDictionary
  xmlns="http://schemas.microsoft.com/winfx/2006/xaml/presentation"
  xmlns:x="http://schemas.microsoft.com/winfx/2006/xaml">
  <Color x:Key="1">White</Color>
  <Color x:Key="2">Black</Color>
</ResourceDictionary>
```

This leverages the XAML Key keyword (defined in the secondary XML namespace), which is processed specially and enables us to attach a key to each Color value. (The Color type does not define a Key property.) Therefore, the XAML is equivalent to the following C# code:

```
Windows.UI.Xaml.ResourceDictionary d = new Windows.UI.Xaml.ResourceDictionary();
Windows.UI.Color color1 = Windows.UI.Colors.White;
Windows.UI.Color color2 = Windows.UI.Colors.Black;
d.Add("1", color1);
d.Add("2", color2);
```

Note that the value specified in XAML with x:Key is treated as a string unless a markup extension is used; no type conversion is attempted otherwise.

More Type Conversion

Plain text can often be used as the child of an object element, as in the following XAML declaration of SolidColorBrush:

```
<SolidColorBrush>White</SolidColorBrush>
```

As explained earlier, this is equivalent to the following:

```
<SolidColorBrush Color="White"/>
```

even though Color has not been designated as a content property. In this case, the first XAML snippet works because a type converter exists that can convert strings such as "White" (or "white" or "#FFFFFF") into a SolidColorBrush object.

Although type converters play a huge role in making XAML readable, the downside is that they can make XAML appear a bit "magical," and it can be difficult to understand how it maps to instances of objects. Using what you know so far, it would be reasonable to assume that you can't declare an instance of a class in XAML if it has no default constructor. However, even though the `Windows.UI.Xaml.Media.Brush` base class for `SolidColorBrush`, `LinearGradientBrush`, and other brushes has no constructors at all, you can express the preceding XAML snippets as :

```xaml
<Brush>White</Brush>
```

because the type converter for `Brushes` understands that this is still `SolidColorBrush`.

The Extensible Part of XAML

Because XAML was designed to work with the .NET type system, you can use it with just about any object, including ones you define yourself. It doesn't matter whether these objects have anything to do with a user interface. However, the objects need to be designed in a "declarative-friendly" way. For example, if a class doesn't have a default constructor and doesn't expose useful instance properties, it's not going to be directly usable from XAML. A lot of care went into the design of the APIs in the `Windows.UI.Xaml` namespace—above and beyond the usual design guidelines—to fit XAML's declarative model.

To use an arbitrary .NET class (with a default constructor) in XAML, simply include the proper namespace with `using` syntax. The following XAML does this with an instance of `System.Net.Http.HttpClient` and `System.Int64`:

```xaml
<ListBox xmlns="http://schemas.microsoft.com/winfx/2006/xaml/presentation">
  <ListBox.Items>
    <sysnet:HttpClient xmlns:sysnet="using:System.Net.Http"/>
    <sys:Int64 xmlns:sys="using:System">100</sys:Int64>
  </ListBox.Items>
</ListBox>
```

> The XAML language namespace defines keywords for a few common primitives so you don't need to separately include the System namespace: `x:Boolean`, `x:Int32`, `x:Double`, and `x:String`.

XAML Processing Rules for Object Element Children

You've now seen the three types of children for object elements. To avoid ambiguity, any valid XAML parser follows these rules when encountering and interpreting child elements:

1. If the type implements `IList`, call `IList.Add` for each child.
2. Otherwise, if the type implements `IDictionary`, call `IDictionary.Add` for each child, using the `x:Key` attribute value for the key and the element for the value.

• • •

3. Otherwise, if the parent supports a content property (indicated by `Windows.UI.Xaml.Markup.ContentPropertyAttribute`) and the type of the child is compatible with that property, treat the child as its value.

4. Otherwise, if the child is plain text and a type converter exists to transform the child into the parent type (*and* no properties are set on the parent element), treat the child as the input to the type converter and use the output as the parent object instance.

5. Otherwise, treat it as unknown content and raise an error.

Rules 1 and 2 enable the behavior described in the earlier "Collection Items" section, rule 3 enables the behavior described in the section "The Content Property," and rule 4 explains the often-confusing behavior described in the "More Type Conversion" section.

Mixing XAML with Procedural Code

XAML-based Windows Store apps are a mix of XAML and procedural code like C#. This section covers the two ways that XAML and procedural code can be mixed together: dynamically loading and parsing XAML yourself, or leveraging the built-in support in Visual Studio projects.

Loading and Parsing XAML at Runtime

The `Windows.UI.Xaml.Markup` namespace contains a simple `XamlReader` class with a simple static `Load` method. `Load` can parse a string containing XAML, create the appropriate objects, and return an instance of the root element. So, with a string containing XAML content somewhat like `MainPage.xaml` from the preceding chapter, the following code could be used to load and retrieve the root `Page` object:

```
string xamlString = …;
// Get the root element, which we know is a Page
Page p = (Page)XamlReader.Load(xamlString);
```

After `Load` returns, the entire hierarchy of objects in the XAML file is instantiated in memory, so the XAML itself is no longer needed. Now that an instance of the root element exists, you can retrieve child elements by making use of the appropriate content properties or collection properties. The following code assumes that the `Page` has a `StackPanel` object as its content, whose fifth child is a Stop button:

```
string xamlString = …;
// Get the root element, which we know is a Page
Page p = (Page)XamlReader.Load(xamlString);
// Grab the Stop button by walking the children (with hard-coded knowledge!)
StackPanel panel = (StackPanel)p.Content;
Button stopButton = (Button)panel.Children[4];
```

With a reference to the `Button` control, you can do whatever you want: set additional properties (perhaps using logic that is hard or impossible to express in XAML), attach event handlers, or perform additional actions that you can't do from XAML, such as calling its methods.

Of course, the code that uses a hard-coded index and other assumptions about the user interface structure isn't satisfying, because simple changes to the XAML can break it. Instead, you could write code to process the elements more generically and look for a Button element whose content is a "Stop" string, but that would be a lot of work for such a simple task. In addition, if you want the Button to contain graphical content, how can you easily identify it in the presence of multiple Buttons?

Fortunately, XAML supports naming of elements so they can be found and used reliably from procedural code.

Naming XAML Elements

The XAML language namespace has a Name keyword that enables you to give any element a name. For the simple Stop button that we're imagining is embedded somewhere inside a Page, the Name keyword can be used as follows:

```
<Button x:Name="stopButton">Stop</Button>
```

With this in place, you can update the preceding C# code to use Page's FindName method that searches its children (recursively) and returns the desired instance:

```
string xamlString = …;
// Get the root element, which we know is a Page
Page p = (Page)XamlReader.Load(xamlString);
// Grab the Stop button, knowing only its name
Button stopButton = (Button)p.FindName("stopButton");
```

FindName is not unique to Page; it is defined on FrameworkElement, a base class for many important classes in the XAML UI Framework.

Visual Studio's Support for XAML and Code-Behind

Loading and parsing XAML at runtime can be interesting for some limited dynamic scenarios. Windows Store projects, however, leverage work done by MSBuild and Visual Studio to make the combination of XAML and procedural code more seamless. When you compile a project with XAML files, the XAML is included as a resource in the app being built and the plumbing that connects XAML with procedural code is generated automatically.

> **• • •**
> **Naming Elements Without x:Name**
>
> The x:Name syntax can be used to name elements, but FrameworkElement also has a Name property that accomplishes the same thing. You can use either mechanism on such elements, but you can't use both simultaneously. Having two ways to set a name is a bit confusing, but it's handy for these classes to have a Name property for use by procedural code. In addition, sometimes you want to name an element that doesn't derive from FrameworkElement (and doesn't have a Name property), so x:Name is necessary for such cases.

The automatic connection between a XAML file and a code-behind file is enabled by the `Class` keyword from the XAML language namespace, as seen in the preceding chapter. For example, `MainPage.xaml` had the following:

```
<Page x:Class="HelloRealWorld.MainPage" …>
  …
</Page>
```

This causes the XAML content to be treated as a partial class definition for a class called `MainPage` (in the `HelloRealWorld` namespace) derived from `Page`. The other pieces of the partial class definition reside in auto-generated files as well as the `MainPage.xaml.cs` code-behind file. Visual Studio's Solution Explorer ties these two files together by making the code-behind file a subnode of the XAML file, but that is an optional cosmetic effect enabled by the following XML inside of the `.csproj` project file:

```
<Compile Include="MainPage.xaml.cs">
  <DependentUpon>MainPage.xaml</DependentUpon>
</Compile>
```

You can freely add members to the class in the code-behind file. And if you reference any event handlers in XAML (via event attributes such as `Click` on `Button`), this is where they should be defined.

Whenever you add a page to a Visual Studio project (via **Add New Item…**), Visual Studio automatically creates a XAML file with `x:Class` on its root, creates the code-behind source file with the partial class definition, and links the two together so they are built properly.

The additional auto-generated files alluded to earlier contain some "glue code" that you normally never see and you should never directly edit. For a XAML file named `MainPage.xaml`, they are:

→ `MainPage.g.cs`, which contains code that attaches event handlers to events for each event attribute assigned in the XAML file.

→ `MainPage.g.i.cs`, which contains a field definition (private by default) for each named element in the XAML file, using the element name as the field name. It also contains an `InitializeComponent` method that the root class's constructor must call in the code-behind file. This file is meant to be helpful to IntelliSense, which is why it has an "i" in its name.

The "g" in both filenames stands for *generated*. Both generated source files contain a partial class definition for the same class partially defined by the XAML file and code-behind file.

If you peek at the implementation of `InitializeComponent` inside the auto-generated file, you'll see that the hookup between C# and XAML isn't so magical after all. It looks a lot like the code shown previously for manually loading XAML content and grabbing named elements from the tree of instantiated objects. Here's what the method looks like for the preceding chapter's MainPage if a Button named stopButton were added to it:

```
public void InitializeComponent()
{
  if (_contentLoaded)
    return;

  _contentLoaded = true;
  Application.LoadComponent(this, new System.Uri("ms-appx:///MainPage.xaml"),
    Windows.UI.Xaml.Controls.Primitives.ComponentResourceLocation.Application);

  stopButton = (Windows.UI.Xaml.Controls.Button)this.FindName("stopButton");
}
```

The LoadComponent method is much like XamlReader's Load method, except it works with a reference to an app's resource file.

> To reference a resource file included with your app, simply use a URI with the format "ms-appx:///relative path to file". XAML files are already treated specially, but adding a new resource file to your app is as simple as adding a new file to your project with a **Build Action** of **Content**. Chapter 13, "Images," shows how to use resources such as image files with the Image element.

XAML Binary Format

By default, your app's package does not contain your .xaml source files but rather binary .xbf files known as XAML binary format. These files contain optimized node streams representing the original XAML content, which results in a startup performance improvement of up to 25% thanks to removing the need to load and parse XAML at run-time. This feature is new to Windows 8.1 and Visual Studio 2013.

XAML Keywords

The XAML language namespace (http://schemas.microsoft.com/winfx/2006/xaml) defines a handful of keywords that must be treated specially by any XAML parser. They mostly control aspects of how elements get exposed to procedural code, but several are useful independent of procedural code. You've already seen some of them (such as Key, Name, and Class), but Table 2.2 lists all the ones relevant for Windows Store apps. They are listed with the conventional x prefix because that is how they usually appear in XAML and in documentation.

Special Attributes Defined by the W3C   **• • •**

In addition to keywords in the XAML language namespace, XAML also supports two special attributes defined for XML by the World Wide Web Consortium (W3C): `xml:space` for controlling whitespace parsing and `xml:lang` for declaring the document's language and culture. The `xml` prefix is implicitly mapped to the standard XML namespace; see `http://www.w3.org/XML/1998/namespace`.

TABLE 2.2   Keywords in the XAML Language Namespace, According to the Conventional x Namespace Prefix

Keyword	Valid As	Meaning
x:Boolean	An element	Represents a `System.Boolean`.
x:Class	Attribute on root element	Defines a namespace-qualified class for the root element that derives from the element type.
x:Double	An element	Represents a `System.Double`.
x:FieldModifier	Attribute on any nonroot element but must be used with `x:Name` (or equivalent)	Defines the visibility of the field to be generated for the element (which is private by default). The value must be specified in terms of the procedural language (for example, `public`, `private`, and `internal` for C#).
x:Int32	An element	Represents a `System.Int32`.
x:Key	Attribute on an element whose parent is a dictionary	Specifies the key for the item when added to the parent dictionary.
x:Name	Attribute on any nonroot element but must be used with `x:Class` on root	Chooses a name for the field to be generated for the element, so it can be referenced from procedural code.
x:Null	An element or an attribute value as a markup extension	Represents a `null` value.
x:StaticResource	An element or an attribute value as a markup extension	References a XAML resource.
x:String	An element	Represents a `System.String`.
x:Subclass	Attribute on root element and must be used with `x:Class`	Specifies a subclass of the `x:Class` class that holds the content defined in XAML. This is only needed for languages without support for partial classes, so there's no reason to use this in a C# XAML project.
x:TemplateBinding	An element or an attribute value as a markup extension	Binds to an element's properties from within a template, as described in Chapter 18.
x:ThemeResource	An element or an attribute value as a markup extension	References a theme-specific XAML resource
x:Uid	Attribute on any element	Marks an element with an identifier used for localization.

Summary

You have now seen how XAML fits in with the rest of an app's code and, most importantly, you now have the information needed to translate most XAML examples into a language such as C# and vice versa. However, because type converters and markup extensions are "black boxes," a straightforward translation is not always going to be obvious.

As you proceed further, you might find that some APIs can be a little clunky to use in C# because their design is often optimized for XAML use. For example, the XAML UI Framework exposes many small building blocks to help enable rich composition, so some scenarios can involve manually creating a lot of objects. Besides the fact the XAML excels at expressing deep hierarchies of objects concisely, Microsoft spent more time implementing features to effectively hide intermediate objects in XAML (such as type converters) rather than features to hide them from procedural code (such as constructors that create inner objects on your behalf).

In some areas (such as complicated paths and shapes), typing XAML by hand isn't practical. In fact, the trend from when XAML was first introduced in beta form has been to remove some of the handy human-typeable shortcuts in favor of a more robust and extensible format that can be supported well by tools. But I still believe that being familiar with XAML and seeing the APIs through both procedural and declarative perspectives is the best way to learn the technology. It's like understanding how HTML works without relying on a visual tool.

Classes in the XAML UI Framework have a deep inheritance hierarchy, so it can be hard to get your head wrapped around the significance of various classes and their relationships. A handful of fundamental classes are referenced often and deserve a quick explanation before we get any further in the book. The Page class, for example, derives from a UserControl class which derives from all of the following classes, in order from most to least derived:

→ **Control**—The base class for familiar controls such as Button and ListBox. Control adds many properties to its base class, such as Foreground, Background, and FontSize, as well as the ability to be given a completely new visual template. Part IV, "Understanding Controls," examines the built-in controls in depth.

→ **FrameworkElement**—The base class that adds support for styles, data binding, XAML resources, and a few common mechanisms such as tooltips and context menus.

→ **UIElement**—The base class for all visual objects with support for routed events, layout, and focus. These features are discussed in Chapter 4, "Layout," and Chapter 5, "Interactivity."

→ **DependencyObject**—The base class for any object that can support dependency properties, also discussed in Chapter 5.

→ **Object**—The base class for all .NET classes.

Throughout the book, the simple term *element* is used to refer to an object that derives from UIElement or FrameworkElement. The distinction between UIElement and FrameworkElement is not important because the framework doesn't include any other public subclasses of UIElement.

Chapter 3

SIZING, POSITIONING, AND TRANSFORMING ELEMENTS

When building an app, one of the first things you must do is arrange a bunch of elements in its window. This sizing and positioning of elements is called *layout*. XAML apps are provided a feature-rich layout system that covers everything from placing elements at exact coordinates to building experiences that scale and rearrange across a wide range of screen resolutions and aspect ratios. This is essential for handling the diversity of Windows devices, as well as intelligently handling when your app isn't the only one on the screen.

In XAML apps, layout boils down to interactions between parent elements and their child elements. Parents and their children work together to determine their final sizes and positions. Although parents ultimately tell their children where to render and how much space they get, they are more like collaborators than dictators; parents also *ask* their children how much space they would like before making their final decision.

Parent elements that support the arrangement of multiple children are known as *panels*, and they derive from a class called Panel. All the elements involved in the layout process (both parents and children) derive from UIElement.

Because layout is such an important topic, this book dedicates three chapters to it. This chapter focuses on the children, examining the common ways that you can control layout on a child-by-child basis. Several properties control these aspects, most of which are summarized in Figure 3.1 for an arbitrary element inside an arbitrary panel. Size-related properties are shown in blue, and position-related properties are shown in red. In addition, elements can have transforms applied to them (shown in green) that can affect both size and position.

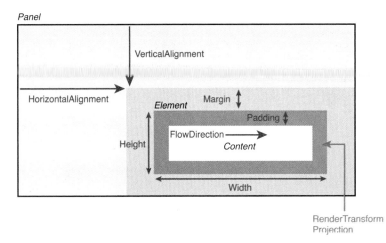

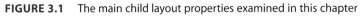

FIGURE 3.1   The main child layout properties examined in this chapter

The next chapter continues the layout story by examining the variety of built-in parent panels, each of which arranges its children in unique ways. Creating custom panels is an advanced topic reserved for Chapter 28, "Layout with Custom Panels."

Controlling Size

Every time layout occurs, such as when an app's window is resized or the screen is rotated, child elements tell their parent panel their desired size. Elements tend to *size to their content*, meaning that they try to be large enough to fit their content and no larger. This size can be influenced on individual instances of children via several straightforward properties.

Height and Width

All `FrameworkElement`s have simple `Height` and `Width` properties (of type `double`), and they also have `MinHeight`, `MaxHeight`, `MinWidth`, and `MaxWidth` properties that can be used to specify a range of acceptable values. Any or all of these can be easily set on elements in C# or in XAML.

An element naturally stays as small as possible, so if you use `MinHeight` or `MinWidth`, it is rendered at that height/width unless its content forces it to grow. In addition, that growth can be limited by using `MaxHeight` and `MaxWidth`—as long as these values are larger than their `Min` counterparts. When using an explicit `Height` and `Width` at the same time as their `Min` and `Max` counterparts, `Height` and `Width` take precedence as long as they are in the range from `Min` to `Max`. The default value of `MinHeight` and `MinWidth` is `0`, and the default value of MaxHeight and MaxWidth is Double.PositiveInfinity (which can be set in XAML as simply "Infinity").

> **(!) Avoid setting explicit sizes!**
>
> Giving controls explicit sizes makes it difficult to adapt to different screen sizes and orientations, and could cause text to be cut off if you ever translate it into other languages, as demonstrated in Chapter 1, "Hello, *Real* World!" Therefore, you should avoid setting explicit sizes unless absolutely necessary. Fortunately, setting explicit sizes is rarely necessary, thanks to the panels described in the next chapter.

To complicate matters, FrameworkElement also contains a few more size-related properties:

→ DesiredSize (inherited from UIElement)

→ RenderSize (inherited from UIElement)

→ ActualHeight and ActualWidth

Unlike the other six properties that are *input* to the layout process, however, these are read-only properties representing *output* from the layout process. An element's DesiredSize is calculated during layout, based on other property values (such as the aforementioned Width, Height, Min*XXX*, and Max*XXX* properties) and the amount of space its parent currently gives it. It is used internally by panels.

RenderSize represents the final size of an element after layout is complete, and ActualHeight and ActualWidth are exactly the same as RenderSize.Height and RenderSize.Width, respectively. That's right: Whether an element specified an explicit size, specified a range of acceptable sizes, or didn't specify anything at all, the behavior of the parent can alter an element's final size on the screen. These three properties are, therefore, useful for advanced scenarios in which you need to programmatically act on an element's size. The values of all the other size-related properties, on the other hand, aren't very interesting to base logic on. For example, when not set explicitly, the value of Height and Width are Double.NaN, regardless of the element's true size.

> **Be careful when writing code that uses `ActualHeight` and `ActualWidth` (or `RenderSize`)!**
>
> Every time the layout process occurs, it updates the values of each element's `RenderSize` (and, therefore, `ActualHeight` and `ActualWidth` as well). However, you can't rely on the values of these properties at all times. It's safe to rely on their values within an event handler for the `LayoutUpdated` event defined on `FrameworkElement`. At the same time, you must not alter layout from within a `LayoutUpdated` handler. If you do, an exception will be thrown pointing out that you introduced a cycle.
>
> `UIElement`'s `void InvalidateLayout` method forces any pending layout updates to occur, but you should avoid using this method. Besides the fact that frequent calls to `UpdateLayout` can harm performance because of the excess layout processing, there's no guarantee that the elements you're using properly handle the potential reentrancy in their layout-related methods.

Margin and Padding

`Margin` and `Padding` are two similar properties that are also related to an element's size. All `FrameworkElements` have a `Margin` property, and all `Controls` (plus many other elements) have a `Padding` property. Their only difference is that `Margin` controls how much extra space gets placed around the *outside* edges of the element, whereas `Padding` controls how much extra space gets placed around the *inside* edges of the element.

Both `Margin` and `Padding` are of type `Thickness`, an interesting class that can represent one, two, or four `double` values. Here is how the values are interpreted when set in XAML:

→ When set to a list of **four values**, the numbers represent the left, top, right, and bottom edges, respectively.

→ When set to a list of **two values**, the first number is used for the left and right edges and the second number is used for the top and bottom edges. So `"12,24"` is a shortcut way of specifying `"12,24,12,24"`.

→ When set to a **single value**, it is used for all four sides. So `"12"` is a shortcut way of specifying `"12,12"`, which is a shortcut for `"12,12,12,12"`.

→ Negative values may be used for margins (and often are), but are not allowed for padding.

→ The commas are optional. You can use spaces instead of, or in addition to, commas. `"12,24"` is the same as `"12 24"` and `"12, 24"`.

When creating a `Thickness` in C#, you can use its constructor that accepts either a single value or all four values:

```
this.TextBox.Margin = new Thickness(12);          // Margin="12" in XAML
this.TextBox.Margin = new Thickness(12,24,12,24); // Margin="12,24" in XAML
```

Note that the handy two-number syntax is a shortcut only available through XAML. Thickness does not have a two-parameter constructor.

FIGURE 3.2   Size matters when it comes to the device's screen, due to the automatic scaling called out in the "Display" dropdown.

The effect of this scaling can be easily seen with the following XAML placed in a Page:

```xaml
<StackPanel HorizontalAlignment="Left">
  <Rectangle Fill="Red" Height="100" Width="1000"/>
  <TextBlock Name="textBlock" FontSize="40"/>
</StackPanel>
```

with code-behind that sets the TextBlock's Text to the Page's current dimensions as reported by the XAML UI Framework:

```csharp
this.textBlock.Text = "Page size: " + this.ActualWidth + "x" + this.ActualHeight;
```

Figure 3.3 shows the result on two different simulator settings. In both cases, the red Rectangle is 1,000 units long as far as your code is concerned. However, it gets scaled larger on the smaller screen (and the Page's reported bounds are now smaller than the true resolution). Depending on the screen, a user can also bump up the scale from 100% to 140% or 140% to 180% by selecting the "Change the size of apps on the displays that can support it" option in the "Display" section of the PC Settings app.

23" screen at 1920x1080 (100% scale)

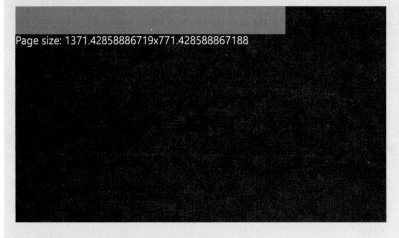

10.6" screen at 1920x1080 (140% scale)

FIGURE 3.3   The same page at the same resolution, but under two different simulator screen sizes

Controlling Position

This section doesn't discuss positioning elements with (X,Y) coordinates, as you might expect. Parent panels define their own unique mechanisms for enabling children to position themselves, and those are discussed in the next chapter. A few mechanisms are common to all FrameworkElement children, however, and that's what this section examines. These mechanisms are related to alignment and a concept called *flow direction*.

Alignment

The HorizontalAlignment and VerticalAlignment properties enable an element to control what it does with any extra space that its parent panel gives it. Each property has a corresponding enumeration with the same name, giving the following options:

→ **HorizontalAlignment**—Left, Center, Right, and Stretch

→ **VerticalAlignment**—Top, Center, Bottom, and Stretch

Stretch is the default value for both properties, although various controls override the setting. The effects of HorizontalAlignment can easily be seen by placing a few Buttons in a StackPanel (a panel described further in the next chapter) and marking them with each value from the enumeration:

```
<StackPanel>
  <Button HorizontalAlignment="Left" Content="Left" Background="Red"/>
  <Button HorizontalAlignment="Center" Content="Center" Background="Orange"/>
  <Button HorizontalAlignment="Right" Content="Right" Background="Green"/>
  <Button HorizontalAlignment="Stretch" Content="Stretch" Background="Blue"/>
</StackPanel>
```

Notice that an enumeration value such as HorizontalAlignment.Left is able to be specified in XAML as simply Left. This is thanks to a type converter that is able to handle any enumeration. The rendered result appears in Figure 3.4.

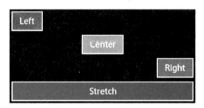

FIGURE 3.4 The effects of HorizontalAlignment on Buttons in a StackPanel

These two properties are useful only when a parent panel gives the child element more space than it needs. For example, adding VerticalAlignment values to elements in the StackPanel used in Figure 3.4 would make no difference, because each element is already given the exact amount of height it needs (no more, no less).

Interaction Between Stretch Alignment and Explicit Element Size

When an element uses Stretch alignment (horizontally or vertically), an explicit Height or Width setting still takes precedence. MaxHeight and MaxWidth also take precedence, but only when their values are smaller than the natural stretched size. Similarly, MinHeight and MinWidth take precedence only when their values are *larger* than the natural stretched size. When Stretch is used in a context that constrains the element's size, it acts like an alignment of Center (or Left if the element is too large to be centered in its parent).

Content Alignment

In addition to HorizontalAlignment and VerticalAlignment properties, the Control class also has Horizontal**Content**Alignment and Vertical**Content**Alignment properties. These properties determine how a control's *content* fills the space *within* the control. (Therefore, the relationship between alignment and content alignment is somewhat like the relationship between Margin and Padding.)

The content alignment properties are of the same enumeration types as the corresponding alignment properties, so they provide the same options. However, the default value for HorizontalContentAlignment is Left, and the default value for VerticalContentAlignment is Top. Some elements implicitly choose different defaults. Buttons, for example, center their content in both dimensions by default.

Figure 3.5 demonstrates the effects of HorizontalContentAlignment, simply by taking the previous XAML snippet and changing the property name as follows:

```
<StackPanel>
  <Button HorizontalContentAlignment="Left" HorizontalAlignment="Stretch"
          Content="Left" Background="Red"/>
  <Button HorizontalContentAlignment="Center" HorizontalAlignment="Stretch"
          Content="Center" Background="Orange"/>
  <Button HorizontalContentAlignment="Right" HorizontalAlignment="Stretch"
          Content="Right" Background="Green"/>
  <Button HorizontalContentAlignment="Stretch" HorizontalAlignment="Stretch"
          Content="Stretch" Background="Blue"/>
</StackPanel>
```

Each Button also has its HorizontalAlignment set to Stretch rather than its default of Left so the differences in HorizontalContent-Alignment are visible. Without this, each Button would auto-size to its content and there would be no extra space for the content to move within.

FIGURE 3.5   The effects of HorizontalContentAlignment on Buttons in a StackPanel

In Figure 3.5, the Button with HorizontalContentAlignment="Stretch" might not appear as you expected. Its inner TextBlock is technically stretched, but it's meaningless because TextBlock (which is not a Control) doesn't have the same notion for stretching its inner text. For other types of content, Stretch can indeed have the intended effect.

FlowDirection

FlowDirection is a property on FrameworkElement (and several other classes) that can reverse the way an element's inner content flows. It applies to some panels and their arrangement of children, and it also applies to the way content is aligned inside child controls. The property is of type FlowDirection, with two values: LeftToRight (FrameworkElement's default) and RightToLeft.

The idea of FlowDirection is that it should be set to RightToLeft when the current culture corresponds to a language that is read from right to left. This reverses the meaning of left and right for settings such as content alignment. The following XAML demonstrates this, with Buttons that force their content alignment to Top and Left but then apply each of the two FlowDirection values:

```xml
<StackPanel>
  <Button FlowDirection="LeftToRight"
          HorizontalContentAlignment="Left" Width="320"
          Background="Red">LeftToRight</Button>
  <Button FlowDirection="RightToLeft"
          HorizontalContentAlignment="Left" Width="320"
          Background="Orange">RightToLeft</Button>
</StackPanel>
```

The result is shown in Figure 3.6.

Notice that FlowDirection does not affect the flow of letters within these Buttons. English letters always flow left to right, and Arabic letters always flow right to left, for example. But

FIGURE 3.6   The effects of FlowDirection on Buttons with Left content alignment

FlowDirection reverses the notion of left and right for other pieces of the user interface, which typically need to match the flow direction of letters.

You must explicitly set FlowDirection to match the current culture, but fortunately you can do this on a single, top-level element. Windows doesn't automatically change FlowDirection on your behalf in order for the behavior to be predictable and easily testable. The idea is that you should specify FlowDirection appropriately inside the .resw file for each distinct culture you support. For example, if you include a resource with the name Root.FlowDirection, then you can mark a Page's root element with x:Uid="Root" to control FlowDirection on a per-culture basis. The resource just needs to be given the value of LeftToRight or RightToLeft.

Applying 2D Transforms

The XAML UI Framework contains a handful of built-in two-dimensional transform classes (derived from Transform) that enable you to change the size and position of elements independently from the previously discussed properties. Some also enable you to alter elements in more exotic ways, such as by rotating or skewing them.

All UIElements have a RenderTransform property that can be set to any Transform in order to change its appearance *after* the layout process has finished (immediately before the element is rendered). They also have a handy RenderTransformOrigin property that represents the starting point of the transform (the point that remains stationary). Figure 3.7 demonstrates the impact of setting `RenderTransformOrigin` to five different (x,y) values when used with one of the `Transform` objects that performs rotation.

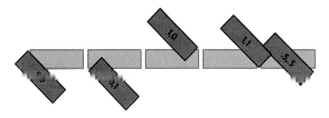

FIGURE 3.7   Five common `RenderTransformOrigins` used on rotated `Buttons` rendered on top of unrotated `Buttons`

`RenderTransformOrigin` can be set to a `Windows.Foundation.Point`, with (0,0) being the default value. This represents the top-left corner, shown by the first button in Figure 3.7. An origin of (0,1) represents the bottom-left corner, (1,0) is the top-right corner, and (1,1) is the bottom-right corner. You can use numbers greater than 1 to set the origin to a point outside the bounds of an element, and you can use fractional values. Therefore, (.5,.5) represents the middle of the object. The reason the corner-pivoting appears slightly off in Figure 3.7 is an artifact of the default appearance of `Buttons`. They have an invisible three-pixel-wide region around their visible rectangle. If you imagine each button extending three pixels in each direction, the pivoting of the first four buttons would be exactly on each corner.

The value for `RenderTransformOrigin` can be specified in XAML with two comma-delimited numbers (and no parentheses). For example, a `Button` rotated around its center, like the one at the far right of Figure 3.7, can be created as follows:

```
<Button RenderTransformOrigin=".5,.5">
  <Button.RenderTransform>
    <RotateTransform Angle="45"/>
  </Button.RenderTransform>
</Button>
```

This section looks at all the built-in 2D transforms, all in the `Windows.UI.Xaml.Media` namespace:

→ `RotateTransform`

→ `ScaleTransform`

→ `SkewTransform`

→ `TranslateTransform`

→ `CompositeTransform`

→ `TransformGroup`

→ `MatrixTransform`

RotateTransform

RotateTransform, which was just demonstrated, rotates an element according to the values of three double properties:

→ **Angle**—Angle of rotation, specified in degrees (default value – 0)

→ **CenterX**—Horizontal center of rotation (default value = 0)

→ **CenterY**—Vertical center of rotation (default value = 0)

The default (CenterX,CenterY) point of (0,0) represents the top-left corner.

> **What's the difference between using the CenterX and CenterY properties on transforms such as RotateTransform versus using the RenderTransformOrigin property on UIElement?**
>
> When a transform is applied to a UIElement, the CenterX and CenterY properties at first appear to be redundant with RenderTransformOrigin. Both mechanisms control the origin of the transform.
>
> However, CenterX and CenterY enable absolute positioning of the origin rather than the relative positioning of RenderTransformOrigin. Their values are specified as logical pixels, so the top-right corner of an element with a Width of 20 would be specified with CenterX set to 20 and CenterY set to 0 rather than the point (1,0). Also, when multiple RenderTransforms are grouped together (described later in this chapter), CenterX and CenterY on individual transforms enables more fine-grained control. Finally, the individual double values of CenterX and CenterY are easier to use with data binding than the Point value of RenderTransformOrigin.
>
> That said, RenderTransformOrigin is generally more useful than CenterX and CenterY. For the common case of transforming an element around its middle, the relative (.5,.5) RenderTransformOrigin is easy to specify in XAML, whereas accomplishing the same thing with CenterX and CenterY would require writing some C# code to calculate the absolute offsets.
>
> Note that you can use RenderTransformOrigin on an element simultaneously with using CenterX and CenterY on its transform. In this case, the two X values and two Y values are combined to calculate the final origin point.

Whereas Figure 3.7 shows rotated Buttons, Figure 3.8 demonstrates what happens when RotateTransform is applied *to the inner content* of a Button. To achieve this, the simple string that typically appears inside a Button is replaced with an explicit TextBlock as follows:

```
<Button Background="Orange">
  <TextBlock RenderTransformOrigin=".5,.5">
   <TextBlock.RenderTransform>
     <RotateTransform Angle="45"/>
   </TextBlock.RenderTransform>
     45°
  </TextBlock>
</Button>
```

FIGURE 3.8   Using RotateTransform on the content of a Button

ScaleTransform

ScaleTransform enlarges or shrinks an element horizontally, vertically, or in both directions. This transform has four straightforward double properties:

→ **ScaleX**—Multiplier for the element's width (default value = 1)

→ **ScaleY**—Multiplier for the element's height (default value = 1)

→ **CenterX**—Origin for horizontal scaling (default value = 0)

→ **CenterY**—Origin for vertical scaling (default value = 0)

A ScaleX value of 0.5 shrinks an element's rendered width in half, whereas a ScaleX value of 2 doubles the width. CenterX and CenterY work the same way as with RotateTransform.

Listing 3.1 applies ScaleTransform to three Buttons in a StackPanel, demonstrating the ability to stretch them independently in height or in width. Figure 3.9 shows the result.

LISTING 3.1   Applying ScaleTransform to Buttons in a StackPanel

```
<StackPanel Width="200">
  <Button Background="Red">No Scaling</Button>
  <Button Background="Orange">
  <Button.RenderTransform>
    <ScaleTransform ScaleX="2"/>
  </Button.RenderTransform>
    X</Button>
  <Button Background="Yellow">
  <Button.RenderTransform>
    <ScaleTransform ScaleX="2" ScaleY="2"/>
  </Button.RenderTransform>
    X + Y</Button>
  <Button Background="Lime">
  <Button.RenderTransform>
    <ScaleTransform ScaleY="2"/>
  </Button.RenderTransform>
    Y</Button>
</StackPanel>
```

Figure 3.10 displays the same Buttons from Listing 3.1 (and Figure 3.9) but with explicit CenterX and CenterY values set. The point represented by each pair of these values is displayed in each Button's text. Notice that the lime Button isn't moved to the left like the orange Button, despite being marked with the same CenterX of 70. That's because CenterX is relevant only when ScaleX is a value other than 1, and CenterY is relevant only when ScaleY is a value other than 1.

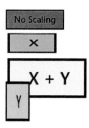

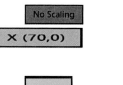

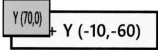

FIGURE 3.9 The scaled Buttons from Listing 3.1

FIGURE 3.10 The Buttons from Listing 3.1 but with explicit scaling centers

How do transforms such as ScaleTransform affect FrameworkElement's ActualHeight and ActualWidth properties or UIElement's RenderSize property?

Applying a transform to FrameworkElement never changes the values of these properties. Therefore, because of transforms, these properties can "lie" about the size of an element on the screen. For example, all the Buttons in Figures 3.9 and 3.10 have the same ActualHeight, ActualWidth, and RenderSize.

Such "lies" might surprise you, but they're usually for the best. The point of transforms is to alter an element's appearance without the element's knowledge. Giving elements the illusion that they are being rendered normally enables arbitrary controls to be plugged in and transformed without special handling.

How does ScaleTransform affect Margin and Padding?

Padding is scaled along with the rest of the content (because Padding is internal to the element), but Margin does not get scaled. As with ActualHeight and ActualWidth, the numeric Padding property value does not change, despite the visual scaling.

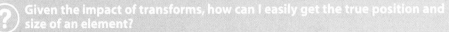

Given the impact of transforms, how can I easily get the true position and size of an element?

Sometimes you do really need to know an element's final position and size, taking into account the effects from transforms. For example, several Windows Runtime APIs require the position or bounds of an on-screen element so Windows can display system UI in the right spot. You can get a window-relative position that accounts for all transforms as follows:

```
static Point GetPositionInWindow(FrameworkElement element)
{
  GeneralTransform transform = element.TransformToVisual(null);
  return transform.TransformPoint(new Point() /* Represents 0,0 */);
}
```

You can get the bounding rectangle as follows:

```
static Rect GetBoundsInWindow(FrameworkElement element)
{
  GeneralTransform transform = element.TransformToVisual(null);
  return transform.TransformBounds(
    new Rect(0, 0, element.ActualWidth, element.ActualHeight));
}
```

SkewTransform

SkewTransform slants an element according to the values of four `double` properties:

➔ **AngleX**—Amount of horizontal skew (default value = 0)

➔ **AngleY**—Amount of vertical skew (default value = 0)

➔ **CenterX**—Origin for horizontal skew (default value = 0)

➔ **CenterY**—Origin for vertical skew (default value = 0)

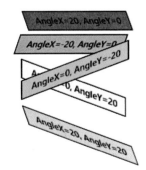

These properties behave much like the properties of the previous transforms. Figure 3.11 demonstrates SkewTransform applied as a RenderTransform on several Buttons, using the default center of the top-left corner.

FIGURE 3.11   SkewTransform applied to Buttons in a StackPanel

TranslateTransform

TranslateTransform simply moves an element according to two `double` properties:

→ **X**—Amount to move horizontally (default value = `0`)

→ **Y**—Amount to move vertically (default value = `0`)

TranslateTransform is an easy way to "nudge" elements one way or another. Most likely, you'd do this dynamically based on user actions (and perhaps in an animation). With all the panels described in the next chapter, it's unlikely that you'd need to use TranslateTransform to arrange a static user interface.

Combining Transforms

If you want to transform an element multiple ways simultaneously, such as rotate *and* scale it, a few different options are available:

→ CompositeTransform

→ TransformGroup

→ MatrixTransform

CompositeTransform

The CompositeTransform class is the easiest way to combine transforms. It has all the properties of the previous four transforms, although some have slightly different names: Rotation, ScaleX, ScaleY, SkewX, SkewY, TranslateX, TranslateY, CenterX, and CenterY.

Figure 3.12 shows several transforms being applied to a single Button as follows:

```
<Button Background="Orange">
  <Button.RenderTransform>
    <!-- The composite transform order is always
         scale, then skew, then rotate, then translate -->
    <CompositeTransform Rotation="45" ScaleX="5" ScaleY="1" SkewX="30"/>
  </Button.RenderTransform>
  OK
</Button>
```

It can be handy to always use CompositeTransform instead of the previous transforms, even if you're only performing one type of transform.

TransformGroup

CompositeTransform always applies its transforms in the same order: scale, skew, rotate, and then translate. If you require a nonstandard order, you can use a TransformGroup instead then put its child transforms in any order. For example, the following XAML looks like it might have the same effect as the previous XAML, but Figure 3.13 shows that the result is much different:

FIGURE 3.12   A Button scaled, skewed, and rotated with a single CompositeTransform

```
<Button Background="Orange">
  <Button.RenderTransform>
    <TransformGroup>
      <!-- First rotate, then scale, then skew! -->
      <RotateTransform Angle="45"/>
      <ScaleTransform ScaleX="5" ScaleY="1"/>
      <SkewTransform AngleX="30"/>
    </TransformGroup>
  </Button.RenderTransform>
  OK
</Button>
```

TransformGroup is just another Transform-derived class, so it can be used wherever any transform is used.

FIGURE 3.13   This time, the Button is rotated, scaled, and then skewed

For maximum performance, the system calculates a combined transform out of a TransformGroup's children and applies it as a single transform, much as if you had used CompositeTransform. Note that you can apply multiple instances of the same transform to a TransformGroup. For example, applying two separate 45° RotateTransforms would result in a 90° rotation.

MatrixTransform

MatrixTransform is a low-level mechanism that can be used to represent all combinations of rotation, scaling, skewing, and translating. MatrixTransform has a single Matrix property (of type Matrix) representing a 3x3 affine transformation matrix. (*Affine* means that straight lines remain straight.) Its Matrix property has the following subproperties representing 6 values in a 3x3 matrix:

$$
\begin{bmatrix}
\text{M11} & \text{M12} & 0 \\
\text{M21} & \text{M22} & 0 \\
\text{OffsetX} & \text{OffsetY} & 1
\end{bmatrix}
$$

The final column's values cannot be changed.

MatrixTransform's String Syntax

`MatrixTransform` is the only transform that can be specified as a simple string in XAML. For example, you can translate a `Button` 10 units to the right and 20 units down with the following syntax:

```
<Button RenderTransform="1,0,0,1,10,20"/>
```

The comma-delimited list represents the `M11`, `M12`, `M21`, `M22`, `OffsetX`, and `OffsetY` values, respectively. The values `1`, `0`, `0`, `1`, `0`, `0` give you the identity matrix (meaning no transform is done), so making `MatrixTransform` act like `TranslateTransform` is as simple as starting with the identity matrix and then using `OffsetX` and `OffsetY` as `TranslateTransform`'s X and Y values. Scaling can be done by treating the first and fourth values (the 1s in the identity matrix) as `ScaleX` and `ScaleY`, respectively. Rotation and skewing are more complicated because they involve `sin`, `cos`, and angles specified in radians.

If you're comfortable with the matrix notation, representing transforms with this concise (and less-readable) syntax can be a time saver when you're writing XAML by hand.

Applying 3D Transforms

Although you can use DirectX in a XAML app to work with a full 3D graphics engine, the XAML UI Framework does not directly expose full 3D capabilities. It does, however, enable you to perform the most common 3D effects with *perspective transforms*. These transforms escape the limitations of the 2D transforms by enabling you to rotate and translate an element in any or all of the three dimensions.

Perspective transforms are normally done with a class called `PlaneProjection`, which defines `RotationX`, `RotationY`, and `RotationZ` properties. The X and Y dimensions are defined as usual, and the Z dimension extends into and out of the screen, as illustrated in Figure 3.14. X increases from left-to-right, Y increases from top-to-bottom, and Z increases from back-to-front.

FIGURE 3.14   The three dimensions, relative to the screen

Although plane projections act like transforms, they derive from a class called `Projection` rather than `Transform`. Therefore, one cannot be assigned to an element via its `RenderTransform` property, but rather a separate property called `Projection`. The following plane projections are marked on playing card images, producing the result in Figure 3.15:

```
<StackPanel Orientation="Horizontal">
  <Image Source="Images/CardHA.png" Width="150" Margin="12">
    <Image.Projection>
      <PlaneProjection RotationX="55"/>
    </Image.Projection>
  </Image>
  <Image Source="Images/CardH2.png" Width="150">
    <Image.Projection>
      <PlaneProjection RotationY="55"/>
    </Image.Projection>
  </Image>
  <Image Source="Images/CardH3.png" Width="150" Margin="36">
    <Image.Projection>
      <PlaneProjection RotationZ="55"/>
    </Image.Projection>
  </Image>
```

```
  <Image Source="Images/CardH4.png" Width="150" Margin="48">
    <Image.Projection>
      <PlaneProjection RotationX="30" RotationY="30" RotationZ="30"/>
    </Image.Projection>
  </Image>
</StackPanel>
```

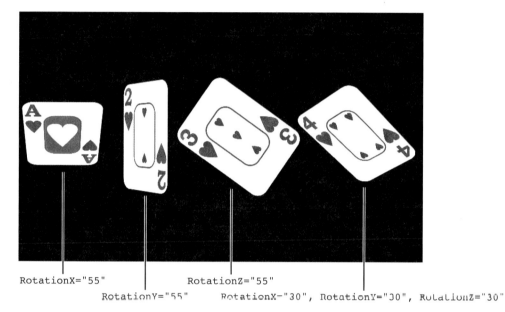

RotationX="55"   RotationZ="55"

        RotationY="55"   RotationX="30", RotationY="30", RotationZ="30"

FIGURE 3.15   Using a plane projection to rotate the card around the X, Y, and Z axes, then all three axes

Notice that rotating around only the Z axis is like using a 2D RotateTransform, although the direction is reversed.

Much like the 2D transform classes, PlaneProjection defines additional properties for changing the center of rotation: CenterOfRotationX, CenterOfRotationY, and CenterOfRotationZ. The first two properties are relative to the size of the element, on a scale from 0 to 1. The CenterOfRotationZ property is always in terms of absolute (logical) pixels, as elements never have any size in the Z dimension to enable a relative specification.

PlaneProjection defines six properties for translating an element in any or all dimensions. GlobalOffsetX, GlobalOffsetY, and GlobalOffsetZ apply the translation after the rotation, so the offsets are relative to the global screen coordinates. LocalOffsetX, LocalOffsetY, and LocalOffsetZ apply the translation before the rotation, causing the rotation to be relative to the rotated coordinate space.

•••

`Matrix3DProjection`

One other type of projection exists that can be assigned to an element's `Projection` property: `Matrix3DProjection`, which also derives from the `Projection` base class. This is a low-level construct that enables you to specify the projection as a 4x4 3D transformation matrix. This can be handy if you are already working with 3D transformation matrices, otherwise the simpler `PlaneProjection` is all you need to use.

Summary

That concludes our tour of the layout properties that child elements can use to influence the way they appear on the screen. Although you can experiment with them by manually typing XAML and observing the results, tools such as Blend and the Visual Studio designer make it even easier to get a feel for how values for complicated properties such as `RenderTransform` and `Projection` effect any element.

The most important part of layout, however, is the parent panels. This chapter repeatedly uses a simple `StackPanel` for simplicity, but the next chapter formally introduces this panel and all the other panels as well.

Chapter 4

LAYOUT

Layout is a critical component of an app's usability on a
wide range of devices, but without good platform support,
getting it right can be difficult. Arranging the pieces of a
user interface with static pixel-based coordinates and static
pixel-based sizes can work in limited environments, such as
in Windows Phone 7.x apps in which all devices are guaranteed to have the same screen resolution. However, such
interfaces start to crumble under the diversity enabled by
Windows.

Windows apps can run on anything from small tablets to
enormous HDTVs or projector screens. More importantly,
the resolution, DPI, and aspect ratios on these devices can
all vary greatly. Furthermore, users expect most apps to
gracefully handle different orientations and sharing the
screen with other windows, both of which can greatly
change an app's ideal layout. Apps that don't take advantage of the space given to them are frustrating to use. But
the space given an app isn't the only factor to consider
when it comes to layout. Content that changes in unpredictable ways (such as text being translated into different
languages or dynamically-downloaded content) also
requires flexible layout.

The first step to mastering layout is knowing how to
retrieve the size of the current screen and the space the
user has given to your app's window, as well as how to
know when either of these change. This chapter begins
with this topic. What you do based on this information,
and whether you even care to take explicit actions, is
highly dependent on your user interface and your goals.

The bulk of the chapter examines an important feature in the XAML UI Framework that helps you tackle challenging layout: *panels*. In some cases, smart use of panels can make the same XAML adjust gracefully to all the different shapes and sizes your app could become, avoiding the need to do the sort of window size detection covered first. More likely, panels can at least help you minimize the amount of manual UI adjustments needed in response to changing conditions.

Finally, this chapter ends with a discussion on strategies to deal with *content overflow*—in other words, what happens when parents and children can't agree on the use of available space. As with panels, the techniques discussed in this section, such as scrolling and scaling, can reduce the amount of manual work you need to do to handle the diversity of sizes and views.

Discovering Your Window Size and Location

You might want to make several adjustments to your user interface depending on the exact dimensions given to your app or simply whether your app is currently taller than it is wide (caused by the portrait orientation or by sharing the screen with other windows). Perhaps you need to scale elements, add/remove them, or rearrange them. Apps with multi-column user interfaces often reduce then eliminate columns as their window size shrinks. Apps often switch between horizontal scrolling and vertical scrolling of the same content depending on whether their window is portrait-shaped or landscape-shaped.

You can discover the size of your window at any time with the `Window.Current.Bounds` property of type `Windows.Foundation.Rect`. Because the size of your window can change at any time (most likely due to sharing the screen or an orientation change rather than a resolution change), it's important to be notified of any changes if you do indeed need to make adjustments. You can accomplish this by attaching an event handler to the `Window.Current.SizeChanged` event. The `WindowSizeChangedEventArgs` instance passed to the handler has a `Size` property that's equivalent to `Window.Current.Bounds`, so there are two ways to get the size of your window inside such handlers.

Note that all `FrameworkElements` have a `LayoutUpdated` event that gets raised whenever their layout is invalidated. If you attach a `LayoutUpdated` event handler to the root element that is set as the window's content (`Window.Current.Content`), then that suffices as an alternative to a

> **① Remember to detach event handlers!**
>
> Because an app's window but might potentially have multiple pages whose code attaches a `SizeChanged` event handler, remember to detach each handler when appropriate to avoid keeping pages alive longer than desired!

`SizeChanged` handler. Alternatively, if the window's content is a `Frame` (as it always is unless you've altered the Visual Studio-generated `App.xaml.cs`), then you could attach a handler to each `Page`'s `LayoutUpdated` event. This could be simpler to manage in a multi-page app. Furthermore, inside a `LayoutUpdated` event handler, you can discover the current size of your window by inspecting the root's `ActualWidth` and `ActualHeight` properties. These properties are equivalent to `Window.Current.Bounds.Width` and `Window.Current.Bounds.Height`.

> Note that `Windows.Current.Bounds` is a property of type `Windows.Foundation.Rect` rather than `Windows.Foundation.Size`. This means that it exposes `Left` and `Top` properties in addition to `Width` and `Height`. All four values accurately represent the app's position on the screen, so you can figure out whether you're adjacent to a certain edge of the screen when sharing the screen with other windows. It makes sense for certain apps to take advantage of this knowledge, such as a piano app in which the keys should always face a physical edge if possible. Windows 8.1 introduces two new APIs for discovering this in a more straightforward manner: `ApplicationView.GetForCurrentView().AdjacentToLeftDisplayEdge` and `ApplicationView.GetForCurrentView().AdjacentToRightDisplayEdge`.

> **Can my app span multiple screens?**
>
> Yes and no. For a Windows Store app, its window can only reside on one screen at a time, but it may show multiple windows. Each window may reside on any screen. Therefore, the only way to span screens is for the user to arrange your app's windows as such. This keeps things simple for developers, because all size-related APIs describe the size of a single window rather than the app. Because each screen may have a distinct resolution and scale factor applied, you don't have to worry about heterogeneous conditions for a single window instance.

Choosing a Minimum Width

By default, an app's window can be no narrower than 500 logical pixels. You can, however, optionally support narrower widths all the way down to 320 logical pixels. You do this by changing the **Minimum width** value on the **Application** tab of your app manifest to "320 px." This is necessary so Windows knows to allow the user more flexibility in resizing your window when it is sharing the screen with another window.

Apps that choose to support the "narrow mode" down to 320 pixels typically do so because they've got content that a user likely wants to monitor or interact with while performing other tasks. Classic examples are a chat program or any kind of news feed (perhaps from Facebook or Twitter). Because this is an app-wide setting, it applies to all of an app's windows. If you choose to support "narrow mode" in your app, you are free to decide when to transition your UI into its narrow view. Because the user can fluidly resize your window to any width above 320, you could choose to make the transition at a width of 400 pixels, for example.

Note that the 320 and 500 numbers represent logical pixels. This means that the shape of an app at its minimum width ends up being different on two screens with the same resolution but different DPI. You can see this in Visual Studio's simulator. If you resize an app down to 320-pixels-wide on the 23" screen with 1920x1080 resolution, `Windows.Current.Bounds` reports a size of 320x1080 as you'd expect because it's a 96-DPI screen. But on the 207-DPI 10.6" screen with the same resolution, the pixels are scaled up 40% from a smaller logical resolution of 1371.429x771.4286. Therefore, if you do the same resize action on this higher-DPI screen with the same resolution, the app looks "fatter," and `Windows.Current.Bounds` reports a size of 320x771.4286. The constant logical width of 320 results in a wider app because the logical screen width is smaller.

What about minimum window *height*?

Because users cannot vertically resize Windows Store apps (at least as of Windows 8.1), a window's height always matches the screen height. The height can change, of course, if the screen's orientation changes or if the window is moved to a different screen. The lowest supported screen resolution for Windows Store apps is 1024x768, so the minimum window height is 768 logical pixels.

If you support "narrow mode," checking for a window width of less than 500 is a natural way to adjust your UI for the limited space. For example:

```
Window.Current.SizeChanged += Window_SizeChanged;
…
void Window_SizeChanged(object sender, WindowSizeChangedEventArgs e)
{
  if (e.Size.Width < 500)
  {
    // Optimize the UI for "narrow mode"
    …
  }
  else
  {
    // Optimize the UI for "normal mode"
    …
  }
}
```

Design guidelines recommend reducing margins in addition to reducing the size of most elements in this mode, as well as ensuring you're using vertical scrolling for any lists. It's okay for your app's functionality to be limited in this mode. The idea is that if the user requires full functionality, he or she will resize your window to make it bigger.

These are now deprecated in order to support the new flexible window-resizing approach exposed by Windows 8.1. Windows 8 only supported three window sizes (known as *view states*):

→ **Fullscreen**, which occupied the entire screen

→ **Snapped**, which is always 320 logical pixels wide

→ **Filled**, which is the remainder of the screen once a different app has been snapped (1024 or more logical pixels wide)

In addition to not supporting fluid window resizing, Windows 8 only supports up to 2 Windows Store apps on the screen at once, whereas Windows 8.1 supports up to 4, depending on characteristics of the screen. Whereas the Windows Store requires all Windows 8 apps to support the 320-pixel-wide snapped mode and behave reasonably, Windows 8.1 apps do not.

In terms of APIs, using the `ApplicationView.Value` property or the `ApplicationView.TryUnsnap` method from the `Windows.UI.ViewManagement` namespace in a Windows 8.1 app produces compiler warnings. On Windows 8.1, `TryUnsnap` now does nothing and always returns `false`. When upgrading an app from Windows 8 to Windows 8.1, you should remove code related to view states and instead adjust your user interface based on the current window width.

Because apps on Windows 8 were never rendered at a width between 320 and 1024 logical pixels in landscape orientation, apps that have not yet been retargeted to Windows 8.1 get *pillarboxed* when the user resizes them to a width between these values, as shown in Figure 4.1. (*Pillarboxing* is simply "vertical letterboxing," in which gray bars appear on the left and right sides.) Simply recompiling your app for Windows 8.1 will remove the pillarboxing compatibility mode and enable it to resize smoothly from either 320 or 500 pixels upward. Of course, you must verify that your app behaves appropriately for all these window sizes.

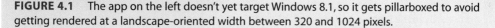

FIGURE 4.1   The app on the left doesn't yet target Windows 8.1, so it gets pillarboxed to avoid getting rendered at a landscape-oriented width between 320 and 1024 pixels.

Discovering the Current Orientation

Windows can tell you which of the four possible orientations your window's screen is in:

→ **Landscape** (horizontal)

→ **Landscape-flipped** (horizontal but upside down)

→ **Portrait** (vertical, with the hardware Start button on the left)

→ **Portrait-flipped** (vertical, with the hardware Start button on the right)

It's hard to imagine a valid reason for adjusting a user interface based on flipped versus nonflipped, other than some kind of tutorial that wants to place an arrow pointing to the hardware Start button. Nevertheless, if you care about distinguishing between any orientations, you can discover the current orientation via the static `Windows.Graphics.Display.DisplayProperties.CurrentOrientation` property. This property is a `DisplayOrientations` enumeration with the four possible values plus `None`. The reason for the `None` value (and the plural name) is that it's also the type of a static `AutoRotationPreferences` property on the same class that reveals the app's setting for "supported rotations" in the package manifest, as described in Chapter 1, "Hello, *Real World!*" In this case, it's used like a flags enumeration in which any or all of the four valid orientations could be set. For properties such as `CurrentOrientation`, however, the value is always exactly one (non-`None`) value.

To be notified of changes to the `CurrentOrientation` property, you can attach a handler to the static `Windows.Graphics.Display.DisplayProperties.OrientationChanged` event. Because `OrientationChanged` is a static event, you should be careful to detach event handlers if your app might attach several of them. Also, because the timing between `SizeChanged` and `OrientationChanged` is unpredictable, you should not look at `Window.Current.Bounds` inside an `OrientationChanged` handler.

> Although detecting screen orientation is included in this chapter for completeness, most apps should not change their window layout based on the screen orientation. Instead, layout decisions should be based on the size and aspect ratio of the *window*. For example, Microsoft recommends switching from horizontal scrolling to vertical scrolling when the window's height is greater than its width, regardless of whether this happens due to a portrait-oriented screen or a landscape-oriented screen being shared by multiple windows. This detection can be done with code such as the following:

```
Window.Current.SizeChanged += Window_SizeChanged;
…
void Window_SizeChanged(object sender, WindowSizeChangedEventArgs e)
{
  if (e.Size.Height > e.Size.Width)
  {
    // Optimize the UI for a "portrait window"
```

```
    …
  }
  else
  {
    // Optimize the UI for a "landscape window"

    …
  }
}
```

The static `Windows.Graphics.Display.DisplayProperties` class exposes several interesting characteristics about the current screen in addition to its current orientation: Its native orientation (the primary way it is designed to be held/viewed), the scale factor applied to all non-desktop UI (100%, 140% or 180%), its DPI, whether stereoscopic 3D is enabled, and its International Color Consortium (ICC) color profile. The latter three also have corresponding property-change events.

The scale factor, exposed by `DisplayProperties.ResolutionScale` represents the mapping between logical and physical pixels. It is a property of the enumeration type `ResolutionScale`. For example, in the earlier example of the 207-DPI 10.6" screen with 1920x1080 resolution in which the pixels are scaled up 40%, the value of `ResolutionScale` is `ResolutionScale.Scale140Percent`.

Panels

A panel (any class that derives from `Panel`) can contain children and arrange them in specific ways. The XAML UI Framework contains several panels, and you can create your own. This section examines the four main built-in panels, all in the `Windows.UI.Xaml.Controls` namespace:

→ `Canvas`

→ `StackPanel`

→ `Grid`

→ `VariableSizedWrapGrid`

Canvas

`Canvas` is the most basic panel, because it supports only the "classic" notion of positioning elements with explicit coordinates. You can position elements in a `Canvas` by using its `Left` and `Top` properties. These properties are special *attached properties* that can be *attached* to other elements. Listing 4.1 demonstrates this, with attached property syntax seen in Chapter 1 with automation properties.

LISTING 4.1   Buttons Arranged in a Canvas

```
<Page …>
  <Canvas x:Name="canvas">
    <Button Background="Red">Left=0, Top=0</Button>
    <Button x:Name="b" Canvas.Left="25" Canvas.Top="25"
            Background="Orange">Left=25, Top=25</Button>
  </Canvas>
</Page>
```

When the XAML parser encounters this Canvas.Left and Canvas.Top syntax, it requires that Canvas (sometimes called the *attached property provider*) have static methods called SetLeft and SetTop that can set the value accordingly. Therefore, the declaration of the Button named b in Listing 4.1 is equivalent to the following C# code:

```
Button b = new Button();
Canvas.SetLeft(b, 25);
Canvas.SetTop(b, 25);
b.Background = new SolidColorBrush(Color.Orange);
b.Content = "Left=25, Top=25";
canvas.Children.Add(b);
```

Although the XAML in Listing 4.1 nicely represents the logical attachment of Left and Top to Canvas, the C# code reveals that there's no real magic here—just a method call that associates an element with an otherwise unrelated property. One of the interesting things about the attached property abstraction is that no .NET property is a part of it! Note also that Canvas, like all panels, has a Children collection of UIElements. Adding a child element in XAML is equivalent to adding it to its Children collection.

The Canvas.Left and Canvas.Top values serve as margins (to which the element's own Margin values are added). If an element doesn't use either of these attached properties (leaving them with their default value of Double.NaN), it is placed in the top-left corner of the Canvas (the equivalent of setting Left and Top to 0). Figure 4.2 demonstrates this with the rendered result of the XAML in Listing 4.1.

Attached Properties •••

Although attached properties, sometimes called *attachable properties*, are a general-purpose mechanism, they were designed with the needs of layout panels in mind. Various Panel-derived classes define attached properties for controlling how their children are arranged. This way, each Panel can apply its own custom behavior to arbitrary children without requiring all possible child elements to be burdened with their own set of relevant properties. It also enables systems such as layout to be easily extensible, because anyone can write a new Panel with custom attached properties.

FIGURE 4.2   The Buttons in a Canvas from Listing 4.1

Table 4.1 evaluates the way that some of the child layout properties discussed in the preceding chapter apply to elements inside a Canvas.

TABLE 4.1   Canvas's Interaction with Child Layout Properties

Property	Usable Inside Canvas?
Margin	Partially. On the two sides used to position the element (Top and Left), the relevant two out of four margin values are added to the attached property values. Right and Bottom have no effect.
HorizontalAlignment and VerticalAlignment	No. Elements are given only the exact space they need.

The default Z order (defining which elements are "on top of" other elements) is determined by the order in which the children are added to the parent. In XAML, this is the order in which children are listed in the file. Elements added later are placed on top of elements added earlier. That is why, in Figure 4.2, the orange Button is on top of the red Button. This is relevant not just for the built-in panels that enable elements to overlap (such as Canvas) but whenever a RenderTransform causes an element to overlap another (as shown in Figures 3.9, 3.10, and 3.11 in the preceding chapter).

However, you can customize the Z order of any child element by marking it with the ZIndex attached property that is defined on Canvas. ZIndex is an integer with a default value of 0 that you can set to any number (positive or negative). Elements with larger ZIndex values are rendered on top of elements with smaller ZIndex values, so the element with the smallest value is in the back, and the element with the largest value is in the front. In the following example, ZIndex causes the red button to be on top of the orange button, despite being an earlier child of the Canvas:

```
<Canvas>
  <Button Canvas.ZIndex="1" Background="Red">On Top!</Button>
  <Button Background="Orange">On Bottom with a Default ZIndex=0</Button>
</Canvas>
```

If multiple children have the same ZIndex value, the order is determined by their order in the panel's Children collection, as in the default case.

Therefore, programmatically manipulating Z order is as simple as adjusting the ZIndex value. To cause the preceding red Button to be rendered behind the orange Button, you can set the attached property value to any number less than or equal to zero. The following line of C# does just that (assuming that the red button's name is redButton):

```
Canvas.SetZIndex(redButton, 0);
```

Although ZIndex is defined on Canvas, this mechanism works with all panels!

Although Canvas is too primitive a panel for creating flexible user interfaces, it is the most lightweight panel. So, you should keep it in mind for maximum performance when you need precise control over the placement of elements. Games, for example, tend to use Canvas because each element requires a precise position (perhaps calculated by a physics engine). The otherwise statically-placed content can still scale as needed simply by applying a transform to the Canvas or a parent element.

StackPanel

StackPanel is a popular panel because of its simplicity and usefulness. As its name suggests, it simply stacks its children sequentially. Many examples in previous chapters use StackPanel because it doesn't require the use of any attached properties to get a reasonable-looking user interface. In fact, StackPanel is one of the few panels that doesn't define any of its own attached properties!

With no attached properties for arranging children, you just have one way to customize the behavior of StackPanel—setting its Orientation property to Horizontal or Vertical. Vertical is the default Orientation. Figure 4.3 shows simple Buttons in two StackPanels with only their Orientation set.

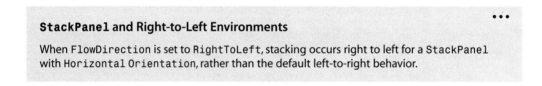

Orientation="Vertical" (default)   Orientation="Horizontal"

FIGURE 4.3   Buttons in a StackPanel, using both Orientations

• • •

StackPanel and Right-to-Left Environments

When FlowDirection is set to RightToLeft, stacking occurs right to left for a StackPanel with Horizontal Orientation, rather than the default left-to-right behavior.

Table 4.2 evaluates the way that some of the child layout properties apply to elements inside a StackPanel.

TABLE 4.2   StackPanel's Interaction with Child Layout Properties

Property	Usable Inside StackPanel?
Margin	Yes. Margin controls the space between an element and the StackPanel's edges as well as space between elements.
HorizontalAlignment and VerticalAlignment	Partially, because alignment is effectively ignored in the direction of stacking (children get the exact amount of space they need). For Orientation="Vertical", VerticalAlignment is meaningless. For Orientation="Horizontal", HorizontalAlignment is meaningless.

Grid

Grid is the most versatile panel and probably the one you'll use most often. (Visual Studio and Blend use Grid by default, even when you create a Blank App project.) It enables you to arrange its children in a multirow and multicolumn fashion, and it provides a number of features to control the rows and columns in interesting ways. Working with Grid is like working with a table or CSS grid in HTML.

Listing 4.2 uses Grid to build a user interface somewhat like the Windows Start screen. It defines a 7x8 Grid and arranges children in many of its cells.

LISTING 4.2   First Attempt at a Start Screen Clone Using a Grid

```
<Grid Background="#1D1D1D">

  <!-- Define seven rows: -->
  <Grid.RowDefinitions>
    <RowDefinition/> <!-- The area above the tiles -->
    <RowDefinition/> <!-- Tile row #1 -->
    <RowDefinition/> <!-- Tile row #2 -->
    <RowDefinition/> <!-- Tile row #3 -->
    <RowDefinition/> <!-- Tile row #4 -->
    <RowDefinition/> <!-- Tile row #5 -->
    <RowDefinition/> <!-- The area below the tiles -->
  </Grid.RowDefinitions>

  <!-- Define eight columns: -->
  <Grid.ColumnDefinitions>
    <ColumnDefinition/> <!-- Left margin -->
    <ColumnDefinition/> <!-- Tile column #1 -->
    <ColumnDefinition/> <!-- Tile column #2 -->
    <ColumnDefinition/> <!-- Tile column #3 -->
    <ColumnDefinition/> <!-- Tile column #4 -->
    <ColumnDefinition/> <!-- The user's name -->
```

```
    <ColumnDefinition/> <!-- The user's photo -->
    <ColumnDefinition/> <!-- Right margin -->
  </Grid.ColumnDefinitions>

  <!-- The "Start" text -->
  <TextBlock Grid.Row="0" Grid.Column="1" FontSize="54" FontFamily="Segoe UI"
             FontWeight="Light" VerticalAlignment="Center" Margin="0,0,0,26">
      Start
  </TextBlock>

  <!-- The simulated live tiles -->
  <Rectangle Grid.Row="1" Grid.Column="1" Margin="4" Fill="DodgerBlue"/>
  <Rectangle Grid.Row="1" Grid.Column="3" Margin="4" Fill="Coral"/>
  <Rectangle Grid.Row="2" Grid.Column="1" Margin="4" Fill="PaleVioletRed"/>
  <Rectangle Grid.Row="2" Grid.Column="3" Margin="4" Fill="LimeGreen"/>
  <Rectangle Grid.Row="3" Grid.Column="1" Margin="4" Fill="White"/>
  <Rectangle Grid.Row="3" Grid.Column="3" Margin="4" Fill="DodgerBlue"/>
  <Rectangle Grid.Row="4" Grid.Column="1" Margin="4" Fill="LimeGreen"/>
  <Rectangle Grid.Row="4" Grid.Column="3" Margin="4" Fill="Yellow"/>
  <Rectangle Grid.Row="4" Grid.Column="4" Margin="4" Fill="PaleVioletRed"/>
  <Rectangle Grid.Row="5" Grid.Column="1" Margin="4" Fill="Tan"/>
  <Rectangle Grid.Row="5" Grid.Column="3" Margin="4" Fill="DodgerBlue"/>
  <Rectangle Grid.Row="5" Grid.Column="4" Margin="4" Fill="LimeGreen"/>

  <!-- The current user's name and photo -->
  <TextBlock Grid.Row="0" Grid.Column="5" FontSize="28" FontFamily="Segoe UI"
             FontWeight="Light" HorizontalAlignment="Right"
             VerticalAlignment="Center" Margin="0,0,8,28">
      Adam Nathan
  </TextBlock>
  <Image Grid.Row="0" Grid.Column="6" Source="profile.png"
         VerticalAlignment="Center" Stretch="None" Margin="0,0,0,26"/>
</Grid>
```

For the basic usage of Grid, you define the number of rows and columns by adding that number of RowDefinition and ColumnDefinition elements to its RowDefinitions and ColumnDefinitions properties. (This is a little verbose but handy for giving individual rows and columns distinct sizes.) You can then position child elements in the Grid using its Row and Column attached properties, which are zero-based integers. When you don't explicitly specify any rows or columns, a Grid is implicitly given a single cell. And when you don't explicitly set Grid.Row or Grid.Column on child elements, the value 0 is used for each.

Grid cells can be left empty, and multiple elements can appear in the same Grid cell. In this case, elements are simply rendered on top of one another according to their Z order.

As with Canvas, child elements in the same cell don't interact with each other in terms of layout; they simply overlap.

Figure 4.4 shows the result of Listing 4.2 in the Visual Studio XAML designer, because the designer's grid lines help to put the visuals in context.

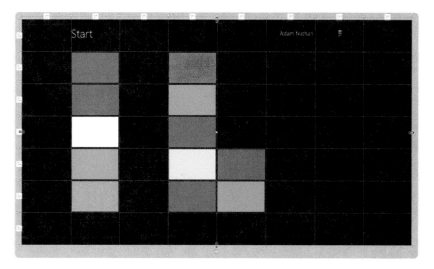

FIGURE 4.4   The first attempt at a Start screen is not satisfactory.

There are a few noticeable problems with Figure 4.4: The first row should have more vertical space, the user name and photo have too much horizontal space, and the spacing and shape of the pseudo-tiles (Rectangle elements) don't look right. In fact, most of the tiles are intended to appear in their wide mode. All of these problems are caused by the fact that every row has the same height, every column has the same width, and every element is confined to a single cell. Fortunately, we can solve all of these problems with some explicit Heights and Widths on RowDefinition and ColumnDefinition, respectively, and two more attached properties defined by Grid: RowSpan and ColumnSpan. Listing 4.3 applies these changes.

LISTING 4.3   An Improved Start Screen Clone

```
<Grid Background="#1D1D1D">

  <!-- Define seven rows: -->
  <Grid.RowDefinitions>
    <RowDefinition Height="180"/> <!-- The area above the tiles -->
    <RowDefinition Height="128"/> <!-- Tile row #1 -->
    <RowDefinition Height="128"/> <!-- Tile row #2 -->
    <RowDefinition Height="128"/> <!-- Tile row #3 -->
    <RowDefinition Height="128"/> <!-- Tile row #4 -->
    <RowDefinition Height="128"/> <!-- Tile row #5 -->
```

```
    <RowDefinition/>                  <!-- The area below the tiles -->
  </Grid.RowDefinitions>

  <!-- Define eight columns: -->
  <Grid.ColumnDefinitions>
    <ColumnDefinition Width="116"/> <!-- Left margin -->
    <ColumnDefinition Width="128"/> <!-- Tile column #1 -->
    <ColumnDefinition Width="128"/> <!-- Tile column #2 -->
    <ColumnDefinition Width="128"/> <!-- Tile column #3 -->
    <ColumnDefinition Width="120"/> <!-- Tile column #4 -->
    <ColumnDefinition/>                  <!-- The user's name -->
    <ColumnDefinition Width="40"/>  <!-- The user's photo -->
    <ColumnDefinition Width="46"/>  <!-- Right margin -->
  </Grid.ColumnDefinitions>

  <!-- The "Start" text -->
  <TextBlock Grid.Row="0" Grid.Column="1" FontSize="54" FontFamily="Segoe UI"
             FontWeight="Light" VerticalAlignment="Center" Margin="0,0,0,26">
    Start
  </TextBlock>

  <!-- The simulated live tiles -->
  <Rectangle Grid.Row="1" Grid.Column="1" Grid.ColumnSpan="2" Margin="4"
             Fill="DodgerBlue"/>
  <Rectangle Grid.Row="1" Grid.Column="3" Grid.ColumnSpan="2" Margin="4"
             Fill="Coral"/>
  <Rectangle Grid.Row="2" Grid.Column="1" Grid.ColumnSpan="2" Margin="4"
             Fill="PaleVioletRed"/>
  <Rectangle Grid.Row="2" Grid.Column="3" Grid.ColumnSpan="2" Margin="4"
             Fill="LimeGreen"/>
  <Rectangle Grid.Row="3" Grid.Column="1" Grid.ColumnSpan="2" Margin="4"
             Fill="White"/>
  <Rectangle Grid.Row="3" Grid.Column="3" Grid.ColumnSpan="2" Margin="4"
             Fill="DodgerBlue"/>
  <Rectangle Grid.Row="4" Grid.Column="1" Grid.ColumnSpan="2" Margin="4"
             Fill="LimeGreen"/>
  <Rectangle Grid.Row="4" Grid.Column="3" Margin="4" Fill="Yellow"/>
  <Rectangle Grid.Row="4" Grid.Column="4" Margin="4" Fill="PaleVioletRed"/>
  <Rectangle Grid.Row="5" Grid.Column="1" Grid.ColumnSpan="2" Margin="4"
             Fill="Tan"/>
  <Rectangle Grid.Row="5" Grid.Column="3" Margin="4" Fill="DodgerBlue"/>
  <Rectangle Grid.Row="5" Grid.Column="4" Margin="4" Fill="LimeGreen"/>

  <!-- The current user's name and photo -->
  <TextBlock Grid.Row="0" Grid.Column="5" FontSize="28" FontFamily="Segoe UI"
```

```
                FontWeight="Light" HorizontalAlignment="Right"
                VerticalAlignment="Center" Margin="0,0,8,28">
        Adam Nathan
    </TextBlock>
    <Image Grid.Row="0" Grid.Column="6" Source="profile.png"
            VerticalAlignment="Center" Stretch="None" Margin="0,0,0,26"/>
</Grid>
```

RowSpan and ColumnSpan have a value of 1 by default and can be set to any number greater than 1 to make an element span that many rows or columns. (If a value greater than the number of rows or columns is given, the element simply spans the maximum number that it can.) Figure 4.5 demonstrates the improved result from Listing 4.3, again in the Visual Studio XAML designer.

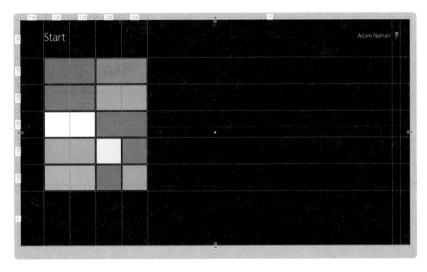

FIGURE 4.5   Using RowSpan, ColumnSpan, and some explicit row/column sizes improves the appearance of the Start screen clone.

Table 4.3 evaluates the way that some of the child layout properties apply to elements inside a Grid.

TABLE 4.3   Grid's Interaction with Child Layout Properties

Property	Usable Inside Grid?
Margin	Yes. Margin controls the space between an element and the edges of its cell.
HorizontalAlignment and VerticalAlignment	Yes. Unlike with the previous panels, both directions are completely usable unless an autosized cell causes an element to have no extra room. Therefore, by default, most elements completely stretch to fill their cells.

Sizing the Rows and Columns

The hardcoded row heights and column widths in the Start screen example work for certain resolutions, but more work would need to be done to make the UI flexible enough to handle all possible resolutions. This could be done with code-behind that checks the current screen size and adjust values accordingly, but Grid exposes sophisticated sizing options that can sometimes make such code unnecessary.

Unlike almost all other Height and Width properties, RowDefinition's and ColumnDefinition's corresponding properties are of type GridLength rather than double. This way, Grid can uniquely support three different types of RowDefinition and ColumnDefinition sizing:

→ **Absolute sizing**—Setting Height or Width to a numeric value representing logical pixels (like all other Height and Width values). Unlike the other types of sizing, an absolute-sized row or column does not grow or shrink as the size of the Grid or size of the elements changes. In Figure 4.5, all but one row and one column use absolute sizing.

→ **Autosizing**—Setting Height or Width to Auto (case insensitive), which gives child elements the space they need and no more (like the default setting for other Height and Width values). For a row, this is the height of the tallest element, and for a column, this is the width of the widest element. This is a better choice than absolute sizing whenever text is involved to be sure it doesn't get cut off because of localization.

→ **Proportional sizing (sometimes called *star sizing*)**—Setting Height or Width to special syntax to divide available space into equal-sized regions or regions based on fixed ratios. A proportional-sized row or column grows and shrinks as the Grid is resized.

Absolute sizing and autosizing are straightforward, but proportional sizing needs more explanation. It is done with *star syntax* that works as follows:

→ When a row's height or column's width is set to *, it occupies all the remaining space.

→ When multiple rows or columns use *, the remaining space is divided equally between them.

→ Rows and columns can place a coefficient in front of the asterisk (like 2* or 5.5*) to take proportionately more space than other columns using the asterisk notation. A column with width 2* is always twice the width of a column with width * (which is shorthand for 1*) *in the same* Grid. A column with width 5.5* is always twice the width of a column with width 2.75* *in the same* Grid.

The "remaining space" is the height or width of the Grid minus any rows or columns that use absolute sizing or autosizing. Figure 4.6 demonstrates these different scenarios with simple columns in a Grid.

The default height and width for Grid rows and columns is *. That's why the last row and the username column in Figure 4.5 occupy all remaining space.

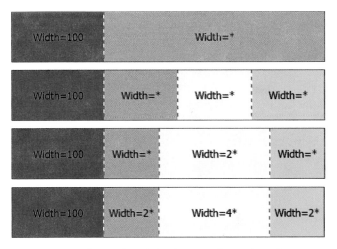

FIGURE 4.6   Proportional-sized Grid columns in action

Why doesn't Grid provide built-in support for percentage sizing, like in HTML and CSS?

The most common use of percentage sizing—setting the width or height of an item to 100%—is handled by setting an element's HorizontalAlignment or VerticalAlignment property to Stretch inside most panels. For more complicated scenarios, Grid's proportional sizing effectively provides percentage sizing, but with a syntax that takes a little getting used to. For example, to have a column always occupy 25% of a Grid's width, you can mark it with * and ensure that the remaining columns have a total width of 3*.

Microsoft chose this syntax so developers wouldn't have to worry about keeping the sum of percentages equal to 100 as rows or columns are dynamically added or removed. In addition, the fact that proportional sizing is specified relative to the remaining space (as opposed to the entire Grid) makes its behavior more understandable than an HTML table when mixing proportional rows or columns with fixed-size rows or columns.

How can I give Grid cells background colors, padding, and borders, as with cells of an HTML table?

There is no intrinsic mechanism to give Grid cells such properties, but you can simulate them easily, thanks to the fact that multiple elements can appear in any Grid cell. To give a cell a background color, you can simply plop in a Rectangle with the appropriate Fill (as in Figures 4.3 and 4.4) or a Border with the appropriate Background, which stretches to fill the cell by default. To give a cell padding, you can use autosizing and set the Margin on the appropriate child element. For borders, you can again use a Rectangle but give it an explicit Stroke of the appropriate color, or you can use a Border element and set its BorderBrush appropriately. The latter is preferred for performance reasons.

Just be sure to add such Rectangles or Borders to the Grid *before* adding any of the other children (or explicitly mark them with the ZIndex attached property), so their Z order puts them behind the main content.

• • •

Using GridLength from Procedural Code

In XAML, a type converter converts strings such as "100", "auto", and "2*" to GridLength structures. From C#, you can use one of two constructors to construct the appropriate GridLength. The key is a GridUnitType enumeration that identifies which of the three types of values you're creating.

For absolute sizing, you can use the constructor that takes a simple double value (such as 100):

```
GridLength length = new GridLength(100);
```

or you can use another constructor that accepts a GridUnitType value:

```
GridLength length = new GridLength(100, GridUnitType.Pixel);
```

In both examples, the length is 100 logical pixels.

Double.NaN isn't a supported value for the GridLength constructors, so for autosizing you must use GridUnitType.Auto:

```
GridLength length = new GridLength(0, GridUnitType.Auto);
```

The number passed as the first parameter is ignored. However, the preferred approach is to use the static GridLength.Auto property, which returns an instance of GridLength just like the one created by the preceding line of code. For proportional sizing, you can pass a number along with GridUnitType.Star:

```
GridLength length = new GridLength(2, GridUnitType.Star);
```

This example is equivalent to specifying 2* in XAML. You can pass 1 with GridUnitType.Star to get the equivalent of *.

> In addition to Height, RowDefinition exposes MinHeight and MaxHeight properties (of type double, as usual) to provide more options of creating flexible layout. Similarly, ColumnDefinition exposes MinWidth and MaxWidth properties of type double.

Comparing Grid to Other Panels

Grid is the best choice for most complex layout scenarios because it can do everything done by the previous panels and more. Grid can also accomplish layout that would otherwise require multiple panels. To demonstrate that Grid is usually the best choice, it's interesting to see how to mimic the behavior of other panels with Grid, knowing that you can take advantage of Grid's extra features at any time.

Mimicking Canvas with Grid

If you leave Grid with a single row and column and set the HorizontalAlignment and VerticalAlignment of all children to values other than Stretch, the children get added to the single cell just as they do in a Canvas. Setting HorizontalAlignment to Left and VerticalAlignment to Top is like setting Canvas.Left and Canvas.Top to 0. Applying Margin values to each element can give you the same effect as setting Canvas's attached properties to the same values. This is what the Visual Studio designer does when the user places and moves items on the design surface.

Mimicking StackPanel with Grid

A single-column Grid with autosized rows looks just like a vertical StackPanel when each element is manually placed in consecutive rows. Similarly, a single-row Grid with auto-sized columns looks just like a horizontal StackPanel when each element is manually placed in consecutive columns.

VariableSizedWrapGrid

VariableSizedWrapGrid is not as versatile as Grid, but it can do one trick that Grid cannot: wrap its elements when there's not enough space. Although its name ends in "Grid," VariableSizedWrapGrid is more like a StackPanel than a Grid. It stacks its children vertically (by default) or horizontally based on its Orientation property, and it doesn't define any attached properties for placing items in specific rows or columns. The stack simply wraps into new rows/columns as needed.

Figure 4.7 demonstrates how the following VariableSizedWrapGrid placed directly in a Page handles various layout conditions that can be inflicted by a user. It contains 10 buttons that differ only by Background and Content:

```
<Page …>
    <VariableSizedWrapGrid Orientation="Horizontal" Background="Brown">
        <Button FontSize="50" Width="200" Background="#0000ff">0</Button>
        …
    </VariableSizedWrapGrid>
</Page>
```

This panel is useful for displaying an indeterminate number of items with a more interesting layout than a simple list, much like the Windows file picker. There's no guarantee that every child element can be viewed, as with the last configuration in Figure 4.7. In this example, the app should probably add scrolling behavior. Scrolling is covered later in this chapter.

Fullscreen landscape

Fullscreen portrait

Sharing the screen with a small window

Sharing the screen with a large window

FIGURE 4.7   The horizontal `VariableSizedWrapGrid` shifts the placement of its children as the available horizontal space changes.

`VariableSizedWrapGrid` defines two attached properties that can be placed on its children: `RowSpan` and `ColumnSpan`. As with `Grid`, this enables a single element to span multiple rows/columns. Figure 4.8 is an update to Figure 4.7 that demonstrates this. The `Button` labeled "2" has been marked with:

> Although `Grid` looks like it can practically do it all, `StackPanel` and `VariableSizedWrapGrid` are better choices when dealing with an indeterminate number of child elements (typically as an items panel for an items control, described in Chapter 11, "Items Controls").

```
VariableSizedWrapGrid.RowSpan="2"
```

And the `Button` labeled "8" has been marked with:

```
VariableSizedWrapGrid.ColumnSpan="2"
```

In addition to their change to shades of green (for emphasis), the Button with "2" has been given a VerticalAlignment of Stretch so it can take advantage of the extra space given to it. Similarly, the Button with "8" has been given a Width of 400 rather than 200.

Fullscreen landscape

Fullscreen portrait

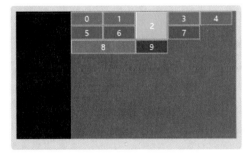

Sharing the screen with a small window

Sharing the screen with a large window

FIGURE 4.8   The use of RowSpan and ColumnSpan changes the wrapping behavior compared to Figure 4.7.

In addition to the two attached properties, VariableSizedWrapGrid defines six properties for controlling its behavior:

→ **Orientation**—This is just like StackPanel's property, and Vertical is the default. Vertical is the way most apps arrange their elements: stacked top to bottom and then wrapped left to right. Horizontal is the opposite, as demonstrated in Figures 4.7 and 4.8: stacked left to right and then wrapped top to bottom.

→ **ItemHeight**—A uniform height for all child elements. The way each child fills that height depends on its own VerticalAlignment, Height, and so forth. Any elements taller than ItemHeight get clipped.

→ **ItemWidth**—A uniform width for all child elements. The way each child fills that width depends on its own HorizontalAlignment, Width, and so forth. Any elements wider than ItemWidth get clipped.

→ **MaximumRowsOrColumns**—An integer that forces wrapping after a specific number of rows or columns, based on the orientation. When Vertical, you can think of this property as "Maximum Down." When Horizontal, you can think of this property as "Maximum Columns." When left as its default value of -1, wrapping happens automatically based on the space given to the panel.

→ **VerticalChildrenAlignment**—Can be set to Top (the default), Center, Bottom, or Stretch. This matters only if ItemHeight or RowSpan is set in such a way to give a child more space than its natural height.

→ **HorizontalChildrenAlignment**—Can be set to Left (the default), Center, Right, or Stretch. This matters only if ItemWidth or ColumnSpan is set in such a way to give a child more space than its natural width.

> **(?) Why does VariableSizedWrapGrid have such a verbose name, rather than something simple like WrapGrid?**
>
> It's given the lengthy name because there already is a WrapGrid panel that has all the features of VariableSizedWrapGrid except for the RowSpan and ColumnSpan attached properties (the "variable sized" feature). It also has an extra feature that VariableSizedWrapGrid does not: virtualization support, which is a performance optimization for large numbers of items.
>
> The reason that WrapGrid is not covered in this chapter is because it is permitted to be used only inside an items control, which is a topic in Chapter 11.

> **•••**
>
> **VariableSizedWrapGrid and Right-to-Left Environments**
>
> When FlowDirection is set to RightToLeft, wrapping occurs right to left for a VariableSizedWrapGrid with Vertical Orientation, and stacking occurs right to left for a VariableSizedWrapGrid with Horizontal Orientation.

Table 4.4 evaluates the way that some of the child layout properties apply to elements inside a VariableSizedWrapGrid.

TABLE 4.4 `VariableSizedWrapGrid`'s Interaction with Child Layout Properties

Property	Usable Inside `VariableSizedWrapGrid`?
`Margin`	Yes. Margins are included when `VariableSizedWrapGrid` calculates the size of each item for determining default stack widths or heights.
`HorizontalAlignment` and `VerticalAlignment`	Partially. Alignment can be used in the opposite direction of stacking, just like with `StackPanel`. But alignment can also be useful in the direction of stacking when `VariableSizedWrapGrid`'s `ItemHeight` or `ItemWidth` gives an element extra space to align within.

Handling Content Overflow

The built-in panels make their best effort to accommodate the size needs of their children. But sometimes they are forced to give children smaller space than they would like, and sometimes children refuse to render completely within that smaller space. For example, perhaps an element is marked with an explicit width that's wider than the containing panel. Or perhaps an element contains so many children that they can't all fit on the screen. In such cases, a content overflow problem exists.

You can deal with content overflow by using several different strategies:

→ Clipping

→ Scrolling

→ Scaling

→ Wrapping

→ Trimming

The first three strategies are examined in this section. You've already seen examples of wrapping with `VariableSizedWrapGrid`. Trimming refers to a more intelligent form of clipping, and it is supported only for text by `TextBlock` and `RichTextBlock`. These elements have a `TextTrimming` property that can be set to `None` (the default), `CharacterEllipsis`, or `WordEllipsis`.

Clipping

Clipping (that is, truncating or cropping) children is the default way that panels handle them when they are too large. Clipping can happen at the edges of a panel or within a panel (such as at the edges of a `Grid` cell). This behavior can be controlled to some degree, however.

The following 2x2 `Grid` contains two `TextBlocks`. The top one gets clipped by the right edge of its cell, but the bottom one does not. That's because a `Canvas` ignores any size constraints that its parent tries to impose. Furthermore, a Canvas, unlike other panels, never clips its children. Figure 4.9 shows what this XAML looks like in the Visual Studio designer:

```
<Page …>
  <Grid Width="200" Height="200"
        Background="{ThemeResource ApplicationPageBackgroundThemeBrush}">
    <Grid.RowDefinitions>
      <RowDefinition/>
      <RowDefinition/>
    </Grid.RowDefinitions>
    <Grid.ColumnDefinitions>
      <ColumnDefinition/>
      <ColumnDefinition/>
    </Grid.ColumnDefinitions>
    <!-- Top TextBlock -->
    <TextBlock Grid.Row="0">This text doesn't fit in the cell.</TextBlock>
    <!-- Bottom TextBlock -->
    <Canvas Grid.Row="1">
      <TextBlock>This text doesn't fit in the cell.</TextBlock>
    </Canvas>
  </Grid>
</Page>
```

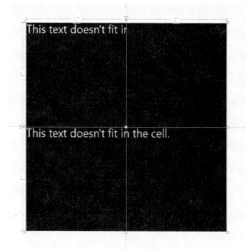

FIGURE 4.9   Placing the bottom TextBlock in a Canvas avoids the clipping done by the Grid cell.

Although Canvas can be used as an intermediate element to prevent clipping in other panels, increasing an element's RowSpan and/or ColumnSpan is usually the best way to enable it to "bleed" into adjacent cells when trying to prevent clipping in a Grid.

Clipping occurs before RenderTransforms are applied!

When enlarging an element with ScaleTransform as a RenderTransform, the element can easily surpass the bounds of the parent panel yet doesn't get clipped (unless it reaches the edge of the page). *Shrinking* an element with ScaleTransform as a RenderTransform is more subtle. If the unscaled element would have been clipped because it exceeds its parent's bounds, the scaled element is still clipped exactly the same way, even if the entire element can fit! That's because clipping is part of the layout process and already determined by the time RenderTransform is applied. Figure 4.10 demonstrates this by applying a ScaleTransform to the top TextBlock with a ScaleX value of .7.

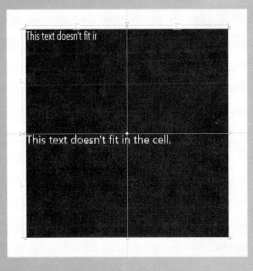

FIGURE 4.10   Even when a transform squishes the top text, it is still clipped as if no transform has been applied.

Scrolling

For most apps, the ability to scroll through content that is too large to view all at once is critical. The XAML UI Framework makes this easy because all you need to do is wrap an element in a ScrollViewer control, and the element instantly becomes scrollable. ScrollViewer makes use of ScrollBar controls and hooks them up to your content automatically. Internally, it supports *independent input*—processing input on a background thread—for smooth motion that doesn't get bogged down by activity on the UI thread.

ScrollViewer has a Content property that can be set to a single item, typically an entire panel. Because Content is ScrollViewer's content property in the XAML sense, you can place the item requiring scrolling as its child element. Here's an example:

```
<Page …>
  <ScrollViewer>
    <StackPanel>
      …
    </StackPanel>
  </ScrollViewer>
</Page>
```

Figure 4.11 shows the Page containing the simple StackPanel, with and without a ScrollViewer.

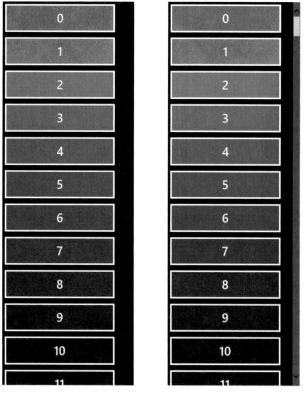

No ScrollViewer   Wrapped in a ScrollViewer

FIGURE 4.11   ScrollViewer enables scrolling of an element that is larger than the space given to it.

The ScrollBar controls act like standard scrollbars. They appear only when the app has focus and the mouse pointer moves over the app. They respond to a variety of input, such as arrow keys for fine-grained scrolling, Page Up and Page Down for coarser scrolling, and Ctrl+Home or Ctrl+End to jump to the beginning or end, respectively, when the ScrollViewer has keyboard focus. Touch manipulation also works as expected on the entire scrollable area when running on a device that supports it.

Customizing ScrollViewer

Scrolling is vertical-only by default, which is a poor choice for Windows Store apps because they typically scroll in a horizontal direction instead. If the StackPanel in Figure 4.11 were marked with a Horizontal Orientation instead, you would see only the left-most part of it, but there would still be a vertical-only scrollbar that had no effect (because all the content fits on the screen in the vertical dimension).

Fortunately, ScrollViewer exposes several properties and methods for customizing its scrolling. Its two most important properties are VerticalScrollBarVisibility and HorizontalScrollBarVisibility. Both of these properties are of type ScrollBarVisibility, an enumeration that defines four distinct states specific to its two scrollbars:

→ **Visible**—The scrollbar is always visible in the appropriate contexts (for example, when an app has focus and a mouse pointer moves over it), regardless of whether it's needed. When it's not needed, it has a disabled look and doesn't respond to input. (But this is different from the ScrollBarVisibility value called Disabled.)

→ **Auto**—The scrollbar is visible if the content is big enough to require scrolling in that dimension. Otherwise, the scrollbar is never visible.

→ **Hidden**—The scrollbar is always invisible but still logically exists, in that scrolling can still be done with touch and with arrow keys. Therefore, the content is still given all the length it wants in that dimension. This mode should be avoided because the scrollable behavior isn't obvious without the scrollbar.

→ **Disabled**—The scrollbar is not only invisible but it doesn't exist, so scrolling is not possible via any input method. In this case, the content is given only the length of its parent rather than all the length it wants.

The default value for VerticalScrollBarVisibility is Visible, and the default value for HorizontalScrollBarVisibility is Disabled.

Depending on the content inside ScrollViewer, the subtle difference between Hidden and Disabled can be not so subtle. For example, Figure 4.12 shows two different Pages containing a ScrollViewer with the same VariableSizedWrapGrid. The only difference is that in one Page the ScrollViewer has VerticalScrollBarVisibility set to Disabled, and in the other page the ScrollViewer has it set to Hidden. (In both cases, HorizontalScrollBarVisibility is set to Visible.)

VerticalScrollBarVisibility=Hidden, HorizontalScrollBarVisibility=Visible

0	15	30	45	60	75	90	105	120	135	150	1
1	16	31	46	61	76	91	106	121	136	151	1
2	17	32	47	62	77	92	107	122	137	152	1
3	18	33	48	63	78	93	108	123	138	153	1
4	19	34	49	64	79	94	109	124	139	154	1
5	20	35	50	65	80	95	110	125	140	155	1
6	21	36	51	66	81	96	111	126	141	156	1
7	22	37	52	67	82	97	112	127	142	157	1
8	23	38	53	68	83	98	113	128	143	158	1
9	24	39	54	69	84	99	114	129	144	159	1
10	25	40	55	70	85	100	115	130	145	160	1
11	26	41	56	71	86	101	116	131	146	161	1
12	27	42	57	72	87	102	117	132	147	162	1
13	28	43	58	73	88	103	118	133	148	163	1
14	29	44	59	74	89	104	119	134	149	164	1

VerticalScrollBarVisibility=Disabled, HorizontalScrollBarVisibility=Visible

FIGURE 4.12   Although the vertical scrollbar is invisible in both cases, the different values for VerticalScrollBarVisibility drastically alter the layout of the VariableSizedWrapGrid.

In the Hidden case, the panel is given as much height as it desires (the same as if VerticalScrollBarVisibility were set to Visible or Auto), so it makes use of it and arranges all children on the same column. In this arrangement, the visible horizontal scrollbar is useless because no scrolling can be done in that direction. However, vertical scrolling can be done with touch or a keyboard, even though no vertical scrollbar is visible.

In the Disabled case, the VariableSizedWrapGrid is given only the height of the Page, so wrapping occurs as if no ScrollViewer existed. In this case, the horizontal scrollbar works as expected.

How can I trigger code to execute when a scrollbar appears or disappears?

Because even a "visible" scrollbar is sometimes not visible on the screen, ScrollViewer defines a separate pair of visibility properties—ComputedHorizontalScrollBarVisibility and ComputedVerticalScrollBarVisibility—that reveal the *actual* visibility at any point in time. The next chapter explains how you can write event handlers to detect when the values of properties such as these change.

ScrollViewer contains methods for programmatically scrolling to a specific horizontal or vertical offset, as well as many properties that reveal the size of *extent* (all inner content), the size of the *viewport* (the viewable region), and the size of the remaining scrollable area (the difference between the extent and the viewport). In addition, it has some properties that warrant an explanation:

→ **HorizontalScrollMode** and **VerticalScrollMode** can be set to Disabled to prevent the default *overscroll effect*: content temporarily pushed past the end when scrolling via touch. When set to Auto, scrolling is considered to be on "rails." This means that if you move your finger or mouse pointer in an *almost* horizontal or *almost* vertical motion, the scrolling snaps to one dimension as if you're moving perfectly horizontal or perfectly vertical.

→ **IsHorizontalScrollChainingEnabled** and **IsVerticalScrollChainingEnabled** are Boolean properties that enable a scrolling action to be transferred from a child element to its parent once the child scrolling has reached the end. This applies to mouse wheel scrolling as well as touch.

→ **IsScrollInertiaEnabled** can be set to false to disable the additional scrolling that happens based on the acceleration when scrolling is done via touch.

→ **LeftHeader** and **TopHeader**, new to Windows 8.1, can be set to docked elements that remain stationary while the rest of the content scrolls. This enables you to create an experience similar to frozen rows/columns in Excel.

The remaining properties exist to support *snap points*.

Snap Points

Snap points are "magnetic" spots that enable items in an otherwise freely scrollable region to snap into place. This technique is commonly used on phones or tablets to enable swiping through something like a series of photos while ensuring that a single photo is entirely visible after the swipe. The Windows Photos app behaves this way (after tapping on a photo to make it fill the screen), although it does this with a more sophisticated control built on top of ScrollViewer: FlipView, discussed in Chapter 11.

If you want to enable snap points with only one item visible on the screen at a time, then FlipView is a much better choice. But if you want to enable them while viewing multiple items on the screen at the same time, then you can use ScrollViewer with its HorizontalSnapPointsType and/or VerticalSnapPointsType properties set appropriately.

HorizontalSnapPointsType and VerticalSnapPointsType can be independently set to one of the following values from a SnapPointsType enumeration:

→ **None**—Snapping is disabled.

→ **MandatorySingle**—The ScrollViewer always snaps to the next snap point when scrolling completes, regardless of how much inertia there is.

→ **Mandatory**—The ScrollViewer always snaps to a snap point when scrolling completes, but it may scroll past several snap points depending on how much inertia there is.

→ **OptionalSingle**—Like MandatorySingle, but the user can also position the ScrollViewer at an arbitrary spot by carefully dragging it (without flicking).

→ **Optional**—Like Mandatory, but the user can also position the ScrollViewer at an arbitrary spot by carefully dragging it (without flicking). This is the default value.

The following XAML enables snapping to the Rectangle boundaries inside the StackPanel:

```
<ScrollViewer HorizontalScrollBarVisibility="Visible"
              HorizontalSnapPointsType="Mandatory">
  <StackPanel Orientation="Horizontal">
    <Rectangle Fill="Red" Height="200" Width="200"/>
    <Rectangle Fill="Red" Height="200" Width="200"/>
    ...
  </StackPanel>
</ScrollViewer>
```

Support for this snapping behavior is built directly into panels such as StackPanel. Note that there's no requirement that the items all have the same size. By default, horizontal snapping is done with the left edge of the app and the left edge of the closest item. Vertical snapping is done with the top edge of the app and the top edge of the closest item. This can be customized, however, by setting ScrollViewer's HorizontalSnapPointsAlignment and/or VerticalSnapPointsAlignment properties to one of the following values:

→ **Near**—The default behavior. Left-edge snapping for horizontal scrolling and top-edge snapping for vertical scrolling.

→ **Far**—The opposite of near. Right-edge snapping (the right edge of the app and the right edge of the closest item) for horizontal scrolling and bottom-edge snapping (the bottom edge of the app and the bottom edge of the closest item) for vertical scrolling.

> ⓘ **Snap points affect only touch manipulation!**
>
> When a snap-point-enabled ScrollViewer is scrolled via mouse or keyboard, the snap points have no effect. This limitation may be removed in a future version of Windows.

→ **Center**—Snaps the center of the app with the center of the closest item.

Scaling

Although scrolling is a popular and long-standing way to deal with large content, dynamically shrinking or enlarging content to "just fit" in a given space is more appropriate for several scenarios. For example, it doesn't make sense for most games to change the shape of their game surface. Whether the game board or playing field must maintain a specific aspect ratio, or you want to avoid giving widescreen players an unfair advantage by seeing more of the scrolling world ahead, the typical approach is to scale up the game surface as much as possible and use letterboxing to fill any extra space (or perhaps show extra UI elements like game stats). If your app uses vector graphics, then you can scale to your heart's content. If it uses bitmaps, as many games do, then you might have to place an upper limit on any scaling done, and/or provide multiple sizes of the bitmap assets.

The XAML UI Framework makes scaling extremely easy, in more ways than the transforms seen in the preceding chapter. An element called `Viewbox` can be used to automatically scale content in a few different ways. And the `ScrollViewer` we just examined also has support for interactive zooming.

Viewbox

`ScaleTransform` can scale elements *relative to their own size*, but it doesn't provide a mechanism to scale elements *relative to the available space* without writing some custom code. Fortunately, the `Viewbox` element provides an easy mechanism to scale arbitrary content within a given space.

`Viewbox`, like `ScrollViewer`, can have only one child element. By default, `Viewbox` stretches in both dimensions to fill the space given to it. But it also has a `Stretch` property to control how its single child gets scaled within its bounds. The property is a `Stretch` enumeration, which has the following values:

→ **None**—No scaling is done. This is the same as not using `Viewbox` at all.

→ **Fill**—The child's dimensions are set to equal the `Viewbox`'s dimensions. Therefore, the child's aspect ratio is not necessarily preserved.

→ **Uniform**—The child is scaled as large as it can be while still fitting entirely within the `Viewbox` and preserving its aspect ratio. Therefore, there will be extra space in one dimension if its aspect ratio doesn't match. This is the default value.

→ **UniformToFill**—The child is scaled to entirely fill the `Viewbox` while preserving its aspect ratio. Therefore, the content will be cropped in one dimension if its aspect ratio doesn't match.

These options are demonstrated in Figure 4.13 using some XAML-based clipart created by the amazing Daniel Cook from lostgarden.com. This is not an image, but rather many vector shapes that scale without degradation.

Stretch=None   Stretch=Fill

Stretch=Uniform   Stretch=UniformToFill

FIGURE 4.13   Each of the four values for Viewbox's Stretch property changes the girl's layout.

A second property of Viewbox controls whether you want to use it only to shrink content or enlarge content (as opposed to doing either). This property is called StretchDirection, and it is a StretchDirection enumeration with the following values:

→ **UpOnly**—Enlarges the content, if appropriate. If the content is already too big, Viewbox leaves the current content size as is.

→ **DownOnly**—Shrinks the content, if appropriate. If the content is already small enough, Viewbox leaves the current content size as is.

→ **Both**—Enlarges or shrinks the content, whichever is needed to get the stretching described earlier. This is the default value.

It's amazing how easy it is to choose between a scrolling strategy and a scaling strategy for dealing with large content. Just wrap the same content in either a ScrollViewer or Viewbox!

> **Viewbox removes all wrapping!**
>
> Viewbox is handy for many situations, but it's not a good choice for content you'd normally like to wrap. That's because the content is given as much space as it needs in both directions before it is potentially scaled. Figure 4.14 demonstrates this by using the VariableSizedWrapGrid with ten Buttons from Figure 4.7, but wrapping it in a Viewbox.
>
> No matter the orientation, the result is a single line of content that could potentially be much smaller than you would have liked. Giving Viewbox a StretchDirection of UpOnly rather than the default of Both doesn't help either. The layout of Viewbox's content happens before any potential scaling. Therefore, UpOnly prevents the Buttons from shrinking, but they are still arranged in a single line, as shown in Figure 4.15.

FIGURE 4.14   The VariableSizedWrapGrid used in Figure 4.7 has no need to wrap when placed in a Viewbox.

FIGURE 4.15   Giving the Viewbox from Figure 4.14 a StretchDirection="UpOnly" prevents the Buttons from shrinking but doesn't affect the inner VariableSizedWrapGrid's layout.

The result of this is similar to the use of VerticalScrollBarVisibility="Hidden" in Figure 4.12, except that there's no way to scroll to the remaining content in this case, even with the keyboard.

Interactive Zooming with `ScrollViewer`

`ScrollViewer` can do another trick besides scrolling: By default, it enables pinch-to-zoom touch gestures on its content. If you don't want this behavior, you can set its `ZoomMode` property to `Disabled` rather than its default value of `Enabled`.

If you want to customize how far the content can be zoomed in or out, then set `ScrollViewer`'s `MinZoomFactor` and `MaxZoomFactor` properties, which have default values of .1 and 10, respectively. `ScrollViewer` also exposes zoom-specific customizations that work just like the similarly named properties for customizing scrolling: `IsZoomChainingEnabled`, `IsZoomInertiaEnabled`, and `ZoomSnapPointsType`.

You can programmatically retrieve the current zoom factor with the read-only `ZoomFactor` property, and you can add zoom snap points to the `ZoomSnapPoints` property.

Summary

With all the features described in this chapter and the preceding chapter, you can control layout in many interesting ways. This isn't like the old days, where your only options were pretty much just choosing a size and choosing an (X,Y) point on the screen. This chapter covered all the built-in panels that you would use directly in a page, but there are some additional ones that are meant for more limited contexts. They are described in Chapter 11.

The built-in panels—notably `Grid`—are a key part of enabling rapid development of apps that can be tailored to screens of all shapes and sizes. But one of the most powerful aspects of XAML layout is that parent panels can themselves be children of other panels. Although each panel was examined in isolation in this chapter, panels can be nested to provide impressive versatility. As you'll see in Chapter 11, controls such as `ListBox` use such panels to arrange their own items, and you can swap in arbitrary other panels to radically change their appearance without losing all their behaviors.

Chapter 5

In This Chapter

- Dependency Properties
- Routed Events
- Commands

INTERACTIVITY

Now that you know how to arrange your app's user interface, it's time to make it interactive. This chapter covers a few pieces of important plumbing in the XAML UI Framework—dependency properties, routed events, and commands. Much like the relationship between the two preceding chapters, this chapter provides the foundation for the input events discussed in the next chapter.

The topics in this chapter are some of the main culprits responsible for the framework's steep learning curve. Becoming familiar with these concepts now enables you to approach the rest of this book (or any other documentation) with confidence. Dependency properties and routed events are at the core of the entire design of the XAML UI Framework.

Dependency Properties

Classes in the XAML UI Framework expose several properties, because properties are easy to set in XAML. Many of these properties are a special kind called a *dependency property* that enable styling, automatic data binding, animation, and more. You might first meet this concept with skepticism, because it complicates the picture of types having simple fields, properties, methods, and events. But when you understand the problems that dependency properties solve, you will probably start to like them.

A dependency property *depends* on multiple providers for determining its value at any point in time. These providers could be an animation continuously changing its value, a parent element whose property value propagates down to its children, and so on. Arguably the biggest feature of a dependency property is its built-in ability to provide change notification.

The motivation for adding such intelligence to properties is to enable rich functionality directly from declarative markup. Because the key to a class's declarative-friendly design is heavy use of properties, Button, for example, has 71 public instance properties (61 of which are inherited from Control and its base classes)! Properties can be easily set in XAML—directly or by using a design tool—without any procedural code. Without the extra plumbing in dependency properties, however, it would be hard for the simple action of setting properties to get the desired results without the need to write additional code.

In this section, we briefly look at the implementation of a dependency property to make this discussion more concrete, and then we dig deeper into some of the ways that dependency properties add value on top of plain properties:

→ Change notification

→ Property value inheritance

→ Support for multiple providers

Understanding most of the nuances of dependency properties is usually not important unless you're creating a custom control. However, all developers need to be aware of what dependency properties are and how they work. For example, you can only style and animate dependency properties. After working with XAML for a while, you might find yourself wishing that *all* properties would be dependency properties!

A Dependency Property Implementation

In practice, dependency properties are just normal properties hooked into some extra infrastructure. This is all accomplished via APIs in the XAML UI Framework; no programming languages (other than XAML) have an intrinsic understanding of a dependency property.

Listing 5.1 demonstrates how ButtonBase, the base class of Button, effectively implements one of its dependency properties called IsPressed.

LISTING 5.1   A Standard Dependency Property Implementation

```
public class ButtonBase : ContentControl
{
  // The dependency property
  public static readonly DependencyProperty IsPressedProperty =
    DependencyProperty.Register("IsPressed", typeof(bool), typeof(ButtonBase),
      new PropertyMetadata(false, OnIsPressedChanged));
```

```
// A .NET property wrapper (optional)
public bool IsPressed
{
  get { return (bool)GetValue(ButtonBase.IsPressedProperty); }
  set { SetValue(ButtonBase.IsPressedProperty, value); }
}

// A property changed callback (optional)
static void OnIsPressedChanged(
  DependencyObject o, DependencyPropertyChangedEventArgs e) { … }
…
}
```

The static `IsPressedProperty` field is the actual dependency property, represented by the `DependencyProperty` class. By convention, all `DependencyProperty` fields are public, static, and have a `Property` suffix. Several pieces of infrastructure require that you follow this convention: localization tools, XAML loading, and more. This is why the MSDN documentation for so many classes in the XAML UI Framework lists all the annoying *XXX*`Property` members with boilerplate descriptions!

Dependency properties are usually created by calling the static `DependencyProperty.Register` method, which requires a name (`IsPressed`), a property type (`bool`), and the type of the class claiming to own the property (`ButtonBase`). Optionally (via different overloads of `Register`), you can pass callbacks for handling property value changes and/or setting its initial value. `ButtonBase` calls an overload of `Register` to give the dependency property a default value of `false` and to attach a delegate for change notifications.

Finally, the traditional .NET property called `IsPressed` implements its accessors by calling `GetValue` and `SetValue` methods inherited from `DependencyObject`, the low-level base class from which all classes with dependency properties must derive. `GetValue` returns the last value passed to `SetValue` or, if `SetValue` has never been called, the default value registered with the property. The `IsPressed` .NET property (sometimes called a *property wrapper* in this context) is not strictly necessary; consumers of `ButtonBase` or a derived class like `Button` could directly call the `GetValue`/`SetValue` methods because they are exposed publicly. But the .NET property makes programmatic reading and writing of the property much more natural for consumers, and it enables the property to be set via XAML.

> Visual Studio has a snippet called propdp that automatically expands into a definition of a dependency property, which makes defining one much faster than doing all the typing yourself.

On the surface, Listing 5.1 looks like an overly verbose way of representing a simple Boolean property. However, because GetValue and SetValue internally use an efficient sparse storage system and because IsPressedProperty is a static field (rather than an instance field), the dependency property implementation saves per-instance memory compared to a typical property. If all the properties on XAML-based controls were wrappers around instance fields (as most properties are), they would consume a significant amount of memory because of all the local data attached to each instance. Having 71 fields for each Button, not to mention the fields for all the other controls, would add up quickly! Instead, almost all of Button's public properties are dependency properties.

> **(!) Property wrappers are bypassed at runtime when setting dependency properties in XAML!**
>
> Although the XAML compiler depends on the property wrapper at compile time, at runtime, the underlying GetValue and SetValue methods are called directly! Therefore, to maintain parity between setting a property in XAML and in C#, it's crucial that property wrappers not contain any logic in addition to the GetValue/SetValue calls. If you want to add custom logic, that's what the registered callbacks are for. All built-in property wrappers abide by this rule, so this warning is for anyone writing a custom class with its own dependency properties.

The benefits of the dependency property implementation extend to more than just memory usage, however. The implementation centralizes and standardizes a fair amount of code and enables the three features listed earlier that we now examine one-by-one.

Change Notification

Change notification is mostly leveraged internally by the system (for features such as animation). Whenever the value of a dependency property changes, a number of actions are automatically triggered. In Listing 5.1, OnIsPressedChanged gets called automatically whenever anyone changes the value of IsPressed.

Property Value Inheritance

The term *property value inheritance* (or *property inheritance* for short) doesn't refer to traditional object-oriented class-based inheritance but rather the flowing of property values down the tree of elements. An example of this can be seen with the following XAML:

```
<Page …
    FontSize="200" FontStyle="Italic" FontWeight="Bold" Foreground="Red">
    <StackPanel>
        <TextBlock>Guess my appearance!</TextBlock>
        <TextBlock FontSize="40">Guess my appearance!</TextBlock>
        <CheckBox>Guess my appearance!</CheckBox>
        <Button>Guess my appearance!</Button>
    </StackPanel>
</Page>
```

This sets four text-related properties on the root page that are meant to be inherited by the text in the TextBlock, CheckBox, and Button descendants. For the most part, these settings flow all the way down the tree and are inherited by these elements. The second TextBlock's FontSize does not change because it is explicitly marked with a FontSize of 40, overriding the inherited value of 200. The inherited FontStyle setting of Italic, on the other hand, affects all four elements because none of them have this set explicitly.

Still, it's hard to guess the resultant appearance of all four elements in this situation. Figure 5.1 shows the result.

FIGURE 5.1   The four text-related property values set on the root Page aren't consistently inherited by its elements.

The first TextBlock successfully inherits all four property values, and the second one inherits all three that aren't locally set with a different value. However, the CheckBox inherits only Bold and Italic, and the Button inherits only Italic! What's going on? The behavior of property value inheritance can be subtle in cases like this for two reasons:

→ Not every dependency property participates in property value inheritance.

→ Other higher-priority sources might set the property value, as explained in the next section.

In this case, the latter reason is to blame. A few controls, such as Button and CheckBox, internally set some of their font properties to match current system settings. The result can be especially confusing because such controls end up "swallowing" any inheritance from proceeding further down the element tree. For example, if you add a TextBlock as an explicit child of the CheckBox or Button, its FontSize and Foreground properties would be set to their default values, unlike the other TextBlocks.

Support for Multiple Providers

Many powerful mechanisms independently attempt to set the value of dependency properties. Without a well-defined mechanism for handling these disparate property value providers, the system would be a bit chaotic, and property values could be unstable. Of course, as their name indicates, dependency properties were designed to depend on these providers in a consistent and orderly manner.

The following list reveals the property value providers that can set the value of most dependency properties, in order from highest to lowest precedence:

1. Active animations

2. Local value

3. Template properties

4. Style setters

5. Property value inheritance

6. Default value

You've already seen some of the property value providers, such as property value inheritance (#5). *Local value* (#2) technically means any call to `DependencyObject.SetValue`, but this is typically seen with a simple property assignment in XAML or C# (because of the way dependency properties are implemented, as shown previously with `ButtonBase.IsPressed`). *Default value* (#6) refers to the initial value registered with the dependency property, which naturally has the lowest precedence.

If one or more animations are running, they have the power to alter the current property value or completely replace it. Therefore, animations (the topic of Chapter 17, "Animation") can trump all other property value providers—even local values! This is often a stumbling block for people who are new to XAML. The other providers, which involve styles and templates, are explained further in Chapter 18, "Styles, Templates, and Visual States."

This order of precedence explains why some of `CheckBox`'s and `Button`'s property values were not impacted by property value inheritance in Figure 5.1. The setting of these two controls' font properties to match system settings is done via style setters (#4). Although this has precedence over property value inheritance (#5), you can still override these font settings using any mechanism with a higher precedence, such as setting local values on `CheckBox` and/or `Button`.

Clearing a Local Value

If you ever want to clear a locally set property value and let the system set the value from the relevant provider with the next highest precedence, explicitly setting the property to its default value isn't good enough. It's still a local value that overrides everything else. Instead, you must use DependencyObject's ClearValue method. This can be called on a TextBlock tb as follows in C#:

```
tb.ClearValue(TextBlock.FontSizeProperty);
```

(TextBlock.FontSizeProperty is the static DependencyProperty field.) After calling ClearValue, the local value is removed from the equation when the base value is recalculated.

Attached Properties

The preceding chapter used many attached properties. Attached properties are a special form of dependency properties, so this section looks at how to implement one. It turns out that it's quite simple.

Recall that setting Canvas.Left on an element in XAML is equivalent to calling Canvas's static SetLeft method. Internally, methods such as SetLeft simply call the same DependencyObject.SetValue method that a normal dependency property accessor calls, but on the passed-in element (that derives from DependencyObject):

```
public static void SetLeft(UIElement element, double value)
{
  element.SetValue(Canvas.LeftProperty, value);
}
```

Similarly, attached properties also define a static Get*XXX* method (where *XXX* is the name of the property) that calls the familiar DependencyObject.GetValue method:

```
public static double GetLeft(UIElement element)
{
  return (double)element.GetValue(Canvas.LeftProperty);
}
```

As with property wrappers for normal dependency properties, these Get*XXX* and Set*XXX* methods must not do anything other than make a call to GetValue and SetValue.

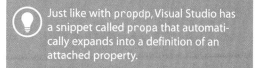
Just like with propdp, Visual Studio has a snippet called propa that automatically expands into a definition of an attached property.

The attached property field, Canvas.LeftProperty in this example, must be registered with DependencyProperty.Register**Attached** instead of DependencyProperty.Register.

···

Attached Properties as an Extensibility Mechanism

Similar to previous Microsoft frameworks, FrameworkElement defines a Tag property (of type System.Object) that enables you to store arbitrary custom data in any element. But attached properties are a more powerful and flexible mechanism for attaching custom data to any object deriving from DependencyObject. It's often overlooked that attached properties even enable you to effectively add custom data to instances of sealed classes!

A further twist to the story of attached properties is that although setting them in XAML relies on the presence of the static SetXXX method, you can bypass this method in C# and call DependencyObject.SetValue directly. This means that you can use any dependency property as an attached property in C#. For example, the following code attaches Viewbox's StretchDirection property to a Button and assigns it a value of UpOnly:

```
// Attach an unrelated property to a Button and set its value:
button.SetValue(Viewbox.StretchDirectionProperty, StretchDirection.UpOnly);
```

Although this seems nonsensical, and it certainly doesn't magically enable new stretching functionality on this Button, you have the freedom to consume this property value in a way that makes sense to your app.

There are more realistic ways to extend elements in this manner. FrameworkElement's Tag property is a dependency property, so you can attach it to an instance of any DependencyObject that doesn't already have its own Tag property. For example, PlaneProjection is a sealed class without a Tag property (because it is not a FrameworkElement). Yet the following code attaches custom data to a PlaneProjection instance:

```
PlaneProjection projection = new PlaneProjection();
projection.SetValue(FrameworkElement.TagProperty, "my custom data");
```

This is just one of the ways to achieve extensibility without the need for traditional inheritance.

Routed Events

Just as the XAML UI Framework's dependency properties add infrastructure and features on top of the simple notion of properties, *routed events* add infrastructure and features on top of the simple notion of events. Routed events are events that are designed to work well with a tree of elements.

XAML is natural for representing a user interface because of its hierarchical nature. But regardless of whether elements in a user interface are expressed in XAML or C#, they form a tree based on their parent/child relationships.

When a routed event is raised by an element, it travels up the element tree to the root, getting raised on each element in a simple and consistent fashion, without the need for any custom code. This process is known as *event bubbling*. In fact, you can think of the term "routed event" as a fancy way of saying "bubbling event." When routed events were introduced in WPF, you could choose one of three routing strategies: bubbling, tunneling (travel downward), or direct. In Windows Store apps, there is no choice, so the "routed" name is mostly a historical artifact.

Event bubbling helps most applications remain oblivious to details of the visual tree, which is good for restyling and is crucial to successful element composition. For example, consider the media-player-style Stop `Button` in Chapter 2, "Mastering XAML." A user might tap directly on the `Rectangle` inside the `Button`, but the event bubbles up to the `Button`, enabling it to react appropriately. (Yet if you want to detect taps directly on the `Rectangle` for some reason, you have the freedom to do so as well.) Without routed events, producers of the inner content or consumers of the `Button` would have to write code to patch everything together.

The Visual Tree

Different elements publicly expose their child(ren) in different ways, such as a `Content` versus `Child` versus `Children` property, but internally they all use the same protected members on `UIElement` to inform the system of the formal relationship. This formal element tree is also sometimes referred to as the *visual tree*. It usually contains intermediate elements that aren't explicitly constructed in your XAML or C#, but are an artifact of an element's current visual template (discussed in Chapter 18).

You can see this for yourself by inspecting the visual tree with a `VisualTreeHelper` class that exposes static `GetChildCount`, `GetChild`, and `GetParent` methods. The following recursive method prints a simple representation of a visual tree to the debugger's output window:

```
static void PrintVisualTree(int depth, DependencyObject obj)
{
  // Print the object with preceding spaces that represent its depth
  Debug.WriteLine(new string(' ', depth) + obj);

  // Recursive call for each child
  for (int i = 0; i < VisualTreeHelper.GetChildrenCount(obj); i++)
    PrintVisualTree(depth + 1, VisualTreeHelper.GetChild(obj, i));
}
```

Imagine that you have the following trivial `MainPage.xaml`:

```
<Page x:Class="Chapter5.MainPage" …>
  <Viewbox>
    <Button>Tap me</Button>
  </Viewbox>
</Page>
```

Calling `PrintVisualTree(0, this)` in `MainPage`'s code-behind file (which must be done *after* layout has occurred at least once, such as in a handler for `MainPage`'s `Loaded` event) produces the following output:

```
Chapter5.MainPage
 Windows.UI.Xaml.Controls.Viewbox
  Windows.UI.Xaml.Controls.Border
   Windows.UI.Xaml.Controls.Button
    Windows.UI.Xaml.Controls.Grid
     Windows.UI.Xaml.Controls.Border
      Windows.UI.Xaml.Controls.ContentPresenter
       Windows.UI.Xaml.Controls.Grid
        Windows.UI.Xaml.Controls.TextBlock
      Windows.UI.Xaml.Shapes.Rectangle
      Windows.UI.Xaml.Shapes.Rectangle
```

Because they enable you to peer inside the deep composition of elements, visual trees can be surprisingly complex. The Border element wrapping the Button is a "visual implementation detail" of Viewbox, and the elements inside Button are its own visual implementation details. Notice that Button internally uses two Grids to arrange its content! The deepest child, the TextBlock, is what renders the "Tap me" string inside the Button.

Fortunately, although visual trees are an essential piece of infrastructure, you often don't need to worry about them unless you're radically restyling controls. Code such as PrintVisualTree should be used only for experimentation, or if you're writing some sort of visual tree inspection tool. That's because depending on a specific visual tree at runtime breaks one of the framework's core tenets—the separation of look and logic. When someone restyles a control such as Viewbox or Button using the techniques described in Chapter 18, the contents of the visual tree can radically change. You should not write code that would fail in such a condition.

A Routed Event in Action

Routed events have several similarities with dependency properties. Just as dependency properties are represented as public static DependencyProperty fields with a conventional Property suffix, routed events are represented as public static RoutedEvent fields with a conventional Event suffix. A routed event is registered somewhat like a dependency property, and a corresponding normal event—or *event wrapper*—is defined to enable more familiar use from C# and adding a handler in XAML with event attribute syntax. In most cases, routed events don't look very different from normal events. As with dependency properties, no programming languages (other than XAML) have an intrinsic understanding of the *routed* designation. The extra support is based on a handful of APIs.

Routed events have one important difference from dependency properties, however. You cannot define your own. In fact, the entire XAML UI Framework defines only 23 routed events—and they all live on UIElement! All these events are related to user input (touch, mouse, pen, or keyboard) and are covered in depth in the next chapter. Let's briefly look at one example now.

The PointerReleased routed event is raised when a press of a finger, mouse button, or pen is finished. (For the finger example, it means the finger has stopped making contact with the screen.) The XAML in Listing 5.2 handles this event on the root Page element.

LISTING 5.2   Leveraging Event Bubbling to Handle Events on the Root Page

```
<Page x:Class="Chapter5.MainPage" PointerReleased="MainPage_PointerReleased" …>
  <Grid Background="Blue">
    <Rectangle Fill="Red" Width="100" Height="100"/>
  </Grid>
</Page>
```

The MainPage_PointerReleased event handler referenced in Listing 5.2 is defined in a code-behind file:

```
void MainPage_PointerReleased(object sender, PointerRoutedEventArgs e)
{
  …
}
```

Regardless of where the finger, mouse pointer, or pen is when the event occurs (as long as it's somewhere over the Page), the Page-level handler gets called thanks to event bubbling. If the handler is attached on the Rectangle instead, then only releases directly on top of the Rectangle would cause the handler to be called. If the handler is attached on the Rectangle *and* the Page, then it would get called twice when the release happens on top of the Rectangle.

Handlers for all routed events have a signature matching the pattern for general .NET event handlers: The first parameter is a System.Object typically named sender, and the second parameter (typically named args or e) is a class that derives from RoutedEventArgs. The sender parameter passed to a handler is always the element to which the handler was attached. RoutedEventArgs, the base class of the e parameter, is a subclass of EventArgs that exposes one property called OriginalSource. OriginalSource is the element that originally raised the event. Because of bubbling, the sender and OriginalSource can easily be different elements (although the sender would be an ancestor of OriginalSource). For Listing 5.2, the sender passed to MainPage_PointerReleased would always be the Page, but the OriginalSource would either be the Grid or the Rectangle.

Halting Bubbling

None of the routed events directly pass a RoutedEventArgs instance to its handlers, but rather a derived type such as the PointerRoutedEventArgs class seen in the preceding example. These classes add event-specific properties above and beyond the OriginalSource property, but they all share one extra property in common: Handled.

Handled is a Boolean property that is not meant to be inspected, but rather set. A handler can set to it to true to mark the event as "handled," which halts the bubbling. In the code-behind file for Listing 5.2, if MainPage_PointerReleased set e.Handled to true, then it wouldn't end up being called multiple times even if the handler were attached to all three elements.

Several controls internally handle low-level routed events (preventing their bubbling) and take some alternate action. For example, Button (via its ButtonBase base class) handles PointerPressed, PointerReleased and KeyUp routed events (the latter only when the released key is Enter or the Spacebar), and then raises its own (non-routed) Click event. This is done to provide a single event for the logical action of clicking a Button, even if the "click" was done via a keyboard shortcut.

As a result, PointerPressed and PointerReleased (and sometimes KeyUp) get swallowed when such events originate from within a Button. If you add a Button to the Page in Listing 5.2 and then tap the Button, the MainPage_PointerReleased does *not* get called upon the release. Incidentally, if the goal is to detect taps anywhere on a Page, you should attach a handler to the routed Tapped event instead of PointerReleased because the latter gets raised at the end of basically any gesture (such as a swipe). And Button doesn't prevent the bubbling of the Tapped event.

•••

Halting a Routed Event Is an Illusion

Although setting Handled to true in a routed event handler appears to stop the bubbling, individual handlers further up the tree can opt to receive the events anyway! This can be done only from procedural code, using an AddHandler method defined on UIElement.

AddHandler, and a companion RemoveHandler method, are analogous to DependencyObject's GetValue and SetValue methods. They are an alternate way to attach/detach event handlers to an element—for its routed events only.

AddHandler has three parameters: a RoutedEvent object that identifies the event (one of the static fields on UIElement with an Event suffix), the delegate for handling the event, and a Boolean handledEventsToo value. If you pass true for handledEventsToo, then the handler gets invoked regardless of anyone's attempt to halt bubbling.

For example, imagine that the code-behind file for Listing 5.2 leveraged this trick to attach the same event handler to the Page:

```
public MainPage()
{
  InitializeComponent();
  this.AddHandler(UIElement.PointerReleasedEvent,
    new PointerEventHandler(MainPage_PointerReleased), true);
}
```

If the page also contained a Button, this handler would now be notified about PointerReleased events occurring from within the Button because its internal handling of PointerReleased is ignored.

The use of AddHandler (and RemoveHandler) is interesting only for doing this handledEventsToo trick. Otherwise, you can just use the standard += and -= C# syntax for attaching/detaching event handlers, or attach the handlers in XAML.

> **Don't be fooled by events that claim to be routed events!**
>
> You might be surprised to read that the XAML UI Framework contains only 23 routed events, because *tons* of events in the framework use a RoutedEventHandler or similar delegate type that passes a RoutedEventArgs (or derived) instance to its event handlers. This is pervasive in controls, such as Button's Click event, any items control's SelectionChanged event, and TextBox's TextChanged event, to name a few. And nothing prevents you from defining your own .NET events that use the RoutedEventHandler delegate type. Yet none of these events (other than the 23 on UIElement) are actually routed events!
>
> For compatibility with Silverlight, the XAML UI Framework misrepresents many events in this manner. Silverlight had originally done this so the tools that targeted WPF (such as Visual Studio's designer and Blend) would automatically work with Silverlight, and so WPF code could be more easily ported to Silverlight. (In WPF, all these events are routed events, and third parties can define their own.) However, the result is confusing for anyone who understands what routed events are and tries to take advantage of their unique features! Just remember that if there is no corresponding static RoutedEvent field, then the event is not routed.
>
> By the way, this overuse of RoutedEventArgs is the reason that it doesn't define a Handled property despite the fact that halting the bubbling is a standard feature of routed events. Instead, the property is placed on every relevant RoutedEventArgs-derived class that is used by *real* routed events!

Commands

Although events are widely used in Windows Store apps, it's good to be aware of built-in support for *commands*, a more abstract and loosely coupled version of events. Whereas events are tied to details about specific user actions (such as a Button being clicked or a ComboBoxItem being selected), commands represent actions independent from their user interface exposure—a logical notion like Open or Refresh. An app might want to expose such actions through many mechanisms simultaneously: Buttons in an app bar, keyboard shortcuts, and so on.

You could handle the multiple exposures of the same commands with events fairly well. For example, you could define a generic Refresh event handler and attach each handler to the appropriate events on the relevant elements (the Click event on a Button, a KeyDown event that detects a specific keyboard shortcut, and so on). In addition, you'd probably want to enable and disable the appropriate controls whenever the Refresh action is invalid. This two-way communication gets a bit more cumbersome, especially if you don't want to hard-code a list of controls that need to be updated.

Commands are designed to make such scenarios easy. The support reduces the amount of code you need to write (and in some cases eliminates all procedural code), and it gives you more flexibility to change your user interface without breaking the underlying logic. They are a core part of the Model-View-ViewModel (MVVM) pattern, a popular pattern for structuring code in XAML-based projects. MVVM is focused on keeping a strong separation between the user interface (view), behaviors (view model), and underlying data

(model). Following an MVVM architecture means avoiding—sometimes completely elimi-
nating—code-behind files! Commands, along with data binding (discussed in Chapter 19,
"Data Binding"), make this possible.

> This book doesn't delve into the MVVM pattern, because there are entire books dedicated
> to the topic, but the following are good resources for learning more:
>
> → http://msdn.microsoft.com/en-us/magazine/dd419663.aspx (an article based on WPF)
>
> → http://joeroliberty.com/2010/05/08/mvvm-its-not-kool-aid-3 (a blog post based on
>   Silverlight)

So what exactly is a command? It's any object implementing the ICommand interface from
the System.Windows.Input namespace, whose name is an artifact left over from WPF and
Silverlight. ICommand defines three simple members:

→ **Execute**—The method that executes the command-specific logic

→ **CanExecute**—A method that returns true if the command is enabled or false if it is
  disabled

→ **CanExecuteChanged**—An event that is raised whenever the value of CanExecute
  changes

If you want to create a Refresh command, you could define and implement a
RefreshCommand class implementing ICommand, find a place to store it (perhaps as a static
field on your App class), call Execute from relevant event handlers (when CanExecute
returns true), and handle the CanExecuteChanged event to toggle the IsEnabled property
on the relevant pieces of user interface. This doesn't sound much better than simply using
events, however, unless you're devoted to following a pattern such as MVVM.

One thing that makes this more palatable is that all Buttons (via ButtonBase) and
MenuFlyoutItem have a Command property that can be set to any ICommand (plus a
CommandParameter property whose value gets passed to ICommand.Execute). When any
Button with a non-null Command is clicked, it automatically invokes the command's
Execute method (when CanExecute returns true). In addition, such Buttons automatically
keep their value for IsEnabled synchronized with the value of CanExecute by leveraging
the CanExecuteChanged event.

Although WPF and Silverlight expose several built-in command objects for common
actions (such as Cut, Copy, and Paste), no such objects are included in the XAML UI
Framework for Windows Store apps.

Summary

In this chapter, you learned about all the core plumbing that enables rich interactivity and the ways in which these mechanisms are optimized for hierarchical elements in a user interface. With multiple types of properties, multiple types of events, and surprisingly complex visual trees, the landscape isn't quite as simple as you might have expected. Hopefully you can now appreciate some of the value of these mechanisms. Throughout the rest of the book, these concepts generally fade into the background as we focus on accomplishing specific development tasks.

Chapter 6

HANDLING INPUT: TOUCH, MOUSE, PEN, AND KEYBOARD

When creating a Windows Store app, one particular task might sound daunting: You must make the app work well regardless of whether the user is leveraging a touchscreen, a mouse, a hardware keyboard, the software keyboard, or even a stylus (referred to as a *pen* in this chapter). No other platform has the same kind of expectations for its apps to the degree that Windows does.

Fortunately, a lot of care went into making this task much easier than you might imagine. You can use the following three-part strategy to deal with the wide range of input devices:

→ As much as possible, leverage the interactions already built into the framework's controls. They are designed to work well with all input types, and in a manner that's consistent with user expectations.

→ For custom interactions, Microsoft's guidance is to "code for touch, because you'll get the right behavior for mouse and pen for free." This chapter shows you how that can happen.

→ Consider creating optimized experiences for specific input devices if it makes sense for your app. For example, a productivity app should provide useful keyboard shortcuts, and a drawing app should leverage extra features that only a pen can provide.

The first part of this strategy is the topic of Part IV, "Understanding Controls," but the latter two are the focus of this chapter.

> **(?) How do I handle input from a game controller?**
>
> Windows Store apps can support Xbox-compatible game controllers, although this is exposed to developers via XInput, a C++ DirectX API. That's not a problem, however, because the nature of the Windows Runtime makes it straightforward to expose such functionality to a C# XAML app.
>
> The Windows SDK sample at http://code.msdn.microsoft.com/windowsapps/XInput-and-JavaScript-c72fe535 wraps XInput in a simple C++ Windows Runtime component that can be consumed from C#. (The sample happens to show it used from JavaScript.)

Touch Input

Windows Store apps can leverage a large number of events that enable any kind of touch interaction imaginable. (Note that the term *touch* includes touching with more than one finger simultaneously, which is sometimes called *multitouch*.) This rich functionality is exposed through UIElement, so it is pervasive as well as flexible. It's worth noting that because of the rich built-in behaviors of the built-in controls, certain types of apps don't ever need to directly interact directly with any of these events. Controls such as ScrollViewer, as seen in Chapter 4, "Layout," handle a number of touch events on your behalf and already do what you (and users) expect them to do.

Touch events can be separated into three categories:

→ **Pointers**—The lowest-level raw events

→ **Gestures**—Higher-level events for motions calculated from the pointer events

→ **Manipulations**—Complex gestures that stream information to an app while the gesture is still being performed

As you'll see, all three categories are relevant for more types of input than just touch. Also note that although the touch digitizer is typically integrated into the screen, it can be part of an external device as well (such as the Microsoft Touch Mouse). This section occasionally uses the terms *screen* and *digitizer* interchangeably.

Pointers

Input for Windows Store apps is consolidated into a concept called a *pointer*. No, this isn't a C++-style pointer, it's an abstraction for three separate kinds of input: touch, mouse, and pen. This enables an app to use a single set of APIs for the things that touch, mouse, and pen have in common, which is quite a bit.

The pointer abstraction involves four main classes: PointerDevice, Pointer, PointerPoint, and PointerPointProperties. Figure 6.1 demonstrates their meaning and relationship. A single PC can (and often does) have multiple `PointerDevices`, each `PointerDevice` can support multiple `Pointers` (such as five fingers for touch), and each `Pointer` can generate a series of `PointerPoints`.

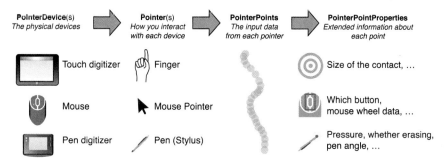

| PointerDevice(s)
The physical devices | | Pointer(s)
*How you interact
with each device* | | PointerPoints
*The input data
from each pointer* | | PointerPointProperties
*Extended information about
each point* |

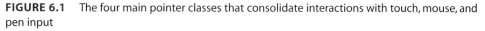

FIGURE 6.1   The four main pointer classes that consolidate interactions with touch, mouse, and pen input

PointerDevice

`PointerDevice` (in the `Windows.Devices.Input` namespace) exposes low-level properties that reveal many details about the hardware. The most interesting ones are `MaxContacts` for the maximum number of simultaneous pointers supported (1 for a mouse and 5 for many touch digitizers) and `PointerDeviceType`, which is set to either `Touch`, `Mouse`, or `Pen`. It also exposes two static methods: one for enumerating all current `PointerDevices`, and one that returns the `PointerDevice` responsible for a specific `Pointer`. For example, a Surface Pro returns three `PointerDevices` (one of each type) when a Touch Cover or Type Cover (with its built-in trackpad) is connected.

The `Windows.Devices.Input` namespace also contains a `TouchCapabilities` class that is awkward to use but provides shortcuts to information you can otherwise glean by enumerating all `PointerDevices`. After instantiating a `TouchCapabilities` object, you can check whether the current PC has *any* digitizer (touch or pen) with its `TouchPresent` property whose value is 1 for `true` or 0 for `false`. You can also check its `Contacts` property, which returns the minimum `MaxContacts` value from all current touch and pen `PointerDevices`.

Pointer

The `Pointer` class is simple. It exposes four properties. The main one, `PointerId`, is a `uint` that uniquely identifies it. This is helpful for tracking individual fingers, for example, when multiple fingers are raising events simultaneously. Its `PointerDeviceType` property exposes the same information as the same-named property from `PointerDevice`. The remaining two properties, `IsInContact` and `IsInRange`, are duplicated on the `PointerPoint` and `PointerPointProperties` classes, and they are described in the next two sections.

PointerPoint

The PointerPoint class is much more than a simple coordinate on the screen. It exposes the following properties:

→ **Position**—The coordinates expressed as a Windows.Foundation.Point. Windows occasionally adjusts Position automatically due to a feature called *touch input prediction*. This attempts to compensate for inaccurate touches. For example, if a user taps near a hyperlink, Windows will likely adjust Position to be directly on the hyperlink.

→ **RawPosition**—The coordinates directly reported by the input device. Unlike Position, RawPosition does not get adjusted by touch input prediction.

→ **IsInContact**—Whether the pointer is currently touching the digitizer.

→ **Timestamp**—Occurrence of this input, in terms of milliseconds since boot time.

→ **FrameId**—An ID that groups multiple touches that should be treated as a unit.

→ **Properties**—A PointerPointProperties instance containing extra information.

→ **PointerId**—The numeric ID of the Pointer responsible for this PointerPoint.

→ **PointerDevice**—The PointerDevice responsible for the Pointer.

PointerPoint exposes a static GetCurrentPoint method that enables you to get the current PointerPoint for any Pointer (identified by its ID) at any time. It also exposes a static GetIntermediatePoints method described later in this chapter.

PointerPointProperties

The PointerPointProperties instance exposed by PointerPoint is a treasure trove of information. Most of it is specific to mouse and pen devices (and, therefore, described later), but the following properties are relevant for touch:

→ **ContactRect**—The bounding rectangle of the contact area (for digitizers that support giving this information). Be careful about relying exclusively on this data, however, because some digitizers report a zero-sized rectangle. Like PointerPoint. Position, this data can be adjusted by touch input prediction.

→ **ContactRectRaw**—The raw version of ContactRect. Like PointerPoint.RawPosition, this is unaffected by touch input prediction.

→ **IsInRange**—Reports whether the finger is close to the touch digitizer but not quite touching it. (If the touch digitizer supports this kind of z-axis detection.)

→ **IsPrimary**—Whether this input belongs to the primary Pointer (the first one that made contact out of the ones currently in contact with the digitizer).

→ **TouchConfidence**—false if the contact got rejected by the PointerDevice, because it seems to be an accidental touch.

Pointer Events

With all the background out of the way, it's now time to see the primary way your code can be exposed to these pointer classes. The pointer events are all routed events and all exposed by UIElement, so every visual element on your pages can raise them, and they bubble up through the element tree. The following pointer events are relevant to touch:

→ **PointerPressed**—Raised when a Pointer first makes contact with the element.

→ **PointerMoved**—Raised continuously as a Pointer moves over the element.

→ **PointerReleased**—Raised when a previously pressed Pointer releases contact under normal circumstances.

→ **PointerEntered**—Raised when a Pointer first enters the element's bounds.

→ **PointerExited**—Raised when a Pointer leaves the element's bounds.

→ **PointerCanceled**—Raised when the Pointer is lost due to an unusual reason, such as the user rotating the device or disconnecting the relevant (external) PointerDevice.

→ **PointerCaptureLost**—Raised when pointer capture, explained in the next section, terminates.

When multiple Pointers (fingers) are in contact simultaneously, the pointer events get raised for each one independently. Handlers for all pointer events are given an instance of PointerRoutedEventArgs, which contains the following:

→ **GetPosition**—A method that returns the relevant PointerPoint.

→ **Pointer**—The Pointer instance that generated the event (although the PointerPoint already reveals its ID, which is often all you need to know).

→ **GetIntermediatePoints**—An advanced method that returns a collection of PointerPoints that

> **⚠ When a pointer is pressed, it is not always released!**
>
> Every PointerPressed event is *usually* paired with an eventual PointerReleased event, but not always. If a specific PointerReleased is never raised, then a PointerCanceled or PointerCaptureLost event would be released instead. (Although in certain scenarios, both PointerReleased *and* PointerCaptureLost can be raised.)
>
> Most of the time, it makes sense to attach the same PointerReleased handler to PointerCanceled and PointerCaptureLost so you consider the action "done" even if it terminates abnormally. Some apps, however, might want to commit an action only on PointerReleased and *undo* it on PointerCanceled.

might have accumulated between the current PointerMoved event and the previous one raised. That's right, the data from touch and pen digitizers can be so high-resolution that the stream of input gets coalesced into lower-resolution chunks for performance reasons. (Mice are already low-resolution so GetIntermediatePoints always returns an empty collection when the PointerDevice is a mouse.) Therefore, this enables you to get the highest-resolution data possible and is typically passed along to the `GestureRecognizer` described in the upcoming "Gestures" section.

→ **`Handled`**—Can be set to `true` to "halt" bubbling, as described in the preceding chapter.

→ **`KeyModifiers`**—Reveals if certain keyboard keys were pressed at the time of the event, described further in the "Keyboard Input" section.

`GetPosition` is a method rather than a simple property because it enables you to get the position in more than one way: either relative to the top-left corner of the current window, or relative to the top-left corner of any rendered `UIElement`. To get the window-relative position, you can pass `null` as the single parameter to `GetPosition`. To get an element-relative position, you pass the desired element as the parameter. The latter approach is much more common, especially because it automatically accounts for any transforms applied to the passed-in element (or an ancestor).

Capturing `Pointers`

Suppose you want to support dragging and dropping of `UIElements`. It's easy to imagine using the `PointerPressed`, `PointerMoved`, and `PointerReleased`/`PointerCanceled` events to implement drag-and-drop. You could start a drag action by setting a Boolean variable inside an element's `PointerPressed` handler, move the element to remain under the pointer if the Boolean is `true` inside its `PointerMoved` handler, and then clear the Boolean inside its `PointerReleased` (and `PointerCanceled`) event to end the dragging. It turns out that this simple scheme isn't quite good enough, however, because it's easy to move your finger/mouse/pen too fast or move the dragged element under another element, causing the element you're trying to drag to separate from the `Pointer` and get left behind.

To solve this problem, `UIElements` support *capturing* and *releasing* any `Pointer`. When an element captures one, it receives all its pointer events, even when the `Pointer` is not within its bounds. Actually, even when the `Pointer` is outside the bounds of the app (when it is sharing the screen with other windows)!

When an element releases a `Pointer` from its capture, the event behavior returns to normal. Capture and release can be done with two simple methods defined on `UIElement`—`CapturePointer` and `ReleasePointerCapture`, both of which have a single `Pointer` argument. In addition, a parameterless `ReleasePointerCaptures` method releases all `Pointers` captured by the element, and a read-only `PointerCaptures` property gives you a list of its currently-captured `Pointers`.

Therefore, for a drag-and-drop implementation, you should capture the `Pointer` inside a handler for `PointerPressed` and release it inside a handler for `PointerReleased` (and the two similar events). The only thing left to figure out is the best way to actually move the element inside `PointerMoved`, and that depends on its parent `Panel`. Listing 6.1 demonstrates such an implementation in order to create a page with a draggable red square. It is the code-behind file for the following simple `MainPage.xaml` content:

```
<Page x:Class="Chapter6.MainPage" …>
  <Canvas Background="{ThemeResource ApplicationPageBackgroundThemeBrush}">
    <Rectangle x:Name="shape" Fill="Red" Width="100" Height="100" />
  </Canvas>
</Page>
```

LISTING 6.1   `MainPage.xaml.cs:` Performing Simple Drag and Drop

```
using System;
using Windows.UI.Input;
using Windows.UI.Xaml.Controls;
using Windows.UI.Xaml.Input;

namespace Chapter6
{
  public sealed partial class MainPage : Page
  {
    public MainPage()
    {
      InitializeComponent();

      // Event for beginning drag
      shape.PointerPressed += Shape_PointerPressed;

      // Event for dragging
      shape.PointerMoved += Shape_PointerMoved;

      // All the events that should terminate the drag
      shape.PointerReleased += Shape_PointerReleased;
      shape.PointerCanceled += Shape_PointerReleased;
      shape.PointerCaptureLost += Shape_PointerReleased;
    }

    void Shape_PointerPressed(object sender, PointerRoutedEventArgs e)
    {
      shape.CapturePointer(e.Pointer);
    }

    void Shape_PointerMoved(object sender, PointerRoutedEventArgs e)
    {
      // Only move the shape if one pointer is currently pressed
      if (shape.PointerCaptures != null && shape.PointerCaptures.Count == 1)
      {
        PointerPoint point = e.GetCurrentPoint(null);
```

LISTING 6.1   Continued

```
      // Center the shape under the pointer
      Canvas.SetLeft(shape, point.Position.X - (shape.ActualWidth / 2));
      Canvas.SetTop(shape, point.Position.Y - (shape.ActualHeight / 2));
    }
  }

  void Shape_PointerReleased(object sender, PointerRoutedEventArgs e)
  {
    shape.ReleasePointerCapture(e.Pointer);
  }
 }
}
```

There are several things to note about Listing 6.1:

→ With the availability of the PointerCaptures property, we don't need to define a separate isDragging variable to be set on PointerPressed and cleared on PointerReleased. The code in the PointerMoved handler is able to conditionalize its logic on the state of capture.

→ It's important that all capture APIs are used directly on the shape field because that element is where the event handlers are attached. If Shape_PointerPressed accidentally called **this**.CapturePointer instead, then Shape_PointerMoved and Shape_PointerReleased would not be called subsequently because the Page would capture all the events!

→ In the PointerReleased handler, the call to ReleasePointerCapture causes the PointerCaptureLost event to be raised, which invokes PointerReleased again. That's okay, because ReleasePointerCapture is a no-op if the passed-in Pointer isn't captured.

→ This simplistic drag-and-drop is a bit different from "official" dragging and dropping because it doesn't reject the input if multiple Pointers are in contact simultaneously. It does, however, prevent dragging when multiple Pointers are in contact *with the shape* simultaneously (by checking for exactly one captured Pointer). Otherwise, if you touch the Rectangle with two fingers simultaneously and pull them apart, the shape's position would rapidly oscillate between each finger's position due to Shape_PointerMoved being called for each Pointer in turn.

> **(!) UIElement.PointerCaptures can be null!**
>
> Before any capturing is done, an element's PointerCaptures property is null. When capture happens, it becomes a collection with a nonzero Count. After capture has been released, however, it stays non-null. It becomes an empty collection with a Count of 0. This is why the PointerMoved handler in Listing 6.1 must check for both conditions when determining whether an element is currently capturing any Pointers.

→ If you were to try this same example with a `Button` instead of a `Rectangle`, you would need to attach `Shape_Pressed` and `Shape_Released` with the `AddHandler` method instead of `+=`, and with `true` passed for the `handledEventsToo` parameter. This is due to the halting of event bubbling described in the preceding chapter.

Hit Testing

Although one element's capture can prevent another element from raising pointer events that it otherwise would, there are several other conditions that can cause an element directly underneath a `Pointer` to not raise such events. An element meeting all these conditions is said to be *hit-testable*, although *hittable* would be a slightly better term.

A `UIElement` is hit-testable when the following are all true:

→ Its `Visibility` property is set to `Visible` (which it is by default).

→ It must render something. This means having a nonzero `ActualWidth` and `ActualHeight`, and for many elements this also means having a non-null `Background` or `Fill`. (A Transparent `Background` or `Fill` is fine.)

→ Its `IsHitTestVisible` property is set to `true` (which it is by default).

→ For a `Control`, its `IsEnabled` property is set to `true` (which it is by default).

The `IsHitTestVisible` property is a separate knob that enables you to have an element stay visible but not respond to any input. A `Control`'s `IsEnabled` property exists to not only make it unhittable, but visually indicate that with a disabled appearance. The hit-testability of an element is filled with subtleties, as the warnings in this section point out.

> **(?) Why does `UIElement` define a `Visibility` property that's a two-value enumeration (`Visible` or `Collapsed`) rather than a simple Boolean `IsVisible` property?**
>
> Code would be simpler to write if it was a Boolean property, but this decision is the unfortunate result of what I like to call *viral compatibility*. It was defined this way in Windows 8 to be compatible with Silverlight-based Windows Phone apps, which use the same property. Easy porting from Windows Phone apps to Windows Store apps and vice versa is important to Microsoft as well as developers, so this is understandable.
>
> But why did Silverlight for Windows Phone define it this way? To be compatible with the original Silverlight platform (for the desktop and the Web). Why did Silverlight define it this way? To be mostly compatible with WPF, which defined `Visibility` as a *three-value* enumeration: `Visible`, `Collapsed`, and `Hidden` (which means invisible but still participating in layout, much like a `Visible` element with its `Opacity` set to 0).
>
> This is basically the same situation as the routed events confusion described in the preceding chapter. It's great that Microsoft values compatibility so much, and your Windows Store apps will benefit from this principle for years to come. This is one case, however, where I wish the chain would have been broken somewhere along the line.

> ! **Transparent regions raise input events, but null regions do not!**
>
> If an element's Background or Fill is left at its default null value, then its background region (with no other content) never raises any input events. If you set either property to Transparent, however, the result looks identical but it now raises such events everywhere in its bounds. Along those lines, setting an element's Opacity to 0 does not affect its event-related behavior at all, unlike setting its Visibility to Collapsed.
>
> Elements with non-vector-based content—Image and MediaElement—are hit-testable on their entire bounds even if they contain transparent content (via the alpha channel). You can think of them as always having a Background set to Transparent. The same is true for TextBlock, which has no Background or Fill property either.

> ! **Setting a Page's Background has no effect!**
>
> Despite inheriting a Background property from Control, setting a Page's Background does nothing. Its child element (almost always a Panel) must be given one instead. This is important not just for the visual appearance of a Page but its hit-testability as well. An empty page raises no input events, acting as if its Background is always set to null.

> ! **The true bounds of a Canvas can result in confusing hit-testing behavior!**
>
> Because a Canvas's children can be rendered outside its bounds, it's easy to forget that it has a default actual size of zero in situations for which it doesn't get stretched (such as being placed inside a StackPanel). Because pointer events for Canvas itself (ignoring events bubbled up from any children) get raised only within its bounds (and only then when it has a non-null Background), you can run into situations in which Canvas-level pointer events are raised only for its children.

The *hit-testable* term implies that you can in fact *test* an element for its *hittability*. Checking all its relevant properties (and keeping in mind special rules for certain elements) isn't enough, because the element could still be obscured by an element above it that blocks all its input. Fortunately, you can easily test an element's hittability with the VisualTreeHelper.FindElementsInHostCoordinates method, which has several overloads.

Calling FindElementsInHostCoordinates means asking for all hittable elements that intersect a specific Point or Rect, passed as the first parameter. The second parameter is the element to use as the root of the search, enabling you to scope the question to a specific subtree of elements. Note that the Point or Rect is relative to the passed-in root element. (This element is the "host" mentioned in the method's name.) As with the element passed to GetCurrentPoint, this takes relevant transforms into account.

FindElementsInHostCoordinates has overloads that accept a third parameter: a Boolean includeAllElements that, when true, ignores hit-testability and simply returns all elements in the subtree that intersect the coordinate or region. The collection of returned elements is ordered from top to bottom, so the topmost element that would truly be "hit" by relevant input is the 0th element.

Tracking Multiple Pointers

Listing 6.2 demonstrates responding to and tracking multiple Pointers, using the following simple MainPage.xaml:

```xml
<Page x:Class="Chapter6.MainPage" …>
  <Canvas x:Name="canvas" Background="BlueViolet"/>
</Page>
```

It displays the ID of each pointer currently in contact and keeps it centered under each pointer's location, as shown in Figure 6.2 on a device that supports at least five simultaneous touch points.

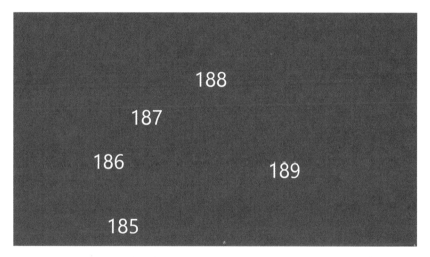

FIGURE 6.2 Pressing five fingers on the screen shows five Pointer IDs at the right locations.

LISTING 6.2 MainPage.xaml.cs: Tracking Multiple Pointers

```csharp
using System.Collections.Generic;
using Windows.UI.Input;
using Windows.UI.Xaml.Controls;
using Windows.UI.Xaml.Input;

namespace Chapter6
{
  public sealed partial class MainPage : Page
  {
    public MainPage()
```

LISTING 6.2   Continued

```
{
  InitializeComponent();
}


// Keep track of which TextBlocks are used for which Pointers
Dictionary<uint, TextBlock> textBlocks = new Dictionary<uint, TextBlock>();


protected override void OnPointerPressed(PointerRoutedEventArgs e)
{
  canvas.CapturePointer(e.Pointer);

  // Create a new TextBlock for this new Pointer
  TextBlock textBlock = new TextBlock {
    Text = e.Pointer.PointerId.ToString(), FontSize = 80 };

  PlaceTextBlockUnderPointerPoint(textBlock, e.GetCurrentPoint(canvas));

  // Keep track of the TextBlock and add it to the canvas
  textBlocks[e.Pointer.PointerId] = textBlock;
  canvas.Children.Add(textBlock);
}

protected override void OnPointerMoved(PointerRoutedEventArgs e)
{
  // Only do this if this Pointer is currently pressed
  if (textBlocks.ContainsKey(e.Pointer.PointerId))
  {
    // Retrieve the right TextBlock
    TextBlock textBlock = textBlocks[e.Pointer.PointerId];

    PlaceTextBlockUnderPointerPoint(textBlock, e.GetCurrentPoint(canvas));
  }
}

protected override void OnPointerReleased(PointerRoutedEventArgs e)
{
  // Remove the TextBlock from the canvas and the dictionary
  if (textBlocks.ContainsKey(e.Pointer.PointerId))
  {
    canvas.Children.Remove(textBlocks[e.Pointer.PointerId]);
    textBlocks.Remove(e.Pointer.PointerId);
    canvas.ReleasePointerCapture(e.Pointer);
  }
}
```

```
  protected override void OnPointerCanceled(PointerRoutedEventArgs e)
  {
    OnPointerReleased(e);
  }

  protected override void OnPointerCaptureLost(PointerRoutedEventArgs e)
  {
    OnPointerReleased(e);
  }

  void PlaceTextBlockUnderPointerPoint(TextBlock textBlock, PointerPoint point)
  {
    Canvas.SetLeft(textBlock, point.Position.X - (textBlock.ActualWidth / 2));
    Canvas.SetTop(textBlock, point.Position.Y - (textBlock.ActualHeight / 2));
  }
 }
}
```

Here are a few notes about Listing 6.2:

→ The implementation is not much different from the drag-and-drop example in Listing 6.1. The main difference is that the elements being dragged (TextBlocks, in this case) are dynamically created and added to the Canvas on PointerPressed and then removed on PointerReleased. For this reason, the events being handled are at the root Page level rather than on the draggable elements.

→ Rather than attaching event handlers to the relevant Page events, Listing 6.2 overrides the corresponding OnXXX methods instead. Often, a class that exposes an event XXX also exposes an OnXXX method that subclasses can override. Either approach can be used, and the result is the same. Note that the base implementation of each method is responsible for raising the corresponding event, so if you still want the event to be raised to any consumers of the object, you should invoke the base method inside the override.

→ Listing 6.2 performs pointer capture, although it's not strictly necessary because of the handling done at the Page level. There is one benefit, however. It keeps the TextBlock "attached" to its finger when the app is sharing the screen with other windows and the finger travels over another window (as long as the finger stays on screen).

Gestures

From the pointer events alone, it would take quite a bit of code to reliably detect user gestures such as press-and-hold, cross-slide item selection, and double taps. Even detecting a proper tap is more complicated than you might think. Furthermore, having apps write such code would be a recipe for disastrous user experiences because of the lack of consistency that would result.

Fortunately, Windows has a *gesture recognizer* that performs calculations based on the raw pointer events and raises appropriate additional events when it recognizes standard gestures. For example, if a user briefly touches a finger on a touchscreen then releases it, we already know that this causes a `PointerPressed` event to be raised followed by a `PointerReleased` event. However, if the timeframe between the two events is short enough, *and* if the amount of finger motion between the two events is small enough (so it doesn't appear to be a swipe or slide), *and* if only one finger is in contact the whole time, then the gesture recognizer raises a `Tapped` event. This higher-level event is what most apps consume.

This mechanism not only provides consistency for gestures among all apps, but with all system UI as well, such as the Start screen. And because it operates on pointers, it applies to touch, mouse, and pen. Figure 6.3 displays the basic Windows touch gestures and what they are intended to mean.

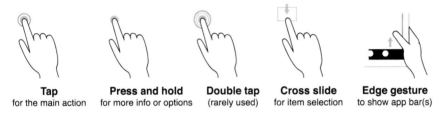

| Tap | Press and hold | Double tap | Cross slide | Edge gesture |
| for the main action | for more info or options | (rarely used) | for item selection | to show app bar(s) |

FIGURE 6.3   The basic Windows gestures

The gesture recognizer does a lot of work to account for sloppy user interaction and characteristics of the current device (such as the frequency of raw input and the physical size of the screen). Therefore, even if you are creating custom gesture support for your app, you should build it on top of the standard gesture recognizer rather than creating your own math engine that does all gesture detection from scratch.

You can interact with the gesture recognizer directly via the `Windows.UI.Input.GestureRecognizer` class, but you often don't need to do this because `UIElement` already does it for you. Instead, you can simply leverage gesture events exposed on all `UIElements`.

GestureRecognizer

Let's take a quick look at the Windows Runtime `GestureRecognizer` class for completeness. You might want to use it for advanced scenarios. For example, it exposes properties that enable you to tweak its settings: distance thresholds for detecting a cross slide (via its `CrossSlideThresholds` property), whether visual feedback is shown for gestures (via its `ShowGestureFeedback` property, `true` by default), and so on. Ignoring the more complex manipulations covered later, `GestureRecognizer` recognizes the following gestures and raises the following events relevant for touch (all single-finger only):

→ **Tapped**—Raised for a simple tap

→ **RightTapped**—Raised for a right tap (for touch, this is a released press-and-hold gesture)

→ **Holding**—Raised during the stages of press-and-hold

→ **CrossSliding**—Raised during the stages of a swipe within an area that scrolls in the perpendicular direction (used for selection and only for touch)

GestureRecognizer also recognizes double taps, but it doesn't expose an event for this. Instead, inside a Tapped event handler, you can check the TapCount property of the passed-in TappedEventArgs instance, which is set to 1 for a single tap or 2 for a double tap.

> Some of the system settings that impact gesture recognition, such as the maximum time between taps for a double tap, or the minimum pressing time for a press-and-hold, are exposed by read-only properties on the Windows.UI.ViewManagement.UISettings class.

Each of the GestureRecognizer events has a unique EventArgs type passed to its handlers, but they all have two properties in common: PointerDeviceType (revealing whether the source is Touch, Mouse, or Pen) and Position (of type Point).

If you want to interact with the GestureRecognizer directly, you must

> **What does the RightTapped event mean for touch input?**
>
> It doesn't mean using your right hand! For touch, RightTapped is raised after releasing a single-finger press-and-hold gesture, because logically that action should do the same thing as a right click from a mouse.

instantiate one, tell it which events you're interested in, attach handlers to those events, and, most importantly, pass it PointerPoints at all the appropriate times. Listing 6.3 demonstrates this in the code-behind file for a hypothetical MainPage.

LISTING 6.3   MainPage.xaml.cs: How to Make GestureRecognizer Raise Its Events

```
using Windows.System;
using Windows.UI.Input;
using Windows.UI.Xaml.Controls;
using Windows.UI.Xaml.Input;

namespace Chapter6
{
  public sealed partial class MainPage : Page
  {
    GestureRecognizer gestureRecognizer;

    public MainPage()
    {
      this.InitializeComponent();
```

LISTING 6.3   Continued

```
  // Initialize gesture recognizer
  gestureRecognizer = new GestureRecognizer();
  gestureRecognizer.GestureSettings = GestureSettings.Tap |
    GestureSettings.RightTap | GestureSettings.DoubleTap |
    GestureSettings.HoldWithMouse | GestureSettings.CrossSlide;

  // Attach handlers for recognized gestures (not shown in this listing)
  gestureRecognizer.Tapped += GestureRecognizer_Tapped;
  gestureRecognizer.RightTapped += GestureRecognizer_RightTapped;
  gestureRecognizer.Holding += GestureRecognizer_Holding;
  gestureRecognizer.CrossSliding += GestureRecognizer_CrossSliding;
}

//
// Handlers for recognized gestures:
//
…

//
// Forward all pointer input to the gesture recognizer so it can do its job:
//

protected override void OnPointerPressed(PointerRoutedEventArgs e)
{
  CapturePointer(e.Pointer);
  gestureRecognizer.ProcessDownEvent(e.GetCurrentPoint(this));
}

protected override void OnPointerMoved(PointerRoutedEventArgs e)
{
  // Pass all intermediate potentially-coalesced points:
  gestureRecognizer.ProcessMoveEvents(e.GetIntermediatePoints(this));
}

protected override void OnPointerReleased(PointerRoutedEventArgs e)
{
  gestureRecognizer.ProcessUpEvent(e.GetCurrentPoint(this));
  ReleasePointerCapture(e.Pointer);
}

protected override void OnPointerCanceled(PointerRoutedEventArgs e)
{
  OnPointerReleased(e);
}
```

LISTING 6.3   Continued

```
  protected override void OnPointerCaptureLost(PointerRoutedEventArgs e)
  {
    OnPointerReleased(e);
  }


  // This is for mouse only, but here for completeness:
  protected override void OnPointerWheelChanged(PointerRoutedEventArgs e)
  {
    bool isShiftKeyDown = ((e.KeyModifiers & VirtualKeyModifiers.Shift) ==
                           VirtualKeyModifiers.Shift);
    bool isControlKeyDown = ((e.KeyModifiers & VirtualKeyModifiers.Control) ==
                             VirtualKeyModifiers.Control);

    gestureRecognizer.ProcessMouseWheelEvent(e.GetCurrentPoint(this),
      isShiftKeyDown, isControlKeyDown);
  }
 }
}
```

For performance reasons, Listing 6.3 tells the gesture recognizer to look only for the specific gestures being handled by the app. Notice the use of the oddly named GestureSettings.HoldWithMouse flag. This detects press-and-hold for a mouse as well as touch and pen. If you want only press-and-hold to be detected for touch and pen, you can use the GestureSettings.Hold flag instead. Also notice the use of GetIntermediatePoints inside OnPointerMoved. GestureRecognizer's ProcessMoveEvents method is designed for this, because it wants the highest-resolution data possible.

The Holding event acts like three events combined into one. Event handlers are given a value from a HoldingState enumeration with three possible values: Started, Completed, and Canceled. The event is raised with the Started value as soon as the sole finger has been pressing long enough in a relatively stationary position. The event is raised with the Completed event once the finger is lifted.

If the finger ends up moving too much before breaking contact or a second finger makes contact, then it is raised with Canceled instead. (Interestingly, if anything unusual happens, such as the screen rotating or a pen getting close to the screen, the event is sometimes raised with Completed rather than Canceled.) If GestureRecognizer is told to detect right taps, RightTapped is raised immediately after a Completed Holding event (but for touch only, because mice and pens have a distinct way to generate a right tap).

> **! Avoid using GestureRecognizer with built-in controls such as Button and ListBox!**
>
> You can run into cases in which logic inside certain controls interferes with GestureRecognizer logic. This sometimes surfaces as an exception complaining that the pointer is already in use. GestureRecognizer is designed to be used with simple shapes (covered in Chapter 16, "Vector Graphics") or custom controls.

Although the `CrossSliding` event is supposed to be raised for perpendicular swiping, `GestureRecognizer` has no idea which direction is perpendicular, or whether the swipe is done in a scrollable region. It's up to the consumer to figure this out. In reality, `GestureRecognizer` simply recognizes a vertical swipe gesture (because scrolling is usually done horizontally). You can change it to recognize horizontal swipes instead by setting `GestureRecognizer`'s `CrossSlideHorizontally` property to `true`. Like `Holding`, `CrossSliding` reports many different states to event handlers with a `CrossSlidingState` enumeration. The typical pattern is an event raised with a `Started` state, followed by many with a `Dragging` state, followed by one with a `Completed` state.

EdgeGesture

You might have noticed that one of the gestures in Figure 6.3 isn't reported by `GestureRecognizer`: the *edge gesture*, a swipe from the top or bottom edge of the screen. This gesture is meant to toggle the visibility of a bottom and/or top app bar. (The equivalent gestures on the left and right edges are not exposed to apps, because these are reserved for app switching and the charms bar.)

The edge gesture is exposed by a dedicated `EdgeGesture` class in the `Windows.UI.Input` namespace that internally uses `GestureRecognizer` to recognize a vertical slide but filters it based on its position. The reason this is a separate class is that it responds to keyboard shortcuts in addition to pointer input. (Pressing either Windows+Z or the context menu key is treated as an edge gesture.)

To use `EdgeGesture`, you first call its static `GetForCurrentView` method to obtain an instance. This is typically done in `App.xaml.cs` in an overridden implementation of `Application.OnWindowCreated`. That way, each window in your app, if there are multiple, handles this appropriately. The next part of this book discusses `OnWindowCreated` and related functionality.

Once you have an instance of `EdgeGesture` returned by `GetForCurrentView`, you can handle its three events:

→ **Starting**—Raised when a matching gesture has started, but it's still possible the pointer will move in such a way that cancels the gesture.

→ **Completed**—Raised when the gesture has successfully completed (the finger has lifted or the key has been pressed).

→ **Canceled**—Raised after `Starting` if the gesture doesn't end up being an edge gesture after all. For example, if a finger swipes up from the bottom edge but turns around and swipes back down, `Canceled` is raised.

Handlers for these events are given an `EdgeGestureEventArgs` instance with a single property called `Kind`. This is an `EdgeGestureKind` enumeration, which is basically the same as `PointerDeviceType` except it includes a value for `Keyboard`. Confusingly, its only values are `Touch`, `Mouse`, and `Keyboard`, so an edge gesture made by a pen is reported as `Touch` instead.

When you use an AppBar or CommandBar control, covered in Part IV, it automatically detects edge gestures and shows/hides accordingly. Therefore, you normally don't need to handle this event directly.

EdgeGesture events cannot currently be raised by mouse input!
This is a bug specific to XAML apps and is still not fixed in Windows 8.1.

UIElement Gesture Events

Listing 6.3 contains a lot of boilerplate code for something that is so common. That's why UIElement internally interacts with GestureRecognizer and exposes its own gesture events. With these convenient events, you don't have to do anything other than attach handlers. Plus, unlike the GestureRecognizer events, the UIElement events are routed events.

The basic UIElement single-finger gesture events should look familiar:

→ **Tapped**—Raised for a simple tap

→ **RightTapped**—Raised for a right tap (for touch, this is a released press-and-hold gesture)

→ **DoubleTapped**—Raised for a double tap

→ **Holding**—Raised during the stages of press-and-hold

These map closely to the GestureRecognizer events discussed in the preceding section. Note the addition of a DoubleTapped event, which is a much simpler and consistent way to handle this gesture. However, there are no events for the cross slide or edge gesture. That's because most scenarios are covered by built-in controls that internally handle this event from GestureRecognizer, so it would have been overkill to provide such events on UIElement.

Analogous to GestureRecognizer's GestureSettings flags, UIElement exposes several properties for toggling the recognition of specific gestures: IsTapEnabled, IsRightTapEnabled, IsDoubleTapEnabled, and IsHoldingEnabled. However, unlike with GestureRecognizer, these are all enabled (true) by default.

Manipulations

A more complex class of gestures, known as *manipulations*, can also be detected and reported by the Windows gesture recognizer. These are meant to handle panning, rotating, and zooming, as shown in Figure 6.4.

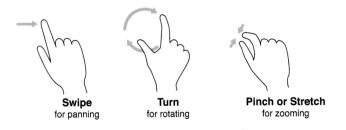

Swipe
for panning

Turn
for rotating

Pinch or Stretch
for zooming

FIGURE 6.4   The more complex Windows gestures known as manipulations

Although the use of more than one finger is unique to manipulations, the biggest differences between these gestures and the previously discussed ones are:

→ Manipulations provide a continuous stream of information (although still in the form of raised events) while the gesture is being performed

→ Manipulations can be done while other fingers are touching the screen. For example, unlike a cross slide, a swipe is still a swipe even if many fingers are doing it.

→ Manipulations can be combined. You can swipe, turn, and pinch/stretch simultaneously with the same two fingers.

Logically, these actions are straightforward to apply to elements, because their concepts map exactly to applying a `TranslateTransform`, `RotateTransform`, and/or `ScaleTransform`. Detecting *when* you should apply these transforms and with *what values* would be an entirely different story, however, if it weren't for the following manipulation events exposed by `UIElement`:

→ `ManipulationStarting` and `ManipulationStarted`

→ `ManipulationDelta`

→ `ManipulationInertiaStarting`

→ `ManipulationCompleted`

These events are also exposed by `GestureRecognizer`, although there is no `ManipulationStarting` event and `ManipulationDelta` is named `ManipulationUpdated` instead. Unlike our examination of the simpler gesture events, this section focuses on the `UIElement` events.

These events combine the information from independent fingers and package the data in an easy-to-consume form. Unlike the basic gestures, elements must opt into the manipulation events. For a `UIElement` to raise them, its

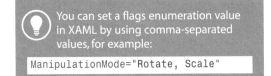

You can set a flags enumeration value in XAML by using comma-separated values, for example:

`ManipulationMode="Rotate, Scale"`

ManipulationMode property must be set appropriately on itself or a parent. This property is a flags enumeration that can be set to a list of specific manipulations bitwise-ORed together, or All or None.

Using Manipulation Events

ManipulationStarting gets raised as soon as *any* input is detected, followed by ManipulationStarted, which gets raised the instant that the recognizer detects that a translation, rotation, or scale is underway. ManipulationDelta gets raised for each PointerMoved raised during this process, and ManipulationCompleted gets raised after PointerReleased is raised for *all* fingers.

The ManipulationDelta event gives you rich information about how the element is expected to be translated/rotated/scaled. You can then apply this data directly to the relevant transforms. The ManipulationDeltaRoutedEventArgs instance passed to handlers contains a Delta property of type ManipulationDelta that exposes the following properties:

→ **Translation**—A Point property with X and Y values.

→ **Scale**—A float property representing the distance change as a percentage. For example, doubling the distance would report a value of 1.0.

→ **Rotation**—A float property that specifies the angle in degrees.

→ **Expansion**—A float property that is redundant with Scale, but it reports the difference in terms of absolute logical pixels instead of a relative value.

Actually, ManipulationDeltaRoutedEventArgs has *two* properties of type ManipulationDelta. Delta reports the changes compared to the last time the event was raised, but Cumulative reports the changes compared to when ManipulationStarted was raised. So no matter how you prefer to consume the data, there should be a way that pleases you! You can also instantly halt the manipulation by calling ManipulationDeltaRoutedEventArgs's Complete method.

Listing 6.4 contains the code-behind file for the following Page, making it possible to move, rotate, and zoom the contained photo with standard swipe, rotate, and pinch gestures:

```
<Page x:Class="Chapter6.MainPage" …>
  <Canvas Background="Crimson">
    <Image Source="photo.png" RenderTransformOrigin=".5,.5"
           ManipulationMode="All"
           ManipulationStarted="Image_ManipulationStarted"
           ManipulationDelta="Image_ManipulationDelta">
      <Image.RenderTransform>
        <CompositeTransform x:Name="transform"/>
      </Image.RenderTransform>
    </Image>
  </Canvas>
</Page>
```

The result is shown in Figure 6.5.

LISTING 6.4   `MainPage.xaml.cs:` Handling Manipulation Events to Enable Panning, Rotating, and Zooming

```
using Windows.Foundation;
using Windows.UI.Xaml.Controls;
using Windows.UI.Xaml.Input;

namespace Manipulation
{
  public sealed partial class MainPage : Page
  {
    // The transform state at the beginning of the current gesture:
    Point startingTranslation;
    double startingRotation;
    double startingScale;

    public MainPage()
    {
      InitializeComponent();
    }

    void Image_ManipulationStarted(object sender,
                              ManipulationStartedRoutedEventArgs e)
    {
      // Capture the initial state so Cumulative values can be added to these:
      startingTranslation = new Point { X = transform.TranslateX,
                                  Y = transform.TranslateY };
      startingRotation = transform.Rotation;
      startingScale = transform.ScaleX; // Same as ScaleY
    }

    void Image_ManipulationDelta(object sender,
                              ManipulationDeltaRoutedEventArgs e)
    {
      // Update the transform
      transform.TranslateX = startingTranslation.X + e.Cumulative.Translation.X;
      transform.TranslateY = startingTranslation.Y + e.Cumulative.Translation.Y;
      transform.Rotation = startingRotation + e.Cumulative.Rotation;
      transform.ScaleX = transform.ScaleY = startingScale * e.Cumulative.Scale;
    }
  }
}
```

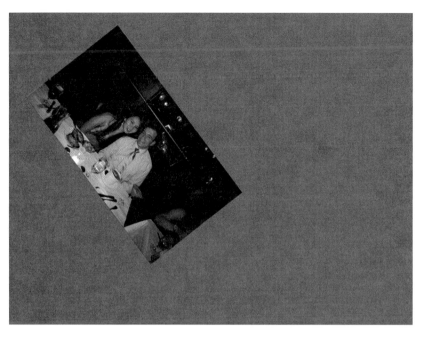

FIGURE 6.5   Enabling panning, rotating, and zooming on an Image by handling the ManipulationStarted and ManipulationDelta events

The Image conveniently has a CompositeTransform applied as its RenderTransform, so the code inside the ManipulationDelta handler needs only to update the transform's properties with data from the ManipulationDeltaRoutedEventArgs instance. Note that setting them to the Cumulative values isn't enough because these values are only deltas from the start of the *current* gesture, and previous gestures might have already transformed the element. That's why the ManipulationStarted event is also handled. By adding the deltas to the pre-gesture values, each new gesture adds on to the previous one. When you use the manipulation events, pointer capture occurs automatically, so you don't have to worry about manual capture and release.

> (!) **If possible, use ScrollViewer's built-in panning and zooming functionality rather than handling manipulation events!**
>
> ScrollViewer's panning and zooming support, described in Chapter 4, is implemented with a second thread to produce the smoothest possible performance. In contrast, handling the manipulation events and setting corresponding transforms must be done on the UI thread. This can cause noticeable lags, depending on what else is happening on the UI thread.
>
> Interestingly, the manipulation events still get raised when ScrollViewer panning and zooming occurs, but you can't stop the manipulation because of the use of a separate thread. You can still act upon this information, however, to keep other elements in sync.

Inertia

Manipulation events include support for giving objects inertia, so they can gradually slow to a stop when a gesture is done rather than stopping instantly. This makes the gestures feel more realistic and make it easy to support things like "flicking" an object to make it move a distance based on the speed of the flick.

Inertia is enabled based on the value of `ManipulationMode`. Therefore, when it is set to `All`, as in the XAML for Listing 6.4, it is enabled. With the `Photo_ManipulationDelta` implementation in Listing 6.4, everything works as expected "for free" because the passed-in values are calculated accordingly. Note that when `ManipulationDelta` is raised in response to inertia, the passed-in `ManipulationDeltaRoutedEventArgs` instance's `IsInertial` property is set to `true`.

Between the stream of `ManipulationDelta` events raised due to actual input and the stream of `ManipulationDelta` events raised due to inertia, the `ManipulationInertiaStarting` event is raised. This gives you an opportunity to customize the inertia. Note that `ManipulationCompleted` is not raised until *all* `ManipulationDelta` events are raised, including ones due to inertia.

If you want the photo manipulation example to work the same way but without inertia, you can change the following attribute in XAML:

```
ManipulationMode="All"
```

to:

```
ManipulationMode="TranslateX, TranslateY, Rotate, Scale"
```

This explicitly sets all the relevant `ManipulationMode` values, but without the three inertia values (`TranslateInertia`, `RotateInertia`, `ScaleInertia`).

Mouse Input

One of the biggest shocks to a WPF or Silverlight developer learning about Windows Store apps is often, "Hey, where are the mouse events?" And now you know the answer: Mouse events are, for the most part, the same pointer events and gesture events used for touch. If you look back at these events, you'll see that they map to the behavior of a mouse. Furthermore, even mouse dragging is treated as translation and holding Ctrl while scrolling the mouse wheel is treated as zooming in the manipulation events.

Of course, there are some mouse-specific APIs exposed for cases in which the common abstraction isn't rich enough, which this section discusses. Let's quickly go through the same areas covered by the "Touch Input" section but examine only the mouse-specific APIs.

MouseDevice and MouseCapabilities

In addition to the generic `PointerDevice` class, the `Windows.Devices.Input` namespace contains a `MouseDevice` class with two interesting members:

→ A static `GetForCurrentView` method that returns the current `MouseDevice` if one exists (or the primary one if there is more than one mouse)

→ A `MouseMoved` event that is just like `PointerMoved`, but raised only for pointer movement from this specific mouse

So there still is one "mouse event" in the framework—it's just a little hard to find! Note that the `MouseDevice` class has no relation to `PointerDevice` other than its similar name.

Similar to `TouchCapabilities`, an awkward `MouseCapabilities` class provides information about any connected mice. After instantiating a `MouseCapabilities` object, you can check a number of pseudo-Boolean properties whose values are 1 for `true` or 0 for `false`: `MousePresent` tells you whether a mouse is attached, `HorizontalWheelPresent` and `VerticalWheelPresent` properties tell you whether any attached mouse supports a horizontal/vertical scroll wheel, and `SwapButtons` tells you whether any attached mouse has reversed left and right buttons. In addition, its `NumberOfButtons` property is a `uint` that reveals how many buttons the mouse has (or the *maximum* number if multiple mice are present).

Revisiting Pointer Events and `PointerPointProperties`

There's one pointer event that was omitted from the discussion in the "Touch Input" section because it is specific to a mouse (or perhaps a fancy pen): `PointerWheelChanged`. Handlers for `PointerWheelChanged` are given the same `PointerRoutedEventArgs` instance as all the other pointer events, but they can retrieve the `PointerPointProperties` object (via `PointerPoint.Properties`) to get the following additional details about the event:

→ **IsHorizontalMouseWheel**—This is true if `PointerWheelChanged` is triggered by a horizontal mouse wheel, and `false` if triggered by a vertical mouse wheel.

→ **MouseWheelDelta**—Reveals how much the wheel position changed since the last time the event was raised (in terms of "notches" or some hardware-specific distance threshold).

It turns out that many of the properties exposed by `PointerPointProperties` are mouse (or pen)-specific, and you might want to inspect them in response to *any* pointer event. Mice can have up to five standard buttons recognized by Windows (left, middle, right, and two *extended buttons*) so it can be crucial to know which button is pressed/released beyond the basic information conveyed by `Tapped` vs. `RightTapped` events. The following `PointerPointProperties` properties enable this:

> **Where is the event for handling the pressing of a mouse's middle button?**
>
> Information about the middle mouse button, if it exists, and any other buttons are exposed via `PointerPointProperties`. You can handle an event such as `Tapped` then determine which button was pressed by looking at the associated `PointerPoint`.

→ `IsLeftButtonPressed`, `IsMiddleButtonPressed`, `IsRightButtonPressed`, `IsXButton1Pressed`, and `IsXButton2Pressed`—These Boolean properties tell you which buttons are depressed at the time of the event.

→ `PointerUpdateKind`—An enumeration value that tells you which of the five mouse buttons was just pressed or released to trigger the current event (if applicable).

> Although all the pointer events described in the "Touch Input" section also apply to mice, they can behave slightly differently. For example, don't forget that whereas `PointerMoved` (and `PointerEntered`/`PointerExited`) events get raised only between `PointerPressed` and `PointerReleased` (or equivalent) events for touch, this is not the case for a mouse pointer. If you write code that relies on the touch-specific ordering of events (for example, do some initialization in a `PointerPressed` handler required by the `PointerMoved` handler), you could easily write an app that crashes as soon as it is used with a mouse!

Revisiting `GestureRecognizer`

`GestureRecognizer` has one mouse (and pen)-specific event not covered previously: `Dragging`. Whereas a single-finger touch-based swipe gesture generates series of `CrossSliding` events depending on its direction, the same motion from a mouse with any button down (or from a pen while in contact) generates a series of `Dragging` events instead.

Like `CrossSliding`, `Dragging` reports many different states to event handlers with an enumeration—this time called `DraggingState`. The pattern is the same: an event raised with a `Started` state, followed by many with a `Continuing` state, followed by one with a `Completed` state. Unlike `CrossSliding`, `Dragging` is reported for any direction.

> **Why is the Dragging event not applicable for touch?**
>
> This decision was made to better handle the common ways in which touch is used, such as swiping anywhere on a surface to pan it without worrying about accidentally dragging-and-dropping an item inside that surface. You could, of course, still choose to implement touch-based dragging using either the raw pointer events or the translation manipulation events, because neither set of events discriminates based on the pointer device. And if you care about inertia, you'd want to use the manipulation events rather than the `Dragging` event anyway.
>
> Note that the `ListView` and `GridView` controls covered in Part IV of this book do support touch-based dragging of their items thanks to their own internal logic. They expose a `CanDragItems` property that enables you to opt-in to this support. To avoid confusing a swipe-to-pan gesture with a dragging gesture, this built-in dragging support must be initiated with a cross slide gesture (in the direction perpendicular to panning).

Revisiting `UIElement` Gesture Events

`UIElement` exposes some additional mouse (and pen)-specific gesture routed events that are all related to the lower-level `Dragging` event:

→ **DragOver** and **Drop**—Maps to Dragging events with states of Started/Continuing and Completed, respectively

→ **DragEnter** and **DragLeave**—Like PointerEntered and PointerExited, but raised only when dragging (meaning a mouse button is depressed)

These events only work in limited contexts, however. To see them raised on a drop target, its AllowDrop property (or an ancestor's) must be set to true. Furthermore, the drop source must be made draggable. For example, it could be an element inside a GridView (covered in Chapter 11, "Items Controls") with its CanDragItems property set to true.

UIElement's Holding event is never raised for mouse input!

UIElement internally uses GestureRecognizer with the Hold setting rather than the HoldWithMouse setting. Therefore, RightTapped is a much better event to use than Holding. It covers the press-and-hold case for touch while also behaving reasonably for mouse and pen. This is a bug that could be fixed in a future version of Windows. In the meantime, if you want a mouse-enabled press-and-hold experience, you can interact with GestureRecognizer directly.

Pen Input

Windows includes fantastic support for pen input. Although Figure 6.1 shows a pen digitizer as an external device, it can be integrated directly into the screen just like a touch digitizer. Indeed, this is how tablets such as the Surface Pro work. So when you read *digitizer* in this section, you can typically think *screen*.

By now, it has been drilled into your head that the pointer, gesture, and manipulation events work great for pen input. Furthermore, it should come as no surprise that from these events, you can access pen-specific information to interact with pen-specific tricks: pressure sensitivity, eraser mode, and more.

Note that when a pen is in use, touch input is ignored. This is an important part of a *palm rejection* feature, which makes it easier to write on a screen without worrying about touching the screen at the same time.

There is no PenDevice or PenCapabilities class analogous to MouseDevice and MouseCapabilities. And there are no additional events you haven't already seen from the "Touch Input" and "Mouse Input" sections. There are, however, many properties on PointerPointProperties that are pen-specific:

→ **IsBarrelButtonPressed**—This is true if the button along the side of the pen's body is depressed during the event.

→ **IsEraser**—This is true if the input is from the "eraser" on the rear of the pen.

→ **IsInRange**—This is true if the pen is close to the digitizer but not quite touching it. (Although this was already mentioned in the "Touch Input" section, I'm listing it again here because it's commonly used with pens.)

→ **IsInverted**—This is true if the rear of the pen is being used instead of the front. (Unlike IsEraser, this can be true even when the pen is not touching the digitizer. IsEraser requires contact.)

→ **Pressure**—A float value from 0.0 to 1.0 that indicates how hard the pen is pressed against the digitizer (or 0.5 if pressure sensitivity isn't supported).

→ **Orientation**—A float value that reveals the angle that the pen is held, in terms of degrees relative to the z-axis (perpendicular to the digitizer).

→ ⎯ ⎯⎯⎯⎯ ⎯⎯⎯⎯⎯⎯ float value that represents an angle in degrees. This value, however, changes as the pen is spun in-place in the user's fingers (independent of the pen's Orientation).

→ **XTilt**—A float value revealing the angle (in degrees) of how much the pen is tilted to the left or right. The value is negative when tilted to the left and positive when tilted to the right.

→ **YTilt**—A float value revealing the angle (in degrees) of how much the pen is tilted to the top or bottom. The value is negative when tilted down (toward the user) and positive when tilted up (away from the user).

(!) Pens typically generate PointerMoved events even when they aren't touching the digitizer!

Because a typical pen digitizer supports the detection of pen input when the pen is *in range* but not *in contact*, pen motion acts more like a mouse than a finger. When PointerMoved events are raised, you cannot assume that the pen is in contact with the digitizer. You can, however, check the IsInRange and IsInContact properties to figure out exactly what is going on.

(?) What does the RightTapped event mean for pen input?

A pen can perform a right tap by tapping the digitizer with its barrel button depressed. Unlike touch, RightTapped is not raised if you attempt to do a press-and-hold gesture with a pen. (Although unlike a mouse, press-and-hold with a pen does raise UIElement's Holding event.)

(💡) All properties exposed by PointerPointProperties use smart default values so they behave reasonably when not supported by the current PointerDevice. Even if you act on some pen-specific properties such as Pressure, you typically can do it unconditionally rather than having to check the PointerDeviceType.

Rendering Handwriting

If you're adding special support for pen in your app, then you likely want to render the strokes that the user is writing or drawing with the pen. The highest-performance way to do this is to leverage a class called CoreIndependentInputSource in conjunction with SwapChainPanel to render the strokes with DirectX. That way, you can receive and process the input on a background thread and not be impacted by activity on the UI thread. (See Chapter 26, "Integrating DirectX," for more information.)

The easiest way to render the strokes, however, is with the help of a Windows Runtime class called InkManager. InkManager keeps track of strokes, manages the ability to erase and select them, enables the data to be saved to and loaded from a stream, and even exposes handwriting recognition capabilities! All you need to do is feed an InkManager the appropriate raw pointer data received by the PointerPressed, PointerMoved, and PointerReleased family of events. Note that InkManager itself does not provide any rendering capabilities. Therefore, the role InkManager plays is very similar to the role of GestureRecognizer examined earlier.

Listing 6.5 performs basic rendering of pen strokes by handling pointer events, updating InkManager, and adding elements to a Canvas that are covered in Chapter 16. Therefore, don't focus on the drawing details but rather the pattern of using InkManager. This code-behind file corresponds to the following simple XAML file:

```
<Page x:Class="Chapter6.MainPage"
  xmlns="http://schemas.microsoft.com/winfx/2006/xaml/presentation"
  xmlns:x="http://schemas.microsoft.com/winfx/2006/xaml">
  <Canvas Name="canvas" Background="Gray" />
</Page>
```

The Canvas is given an explicit background to make it hittable and therefore receive the input events.

LISTING 6.5   MainPage.xaml.cs: Rendering Ink Strokes on a Canvas

```
using System;
using Windows.Devices.Input;
using Windows.Foundation;
using Windows.UI;
using Windows.UI.Input;
using Windows.UI.Input.Inking;
using Windows.UI.Xaml.Controls;
using Windows.UI.Xaml.Input;
using Windows.UI.Xaml.Media;
using Windows.UI.Xaml.Shapes;
```

LISTING 6.5   Continued

```csharp
namespace Chapter6
{
  public sealed partial class MainPage : Page
  {
    // Keeps track of the ink stroke data and can perform handwriting recognition
    InkManager inkManager = new InkManager();

    // Used for drawing strokes on the screen
    PathFigure currentFigure;

    public MainPage()
    {
      this.InitializeComponent();
      this.canvas.PointerPressed += Canvas_PointerPressed;
      this.canvas.PointerMoved += Canvas_PointerMoved;
      this.canvas.PointerReleased += Canvas_PointerReleased;
      this.canvas.PointerCanceled += Canvas_PointerReleased;
      this.canvas.PointerCaptureLost += Canvas_PointerReleased;
    }

    void Canvas_PointerPressed(object sender, PointerRoutedEventArgs e)
    {
      if (e.Pointer.PointerDeviceType == PointerDeviceType.Pen)
      {
        // Tell the InkManager about the PointerPressed event
        this.inkManager.ProcessPointerDown(e.GetCurrentPoint(this));

        // Set up a new shape to render the strokes between pointer down and up
        PathGeometry geometry = new PathGeometry();
        this.currentFigure = new PathFigure();
        geometry.Figures.Add(this.currentFigure);
        Path path = new Path { Data = geometry, StrokeThickness = 8,
                               Stroke = new SolidColorBrush(Colors.Yellow) };

        // Add the (currently-empty) shape to the Canvas
        this.canvas.Children.Add(path);
      }
    }

    void Canvas_PointerMoved(object sender, PointerRoutedEventArgs e)
    {
      if (e.Pointer.PointerDeviceType == PointerDeviceType.Pen)
      {
        if (e.Pointer.IsInContact)
        {
```

LISTING 6.5   Continued

```csharp
      // Only do this when a pen is in use, and when it is making contact
      PointerPoint pointerPoint = e.GetCurrentPoint(this);

      // Tell the InkManager about the PointerMoved event.
      // Returns a Point when inking or selecting, or a Rect when erasing.
      object update = this.inkManager.ProcessPointerUpdate(pointerPoint);

      if (this.inkManager.Mode == InkManipulationMode.Inking)
      {
        DrawStroke((Point)update);
      }
      else if (this.inkManager.Mode == InkManipulationMode.Erasing)
      {
        Rect rect = (Rect)update;
        // The erasure is only successful if the invalidation Rect is nonzero
        if (rect.Height > 0 || rect.Width > 0)
        {
          RemoveErasedStrokes(rect);
        }
      }
    }
  }
}

void Canvas_PointerReleased(object sender, PointerRoutedEventArgs e)
{
  if (e.Pointer.PointerDeviceType == PointerDeviceType.Pen)
  {
    // Tell the InkManager about the PointerPressed event
    this.inkManager.ProcessPointerUp(e.GetCurrentPoint(this));
  }
}

void DrawStroke(Point point)
{
  if (this.currentFigure.Segments.Count == 0)
  {
    // Set the starting point
    this.currentFigure.StartPoint = point;
  }

  // Add a line segment from the previous point to the current point
  this.currentFigure.Segments.Add(new LineSegment { Point = point });
}
```

LISTING 6.5   Continued

```
void RemoveErasedStrokes(Rect invalidationRect)
{
  // Just compare the segments from the current InkStrokes tracked by the
  // InkManager (which has at least one newly-erased stroke) to the segments
  // drawn on the screen, and remove any drawn segments that no longer
  // correspond to strokes managed by the InkManager.
  // Note that this ignores the passed-in invalidation rectangle.
  int pathIndex = 0, pathSegmentIndex = 0;
  Path currentPath = (Path)this.canvas.Children[pathIndex];
  PathSegmentCollection currentPathSegments =
    ((PathGeometry)currentPath.Data).Figures[0].Segments;
  LineSegment currentPathSegment =
    (LineSegment)currentPathSegments[pathSegmentIndex];

  foreach (InkStroke stroke in this.inkManager.GetStrokes())
  {
    foreach (InkStrokeRenderingSegment inkSegment in
      stroke.GetRenderingSegments())
    {
      if (currentPathSegment.Point != inkSegment.Position)
      {
        // This has been erased, so remove it from the path
        currentPathSegments.Remove(currentPathSegment);

        // If this was the first segment in the path,
        // update the StartPoint to match the new first segment
        if (pathSegmentIndex == 0 && currentPathSegments.Count > 0)
        {
          ((PathGeometry)currentPath.Data).Figures[0].StartPoint =
            ((LineSegment)currentPathSegments[0]).Point;
        }

        // Account for the removed path segment
        pathSegmentIndex--;
      }

      // Update all the "current" references for the next iteration
      pathSegmentIndex++;
      if (pathSegmentIndex == currentPathSegments.Count)
      {
        // We've reached the end of this path
        pathIndex++;
        pathSegmentIndex = 0;
        if (pathIndex < this.canvas.Children.Count)
        {
          currentPath = (Path)this.canvas.Children[pathIndex];
```

LISTING 6.5   Continued

```
                    currentPathSegments =
                        ((PathGeometry)currentPath.Data).Figures[0].Segments;
                    currentPathSegment =
                        (LineSegment)currentPathSegments[pathSegmentIndex],
                }
            }
        }
    }
}
}
```

There are several things to note about this listing:

→ If you want this code to work with a mouse as well, simply remove the check for the PointerDeviceType at the beginning of the three event handlers.

→ InkManager's ProcessPointerUpdate method is unusual. It returns different (and unrelated) objects depending on whether the pen is in an erasing mode. When inking (or selecting), it returns a Point that matches the passed-in PointerPoint's Position. When erasing, it returns a Rect that represents an area encompassing any erased strokes (so drawing logic can take advantage of this data). If no strokes get erased by the update, it returns a zero-sized Rect. If you use this code with mouse input, it will always appear to be in inking mode.

→ An improvement to Canvas_PointerReleased would be to handle a precise tap (in which PointerPressed is raised then PointerReleased, without any PointerMoved in-between). In this case, the InkManager is told about the "dot" but nothing is drawn on the screen because DrawStroke is only called inside Canvas_PointerMoved.

→ Inside DrawStroke, a simple LineSegment is used to connect each point to the previous one. For better rendering, more data from the pen (such as the amount of pressure) could be used, but this would require many changes in the way the vector graphic elements are currently being used.

→ The most complicated part of this code deals with removing visuals from the screen in the event that strokes are erased. In fact, this erasure feature is currently the only reason this listing even needs InkManager. If we didn't want to support direct erasing from the pen, this listing could have removed all use of InkManager and perform the drawing of strokes the same way, based on the data already given by the pointer events.

→ InkManager can be used more deeply to improve the rendering of ink strokes. It automatically calculates Bézier curves that can be used to produce a smoother drawing and exposes them on the relevant InkStrokeRenderingSegment objects. For example, you could discard the current drawing inside Canvas_PointerReleased then iterate through InkManager's collection of strokes, as done in RemoveErasedStrokes, to replace it with a better drawing. Chapter 16 discusses Bézier curves and how to draw them.

Figure 6.6 shows the result of running this code then receiving user input.

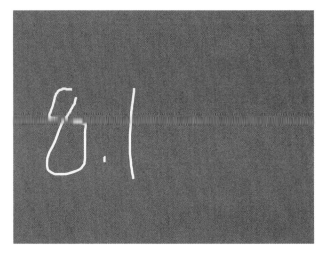

FIGURE 6.6   With the code from Listing 6.5, pen strokes can be rendered in a `Canvas`.

Handwriting Recognition

`InkManager`'s most amazing trick is arguably the ability to perform handwriting recognition. Even more so than `GestureRecognizer`, this is rocket science that you likely do not want to build yourself. The handwriting recognition is the same great functionality exposed by the Windows software keyboard, and is supported for 33 languages. For many apps, letting the software keyboard handle handwriting recognition is good enough and requires no additional effort. The app simply receives input text as if it were typed. For apps that desire a more integrated handwriting recognition experience, however, `InkManager` makes it possible.

Because Listing 6.5 is already feeding `InkManager` the appropriate pointer data at the appropriate times, adding handwriting recognition is a very small addition to the code. First, let's update the XAML to include a `ListView` that will display a list of recognition guesses from `InkManager` alongside the hand-written text and use a `Grid` to display the `Canvas` and `ListView` side-by-side:

```
<Page x:Class="Chapter6.MainPage"
  xmlns="http://schemas.microsoft.com/winfx/2006/xaml/presentation"
  xmlns:x="http://schemas.microsoft.com/winfx/2006/xaml">
  <Grid>
    <Grid.ColumnDefinitions>
      <ColumnDefinition />
      <ColumnDefinition Width="Auto" />
    </Grid.ColumnDefinitions>
    <Canvas Name="canvas" Background="Gray" />
```

```
    <ListView Name="listView" Grid.Column="1" FontSize="50"
            Header="Recognized text:" />
  </Grid>
</Page>
```

We can then trigger recognition to happen on every `PointerReleased` event by adding the following call to Listing 6.5:

```
void Canvas_PointerReleased(object sender, PointerRoutedEventArgs e)
{
  if (e.Pointer.PointerDeviceType == PointerDeviceType.Pen)
  {
    // Tell the InkManager about the PointerPressed event
    this.inkManager.ProcessPointerUp(e.GetCurrentPoint(this));

    RecognizeStrokes();
  }
}
```

`RecognizeStrokes` can then be implemented as follows:

```
// Perform handwriting recognition and display all recognition guesses
async Task RecognizeStrokes()
{
  listView.Items.Clear();

  foreach (InkRecognitionResult result in
    await this.inkManager.RecognizeAsync(InkRecognitionTarget.All))
  {
    foreach (string candidate in result.GetTextCandidates())
    {
      // Display the candidate string
      listView.Items.Add(
        new ListViewItem { Content = candidate, FontSize = 50 });
    }
  }
}
```

InkManager's handwriting recognition API is `RecognizeAsync`, which returns a collection of `InkRecognitionResults`, one for each recognized word in the order it was written. Each `InkRecognitionResult` provides a collection of candidate strings that represent a guess for what is written in order from highest to lowest confidence. Inside `RecognizeStrokes`, all candidates from all `InkRecognitionResults` are simply added to the `ListView` as a flat list of items for demonstration purposes. Like any potentially long-running API in the Windows Runtime, `RecognizeAsync` runs asynchronously and therefore is called with an `await` keyword inside a method decorated with `async`. Chapter 8, "Threading, Windows, and Pages," discusses asynchronous operations in more detail.

When you call `RecognizeAsync`, you must pass one of the following
`InkRecognitionTarget` enumeration values:

→ **All**—All strokes tracked by `InkManager` are given to the recognition algorithm

→ **Selected**—Only the selected strokes are given to the recognition algorithm

→ **Recent**—Only the strokes added after the preceding call to `RecognizeAsync` are given
   to the recognition algorithm, which is handy for incremental recognition within a
   large amount of handwriting

By default, `InkManager` performs recognition with the user's default language, but you can
override this by calling `SetDefaultRecognizer` with an `InkRecognizer` instance that you
can obtain from `InkManager`'s `GetRecognizers` method.

Figure 6.7 shows the result of running the code from Listing 6.5 with the additions from
this section. The first result is indeed the correct answer.

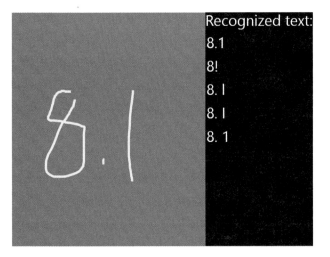

FIGURE 6.7   `InkManager` enables you to recognize handwriting directly within your app.

Keyboard Input

In contrast to the other areas, the keyboard input APIs look traditional—and even
simpler—compared to past Microsoft technologies. Although an app might be used with a
software keyboard or hardware keyboard, the resulting input looks identical.

Because keyboard input is not tied into pointer events, and because gestures and manipulations are based on pointers, users cannot automatically perform standard gestures with a
keyboard. The one exception is the edge gesture, discussed earlier, which is automatically
invoked by Windows+Z or the context menu key. When this happens, only the
`EdgeGesture.Completed` event is raised because there's no way to start then cancel the
gesture in this fashion.

> **How can I tell whether a hardware keyboard is present?**
>
> You can instantiate a KeyboardCapabilities class from the Windows.Devices.Input namespace and check the value of its one and only property: KeyboardPresent. Its value is 1 for true or 0 for false. Although it's not mentioned in its name, this refers to the *hardware* keyboard. On a device with a touchscreen, the software keyboard is always available when the hardware keyboard is not.

UIElement Keyboard Events

UIElement exposes two simple routed events for keyboard input: KeyDown and KeyUp. The EventArgs parameter passed to keyboard event handlers is a KeyRoutedEventArgs instance that contains the following properties:

→ **Key**—The key that was pressed or released. This property is of type Windows. System.VirtualKey, a large enumeration of every possible key.

→ **KeyStatus**—Reports extended information for certain keys.

→ **Handled**—The typical routed event property that can "halt" bubbling.

The KeyStatus property is a Windows.UI.Core.CorePhysicalKeyStatus structure. In case you didn't get all the hints from its name, this is "core" information that is needed only for advanced scenarios. It exposes the following properties:

→ **RepeatCount**—Tracks the number of times the KeyDown event gets repeated for a single, prolonged key press. For example, when you hold down the spacebar long enough, a flurry of KeyDown events are raised before KeyUp is raised.

→ **ScanCode**—The key's numeric scan code.

→ **IsExtendedKey**—Whether the key maps to an extended ASCII character.

→ **IsMenuKeyDown**—Whether the Alt key is depressed at the time this event is raised.

→ **IsKeyReleased** and **WasKeyDown**— Provide extra information about the key's status.

Although the software keyboard causes KeyDown and KeyUp events to be raised just like a hardware keyboard, the software keyboard does not raise these events for a few reserved combinations: Ctrl+A (select all), Ctrl+Z (undo), Ctrl+X (cut), Ctrl+C (copy), and Ctrl+V (paste).

> **! UIElement keyboard events are raised only when the element has focus!**
>
> Sometimes an element has focus automatically, but sometimes you need to take explicit action. The upcoming "Focus" section explains more.
>
> Alternatively, you can be notified of every keystroke regardless of focus by attaching a handler to the lower-level AcceleratorKeyActivated event available from Window.Current.CoreWindow. Dispatcher. The event is named as such because keyboard shortcuts (also called accelerator keys) only make sense if they are able to work without focus requirements.

> ### (!) In the keyboard APIs, the "menu" refers to the Alt key!
>
> Members such as VirtualKey.Menu and CorePhysicalKeyStatus.IsMenuKeyDown refer to the Alt key. Although this naming seems like an odd break from .NET tradition, it is consistent with the old VK_MENU constant from Win32. Therefore, this name is an artifact of VirtualKey being a Windows Runtime API (designed by the Windows team) rather than a .NET API. The same can be said for why the enumeration is named **Virtual**Key rather than simply Key. However, you can think of the Alt key as "the key used to reveal the menu in several desktop apps" as a way to justify its Menu name.
>
> Note that the context menu key, which not all keyboards have, is exposed with another confusing name: VirtualKey.Application.

Getting Key States at Any Time

If the KeyDown, KeyUp, and AcceleratorKeyActivated events were all you had to work with, detecting key combinations (such as Alt+G) would be awkward. Each key is reported one-at-a-time, so you would need a member variable representing the state of Ctrl to set on KeyDown and clear on KeyUp. Then you could check its value when receiving another event for the letter G.

Fortunately, there are two methods for determining the state of any key at any time: GetKeyState and GetAsyncKeyState. These methods are tucked away in Window.Current.CoreWindow, a surprisingly obscure place for an important feature. This is not just useful for key combinations, but for code that isn't driven by input events, such as a game loop.

With both GetKeyState and GetAsyncKeyState, you can simply pass in a VirtualKey value, and you get back one or more values from a CoreVirtualKeyStates enumeration:

→ **None**—The key is not pressed.

→ **Down**—The key is pressed.

→ **Locked**—The key is engaged in a locked state, such as Caps Lock, although this often shows up for regular keys when held down as part of a key combination.

> ### (!) CoreVirtualKeyStates is a flags enumeration!
>
> Not only is it a flags enumeration, but it is common for a combined state of Down and Locked to be reported for any key held down as part of a key combination. Therefore, to be safe, you should always test for specific values with Boolean logic rather than equality.

The following code uses a DispatcherTimer (discussed in Chapter 17, "Animation") in a Page's constructor to continuously check the state of the Alt and G keys in order to report when Alt+G is pressed:

```
public MainPage()
{
  InitializeComponent();

  // Start a timer that continuously invokes the delegate on the UI thread:
  DispatcherTimer timer = new DispatcherTimer();
  timer.Tick += delegate
  {
    CoreVirtualKeyStates menuState =
      Window.Current.CoreWindow.GetKeyState(VirtualKey.Menu);
    CoreVirtualKeyStates gState =
      Window.Current.CoreWindow.GetKeyState(VirtualKey.G);

    if ((menuState & CoreVirtualKeyStates.Down) == CoreVirtualKeyStates.Down &&
        (gState & CoreVirtualKeyStates.Down) == CoreVirtualKeyStates.Down)
    {
      // Alt+G is pressed
    }
  };
  timer.Start();
}
```

The preceding code is meant to simulate a game loop, but the following code is a variation that checks the state of the keyboard only when the KeyDown event is raised. It leverages the KeyDown event to detect when G is pressed, then checks whether the Alt key is also pressed at the same time:

```
protected override void OnKeyDown(KeyRoutedEventArgs e)
{
  if (e.Key == VirtualKey.G)
  {
    CoreVirtualKeyStates menuState =
      Window.Current.CoreWindow.GetKeyState(VirtualKey.Menu);

    if ((menuState & CoreVirtualKeyStates.Down) == CoreVirtualKeyStates.Down)
    {
        // Alt+G is pressed
    }
  }
}
```

If the Alt key is indeed pressed, then OnKeyDown would have already been called for that key, which would have been ignored at the time. This is a much simpler approach than tracking the state of each key across multiple KeyDown and KeyUp events.

What's the difference between `CoreWindow.GetKeyState` and `CoreWindow.GetAsyncKeyState`?

Their names are confusing, especially because they have identical signatures, but they are named after Win32 APIs with the same names. `GetKeyState` represents the state of a key at the time of a relevant input event, whereas `GetAsyncKeyState` represents the state of a key *right now*. Most of the time, `GetKeyState` is the right choice for apps.

How do I find out whether the *left* or *right* Alt, Ctrl, or Shift key was pressed?

Although the KeyDown and KeyUp events report the generic `VirtualKey.Menu`, `VirtualKey.Control`, and `VirtualKey.Shift` values, the `VirtualKey` enumeration does contain separate values for LeftMenu versus RightMenu, LeftControl versus RightControl, and LeftShift versus RightShift (as well as LeftWindows versus RightWindows). You can pass these more specific values to `GetKeyState` or `GetAsyncKeyState` to find out which one is currently pressed, or if both are pressed.

`GetKeyState` and `GetAsyncKeyState` can be used to get the state of mouse buttons on-demand as well, because the `VirtualKey` enumeration includes values for LeftButton, MiddleButton, RightButton, XButton1, and XButton2. However, if the left and right mouse buttons are logically swapped, these methods are not aware of it. Asking about LeftButton and RightButton always returns information about the physical left and right buttons, respectively.

Keyboard Modifiers in Pointer Events

Although the keyboard events are not pointer events, the pointer events do report some information about the current state of the keyboard via the `PointerRoutedEventArgs`. `KeyModifiers` property. The idea is that certain special keys are pressed to "modify" another gesture.

The property is of type `Windows.System.VirtualKeyModifiers`, another enumeration. It reveals whether certain keys are currently pressed: Control, Shift, Windows, Menu (the Alt key), or None. Naturally, this is a flags enumeration because any number of these can be pressed simultaneously. Therefore, you don't want to check for equality unless you care about the state of every modifier key. For example, the following code checks whether Alt is pressed while the pointer is moving but doesn't rule out Shift+Alt or Ctrl+Alt, and so on:

```
protected override void OnPointerMoved(PointerRoutedEventArgs e)
{
  if ((e.KeyModifiers & VirtualKeyModifiers.Menu) == VirtualKeyModifiers.Menu)
  {
```

```
    // Alt is pressed, potentially also with Ctrl, Shift, and/or Windows
  }
}
```

On the other hand, the following code checks for Alt and nothing else:

```
protected override void OnPointerMoved(PointerRoutedEventArgs e)
{
  if (e.KeyModifiers == VirtualKeyModifiers.Menu)
  {
    // Alt is the only modifier pressed
  }
}
```

Focus

As mentioned previously, a UIElement receives keyboard input (and raises keyboard events) only if it has focus. For that to happen, it must first be *eligible* for focus, which means it must:

→ Be enabled (IsEnabled=true)

→ Be visible (Visibility=Visible)

→ Be hit-testable (HitTestVisible=true)

→ Be included in tab navigation (IsTabStop=true)

This list of requirements usually isn't a big burden because the four properties listed are true by default.

Focus can be given only to Controls (indeed, some of the properties in this list are defined only by Control), so keyboard events can't originate from *any* UIElement despite being defined by UIElement. They can be handled on non-Control UIElements *containing* Controls, however, thanks to event bubbling..

Out of the set of focus-eligible Controls, the first one is given focus by default (although sometimes knowing which one is first can be tricky). The user can change which Control has focus by pressing the Tab key. This cycles through each eligible control, and also shows a system-defined *focus rectangle* (that unsightly dotted rectangle) around the control. Tapping a Control also gives it focus, so focus isn't *just* about the keyboard. You can modify the natural tab order by setting any Control's TabIndex property to an integer. This works much like Canvas's ZIndex property. Having an appropriate tab order is critical for a good keyboard navigation experience, but it's even more important

An app can have at most one element with focus at any point in time. To discover which element, if any, currently has focus, you can call the static FocusManager.GetFocusedElement method. GetFocusedElement is FocusManager's only public member.

for users who rely on the Windows Narrator to read the contents of your user interface in a sensible way.

You can programmatically get and set an element's focus state with two APIs on UIElement: a FocusState property and a Focus method.

FocusState is a read-only property. It is an enumeration value that not only reveals whether an element has focus, but *how* it got focus. In addition to its Unfocused value, it has three possible "focused" values: Keyboard, Pointer, and Programmatic. The last value refers to calls to Focus.

Calling the Focus method *attempts* to set an element's focus, because it might not be eligible for focus. (It's also possible to call Focus too early, such as on a Page before its OnNavigatedTo method is called.) Therefore, it returns true if successful, and false otherwise. It's odd, but you must pass Focus a FocusState value. Typically, you would pass Programmatic, but with the other values you can mimic keyboard or pointer focus for a rare case in which code depends on the type of focus given.

UIElement defines GotFocus and LostFocus events that are raised when focus changes. These are its only two events that are *not* routed events (even though its handler's signatures use RoutedEventArgs, as explained in the preceding chapter).

Summary

Although this chapter is structured in terms that developers are used to thinking about—touch, mouse, pen, and keyboard—you've now seen the *two* primary types of input received by elements—pointer input and keyboard input. You also examined all the standard gestures—including the more complex gestures known as manipulations—that Windows automatically and consistently recognizes based on the raw pointer input. Of course, you're free to develop your own gestures based on the same pointer input that is normally fed to GestureRecognizer, such as an iOS-style four-finger swipe. You could support this while still leveraging the work done by GestureRecognizer by using four GestureRecognizer instances and being careful to feed data from one finger to each instance by filtering on each Pointer's PointerId.

By finishing this chapter, you also reached a milestone in understanding XAML apps. Although it has the simple name of "Building an App," Part II is technically all about what the core UIElement class has to offer. UIElement defines a ton of members, but they all enable layout and input. Now that you have learned practically everything there is to learn about UIElement, we can move much faster through the features available to XAML apps.

Chapter 7

APP LIFECYCLE

Compared to desktop apps, Microsoft has chosen a much different approach for how and when Windows Store apps run. The result is much more like apps on a smartphone or competing tablet platforms. To the user, the experience of downloading an app from the Windows Store is obviously different than installing a desktop app. Being able to trust that you can delete an unwanted app is also a refreshing change. (When a user deletes a Windows Store app, all of its local data is removed as well. However, if the app ever created user data, such as in the Documents, Music, Pictures, or Videos libraries, that data is kept intact.) Windows Store apps also tend to do a good job at remembering a user's *session*—coming back however the user had left it, even after rebooting or perhaps even when launching the app from a different device.

The scheme of how and when Windows Store apps run, also referred to as their *lifecycle*, enables some of this. But the most important features that are enabled by the app lifecycle are better performance and better battery life, because an offscreen app typically is not running, even though most users might not realize this.

Whereas a desktop app can be in one of two execution states at any time, *running* or *not running*, Windows Store apps have a third possible state: *suspended*. A suspended app is basically paused; it is still in memory, but all of its threads have been suspended. (The Windows kernel ensures that an app can't be suspended in a critical section that could cause a system-wide deadlock.)

This third state is useful for preventing inactive apps from hogging additional resources. The goal is for the app (or apps) in the foreground to have the luxury of as much computing power as possible, and to enable better battery life by running less. At the same time, a suspended app can switch back to the running state quickly.

Many different situations can cause an app to transition from one state to another, and the `Application` class (the base class of a project's `App` class defined in `App.xaml` and `App.xaml.cs`) exposes events or virtual methods that enable you to detect most of these transitions. Figure 7.1 displays the three execution states with all possible transitions. The four green arrows represent transitions that have corresponding notifications. These notifications (either events or On*XXX* virtual methods) all live on the `Application` class. The two red, textured arrows represent transitions that happen without notifying the app.

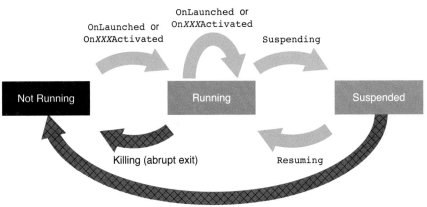

FIGURE 7.1   The three execution states, all possible transitions, and corresponding `Application` notifications

Figure 7.1 shows that there are six basic actions that can cause an app to transition among the three execution states:

→ Launching

→ Activating

→ Suspending

→ Resuming

→ Killing

→ Terminating

In the face of all this, your goal should be to provide a typical user experience with the following characteristics:

→ **After the user switches away from an app, bringing it back should return the app just how the user left it.** Although if it shows automatically updating content like a Twitter feed, it should certainly refresh it. To most users, there is no meaningful distinction between an offscreen app that is still running versus a suspended app versus a suspended app that is later terminated. (Although in the terminated case, the user needs to explicitly launch the app again to bring it back.) Either way, the app should keep track of the user's session.

→ **After the user explicitly closes an app, launching it again should give the user a "fresh" session.** Users have a few ways to close an app, such as performing a big swipe down from the top edge of the screen or pressing Alt+F4.

To enable this pattern, an app must save any session state when suspending, and then restore it when appropriate. The rest of this section discusses when it is appropriate, because the correct approach can be subtle.

These are just guidelines, of course. For some apps, it might make sense to always maintain the same session no matter what. For other apps, it might make sense to start the app fresh if a long amount of time has passed after it was previously suspended or terminated. And for others, it might sense to give the user a choice of whether to resume where he or she left off or to start over with a fresh session. (For games, this would likely already be a choice presented to the user on a "paused screen," so it could simply present the same screen when returning in this fashion.)

Let's now examine the six actions and how to respond to them. Instead of the order listed previously, it's easiest to start with the two different ways to exit the *running* state (Killing versus Suspending), then the two ways to exit the *suspended* state (Resuming versus Terminating), and finally the two ways to exit the *not running* state (Launched versus Activated). After this, we look at a helper class called for managing session state called `SuspensionManager` as well as ways for one app to launch another app.

> The typical app lifecycle can be enhanced in two ways. Apps can run in the background using background tasks. Apps can also *appear* to run in the background when using live tiles (discussed in Chapter 25, "Thinking Outside the App: Live Tiles, Notifications, and the Lock Screen").

Killing

An app transitions from *running* directly to *not running* (the red "Killing" arrow in Figure 7.1) only when it is forced to do so, as with the following conditions:

→ The user signs out (which includes shutting down or restarting the computer) and the app hasn't already been suspended.

→ The user invokes "End task" in Task Manager, or an equivalent command in a command-line tool such as TaskKill.

→ The app hangs, or the code it executes in response to suspension takes longer than 5 seconds, or the code it executes in response to launch/activation (while the splash screen is showing) takes longer than 15 seconds.

→ The app is under the debugger's control and the developer ends the process in Visual Studio.

→ The app calls Application's Exit method (Application.Current.Exit).

It should not be a surprise that there's no way for an app to respond to these exceptional conditions. After this happens, any session state persisted by the app should be ignored by future launches because it could be corrupted.

> If your app "crashes" (throws an unhandled exception for an unknown reason), don't attempt to handle it and provide a message to the user. The best user experience is to let the app exit quickly. Windows will send a "problem report" to Microsoft if the user consents, and you can view the details of these reports via your dashboard on the Windows Dev Center website.

> **Do not call Application's Exit method!**
> Apps that attempt to kill themselves are likely to not get accepted into the Windows Store, especially if they show an explicit close button in their user interface. Apps should instead let Windows manage their lifetime, and let users perform the standard "close" gestures.

Suspending

Whereas *killing* is the rude and rare way for an app to stop running, *suspending* is the gentle and common way. Immediately before suspension occurs, Application's Suspending event is raised. This is the time for an app to save any necessary session state, because it's possible the app will be terminated (without any notification) before it ever runs again. This is also the time to release any files, devices, or other exclusive resources so other apps can use them while your app is suspended. (Remember that suspending an app just pauses it, much like pausing it in a debugger, so resources don't get automatically released in this state unless they are treated specially by Windows.)

A user cannot directly suspend an app. Instead, an app is suspended by Windows for one of three different conditions:

→ Five seconds after it has been removed from the screen and replaced with another active app (the Start screen doesn't count), as long as it wasn't removed by a "close" gesture (such as the big swipe or Alt+F4).

→ When Windows enters a low-power mode. This is a heuristic influenced by a number of factors. On devices that support it, this means the *connected standby* mode in which drivers and background tasks still run.

→ Ten seconds after the user performs a "close" gesture.

For the first condition, the five-second delay and the caveats exist to optimize fast app-switching. For the last condition, the ten-second delay enables faster relaunching/reactivating of the app during that window of time (presumably when closing it was an accident), and the suspension is done to give the app a chance to do any of its typical state-saving, resource-releasing, or other bookkeeping. (After this suspension, Windows automatically closes the app.) You can see this ten-second delay by closing any app and watching its entry in Task Manager. This also explains why the Visual Studio debugger takes a long time to stop debugging (ten seconds, to be exact) when you close an app currently being debugged.

This behavior for when a user explicitly closes an app is a bit strange, because in this case the app is supposed to ignore any saved session state the next time it is launched. However, this behavior means that the app doesn't have to go out of its way to perform the same "shutdown" logic for suspending versus closing.

If the user launches or activates the app within ten seconds of closing it, then the pending suspension gets cancelled! The existing app instance's OnLaunched or OnXXXActivated method is called, and the app should pretend it is a fresh instance even though it is not. Again, this is okay because the app should provide a fresh session after being explicitly closed by a user anyway.

(?) How do I make my game automatically pause as soon as the user closes or switches away from it?

The Suspending event is certainly no good for this, because the game would continue for at least five seconds! Although no Application event is raised as soon as the user closes or switches away from an app, there are two such events defined on the host Window (accessed via the static Window.Current property). Its Activated event is instantly raised whenever an app gains *or loses* focus, and you can tell which happened by checking the passed-in WindowActivationState property. Its VisibilityChanged event is instantly raised whenever it becomes visible or invisible, and you can tell which happened by checking the passed-in VisibilityChangedEventArgs.Visible property. These events provide a perfect opportunity to react immediately. Activated is more appropriate for pausing a game, because it also gets raised when the user places multiple windows on the screen or resizes windows. VisibilityChanged does not get raised in this scenario. SizeChanged gets raised, but only once the user is done dragging the window divider and lets go, which is a little late to pause a game.

Handling the Suspending Event

Visual Studio-generated projects handle Application's Suspending event in a handler called OnSuspending in App.xaml.cs. In a Blank App project, however, it's waiting for you to do something useful:

```
private void OnSuspending(object sender, SuspendingEventArgs e)
{
  var deferral = e.SuspendingOperation.GetDeferral();
  //TODO: Save application state and stop any background activity
  deferral.Complete();
}
```

The SuspendingEventArgs instance has a single SuspendingOperation property that exposes the GetDeferral method used in this snippet and a Deadline property that tells you how long you have to finish your logic in response to this event (currently five seconds).

As for the actual work, you should serialize any relevant data into a local file using the application data APIs covered in Chapter 20, "Working with Data." However, the SuspensionManager class covered later in this chapter does a lot of this work on your behalf, so you can just use it instead.

> Microsoft recommends that you persist state incrementally right when it changes, if possible, rather than waiting for the Suspending event to do this work. If you can do this with all of your relevant state, then you don't even need to handle the Suspending event.

Deferral

As with the preceding code snippet, the code inside a Suspending event handler is often sandwiched between a call to GetDeferral and a call to the returned object's Complete method. (The returned object is a SuspendingDeferral and Complete is its only method.) This is needed only if the code you execute is asynchronous. In this case, it tells the system to wait until you call Complete *or until the Deadline passes*. Using a deferral does *not* enable you to escape the five-second requirement!

The reason this deferral mechanism is needed is that as soon as you await, the current thread of execution returns to the system code that raised the event. Without this mechanism, the system would think you were done with your suspension logic and would instantly suspend the app without giving the asynchronous code a chance to finish.

In theory, you can omit the calls to GetDeferral and Complete if the code is completely synchronous. In practice, this usually doesn't happen, because code that persists state outside the app's own memory is usually asynchronous. The application data APIs do include synchronous *application settings* APIs, but the recommendation for persisting session state is to use a file rather than settings. Files give you more flexibility in data persistence than settings, as explained in Chapter 20.

Resuming

An app is resumed (changed from *suspended* to *running*) as soon as it is brought back on-screen. This raises Application's Resuming event. However, an app often doesn't need to handle Resuming, because there's usually nothing that needs to be done. After all, the app stayed in memory the whole time with all its variables intact, so it can just continue where it left off. Suspending is like pausing an app in a debugger, and resuming is like unpausing it.

However, if an app previously released any exclusive resources in a handler for Suspending, these likely need to be obtained again in a handler for Resuming. In addition, if an app shows auto-updating information, this might be a good time to force it to refresh.

> If you persist a timestamp when your app is suspended, then you can check it within events such as Resuming to determine whether it's appropriate for your app to take certain actions such as refreshing its data.

Terminating

"Terminating" sounds bad, but it's not. Unlike killing, it's the graceful way for an app to enter the *not running* state. Whereas killing covers all the ways in which a running app suddenly stops running, termination can happen only to an app that is successfully suspended.

Windows tries to keep as many suspended apps in memory as possible, but when memory is tight (or the user is signing out), it must start terminating. There is no notification for this. After all, the terminated app isn't running at the time! That's okay, because each app should have prepared for this when it was being suspended. Because of this, you should think about termination as a "deeper" suspension, almost like putting Windows itself in hibernation mode rather than sleep mode. The next time a terminated app is launched, it is expected to continue where the user left off. That's because the user never explicitly closed the app.

> You can easily test the suspending, resuming, and terminating actions when debugging an app in Visual Studio. The "Debug Location" toolbar, shown in Figure 7.2, enables you to trigger these conditions, although instead of using the term *Terminate*, it uses *Suspend and shutdown*. This, of course, is an accurate description of what it means to terminate an app.

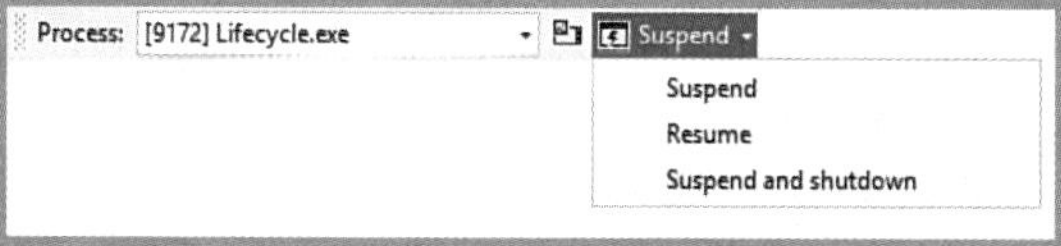

FIGURE 7.2   The "Debug Location" toolbar in Visual Studio enables you to suspend, resume, and terminate ("Suspend and shutdown") an app so you can easily test your handling of these actions.

> **How does Windows decide which suspended app to terminate under a low memory condition?**
>
> It is *not* a first-in, first-out algorithm. Instead, Windows targets the apps based on heuristics. Apps that use the most memory, processor cycles, power, and so on, are likely to be targeted first.

Launching

An app starts out in the *not running* state. It can transition to *running* in one of two ways:

→ **Launching**—The user clicks its primary tile, a secondary tile (if the app has any), or performs an equivalent action, such as clicking the app in the "Apps" list. These conditions cause `Application.OnLaunched` to be called.

→ **Activating**—The user invokes the app as the target of a contract (if it supports any), such as entry points in the Share charm. This causes an `Application.OnXXXActivated` method to be called instead.

As seen in Chapter 1, "Hello, *Real* World!" the Visual Studio-generated `App.xaml.cs` overrides `OnLaunched` in order to initialize the app's content and navigate to the main `Page`. Nothing is done for the "activating" cases, because that is for specialized features that need to be explicitly added to a project.

Inside `OnLaunched`, you must initialize the app's content based on the previous execution state (explained in a moment), and call `Window.Current.Activate` in order to dismiss the splash screen. The call to `Activate` must be made within 15 seconds, otherwise Windows might kill your app. This is why many apps choose to show an extended splash screen that mimics the real one (typically with an added `ProgressRing`), because if initialization involves network access, you can never be sure how long that will take. Another, perhaps more satisfying approach, is to show your initial user interface in some sort of "empty" form with indicators that its content is still loading.

When you call `Window.Current.Activate`, the `Window`'s `Activate` event is raised. Note that this *window activation* concept is completely different from *app activation*. A `Window` is activated whenever it is given focus and deactivated whenever it loses focus.

> **Window's `Activated` event gets raised when the `Window` gets activated *or deactivated*!**
>
> The event should have been called `ActivatedChanged`. In the `WindowActivatedEventArgs` instance passed to handlers, you can check the `WindowActivationState` property for one of three values: `PointerActivated`, `CodeActivated`, or `Deactivated`.
>
> As a previous FAQ alluded, this event basically gets raised hand-in-hand with `Window`'s `VisibilityChanged` event, because a Windows Store app's window typically becomes visible at the same time it gets focus, and becomes invisible at the same time it loses focus. The exception is when multiple windows are sharing the screen. In that case, the user can switch focus between the two visible windows, which causes `Activated` to get raised, but not `VisibilityChanged`.

LaunchActivatedEventArgs

The LaunchActivatedEventArgs instance passed to OnLaunched exposes the following properties:

→ **SplashScreen**—Exposes the location of the image inside the splash screen and a separate Dismissed event for when it goes away. This is helpful for providing your own extended splash screen that mimics the real one, which is highly recommended.

→ **PreviousExecutionState**—Reveals what the app was previously doing with a value from an ApplicationExecutionState enumeration. This is critical information needed for you to handle the launch correctly. Although this enumeration contains the three expected values of NotRunning, Running, and Suspended, it also includes two variations of NotRunning: Terminated and ClosedByUser.

→ **Arguments** and **TileId**—Strings that are only non-null when an app is launched from a secondary tile. As shown in Chapter 25, an app can associate two such strings with any additional tiles that are created.

→ **ActivationKind**—An enumeration value always set to Launch. This is an artifact of the IActivatedEventArgs interface that LaunchActivatedEventArgs implements.

Properly Reacting to PreviousExecutionState

You can see the proper pattern for handling launch by looking at the OnLaunched implementation in a Visual Studio-generated App.xaml.cs file:

```
protected override void OnLaunched(LaunchActivatedEventArgs args)
{
#if DEBUG
  if (System.Diagnostics.Debugger.IsAttached)
  {
    this.DebugSettings.EnableFrameRateCounter = true;
  }
#endif

  Frame rootFrame = Window.Current.Content as Frame;

  // Do not repeat app initialization when the Window already has content,
  // just ensure that the window is active
  if (rootFrame == null)
  {
    // Create a Frame and navigate to the first page
    var rootFrame = new Frame();

    if (args.PreviousExecutionState == ApplicationExecutionState.Terminated)
    {
```

```
    //TODO: Load state from previously suspended application
  }

  // Place the frame in the current Window
  Window.Current.Content = rootFrame;
}

if (rootFrame.Content == null)
{
  // When the navigation stack isn't restored, navigate to the first page
  if (!rootFrame.Navigate(typeof(MainPage), args.Arguments))
  {
    throw new Exception("Failed to create initial page");
  }
}

// Ensure the current Window is active
Window.Current.Activate();
}
```

This can be summarized as, "Just show the current `Window` if it has already been initialized (meaning the app is already running), restore session state if the app was previously terminated, and otherwise create a fresh session." This, of course, sounds strange, especially if you're not familiar with the app lifecycle. Common questions are:

→ Why would the app already be running?

→ Why do we restore state in the `Terminated` case and don't do anything special for the `Suspended` case?

The answers lie in the meaning of each `PreviousExecutionState` value, which can *still* be subtle even if you've read and understood everything thus far!

`PreviousExecutionState` is **Running** only when the launch is caused by the clicking of a secondary tile (or the app has been *activated* by a contract instead of launched). This is the odd-looking transition from *running* to *running* in Figure 7.1. The app never stops running, but this event gives it a chance to respond to whatever clicking the secondary tile is supposed to enable. Although this code path doesn't get executed for an app that doesn't explicitly support secondary tiles or contract targets, the default Visual Studio implementation simply shows the current `Window`. This is the correct behavior for apps with secondary tiles as well, because such apps should check for this (via `args.Arguments` and/or `args.TileId`) and update its user interface appropriately, regardless of `PreviousExecutionState`.

A `PreviousExecutionState` of **Suspended** is not normally seen inside `OnLaunched` because this doesn't get called by an app resuming! This occurs only when a secondary tile has been clicked (or the app has been activated by a contract) and the app was suspended at the time rather than running. In this case, the `Resuming` event is raised immediately before `OnLaunched` is called.

A PreviousExecutionState of **Terminated** means that the app was previously successfully suspended and then later terminated. Therefore, as part of this launch, any session state persisted during suspension should be restored in addition to the normal initialization. This is the only time session state ever needs to be manually restored.

A PreviousExecutionState of **ClosedByUser** means just that. Although this means the app was eventually suspended and terminated just as in the Terminated case, ClosedByUser is only reported when the original suspension was caused by a user's "close" gesture. Therefore, even though there is likely persisted session state that *could* be restored, it should normally not be. This enables you to follow the convention that when a user closes an app, the next launch should appear like a fresh instance.

That only leaves the PreviousExecutionState of **NotRunning**. Because this doesn't include terminating and normal closing, this is reported when one of the following is true:

→ The app was previously killed

→ This is the first time the user has run the app

→ The app was previously closed by the user *within the last ten seconds*

Here's that odd ten-seconds-after-closing-an-app condition again. When the user quickly relaunches the app after closing it, which cancels the pending suspension and termination, the previous state is reported as NotRunning rather than ClosedByUser! This is therefore indistinguishable from your app being killed!

This quirky behavior is one reason why it's good to follow the guideline of starting with a fresh session after an app is closed by the user. As long as you never handle ClosedByUser differently than NotRunning, you'll be fine. Otherwise, a closed app would exhibit different behavior when reopened after 9 seconds versus 11 seconds!

> ! **Do not restore session state when PreviousExecutionState is NotRunning!**
> Even if you decide to act differently than the guidelines, you need to be careful about attempting to restore session state when PreviousExecutionState is NotRunning, because the most likely reason for this (other than the first ever launch of the app) is that the app previously crashed. And if you do a great job at restoring that session, then your app might crash again! When this happens, the user might not be able to successfully launch your app again without uninstalling and reinstalling it, which would wipe out the corrupt session state.

Activating

Application provides a family of methods that you can override for different activation conditions, covering six specific cases and a catch-all for the rest:

→ OnCachedFileUpdaterActivated

→ OnFileActivated

➔ OnFileOpenPickerActivated

➔ OnFileSavePickerActivated

➔ OnSearchActivated

➔ OnShareTargetActivated

➔ OnActivated

When an app is activated for one of these six special cases, *only* the more specific method is invoked. OnActivated is reserved for any cases not covered by the first six. (These six are singled out mostly for historical reasons.) The IActivatedEventArgs instance passed to OnActivated exposes the same Kind, PreviousExecutionState, and SplashScreen properties mentioned in the preceding section. For OnActivated,

Application also exposes an OnWindowCreated method that is called every time an app's Window is created, regardless of how it was launched/activated. This method is the right place to consolidate logic that needs to be shared among all launch and activation code paths, rather than duplicating the logic in each of the relevant OnXXX methods. For example, OnWindowCreated is a great place to cache the result from any call to static GetForCurrentView methods that are pervasive throughout the Windows Runtime, such as EdgeGesture.GetForCurrentView shown in the preceding chapter.

however, checking Kind (of type ApplicationKind) is needed in order to understand what just happened. The ApplicationKind enumeration contains 16 choices, although only nine are relevant for OnActivated because six are handled by the more specific OnXXXActivated methods, and one (Launch) is handed by OnLaunched.

Launch Versus Activation

Although XAML apps treat launching and activating as two different concepts, the core of Windows considers launching to be *one type* of activation. Viewed this way, OnLaunched is just a seventh specialization of OnActivated (that could have been named OnLaunchActivated to match the naming of the other six OnXXXActivated methods).

This helps to explain a number of things:

➔ Why the name of the type passed to OnLaunched is called Launch**Activated**EventArgs.

➔ Why LaunchActivatedEventArgs exposes a useless Kind property always set to Launch. (Similarly, SearchActivatedEventArgs exposes a Kind property always set to Search, and so on.) These specialized types all derive from IActivatedEventArgs, which includes the Kind property.

➔ Why documentation often talks about "activation" when they are referring to launching and/or activation.

The other six OnXXXActivated methods are also specific to XAML apps. This not only enables more concise implementations, but it enables the XAML UI Framework to directly present you with customized EventArgs objects for each one.

The various types of activations are covered in Chapter 21, "Supporting Charms," and Chapter 22, "Leveraging Contracts."

Managing Session State with `SuspensionManager`

Session state is a set of app-specific data that captures things such as which item in a list is currently selected, which page of an article is being viewed, or the current scrollbar position. Unlike user data, such as an email message currently being composed inside your app, it's usually okay if session data somehow gets lost. It provides great value for keeping the user in context across multiple physical executions of an app. But if the user accidentally closes an app by swiping downward instead of sideways, it's usually not worth making an effort to expose the option to restore it on next launch. (The biggest exception to this is probably the user's session in a game. That tends to be highly valued data, yet isn't typically stored in a user-managed storage location.)

A Scheme for Representing Session State

Session state is typically represented as a `Dictionary` with `string` keys and arbitrary values, such as the following:

```
static Dictionary<string, object> sessionState = new Dictionary<string, object>();
```

Session state values are therefore typically set and retrieved as follows:

```
// Store a value
sessionState["CurrentIndex"] = 5;

// Retrieve a value
if (sessionState.ContainsKey("CurrentIndex"))
  index = (int)sessionState["CurrentIndex"];
```

Because this data must be persisted somewhere, the only requirement for the values is that they are serializable. The `Dictionary` could be persisted as follows, using the best practice of writing it into a local file private to the app:

```
public static async Task SaveAsync()
{
  // Serialize synchronously to avoid asynchronous access to shared state
  MemoryStream memoryStream = new MemoryStream();
  DataContractSerializer serializer = new DataContractSerializer(
    typeof(Dictionary<string, object>));
  serializer.WriteObject(memoryStream, sessionState);

  // Write the data to a local app data file
  StorageFile file = await ApplicationData.Current.LocalFolder.CreateFileAsync(
    "_sessionState.xml", CreationCollisionOption.ReplaceExisting);
  using (Stream fileStream = await file.OpenStreamForWriteAsync())
```

```
  {
    memoryStream.Seek(0, SeekOrigin.Begin);
    await memoryStream.CopyToAsync(fileStream);
    await fileStream.FlushAsync();
  }
}
```

This uses the .NET DataContractSerializer, which serializes the data as XML.

Session state could then be restored as follows:

```
public static async Task RestoreAsync()
{
  sessionState = new Dictionary<string, object>();

  // Read previously-persisted data from the file
  StorageFile file = await ApplicationData.Current.LocalFolder.GetFileAsync(
    "_sessionState.xml");
  if (file != null)
  {
    using (IInputStream inputStream = await file.OpenSequentialReadAsync())
    {
      // Deserialize
      DataContractSerializer serializer =
        new DataContractSerializer(typeof(Dictionary<string, object>));
      sessionState = (Dictionary<string, object>)serializer.ReadObject(
        inputStream.AsStreamForRead());
    }
  }
}
```

Introducing SuspensionManager

A SuspensionManager class exists that can do all this saving and restoring work (and a bit more) for you. It exposes a SessionState property that is the same type of Dictionary used in the previous snippets, as well as similar SaveAsync and RestoreAsync methods.

To use this, you must call RestoreAsync inside OnLaunched for the previously terminated condition:

```
if (args.PreviousExecutionState == ApplicationExecutionState.Terminated)
{
  // Restore the saved session state only when appropriate
  await SuspensionManager.RestoreAsync();
}
```

You can set and retrieve session state values as follows:

```
// Store a value
SuspensionManager.SessionState["CurrentIndex"] = 5;

// Retrieve a value
if (SuspensionManager.SessionState.ContainsKey("CurrentIndex"))
  index = (int)SuspensionManager.SessionState["CurrentIndex"];
```

You must also call SaveAsync inside your handler for `Application`'s Suspending event:

```
async void OnSuspending(object sender, SuspendingEventArgs e)
{
  // The deferral is needed due to the async nature of SaveAsync
  var deferral = e.SuspendingOperation.GetDeferral();
  await SuspensionManager.SaveAsync();
  deferral.Complete();
}
```

This is all very natural. The only odd thing is how you include `SuspensionManager` in your app. It is *not* part of any standard libraries. Instead, you can copy the code from most of the official Windows SDK samples at http://code.msdn.microsoft.com. Or, depending on what you do in Visual Studio, Visual Studio will automatically add the code to your project. For example, if you add a new "Basic Page" to your project instead of a "Blank Page," Visual Studio will also add `SuspensionManager.cs` to your project's Common folder. That's because the generated page uses a `NavigationHelper` class (whose source also gets included in your project) that internally leverages `SuspensionManager`. Similarly, if you select a project template other than "Blank App" when creating a new project, `SuspensionManger.cs` will be included in the project *and* the relevant calls to it will be made inside `App.xaml.cs`.

> (!) **Don't forget to add the calls to SuspensionManager's RestoreAsync and SaveAsync methods to App.xaml.cs!**
>
> If you start with a Blank App project in Visual Studio, the calls to SuspensionManager do *not* get automatically added to App.xaml.cs, even if you later add an item that automatically includes SuspensionManager.cs in your project.

> (💡) You can leverage session state as a cache. For example, if your app makes a network request when launched, consider caching the resultant data and using it instead of a live network request when appropriate. (In Windows 8.1, you can also leverage an automatic caching feature supported by Windows.Web.Http.HttpClient, as discussed in Chapter 20.) Apps using data binding can consider caching the entire data context as a single entry in one of the dictionaries. (See Chapter 19, "Data Binding.")

Programmatically Launching Apps

Apps aren't always launched by the user; one app can launch another with the
`Windows.System.Launcher` class. The apps that are launched can be other Windows Store
apps or even desktop apps! However, you cannot pick an arbitrary app and launch it. The
target app must have registered a specific URI scheme for this to work.

> (?) **Is there any way for a Windows Store app to launch a specific app with specific command-line parameters?**
>
> Only if the target app has registered an appropriate URI scheme to support this.

Launching an App for a File

The following code shoes how to launch the default app for viewing PNG files using
Launcher's LaunchFileAsync method:

```
async Task LaunchOtherApp()
{
  StorageFile file = await Package.Current.InstalledLocation.GetFileAsync(
                           @"Assets\Logo.png");
  if (file != null)
  {
    // Launch the default image viewer (which could be a desktop app)
    bool success = await Launcher.LaunchFileAsync(file);
    if (!success)
    {
      …
    }
  }
}
```

This code uses a handy API accessible via `Windows.ApplicationModel.Package` that
provides access to files packaged with your app.

> (!) **When launching another app, your app must already be visible!**
>
> This requirement helps to avoid user confusion. It means that attempting to launch an app
> inside a Page's OnNavigatedTo method doesn't work reliably. Instead, you should use
> Launcher only in response to some user input.

Launching an App for a URI

The following code shows how to launch the default Web browser using Launcher's
LaunchUriAsync method:

```
async Task LaunchOtherApp()
{
    // Launch the default Web browser (which could be a desktop app)
    bool success = await Launcher.LaunchUriAsync(new Uri("http://pixelwinks.com"));
    if (!success)
    {
        …
    }
}
```

When you launch an app for a URI, the file type no longer matters. For example, if you call LaunchUriAsync with http://blog.adamnathan.net/images/logo.png, it still launches the default web browser rather than the default image viewer because the URI scheme is http. If the URI starts with mailto:, then the default mail program is used.

Custom URI schemes are supported as well as the standard ones. The Maps app has registered the bingmaps scheme (documented at http://bit.ly/Qc8rC3). If you launch bingmaps:///, then the app shows the map at the user's previous location, but this behavior can be customized via many query string parameters. For example, you can launch a map of donut shops in Seattle with bingmaps: ///?q=donuts&where=seattle.

> ! **To use LaunchUriAsync with an intranet URI, your app must have the "Home or Work Networking" capability!**
>
> This fact can cause people to waste a lot of time debugging, because when you try to call LaunchUriAsync with an intranet URI and no such capability, it returns false with no extra information!

You may *not* use URIs beginning with file: with LaunchUriAsync. You must find a way to get an appropriate StorageFile object and call LaunchFileAsync instead.

> ? **How can I launch a custom app (that I also wrote)?**
>
> You should invent a custom URI scheme and register your second app to handle it (see Chapter 22). Your first app can then launch it with a URI beginning with that custom scheme. This works out nicely even if the user doesn't have the second app installed, because calling LaunchUriAsync with an unknown scheme presents the user interface shown in Figure 7.3.
>
> No apps are installed to open this type of link (mycustomscheme)
>
> Look for an app in the Store

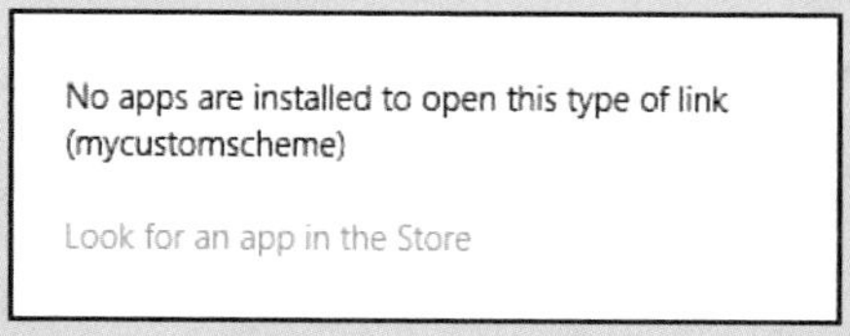

FIGURE 7.3   The result of attempting to launch a URI with an unknown scheme (mycustomscheme://...)

Customizing App Launch

Both LaunchFileAsync and LaunchUriAsync methods have an overload that accepts a
LauncherOptions instance for additional customization. For example, if you set its
DisplayApplicationPicker property to
true, it will present the user with the
typical choose-an-app user interface
shown in Figure 7.4. This also gives the
user the ability to tap elsewhere to
~~cancel the opening of the file altogether~~

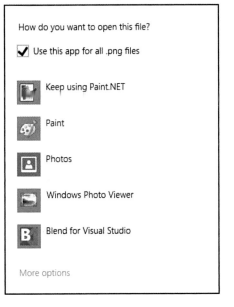

By default, the user interface in Figure
7.4 is shown in the center of the *screen*
(so potentially not even over the app's
bounds if there are multiple windows
sharing the screen). However, you can
control its position by setting one or
more subproperties on LauncherOption's
UI property. InvocationPoint can be set
to a Point representing where the user
performed the action that triggered the
Launcher call. Or SelectionRect can be
set to a similar Rect. (SelectionRect
overrides InvocationPoint.) When you
do this, the placement of the application picker is similar to the placement of
a context menu. You can also customize
the placement by setting

FIGURE 7.4   The user interface shown when
you set LauncherOptions.Display
ApplicationPicker to true

PreferredPlacement to Above, Below, Left, or Right, which is relative to InvocationPoint
or SelectionRect and will be respected as long as there is enough room on the screen.

The following code demonstrates the use of this LauncherOptions object.

```
LauncherOptions options = new LauncherOptions();
options.DisplayApplicationPicker = true;
options.UI.InvocationPoint = new Point(100, 400);
options.UI.PreferredPlacement = Placement.Below;
…
bool success = await Launcher.LaunchFileAsync(file, options);
```

With LauncherOption's FallbackUri property, you can provide an alternate URI if no
app is available to launch the main URI. With its PreferredApplicationDisplayName
and PreferredApplicationPackageFamilyName properties, you can help Windows suggest
the right app to users when they click the "Look for an app in the Store" link shown in
Figure 7.3.

Note that the positioning of the application picker can be relevant even if you don't set
DisplayApplicationPicker to true, because it also gets shown if no appropriate app is
installed.

In Windows 8.1, you can influence how much screen real estate your app occupies after the second app is launched. By default, your app and the new app split the available space 50/50, but you can control this by setting LauncherOption's DesiredRemainingView property to one of the following ViewSizePreference enumeration values: UseHalf, Default (the same as UseHalf), UseLess (than 50%), UseMore (than 50%), UseMinimum (320 or 500 pixels), or UseNone (your window is removed from the screen). These sizes refer to *your* current window, not the new window created for the launched app.

Windows doesn't guarantee that your preference will be respected, as it depends on factors such as the screen resolution, screen orientation, and the number of apps on the screen. In addition, the target app can specify its own preference in its package manifest, even separately for each supported URI scheme and file type. Visual Studio's package manifest designer exposes this in a **Desired view** dropdown.

Summary

If you're familiar with the lifecycle of Windows Phone apps, the lifecycle of Windows Store apps looks deceivingly similar. The biggest difference is that suspending just pauses an in-memory app, whereas Windows Phone's *tombstoning* actually removes the app from memory, wiping out anything that wasn't explicitly persisted.

This chapter thoroughly examined the application lifecycle, but here is a concise summary of how to deal with the various execution states and transition actions:

→ When **launched**:

  → Check whether the app is already running. If so, simply show the currently-hidden Window (with its Activate method).

  → If the app was previously terminated, restore the user's session state (quickly!).

  → Initialize (quickly!) and show your own custom "extended splash screen" if you might need more than 15 seconds.

  → React to specifics of the tile if a secondary tile was clicked.

→ When **activated**, follow the rules for launching, but also respond to the specific request regardless of the previous execution state.

→ While **running**, save user data incrementally.

→ When **suspended**:

  → Assume you'll be terminated, so save session state (quickly!).

  → Release any exclusive resources.

  → Consider updating your app's tile with current information (see Chapter 25).

→ When **resumed**, do nothing (unless some state was destroyed upon suspension that needs to be restored, such as the release of exclusive resources).

An important distinction made in these guidelines is the difference between:

→ **User data**—User-configurable settings, user-generated files, or other data that should be remembered indefinitely

→ **Session state**—Transient state, like a partially filled form for creating a new item that has not yet been saved

The management of user data should be done completely independently from an app's lifecycle and the Suspending event

Chapter 8

THREADING, WINDOWS, AND PAGES

This chapter begins by examining a very important topic, although one that many developers take for granted: the threading model for Windows Store apps. This background is especially helpful for the advanced feature of writing an app that displays multiple windows, which is the second topic in this chapter. Both of these topics generally apply to any type of Windows Store app. The third and final topic—navigating between a window's pages—is XAML-specific. It is also a feature leveraged by just about every real-world XAML app.

Understanding the Threading Model for Windows Store Apps

Windows Store apps have two types of threads that can run your code: UI threads and background threads. (Other types of threads exist, but they are implementation details.) As much as possible, a UI thread should be kept free to process input and update UI elements. Therefore, long-running work should always be scheduled on a background thread.

Typically, an app has a single UI thread, but each window has its own UI thread. Therefore, an app with multiple windows (covered in the upcoming "Displaying Multiple Windows" section) has multiple UI threads. If you have a long-running computation to perform, which therefore isn't appropriate for a UI thread, you don't get to explicitly create a background thread for the task. Instead, you schedule it via a static `RunAsync` method on the `Windows.System.Threading.ThreadPool` class. Windows manages all background threads for you.

There is always a main UI thread, even if the corresponding main window has not yet been shown. For example, if an app is activated via a contract such as the File Picker contract (see Chapter 22, "Leveraging Contracts"), the app typically displays a special file-picking window and never displays its main window. Yet the app has two UI threads running in this scenario, so your code can always count on global state created by the main thread.

UI objects must be created and called on a UI thread. This includes every class deriving from `DependencyObject`, which is most classes in the XAML UI Framework. Outside of the XAML UI Framework, most Windows Runtime objects can be created and used on any thread, and you control their lifetime. This makes them very natural to use in C# without worrying about threading or COM-style apartments. Such objects are called *agile objects*.

ASTA Threads

In documentation and error messages, UI threads are sometimes referred to as *ASTA threads*. ASTA stands for App Single-Threaded Apartment, which is a nod to COM's notion of single-threaded apartments (STA).

ASTA threads are similar to COM's STA threads in that they provide an easy-to-program, single-threaded experience. But they have an enhancement that COM's STA threads do not: they are not reentrant, unless the incoming call is logically connected to the one in progress. In other words, if you make a call from a UI thread to another thread (or process), and that thread needs to call back to the UI thread, the Windows Runtime does a lot of work to track this and allow it. On the other hand, arbitrary code is prevented from calling into the UI thread while it is doing work. This prevents a huge class of bugs that plague desktop apps, and means that UI objects generally don't need locking to protect themselves. The Windows Runtime also prevents UI threads from calling each other directly, as that would be prone to deadlock.

Awaiting an Asynchronous Operation

Windows Runtime APIs are designed to make it really hard to block a UI thread. Whenever the Windows Runtime exposes a potentially-long-running operation, it does so with an asynchronous method that performs its work on a background thread. You can easily identify such methods by their `Async` suffix. And they are everywhere. For example, showing a `MessageDialog` (discussed in Chapter 15, "Other Controls") requires a call to `ShowAsync`:

```
CoreWindowDialog dialog = new MessageDialog("Title");
IAsyncOperation<IUICommand> operation = dialog.ShowAsync();
// The next line of code runs in parallel with ShowAsync's background work
MoreCode();
```

Asynchronous methods in the Windows Runtime return one of several interfaces such as IAsyncOperation or IAsyncAction. Asynchronous methods in .NET return a Task. These are two different abstractions for the same set of asynchronous patterns. The System.WindowsRuntimeSystemExtensions class provides several AsTask extension methods for converting one of these interfaces to a Task, as well as AsAsyncOperation and AsAsyncAction extension methods for converting in the opposite direction.

In the preceding code snippet, when ShowAsync is called in this manner, the call returns immediately. The next line of code can run in parallel with the work being done by MessageDialog on a different thread. When ShowAsync's work is done (because the user dismissed the dialog or clicked one of its buttons), MessageDialog communicates what happened with an IUICommand instance. To get this result, the preceding code must set operation's Completed property to a delegate that gets called when the task has finished. This handler can then call operation's GetResults method to retrieve the IUICommand.

Of course, such code is pretty cumbersome to write, and the proliferation of asynchronous methods would result in an explosion of such code if it weren't for the C# await language feature. When a method returns one of the IAsync*XXX* interfaces or a Task, C# enables you to hide the complexity of waiting for the task's completion. For the ShowAsync example, the resulting code can look like the following:

```
async Task ShowDialog()
{
  MessageDialog dialog = new MessageDialog("Title");
  IUICommand command = await dialog.ShowAsync();
  // The next line of code does not run until ShowAsync is completely done
  MoreCodeThatCanUseTheCommand(command);
}
```

When the ShowAsync call is made in this manner, the current method's execution stops—*without blocking the current thread*—and then resumes once the task has completed. This enables the code to retrieve the IUICommand object as if ShowAsync had synchronously returned it, rather than having to retrieve it from an intermediate object in a convoluted fashion. You can only use the await keyword in a method that is marked with an async keyword. The async designation triggers the C# compiler to rewrite the method's implementation as a state machine, which is necessary for providing the handy await illusion. Due to the way this is implemented, the compiler does not allow you to await within a catch block.

People commonly refer to this pattern as "awaiting a method," but you're actually awaiting the returned IAsync*XXX* or Task object. As before, the method actually returns promptly. This is clearer if the preceding code is expanded to the following equivalent code:

```
async Task ShowDialog()
{
  MessageDialog dialog = new MessageDialog("Title");
  IAsyncOperation<IUICommand> operation = dialog.ShowAsync();
```

```
IUICommand command = await operation;
// The next line of code does not run until the operation is done
MoreCodeThatCanUseTheCommand(command);
}
```

It's also worth noting that the async designation does not appear in the metadata for a method when it is compiled. It is purely an implementation detail. Again, you're not awaiting a method; it simply happens to return a data type that supports being awaited.

Notice that the sample ShowDialog method returns a Task, which seems wrong because the method does not appear to return anything. However, the async-triggered rewriting done by the C# compiler does indeed return a Task object. This enables an asynchronous operation to be chained from one caller to the next. Because ShowDialog returns a Task, its caller could choose to await it.

If an async method actually returns something in its visible source code, such as the command object in the preceding code, then it must return Task<T>, where T is the type of the object being returned. In this example, it would be Task<IUICommand>. The C# compiler enforces that an async method must either return Task, Task<T>, or void. This means that ShowDialog could be rewritten with async void instead of async Task and it would still compile. You should avoid this, however, because it breaks the composition of asynchronous tasks.

> ## (!) Avoid defining an async method with a void return type!
>
> If you do this, your callers cannot await or otherwise leverage an operation returned by your method (because it doesn't return anything), which makes it harder for their code to behave correctly. This cannot be avoided on methods that must match a delegate signature, such as a Button's Click handler. That is not a cause for concern, however, because nobody other than the framework should be calling such methods.

> ## (!) Do not use Task.Wait!
>
> The .NET Task object provides many useful abstractions for cancellation and advanced control flow. You can also schedule your own long-running task via Task.Run, which directly returns a Task, rather than using ThreadPool.RunAsync, which returns an IAsyncAction instead. (Task.Run should really be called Task.RunAsync.)
>
> One feature that you should avoid is Task's Wait method. Although Waiting for a task to complete sounds similar to awaiting the task to complete, the Wait method blocks the current thread. Besides defeating the purpose of the background work, for cases such as showing a MessageDialog, this causes a deadlock:
>
> ```
> void ShowDialog()
> {
>   MessageDialog dialog = new MessageDialog("Title");
>   dialog.ShowAsync().AsTask().Wait(); // DEADLOCK!
> }
> ```

> You can leverage the nice `await` control flow for APIs that don't return a `Task` or `IAsyncXXX` by wrapping the use of the APIs with an object called `TaskCompletionSource`. This has a `Task` property that you can return to your callers, and methods that you can call at the appropriate time to signal that the `Task` has completed, failed, or been canceled. `TaskCompletionSource` is used later in this chapter to provide a nice way to create and show additional windows.

Transitioning Between Threads

Occasions often arise when one thread needs to schedule work to be executed on another thread. For example, although events on XAML objects are raised on the same UI thread that created the object, this is usually not the case for non-UI objects in the Windows Runtime. Instead, they are raised on whatever background thread happens to be doing the work.

An example of this can be seen with the events defined by `MediaCapture`, a class described in Chapter 14, "Audio, Video, and Speech." The following code incorrectly tries to update the UI to notify the user about a failure to capture video from the PC's camera:

```
// A handler for MediaCapture's Failed event
void Capture_Failed(MediaCapture sender, MediaCaptureFailedEventArgs e)
{
  // This throws an exception:
  this.textBlock.Text = "Failure capturing video.";
}
```

The exception thrown explains, "The application called an interface that was marshalled for a different thread. (Exception from HRESULT: 0x8001010E (RPC_E_WRONG_THREAD))."

With `DependencyObject`'s `Dispatcher` property of type `CoreDispatcher`, however, you can marshal a call back to the proper UI thread needed to update the `TextBlock`. It can be used as follows:

```
// A handler for MediaCapture's Failed event
async void Capture_Failed(MediaCapture sender, MediaCaptureFailedEventArgs e)
{
  await this.Dispatcher.RunAsync(CoreDispatcherPriority.Normal, () =>
  {
    // This now works, because it's running on the UI thread:
    this.textBlock.Text = "Failure capturing video.";
  });
}
```

Here, an anonymous method is used for `RunAsync`'s second parameter (which must be a parameterless `DispatchedHandler` delegate) to keep the code as concise as possible. The code must be scheduled to run at one of the following priorities, from highest to lowest:

High (which should never be used by app code), Normal, Low, and Idle (which waits until the destination thread is idle with no pending input).

This CoreDispatcher mechanism is also how one window can communicate with another window. Each Window, along with related Windows Runtime abstractions, expose a Dispatcher property that can schedule a delegate to run on its own UI thread.

Displaying Multiple Windows

People don't normally think about a window when it comes to a Windows Store app, given that there is no window chrome. Nevertheless, the content displayed by a Windows Store app is indeed hosted in a window. Not only that, but an app can use multiple windows simultaneously.

Although they are called *windows* in XAML-specific APIs, windows are often called *views* in Windows Runtime APIs. In Windows Runtime terminology, a view is the union of a window and its UI thread.

Apps show a primary window when activated, but you can create and show any number of secondary windows. You create a secondary window by calling CoreApplicationView.CreateNewView. This returns a CoreApplicationView instance representing the new window and its UI thread, but you can't interact with it yet. You must wait for Application.OnWindowCreated to be called, which occurs on the new UI thread. On this thread, you can initialize the window much like you would initialize your primary window. Once it is initialized, you can show it with an ApplicationViewSwitcher class—back on the original UI thread.

Because of the convoluted control flow, this is a perfect opportunity to use the TaskCompletionSource type mentioned earlier in this chapter. Listing 8.1 adds an await-friendly CreateWindowAsync method to App.xaml.cs, inspired by the Multiple Views Sample project provided by the Windows SDK.

LISTING 8.1   App.xaml.cs: Providing an await-friendly CreateWindowAsync Method

```
using System;
using System.Collections.Concurrent;
using System.Threading.Tasks;
using Windows.ApplicationModel;
using Windows.ApplicationModel.Activation;
using Windows.ApplicationModel.Core;
using Windows.UI.Xaml;
using Windows.UI.Xaml.Controls;

namespace MultipleWindows
{
  sealed partial class App : Application
  {
    // The pending tasks created by CreateWindowAsync
```

```
ConcurrentQueue<TaskCompletionSource<Window>> taskWrappers
  = new ConcurrentQueue<TaskCompletionSource<Window>>();

// Create a new window.
// This wrapper method enables awaiting.
public Task<Window> CreateWindowAsync()
{
  // Create a Task that the caller can await
  TaskCompletionSource<Window> taskWrapper
    = new TaskCompletionSource<Window>();
  this.taskWrappers.Enqueue(taskWrapper);

  // Create the secondary window, which calls Application.OnWindowCreated
  // on its own UI thread
  CoreApplication.CreateNewView();

  // Return the Task
  return taskWrapper.Task;
}

protected override void OnWindowCreated(WindowCreatedEventArgs args)
{
  CoreApplicationView view = CoreApplication.GetCurrentView();
  if (!view.IsMain)
  {
    // This is a secondary window, so mark the in-progress Task as complete
    // and "return" the relevant XAML-specific Window object
    TaskCompletionSource<Window> taskWrapper;
    if (this.taskWrappers.TryDequeue(out taskWrapper))
      taskWrapper.SetResult(args.Window);
    else
      throw new InvalidOperationException();
  }
}

...
  }
}
```

The code inside OnWindowCreated can easily check whether it is being invoked for the main window or a secondary window by obtaining the current CoreApplicationView and examining its IsMain property.

Listing 8.2 shows the code-behind for the following MainPage.xaml that leverages CreateWindowAsync to show a new window every time its Button is clicked:

```
<Page x:Class="MultipleWindows.MainPage" …>
  <Viewbox>
    <Button Click="Button_Click">Show a New Window</Button>
  </Viewbox>
</Page>
```

LISTING 8.2   MainPage.xaml.cs: Using CreateWindowAsync to Create Then Show a
New Window

```
using System;
using Windows.UI.Core;
using Windows.UI.ViewManagement;
using Windows.UI.Xaml;
using Windows.UI.Xaml.Controls;

namespace MultipleWindows
{
  public sealed partial class MainPage : Page
  {
    public MainPage()
    {
      InitializeComponent();
    }

    async void Button_Click(object sender, RoutedEventArgs e)
    {
      int newWindowId = 0;

      // Create the new window with our handy helper method
      Window newWindow = await (App.Current as App).CreateWindowAsync();

      // Initialize the new window on its UI thread
      await newWindow.Dispatcher.RunAsync(CoreDispatcherPriority.Normal, () =>
      {
        // In this context, Window.Current is the new window.
        // Navigate its content to a different page.
        Frame frame = new Frame();
        frame.Navigate(typeof(SecondPage));
        Window.Current.Content = frame;

        // Set a different title
        ApplicationView.GetForCurrentView().Title = "NEW";

        newWindowId = ApplicationView.GetApplicationViewIdForWindow(
                        newWindow.CoreWindow);
      });
```

```
      // Back on the original UI thread, show the new window alongside this one
      bool success =
         await ApplicationViewSwitcher.TryShowAsStandaloneAsync(newWindowId);
    }
  }
}
```

Once `Button_Click` retrieves the new `Window` instance, which actually came from App's `OnWindowCreated` method, it can schedule its initialization on its UI thread. It `awaits` this work's completion, because the next step requires a window ID that must be retrieved from that window's UI thread. With the ID, the original code can then call `ApplicationViewSwitcher.TryShowAsStandaloneAsync` to show the new window.

Figure 8.1 shows the result after the user clicks the `Button` twice, assuming that `SecondPage.xaml`, which is used for each secondary window, contains nothing but a `Page` with a red `Grid`.

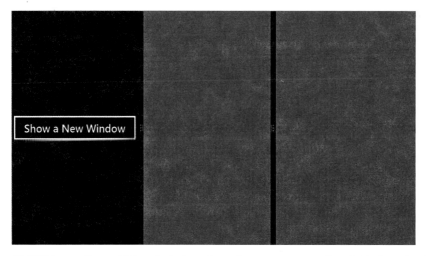

FIGURE 8.1   Two additional windows from the same app are placed side-by-side after `Button_Click` executes twice.

To a user, these windows appear almost no different than three distinct apps. When the windows are offscreen, their entries in the switcher user interface reveal their relationship. It also shows the custom title, as you can see in Figure 8.2.

`TryShowAsStandaloneAsync` has overloads that enable you to specify a `ViewSizePreference` for the target window or for both windows, just like when launching an app. You can also swap one window with another in-place by calling `SwitchAsync` instead of `TryShowAsStandaloneAsync`.

> For several Windows Runtime classes, you obtain an instance by calling their
> static Get(ForCurrentView) methods. Such objects are designed to have a single instance per window. In other words, they are not agile. If you have multiple windows, you should make sure to use the appropriate instance from each UI thread.

FIGURE 8.2   When offscreen, the three windows all reveal their host app in the switcher.

Navigating Between Pages

Although simple apps might have only one Page per window, most windows in real-world apps leverage multiple Pages. The XAML UI Framework contains quite a bit of functionality to make it easy to navigate from one page to another (and back), much like in a Web browser. Visual Studio templates also give you a lot of code in a Common folder to handle many small details, such as applying standard keyboard navigation to page navigation, and automatic integration of session state.

Although a Blank App project is given a single page by default, you can add more pages by right-clicking the project in Solution Explorer then selecting **Add**, **New Item…**, and one of the many Page choices. The different choices are mostly distinguished by different preconfigured layouts and controls.

In addition, if you create a Grid App, Hub App, or Split App project, these are already set up as apps with a multi-Page window. Figure 8.3 shows the behavior of the Split App project before any customizations are made. Selecting a group on the first Page (ItemsPage) automatically navigates to its details on the second page (SplitPage). When the user clicks the back button in the top left corner, the window navigates back to the first page.

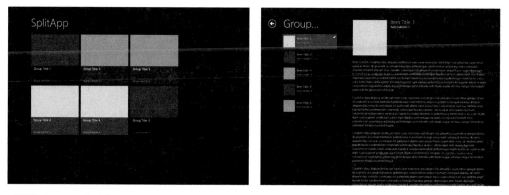

FIGURE 8.3   A Split App project contains two pages: one that shows groups, and one that shows the items inside each group.

Basic Navigation and Passing Data

Although it's natural to think of a Page as the root element of a window (especially for single-page windows), all Pages are contained in a Frame. Frame provides several members to enable Page-to-Page navigation. It is often accessed from the Frame property defined on each Page.

To navigate from one page to another, you call Frame's Navigate method with the type (*not* an instance) of the destination page. An instance of the new page is automatically created and navigated to, complete with a standard Windows animation.

For example, when an item is clicked in a Split App's ItemsPage, it navigates to a new instance of SplitPage as follows:

```
void ItemView_ItemClick(object sender, ItemClickEventArgs e)
{
  // Navigate to the appropriate destination page, configuring the new page
  // by passing required information as a navigation parameter
  var groupId = ((SampleDataGroup)e.ClickedItem).UniqueId;
  this.Frame.Navigate(typeof(SplitPage), groupId);
}
```

Navigate has two overloads, one that accepts only the type of the destination page, and one that also accepts a custom System.Object that gets passed along to the destination page. In this case, this second parameter is used to tell the second page which group was just clicked. If you use SuspensionManager in your project, its automatic management of navigation state means that whatever you pass as the custom Object for Navigate must be serializable.

The target SplitPage receives this custom parameter via the NavigationEventArgs instance passed to the Page's OnNavigatedTo method. It exposes the object with its Parameter property.

A call to Navigate raises a sequence of events defined on Frame. First is Navigating, which happens before the navigation begins. It enables the handler to cancel navigation by setting the passed-in NavigatingCancelEventArgs instance's Cancel property to true. Then, if it isn't canceled, one of three events will be raised: Navigated if navigation completes successfully, NavigationFailed if it fails, or NavigationStopped if Navigate is called again before the current navigation finishes.

Page has three virtual methods that correspond to some of these events. OnNavigatingFrom enables the current page to cancel navigation. OnNavigatedFrom and OnNavigatedTo correspond to both ends of a successful navigation. If you want to respond to a navigation failure or get details about the error, you must handle the events on Frame.

Navigating Forward and Back

Just like a Web browser, the Frame maintains a back stack and a forward stack. In addition to the Navigate method, it exposes GoBack and GoForward methods. Table 8.1 explains the behavior of these three methods and their impact on the back and forward stacks.

TABLE 8.1   Navigation Effects on the Back and Forward Stacks

Action	Result
Navigate	Pushes the current page onto the back stack, empties the forward stack, and navigates to the desired page
GoBack	Pushes the current page onto the forward stack, pops a page off the back stack, and navigates to it
GoForward	Pushes the current page onto the back stack, pops a page off the forward stack, and navigates to it

GoBack throws an exception when the back stack is empty (which means you're currently on the window's initial page), and GoForward throws an exception when the forward stack is empty. If a piece of code is not certain what the states of these stacks are, it can check the Boolean CanGoBack and CanGoForward properties first. Frame also exposes a BackStackDepth readonly property that reveals the number of Pages currently on the back stack.

Therefore, you could imagine implementing Page-level GoBack and GoForward methods as follows:

```
void GoBack()
{
  if (this.Frame != null && this.Frame.CanGoBack) this.Frame.GoBack();
}

void GoForward()
{
  if (this.Frame != null && this.Frame.CanGoForward) this.Frame.GoForward();
}
```

For advanced scenarios, the entire back and forward stacks are now exposed in Windows 8.1 as BackStack and ForwardStack properties, which are both a list of PageStackEntry instances. With this, you can completely customize the navigation experience, and do things such as removing Pages from the back stack that are meant to be transient.

> ### How do I pass data from one page to another when navigating backward?
>
> Sometimes an app uses a scheme that navigates to a new page in order to have the user select something or fill out a form, and then that data needs to be communicated *back* to the original page when the new page is dismissed. You've already seen how to pass data to the next page when calling Navigate, but there is no equivalent mechanism for passing data to the preceding page when calling GoBack. (The same is true for GoForward.)
>
> Instead, you must find a shared place to store the data where both pages know to look. For example, this could be your own static member on one of your classes, or perhaps even session state might be appropriate to use for this.

> ...
>
> ### Frame's Content Property
>
> Instead of calling Navigate, you can place content in a Frame by setting its Content property. (This is what the Visual Studio-generated code in App.xaml.cs does.) This is much different than calling Navigate, however, because doing so clears the back and forward stacks. It also doesn't trigger the typical navigation animation.
>
> Furthermore, the Frame control can hold arbitrary content via its Content property. This is not a normal thing to do, but using Frame in this way enables hosting the content in an isolated fashion. For example, properties that would normally be inherited down the element tree stop when they reach the Frame. In this respect, Frame acts like a frame in HTML.

Page Caching

By default, Page instances are *not* kept alive on the back and forward stacks; a new instance gets created when you call GoBack or GoForward! This means you must take care to remember and restore their state, although you will probably already have code to do this in order to properly handle suspension.

You can change this behavior on a Page-by-Page basis by setting Page's NavigationCacheMode property to one of the following values:

- → **Disabled**—The default value that causes the page to be recreated every time.

- → **Required**—Keeps the page alive and uses this cached instance every time (for GoForward and GoBack, not for Navigate).

- → **Enabled**—Keeps the page alive and uses the cached instance only if the size of the Frame's cache hasn't been exceeded. This size is controlled by Frame's CacheSize property. This property represents a number of Pages and is set to 10 by default

Using Required or Enabled can result in excessive memory usage, and it can waste CPU cycles if an inactive Page on the stack is doing unnecessary work (such as having code running on a timer). Such pages can use the OnNavigatedFrom method to pause its processing and the OnNavigatedTo method to resume it, to help mitigate this problem.

When you navigate to a Page by calling Navigate, you get a new instance of it, regardless of NavigationCacheMode. No special relationship exists between two instances of a Page other than the fact that they happen to come from the same source code. You can leverage this by reusing the same type of Page for multiple levels of a navigation hierarchy, each one dynamically initialized to have the appropriate content. However, if you want every instance of the same page to act as if it's the same page (and "remember" its data from the previously-seen instance), then you need to manage this yourself, perhaps with static members on the relevant Page class.

NavigationHelper

If you add any Page more sophisticated than a Blank Page to your project, it uses a NavigationHelper class whose source also gets included in your project. For convenience, NavigationHelper defines GoBack and GoForward methods just like the ones implemented earlier. It also adds standard keyboard and mouse shortcuts for navigation. It enables navigating back when the user presses Alt+Left and navigating forward when the user presses Alt+Right. For a mouse, it enables navigating back if XButton1 is pressed and forward if XButton2 is pressed. These two buttons are the browser-style previous and next buttons that appear on some mice.

NavigationHelper also hooks into some extra functionality exposed by SuspensionManager in order to automatically maintain navigation history as part of session state. To take advantage of this, you need to call one more method inside OnLaunched (or OnWindowCreated) to make SuspensionManager aware of the Frame:

```
var rootFrame = new Frame();
SuspensionManager.RegisterFrame(rootFrame, "AppFrame");
```

Each Page should also call NavigationHelper's OnNavigatedTo and OnNavigatedFrom methods from its overridden OnNavigatedTo and OnNavigatedFrom methods, respectively, and handle NavigationHelper's LoadState and SaveState events for restoring/persisting state. LoadState handlers are passed the "navigation parameter" object (the second parameter passed to the call to Navigate, otherwise null) as well as the session state Dictionary. SaveState handlers are passed only the session state Dictionary.

When you create a Grid App, Hub App, or Split App project, all these changes are applied automatically. Internally, this works in part thanks to a pair of methods exposed by Frame—GetNavigationState and SetNavigationState—that conveniently provide and accept a serialized string representation of navigation history.

> If your app does any navigation, you should use NavigationHelper (or copy its code) to handle the standard keyboard and mouse shortcuts.

Other Ways to Use Frame

Not every app needs to follow the pattern of a Window hosting a Frame that hosts Page(s). A Window's content doesn't have to be a Frame, and you can embed Frames anywhere UIElements can go. We can demonstrate this by modifying a Split App project to set the Window's Content to a custom Grid subclass that we create. Imagine this is called RootGrid, and it must be constructed with a Frame that it wants to dynamically add to its Children collection. It would be used in App.xaml.cs as follows:

```
// Instead of Window.Current.Content = rootFrame:
Window.Current.Content = new RootGrid(rootFrame);
```

RootGrid can be added to the project as a pair of XAML and code-behind, shown in Listings 8.3 and 8.4.

LISTING 8.3   RootGrid.xaml: A Simple Grid Expecting to Contain a Frame

```
<Grid x:Class="Chapter8.RootGrid" Background="Blue"
  xmlns="http://schemas.microsoft.com/winfx/2006/xaml/presentation"
  xmlns:x="http://schemas.microsoft.com/winfx/2006/xaml">
  <!-- A 3x3 Grid -->
  <Grid.RowDefinitions>
    <RowDefinition/>
    <RowDefinition/>
    <RowDefinition/>
  </Grid.RowDefinitions>
  <Grid.ColumnDefinitions>
    <ColumnDefinition/>
    <ColumnDefinition/>
    <ColumnDefinition/>
  </Grid.ColumnDefinitions>
  <!-- Two Buttons to interact with a Frame -->
  <Button Name="BackButton" Grid.Row="1" HorizontalAlignment="Center"
    Click="BackButton_Click">Back</Button>
  <Button Name="ForwardButton" Grid.Row="1" Grid.Column="2"
    HorizontalAlignment="Center" Click="ForwardButton_Click">Forward</Button>
</Grid>
```

LISTING 8.4   RootGrid.xaml.cs: The Code-Behind That Places the Frame and Interacts with It

```
using Windows.UI.Xaml;
using Windows.UI.Xaml.Controls;
using Windows.UI.Xaml.Navigation;

namespace Chapter8
{
  public sealed partial class RootGrid : Grid
```

```
{
  Frame frame;

  public RootGrid(Frame f)
  {
    InitializeComponent();
    this.frame = f;

    // Add the Frame to the middle cell of the Grid
    Grid.SetRow(this.frame, 1);
    Grid.SetColumn(this.frame, 1);
    this.Children.Add(this.frame);

    this.frame.Navigated += Frame_Navigated;
  }

  void Frame_Navigated(object sender, NavigationEventArgs e)
  {
    if (this.frame != null)
    {
      // Keep the enabled/disabled state of the buttons relevant
      this.BackButton.IsEnabled = this.frame.CanGoBack;
      this.ForwardButton.IsEnabled = this.frame.CanGoForward;
    }
  }

  void BackButton_Click(object sender, RoutedEventArgs e)
  {
    if (this.frame != null && this.frame.CanGoBack)
      this.frame.GoBack();
  }

  void ForwardButton_Click(object sender, RoutedEventArgs e)
  {
    if (this.frame != null && this.frame.CanGoForward)
      this.frame.GoForward();
  }
}
}
```

By placing the Frame in its middle cell, RootGrid is effectively applying a thick blue border to the Frame that persists even as navigation happens within the Frame. (When used this way, Frame seems more like an iframe in HTML.) The simple back and forward Buttons in RootGrid are able to control the navigation (and enable/disable when appropriate) thanks to the APIs exposed on Frame. This unconventional window is shown in Figure 8.4, after navigating to the second page.

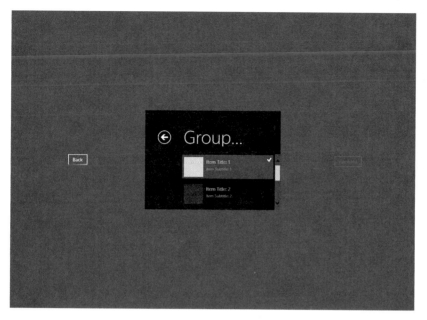

FIGURE 8.4   A Frame doesn't have to occupy all the space in an app's window.

Although this specific use of Frame doesn't seem practical, you can do some neat things with a similar approach. One example would be to have a Page that always stays on screen containing a fullscreen Frame that navigates to various Pages. The reason this is compelling is that the outer Page can have app bars that are accessible regardless of what the current inner Page is. (App bars are discussed in Chapter 10, "Content Controls.")

If you decide you want your Page to truly be the root content in your app's Window, you can change the code in App.xaml.cs to eliminate the hosting Frame. This can work fine, but with no Frame, you don't get the navigation features.

Summary

The design of the Windows Runtime, combined with slick C# language support, could lead one to think, "Threading model? I didn't realize Windows Store apps *had* a threading model." In C#, you get to enjoy the benefits of writing an app that largely feels single-threaded, but has all the power of asynchronous code (and a number of parallelism mechanisms employed internally by the Windows Runtime).

Supporting multiple windows within a single app is one area where the code you write can become awkward, but the model of having each window run on a separate UI thread maximizes an app's responsiveness.

The navigation features enabled by `Frame` and `Page`, although specific to XAML, are similar in spirit to the type of navigation features supported for HTML-based Windows Store apps. Unlike traditional Windows desktop apps, it is quite common for Windows Store apps to expose a user interface centered around navigating to different pages. For example, all the Bing apps except Maps use multiple pages.

Chapter 9

THE MANY WAYS TO EARN MONEY

The app model for Windows Store apps includes the capability to support many *business models* in the Windows Store. Windows Store apps have three easy-to-integrate options for making money. An app can use any or all of the following approaches:

→ Earning revenue by showing advertisements

→ Charging for the app itself

→ Providing in-app purchases

Ads are typically used by free apps, as users who pay for an app are likely to be annoyed by them. Traditional pay-to-install apps can be enhanced with one of two types of free trials, which can help drive a lot of additional usage and a lot of additional revenue. Using in-app purchases to enable features in an otherwise-free app is the *freemium* business model that has gained a lot of popularity. In-app purchases enable a number of interesting scenarios, whether the app itself is free or not. A common mixture of these business models is to expose an in-app purchase that enables the user to remove the ads from the app.

The Windows Store allows you to use a third-party payment system, as long as the transactions comply with the App Developer Agreement (http://go.microsoft.com/fwlink/p/?LinkID=221922). The Windows Store doesn't charge any fees for such transactions. However, there is a lot of benefit to using the built-in payment system, despite the 30% fee on app sales and in-app purchases (which is reduced to 20% once an app reaches $25,000 in total sales). New markets and payment types are continually being added. The Windows Store now supports gift cards and Alipay (the leading online payment provider in China) in addition to credit cards and PayPal. Once a user configures a payment method, that information roams to any device he or she is signed into. Therefore, there is almost no friction when users make purchases with the Windows Store payment system. The Windows Store also gives Windows 8.1 apps more flexibility when it comes to in-app purchases.

It may be obvious, but all the features covered in this chapter require your app to have the Internet (Client) capability in order to work correctly.

> **How do I support a subscription business model?**
>
> The Windows Store does not yet have support for subscriptions, so for now you must use a third-party provider or mimic the experience with in-app purchases. In-app purchases of the *expiring durable* type (described later in this chapter) are a good fit for supporting a subscription-style experience. The one key feature that is missing is the auto-renewal (with the corresponding automatic charge) that you, as a developer, would undoubtedly love to exploit.

Adding Advertisements to Your App

Many ad platforms exist that can be integrated into your app. Some pay you when an ad is shown to your user (paying per *impression*) and some pay you when a user taps on the ad (paying per *click*). In this section, we look at integrating ads from Microsoft Advertising pubCenter into a Windows Store app.

Using pubCenter to show ads has several nice aspects: It pays per impression, it's easy to manage through http://pubcenter.microsoft.com and the Windows Dev Center dashboard, it's designed to serve ads to Windows Store (and Windows Phone) apps, and Visual Studio 2013 introduces built-in integration for pubCenter.

Defining Ad Units in pubCenter

First, make sure you have signed up with pubCenter at http://pubcenter.microsoft.com with the same Microsoft Account that you use to submit Windows Store apps. You can register apps and define ad units on the website, but it's easier to leverage the new wizard for this in Visual Studio 2013.

Imagine that you have created a new Blank App XAML project in Visual Studio. From the **Project** menu (or your project's context menu), select **Add Connected Service**... to bring up the Services Manager dialog. In the **Microsoft Ads** section, click the **Sign in** link to sign into pubCenter, then click the **Create application** link to bring up the dialog shown in Figure 9.1. In here, you give pubCenter a name and category for your app and define any number of ad units.

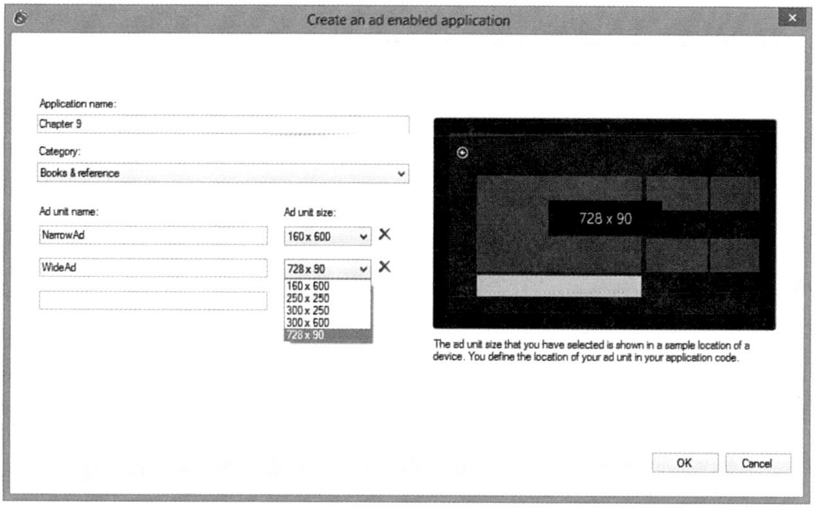

FIGURE 9.1 You can add Windows Store apps to pubCenter and define ad units directly from within Visual Studio 2013.

After pressing the OK button, your definition of the app and its ad units appears in a list in the Services Manager dialog. You can edit this at any time, either via this dialog or the pubCenter website. Figure 9.2 shows that if you visit the pubCenter website after pressing OK, you can see the same information, although with an app ID and ad unit IDs that are hidden from the Visual Studio experience.

When you press OK once more to dismiss the Services Manager dialog in Visual Studio, a reference to the "Microsoft Advertising SDK for Windows 8.1 (Xaml)" extension is automatically added to your project. This appears in Solution Explorer as "MSAdvertisingXaml." Visual Studio also presents you with an AdSamplePage.xaml.txt file that demonstrates how to display each ad unit you just defined in XAML. For the values chosen in Figure 9.1, the text file looks as follows:

```
<Page x:Class="My_Ad_Funded_Windows_XAML_App.MainPage"
  xmlns="http://schemas.microsoft.com/winfx/2006/xaml/presentation"
  xmlns:x="http://schemas.microsoft.com/winfx/2006/xaml"
  xmlns:local="using:TestAdApp"
  xmlns:d="http://schemas.microsoft.com/expression/blend/2008"
  xmlns:mc="http://schemas.openxmlformats.org/markup-compatibility/2006"
  xmlns:UI="using:Microsoft.Advertising.WinRT.UI"
  mc:Ignorable="d">
    <StackPanel Background="{ThemeResource ApplicationPageBackgroundThemeBrush}"
                Orientation="Vertical">
      <UI:AdControl
        ApplicationId="68bc728e-6aba-4b5b-83d3-a01601830827" AdUnitId="137222"
        Width="160" Height="600" Margin="0,0,0,0"
        HorizontalAlignment="Left" VerticalAlignment="Top"/>
```

```
    <UI:AdControl
      ApplicationId="68bc728e-6aba-4b5b-83d3-a01601830827" AdUnitId="137223"
      Width="728" Height="90" Margin="0,0,0,0"
      HorizontalAlignment="Left" VerticalAlignment="Top"/>
  </StackPanel>
</Page>
```

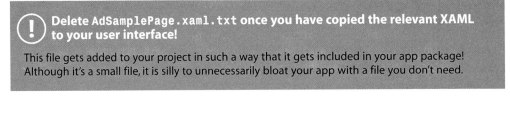

FIGURE 9.2   After adding an app and ad units in Visual Studio, you can manage them on the pubCenter website as well.

> **(!) Delete AdSamplePage.xaml.txt once you have copied the relevant XAML to your user interface!**
>
> This file gets added to your project in such a way that it gets included in your app package! Although it's a small file, it is silly to unnecessarily bloat your app with a file you don't need.

Adding Ads to a Page

The preceding text file, although overly verbose, demonstrates that you use an instance of Microsoft.Advertising.WinRT.UI.AdControl to display an ad to the user. You just need to give it the ApplicationId for your app (the GUID visible on the pubCenter website) and the `AdUnitId` for the relevant ad unit (also visible on the pubCenter website). The following XAML is a cleaned-up version of the two `AdControls`, used with a more appropriate XML namespace and added to the Blank App project's `MainPage.xaml` file:

```
<Page x:Class="Chapter9.MainPage"
  xmlns="http://schemas.microsoft.com/winfx/2006/xaml/presentation"
  xmlns:x="http://schemas.microsoft.com/winfx/2006/xaml"
  xmlns:pubCenter="using:Microsoft.Advertising.WinRT.UI">
  <Grid Background="{ThemeResource ApplicationPageBackgroundThemeBrush}">
    <Grid.RowDefinitions>
      <RowDefinition/>
      <RowDefinition Height="Auto"/>
    </Grid.RowDefinitions>
    <Grid.ColumnDefinitions>
      <ColumnDefinition/>
      <ColumnDefinition Width="Auto"/>
    </Grid.ColumnDefinitions>

    <!-- The NarrowAd ad unit for the Chapter 9 app -->
    <pubCenter:AdControl ApplicationId="68bc728e-6aba-4b5b-83d3-a01601830827"
                         AdUnitId="137222" Width="160" Height="600"
                         Grid.Column="1"/>

    <!-- The WideAd ad unit for the Chapter 9 app -->
    <pubCenter:AdControl ApplicationId="68bc728e-6aba-4b5b-83d3-a01601830827"
                         AdUnitId="137223" Width="728" Height="90"
                         Grid.Row="1"/>
  </Grid>
</Page>
```

With this addition, the result of running the app is shown in Figure 9.3.

Everything is now ready to go. After publishing your app, you can visit pubCenter to monitor the performance of your ads and wait to get paid!

`AdControl` can personalize the ads for the current user, although the user remains in control over this feature. When you use an `AdControl`, a "Microsoft Advertising" link gets automatically placed in the Settings charm for your app. (This is all done via the same APIs available to your own code, covered in Chapter 21, "Supporting Charms.") The link exposes a pane from which the user can enable or disable the ad targeting.

> **(!) All AdControls in your app must use the same `ApplicationId`!**
>
> If you use more than one `ApplicationId` within the same app, only one of those IDs will work at runtime. The controls associated with the other IDs will fail to show any ads.

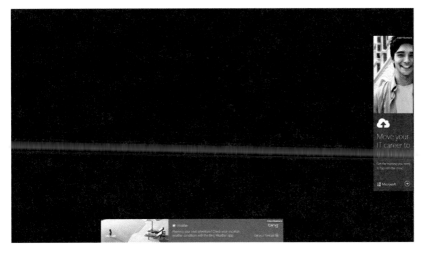

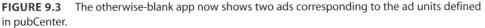

FIGURE 9.3   The otherwise-blank app now shows two ads corresponding to the ad units defined in pubCenter.

> **(!) Avoid changing or reparenting an AdControl!**
>
> Except for the `Latitude` and `Longitude` properties described in the next section, you cannot change any properties of `AdControl` after its initialization. You also should not change an `AdControl`'s parent element once it is added to an element tree. Therefore, don't reuse instances to handle multiple ad units or dynamically add/remove instances from a page.

Advanced `AdControl` Behaviors

Although ad targeting is outside of your control, `AdControl` provides many features that you can use to tweak its behavior. You can control its refresh behavior, provide location information to improve ad relevance, and more.

When the user taps on an ad, it may optionally show an expanded form. In `AdControl` terminology, the user is "engaging" with the ad when this happens. If your app is a game or is playing its own media at the time, this would be a good time to pause it. You can handle `AdControl`'s `IsEngagedChanged` event to catch when this happens, and determine what just happened with `AdControl`'s Boolean `IsEngaged` property. When tapping an ad launches another app like Internet Explorer or the Store, you can rely on `Window`'s `Activated` event, as always, to detect the loss of focus.

By default, an `AdControl` shows a new ad every minute. You can change this by setting its `IsAutoRefreshEnabled` property to `false` (only during initialization, and then you can't change it back). If you do this, you can force it to refresh at any time by calling its `Refresh` method from code-behind. The new ad will appear as soon as it's available. When the refresh happens, whether automatically or due to a `Refresh` call, `AdControl`'s `AdRefreshed` event is raised.

Although you can't dynamically change `IsAutoRefreshEnabled` to `false` after initialization, you *can* call `AdControl`'s `Suspend` method to pause automatic refresh until you call `Resume`. Calling `Suspend` also pauses any animation in the ad and closes it if it is expanded. The latter behavior, however, can be controlled by calling an overload of `Suspend` with a Boolean `closeExpandedAd` parameter. You can call `Suspend` and `Resume` even when `IsAutoRefreshEnabled` is `false` to leverage its ad-pausing and ad-closing behaviors. While an `AdControl` is suspended, revealed by its Boolean `IsSuspended` property, calling `Refresh` does not work.

To help an `AdControl` show more relevant ads, you can set its `Longitude` and `Latitude` properties to the user's current location. If your app is already retrieving the user's position for a non-advertising reason (using the functionality covered in Chapter 23, "Reading from Sensors") then you should set these properties and set them often. Otherwise, you're probably better off ignoring these properties and preventing your app from requesting the Location capability.

Any time `AdControl` attempts to show an ad, many things could go wrong. You can get notified about any errors by handling its `ErrorOccurred` event. The `AdErrorEventArgs` instance passed to handlers reveals what happens via an `Error` property with an `Exception` object representing the failure, as well as an `ErrorCode` property that is set to one of the following values from an `ErrorCode` enumeration:

→ **NoAdAvailable**—There simply isn't the ad inventory to support your request at the moment.

→ **NetworkConnectionFailure**—`AdControl` requires a network connection to retrieve an ad, so this can be a common source of failure.

→ **ServerSideError** and **InvalidServerResponse**—These represent unexpected errors from the Microsoft Advertising service.

→ **ClientConfiguration** and **RefreshNotAllowed**—These represent coding errors in your app, such as using an invalid ID or calling `Refresh` while the `AdControl` is suspended.

→ **Unknown** and **Other**—These are the catch-all values. The `Error` property might reveal more information in these cases.

Whenever a new version of the Microsoft Advertising SDK is released, you should strongly consider downloading it, rebuilding your ad-enabled app with it, then resubmitting your app to the Windows Store. New versions are likely to have fixes and features that can improve your earnings.

Supporting a Free Trial

If you choose a price tier other than "Free" for your app in the Windows Store, then you may optionally choose to offer a free trial. This can be tremendously helpful for selling more copies of your app, and Microsoft recommends it. Although ratings, reviews, and screenshots in the Windows Store can help convince some of your potential customers to make a purchase, many more people likely want to have additional reassurance before spending money on your app. A good trial experience in a good app can provide just that.

The Windows Dev Center dashboard gives you two types of free trials to choose from: time-based trials and unlimited (therefore, feature-differentiated) trials.

> When a user moves from a "trial version" of an app to a "full version," or when a user makes an in-app purchase, the only thing he or she is buying is a *license*. The app bits don't change, so there aren't actually separate versions of an app or separate features that get downloaded (through the Windows Store, anyway). It is the responsibility of your code to properly handle the different licensing conditions and perhaps provide the illusion of separate app versions.

> Paid apps that offer a free trial are more likely to be promoted by Microsoft in the Windows Store than paid apps with no trial. In addition, according to Microsoft and based on data from 2013, about 70% of the top paid apps have free trials, and about 95% of the top grossing apps have free trials.

Time-Based Trials

If you set up a time-based trial in your Windows Dev Center dashboard, you don't need to do any date-based or time-based math in your code. In fact, you don't need to do anything in your code! The Windows Store manages this for you and simply prevents the user from continuing to use your app once the trial expires. The dashboard currently allows you to choose one of four pre-defined time periods: 1 day, 7 days, 15 days, and 30 days. The countdown begins once a user installs your app—on *any* of their devices. Just like a full license, the trial license is per-user and roams accordingly.

Feature-Differentiated Trials

If you want your app to behave differently when it is running under a trial license, you need to write some code. This is typically done with an unlimited trial (the "Trial never expires" option in the Windows Store dashboard), but you can do this with time-based trials as well. For example, you might want to remind a trial user how much time is remaining in their time-based trial. And whether the trial is time-based or not, you probably want to provide a convenient way for them to purchase the full version of your app from directly inside your app.

The first step to executing different code for a trial version versus a full version is understanding the license owned by the current user. You can discover all relevant information about the license via the Windows.ApplicationModel.Store.CurrentApp static class. You check a Boolean CurrentApp.LicenseInformation.IsTrial property and base arbitrary logic off of that. Before using any properties of CurrentApp.LicenseInformation, however, you should ensure CurrentApp.LicenseInformation.IsActive is true. If it is false, then the license has either expired (for a time-based trial), has been revoked, or is somehow missing. For example, when running your app *sideloaded* (not signed and distributed by the Windows Store), as when you're developing your app locally, IsActive is always false. When IsActive is false, you should not enable any features that are meant for paid users or for a limited time only.

The following code summarizes the necessary logic:

```
async Task CheckLicense()
{
  await this.Dispatcher.RunAsync(CoreDispatcherPriority.Normal, () =>
  {
    if (CurrentApp.LicenseInformation.IsActive)
    {
      if (CurrentApp.LicenseInformation.IsTrial)
      {
        // This is the free trial, so adjust the app accordingly.
        …
      }
      else
      {
        // This is the full license, so adjust the app accordingly.
        …
      }
    }
    else
    {
      // The license is invalid or missing. Run in the most limited mode.
      …
    }
  });
}
```

You would typically call a method like CheckLicense during your app's initialization. However, CurrentApp.LicenseInformation also exposes a LicenseChanged event. You should handle this as well and call the same CheckLicense method. That way, if users buy the full license while your app is running—perhaps even on a different PC, you can reward them with an app that instantly responds with its newly-purchased functionality. (You can also revoke features if the license expires while the app is running.)

> **(!) The LicenseChanged event is raised on a background thread!**
>
> This is why the example `CheckLicense` method, which is presumed to be defined on a Page, uses the Page's `Dispatcher` to run the logic on the UI thread. This, of course, isn't needed when you directly call `CheckLicense` from the UI thread during your app's initialization. It also isn't necessary for interacting with `CurrentApp` and `LicenseInformation`, as they are agile objects. However, the presumption is that the `CheckLicense` method will update UI elements based on the current state of the license, which must occur on the UI thread.

The `LicenseInformation` class also exposes an `ExpirationDate` property telling you the exact date and time that the user's time-based trial will expire. With this information, you can implement a motivating message such as, "You only have 4 days remaining before you must purchase this app!" You can easily calculate the number of remaining days as follows:

```
if (CurrentApp.LicenseInformation.IsActive)
{
  if (CurrentApp.LicenseInformation.IsTrial)
  {
    // This is the free trial. Show how many days remain:
    int numDays =
      (CurrentApp.LicenseInformation.ExpirationDate - DateTimeOffset.Now).Days;
    …
  }
}
```

If the trial is unlimited, then `ExpirationDate` is set to a date and time in the past. Therefore, if you're not sure whether your app will use a time-based trial or an unlimited trial, you can protect your logic from being fooled by an unlimited trial by ensuring the time remaining isn't negative. (This condition is unique to an unlimited trial because `IsActive` becomes `false` when a time-based trial expires for real.)

Helping the User Purchase a Full License

Regardless of whether your trial is time-based or unlimited, and whether you change your app's features in trial mode, it's common practice to periodically (and politely) remind trial users to purchase the full license. For this to be most effective, you want to provide some sort of link or button that makes it effortless for them to purchase it from within your app.

One way you could do this is by calling `Launcher.LaunchUriAsync` with `CurrentApp.LinkUri`. This is a link to the appropriate page in the Web-based version of the Windows Store. Even better, you can use a URI with the `ms-windows-store` scheme to launch the appropriate page in the Windows Store app. This URI scheme also supports launching custom search queries in the app, as well as linking to its Updates page. You can find documentation on this scheme at http://bit.ly/T6lNPg.

You can still do better than that, though. The CurrentApp object exposes a method for launching standard a purchasing dialog directly from within your app. You don't even need to worry about populating the contents of the dialog!

Launching a Purchasing Dialog

To launch the standard dialog, call CurrentApp's RequestAppPurchaseAsync method as follows:

```
async Task BuyFullLicense()
{
  try
  {
    // Show the standard purchase dialog
    await CurrentApp.RequestAppPurchaseAsync(false /* XML receipt? */);
    // The purchase probably succeeded, but let the LicenseChanged event handler
    // respond to the change anyway, which verifies that IsActive is true
  }
  catch
  {
    // The user cancelled the action, or there was an error
    // (such as no network connection)
  }
}
```

If the purchase succeeds, the LicenseChanged event is raised, just as when the purchase is made in the Windows Store. Therefore, your handler can still be the only spot in your code where you adjust your app accordingly.

If you pass true to RequestAppPurchaseAsync, it returns an XML-formatted string that is a receipt for the app purchase as well as any in-app purchases that have been made. You can retrieve this same XML string at any later time by calling CurrentApp.GetAppReceiptAsync. The upcoming "Validating Windows Store Receipts" section explains why and how you might examine these receipts.

> **(!) Be prepared for any of CurrentApp's methods to throw an exception!**
>
> Although CurrentApp's properties, such as LicenseInformation, operate on a local cache, its methods all require a working Internet connection. If your app is not resilient to such exceptions, it will not pass Windows Store certification.

Getting Listing Details

When ~~nagging~~ politely asking users to purchase your app, you might want to remind them how inexpensive it is, or display other information from its store listing. This would be dangerous information to hard-code into your app, however. Besides the fact that you might later change your mind about the app's price and change it in the Windows Store, the price and currency varies from region to region.

Fortunately, you can retrieve the details of your app's current listing from `CurrentApp`'s `LoadListingInformationAsync` method. This asynchronously returns a `ListingInformation` object with the following properties:

→ **`CurrentMarket`**—A string containing a BCP-47 language identifier, such as `en-us`, that identifies the region (and therefore price and currency) used for Windows Store transactions.

→ **`Name`** and **`Description`**—Strings for the app's name and description, specific to `CurrentMarket`, as this might vary.

→ **`FormattedPrice`**—The price of the app, specific to `CurrentMarket`. This is thankfully represented as an already formatted string, so all you need to do is display it as-is.

→ **`AgeRating`**—A `uint` representing the minimum appropriate age for customers of the app. Windows Store currently uses values of 3, 7, 12, 16, or 18. This value doesn't change based on `CurrentMarket`. The Windows Dev Center dashboard contains a lot of information about these ratings and their implications.

→ **`ProductListings`**—A collection of `ProductListing` objects representing each available in-app purchase. See the next section for more details.

As with `RequestAppPurchaseAsync`, you should be prepared for `LoadListingInformationAsync` to throw an exception in the case of an error such as no network connectivity.

Supporting In-App Purchases

Your app can leverage two main types of in-app purchases:

→ **Durable products** are permanently owned by the user. Each one may only ever be purchased once by the same user. This is typically used to permanently activate app features or game levels. There is, however, the option to make these expire after a certain amount of time (currently 1, 3, 5, 7, 14, 30, 60, 90, 180, or 365 days). After a durable product expires, the same user may buy it again. This is currently the best approximation of a subscription model offered by the Windows Store.

→ **Consumable products** can be bought over and over. It's up to your app to decide what it means to buy something multiple times, but a common example is a bundle of virtual coins or perhaps a bundle of extra lives in a game. Your app can track how many coins/lives a user has purchased and manage the use of these virtual items independently from the Windows Store.

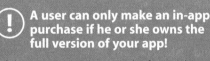

A user can only make an in-app purchase if he or she owns the full version of your app!

If the user currently owns the free trial, in-app purchases do not succeed. In-app purchases work with a free non-trial app, however (i.e. the freemium model).

Consumable products are new to Windows 8.1 and give you a lot of flexibility to customize the purchasing process.

To use in-app purchases, you define them in the "in-app offers" section on the "Services" page for your app inside the Windows Dev Center dashboard. You give each item a Product ID, a price, a type (durable or consumable), and potentially an expiration date. The ID is a name that your code will use to identify the feature, so it must be unique within your app. This ID is not exposed to customers, so you don't need to worry about nice formatting or localization. For example, IDs for a game could be `"LevelPack1"` and `"LevelPack2"`. You get to provide user-visible details for each in-app purchase on the "Description" page for your app in the Windows Dev Center dashboard.

Of course, for each in-app purchase you define in the Windows Store, your app needs code to be able to handle it: both initiating the purchase as well as giving the user what he or she paid for.

> ⚠ **Changing or deleting a Product ID for an in-app purchase in the Windows Dev Center dashboard requires you to resubmit the app for certification!**
>
> This policy is in place to prevent users of the latest version of your app from having a poor experience when trying to purchase something that no longer exists. It is possible to write your app to dynamically retrieve the list of available in-app purchases and handle such changes gracefully, but many apps might not be built this way. Note that consumable products, examined later in this section, give you options to manage a dynamic list of products independently from the list maintained by the Windows Store.

> 💡 The Windows Store enables you to define *free* durable products. This might seem nonsensical, but this can be a very useful concept. Imagine that your app works with virtual coins, and each call to your Web service costs one coin. You would use consumable products that *aren't* free for this. However, it would be nice to give new users a "gift" of 100 coins when they install the app so they get hooked on the functionality that they will later have to purchase. Without managing this through the Windows Store, it would be up to you to prevent users from exploiting your generosity by doing things such as uninstalling then reinstalling your app to get more coins. Instead, you could define a "100 free coins" durable product and instruct the user to accept this gift upon the first use of your app. With this, the Windows Store will enforce that the same user can never receive this gift again, even on separate devices.

Durable Products

The Windows Store manages user licenses for your durable products the same way that it manages the license for your app. As a result, the actions of determining whether a user owns a durable product and initiating a purchase look very similar to the code from the preceding section. This section examines these two actions, as well as retrieving your app's current catalog of products from the Windows Store.

Determining Whether a Product Has Been Purchased

The LicenseInformation object has one more property we haven't examined yet: ProductLicenses. This is what your code must use to check on the current state of an available in-app purchase. Throughout the Windows Store APIs, in-app purchases are called products.

ProductLicenses is a (read-only) Dictionary with string keys and ProductLicense values. The key is the Product ID that identifies the feature in your Windows Dev Center dashboard, chosen by you. Each ProductLicense exposes three simple properties: IsActive, ExpirationDate, and ProductId, which is the same string ID. Again, ExpirationDate is for informational purposes only because IsActive becomes false if the license has expired.

Therefore, the pattern for checking for an in-app purchase's valid license looks much like the pattern for checking on the status of a trial:

```
async Task CheckInAppPurchaseLicenses()
{
  await this.Dispatcher.RunAsync(CoreDispatcherPriority.Normal, () =>
  {
    // Enable the "LevelPack1" feature if appropriate
    if (CurrentApp.LicenseInformation.ProductLicenses["LevelPack1"].IsActive)
    {
      // The feature can be used. If it's a limited-time offer, consider using
      // CurrentApp.LicenseInformation.ProductLicenses["…"].ExpirationDate
      // to help explain that to the user.

      …
    }

    // Enable the "LevelPack2" feature if appropriate
    …
  });
}
```

The same LicenseChanged event applies to in-app purchases as well, so this type of CheckInAppPurchaseLicenses method should also be a handler for LicenseChanged (or called by a method like the previous CheckLicense, if your app supports a trial *and* in-app purchases). Remember that the user can make the purchase from a different device, and you want to react properly to a limited-time purchase's expiration, so handling the event is important.

Initiating a Purchase

There's a reason for the name *in-app purchases*; they not only *can* be bought from within your app, they *must* be bought from within your app! You can trigger such a purchase much like triggering the purchase of the full app license. Instead of calling Request**App**PurchaseAsync, you call Request**Product**PurchaseAsync, which requires the ID for the product being purchased:

```
async Task BuyLevelPack1()
{
  // Only do this if the user doesn't already own the feature
  if (!CurrentApp.LicenseInformation.ProductLicenses["LevelPack1"].IsActive)
  {
    try
    {
      // Show the standard purchase dialog
      await CurrentApp.RequestProductPurchaseAsync(
        "LevelPack1", false /* Don't return an XML receipt */);
      // The purchase probably succeeded, but let the LicenseChanged event handler
      // respond to the change anyway, which verifies that IsActive is true
    }
    catch
    {
      // The user cancelled the action, or there was an error
      // (such as no network connection)
    }
  }
}
```

Request**Product**PurchaseAsync can optionally return the same XML receipt that is optionally returned by Request**App**PurchaseAsync and returned by GetAppReceiptAsync.

The preceding use of RequestProductPurchaseAsync works for both Windows 8 and Windows 8.1 apps, but Windows 8.1 introduces two new overloads of RequestProductPurchaseAsync. Both asynchronously return a PurchaseResults object that contains a ReceiptXml string property as well as a few properties related to consumable products (examined in the next section). One overload only requires the product ID because the receipt is always available in the PurchaseResults object. The other overload is meant for consumable products, so it is described in the "Consumable Products" section.

Displaying Your Catalog

When you present users with a list of available in-app purchases, you should use the ListingInformation object returned by CurrentApp.LoadListingInformationAsync as the data source. Recall that it has a ProductListings property that is a collection of ProductListing objects. Each ProductListing, which represents an available in-app purchase, exposes many properties:

→ **Name**, **Description**, and **FormattedPrice**—These are just like the same-named properties for your app in ListingInformation, and are relative to the current market.

→ **ImageUri**—A representative image for the purchase, if you provided one to the Windows Store.

→ **Keywords** and **Tag**—Additional data that you may have supplied to the Windows Store. Unlike ImageUri, these are not meant to be user-visible.

→ **ProductId**—The unique ID that must be passed along to RequestProductPurchaseAsync.

→ **ProductType**—Either Durable or Consumable, as both types appear in this single collection.

By using these properties, you can avoid hardcoding information into your app that (a) you can dynamically change in the Windows Store and (b) can be customized for the current market. You can use FormattedPrice to tell the user up-front how much each in-app purchase costs in the current market. For durable products, you should combine this information with the user's license

If you've got a large catalog of in-app purchases, you could call LoadListingInformation**By-ProductIds**Async or LoadListing-Information**ByKeywords**Async to retrieve a subset of your catalog. The latter method is only useful if you have defined relevant keywords for your in-app purchases in your Windows Dev Center dashboard.

information, so you can properly indicate which products have already been purchased.

Consumable Products

Because a consumable product can be bought over and over, it doesn't have the same concept of a license that is either active or not. Nor does it have the concept of an expiration date. Therefore, the code shown previously in the "Determining Whether a Product Has Been Purchased" section for durable products does not apply to consumable products. You must implement your own tracking for what the user has purchased and how many. This also means that it's up to you to roam the virtual goods to other devices, if that's something you want to support. Fortunately, Windows makes it easy to roam small amounts of data, as explained in Chapter 20, "Working with Data."

As for initiating a consumable product purchase, the same RequestProductPurchaseAsync method is used, but the details are quite a bit different. This section examines the consumable product purchasing process, and looks at a unique option enabled by consumable products: managing a custom catalog.

Initiating and Fulfilling Purchase

To initiate a consumable product purchase, you should perform the following workflow:

1. Call RequestProductPurchaseAsync, the same as with a durable product.

2. If successful, immediately give the user what he or she paid for. (Unlike with a durable product, don't rely on the LicenseChanged event, because it doesn't apply in this case.)

3. Tell the Windows Store that you have fulfilled the purchase by calling CurrentApp's ReportConsumableFulfillmentAsync method.

The final step is for protection against unexpected problems (such as a loss of network connection or an app crash) that could potentially cause the customer to be charged without your app realizing that the transaction took place. This prevents angry customers and is definitely a win-win situation! Of course, you as the developer are still being trusted to handle other aspects of the purchase correctly.

The following code demonstrates the consumable product purchase workflow with a hypothetical CoinPack product ID:

```
async Task BuyVirtualCoins()
{
  try
  {
    // Show the standard purchase dialog
    PurchaseResults results =
      await CurrentApp.RequestProductPurchaseAsync("CoinPack");

    if (results.Status == ProductPurchaseStatus.Succeeded)
    {
      // The purchase succeeded! Give the user the coins

      ...

      // Report the fulfillment back to the Windows Store
      FulfillmentResult result =
        await CurrentApp.ReportConsumableFulfillmentAsync(
          "CoinPack", results.TransactionId);

      if (result == FulfillmentResult.Succeeded)
      {
        // We're done!
      }
      else
      {
        // Deal with the failure

        ...

      }
    }
  }
  catch
  {
    // There was an error (such as no network connection).
    // Make sure there isn't an unfulfilled purchase.

    ...

  }
}
```

When initiating a purchase of a consumable product, you should call one of the two overloads of RequestProductPurchaseAsync that returns a PurchaseResults object because it exposes a `TransactionId` property that you need in order to report the fulfillment. Note that with the `PurchaseResults`-returning overloads, you can't rely on an exception to indicate failure. You must check its `Status` property, which can be one of the following values from a `ProductPurchaseStatus` enumeration:

→ `Succeeded`—The purchase was successful (although still needs to be fulfilled).

→ `NotFulfilled`—The purchase failed because a previous purchase has not yet been reported as fulfilled to the Windows Store.

→ `AlreadyPurchased`—This failure mode only applies to durable products, as they can only be purchased once.

→ `NotPurchased`—The user cancelled the purchasing process, or the user currently has a trial license (and is therefore ineligible for in-app purchases).

Even if the purchase succeeded, the call to `ReportConsumableFulfillmentAsync` can still fail, so your code should check the returned `FulfillmentResult` enumeration value, which can be one of the following:

→ `Succeeded`—The fulfillment was successful, so you have nothing more to do.

→ `NothingToFulfill`—The purchase has already been fulfilled, or the product ID is invalid, so your code has a logic error.

→ `PurchasePending`—The purchase is not yet final, so it could possibly get reverted. You may wish to prevent the user from consuming their newly-purchased goods until this is resolved.

→ `PurchaseReverted`—The purchase has been reverted, so you should take back your virtual goods.

→ `ServerError`—An unexpected failure prevented the report from being recorded by the Windows Store. You should try again.

---

① A user cannot repurchase the same consumable product until you report it as being fulfilled!

When you see the potential failure conditions from `ReportConsumableFulfillmentAsync`, it might be tempting to wait to grant the user their goods until fulfillment has succeeded. Do not do this! It defeats the whole purpose of reporting fulfillment!

You could find yourself in a situation in which fulfillment can't be reported until a later launch of your app. (For example, perhaps there's a network outage that starts after `RequestProduct-PurchaseAsync` returns but before you call `ReportConsumableFulfillmentAsync`.) Fortunately, you can easily check for unfulfilled purchases at any time (when a network connection is available) by calling `CurrentApp`'s `GetUnfulfilledConsumablesAsync` method. This returns a list of `UnfulfilledConsumable` objects, each with the `ProductId` and `TransactionId` properties that you need in order to fulfill it.

Managing a Custom Catalog

Defining each in-app purchase available to your app in the Windows Dev Center dashboard can be cumbersome, especially if you have a long list of items. It can also be too inflexible to support dynamic catalogs, as changing or removing items requires you to resubmit your app for certification.

The Windows Store has a solution to this problem for Windows 8.1 apps. Without needing to change anything in your dashboard, you can split a single consumable product associated with your app into an arbitrary number of logical products. You can manage your list of logical products independently from the Windows Store, while still using the payment infrastructure provided by the Windows Store. Your list of logical products can be as long as you'd like and you can update it whenever you'd like. Because each logical product needs to be backed by a real consumable product (even if it's the same consumable product used by all), the only requirement is that you have a real consumable product defined in your dashboard for each distinct price point you want to support.

For example, you might define a single "Theme Pack" consumable product in your dashboard priced at $1.49. Rather than presenting your users with the option to buy this generic "Theme Pack," you can present them with options to buy a "Spring Theme Pack," a "Summer Theme Pack," a "Fall Theme Pack," and a "Winter Theme Pack." Each of these would cost $1.49. If you change the price of "Theme Pack" in your dashboard, it would apply to the four logical theme packs.

This support only works with consumable products, because in order for the single product to masquerade as multiple products, it needs the ability to be purchased multiple times. If it doesn't make sense for the user to be able to purchase the same logical product more than once, it is up to you to show the item as purchased in your user interface and prevent duplicate purchases.

For this scheme to work, you need the ability to customize the purchase dialog so the user gets an experience that matches the logical product. This can be done with an overload of `RequestProductPurchaseAsync` that accepts an instance of `ProductPurchaseDisplayProperties`. This class has properties that enable you to customize the product name, description, and image shown by the standard dialog. You can use this as follows:

```
try
{
  string productId = "Theme Pack";        // The ID of the product in the dashboard
  string offerId = "Spring Theme Pack"; // The ID of the logical product,
                                          // which only has meaning to you

  // Show the standard purchase dialog, customized for this logical product
  PurchaseResults results = await CurrentApp.RequestProductPurchaseAsync(
    productId, offerId, new ProductPurchaseDisplayProperties {
      Name = "Spring Theme Pack", Description = "A colorful theme." });
```

```
  if (results.Status == ProductPurchaseStatus.Succeeded)
  {
    …
  }
}
catch
{
  // There was an error (such as no network connection).
  // Make sure there isn't an unfulfilled purchase.
}
```

In the terminology of the Windows Store APIs, logical products are called *offers*. When you customize the purchase dialog, you must also pass along a string ID that is meant to uniquely identify the logical product about to be purchased. This ID has no meaning to the Windows Store, but it flows through the transaction to make it easy for you to track what's going on.

The PurchaseResults object returned by RequestProductPurchaseAsync exposes an OfferId property that matches the string you passed in (at least if the transaction was successful). The XML receipt for a consumable product also includes the matching OfferId. Similarly, each UnfulfilledConsumable object returned by GetUnfulfilledConsumablesAsync exposes an OfferId property that is set appropriately for any unfulfilled logical products. You don't pass the OfferId back to the Windows Store when reporting fulfillment, as it only cares about the real product, but this information can still be useful for your bookkeeping.

> When you take control of your own catalog of virtual products by leveraging OfferIds, you have a lot of flexibility in what you sell and how you sell it. For example, your service could provide the concept of limited edition virtual goods, in which only a certain number can ever be purchased across all users.

Validating Windows Store Receipts

When you check license information within your Windows Store app, you can trust the information returned by the CurrentApp APIs. If you've got your own Web service that integrates with your app, then you might want to leverage the same license information in a number of ways. For example, you could ensure that only users with a valid license for your app can use your service. You could provide features on your website or even in an app on a different platform that are based on the user's purchases through your Windows Store app. Through your service, you could even limit the number of devices from which a user can leverage certain features you provide.

For all of these scenarios to work without the risk of your service being fooled by illegitimate users or falsified information, you service needs a way to get the same trusted license information available to your app. The answer lies in the XML receipts returned by various CurrentApp APIs, because the Windows Store uses the XML Digital Signatures standard (XML-DSIG) to digitally sign each XML document. These digital signatures enable arbitrary code, such as code in your Web service, to verify that any XML receipt was signed by the Windows Store and has not been altered after it was signed.

The typical interaction between your app and your service would be:

1. When performing a purchase, retrieve the XML receipt returned by Request*XXX*PurchaseAsync. (Or get the receipt anytime by calling GetProductReceiptAsync for a specific in-app purchase or GetAppReceiptAsync for the entire app. The latter returns information about all purchased durable products as well.)

2. Send the XML receipt to your service, likely in the body of an HTTP POST request.

3. In your service, verify the receipt's authenticity using an XML-DSIG algorithm.

4. In your service, optionally act upon the license information inside the receipt.

The details of the receipt XML schema are described in MSDN documentation for the CurrentApp methods that produce them. But here is an example of an app receipt for a user that has also purchased a durable product named LevelPack1:

```
<?xml version="1.0" encoding="utf-8"?>
<Receipt Version="1.0" ReceiptDate="2015-09-01T04:30:36Z"
         CertificateId="…" ReceiptDeviceId="…">
  <AppReceipt Id="…" AppId="…"
              PurchaseDate="2015-07-25T02:21:14Z" LicenseType="Full" />
  <ProductReceipt Id="…" AppId="…" ProductId="LevelPack1"
                  PurchaseDate="2015-07-30T07:05:52Z" ProductType="Durable" />
  <Signature xmlns="http://www.w3.org/2000/09/xmldsig#">
    …
  </Signature>
</Receipt>
```

And here is an example of a product receipt after purchasing a consumable product named Theme Pack with an offer ID of Spring Theme Pack:

```
<?xml version="1.0" encoding="utf-8"?>
<Receipt Version="1.0" ReceiptDate="2015-09-01T04:30:36Z"
         CertificateId="…" ReceiptDeviceId="…">
  <ProductReceipt Id="…" AppId="…" ProductId="Theme Pack"
                  PurchaseDate="2015-07-25T02:21:14Z" ProductType="Consumable"
                  OfferId="Spring Theme Pack" />
  <Signature xmlns="http://www.w3.org/2000/09/xmldsig#">
    …
  </Signature>
</Receipt>
```

To verify the receipt's authenticity, you must fetch the public certificate that was used to sign it at https://go.microsoft.com/fwlink/?LinkId=246509&cid=*CertificateId*, where *CertificateId* matches the value of the `CertificateId` attribute inside the XML. With the key in hand, you can use a standard XML-DSIG algorithm to verify the XML's digital signature contained in its `Signature` element. For example, MSDN has a C# example at http://msdn.microsoft.com/en-us/library/ms229950.aspx that leverages the `System.Security.Cryptography.Xml.SignedXml.CheckSignature` method from the .NET Framework.

If verification succeeds, you know you've got a complete and authentic XML document signed by the Windows Store. However, this doesn't protect your service from a "replay attack," in which a single valid XML receipt is used over and over, potentially maliciously shared among many users. Fortunately, like paperwork in the real world, XML receipts from the Windows Store are signed *and dated*. Therefore, you should examine the `ReceiptDate` attribute inside the XML and make sure it is recent, within some threshold that makes sense for the way your app communicates with your service.

Once you have determined that the XML is valid and recent, you can act upon the license information inside the receipt. For an app receipt, this could mean checking whether the current license is a trial license, whether it has expired, what durable products have been purchased, and so on. For a product receipt, this would mean checking what was purchased, whether it has expired, and so on. Although you're interacting with XML to get this information, the logic is similar to using the `LicenseInformation` class in your app code.

From the receipt alone, you cannot track unique users. However, you can leverage properties about some of the IDs that appear inside the receipt. For example, `AppReceipt`'s `Id` value is a hash of the user, the app, and the purchase time. For the purposes of your service, this could suffice as a user ID. `Receipt`'s `ReceiptDeviceId` value is a hash of the user, the app, and the device. Combined with the information from `AppReceipt`'s `Id`, you can track the number of devices used with the same license.

Protecting Yourself Further with the App Specific Hardware ID   •••

If you want your service to identify a specific device with a high degree of confidence, you can use an App Specific Hardware ID (ASHWID) returned by the `Windows.System.Profile.HardwareIdentification.GetPackageSpecificToken` method. To protect user privacy, this identifier changes from app to app. However, for any given app, this identifier stays the same if the hardware stays the same. It's based on the serial numbers of the device's components. In practice, you need to tolerate small changes to this identifier caused by hardware changes such as adding memory or unplugging a USB Bluetooth adapter. See http://aka.ms/WinRT-ASHWID for detailed guidance for using this identifier. Microsoft Office uses a similar approach for protection against piracy.

How do I check if my app is running sideloaded?

This is as simple as checking the value of `CurrentApp.LicenseInformation.IsActive`. When it is `false`, the app does not have a valid Windows Store-signed license. Although this was covered in the "Supporting a Free Trial" section, you can leverage this information independently from any trial support for a bit of extra protection. For example, `AdControl` can leverage `IsActive` to know when to report ad impressions during "real" usage of an app versus the developer running and testing it locally.

Testing Windows Store Features

Testing all the functionality exposed by `CurrentApp` presents a chicken-and-egg problem. When you write a new app that uses these APIs, they will fail because the app has no listing in the Windows Store. For example, if you try to test an in-app purchase in a new app, you'll likely see the dialog shown in Figure 9.4.

FIGURE 9.4   The `CurrentApp` class is not suitable for testing Windows Store interactions because the Windows Store doesn't know anything about it.

Even if you add calls to these APIs to a new version of an already listed app, you're always one step behind the live metadata. Furthermore, it can be difficult to test the various permutations of licenses with your real Microsoft account.

The `Windows.ApplicationModel.Store` namespace has a simple solution for all these problems. It contains a `CurrentApp`**Simulator** class that looks just like `CurrentApp`. Therefore, you can simply replace all references to `CurrentApp` with `CurrentApp`**Simulator** to test your app in every possible situation related to the Windows Store and user licenses.

These two classes don't share a common interface or base class (other than `System.Object`), but you can leverage C#'s alias feature to make switching between the two a one-line change. With the code in this chapter that references `CurrentApp` without a namespace qualification, you probably expect the code to have a standard using statement:

```
using Windows.ApplicationModel.Store;
```

However, you can instead define `CurrentApp` as an alias to the fully-qualified class:

```
using CurrentApp = Windows.ApplicationModel.Store.CurrentApp;
```

That way, changing all uses of CurrentApp to CurrentAppSimulator is as simple as making the following change (to each source file that requires it):

```
using CurrentApp = Windows.ApplicationModel.Store.CurrentAppSimulator;
```

Even better, you could set up your code to always use CurrentAppSimulator in debug builds and always use CurrentApp in release builds:

```
#if DEBUG
  using CurrentApp = Windows.ApplicationModel.Store.CurrentAppSimulator;
#else
  using CurrentApp = Windows.ApplicationModel.Store.CurrentApp;
#endif
```

Your release build is what gets published in the Windows Store (and what gets used in certification testing), so if you do your local testing with a debug build, this conditional compilation produces the right behavior for everyone.

> (!) **Make sure the release build of your app does not use CurrentAppSimulator when you submit it to the Windows Store!**
>
> If it does, your app will fail the certification process. And that's good news, because it would be far worse for such an app to be published to your customers!

Working with CurrentAppSimulator

The first time your app uses CurrentAppSimulator, it automatically generates an XML file in your app's local data folder. This file contains fake metadata corresponding to what would normally be in the Windows Store, as well as the status of the current user's fake licenses. You can open this file directly with Notepad or your favorite text editor by pointing it to %USERPROFILE%\AppData\Local\Packages*PackageFamilyName*\LocalState\ Microsoft\Windows Store\ApiData\WindowsStoreProxy.xml. You can see your project's value of *PackageFamilyName* on the Packaging tab in Visual Studio's package manifest designer. It is derived from your package name (from the same tab), which is set to a GUID by default. Listing 9.1 shows the contents of this auto-generated file.

LISTING 9.1   WindowsStoreProxy.xml: The Default Windows Store Data Used by CurrentAppSimulator

```
<?xml version="1.0" encoding="utf-16" ?>
<CurrentApp>
  <ListingInformation>
    <App>
      <AppId>00000000-0000-0000-0000-000000000000</AppId>
      <LinkUri>
        http://apps.microsoft.com/webpdp/app/00000000-0000-0000-0000-000000000000
```

LISTING 9.1   Continued

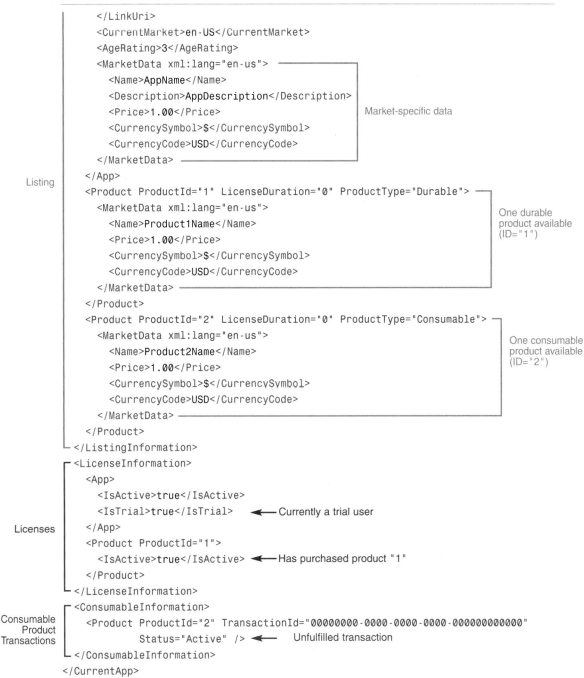

```
      </LinkUri>
      <CurrentMarket>en-US</CurrentMarket>
      <AgeRating>3</AgeRating>
      <MarketData xml:lang="en-us">
        <Name>AppName</Name>
        <Description>AppDescription</Description>
        <Price>1.00</Price>                          Market-specific data
        <CurrencySymbol>$</CurrencySymbol>
        <CurrencyCode>USD</CurrencyCode>
      </MarketData>
    </App>
    <Product ProductId="1" LicenseDuration="0" ProductType="Durable">
      <MarketData xml:lang="en-us">
        <Name>Product1Name</Name>                    One durable
        <Price>1.00</Price>                          product available
        <CurrencySymbol>$</CurrencySymbol>           (ID="1")
        <CurrencyCode>USD</CurrencyCode>
      </MarketData>
    </Product>
    <Product ProductId="2" LicenseDuration="0" ProductType="Consumable">
      <MarketData xml:lang="en-us">
        <Name>Product2Name</Name>                    One consumable
        <Price>1.00</Price>                          product available
        <CurrencySymbol>$</CurrencySymbol>           (ID="2")
        <CurrencyCode>USD</CurrencyCode>
      </MarketData>
    </Product>
  </ListingInformation>
  <LicenseInformation>
    <App>
      <IsActive>true</IsActive>
      <IsTrial>true</IsTrial>         ◄—— Currently a trial user
    </App>
    <Product ProductId="1">
      <IsActive>true</IsActive>       ◄—— Has purchased product "1"
    </Product>
  </LicenseInformation>
  <ConsumableInformation>
    <Product ProductId="2" TransactionId="00000000-0000-0000-0000-000000000000"
             Status="Active" />      ◄——  Unfulfilled transaction
  </ConsumableInformation>
</CurrentApp>
```

Labels in left margin:

Listing

Licenses

Consumable
Product
Transactions

The XML schema maps to the APIs exposed by CurrentApp and CurrentAppSimulator. By default it acts like the current user is an active trial user who has the option to purchase the full license for $1 (which, by the way, is an amount not possible in the Windows Store). The app also has two in-app purchases available. There's a durable product with an ID of 1, but the user has already purchased it. There's also a consumable product with an ID of 2, along with a previous purchase transaction that has yet to be fulfilled. Because the fake user is a trial user, attempting to purchase either product would return NotPurchased. (Even if IsTrial were set to false, calling RequestProductPurchaseAsync with an ID of 1 would return AlreadyPurchased, and calling it with an ID of 2 would return NotFulfilled unless your code first calls ReportConsumableFulfillmentAsync appropriately.)

Of course, the point of this mechanism is to change the XML contents to match your app's listing and its potential in-app purchases, and then test the various conditions. You can freely edit this copy of WindowsStoreProxy.xml in your AppData folder and then launch the app with your customized data in place. (CurrentAppSimulator generates WindowsStoreProxy.xml only if it doesn't already exist.) You can list different products, change which licenses the user has or if they expire, and so on.

The XML schema is documented on the CurrentAppSimulator page on MSDN, along with an XSD file that you can associate with your files in order to get IntelliSense in Visual Studio. The only big gotcha in the schema is that ExpirationDate, a valid subelement for App and Product, must be expressed in the ISO 8601 combined date and time

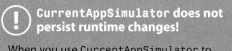

CurrentAppSimulator does not persist runtime changes!

When you use CurrentAppSimulator to make changes to the state of licenses or transactions, this does not get reflected in the XML file on disk. Every time you launch the app, you have a clean slate for testing.

format: *yyyy-mm-dd*T*hh:mm:ss.ss*Z. For example, 11:00AM on February 14, 2018 would be specified as 2018-02-14T11:00:00.00Z.

CurrentAppSimulator has one method that CurrentApp does not have: ReloadSimulatorAsync. You can pass this method an XML file (represented in a StorageFile object) with the same schema as the default WindowsStoreProxy.xml file in order to reinitialize its state. This can make managing your testing much easier (and more automated). See Chapter 20 for more information about working with StorageFile.

Automated Testing

You've seen how CurrentAppSimulator simulates initial Windows Store-related data, but it also simulates interactions with the Windows Store. For example, when you initiate a purchase with CurrentAppSimulator, it launches a purchase dialog geared toward testing, as shown in Figure 9.5. This replaces the real purchase dialog shown (in an error state) in Figure 9.4.

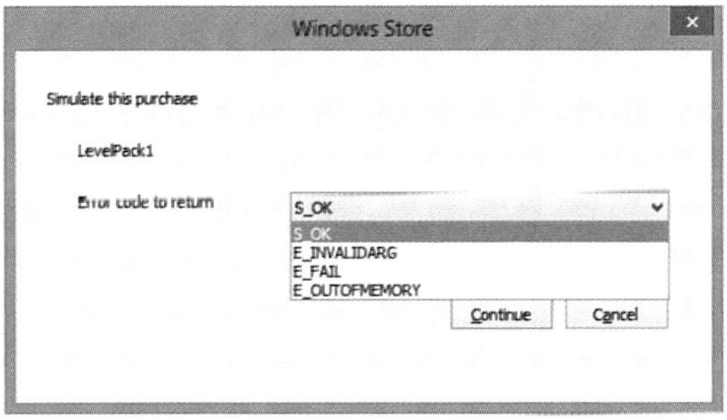

FIGURE 9.5   The purchase dialog shown by `CurrentAppSimulator` may be ugly, but it gets the job done.

The dialog shown in Figure 9.5 corresponds to the user attempting to purchase a `LevelPack1` product. Besides cancelling the purchase with the Cancel button, you can decide whether you want the purchase to succeed or fail. The error codes shown, known as HRESULTs, correspond to the values used by the underlying COM-based API. In case you're not familiar with HRESULTs, `S_OK` is the success return value, and the others are errors. For the purposes of testing your app, choosing any of the error values is equivalent.

This type of simulator interaction isn't great for performing automated testing, but `CurrentAppSimulator` has a solution for that as well. You can add a `Simulation` element to the XML file with a `SimulationMode` set to `Automatic`, and then add subelements that specify what result should be returned by various APIs. For example, the following addition to `WindowsStoreProxy.xml` tells both `RequestProductPurchaseAsync` and `ReportConsumableFulfillmentAsync` to throw an exception (caused by the underlying COM API returning `E_FAIL`):

```
<?xml version="1.0" encoding="utf-16" ?>
<CurrentApp>
  ...
  <Simulation SimulationMode="Automatic">
    <DefaultResponse MethodName="RequestProductPurchaseAsync_GetResult"
                     HResult="E_FAIL"/>
    <DefaultResponse MethodName="ReportConsumableFulfillmentAsync_GetResult"
                     HResult="E_FAIL"/>
  </Simulation>
</CurrentApp>
```

You can intercept the behavior of any `CurrentAppSimulator` method in this fashion, even ones that don't ordinarily produce a dialog (such as `ReportConsumableFulfillmentAsync`). For `RequestProductPurchaseAsync`, however, this XML prevents the dialog from Figure 9.5 from being shown. Note that you must append a `_GetResult` suffix to every `MethodName` value.

Although specifying that a method should return an error HRESULT will reliably make it throw an exception, specifying that it should return S_OK doesn't necessarily mean it will succeed. (The same is true when you manually select S_OK from the dialog in Figure 9.5.) That's because the other elements in the XML impact the behavior. For example, RequestProductPurchaseAsync will still return NotFulfilled if the XML indicates a previous unfulfilled purchase, AlreadyPurchased if you're attempting to purchase a durable product with an active license in the XML, and NotPurchased if the XML indicates that the user is a trial user. ReportConsumableFulfillmentAsync will still return NothingToFulfill if the product ID is invalid or already fulfilled. Therefore, the way to test these non-throwing error conditions is to tweak the other elements in your XML.

The relevant CurrentAppSimulator APIs produce XML receipts, although they do not contain any Signature element and the CertificateId attribute is empty. If you perform proper receipt validation, these receipts will fail validation, as they should!

Summary

With the flexible support for ads, free trials, and in-app purchases, you can come up with all sorts of payment schemes with little effort. When these options are used responsibly with a good app, you have the potential to make a lot of money. It can be mind-boggling to think about the scale of the Windows Store and how easy it is for you to sell software or services around the world.

When using these monetization features, you should plan on monitoring how well they perform and making adjustments accordingly. The Windows Dev Center dashboard and ad platforms such as pubCenter provide a lot of analytics. Experimenting with the timing and placement of ads, the characteristics of a free trial, and the pricing of your app and its features can make an enormous difference to your bottom line.

Chapter 10

CONTENT CONTROLS

XAML would not be nearly as enjoyable to use for writing Windows Store apps without a standard set of controls, so the XAML UI Framework has plenty of standard controls included "in the box." Such controls enable you to quickly assemble common types of user interfaces that can match Windows and other Windows Store apps in both appearance and behavior. These controls are optimized for touch but handle mouse, pen, and keyboard exactly how you'd expect. You've seen a few of them in previous chapters, but this part of the book takes you on a tour of the rest.

The figures in this book typically show controls under the default "dark" theme, which makes them render mostly white. (*Dark* refers to the color of the background they are meant to be placed upon.) However, the built-in controls also support a "light" theme so they can be easily used on top of white or light backgrounds instead. For example, Figure 10.1 displays the default appearance of a Button under both app themes, as well as under the four standard color variations of the high contrast user theme (typically used only by users who need extra help seeing content on the screen). Note that when high contrast is enabled, the app theme (dark versus light) is ignored.

In most cases, the difference in appearance is subtle. Of course, you can give controls a radically different look (based on the current theme or theme-independent) by using custom control templates, as discussed in Chapter 18, "Styles, Templates, and Visual States."

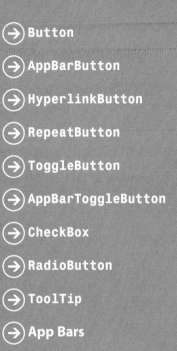

FIGURE 10.1   Button's default appearances under the two app themes and four standard variations of the high contrast user theme

How do the dark, light, and high contrast themes work?

The first thing to understand is that there are two types of themes: those controlled by the app developer (*app themes*) and those controlled by the user (*user themes*). There are only two app themes—*dark* and *light*—and the way to control which one is used by your app is to set the RequestedTheme property on your Application-derived class to either Dark (the default value) or Light (the only other valid value). This is typically done in App.xaml as follows:

```xml
<Application x:Class="MyApp.App"
  xmlns="http://schemas.microsoft.com/winfx/2006/xaml/presentation"
  xmlns:x="http://schemas.microsoft.com/winfx/2006/xaml"
  xmlns:local="using:MyApp"
  RequestedTheme="Light">

  ...
</Application>
```

You can set it in code-behind (the property is an ApplicationTheme enumeration) in case you want to change it based on your own user-exposed setting. However, it must be set only during initialization (before any Window is created), otherwise an exception is thrown.

Windows 8.1 adds the RequestedTheme property to FrameworkElement as well, so any element can override the app-wide theme or the RequestedTheme it would otherwise inherit from an ancestor element. This property is an **Element**Theme enumeration, which adds a third value: Default. This makes the element inherit its theme, and is the default value. Unlike Application.RequestedTheme, FrameworkElement.RequestedTheme can be changed at any time.

The app theme you choose does not make any difference if your app has all custom visuals with custom colors. But when your app uses standard controls with their default templates, or when your app uses theme brushes (such as the ApplicationPageBackgroundThemeBrush background used inside Visual Studio-generated Pages), this choice affects the colors in your app. Note that this scheme differs from Windows Phone, which gives the *user* the power to switch between a dark and light theme that affects all apps that don't hard-code all their colors.

The user can, however, change Windows to a high contrast *user* theme instead of the default *user* theme. This can be done in the PC Settings app under "Ease of Access," in the "High contrast" section (or in the desktop Control Panel). This exposes the four color variations seen in Figure 10.1. Users can customize each relevant color individually. Therefore, even though the user is exposed to four different high contrast "themes," it's best to think of there being only two user themes (default versus high contrast).

When high contrast is used, its color settings override the typical theme colors, making the dark versus light app theme choice irrelevant. This is why Application's property is called **Requested**Theme rather than simply Theme. To put it another way, the two app themes have app-chosen sets of colors for the default user theme, but the high contrast theme has only user-chosen colors.

As with the app themes, a user's high contrast settings affect an app only to the degree it uses standard controls with standard templates, or theme brushes rather than hardcoded colors. You can quickly preview your app under any app or user theme in Visual Studio's XAML designer by changing the values in the "Theme" and "High contrast" drop-downs in the Device tool window.

The built-in controls can be grouped roughly into the following categories, which coincide somewhat with their inheritance hierarchy:

→ Content controls (this chapter)

→ Items controls (Chapter 11)

→ Text (Chapter 12)

→ Images (Chapter 13)

→ Media controls (Chapter 14)

→ All other controls (Chapter 15)

Content controls are controls that are constrained to contain a single item. Content controls all derive from ContentControl, which has a Content property of type Object that contains the single item (as examined with Button in Chapter 2, "Mastering XAML").

Because a content control's single item can be any arbitrary object, the control can contain a potentially large tree of objects. There just can be only one *direct* child. ScrollViewer and Frame, already examined in previous chapters, are both content controls. ScrollViewer's Content is usually set to a Panel such as Grid, so it can contain an arbitrarily complex user interface, and Frame's Content is usually set to a Page, which usually contains a Panel for the same reason.

Content and Arbitrary Objects

Given that a content control's `Content` can be set to any object, it's natural to wonder what happens if you set the content to a non-visual object, such as an instance of `BitArray` or `TimeZoneInfo`. The way it works is fairly simple. All `UIElement`s know how to draw themselves, so if the content derives from `UIElement`, it gets rendered as expected via an internal mechanism. Otherwise, if a data template is applied to the item (as described in Chapter 19, "Data Binding"), that template can provide the rendering behavior on behalf of the object. Otherwise, the content's `ToString` method is called, and the returned text is rendered inside a `TextBlock` control.

Most content controls are buttons—classes deriving from `ButtonBase`. The following sections examine each of them in turn:

→ `Button`

→ `AppBarButton`

→ `HyperlinkButton`

→ `RepeatButton`

→ `ToggleButton`

→ `AppBarToggleButton`

→ `CheckBox`

→ `RadioButton`

We'll also look at three important non-button content controls: `ToolTip`, `AppBar`, and `CommandBar`. One content control—`SettingsFlyout`—is saved for Chapter 21, "Supporting Charms," because design guidelines dictate that you should only use it when supporting the Settings charm.

Button

Buttons are probably the most familiar and essential user interface elements. The `Button` control, pictured in Figure 10.1, has already made several appearances in this book.

Although everyone intuitively knows what a button is, its precise definition (at least for XAML apps) might not be obvious. A button is a content control that can be *clicked*. Note that this is a different concept from being *tapped*. All classes deriving from `UIElement` have a `Tapped` event, but only classes deriving from `ButtonBase` have a `Click` event.

So what's the difference between `Tapped` and `Click` (besides past versus present tense, which is a historical artifact)? `Tapped` is raised only for a simple finger press, mouse button click, or pen tap, but `Click` can be raised from keyboard input as well. As has always been the case with Windows buttons, you can click from the keyboard using the Enter or spacebar keys, if the button has focus. Note that the conditions for `Click` aren't a superset of the conditions for Tapped because of the way mouse input is treated. *Any* mouse button click raises a Tapped event (which often surprises people), whereas only a mouse *left* button click raises a Click event.

> **How can I programmatically click a Button?**
>
> Button, like the other controls, has a peer class in the Windows.UI.Xaml.Automation.Peers namespace to support UI Automation: ButtonAutomationPeer. It can be used as follows with a Button called myButton:
>
> ```
> ButtonAutomationPeer peer = new ButtonAutomationPeer(myButton);
> peer.Invoke(); // This clicks the Button
> ```

Associating a Flyout

A Flyout, new to Windows 8.1, is a piece of UI that acts like a dialog, but has *light dismiss* behavior. That means that tapping outside of its area automatically closes it. Flyouts are typically shown in response to a Button click, so Windows 8.1 also introduces a handy Flyout property on Button that does two things:

1. Automatically attaches the Flyout to the Button so it is positioned appropriately when shown

2. Automatically shows the Flyout (with an appropriate animation) when the Button is clicked

The following XAML demonstrates the use of a Flyout in this manner, and Figure 10.2 shows what this looks like once the Button is clicked:

```
<Button Content="Submit">
  <Button.Flyout>
    <Flyout>
      <StackPanel>
        <TextBlock>Are you sure you want to do this?</TextBlock>
        <Button>Yes</Button>
      </StackPanel>
    </Flyout>
  </Button.Flyout>
</Button>
```

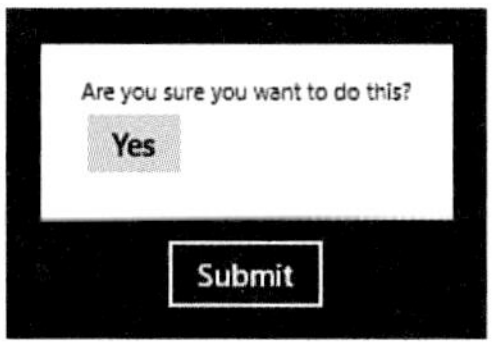

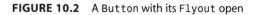

FIGURE 10.2   A Button with its Flyout open

For an example like this, the "Submit" Button likely doesn't need any Click event handler. Instead, it is the "Yes" Button whose Click event must be handled in order to perform the actual submit action. With this UI pattern, there doesn't need to be a "No" or "Cancel" button inside the Flyout. The user cancels the action by tapping elsewhere.

Conceptually, you can think of Flyout as another content control. Internally, it works with a content control called FlyoutPresenter, but Flyout itself is not a content control, nor is it even a Control. Its FlyoutBase base class derives directly from DependencyObject. Because a Flyout is not a UIElement, the same instance can be attached to multiple elements using the StaticResource support examined in Chapter 18.

Flyout, through its FlyoutBase base class, exposes Opening, Opened, and Closed events and a Placement property that enables you to customize where it appears. By default, it appears above the element it is attached to, but you can set Placement to one of the following FlyoutPlacementMode enumeration values: Top, Bottom, Left, Right, or Full. The Full value makes the Flyout appear in the center of the current window. For values other than Full, if there's not enough room in the window for the Flyout to appear in the direction you specify, it will automatically choose a different value that provides enough room.

You can put arbitrary content inside a Flyout, such as a menu, but there is special support for creating menu-based Flyouts thanks to the other subclass of FlyoutBase: MenuFlyout. MenuFlyout is conceptually more like an items control, so we'll take a look at it in the next chapter. The type of Button's Flyout property is actually FlyoutBase, so you can use a MenuFlyout where you would otherwise use Flyout.

In Figure 10.2, the attached Flyout is *not* a child of the Button. Its Parent is null, making it the root of a visual tree completely separate from the Page's visual tree that contains the Button. This subtle fact can be significant because property values and transforms aren't inherited by the Flyout. For example, if the entire Page (or the Button) is marked with a ScaleTransform that magnifies its contents, the Flyout would still appear at its normal size.

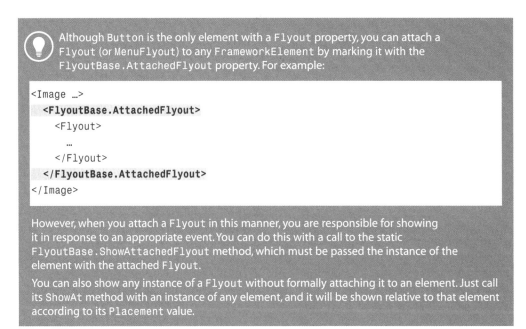

Although Button is the only element with a Flyout property, you can attach a Flyout (or MenuFlyout) to any FrameworkElement by marking it with the FlyoutBase.AttachedFlyout property. For example:

```
<Image ...>
  <FlyoutBase.AttachedFlyout>
    <Flyout>
      ...
    </Flyout>
  </FlyoutBase.AttachedFlyout>
</Image>
```

However, when you attach a Flyout in this manner, you are responsible for showing it in response to an appropriate event. You can do this with a call to the static FlyoutBase.ShowAttachedFlyout method, which must be passed the instance of the element with the attached Flyout.

You can also show any instance of a Flyout without formally attaching it to an element. Just call its ShowAt method with an instance of any element, and it will be shown relative to that element according to its Placement value.

···

Flyouts and App Themes

An astute reader might wonder how the "Yes" Button in Figure 10.2 is able to look different than the "Submit" Button. Flyouts leverage the element-level RequestedTheme property to pull off this trick. It requests Light when the theme is Dark and Dark when the theme is Light, which propagates down to all the elements inside. This very scenario was the motivation for adding this RequestedTheme support in Windows 8.1. Without this trick (or if you explicitly mark the "Yes" Button with RequestedTheme="Dark"), the "Yes" Button would render as white-on-white and therefore not be visible.

ButtonBase Behaviors

Other than the Flyout property, the Button class exposes no additional APIs on top of what it inherits from ButtonBase. In addition to its Click event, ButtonBase exposes IsPointerOver and IsPressed Boolean properties. IsPressed covers keyboard input as well as pointer input, such as holding down the spacebar.

The most interesting feature of ButtonBase, however, is its ClickMode property. This can be set to a value of a ClickMode enumeration to control exactly when the Click event gets raised. Its values are Release (the default), Press, and Hover. Although changing the ClickMode setting on standard buttons would likely confuse users, this capability can be handy for buttons that have been restyled to look like something completely different.

Why does Click correspond to *lifting* a pointer from the screen or keyboard key (by default) rather than *pressing* it?

Although it might sound strange at first, this is standard behavior seen in just about every platform. A benefit of this behavior is that it gives the user a chance to change his or her mind (if he or she presses the wrong button, for example) by dragging a finger, pen, or mouse away from the button instead of simply releasing it.

AppBarButton

AppBarButton, new to Windows 8.1, is a Button that matches the expected style of bottom app bar buttons. (See the "App Bars" section for examples.) Instead of a rectangle containing a single piece of arbitrary content, AppBarButtons are rendered as circles with built-in support for an icon and a label. AppBarButton derives from Button and adds three properties of its own:

→ **Label**—A simple string placed underneath the circle

→ **Icon**—The icon in the circle, represented by an interesting IconElement object that most of this section is dedicated to

→ **IsCompact**—A Boolean that can be set to false to hide the Label and reduce the AppBarButton's padding

Figure 10.3 shows how the following four `AppBarButtons` get rendered:

```
<StackPanel Orientation="Horizontal">
  <AppBarButton Label="Play" Icon="Play"/>
  <AppBarButton Label="Pin to Start" Icon="Pin"/>
  <AppBarButton Label="Like" Icon="Like"/>
  <AppBarButton Label="More" Icon="More"/>
</StackPanel>
```

FIGURE 10.3   AppBarButtons match Windows design guidelines.

The `AppBarButtons` may appear to be spaced far apart, but that extra padding is within the bounds of each one, leaving nice, large (and rectangular) hittable areas that are easy to tap with a finger. Figure 10.4 shows how the same four `AppBarButtons` appear when they each have `IsCompact` set to true.

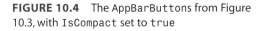

FIGURE 10.4   The AppBarButtons from Figure 10.3, with `IsCompact` set to true

When you use an `AppBarButton` outside of an app bar, such as a back button on the upper left corner of your page, design guidelines state that you should set `IsCompact` to true.

`AppBarButton` is the only subclass of `Button` in the XAML UI Framework. (The other "buttons" in this chapter derive directly from `ButtonBase`.) That means that `AppBarButtons` have the `Flyout` property, but the other controls do not.

Because `AppBarButton` is designed to match design guidelines, several properties inherited from `Button` don't impact its appearance. For example, setting properties such as `Background`, `BorderBrush`, and `BorderThickness` do nothing. Setting `Foreground` works, but it only changes the rendering of the icon and does not affect the label or the circle.

It's funny that `AppBarButton` is a content control, because its `Content` property is not used! It only happens to be a content control because it makes sense for it to derive from `Button` and inherit all its behaviors. You *could* set `Content` to arbitrary content instead of setting `Icon`, but it wouldn't look very good without some effort. You should just use `Icon`. As mentioned previously, `Icon` must be set to an `IconElement`. `IconElement` is a `FrameworkElement` with an additional `Foreground` property, and it serves as the base class for four different types of icons you can use directly:

→ `SymbolIcon`

→ `FontIcon`

→ `PathIcon`

→ `BitmapIcon`

A Trend in XAML Controls

The original designers of XAML and its control model might be horrified at the design of `AppBarButton`. They might say:

→ "`Label` should be a `System.Object` so consumers have more flexibility!"

→ "The `Icon` property should not exist! This control should be leveraging its `Content` property. An `IconElement` could still be used as the value if that's what the consumer desires."

→ "Its default style should not ignore so many properties! If consumers want to increase the thickness of the circle, why shouldn't they be able to set `BorderThickness` accordingly?"

However, users of the control in its current form are likely to say, "Wow! This is so easy to use and get the right look!" This is the general trend with the more recently-introduced XAML controls. They sometimes abandon the pure, completely-flexible model in favor of doing a specific job really well.

SymbolIcon

`SymbolIcon` provides an easy way to use a glyph from the Segoe UI Symbol font. Segoe UI Symbol is like a modern version of the Wingdings font, with many icons matching the style of Windows. `SymbolIcon` has a single `Symbol` property that can be set to a value from the `Windows.UI.Xaml.Controls.Symbol` enumeration to select a glyph via a friendly name. This impressive list of values is shown in Table 10.1.

The XAML for Figure 10.3 shows that a type converter enables you to set `AppBarButton`'s `Icon` property to a simple string. This (case-insensitive) string maps directly to a value from the `Symbol` enumeration. The "Play" button in the preceding XAML could also be rewritten as:

```
<AppBarButton Label="Play">
  <AppBarButton.Icon>
    <SymbolIcon Symbol="Play"/>
  </AppBarButton.Icon>
</AppBarButton>
```

If a value from the `Symbol` enumeration meets your needs, this is the preferred type of icon to use. This not only provides consistency among apps, but font glyphs work nicely because they are vector-based and therefore scale perfectly

TABLE 10.1   The Values from the Symbol Enumeration That Can Be Used for a `SymbolIcon`

Accept	DockRight	Memo	RotateCamera
Account	Document	Message	Save
Add	Download	Microphone	SaveLocal
AddFriend	Edit	More	SelectAll
Admin	Emoji	MoveToFolder	Send
AlignCenter	Emoji2	MusicInfo	SetLockScreen
AlignLeft	Favorite	Mute	SetTile
AlignRight	Filter	NewFolder	Setting
Attach	Find	NewWindow	Shop
AttachCamera	Flag	Next	ShowBcc
Audio	Folder	OneBar	ShowResults
Back	Font	OpenFile	Shuffle
BackToWindow	FontColor	OpenLocal	SlideShow
BlockContact	FontDecrease	OpenPane	SolidStar
Bold	FontIncrease	OpenWith	Sort
Bookmarks	FontSize	Orientation	Stop
BrowsePhotos	Forward	OtherUser	StopSlideShow
Bullets	FourBars	OutlineStar	Street
Calculator	FullScreen	Page	Switch
Calendar	Globe	Page2	SwitchApps
CalendarDay	Go	Paste	Sync
CalendarReply	GoToStart	Pause	SyncFolder
CalendarWeek	GoToToday	People	Tag
Camera	HangUp	Permissions	Target
Cancel	Help	Phone	ThreeBars
Caption	HideBcc	PhoneBook	TouchPointer
CellPhone	Highlight	Pictures	Trim
Character	Home	Pin	TwoBars
Clear	Import	Placeholder	TwoPage
ClearSelection	ImportAll	Play	Underline
Clock	Important	PostUpdate	Undo
ClosedCaption	Italic	PreviewLink	UnFavorite
ClosePane	Keyboard	Previous	UnPin
Comment	LeaveChat	Priority	UnSyncFolder
Contact	Library	ProtectedDocument	Up
Contact2	Like	Read	Upload
ContactInfo	LikeDislike	Redo	Video
ContactPresence	Link	Refresh	VideoChat
Copy	List	Remote	View
Crop	Mail	Remove	ViewAll
Cut	MailFilled	Rename	Volume
Delete	MailForward	Repair	WebCam
Directions	MailReply	RepeatAll	World
DisableUpdates	MailReplyAll	RepeatOne	ZeroBars
DisconnectDrive	Manage	ReportHacked	Zoom
Dislike	Map	ReShare	ZoomIn
DockBottom	MapDrive	Rotate	ZoomOut
DockLeft	MapPin		

FontIcon

FontIcon is a general purpose form of SymbolIcon. Rather than using a predefined font with a fixed list of glyphs, you can use any available font and choose your own character(s). FontIcon enables you to specify a FontFamily, FontSize, FontWeight, and FontStyle. Its Glyph property is just a string, and it can be set to one or more characters. The following XAML demonstrates three uses of FontIcon, shown in Figure 10.5:

```
<AppBarButton Label="Default Font">
  <AppBarButton.Icon>
    <FontIcon FontSize="15" FontWeight="Bold" Glyph="abc"/>
  </AppBarButton.Icon>
</AppBarButton>
<AppBarButton Label="Webdings">
  <AppBarButton.Icon>
    <FontIcon FontFamily="Webdings" Glyph="!"/>
  </AppBarButton.Icon>
</AppBarButton>
<AppBarButton Label="Wingdings with Character Code">
  <AppBarButton.Icon>
    <FontIcon FontFamily="Wingdings" Glyph="&#x004D;"/>
  </AppBarButton.Icon>
</AppBarButton>
```

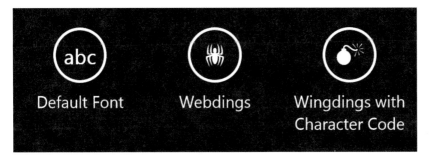

FIGURE 10.5   Three AppBarButtons using FontIcons to get more customized icons

You can browse a font's symbols and get the Unicode value for each one with the Character Map desktop app that ships with Windows, as shown in Figure 10.6. You can then copy and paste characters from Character Map directly into your XAML or, as shown in the preceding XAML, use the XML escape sequence &#x*HexValue*;, where *HexValue* is the Unicode code point shown at the bottom of Character Map for any selected character. Even Segoe UI Symbol contains many interesting icons not covered by the Symbol enumeration, such as the "pig nose" shown in Figure 10.6. You could use a FontIcon with a FontFamily of "Segoe UI Symbol" to easily access these additional icons.

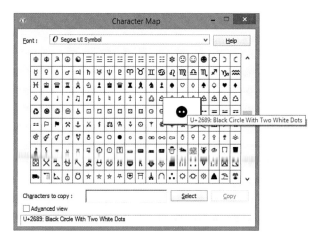

FIGURE 10.6   Browsing potential icons in any font is easy with Character Map.

PathIcon

PathIcon enables you to use completely custom vector artwork as your icon (without having to create your own font with custom glyphs and ship it with your app). It has a single property called Data that can be set to a Geometry. Geometries are covered in Chapter 16, "Vector Graphics," but here's an example of custom vector data that produces the result in Figure 10.7:

```
<AppBarButton Label="Overlapping Triangles">
  <AppBarButton.Icon>
    <PathIcon Data="M 10,10 L 10,25 L 25,25 Z M 30,10 L 10,30 L 30,30 Z"/>
  </AppBarButton.Icon>
</AppBarButton>
```

BitmapIcon

BitmapIcon enables you to use an image file as the source of your icon. Although this is the only type of IconElement that is not vector-based, it does two things to make the image almost as good as vector art:

→ It automatically scales the image to fit inside the circle.

→ It respects transparency and replaces all non-transparent pixels with the appropriate Foreground brush (as long as Foreground is a solid color).

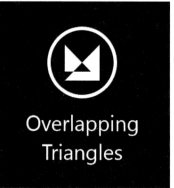

FIGURE 10.7   An AppBarButton using PathIcon to get a completely custom icon

Figure 10.8 demonstrates using the app's large splash screen image as the icon for three AppBarButtons with the following XAML, which varies the Foreground to demonstrate the special treatment of the image content:

```
<AppBarButton Label="Default Foreground">
  <AppBarButton.Icon>
    <BitmapIcon UriSource="Assets/SplashScreen.png"/>
  </AppBarButton.Icon>
</AppBarButton>
<AppBarButton Foreground="Red" Label="Red">
  <AppBarButton.Icon>
    <BitmapIcon UriSource="Assets/SplashScreen.png"/>
  </AppBarButton.Icon>
</AppBarButton>
<AppBarButton Foreground="Aqua" Label="Aqua">
  <AppBarButton.Icon>
    <BitmapIcon UriSource="Assets/SplashScreen.png"/>
  </AppBarButton.Icon>
</AppBarButton>
```

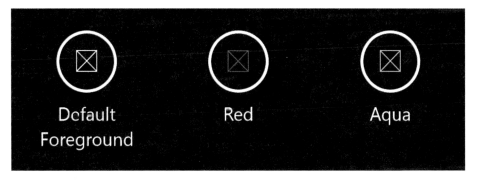

FIGURE 10.8   Three AppBarButtons using the same BitmapIcon with different Foregrounds applied

As with the other three IconElements, these icons change color when the AppBarButton is in its hover or pressed state. Like an Image element, the image file referenced by BitmapIcon can come from a number of places, and there's a way to provide separate images for 100%, 140%, and 180% scales to avoid artifacts when Windows scales content. See Chapter 13, "Images," for more information.

> You can use any IconElement outside an AppBarButton, as it is just another FrameworkElement. This is an especially neat trick for BitmapIcon, because you can leverage its unique "bitmap recoloring" feature elsewhere in your app.

•••

Setting `IconElement`'s Foreground versus `AppBarButton`'s Foreground

Both `AppBarButton` and the `IconElement` base class define a `Foreground` property that customizes the brush used to render the icon. If `Foreground` is set on `IconElement`, it overrides any `AppBarButton` setting. The two properties behave slightly differently, however.

If you set `Foreground="Red"` on an `AppBarButton`, the icon is red except during the hover and pressed states. In the dark theme, the icon becomes white on hover and black when pressed, which is consistent with how app bar buttons usually behave. If you instead set `Foreground="Red"` on any of the four `IconElements`, the icon remains red the entire time, even during the hover and pressed states.

HyperlinkButton

`HyperlinkButton` acts much like a hyperlink in HTML. It is similar to `Button`, but with a different default appearance and one more property: `NavigateUri`. This is the analog to the `AREA` (A) element's `href` attribute in HTML. You can set it to a URL, and when a user clicks the button, it automatically launches the appropriate app to act upon the content. This is equivalent to calling `Launcher.LaunchUriAsync`. For example, if the URL begins with `http://`, the default Web browser opens and shows the page. If it begins with a custom protocol, and an app is installed that can handle it, then that app gets launched appropriately (after prompting the user with a "Did you mean to switch apps?" message). If no such app is installed, then Windows informs the user. Recall that the protocol-handling app can be a desktop app as well as a Windows Store app. That's a pretty neat trick!

Although `HyperlinkButton` has a `Click` event (inherited from `ButtonBase`), there's no need to handle it thanks to its built-in behavior. If you want to perform a custom action, however, you could certainly leave `NavigateUri`'s value unset and perform that action inside a `Click` handler.

Figure 10.9 shows how the following three `HyperlinkButtons` appear:

```
<StackPanel>
  <HyperlinkButton NavigateUri="http://pixelwinks.com">
    This is a HyperlinkButton.
  </HyperlinkButton>
  <HyperlinkButton BorderBrush="AliceBlue" NavigateUri="http://adamnathan.net">
    This is a HyperlinkButton with a border.
  </HyperlinkButton>
  <HyperlinkButton Foreground="Red" NavigateUri="bingmaps:///?q=pizza">
    Any questions?
  </HyperlinkButton>
</StackPanel>
```

Its default appearance differs from `Button` in that its border is invisible and its text (*if* its content is text, of course) is rendered in a shade of purple. This is to distinguish the hyperlink text from regular text, just like blue-colored text in a Web browser.

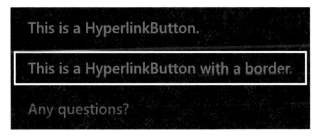

FIGURE 10.9   Examples of `HyperlinkButton`

If you want to use a hyperlink within a larger body of text, you should use a separate `Hyperlink` object inside a `TextBlock` instead. See Chapter 12, "Text," for more details.

Why do the built-in controls use shades of purple as an accent color, and how do I leverage the user's chosen theme colors instead?

As you go through this part of the book, you'll see some controls use purple to accent their otherwise colorless appearance. I can't tell you why *purple* was chosen, but *some* color had to be chosen because the user's theme colors—the background and accent colors chosen via "Personalize" on the Settings charm when the Start screen is visible—aren't exposed to third-party apps. Unlike on Windows Phone, there is no API to retrieve the user-specified accent color. This is an explicit choice by Microsoft rather than a temporary limitation. These colors are reserved for system UI, such as the Start screen, charms bar, and PC Settings app. Apps should use colors consistent with their own branding. For example, the background color used by an app's tile (and presumably its splash screen) is often a great choice to use as an accent color.

You can see all the default colors, defined separately for dark versus light versus high contrast, in `%ProgramFiles(x86)%\Windows Kits\8.1\Include\WinRT\XAML\design\ThemeResources.xaml`. For example, the following entries are all specific to HyperlinkButton:

```
<SolidColorBrush x:Key="HyperlinkButtonBackgroundThemeBrush"
                 Color="Transparent"/>
<SolidColorBrush x:Key="HyperlinkButtonBorderThemeBrush" Color="Transparent"/>
<SolidColorBrush x:Key="HyperlinkDisabledThemeBrush" Color="#66FFFFFF"/>
<SolidColorBrush x:Key="HyperlinkForegroundThemeBrush" Color="#FF9C72FF"/>
<SolidColorBrush x:Key="HyperlinkPointerOverForegroundThemeBrush"
                 Color="#CC9C72FF"/>
<SolidColorBrush x:Key="HyperlinkPressedForegroundThemeBrush"
                 Color="#999C72FF"/>
```

Although the dark and light theme colors are hard-coded, the high-contrast colors use system-defined properties that get updated based on the user's color choices.

Some of these colors can be overridden by setting appropriate properties on the control (such as `Background`, `BorderBrush`, and `Foreground` on `HyperlinkButton`), but others must be overridden by defining new XAML resources with matching key names. Chapter 18 explains how.

RepeatButton

RepeatButton acts like Button except that it continually raises the Click event as long as the button is pressed. The frequency of the raised Click events depends on the values of RepeatButton's Delay and Interval properties, whose default values are both 250 milliseconds. The default look of a RepeatButton is the same as that of Button.

The behavior of RepeatButton might sound strange at first, but it is useful (and standard) for buttons that increment or decrement a value each time they are pressed. For example, the buttons at the ends of a scrollbar exhibit the repeat-press behavior when you press and hold them. Or, if you were to build a numeric "up-down" control, you would likely want to use two RepeatButtons to control the numeric value. RepeatButton is in the Windows.UI.Xaml.Controls.**Primitives** namespace because it is likely that you would use this control only as part of a more sophisticated control rather than use it directly.

ToggleButton

ToggleButton is a "sticky" button that holds its state when it is clicked. Clicking it the first time sets its IsChecked property to true, and clicking it again sets IsChecked to false. The default appearance of ToggleButton is the same as that of Button and RepeatButton, and when IsChecked is true it retains its pressed appearance. It can be used for enabling and disabling features, such as bold/italic/underline buttons on a text editor's toolbar, and is great when space is limited. Otherwise, it's often more appropriate to use a ToggleSwitch control (covered in Chapter 15, "Other Controls") instead.

ToggleButton also has an IsThreeState property that, if set to true, gives IsChecked three possible values: true, false, or null. In fact, IsChecked is of type Nullable <Boolean> (bool? in C#). In the three-state case, the first click sets IsChecked to true, the second click sets it to null, the third click sets it to false, and so on. To vary the order of these state changes, you could create your own subclass and override ToggleButton's OnToggle method to perform your custom logic. Of course, the meaning of this third state is app-specific. Often it is used to represent a mixed state when multiple items are selected, some with the relevant feature on, and some with it off.

In addition to the IsChecked property, ToggleButton defines a separate event for each value of IsChecked: Checked for true, Unchecked for false, and Indeterminate for null.

ToggleButton is also in the Windows.UI.Xaml.Controls.Primitives namespace because it is often isn't used directly. (Its default three-state appearance isn't satisfactory, because the indeterminate state looks no different from the unchecked state.) Instead, its primary role is to be the base class of the next three controls.

AppBarToggleButton

Just like the relationship between AppBarButton and Button, AppBarToggleButton is a ToggleButton that matches the expected style of app bar buttons. It defines the same Label, Icon, and IsCompact properties discussed in the AppBarButton section, but it inherits the sticky IsChecked behavior from ToggleButton. It is also new to Windows 8.1.

Fortunately, unlike its `ToggleButton` base class, this control has a meaningful visual representation of its indeterminate state, should you decide to enable its three-state mode. Figure 10.10 shows the following three `AppBarToggleButtons`, *after* the first one is clicked once and the last one is clicked twice:

```
<StackPanel Orientation="Horizontal">
  <AppBarToggleButton Label="Checked" Icon="Orientation"/>
  <AppBarToggleButton Label="Unchecked" Icon="Orientation"/>
  <AppBarToggleButton IsThreeState="True"
                      Label="Indeterminate" Icon="Orientation"/>
</StackPanel>
```

Before any of these are clicked, they look identical except for their `Labels`.

FIGURE 10.10   The `AppBarToggleButton` control, with all three `IsChecked` states shown

CheckBox

CheckBox, shown in Figure 10.11, is a familiar control. But wait a minute...aren't we in the middle of talking about buttons? Yes, but consider the characteristics of a CheckBox:

→ It has a single piece of *externally supplied* content (so the standard check box doesn't count).

→ It has a notion of being clicked by pointer or keyboard.

→ It retains a state of being checked or unchecked when clicked.

→ It supports a three-state mode, where the state toggles from checked to indeterminate to unchecked.

Does this sound familiar? It should, because a CheckBox is nothing more than a ToggleButton with a different appearance! CheckBox is a simple class deriving from ToggleButton that does little more than override its default style to the visuals shown in Figure 10.11. As with ToggleButton, you should consider using

FIGURE 10.11   The CheckBox control, with all three IsChecked states shown

`ToggleSwitch` instead if you have the space for it and you don't require a three-state mode.

CheckBox Keyboard Support   •••

CheckBox supports one additional behavior that `ToggleButton` does not, for parity with a little-known but long-time feature of Windows check boxes. When a `CheckBox` has focus, pressing the plus (+) key on the number pad checks the control and pressing the minus (–) key on the number pad unchecks the control! Note that this works only if `IsThreeState` hasn't been set to `true`.

RadioButton

`RadioButton` is another control that derives from `ToggleButton`, but it is unique because it has built-in support for mutual exclusion. When multiple `RadioButton` controls are grouped together, only one can be checked at a time. Checking one `RadioButton`—even programmatically— automatically unchecks all others in the same group. In fact, users can't directly uncheck a `RadioButton` by clicking it; unchecking can be done only program-matically. Therefore, `RadioButton` is designed for multiple-choice questions. Figure 10.12 shows the default appear-ance of a `RadioButton`.

FIGURE 10.12   The `RadioButton`, with all three `IsChecked` states shown

The rarely used indeterminate state of a `RadioButton` (`IsThreeState=true` and `IsChecked=null`) is similar to the unchecked state in that a user cannot enable this state by clicking on it; it must be set programmatically. If the `RadioButton` is clicked, it changes to the checked state. But if another `RadioButton` in the same group becomes checked, any indeterminate `RadioButtons` remain in the indeterminate state. As with its base `ToggleButton` class, the indeterminate state looks no different than the unchecked state, so it's an especially confusing option to use in practice.

Placing several `RadioButtons` in the same group is straightforward. By default, any `RadioButtons` that share the same direct parent are automatically grouped together. For example, only one of the following `RadioButtons` can be checked at any point in time:

```
<StackPanel>
  <RadioButton>Option 1</RadioButton>
  <RadioButton>Option 2</RadioButton>
  <RadioButton>Option 3</RadioButton>
</StackPanel>
```

If you need to group `RadioButtons` in a custom manner, however, you can use the `GroupName` property, which is a simple string. Any `RadioButtons` with the same `GroupName` value get grouped together (as long as they have the same root element). Therefore, you can group them across different parents, as shown here:

```
<StackPanel>
  <StackPanel>
    <RadioButton GroupName="A">Option 1</RadioButton>
    <RadioButton GroupName="A">Option 2</RadioButton>
  </StackPanel>
  <StackPanel>
    <RadioButton GroupName="A">Option 3</RadioButton>
  </StackPanel>
</StackPanel>
```

Different parents

Or you can even create subgroups inside the same parent:

```
<StackPanel>
  <RadioButton GroupName="A">Option 1</RadioButton>
  <RadioButton GroupName="A">Option 2</RadioButton>
  <RadioButton GroupName="B">A Different Option 1</RadioButton>
  <RadioButton GroupName="B">A Different Option 2</RadioButton>
</StackPanel>
```

Different groups

Of course, the last example here would be a confusing piece of user interface without an extra visual element separating the two subgroups!

ToolTip

Logically, a tooltip is floating content that appears when you hover over an associated element and disappears when you move the pointer away. (Unlike a `Flyout`, it is meant for hovering only and is noninteractive.) The `ToolTip` control doesn't perform any of this magic, however. It's a simple content control that places its content in a white box with a grey border (in the dark theme). The magic is done by a `ToolTipService` class and its three attached properties. The main one is `ToolTipService.ToolTip`, which enables a `ToolTip` to be attached to any `UIElement` and automatically appear/disappear when appropriate. Figure 10.13 shows a typical `ToolTip` in action, created from the following XAML:

```
<Button>
  +
  <ToolTipService.ToolTip>
    <ToolTip>
      Add New Item
    </ToolTip>
  </ToolTipService.ToolTip>
</Button>
```

Although ToolTips might not seem worthwhile when designing a "touch first" app because typical touch digitizers don't support hovering, they are indeed an important part of a well-designed user interface. In fact, each of the pointer types is able to reveal an attached ToolTip. A mouse pointer can hover over an element, of course, and so

FIGURE 10.13   A ToolTip attached to a Button

can a pen (when it is in range but not in contact). But all three pointer types can do a press-and-hold gesture as well to reveal the ToolTip. Note that when a ToolTip is attached to a Control, it never appears when the Control is disabled (IsEnabled=false).

As with Flyout, a ToolTip is *not* a child of the element it is attached to and does not inherit property values or transforms. However, because ToolTip is a content control, you can directly set various properties such as RenderTransform.

You don't need to use the ToolTip class when setting ToolTipService.ToolTip on an element! The property is of type Object, and if you set it to any non-ToolTip object, the property's implementation automatically creates a ToolTip and uses the property value as the ToolTip's content. Therefore, the XAML for Figure 10.13 could be simplified to the following and give the same result:

```
<Button>
  +
  <ToolTipService.ToolTip>
      Add New Item
  </ToolTipService.ToolTip>
</Button>
```

or it could be simplified further, as follows:

```
<Button Content="+" ToolTipService.ToolTip="Add New Item"/>
```

Of course, if you want to set properties directly on the ToolTip instance (such as its RenderTransform), you'll want to use an explicit element.

Because of the flexibility of content controls, a ToolTip can hold anything you want. Listing 10.1 shows how you might construct a richer one inspired by the kind you find in Microsoft Office apps. The result is shown in Figure 10.14.

LISTING 10.1   A Complex ToolTip

```
<CheckBox>
  CheckBox
  <ToolTipService.ToolTip>
```

LISTING 10.1   Continued

```xml
  <StackPanel>
    <TextBlock FontWeight="Bold" Foreground="Blue">
      The CheckBox
    </TextBlock>
    <TextBlock TextWrapping="Wrap" Width="200">
      CheckBox is a familiar control. But it's not much
      more than a ToggleButton styled differently!
    </TextBlock>
    <StackPanel Orientation="Horizontal" Margin="-10,10,-10,-7"
                Background="Blue">
      <Image Margin="4" Source="Assets/help.png"/>
      <TextBlock VerticalAlignment="Center" Foreground="White"
                 FontWeight="Bold">Press F1 for more help.</TextBlock>
    </StackPanel>
  </StackPanel>
  </ToolTipService.ToolTip>
</CheckBox>
```

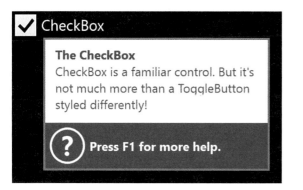

FIGURE 10.14   A rich tooltip is easy to create thanks to the flexibility of content controls.

Although a `ToolTip` can contain interactive controls such as `Buttons`, those controls never get focus, and you can't click or otherwise interact with them. The default inverted background color of a `ToolTip` makes most controls appear invisible anyway, unless you mark them with the opposite `RequestedTheme` value. (`ToolTip` intentionally does not perform the same `RequestedTheme` trick that `FlyoutBase` performs because placing controls inside a `ToolTip` doesn't usually make sense.)

The beginning of this section mentioned that `ToolTipService` defines three attached properties. Besides `ToolTip`, the other two are `Placement` and `PlacementTarget`. `Placement` customizes the `ToolTip`'s desired placement relative to the pointer, similar to `FlyoutBase`'s `Placement` property but with slightly different values: `Top`, `Bottom`, `Left`, `Right`, or `Mouse` (the default value). The last value, which really should be called `Pointer` instead, means *the location of the hovering pointer*. The other values are relative to the *element* rather than the pointer. As with Flyout, if there's not enough room to display the entire ToolTip at the desired location, it will be shown in a different spot. PlacementTarget can be set to an instance of an element if you want the Placement value to be relative to a *different* element than the one under the pointer.

The ToolTip class itself defines Opened and Closed events (and an IsOpen property) in case you want to act on its appearance and disappearance. It also defines several properties for tweaking its placement: HorizontalOffset, VerticalOffset, plus the same Placement and PlacementTarget properties defined on ToolTipService. If both ToolTip and ToolTipService have an explicit value for these, the value on ToolTipService has precedence.

> **How can I forcibly close a ToolTip that is currently showing?**
>
> IsOpen is a read-write property, so set its IsOpen property to false.

App Bars

Most Windows Store apps should leverage one or two app bars that appear from the top and/or bottom of a Page whenever the user performs an edge gesture (an appropriate swipe, right mouse button click, pressing Windows+Z, or pressing the context menu key). Users expect to find additional functionality via this gesture.

The bottom app bar has fairly rigid design guidelines. It should contain a specific style of buttons that trigger context-specific commands, although it can often have a group of buttons that act like RadioButtons for changing the view of the current page. The buttons should be docked to each edge, favoring the right edge. (This is done not only to scale naturally to different resolutions, but to be in a good position for the user's thumbs when holding a tablet.) And the app bar background should match the app's signature color (the color used as its tile background). Figure 10.15 shows bottom app bars from several Microsoft apps.

The top app bar has looser design guidelines. It is often used for navigation to sections of the app, although it could be used for completely custom purposes as well. One common trait among top app bars is that they are usually much taller than a bottom app bar, and they generally don't use the same style of buttons used by bottom app bars. Figure 10.16 shows top app bars from some Microsoft apps.

In Windows 8, the XAML UI Framework introduced an AppBar control. AppBar handles many behaviors users expect from app bars, and could be used for both a bottom app bar and top app bar. However, you had to do a lot of work to produce a bottom app bar that matches design guidelines (especially because AppBarButton and its related controls didn't exist).

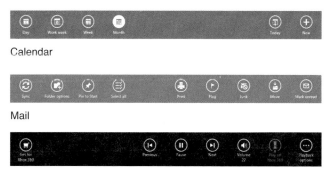

Calendar

Mail

Video

News

FIGURE 10.15   The bottom app bars from four Microsoft apps generally follow the same pattern.

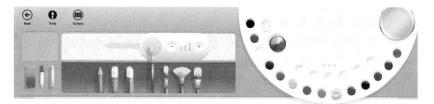

News

Store

Fresh Paint

FIGURE 10.16   The top app bars from three Microsoft apps have much more variation than bottom app bars.

In Windows 8.1, the XAML UI Framework has introduced a second app bar control called CommandBar. It derives from AppBar, but it is designed specifically for bottom app bars. With it, and the AppBarButton family of controls, you can trivially create a first-class bottom app bar that looks and behaves as it should.

This section first explains AppBar, then it examines what CommandBar adds on top of it.

> You should use AppBar for a top app bar and CommandBar for a bottom app bar. If your bottom app bar needs to deviate from the standard behavior, such as hosting an inline TextBox similar to Internet Explorer's bottom app bar, then you should use an AppBar instead.
>
> You can find detailed design guidelines at http://design.windows.com. Included in these guidelines are recommendations on placing buttons in an app bar, including conventions for choosing the left side versus right side.

AppBar

Like ToolTip, the AppBar control adds nothing to its inner content other than enforcing a minimum height and adding some horizontal padding. It does contain automatic behavior for showing and hiding itself, however (unlike ToolTip which relies on ToolTipService for this). An AppBar is invisible by default but automatically animates in and out when an edge gesture is performed (an appropriate swipe, right mouse button click, pressing Windows+Z, or pressing the context menu key).

You can place an AppBar anywhere you'd place other elements, but it is intended to be attached to a Page via Page's TopAppBar or BottomAppBar property. When you attach an AppBar to one of these, it docks to the top or bottom edge, it overlays any content underneath (as expected), and a few of its visual defaults automatically change. For example, when attached to a Page, its default BorderBrush becomes a translucent black instead of Transparent, and its default animation becomes a slide instead of a fade.

The following XAML attaches a simple AppBar containing a Button as the Page's TopAppBar, which produces the result shown in in Figure 10.17:

```
<Page …>
  <Page.TopAppBar>
    <AppBar Background="Green">
      <Button>Home</Button>
    </AppBar>
  </Page.TopAppBar>
  <Grid Background="OrangeRed">
    <TextBlock VerticalAlignment="Top" FontSize="100">Main content</TextBlock>
  </Grid>
</Page>
```

Closed

Open

FIGURE 10.17   When attached to a Page, an AppBar's parent element is null, and it overlays the Page's content.

As with attaching a ToolTip or Flyout to an element, attaching an AppBar to a Page in this manner makes it the root of its own visual tree. Therefore, Page-level transforms and other property values do not impact the AppBar. Unlike with ToolTip, you must always set TopAppBar or BottomAppBar to an explicit AppBar element. (The properties are of type AppBar rather than the generic Object.)

Besides Opened and Closed events and a read-write IsOpen property (just like on ToolTip), AppBar defines a Boolean IsSticky property that is false by default. When set to true, the AppBar, once open, stays open unless the user does an edge gesture to close it or the app programmatically sets IsOpen to false. When false, the AppBar has light dismiss behavior that causes it to automatically close when it loses focus, just like a Flyout. Note that both IsSticky values work as advertised only when an AppBar is properly attached to a Page via TopAppBar or BottomAppBar.

Of course, app bars usually have more than one control inside. Therefore, an AppBar's Content is normally set to an appropriate panel with many things inside. The following AppBar produces a reasonable experience for a top app bar, shown in Figure 10.18. It also overrides the default border that is usually unwanted:

```
<Page …>
  <Page.TopAppBar>
    <AppBar Background="Green" BorderBrush="Transparent">
      <StackPanel Orientation="Horizontal">
        <Button MinWidth="140" Margin="12,0">Home</Button>
        <Button MinWidth="140" Margin="12,0">Your apps</Button>
        <Button MinWidth="140" Margin="12,0">Your account</Button>
      </StackPanel>
    </AppBar>
  </Page.TopAppBar>
  <Grid Background="OrangeRed">
    <TextBlock VerticalAlignment="Top" FontSize="100">Main content</TextBlock>
  </Grid>
</Page>
```

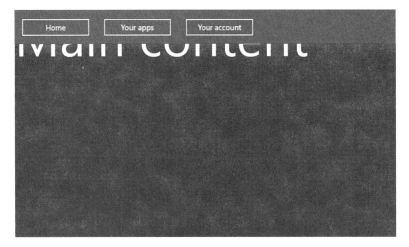

FIGURE 10.18   A more realistic top app bar contains a panel with several controls inside.

How can I use the same AppBar across multiple pages?

You would have to detach it from the current Page and attach it to the next Page when navigating from one to the other. (Because an AppBar is always attached to a Page, it would be more appropriate to call it a *page* bar.) Of course, if the Page with the AppBar(s) contains a Frame that does its own navigation (like an iframe in an HTML page), then you get to keep the single AppBar without ever detaching/reattaching it.

CommandBar

CommandBar, which derives from AppBar, adds two simple properties: PrimaryCommands and SecondaryCommands. Primary commands are automatically stacked on the right, per design guidelines, and secondary commands are stacked on the left. (If FlowDirection is RightToLeft, then the placement of commands is reversed.) The inherited Content property is ignored by CommandBar's default style, so this is another instance of a content control that doesn't really act like a content control. You must populate its content via the two new properties.

Each of these properties is a collection of ICommandBarElements, an interface implemented by three controls:

→ AppBarButton

→ AppBarToggleButton

→ AppBarSeparator

This means that a CommandBar can only contain these three types of elements, unless you create your own objects that implement ICommandBarElement. (This is easy to do, by the way, because the interface only defines a Boolean IsCompact property.) You've already seen the first two elements, and AppBarSeparator is a simple vertical line that can be used to separate groups of buttons.

The following XAML produces the bottom app bar in Figure 10.19:

```
<Page …>
  <Page.BottomAppBar>
    <CommandBar Background="Green" BorderBrush="Transparent">
      <CommandBar.PrimaryCommands>
        <AppBarButton Label="Previous" Icon="Previous"/>
        <AppBarButton Label="Pause" Icon="Pause"/>
        <AppBarButton Label="Next" Icon="Next"/>
        <AppBarButton Label="Volume" Icon="Volume"/>
        <AppBarButton Label="Playback options" Icon="More"/>
      </CommandBar.PrimaryCommands>
      <CommandBar.SecondaryCommands>
        <AppBarButton Label="Buy" Icon="Shop"/>
        <AppBarButton Label="Pin to Start" Icon="Pin"/>
        <AppBarSeparator Foreground="White"/>
        <AppBarButton Label="Select all" Icon="SelectAll"/>
        <AppBarButton Label="Clear selection" Icon="ClearSelection"/>
      </CommandBar.SecondaryCommands>
    </CommandBar>
  </Page.BottomAppBar>
  …
</Page>
```

FIGURE 10.19   A nice-looking bottom app bar is easy to create with CommandBar.

By default, AppBarSeparator renders in a gray color that's hard to see on top of the chosen green background, so its Foreground is explicitly set to White to match the AppBarButtons.

CommandBar overrides its content property to be PrimaryCommands rather than content. Therefore, you can remove the explicit CommandBar.PrimaryCommands property element in XAML and treat the list of buttons as the direct content for CommandBar:

```
<Page …>
  <Page.BottomAppBar>
    <CommandBar Background="Green" BorderBrush="Transparent">
      <AppBarButton Label="Previous" Icon="Previous"/>
      <AppBarButton Label="Pause" Icon="Pause"/>
      <AppBarButton Label="Next" Icon="Next"/>
      <AppBarButton Label="Volume" Icon="Volume"/>
      <AppBarButton Label="Playback options" Icon="More"/>
      <CommandBar.SecondaryCommands>
        <AppBarButton Label="Buy" Icon="Shop"/>
        <AppBarButton Label="Pin to Start" Icon="Pin"/>
        <AppBarSeparator Foreground="White"/>
        <AppBarButton Label="Select all" Icon="SelectAll"/>
        <AppBarButton Label="Clear selection" Icon="ClearSelection"/>
      </CommandBar.SecondaryCommands>
    </CommandBar>
  </Page.BottomAppBar>
  …
</Page>
```

CommandBar has built-in logic for handling the resizing of your window in a way that follows design guidelines. If all of your elements cannot fit within the current CommandBar width, it automatically switches all of them to compact mode by setting their IsCompact properties to true. (This is the reason you can only add ICommandBarElements to CommandBar.) And if they still don't all fit in their compact mode, CommandBar hides all the secondary commands in order to leave room for the (more important) primary commands. This is demonstrated in Figure 10.20 by resizing the window from Figure 10.19 to smaller and smaller widths.

Notice that the secondary commands do not get hidden one-by-one; it's an all-or-nothing proposition. If you want more fine-grained hiding, you would have to do this yourself by toggling the right elements' Visibility at the right times. Of course, for your top app bar, or anywhere you use AppBar instead of CommandBar, you'll need to handle all aspects of intelligent resizing on your own.

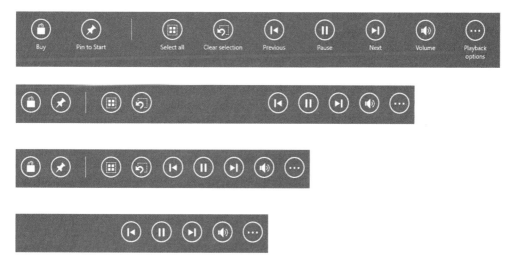

FIGURE 10.20   A CommandBar handles resizing intelligently by automatically switching elements to compact mode then hiding secondary commands if necessary.

Summary

Never before has a button been so flexible! In the XAML UI Framework, Button and most of the other content controls can contain absolutely anything—but they can directly contain only one item. This chapter highlighted what makes each type of Button unique, and examined the three non-Button content controls that haven't been covered earlier in this book. The new elements in Windows 8.1—Flyout and its related objects, AppBarButton and its related elements, and CommandBar—are all about making it easier for you to create the kind of signature Windows experiences that match the built-in apps and Microsoft's design guidelines.

Viewbox, introduced in Chapter 4, "Layout," and a handy element called Border (which supports customizable rounded corners with its CornerRadius property) can often be mistaken for content controls because they directly contain only one item. They are not, however. They derive directly from FrameworkElement, and therefore lack many features given to Control. Instead of a Content property, they have a Child property.

Although XAML apps and HTML apps both have common controls that look and act the same way, they are completely separate implementations with much different exposure to developers. The HTML controls are based on the HTML5 standard and heavily use CSS and JavaScript, whereas the XAML controls expose an object and styling model familiar to WPF and Silverlight developers. This does mean that sometimes one framework gets ahead of the other. (For example, the Windows Library for JavaScript already had a Flyout control in the Windows 8 timeframe.) However, in both cases, they take advantage of hardware acceleration for great performance.

Now, with the tour of content controls complete, it's time to move on to controls that are designed to directly contain more than one item—*items controls*.

Chapter 11

ITEMS CONTROLS

Besides content controls, the other large category of XAML controls is *items controls*, which can contain an unbounded collection of items rather than just a single piece of content. All items controls derive from the abstract ItemsControl class, which, like ContentControl, is a direct subclass of Control.

Although the ItemsControl class doesn't have any notion of selected item(s), all the built-in items controls happen to derive from Selector, a subclass of ItemsControl. Selector adds the following three read/write properties to enable the concept of selection:

→ **SelectedIndex**—A zero-based integer that indicates what item is selected or -1 if nothing is selected. Items are numbered in the order in which they are added to the collection.

→ **SelectedItem**—The actual item instance that is currently selected.

→ **SelectedValue**—The value of the currently selected item. By default this value is the item itself, making SelectedValue identical to SelectedItem. You can set a separate SelectedValuePath property, however, to choose an arbitrary property or expression that should represent each item's value. This expression is known as a *property path*, and is covered in Chapter 17, "Animation."

These properties are automatically kept in sync, so if you set SelectedIndex to -1, SelectedItem becomes null (and vice versa).

Selector also defines an event—SelectionChanged—that makes it easy to detect changes to the current selection, whether it happened via pointer input, keyboard input, or programmatically. There are many ways selection can happen (even with pointer input, it can be a tap or a cross slide), so it's important to use this event for reliable detection rather than input events.

The XAML UI Framework contains five Selectors, and each one is described in this chapter:

- → ComboBox
- → ListBox
- → ListView
- → GridView
- → FlipView

ComboBox and ListBox are classic controls that have been updated for Windows Store apps, but the latter three are specific to Windows Store apps.

This chapter also introduces the SemanticZoom control. It is not a Selector, or even an items control. However, it is designed to be used with controls like ListView and/or GridView, so this is a good place to learn about it. This chapter also looks at MenuFlyout, which acts a lot like an items control in the same way that Flyout acts like a content control.

Before examining each control, however, let's look at two important aspects of all items controls: the items themselves, and an interesting feature known as *items panels*.

Items in the Control

ItemsControl stores its content in an Items property (of type ItemCollection). Each item can be an arbitrary object (System.Object) that by default gets rendered just as it would inside a content control. In other words, any UIElement is rendered as expected, and (ignoring data templates) any other type is rendered as a TextBlock containing the string returned by its ToString method.

The simple ListBox control shown in Chapter 2, "Mastering XAML," is an items control. Whereas Chapter 2 always adds ListBoxItems to the Items collection, the following example adds arbitrary objects to Items instead (all done in XAML for convenience):

```
<ListBox xmlns:sys="using:System">
  <Button>Button</Button>
  <x:Double>1.23</x:Double>
  <sys:EventArgs/>
  <sys:UriBuilder/>
</ListBox>
```

The child elements are implicitly added to the Items collection because Items is a content property. This ListBox, after selecting the first item, is shown in Figure 11.1. The UIElement (Button) is rendered normally and is fully interactive. Note that if the first item were not selected, the Button would look invisible because it would be rendered as white-on-white. The other three objects render according to their ToString methods. (Notice that UriBuilder's ToString reports its URI, http://localhost/ by default, rather than simply returning its type name.)

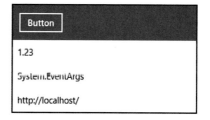

FIGURE 11.1   A ListBox containing arbitrary objects

Item Containers

When elements other than ListBoxItem are placed in a ListBox, each one gets implicitly wrapped in a ListBoxItem. (You can see this from code if you traverse up the visual tree from any of the items.) This is done to preserve some common behaviors and visuals, such as the purple selection highlight seen in Figure 11.1.

ListBoxItem derives from SelectorItem (which derives from ContentControl). Each of the five Selectors has a corresponding *SelectorName*Item class that always wraps each of its items (implicitly if not already done explicitly). ListBox has ListBoxItem, ComboBox has ComboBoxItem, and so on. These classes are called *item containers*. ItemsControl exposes a few advanced properties related to its item containers, enabling customization of their visual style and transition animations.

Although all Selectors already define properties that reveal the currently selected item, SelectorItem also exposes a read/write IsSelected property that can often be a more handy way to discover or change a selection.

As mentioned in Chapter 2, the Items property is read-only. This means that you can add objects to the initially empty collection or remove objects, but you can't point Items to an entirely different collection. ItemsControl has a separate property—ItemsSource—that supports filling its items with an existing arbitrary collection. The use of ItemsSource is examined further in Chapter 19, "Data Binding."

To keep things simple in this chapter and to focus on the controls themselves, the examples fill items controls with visual elements. This is a bit unrealistic, however, especially for large collections of items. The preferred approach is to give items controls nonvisual items (for example, custom business objects) and use data templates to define how each item gets rendered. Furthermore, using data binding (with the ItemsSource property) automatically enables richer items controls features automatically, such as item grouping. Chapter 19 discusses data templates, data binding, and features such as grouping.

Items Panels

The essence of items controls is not their visual appearance but rather their storage of multiple items and, for `Selectors`, the ways in which their items are logically selected. Although all XAML controls can be visually altered by applying a new control template, items controls have a shortcut for replacing just the piece of the control template responsible for arranging its items. This mini-template, called an *items panel*, enables you to swap out the panel used to arrange items while leaving everything else about the control intact. You can apply an items panel to any items control by settings its `ItemsPanel` property.

Conveniently, the panels used to arrange items within an items control are the same kind of panels used everywhere else (classes that derive from `Panel`). For example, a `ListBox` stacks its items vertically. Its default items panel is not quite a `StackPanel`, but rather a panel called **Virtualizing**StackPanel that adds support for UI virtualization. Therefore, the following XAML leverages the `ItemsPanel` property to replace the default arrangement with an explicit `VirtualizingStackPanel` that is told to stack its items horizontally instead:

```
<ListBox>
  <ListBox.ItemsPanel>
    <ItemsPanelTemplate>
      <VirtualizingStackPanel Orientation="Horizontal"/>
    </ItemsPanelTemplate>
  </ListBox.ItemsPanel>
  <ListBoxItem>one</ListBoxItem>
  <ListBoxItem>two</ListBoxItem>
  <ListBoxItem>three</ListBoxItem>
</ListBox>
```

You could use a simple `StackPanel` instead, but you would lose the UI virtualization support. For the most part, you can use all the panels discussed in Chapter 4, "Layout" (or any `Panel`-derived custom panel) as an items panel—except for one. `VariableSizedWrapGrid` contains logic that disallows its use as an items panel. That's because a closely related `WrapGrid` or `ItemsWrapGrid` is meant to be used as an items panel instead.

···

UI Virtualization

UI virtualization refers to the behavior of some panels that optimizes performance when filling an items control with a large number of data objects—not item containers such as `ListBoxItem`. Such panels wrap each item in an item container only when it is on-screen or almost on-screen. When the item moves far enough off-screen, the item container is recycled (able to be used by another item).

The XAML UI Framework ships five virtualizing panels: `VirtualizingStackPanel`, `ItemsStackPanel`, `WrapGrid`, `ItemsWrapGrid`, and `CarouselPanel`. None of these panels work for anything other than an items panel, and the latter three even restrict which controls are allowed to use them. `ItemsStackPanel` and `ItemsWrapGrid` are new to Windows 8.1. They are better versions of `VirtualizingStackPanel` and `WrapGrid`, and are used by `ListView` and `GridView`, respectively, to provide significant performance improvements compared to Windows 8.

How can I get WrapGrid or CarouselPanel to work?

These two panels often entice developers to give them a try, but they are misleading because they work only in limited situations. `WrapGrid`, which is just like `VariableSizedWrapGrid` but with the RowSpan and ColumnSpan features removed (and with UI virtualization support added), can be used as the items panel for controls deriving from `ListViewBase` only. For the built-in controls, that means `ListView` and `GridView` only. The same is true for `ItemsWrapGrid`, the version of `WrapGrid` with better UI virtualization support.

`CarouselPanel`, which supports wrap-around for an infinite scrolling effect, can currently be used as the items panel for `ComboBox` only. It also happens to be `ComboBox`'s default items panel. It enables the list of items to wrap around and provide an infinite scrolling experience, but only when there are enough items and only when touch is used.

Figure 11.2 demonstrates the effect of the preceding XAML that changes the `ListBox`'s item arrangement from vertical to horizontal, as well as a silly variation that uses `Grid` as the items panel.

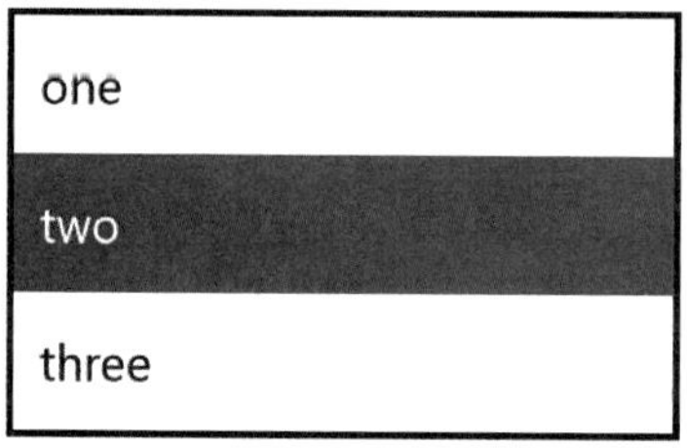

one

two

three

`<VirtualizingStackPanel/>` (default)

one   two   three

`<VirtualizingStackPanel Orientation="Horizontal"/>`

`<Grid/>`

FIGURE 11.2   The effect of various items panels on a simple `ListBox` whose second item is selected

Using <Grid/> as the items panel looks ridiculous because by default it has a single cell, and every item is placed inside it. (It gives the same result as using a Canvas, although you'd need to give the Canvas an explicit height for the inside of the ListBox to even be visible.)

You could, of course, configure the Grid with multiple rows and/or columns. If any items in the ListBox are marked with relevant attached properties, they get respected by the items panel. The following (only slightly less silly) update to the ListBox demonstrates this:

```
<ListBox>
  <ListBox.ItemsPanel>
    <ItemsPanelTemplate>
        <!-- Define a three-row, two-column Grid -->
      <Grid>
        <Grid.RowDefinitions>
          <RowDefinition/>
          <RowDefinition/>
          <RowDefinition/>
        </Grid.RowDefinitions>
        <Grid.ColumnDefinitions>
          <ColumnDefinition/>
          <ColumnDefinition/>
        </Grid.ColumnDefinitions>
      </Grid>
    </ItemsPanelTemplate>
  </ListBox.ItemsPanel>
  <ListBoxItem Grid.Row="2">one</ListBoxItem>
  <ListBoxItem Grid.Row="1" Grid.Column="1">two</ListBoxItem>
  <ListBoxItem>three</ListBoxItem>
</ListBox>
```

The result of applying this unusual items panel is shown in Figure 11.3.

It's worth pointing out that the theoretical elegance of mixing arbitrary Panels with arbitrary items controls does not get fully realized in practice. On the one side, the implementations of some Panels purposely restrict their uses at

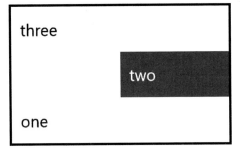

FIGURE 11.3   You can get creative with items panels.

run-time (such as `VariableSizedWrapGrid`, `WrapGrid`, and `CarouselPanel`). On the other side, the implementations of many items controls make assumptions based on their default items panel that don't always play nicely with other `Panel`s. The simple `ListBox` control is the shining example of flexibility. It works perfectly with any `Panel` (even custom ones) as long as the `Panel` itself doesn't purposely restrict its use. That's because `ListBox`'s implementation makes no assumptions about the arrangement of its items. Every other built-in items control, however, acts strangely if you customize its items panel in certain ways. That's because they provide much richer modes of interaction that exploit characteristics of their default items panels.

ComboBox

Now let's look at each items control, one by one. The `ComboBox` control, shown in Figure 11.4 from the following XAML, enables users to select one item from a list:

```
<ComboBox>
  <ComboBoxItem>Small</ComboBoxItem>
  <ComboBoxItem>Medium</ComboBoxItem>
  <ComboBoxItem>Large</ComboBoxItem>
</ComboBox>
```

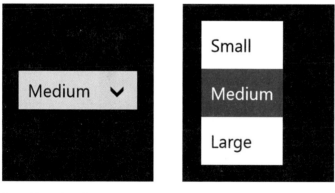

Drop-down closed   Drop-down opened

FIGURE 11.4 The `ComboBox` fits the selection of an item into a small space.

`ComboBox` is a popular control because it doesn't occupy much space. It displays the current selection in a *selection box*, with the rest of the list shown on demand in a *drop-down*. The drop-down can be opened and closed by tapping the control or by pressing Alt+up arrow, Alt+down arrow, or F4 when it has focus. Even when closed, the user can use the up and down arrow keys to change the current selection. When manipulated with touch, the list of items wraps around if there are more than nine, thanks to its use of `CarouselPanel`.

The *drop-down*'s name (much like the downward pointing arrow) is a historical artifact, because it doesn't always drop *downward*. Space permitting, ComboBox attempts to position the list of items such that the selected item stays in the same spot. In Figure 11.4, it would expand upward if "Large" was already selected, or downward if "Small" was selected. (This logic is unfortunately specific to the default items panel's appearance, so changing it can make the drop-down's position look strange.) The drop-down gets only so tall before resorting to scrolling, and this is controllable via the MaxDropDownHeight property.

Starting in Windows 8.1, ComboBox has a Header property that enables you to place custom UI on top, such as a title. The property is of type Object, and it can be used just like the Content property of a content control. This is usually set to a simple string, but it could be set to a UIElement or used in conjunction with the HeaderTemplate property (see Chapter 18, "Styles, Templates, and Visual States"). For example, the following XAML is shown in Figure 11.5:

```
<ComboBox Header="Size">
  <ComboBoxItem>Small</ComboBoxItem>
  <ComboBoxItem>Medium</ComboBoxItem>
  <ComboBoxItem>Large</ComboBoxItem>
</ComboBox>
```

In Windows 8.1, ComboBox also has a PlaceholderText property that can be set to any watermark string. This text appears in the selection box, but only when no item is selected.

ComboBox defines two events—DropDownOpened and DropDownClosed—and a property—IsDropDownOpen—that enable you to act on the drop-down being opened or closed. For example, you can delay the filling of ComboBox items until the drop-down is opened by handling the DropDownOpened event. Note that IsDropDownOpen is a read/write property, so you can set it directly to change the state of the drop-down.

FIGURE 11.5   ComboBox's Header property makes it easy to create standard forms.

How do I make ComboBox *editable*, so the user can type a new value into it?

You can't. ComboBox defines an IsEditable property for some amount of compatibility with WPF and Silverlight, but it is read-only and always returns false. You could construct a custom control that provides such an experience by using a TextBox and an associated MenuFlyout. Or, you could rely on a third-party control like Telerik's ComboBox (http://telerik.com) that acts more like the classic editable variety.

> **How do I make ComboBox respond to keystrokes so the user can type to jump to a specific item?**
>
> This functionality is not provided automatically. You would need to handle keystrokes yourself and adjust the current selection accordingly (or rely on a third-party control). Keep in mind that ComboBox can contain non-textual items, so your logic might need to account for that.

> **When the SelectionChanged event gets raised, how do I get the new selection?**
>
> The SelectionChanged event is designed to handle controls that allow multiple selections, so it can be a little confusing for a single-selection selector such as ComboBox. The SelectionChangedEventArgs type passed to event handlers has two properties of type IList<object>: AddedItems and RemovedItems. AddedItems contains the new selection, and RemovedItems contains the previous selection. You can retrieve a new single selection as follows:
>
> ```
> void ComboBox_SelectionChanged(object sender, SelectionChangedEventArgs e)
> {
>   object newSelection = (e.AddedItems.Count > 0) ? e.AddedItems[0] : null;
>   …
> }
> ```
>
> And, like this code, you should never assume that there's a selected item. Although a user has no way to clear a ComboBox's selection, it can be cleared programmatically.

ListBox

The familiar ListBox control, shown in Figure 11.1, is similar to ComboBox except that all items are displayed directly within the control's bounds, or you can scroll to view additional items if they don't all fit. The most important feature of ListBox is that it can support multiple simultaneous selections. This is controllable via the SelectionMode property, which accepts three values (from a SelectionMode enumeration):

→ **Single**—Only one item can be selected at a time, just like with ComboBox. This is the default value.

→ **Multiple**—Any number of items can be selected simultaneously. Tapping an unselected item adds it to ListBox's SelectedItems collection, and tapping a selected item removes it from the collection. This behavior can be annoying if single-selection is the norm, because changing the selection is a two-step process.

➔ **Extended**—Any number of items can be selected simultaneously, but the behavior is optimized for the single selection case. To select multiple items in this mode, you must hold down Shift (for contiguous items) or Ctrl (for noncontiguous items) while tapping. Note that there is no provision for multiselect in this mode without a keyboard.

Other than the SelectionMode property, ListBox defines a SelectedItems property to support multiselect, a SelectAll method, and a handy ScrollIntoView method that ensures that the passed-in item from its Items collection is visible.

ListBox Properties and Multiple Selection   • • •

Although ListBox has a SelectedItems property that can be used no matter which SelectionMode is used, it still inherits the SelectedIndex, SelectedItem, and SelectedValue properties from Selector that don't fit in with the multiselect model.

When multiple items are selected, SelectedItem points to the first item in the SelectedItems collection (which is the item selected the earliest by the user), and SelectedIndex and SelectedValue give the index and value for that item. But it's best not to use these properties on a control that supports multiple selections. Note that ListBox does *not* define a SelectedIndices or SelectedValues property.

(?) How do I get the items in my items control to have automation IDs, as seen in UI Automation tools?

The easiest way to give any FrameworkElement an automation ID is to set its Name property, because that is used by default for automation purposes. However, if you want to give an element an ID that is different from its name, set the AutomationProperties.AutomationId attached property to the desired string.

The default visual tree for ListBox contains a ScrollViewer, which means you can set some ScrollViewer attached properties on ListBox to impact its behavior. For example, you can enable pinch-and-stretch zooming of its inner content as follows:

```
<ListBox ScrollViewer.ZoomMode="Enabled">
  …
</ListBox>
```

ListView

You can think of `ListView` as a "fancy `ListBox`" optimized for touch and the style of Windows Store apps. Probably the most important difference is the addition of cross slide gesture support for selection—although you can turn that off by setting `IsSwipeEnabled` to `false`. (`IsSwipeEnabled` should have been called `IsCrossSlideEnabled` for consistency with the gesture recognizer.)

Several visual differences are also noticeable compared to `ListBox`. In a `ListView`, items animate in initially, items have a shrink-on-press effect, the margins are different, the selection highlight includes a checkmark, and so on. Figure 11.6 demonstrates these differences using the same `Rectangle` elements as items in both. Note that the background of `ListView` is `Transparent` by default, so the dark color in Figure 11.6 is coming from a parent.

ListBox   ListView

FIGURE 11.6   `ListView` has a number of visual differences compared to `ListBox`.

The odd-looking margin to the right of the `ListView` selection highlight is there for the scrollbar that appears under the right conditions. Unlike in `ListBox`, the selection highlight doesn't extend underneath the scrollbar so the checkmark remains unobscured.

The selection highlight includes a border that overlaps a small amount of the selected item. You can't see its shape in Figure 11.6 because the squares aren't as wide as the ListView, but Figure 11.7 shows its style. It looks exactly like the selection highlight used in the Start screen, file picker, and other Windows-provided UI. As Figure 11.6 reveals, its size is based on the size of the item in the stacking dimension and the size of the ListView in the perpendicular direction.

FIGURE 11.7   The ListView selection highlight is consistent with signature Windows user interfaces, such as the Start screen.

As with ListBox, ListView exposes SelectionMode and SelectedItems properties (the latter to handle multiselect), as well as SelectAll and ScrollIntoView methods. It has many additional features, however, some big and some small. Two small ones are richer ScrollIntoView functionality and support for a header and footer. Four big ones are its selection behavior, item reordering, data virtualization, and incremental item rendering.

Richer ScrollIntoView

ListView has two overloads of ScrollIntoView: the one-parameter version that matches ListBox's version, and one that accepts an extra ScrollIntoViewAlignment enumeration parameter. This provides two options:

→ **Default**—The control scrolls the minimal distance necessary to put the item entirely on the screen. Therefore, if the item is already on the screen, the control won't scroll at all. This provides the same behavior as the simpler overload and the same behavior as ListBox.

→ **Leading**—The control scrolls as much as necessary to make the item the **first** one visible (or as close as possible if there aren't enough items following it). That means the top edge when scrolling vertically, or the left edge when scrolling horizontally (via a custom items panel).

Header and Footer

Like ComboBox, ListView has a Header property of type Object. It also has a Footer property of type Object. These could be set to simple strings, UIElements, or used in conjunction with HeaderTemplate and FooterTemplate properties.

This header (and footer) work differently than the way the header works with ComboBox. Rather than remaining in a stationary position, the header and footer scroll along with the content. Therefore, these properties provide a way to inject a special first and/or last element in the list that doesn't participate in selection.

Selection

In addition to supporting cross-slide selection (when IsSwipeEnabled is left at its default value of true), which applies only to touch input, ListView also supports selection via right tap. Recall that a right tap can not only be done by a mouse or pen, but by a press-and-hold touch gesture as well.

ListView's SelectionMode property is a bit different from ListBox's. The ListView property is of type **ListView**SelectionMode, which adds a None value to the typical Single, Multiple, and Extended options. The default SelectionMode is Single, as with ListBox. When the SelectionMode is None, no item ever gets selected by user input, although the items can still get focus, as shown in Figure 11.8.

FIGURE 11.8   Although no items get selected in a ListView with SelectionMode=None, the second item has focus (and the corresponding focus rectangle).

Although items can be selected programmatically on a ListView with a SelectionMode=None, such items never get rendered with the selection highlight, so the value of doing such a thing is dubious.

The behavior of the Multiple versus Extended SelectionMode is more subtle for ListView than it is for ListBox, but the result is more useful. The behavior is the same as ListBox for the selection gestures shared by both: simple taps and keyboard navigation. However, the ListView-specific selection gestures act in a Multiple fashion even when Extended is used. Although tapping and using arrow keys when SelectionMode=Extended acts in a single-select fashion unless the Shift or Ctrl key is held down, right taps and cross slides toggle the selection state of the relevant item. This means that the use of SelectionMode=Extended gives a traditional multiselect experience (optimized for single selection) when traditional gestures are used, but gives a modern multiselect experience (optimized for multiple selections) when newer gestures are used.

In addition to the normal selection concept enabled by the SelectionChanged event, ListView supports Button-style clicking of its items via a pointer tap or the Enter key (but no spacebar). You must opt into this mode by setting IsItemClickEnabled to true. (Unlike IsSwipeEnabled, it is false by default.) If you do so, pointer taps and Enter key presses no longer affect the current selection. Instead of raising SelectionChanged, they raise an ItemClick event. All the other selection gestures (including pressing the space bar) still affect selection according to the current SelectionMode.

> **Because ListView handles right taps, one with focus prevents those right taps from toggling any app bars!**
>
> However, because it is customary to show a bottom app bar (with context-specific buttons) whenever an item is selected, this will not be a problem if you explicitly toggle the app bar's IsOpen property in the SelectionChanged event handler. Regardless of how the selection change happens, you should show it if there are any selected items and hide it otherwise.

So why would you enable this "item clicking" concept in addition to selection? As weird as it might sound at first, this basically describes the behavior of the Start screen. Normal clicking of a tile doesn't *select* it; it launches the app! Selection of the items, used for tasks such as unpinning or uninstalling an app, is a relatively rare user action reserved for the extended gestures.

Reordering Items

Seemingly by magic, ListView contains automatic support for drag-and-drop reordering of items, much like on the Start screen. As you drag an item around, the other items even move around to get out of the way! This is pictured in Figure 11.9. Just like with the Start screen, dragging starts instantly for mouse or pen, but for touch the drag must start perpendicular to the panning direction to avoid confusion with the typical panning gesture. This can work end-to-end without any of your own C# code, although ListView does have a DragItemStarting event in case you want to add custom behavior.

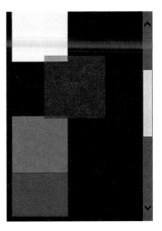

FIGURE 11.9   Dragging the red square to a new spot in the ListView works automatically, but you must explicitly enable this mode.

There's a trick for getting this to work, however. You must set all of the following three properties to true:

```
<ListView CanDragItems="True" CanReorderItems="True" AllowDrop="True">
```

With AllowDrop set to true, you can even drag and drop one of the items from the ListView to a different element.

> **?** **When should I use a ListView?**
>
> You should use ListView for full-featured lists in which space is constrained, such as a side pane, or for the main content when your window is resized to be too small for reasonable horizontal panning. Otherwise, GridView provides the best use of screen real estate.

Data Virtualization

ListView also contains support for *data virtualization*, but that requires data binding, so it is discussed in Chapter 19. Unlike UI virtualization, which is the process of constructing the item containers on-demand, data virtualization is the practice of constructing the underlying items on-demand as well. This can not only be vital for large collections, but modest-sized ones that are slow to retrieve (typically because the source data is online).

Incremental Item Rendering

Incremental item rendering improves the performance of rendering a lot of items, which can greatly improve the experience of scrolling through a long list. When there's not enough time to completely render new items that enter the screen in a given frame, you can prioritize the rendering of the individual elements that make up each item. That way, every item can be at least partially rendered, rather than having only a few items completely rendered and the rest not rendered at all. Taking advantage of this feature involves the use of data templates, so it is covered in Chapter 19 as well.

GridView

If you are familiar with ListView, then you're already familiar with GridView, because it's effectively just a ListView with a different layout that wraps its items into additional columns. ListView and GridView both derive from a class called ListViewBase, and every API discussed in the preceding section actually belongs to ListViewBase! Both ListView and GridView add zero public APIs to their base class besides a default constructor. Therefore, you can think of ListView as nothing more than a ListViewBase with an ItemsStackPanel items panel, and you can think of GridView as nothing more than a ListViewBase with an ItemsWrapGrid items panel. The reality is a bit more complicated, however, because the two classes have different implementation details that rely on their own default items panels.

Because all the behaviors of GridView are covered by the preceding section, this section highlights GridView's visuals. Figure 11.10 compares GridView to ListView using the same Rectangles from Figure 11.6 that compared ListView to ListBox.

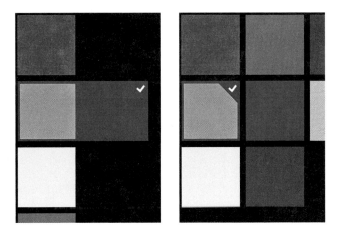

ListView   GridView

FIGURE 11.10   ListView and GridView differ only by the arrangement of their items.

GridView items are stacked vertically, just like in ListView. However, due to the wrapping, the default scrolling/panning direction is horizontal rather than vertical. If the items are not all the same size, the space of the largest item is given to every item. This is demonstrated in Figure 11.11, which contains a red Rectangle that is taller than the rest.

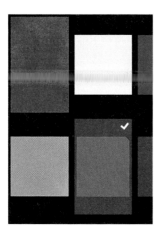

FIGURE 11.11   Every item is given the same amount of space—the size of the largest one.

The automatic item reordering (when you set CanDragItems, CanReorderItems, and AllowDrop to true) works just as well for GridView, as shown in Figure 11.12.

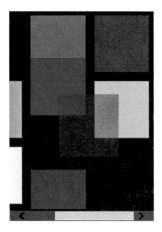

FIGURE 11.12   Drag-and-drop item reordering works seamlessly.

> As with any item arrangement done horizontally, setting FlowDirection to RightToLeft reverses the default behavior. This causes GridView's items to start on the right and wrap toward the left.

FlipView

Despite the similar-sounding name, FlipView has nothing to do with ListView or GridView. It is designed to show only one item at a time, enabling the user to "flip" through items just like flipping pages in a book. Its items are automatically arranged with appropriate margins and snap points to make this work. This control is ideal for any kind of "help" documentation in your app, where each item in the control is a page of text.

FlipView derives directly from Selector and adds no public APIs other than its constructor and a UseTouchAnimationsForAllNavigation property that can be set to false to turn off its animations for mouse, pen, and keyboard input. This means that, unlike the previous three controls, this doesn't enable multiselect. The single selection is the item that is currently visible inside the control.

FlipView automatically supports a number of gestures for navigating its items:

→ With touch, you can swipe back and forth. If you tap (or press and hold) the control, back and/or forward buttons appear that you can tap instead.

→ With a mouse or pen, you can tap the forward and back buttons that appear on hover or when the control has focus.

→ With a keyboard, you can use the left and right arrow keys (or the up and down arrow keys) to navigate back and forward, respectively.

Figures 11.13 and 11.14 illustrate the sequence of flipping from the first item to the second item using two different input techniques. These figures use the same Rectangle items from previous examples. The animated transition in Figure 11.14 can be removed by setting UseTouchAnimationsForAllNavigation to false.

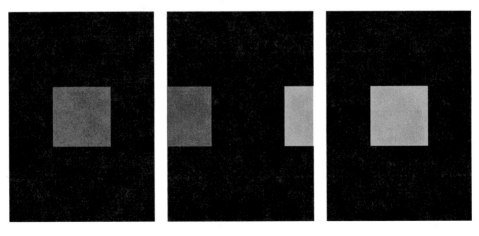

Initial selection   During the swipe   New selection

FIGURE 11.13   Flipping from the red to orange square with a swipe

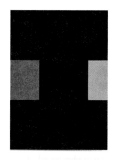

Initial selection   Got focus   During the transition

New selection   Lost focus

FIGURE 11.14   Flipping from the red to orange square with the forward button

You can make a `FlipView` flip vertically rather than horizontally by applying a `StackPanel` (or `VirtualizingStackPanel` or `ItemsStackPanel`) with its default `Vertical Orientation`. The back and forward buttons even render appropriately for this configuration, as shown in Figure 11.15. Furthermore, because the up and down arrow keys are already treated the same way as the left and right arrow keys, keyboard input works naturally as well.

FIGURE 11.15   With a vertically stacking items panel, `FlipView` does all the right things.

SemanticZoom

Whenever this book talks about *zooming*, it's referring to basic optical zooming. *Semantic zooming*, on the other hand, refers to a type of zooming that doesn't necessarily preserve the appearance of the content. Instead, zooming out involves switching to a higher-level view of the content that's more useful for navigating it "at a distance."

The Windows shell exposes semantic zooming in several important places, such as the Start screen, the apps list, the file picker, and the contact picker. Many apps, such as the Photos app, expose it as well. In all cases, there are two distinct views to zoom between. Figure 11.16 shows the two views for the file picker. The zoomed-in view is the default view that shows every file and subfolder in the current folder. The zoomed-out view shows only groupings (one per letter plus a few more). Zooming is done with the same pinch or stretch touch gesture used for optical zooming, although it can also be done with either the mouse wheel or +/- keys while holding down the Ctrl key.

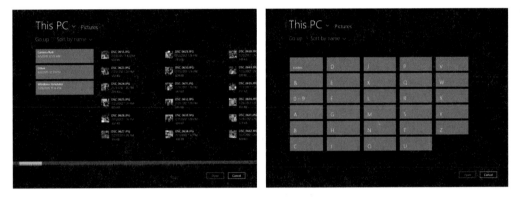

Zoomed-in view   Zoomed-out view

FIGURE 11.16   The Windows file picker uses semantic zoom to great effect.

In contrast, the Start screen's semantic zooming looks similar to an optical zoom, but in the zoomed-out view the tiles are rendered more simply, group names aren't scaled proportionally (so they can still be read easily), and the functionality changes. Instead of being able to manage individual tiles and launch apps, the zoomed-out view enables rearranging groups of tiles.

In both examples, the target action (such as selecting a file or launching an app) cannot be done from the zoomed-out view. Its primary purpose is to provide a quick way to jump to a spot in the zoomed-in view without requiring a lot of scrolling.

For XAML apps, the `SemanticZoom` control provides the infrastructure to expose the same two-level semantic zooming functionality automatically. It has two properties—`ZoomedInView` and `ZoomedOutView`—representing the two different views. `SemanticZoom` is not an items control, but each view must be an object implementing an interface called `ISemanticZoomInformation`. And there are only two classes in the XAML UI Framework that implement this interface: `ListViewBase` and `Hub`. Therefore, the only built-in controls you can use with it are `ListView`, `GridView`, and `Hub` (covered in Chapter 15, "Other Controls").

The following XAML is a simple example of how you could populate the two views of `SemanticZoom`:

```
<SemanticZoom ViewChangeStarted="SemanticZoom_ViewChangeStarted">
  <!-- The default zoomed-in view -->
  <SemanticZoom.ZoomedInView>
    <GridView x:Name="Numbers">
      <GridViewItem>1</GridViewItem>
      <GridViewItem>2</GridViewItem>
      <GridViewItem>3</GridViewItem>
      <GridViewItem>4</GridViewItem>
      <GridViewItem>5</GridViewItem>
      ...
      <GridViewItem>300</GridViewItem>
    </GridView>
  </SemanticZoom.ZoomedInView>

  <!-- The zoomed-out view -->
  <SemanticZoom.ZoomedOutView>
    <ListView>
      <ListViewItem x:Name="Group1">1-100</ListViewItem>
      <ListViewItem x:Name="Group2">101-200</ListViewItem>
      <ListViewItem x:Name="Group3">201-300</ListViewItem>
    </ListView>
  </SemanticZoom.ZoomedOutView>
</SemanticZoom>
```

The zoomed-in view contains the numbers 1-300, and the zoomed-out view merges the items into groups of 100. Both `GridView` and `ListView` are used for demonstration purposes. `GridView` is almost always the most appropriate for the large number of zoomed-in items, and in this case the number of zoomed-out items is small enough to make the choice irrelevant.

This simple XAML is almost all we need. The views animate in and out appropriately based on the standard gestures, and selecting an item in the zoomed-out view automatically transitions back to the zoomed-in view. The one thing that's missing is the ability to keep the two views in sync. For example, when the user selects "101-200" in the zoomed-out view, it should cause the zoomed-in view to scroll to the 101st item. With this XAML alone, however, the zoomed-in view doesn't scroll unless the user scrolls it. That's because the `SemanticZoom` control doesn't understand the *semantics* of the zoomed-out `ListViewItems`.

This can be remedied by writing some code to manually keep the views in sync. `SemanticZoom` exposes both `ViewChangeStarted` and `ViewChangeCompleted` events, so the following `ViewChangeStarted` event handler (already attached in the preceding XAML) updates the zoomed-in view immediately before each transition from zoomed-out to zoomed-in:

```
void SemanticZoom_ViewChangeStarted(object sender,
                                    SemanticZoomViewChangedEventArgs e)
{
  if (e.IsSourceZoomedInView)
  {
    // Do nothing special when zooming out
  }
  else
  {
    // Potentially scroll the zoomed-in view before zooming in
    ListViewItem item = e.SourceItem.Item as ListViewItem;
    if (item == Group1)
    {
      Nums.ScrollIntoView(Nums.Items[0], ScrollIntoViewAlignment.Leading);
    }
    else if (item == Group2)
    {
      Nums.ScrollIntoView(Nums.Items[100], ScrollIntoViewAlignment.Leading);
    }
    else
    {
      Nums.ScrollIntoView(Nums.Items[200], ScrollIntoViewAlignment.Leading);
    }
  }
}
```

Notice that the overload of `ScrollIntoView` is used to enable the `Leading` alignment option (described previously in the "`ListView`" section). This is the appropriate choice for semantic zooming because it matches user expectations of what it means to jump to a specific spot in the list. Notice also that the selected item that triggered the view change is buried in an `Item` subproperty of `SemanticZoomViewChangedEventArgs.SourceItem`. The `SourceItem` property (of type `SemanticZoomLocation`) also includes a `Bounds` property (of type `Rect`), which can be helpful for advanced customizations of the transition or the resultant view.

In the zoomed-in view, `SemanticZoom` automatically shows a little minus `Button` that acts much like the one at the end of the scrollbar when the Windows uses semantic zoom in its own user interfaces. However, unlike in Windows, it is placed above the scrollbar and visible even when the scrollbar is not. If you want to replace this `Button` with your own custom user interface, you can disable it by setting `SemanticZoom`'s `IsZoomOutButtonEnabled` property to `false`. You should be sure to have something equivalent if you do this. The `Button` not only serves as a handy shortcut, but it's a powerful cue that informs the user that zooming is possible for the current content.

> ⚠ **Don't wrap `SemanticZoom` in a `ScrollViewer` (with the same scrolling direction)!**
>
> As always, make sure that a control that is meant to contain scrollable content is itself properly constrained in size. Otherwise, its own content might never scroll. This can impact programmatic scrolling with `ScrollIntoView` in a subtle and confusing way, and `SemanticZoom` is often the motivation for using `ScrollIntoView`.
>
> If `SemanticZoom` is placed in a `ScrollViewer` that scrolls in the same orientation as `SemanticZoom`'s two views, then `SemanticZoom` is given infinite space in the direction scrolling and its views never scroll. This makes all `ScrollIntoView` calls no ops. However, *user-driven* scrolling still appears to work just fine because the *parent* `ScrollViewer` translates the entire `SemanticZoom` control!

MenuFlyout

As the preceding chapter pointed out, both `Flyout` and `MenuFlyout` derive from `FlyoutBase`. Rather than a `Content` property, `MenuFlyout` has an `Items` property. However, unlike items controls, this `Items` property is a collection of `MenuFlyoutItemBase` controls. Therefore, you can only put the following types of built-in controls inside a `MenuFlyout`:

→ **MenuFlyoutItem**—Looks like a standard menu item and acts like a `Button`. Like `Button`, it has a `Click` event and `Command`/`CommandParameter` properties for supporting the loosely-coupled commanding pattern. It is not able to host generic content, however. Instead, its content property is a string property called `Text`.

→ **ToggleMenuFlyoutItem**—Derives from `MenuFlyoutItem` and adds an `IsChecked` property. `IsChecked` is a simple Boolean value, so there's no support for an indeterminate state. It also has no event triggered by the value of `IsChecked` changing. Clicking the item toggles `IsChecked`, so you can check its value in a handler for its `Click` event.

→ **MenuFlyoutSeparator**—Used to visually separate groups of items. It defines no members beyond what it inherits from `Control`.

Figure 11.17 demonstrates a `MenuFlyout` containing all three types of items by attaching it to a `Button` as follows:

```
<Button Content="Show MenuFlyout">
  <Button.Flyout>
    <MenuFlyout>
      <MenuFlyoutItem>One</MenuFlyoutItem>
      <MenuFlyoutItem>Two</MenuFlyoutItem>
      <MenuFlyoutSeparator/>
      <ToggleMenuFlyoutItem IsChecked="True">Three</ToggleMenuFlyoutItem>
    </MenuFlyout>
  </Button.Flyout>
</Button>
```

FIGURE 11.17   The MenuFlyout provides a traditional context menu experience.

Summary

Items controls are vital to understand for just about any XAML app. It's hard to imagine a nontrivial XAML app that doesn't use both content controls and items controls. Unlike content controls, however, there's a lot to learn about items controls! A recurring theme throughout this chapter is the importance of data binding if you're working with a sizable or dynamic list of items. Therefore, items controls will be revisited when it's time to examine data binding in depth.

Chapter 12

TEXT

You've seen TextBlock a number of times in this book, but it's not the only text control available. It also is a much richer control than most people expect. This chapter covers the two "blocks"—TextBlock and RichTextBlock—designed for displaying text, and the analogous two "boxes"—TextBox and RichEditBox—designed for displaying *and editing* text. It also examines the special-purpose PasswordBox that should be used if you ever need to ask the user for a password.

TextBlock

TextBlock contains a number of simple properties for modifying its font: FontFamily, FontSize, FontStyle, FontWeight, and FontStretch. The behaviors of several of these are dependent on characteristics of the font family in use. For example, FontStretch can be set to one of ten enumeration values ranging from UltraCondensed (50% of Normal) to UltraExpanded (200% of Normal) but unless such variations are installed as part of the font family, setting these has no effect. Similarly, the type of the FontWeight property is a funny FontWeight structure with a single double field, but most fonts support only two weights (normal or bold). To simplify the use of FontWeight, the Windows Runtime exposes a FontWeights class with public static fields of appropriately initialized FontWeight instances. There are eleven possible choices, such as Normal, SemiBold, Bold, ExtraBold, Light, SemiLight, and so on.

Independent of the font, TextBlock enables a number of modifications to the way it renders text. The obvious one is the Foreground property that represents the text color, but here are the others:

> If you include a custom font file as content in your app's package, you can reference it with a FontFamily URI such as *RelativePath/FontFile*.ttf#*FontName*.

→ **TextAlignment**—Can be set to Left (the default), Center, Right, or Justify.

→ **TextTrimming**—What should happen to text that doesn't fit within the TextBlock's horizontal bounds. Can be set to None (the default), Clip, WordEllipsis, or CharacterEllipsis. None leaves the text alone, and Clip truncates it at a pixel level, whereas the other two options place an ellipsis at the end. With WordEllipsis, the ellipsis is placed only at the end of whole words, meaning a word is never partially rendered when WordEllipsis is used, with the exception of the first word. If the TextBlock isn't big enough to fit the first whole word, then it will render as many letters as it can in order to make the letters plus the ellipses fit. (And if there's no room for even a single letter plus the ellipsis, it will still render them and allow them to be truncated.) CharacterEllipsis, a new option for Windows 8.1, places an ellipsis after the last full character that fits, regardless of whether it breaks up a word.

→ **TextWrapping**—Controls whether text can wrap onto additional lines. Can be set to NoWrap (the default), Wrap, or WrapWholeWords. WrapWholeWords is a new option as of Windows 8.1. Whereas Wrap breaks up a word at a letter boundary when it doesn't fit (such as for a word longer than the width of the TextBlock), WrapWholeWords refuses to break up any word. Instead, it allows it to be truncated or trimmed at the edge of the TextBlock, depending on the value of TextTrimming.

→ **CharacterSpacing**—The amount of extra space between characters (0 by default) measured in thousandths of an em. (One *em* equals the current FontSize, so em measurements are always relative.) This can be set to a negative value to push letters closer together.

→ **LineHeight**—The height of each line, measured in logical pixels, when TextWrapping is set to enable wrapping. The line height is normally determined automatically, so this property is relevant only when a separate LineStackingStrategy property is set to BlockLineHeight (which means, "respect the LineHeight property value"). At LineHeight's default value of 0, the setting is ignored.

→ Several more properties are covered in the "New Properties in Windows 8.1" section: **MaxLines**, **TextLineBounds**, **OpticalMarginAlignment**, **TextReadingOrder**, and **IsColorFontEnabled**.

Figure 12.1 demonstrates various `CharacterSpacing` values with the following XAML:

```
<StackPanel>
  <TextBlock … CharacterSpacing="-100">SPACING=-100</TextBlock>
  <TextBlock …>SPACING=DEFAULT</TextBlock>
  <TextBlock … CharacterSpacing="100">SPACING=100</TextBlock>
  <TextBlock … CharacterSpacing="500">SPACING=500</TextBlock>
</StackPanel>
```

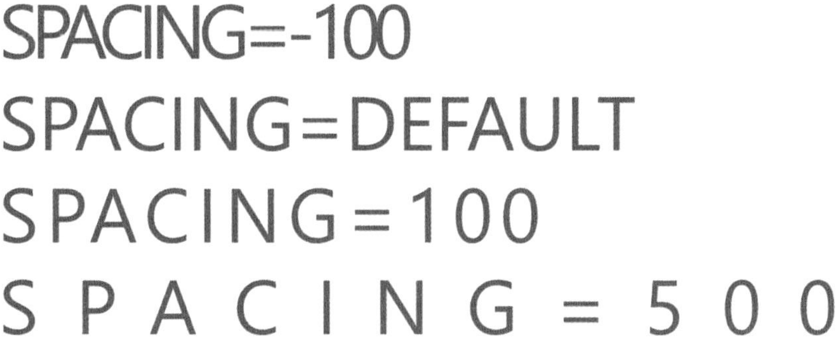

SPACING=-100
SPACING=DEFAULT
SPACING=100
S P A C I N G = 5 0 0

FIGURE 12.1   Using `CharacterSpacing` to adjust the horizontal spacing of text

Figure 12.2 demonstrates a custom `LineHeight` with the following TextBlock:

```
<TextBlock FontSize="100" Width="900" FontWeight="Bold" Foreground="Purple"
  TextWrapping="Wrap" LineStackingStrategy="BlockLineHeight" LineHeight="60">
  THE FONT SIZE IS 100 BUT THE LINE HEIGHT IS 60!
</TextBlock>
```

THE FONT SIZE IS 100 BUT THE LINE HEIGHT IS 60!

FIGURE 12.2   Using `LineHeight` to adjust the vertical spacing of text

Because `CharacterSpacing` and `LineHeight` are numeric dependency properties, you can even animate their values using the techniques from Chapter 17, "Animation."

New Properties in Windows 8.1

As mentioned in the list of properties, five are new to Windows 8.1:

➔ **MaxLines**—Limits the number of lines rendered. The default value of 0 means "no limit."

→ **TextLineBounds**—Customizes the automatic height of each line when TextWrapping is set to enable wrapping. This gives you a lot of customization of line height without resorting to specifying a hardcoded LineHeight value.

→ **OpticalMarginAlignment**—Can be set to TrimSideBearings instead of the default value of None to remove extra horizontal space inherent to the font. This is critical for horizontally aligning text of different sizes without resorting to hacks.

→ **TextReadingOrder**—Can be set to DetectFromContent instead of the default value of Default. This detects the flow direction from the text rather than relying on the FlowDirection property.

→ **IsColorFontEnabled**—Can be set to false to disable the new support for multicolor font glyphs.

TextLineBounds

TextLineBounds can be set to one of four values from the TextLineBounds enumeration. The descriptions of these values use terms demonstrated in Figure 12.3:

→ **Full**—Gives each line the full vertical height possible (from *full top* to *full bottom*). This is the default value.

→ **TrimToBaseline**—Gives each line the height from *full top* to *baseline*.

→ **TrimToCapHeight**—Gives each line the height from *cap height* to *full bottom*.

→ **Tight**—Gives each line the height from *cap height* to *baseline*. This height is the intersection of TrimToBaseline and TrimToCapHeight and is the smallest option.

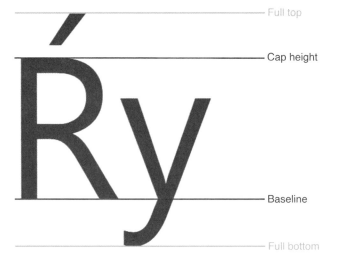

FIGURE 12.3   The meaning of the Full Top, Cap Height, Baseline, and Full Bottom terms

Therefore, Figure 12.4 demonstrates these four TextLineBounds options on the sample Ŕy text using the following XAML:

```
<StackPanel Orientation="Horizontal" Background="Yellow">
  <TextBlock FontSize="100" Foreground="Blue" TextWrapping="Wrap" Width="120"
          TextLineBounds="Full">Ŕy Ŕy</TextBlock>
  <TextBlock FontSize="100" Foreground="Blue" TextWrapping="Wrap" Width="120"
          TextLineBounds="TrimToBaseline">Ŕy Ŕy</TextBlock>
  <TextBlock FontSize="100" Foreground="Blue" TextWrapping="Wrap" Width="120"
          TextLineBounds="TrimToCapHeight">Ŕy Ŕy</TextBlock>
  <TextBlock FontSize="100" Foreground="Blue" TextWrapping="Wrap" Width="120"
          TextLineBounds="Tight">Ŕy Ŕy</TextBlock>
</StackPanel>
```

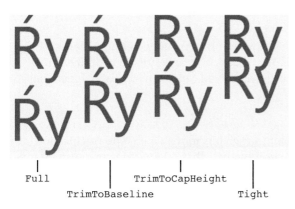

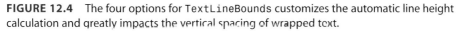

FIGURE 12.4   The four options for TextLineBounds customizes the automatic line height calculation and greatly impacts the vertical spacing of wrapped text.

OpticalMarginAlignment

Getting different-sized text inside TextBlocks to line up on their left edge has traditionally been a big pain, requiring manual margin adjustments to get the desired visual effect. That's because font glyphs have some inherent space on their sides (*"side bearings"*), and this space gets scaled along with the glyphs when you increase the font size. And yet, Windows Store apps often try to horizontally align text of different sizes, such as with a title and subtitle on a page.

This is why Windows 8.1 introduces the OpticalMarginAlignment property that can get rid of these side bearings that cause text alignment to look incorrect. Figure 12.5 demonstrates this by rendering the following StackPanel with and without the OpticalMarginAlignment setting on the two TextBlocks:

```
<StackPanel Background="Yellow">
  <TextBlock FontSize="100" OpticalMarginAlignment="TrimSideBearings"
          Foreground="Blue">Page Title</TextBlock>
  <TextBlock FontSize="40" OpticalMarginAlignment="TrimSideBearings"
          Foreground="Blue">Page Subtitle</TextBlock>
</StackPanel>
```

Page Title Page Title
Page Subtitle   Page Subtitle

Without `TrimSideBearings`   With `TrimSideBearings`

FIGURE 12.1   Setting `OpticalMarginAlignment` to `TrimSideBearings` makes all text crisply align to the left margin of the parent `StackPanel`.

TextReadingOrder

The *reading order* of text (left-to-right or right-to-left) is normally determined by the `FlowDirection` property set on either the `TextBlock` or an ancestor element. By setting `TextReadingOrder` to `DetectFromContent`, however, you can let the actual bidirectional text dictate the proper order.

IsColorFontEnabled

Microsoft has added support for multicolor font glyphs to the OpenType specification, motivated by the popular (and colorful) *emoji* symbols that originated from Japan. Many of these symbols are emoticons, but they also include hearts, holiday-themed pictures, musical instruments, and much more. It's worth noting that this support is vector-based, unlike the bitmap-based emoji support in Apple's and Google's operating systems. Windows 8.1 also comes with a font containing emoji in full color, called Segoe UI Emoji.

In Windows 8.1, `TextBlock` supports multicolor fonts by default, although you can turn it off by setting `IsColorFontEnabled` to `false`. Figure 12.6 demonstrates this with the following two `TextBlock`s:

```
<StackPanel>
  <TextBlock Name="colorTextBlock" FontFamily="Segoe UI Emoji" FontSize="100"/>
  <TextBlock Name="plainTextBlock" FontFamily="Segoe UI Emoji" FontSize="100"
          IsColorFontEnabled="False"/>
</StackPanel>
```

FIGURE 12.6   The bottom `TextBlock` has `IsColorFontEnabled` set to `false`, causing the emoji to be rendered in a single-color style matching the `TextBlock`'s `Foreground`.

Because the emoji glyphs are assigned unusual character codes, these two TextBlocks have their Text assigned in code-behind:

```
// Fill the string with 15 consecutive emoji
string emoji = "";
for (int charCode = 0x1F600; charCode < 0x1F60F; charCode++)
{
  emoji += Char.ConvertFromUtf32(charCode);
}

// Assign the same string to both TextBlocks
colorTextBlock.Text = emoji;
plainTextBlock.Text = emoji;
```

When multicolored glyphs are rendered with the default multicolor support enabled, they use the colors specified inside the font. When multicolor glyphs are rendered with IsColorFontEnabled set to false, they respect the TextBlock's Foreground value.

Text Content

The big secret of TextBlock is that its Text property (of type string) is *not* its content property. Instead, it is a property called Inlines that is a collection of Inline objects. Although the following TextBlock gives the same result as setting the Text property, you're really setting Inlines instead:

```
<!-- TextBlock.Inlines is being set here: -->
<TextBlock>Text in a TextBlock</TextBlock>
```

A type converter makes the value resemble a simple string, but it's actually a collection with one Inline-derived element called Run. Therefore, the preceding XAML is equivalent to the following:

```
<TextBlock><Run Text="Text in a TextBlock"/></TextBlock>
```

which is also equivalent to the following XAML because Text is Run's content property:

```
<TextBlock><Run>Text in a TextBlock</Run></TextBlock>
```

A Run is a chunk of text with identical formatting. Using a single explicit Run doesn't add value, but things can start to get interesting when you use multiple Runs in the same TextBlock. For example, the preceding TextBlock could be expressed as follows:

```
<TextBlock>
  <Run>Text</Run>
  <Run> in</Run>
  <Run> a</Run>
  <Run> TextBlock</Run>
</TextBlock>
```

This doesn't change the rendering behavior compared to the previous XAML. Run, however, has several formatting properties that can override the corresponding properties on the parent TextBlock: FontFamily, FontSize, FontStretch, FontStyle, FontWeight, Foreground, and even CharacterSpacing, FlowDirection, and Language. The following XAML, shown in Figure 12.7, takes advantage of this fact:

```
<TextBlock Foreground="Brown" FontSize="30">
  <Run FontStyle="Italic" FontFamily="Georgia" Foreground="Blue">Rich</Run>
  <Run FontFamily="Comic Sans MS" CharacterSpacing="-200"> Text </Run>
  <Run FontFamily="Arial Black" Foreground="Orange" FontSize="100">in</Run>
  <Run FontFamily="Verdana" FontWeight="Bold" Foreground="Green"> a </Run>
  <Run FontFamily="Courier New" FontWeight="Bold" CharacterSpacing="200">
    TextBlock</Run>
</TextBlock>
```

Rich Text **in** a **T e x t B l o c k**

FIGURE 12.7   Several uniquely formatted Runs inside a single TextBlock

Although this is a silly example, the same technique can be used for something useful like italicizing or underlining a single word in a paragraph. This is much easier than trying to use multiple TextBlocks and worrying about positioning each one correctly. And by using a single TextBlock, you get one consistent behavior for clipping, wrapping, and even text selection across the heterogeneous text.

How can I underline text in a TextBlock?

There is no property on TextBlock for this. Instead, you must use another Inline-derived element called Underline within a TextBlock's content. For example:

```
<TextBlock><Underline>Underlined text</Underline></TextBlock>
```

When you add content to a TextBlock's Inlines property, the (unformatted) content is appended to its Text property. Therefore, it is still valid to programmatically retrieve the value of the Text property when only Inlines is explicitly set. For example, the value of Text is the expected "Rich Text in a TextBlock" string for the TextBlock in Figure 12.7.

TextBlock and Whitespace

When a TextBlock's content is set via the Text property, any whitespace in the string is preserved. When its content is set via Inlines in XAML, however, whitespace is not preserved. Instead, leading and trailing whitespace is ignored, and any contiguous whitespace is coalesced into a single whitespace character (as in HTML).

Explicit Versus Implicit Runs

Although the following TextBlock:

```
<TextBlock>Text in a TextBlock</TextBlock>
```

is equivalent to this:

```
<TextBlock><Run>Text in a TextBlock</Run></TextBlock>
```

the behavior of the type converter is not always straightforward. For example, the following use of another Inline called LineBreak is valid:

```
<TextBlock>Text in<LineBreak/>a TextBlock</TextBlock>
```

whereas the following is not:

```
<TextBlock><Run>Text in<LineBreak/>a TextBlock</Run></TextBlock>
```

The last variation is not valid because Run's content property (Text) is a simple string, and you can't embed a LineBreak element inside a string. The content property of TextBlock (Inlines) is converted to one or more Runs via a type converter that specifically handles LineBreak, which is why the first use of LineBreak works. This type converter makes the following XAML:

```
<TextBlock>Text in<LineBreak/>a TextBlock</TextBlock>
```

equivalent to the following TextBlock containing two Runs, one on each side of the LineBreak:

```
<TextBlock><Run>Text in</Run><LineBreak/><Run>a TextBlock</Run></TextBlock>
```

Text Elements

The Inline class derives from TextElement, a class representing all kinds of text content. Note that TextElements are not UIElements; they do not individually participate in the standard UIElement mechanisms such as layout, input events, and focus. They are specifically for text controls and text-specific layout rules are applied to them.

Two types of TextElements exist—Inlines and Blocks. A Block is a rectangular region, whereas an Inline is a region that flows more freely with text, potentially occupying a nonrectangular space (flowing from the end of one line to the beginning of the next). There are several more types of Inline objects besides the previously seen Run, LineBreak, and Underline. All the relevant classes and their inheritance relationships are shown in Figure 12.8.

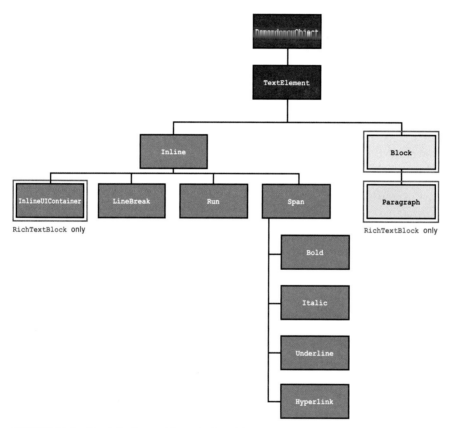

FIGURE 12.8   The inheritance hierarchy involving TextElement

If this seems like an excessive amount of structure, that's because it is! These classes were originally introduced in WPF, and in WPF there are many types of Blocks (and more types of Inlines as well). Some of these classes can be used only by RichTextBlock, so they are discussed in the upcoming "RichTextBlock" section. In addition to Run and the simple LineBreak, the only other type of Inline that you can use inside a TextBlock is Span and its descendants.

Span itself can be used to group text with the same formatting, just like Run. (The previously mentioned formatting properties on Run are defined on TextElement, so they are common to all.) Figure 12.7 would look identical if all of its Run elements were replaced with Span. The difference between Run and Span is that Span supports nested Inlines. It has an `Inlines` content property, just like `TextBlock`, whereas `Run` has only a simple string `Text` content property.

The following XAML demonstrates the nested nature of Spans, rendered in Figure 12.9:

```
<TextBlock FontStyle="Italic">
  <Span Foreground="Brown">
    1
    <Span FontSize="20">
      2
      <Span FontWeight="Bold">3</Span>
      2
    </Span>
    1
  </Span>
</TextBlock>
```

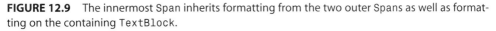

FIGURE 12.9   The innermost Span inherits formatting from the two outer Spans as well as formatting on the containing `TextBlock`.

The `Bold` element is a shortcut for `<Span FontWeight="Bold"/>` and the `Italic` element is a shortcut for `<Span FontStyle="Italic"/>`. The `Underline` element, however, is the only way to get underlined text. The following `TextBlock`, shown in Figure 12.10, demonstrates these Span-derived elements:

```
<TextBlock Foreground="BlueViolet">
  <Italic>Then I said</Italic> "<Bold>stop <Underline>now</Underline></Bold>!"
</TextBlock>
```

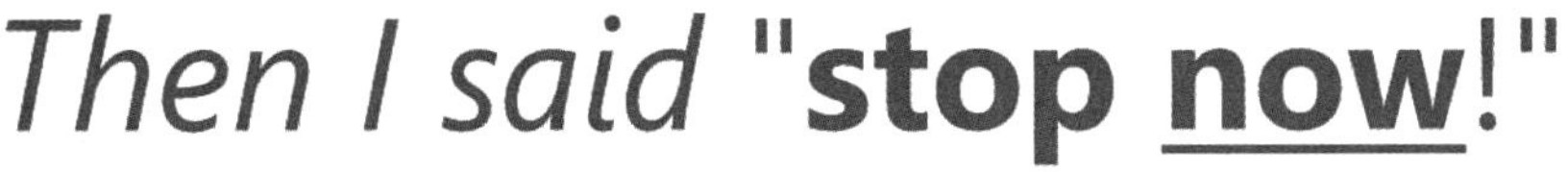

*Then I said "**stop <u>now</u>**!"*

FIGURE 12.10   Using `Italic`, `Bold`, and `Underline` in a single `TextBlock`

The final `Span` subclass is a nifty element called `Hyperlink` that acts like a hyperlink in HTML (and like the `HyperlinkButton` control). You can embed `Hyperlink`s inside a `TextBlock` element and, as with the HTML AREA (or A) tag, the content is automatically rendered as a clickable hyperlink that launches the appropriate app to display the target URI. This target page is specified via `Hyperlink`'s `NavigateUri` property (the analog to the href attribute in HTML).

The launching is done on your behalf via Launcher.LaunchUriAsync (with the default ViewSizePreference option), so the URI scheme determines what app gets launched. For example, the following XAML gets rendered as in Figure 12.11, which shows the experience after the Hyperlink has been clicked:

```
<TextBlock>
  Click <Hyperlink NavigateUri="http://bing.com">here</Hyperlink> to visit Bing.
</TextBlock>
```

FIGURE 12.11   A Hyperlink makes it easy to provide an HTML-style navigation experience with a simple TextBlock.

The default blue rendering of Hyperlink can be customized by setting its Foreground property. Hyperlink supports keyboard focus. Like a Button, it can be clicked by pressing the Enter key when it has focus. It raises a Click event when it is clicked, regardless of how it was done.

> If you want to perform custom navigation, but still like the convenience of Hyperlink's automatic text formatting, you can use Hyperlink with an empty NavigateUri value, then handle Hyperlink's Click event and perform your custom work inside this handler. Strangely, there is no way to cancel the launching inside a Click handler, but an empty NavigateUri prevents the automatic launch from being attempted.

Text Selection

As mentioned previously, TextBlock optionally supports text selection. To enable it, you must set its IsTextSelectionEnabled property to true. When you do this, people using touch input can tap any word to highlight it, and then drag two circle adornments to change the range of the selection. With a mouse or pen, a caret is rendered instead of the typical mouse pointer, and users can do the typical selection gestures of dragging to define the selection range or double tapping to select an entire word. A right tap gesture on the TextBlock (which is press-and-hold for touch input) brings up a context menu with the choices of Copy (only if text is selected) and Select All, shown in Figure 12.12. The standard keyboard shortcuts of Ctrl+C for Copy and Ctrl+A for Select All work as well. Copying is done to the Windows clipboard, so the text can be pasted into desktop apps as well as Windows Store apps. Although the default selection color is used, starting in Windows 8.1, TextBlock enables you to change the color of the selection rectangle with its SelectionHighlightColor property.

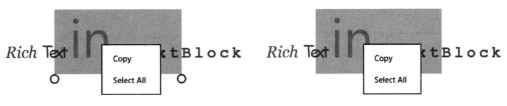

Touch-based selection with extra adornments   Mouse- and pen-based selection

FIGURE 12.12   With IsTextSelectionEnabled=true, text can be selected and copied via several standard gestures.

TextBlock exposes many text selection members based around a TextPointer class that represents a position within its text. In addition to a parameterless SelectAll method, a Select method enables you to programmatically select a specific range of text based on two passed-in TextPointers. TextBlock's readonly ContentStart and ContentEnd properties point to the beginning and end of the entire text content, and from these you can call TextPointer's GetPositionAtOffset method to retrieve a TextPointer pointing to any character you'd like.

> **Can I customize the text selection context menu?**
>
> No, but TextBlock raises a ContextMenuOpening event so you can perform custom actions whenever it gets shown.

Whenever the text selection changes, whether programmatically or from user input, TextBlock's SelectionChanged event is raised. You can retrieve the current text selection in two ways. TextBlock's readonly SelectedText property gives you the content as a string, whereas its readonly SelectionStart and SelectionEnd properties give you TextPointers for the beginning and end of the selection.

TextPointer

The TextPointer class is basically a character offset, but it uses heuristics to remain in the "same" spot in the face of text additions and deletions. Heuristics are needed because the correct behavior can be ambiguous. For example, after text is inserted at the same position as a TextPointer, you could consider the TextPointer to now point immediately before the new text or immediately after. To resolve such ambiguity, TextPointer has a concept of *logical direction*, exposed by a LogicalDirection enumeration with Backward and Forward values. Every TextPointer has a logical direction assigned to it, based either on how the user performed a

selection, or how the `TextPointer` was programmatically obtained. `TextPointer` also
exposes a `GetCharacterRect` method that returns the bounding `Rect` for any character, which
is helpful for overlaying elements on top of text.

The irony is that none of the editable controls currently expose `TextPointer`, so its primary
purpose does not get exercised.

The `Windows.UI.Xaml.Documents.Typography` class exposes several attached
properties that can be placed on text controls to configure advanced OpenType
properties on fonts that support them. For example, if you use the Gabriola font and set
`Typography.StandardLigatures="True"` on a `TextBlock`, you can see a difference in how
"ft" is rendered. As in the Microsoft logo, a single line connects the two letters when ligatures are
used.

RichTextBlock

A typical first reaction to discovering the `RichTextBlock` element is, "Isn't `TextBlock`
already rich?" TextBlock can do a lot when it comes to formatting text, but
RichTextBlock adds two big new tricks:

→ Embedding arbitrary `UIElements` among text

→ Letting text overflow into separate elements, which enables multi-column text or
other custom text layouts

Except for these two features, `TextBlock` and `RichTextBlock` are almost identical. They
expose the same methods, properties, and events, although `RichTextBlock` happens to
have an extra `GetPositionFromPoint` method that returns a `TextPointer` for the passed-in
`Point`. RichTextBlock also has some different defaults: `IsTextSelectionEnabled` is `true`
by default, and `TextWrapping` is `Wrap` by default.

One other difference is that `RichTextBlock`'s content property is called `Blocks` rather than
`Inlines`. Naturally, it holds a collection of `Blocks` rather than `Inlines`. From Figure 12.8,
you can see that this is a convoluted way of saying that `RichTextBlock` must contain a set
of `Paragraphs`.

`Paragraph`'s purpose is to hold a collection of `Inlines`, so it's basically the same as a `Span`
with an automatically inserted `LineBreak` at the end. Although unlike `Span`, `Paragraph`
inherits some extra formatting capabilities from its `Block` base class: `TextAlignment`,
`LineHeight`, `LineStackingStrategy`, and `Margin` properties just like the ones defined on
`TextBlock` and `RichTextBlock`. It also defines a `TextIndent` property that enables you to
indent the first line of text by an amount specified in logical pixels.

Figure 12.13 shows the following two-Paragraph RichTextBlock that demonstrates two TextAlignment settings:

```
<RichTextBlock Foreground="Chocolate">
  <Paragraph TextAlignment="Right">
    This is paragraph #1, which is <Bold>right-aligned</Bold>.
  </Paragraph>
  <Paragraph TextAlignment="Justify">
    This is paragraph #2. It is <Bold>justified</Bold>, which impacts all but the
    last line (and any lines with a LineBreak).
  </Paragraph>
</RichTextBlock>
```

This is paragraph
#1, which is
right-aligned.
This is paragraph
#2. It is **justified**,
which impacts all
but the last line
(and any lines
with a LineBreak).

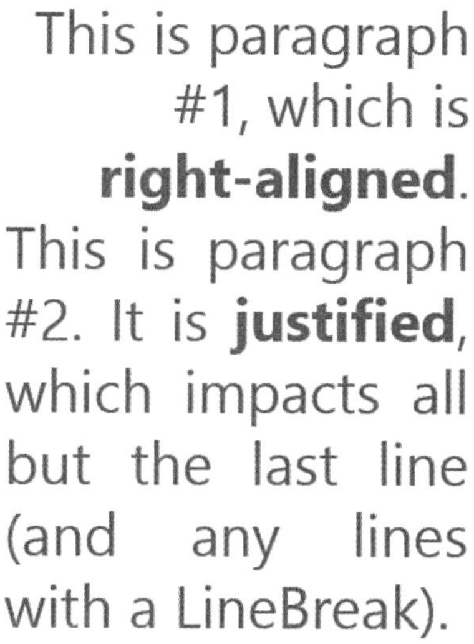

FIGURE 12.13   Each Paragraph in a RichTextBlock can be given different TextAlignments (in addition to other formatting settings).

Embedding UIElements

The fact that RichTextBlock can contain embedded UIElements is not obvious from looking at its APIs. This capability comes from the InlineUIContainer element, which is an Inline. It has a simple Child content property of type UIElement.

Although InlineUIContainer *should* be able to be added to the plain old TextBlock's Inlines collection, doing so fails at runtime. It turns out that InlineUIContainers must be placed within a Block, and this is the reason that this feature is supported only by RichTextBlock.

The capability to embed a UIElement among text means you can insert just about anything: an image, a video, a Panel containing a large tree of elements, and so on. Such elements are fully interactive and can get focus, despite feeling like part of the text.

The following XAML demonstrates `InlineUIContainer` with something a bit unusual. It embeds a `StackPanel` along with its three `RadioButtons`, as shown in Figure 12.14:

```
<RichTextBlock Foreground="OrangeRed" FontSize="20">
  <Paragraph>
    I would like a
    <InlineUIContainer>
      <StackPanel>
        <RadioButton>small</RadioButton>
        <RadioButton IsChecked="True">medium</RadioButton>
        <RadioButton>large</RadioButton>
      </StackPanel>
    </InlineUIContainer> drink, please.
  </Paragraph>
</RichTextBlock>
```

`UIElements` don't get rendered any differently than normal when used in this fashion. In Figure 12.14, the app is using the light theme, which is why the `RadioButtons` look different than they do in Chapter 10, "Content Controls."

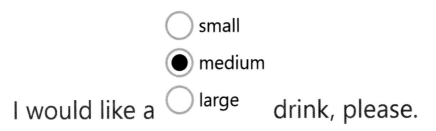

FIGURE 12.14   With `InlineUIContainer`, you can jam just about anything inside a `RichTextBlock`.

Each `InlineUIContainer` can be selected only as an entire unit, and its content is never included on the clipboard when copying a selection; it is simply skipped.

Text Overflow

If you place more text in a `RichTextBlock` (or `TextBlock`) than what fits in its bounds, you could wrap it in a `ScrollViewer` to make it all readable. `RichTextBlock`, however, supports a nifty trick that enables text that doesn't fit to spill into a special element called `RichTextBlock`**Overflow** that you can place anywhere. If the remaining content doesn't all fit in the `RichTextBlockOverflow`, it can spill into another `RichTextBlockOverflow`, and so on.

To enable this feature, all you need to do is set `RichTextBlock`'s `OverflowContentTarget` property to the desired `RichTextBlockOverflow` instance. `RichTextBlockOverflow` has its own `OverflowContentTarget` property so you can keep chaining `RichTextBlockOverflows` to each other. You could use this to create multicolumn text, which is a popular way for

Windows Store apps to display articles, instructions, or other lengthy chunks of text. The following XAML shows how, with the result shown in Figure 12.15:

```xml
<Grid Background="White">
  <!-- Define a three-column grid -->
  <Grid.ColumnDefinitions>
    <ColumnDefinition/>
    <ColumnDefinition/>
    <ColumnDefinition/>
  </Grid.ColumnDefinitions>

  <!-- The single "real" RichTextBlock contains all content and formatting -->
  <RichTextBlock Foreground="Black" FontSize="20" FontFamily="Cambria"
                 Margin="12" OverflowContentTarget="{Binding ElementName=o1}">
    <Paragraph>
      Lorem ipsum dolor sit amet, …
    </Paragraph>

    …
  </RichTextBlock>

  <!-- The 1st overflow element transfers its own overflow -->
  <RichTextBlockOverflow Name="o1" Grid.Column="1" Margin="12"
                         OverflowContentTarget="{Binding ElementName=o2}" />

  <!-- The 2nd overflow element renders as much as it can,
       then truncates its own overflow -->
  <RichTextBlockOverflow Name="o2" Grid.Column="2" Margin="12" />
</Grid>
```

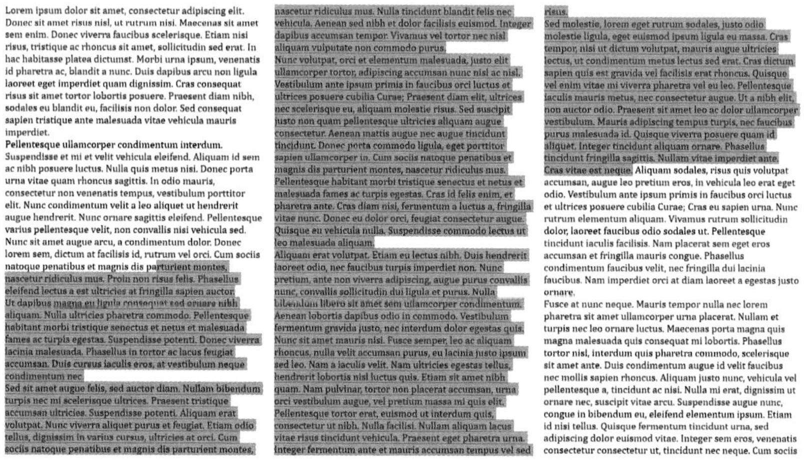

FIGURE 12.15   Three-column text, partially selected, displayed with `RichTextBlock` and two linked `RichTextBlockOverflows`

Notice that text selection works seamlessly across the three disjoint elements as if they are a single RichTextBlock. The one true RichTextBlock is the master; it holds all the text content and formatting settings. Although a RichTextBlockOverflow can choose its own independent settings for standard visual properties like Padding, Margin, or RenderTransform, it can't override any font settings.

If the RichTextBlock was wrapped in a ScrollViewer, it would have no overflow content and the RichTextBlockOverflows would remain empty. Although the OverflowContentTarget property can be easily set to a RichTextBlockOverflow instance in code behind, the preceding XAML uses a simple data binding feature (covered in Chapter 19, "Data Binding") to assign it to an element by its name.

Because each RichTextBlock and RichTextBlockOverflow is a separate element, you can get creative with layout. Figure 12.16 updates the preceding Grid by adding an extra row, moving the first RichTextBlockOverflow to the new row, and interspersing colored Rectangles among the text content. You could use a similar technique to wrap text around an image in a way that adjusts to changing text size or app size. This is more flexible than embedding a UIElement within the text, because its position would be fixed.

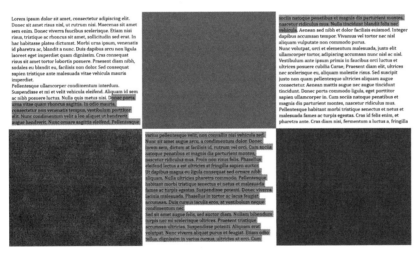

FIGURE 12.16   Text overflow and selection is still seamless no matter where RichTextBlock and its linked RichTextBlockOverflows are placed.

Figure 12.17 shows an extreme use of RichTextBlockOverflows to tightly wrap text around an image. Each line is rendered with one or two separate (and carefully placed!) elements in order to achieve this effect, which is obvious in the part of the figure that shows the content as viewed in the Visual Studio XAML designer. Although the star is nonrectangular, the Image element rendering it is indeed rectangular, so the position of each RichTextBlockOverflow is hard-coded for this specific content. Although the RichTextBlock appears to be in single-line mode (TextWrapping=NoWrap), the overflow feature works only if TextWrapping is left at its default value of Wrap. Therefore, the

RichTextBlock in Figure 12.17, as well as each RichTextBlockOverflow, constrains its Height to make only one line of text fit.

As viewed in Visual Studio's designer   The final result, with some text selected

FIGURE 12.17   Using fine-grained text overflow to carefully avoid content that appears nonrectangular

RichTextBlock's readonly Boolean HasOverflowContent property reveals whether any of its content can overflow, regardless of whether a RichTextBlockOverflow is attached to receive the overflowing content.

TextBox

The TextBox control, pictured in Figure 12.18, enables users to type one or more lines of text. The software keyboard is automatically shown when a TextBox gets focus via touch and hidden when a TextBox loses focus. (This is true even if a hardware keyboard is present.) You can prevent this automatic display of the software keyboard by setting TextBox's PreventKeyboardDisplayOnProgrammaticFocus property to true.

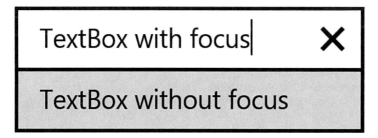

FIGURE 12.18   Two TextBoxes, one with focus and one without

PreventKeyboardDisplayOnProgrammaticFocus is new to Windows 8.1, as well as three other features: a Header property that can be set to any System.Object (although typically text), a PlaceholderText property that can be set to any watermark string (text that only appears when the TextBox has no real text content), and a Paste event that enables you to distinguish pasted text versus typed text. Figure 12.19 demonstrates `Header` and `PlaceholderText` with the following `TextBlock`:

```
<TextBox Header="Name"
        PlaceholderText="Type your name as it appears on your card"/>
```

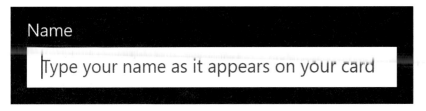

FIGURE 12.19   The `Header` and `PlaceholderText` properties make it easy to create common form-filling user interfaces.

Unlike most other XAML controls, the content of `TextBox` is not stored as a generic `System.Object`. Instead, `TextBox` stores it in a simple string property called `Text` and raises a `TextChanged` event whenever the string changes. Because its text is stored as a simple string, `TextBox` doesn't support formatted text. It does inherit the standard five `FontXXX` properties from `Control`, which apply to all of its text uniformly. Other than that, however, `TextAlignment`, `TextWrapping`, and `IsColorFontEnabled` are the only text-specific formatting properties you can adjust.

When a `TextBox` has content, has focus, and is in its default single-line mode with no wrapping, it contains an "X" button that can be tapped to quickly clear the content, which is especially handy on devices without a hardware keyboard. You can enable `TextBox`'s multiline mode by setting `AcceptsReturn` for true.

···

`AcceptsReturn` versus `TextWrapping`

Setting `AcceptsReturn` to true not only enables typing and pasting newlines, but displaying them as well. In this mode, setting `TextWrapping` to Wrap affects any lines that are too long to display within the width of the `TextBox`.

With `AcceptsReturn` left as false and `TextWrapping` left as NoWrap, a `TextBox` never displays more than one line. If you attempt to set `Text` to a string with a newline, it displays only the first line of text. However, if you set `TextWrapping` to Wrap or WrapWholeWords while `AcceptsReturn` is false, the `TextBox` is in a weird mode in which it can *display* text with newlines, but the user can't press the Enter key to insert one. The only way it can receive newlines is programmatically or by pasting in text with newlines. Needless to say, this is a combination of property values to avoid!

You can limit the length of text that can be typed into a `TextBox` with its `MaxLength` property. Its default value is `0`, which means infinite. Note that you can always programmatically set `Text` to a string longer than `MaxLength` and the `TextBox` will still display it.

Spelling and Text Prediction

TextBox supports two nifty features that are available by setting a corresponding Boolean property to `true`:

→ **IsSpellCheckEnabled**—Places red squiggles under misspelled words and provides a context menu with suggestions and other options. It also autocorrects common mistakes.

→ **IsTextPredictionEnabled**—Suggests a word while you type. This is `true` by default, but it is activated only when input is coming from the software keyboard. (The theory is that it would be more of a distraction than help when typing on a hardware keyboard.)

The spell check functionality, along with autocorrect, provides a similar experience to what you get in Microsoft Office. If you do a touch-based tap or a mouse- or pen-based right tap on a red-underlined word, you get a context menu like the one in Figure 12.20. If you make a common mistake (such as typing "wierd" instead of "weird"), the correction is made automatically, but performing the same gesture gives the user the option to undo the autocorrection and stop doing that specific one in the future.

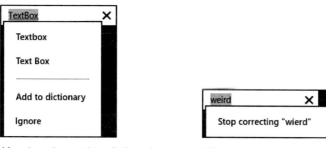

After detecting a misspelled word   After autocorrecting a misspelled word

FIGURE 12.20   Spell check manifests itself in two different ways.

Red squiggles are triggered for more than just spelling errors. For example, if you repeat a word, the second one gets a squiggle with the context menu option of "Delete repeated word."

When you select "Ignore," it applies only to that specific TextBox instance (for the lifetime of the object). The dictionary is provided by Windows, and any words added or ignored apply to all Windows Store apps that use this feature.

Although spell check looks full-featured, it unfortunately isn't quite good enough for serious use due to some annoying behaviors. The spell check for a word isn't done until a character is typed *after* the word (such as punctuation or a space). That means if there's only one word, or if the content ends in a word with no punctuation, its spelling doesn't get checked. Also, when you add a word to the dictionary, it removes the red squiggle from that instance of the word, but it sometimes misses other occurrences, even within the same TextBox! The missed instances have to be perturbed (such as adding a space after each one) in order for their obsolete squiggles to go away. And of course, with no way for the user to view the custom words that were added to the dictionary and remove any that were added by accident, the feature isn't complete.

The text prediction functionality (on by default when using the software keyboard), is demonstrated in Figure 12.21. Tapping the suggestion replaces the word currently being typed with the suggested word.

FIGURE 12.21   With text prediction enabled, the most likely suggestion is presented in a tappable tooltip as you type a word.

? Can I supply a custom context-specific dictionary to use with text prediction?

No. Instead, you can mimic the feature with your own processing of what's being typed in a TextBox, and turn off the built-in text prediction (with IsTextPredictionEnabled= false) so it doesn't interfere with your custom user interface.

Text Selection

TextBox exposes straightforward and familiar members for text selection— SelectionHighlightColor, SelectAll, Select, SelectedText, SelectionStart, SelectionLength, and GetRectFromCharacterIndex. However, unlike TextBlock and RichTextBlock, these are based on simple int character indices rather than TextPointer objects.

In addition to the Select All and Copy commands supported by TextBlock and RichTextBlock, TextBox's editable nature enables it to provide automatic support for Cut, Paste, Undo, and Redo as well. The availability of every command except Select All depends on context, but Figure 12.22 shows the built-in context menu when every command is available.

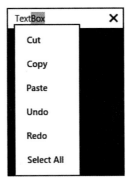

You can remove the editable part of TextBox by setting its IsReadOnly property to true. When you do this, it looks identical, except the content can't be changed by the user and the "X" button never appears. Text selection can still be performed, as well as the Select All and Copy commands, just like with a TextBlock.

FIGURE 12.22   TextBox supports all the standard text commands via a context menu as well as their standard keyboard shortcuts.

InputScope and the Software Keyboard

The software keyboard enables text entry on devices without an active hardware keyboard. It is sometimes referred to as the *on-screen keyboard*, the *touch keyboard*, the *soft keyboard*, the *software input panel*, or even the *input pane*. When any of the editable text controls get focus (TextBox, RichEditBox, or PasswordBox), the software keyboard automatically appears on top of the app by default. (All three editable text controls expose the same PreventKeyboardDisplayOnProgrammaticFocus property for overriding this behavior.) Although it obscures a significant portion of the screen, Windows automatically shifts the contents of a Windows Store app so the control with focus remains visible on the screen.

There are almost no APIs for interacting with the software keyboard. There's just the KeyboardCapabilities.KeyboardPresent property mentioned in Chapter 6, "Handling Input: Touch, Mouse, Pen, and Keyboard," for determining whether a hardware keyboard is being used, and an InputPane class, described in a later "Digging Deeper" sidebar, for customizing how your app responds to it being shown or hidden. Other than these two APIs, the software keyboard is designed such that apps don't need to know or care which type of keyboard is used to enter text, or if a special mode of the software keyboard is used.

Can I force the software keyboard to disappear without requiring the user to tap on something else?

Yes, by programmatically giving focus to a control other than the text-entry control. This is commonly done in response to the user tapping the Enter key, because this key otherwise does nothing except for multiline TextBoxes, which can be frustrating for users.

It's certainly harder for a user to type on the software keyboard compared to a hardware keyboard, but the software keyboard does have its advantages. The user can switch it to a "thumbs mode," which pushes the keys to the edges for easier typing while holding a tablet with two hands. The user can also switch it into "handwriting-recognition mode" so she can write with a pen or finger and have it automatically converted into text. (I'm sure it's also only a matter of time until it has a mode that does speech recognition.) Furthermore, an app can make the keyboard change its display depending on the context. For example, it can show a ".com" button when a TextBox wants a URL, or initially show numbers and symbols when a TextBox wants a number. (That said, my family's first computer, the IBM PCjr, had similar technology that worked on the hardware keyboard: a piece of cardboard that you placed on top in order to relabel keys. That was the best way to play King's Quest.)

You can change the keyboard's display by marking a TextBox with an appropriate *input scope*. An input scope is basically a pre-defined label that can be assigned to a text box's InputScope property. Some examples are Default, Url, and Number. The Number input scope can be assigned in XAML as follows:

```
<TextBox>
  <TextBox.InputScope>
    <InputScope>
```

```
        <InputScope.Names>
          <InputScopeName NameValue="Number"/>
        </InputScope.Names>
      </InputScope>
    </TextBox.InputScope>
</TextBox>
```

Or, thankfully, the much less verbose:

```
<TextBox InputScope="Number"/>
```

The list of allowed input scopes is provided by the `InputScopeNameValue` enumeration. There are 18 possible choices, although most of them are specific to Asian languages. Figure 12.23 shows all the variations that are relevant for American English, with differences from the `Default` layout highlighted in red.

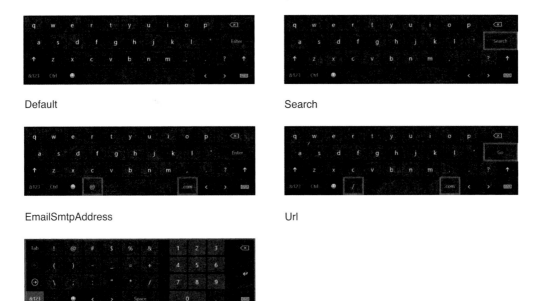

Default   Search

EmailSmtpAddress   Url

Number and TelephoneNumber

FIGURE 12.23   Different keyboard layouts are controlled by `InputScope`.

In Search and Url layouts, the "Search" and "Go" keys are just the Enter key with a different label (much like the old-fashioned cardboard keyboard overlay).

Some input scope values map to the same layout even though you could imagine them having slightly different layouts, such as `Number` versus `TelephoneNumber`. Perhaps a future release of Windows could show a distinct display for `TelephoneNumber` with some smarts regarding the geographic meaning of area codes, but in the meantime the distinct value at least serves as a bit of documentation for other developers or designers working on the app.

The various input scopes impact the keyboard's thumbs mode in a similar fashion as in Figure 12.23, although there are subtle differences (like the Enter key showing a magnifying glass icon rather than the "Search" text when the Search input scope is used). As you might expect, input scopes have no impact on the keyboard's handwriting recognition mode.

You can test the various input scopes with the Visual Studio simulator. Just be sure to change the simulator from "Mouse mode" to "Basic touch mode," because the former makes the simulator act like a hardware keyboard (the one from the host PC running Visual Studio) is always active.

How do I restrict what gets typed into a text box (such as allowing only digits)?

You must write code that manually filters out unwanted characters. Input scopes do not help in this regard, because the user can still find a way to type every possible character regardless of whether the software keyboard or hardware keyboard is used. Input scopes are about providing convenience to the user; they are not about restricting or validating input.

The following KeyDown event handler does a reasonable job of allowing only digits to be entered into a TextBox, handling both the regular number keys as well as the number pad, and not getting fooled by the Shift key. However, it still doesn't protect against pasting in arbitrary text (although the Paste event could be used to guard against that). The reliable approach would be to validate the content *after* it is entered, using a TextChanged event handler.

```
void TextBox_KeyDown(object sender, KeyRoutedEventArgs e)
{
  switch (e.Key)
  {
    case VirtualKey.Number0: case VirtualKey.Number1: case VirtualKey.Number2:
    case VirtualKey.Number3: case VirtualKey.Number4: case VirtualKey.Number5:
    case VirtualKey.Number6: case VirtualKey.Number7: case VirtualKey.Number8:
    case VirtualKey.Number9:
    case VirtualKey.NumberPad0: case VirtualKey.NumberPad1:
    case VirtualKey.NumberPad2: case VirtualKey.NumberPad3:
    case VirtualKey.NumberPad4: case VirtualKey.NumberPad5:
    case VirtualKey.NumberPad6: case VirtualKey.NumberPad7:
    case VirtualKey.NumberPad8: case VirtualKey.NumberPad9:
      if (Window.Current.CoreWindow.GetAsyncKeyState(VirtualKey.Shift)
          != CoreVirtualKeyStates.None)
      {
        // Shift is being pressed! That means we just caught a !, @, #, $, %,
        // ^, &, *, (, or ) pretending to be a digit!
        // This is not allowed. Swallow the keystroke!
```

```
      e.Handled = true;
    }
    else
    {
      // This is allowed. There's nothing more to do!
    }
    break;
  default:
    // This is not allowed. Swallow the keystroke!
    e.Handled = true;
    break;
  }
}
```

The software keyboard has several nice behaviors that you might not be aware of. For example, you can double tap the shift key to turn on Caps Lock and tap it later to turn it off. You can also hold down many keys to get alternatives related to that key. Figure 12.24 shows a few examples of this.

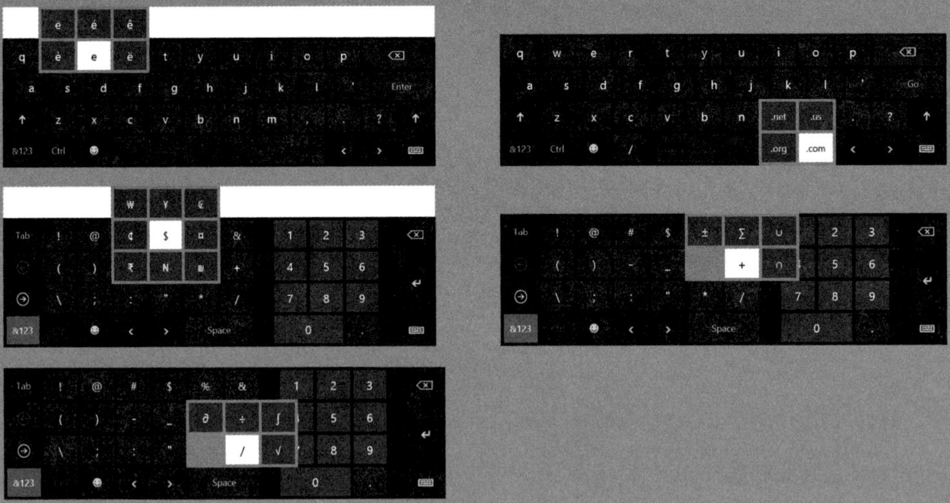

FIGURE 12.24   Many keys can be held down to get related symbols.

Responding to Showing and Hiding the Software Keyboard   •••

For advanced scenarios, Windows.UI.ViewManagement.InputPane exposes two events that are raised immediately before the software keyboard is shown or hidden: Showing and Hiding. It also exposes an OccludedRect property that reveals the exact region of your app that is covered by the software keyboard. To get an instance of InputPane, you call the static InputPane.GetForCurrentView method.

If you want to disable the automatic shifting of your app's content done by Windows to keep the focused TextBox in view, you can handle the Showing event and set the passed-in InputPaneVisibilityEventArgs instance's EnsuredFocusedElementInView property to true. This tells Windows, "Don't bother doing anything because I'm making sure that the right things are remaining in view."

Invoking the Software Keyboard from Custom Controls   •••

It's possible for you to write a custom control that, just like TextBox, RichEditBox, and PasswordBox, automatically invokes the software keyboard when it gets touch-based focus. To do this, your control must have a certain type of UI Automation peer class that you instantiate and return in the control's overridden OnCreateAutomationPeer method. The peer class, which should derive from FrameworkElementAutomationPeer, must implement two interfaces: ITextProvider and IValueProvider. The Windows SDK has an example of this at http://code.msdn.microsoft.com/windowsapps/Touch-keyboard-sample-43532fda.

RichEditBox

RichEditBox is a version of TextBox that enables the display and editing of rich-formatted text. The reason it's called Rich**Edit**Box rather than the more obvious Rich**Text**Box is that it's a thin wrapper over rich text formatting exposed by the Windows Runtime, which is a whole different set of APIs than the XAML-specific rich text formatting APIs. (Perhaps a future version of the XAML UI Framework will contain a RichTextBox control that supports XAML-specific TextElement-based rich formatting, similar to RichTextBlock.) The "rich edit" term also has a long history in Win32.

The implication of this is that interacting with RichEditBox feels a lot less like interacting with a typical XAML control and instead has an API style that betrays its Windows Runtime roots. RichEditBox has a Document property of type ITextDocument rather than BlockCollection. The property is readonly, and there's no public class that implements ITextDocument, so you modify the existing one rather than setting it to a new instance. ITextDocument is one of several Windows Runtime interfaces exposed in the Windows.UI.Text namespace:

→ **ITextDocument**—The top-level interface for all the text content, from which you can modify text, select text, get ranges of text, apply text formatting, control undo behavior, and more. You can even load the content from a stream and save it to a stream, optionally in Rich Text Format (RTF).

→ **ITextSelection**—Represents currently selected text; the Windows Runtime analog to TextPointer.

→ **ITextRange**—Represents a chunk of continuous text, independent from any selection. It enables a number of powerful modifications to the range of text.

→ **ITextParagraphFormat**—Formatting options for one or more paragraphs, such as spacing and indentation, treatment of bulleted and numbered lists, and even control of widows and orphans (see http://wikipedia.org/wiki/Widows_and_orphans).

→ **ITextCharacterFormat**—Formatting options for one or more characters. This includes the same type of formatting seen with TextElements, such as bold, italic, and underline, but includes many more options, such as superscript, subscript, strikethrough, small caps, first-class embedded links, readonly regions, and so on.

RichEditBox isn't designed to be XAML-friendly, so you can place simple text in an instance of the control named richEditBox with C# code such as the following:

```
richEditBox.Document.SetText(TextSetOptions.None, "Initial text");
```

The following initializes the control with RTF-formatted text instead, producing the result in Figure 12.25:

```
richEditBox.Document.SetText(TextSetOptions.FormatRtf,
  @"{\rtf1\pard Initial text with {\b bold} or {\i italic} formatting!}");
```

Initial text with **bold** or *italic* formatting!

FIGURE 12.25   Showing content from an RTF-formatted string in RichEditBox

The following code programmatically changes the format of all the text in the control to "small caps" (small uppercase letters):

```
// Grab the default character format:
ITextCharacterFormat format = richEditBox.Document.GetDefaultCharacterFormat();
// Modify it:
format.SmallCaps = FormatEffect.On;
// Set the modified format as the new default character format:
richEditBox.Document.SetDefaultCharacterFormat(format);
richEditBox.Document.SetText(TextSetOptions.FormatRtf,
  @"{\rtf1\pard Initial text with {\b bold} or {\i italic} formatting!}");
```

Calling SetDefaultCharacterFormat removes existing formatting (such as bold and italic), so SetText is called afterward to preserve that formatting on top of the "small caps" choice.

The `ITextDocument` family of APIs in the `Windows.UI.Text` namespace is powerful. Although the API style might take some getting used to, it makes the rich formatting of `TextBlock` and `RichTextBlock` look like a toy. Its richness is not just in formatting options, but it extends to user interaction as well. For example, it not only supports double tapping with a mouse or pen to select a whole word, but triple tapping with a mouse or pen to select an entire paragraph. This matches the behavior of most text editors, such as Microsoft Word and WordPad.

`RichEditBox` can't do the two `RichTextBlock` tricks of embedding `UIElements` or overflowing into multiple controls, but that shouldn't be a surprise because `ITextDocument` is a Windows Runtime interface and therefore UI-technology-agnostic. Although embedding *interactive* controls (as in Figure 12.14) is not normally needed, the inability to embed images within text is a notable loss.

Because `RichEditBox` natively handles RTF, a user can paste RTF content from the clipboard and have it render perfectly. A user can even paste a lot of content from Microsoft Word and have it look pretty decent. Figure 12.26 shows an example of content from Microsoft Word pasted into a `RichEditBox`.

FIGURE 12.26   Sample content from Microsoft Word pasted into a `RichEditBox`

RichEditBox doesn't look *completely* out of place in the XAML world, however. It does, after all, derive from Control, so it has a long list of familiar properties and behaviors. It also defines several of the same properties as TextBox, such as AcceptsReturn, TextAlignment, TextWrapping, SelectionHighlightColor, IsColorFontEnabled, and IsReadOnly for more familiar control over this small amount of these basic formatting and editing capabilities, InputScope for the same customizations of the software keyboard, the same IsSpellCheckEnabled and IsTextPredictionEnabled features with their quirks, the new Header and PlaceholderText properties, and a ContextMenuOpening event. It also exposes the same SelectionChanged event, although all information about the current selection must be retrieved through the Document (ITextDocument) property.

PasswordBox

PasswordBox is a simple TextBox-style control designed for the entry of a password. Rather than display the text typed in, it displays little circles. Although it doesn't have one by default, you can give it a Windows-style *password reveal button* if you set IsPasswordRevealButtonEnabled to true. This reveals the password while it is pressed, as demonstrated in Figure 12.27.

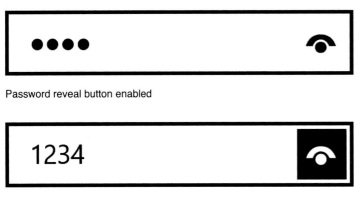

Password reveal button enabled

Password reveal button pressed

FIGURE 12.27   The PasswordBox with IsPasswordRevealButtonEnabled=true

Although it would be a strange thing to do, you can customize the symbol used to mask the password by setting PasswordChar to any character. The default circle is the bullet character (Unicode character 2022). As with the revealed password, it gets displayed in whatever font family is used by the control.

PasswordBox's behavior is intentionally limited. It doesn't support Cut, Copy, Undo, and Redo actions, although it does support Paste. Not surprisingly, it doesn't support spell check or text prediction either! It has no InputScope, so the software keyboard presented to the user is always the same. The keyboard is presented in a special password layout, however. It's like the default one, except with a "Hide keypress" button in place of the left and right arrows, the alternatives for keys (such as the ones shown in Figure 12.24) disabled, and the emoticons mode disabled. The "Hide keypress" button turns off the highlight effect when pressing on-screen keys, which is especially important if you're giving a presentation!

PasswordBox's API is also limited, because an app shouldn't do anything with a password other than pass it along to the service that needs it. Its text is stored in a string property called Password, and a simple PasswordChanged event (with no information about the old or new text) is raised when appropriate. The only other things you can do programmatically are call SelectAll, set properties such as Header, PlaceholderText, MaxLength, and SelectionHighlightColor, or respond to the ContextMenuOpening event. You do not get notified about selection changes, nor is any information about selection exposed, because you should have no reason to care about it.

As much as possible, you should avoid asking the user for a password. Handling it correctly is a burden for you, entering it is a burden for the user, and it requires the user to trust that your app will handle it responsibly.

If the service you must connect to supports any kind of flow with a sign-in webpage, then you can probably leverage the WebAuthenticationBroker in the Windows.Security.Authentication.Web namespace. You give this easy-to-use class a URI representing the appropriate sign-in page on the server, and it presents the user with the page inside system UI that is isolated from your app. Upon its asynchronous return, you get a WebAuthenticationResult with the data you need to continue (which depends on the specifics of the service).

WebAuthenticationBroker not only prevents you from writing a lot of code to deal with OAuth or other authentication protocols, but as of Windows 8.1 it securely stores and shares the authentication cookies with Internet Explorer. This means that if the user has previously signed in, even from Internet Explorer, the sign-in can happen automatically! (If there are additional app-specific permissions that need to be granted, the silent authentication would fail and the appropriate page can be shown.) That is why WebAuthenticationBroker is the best choice. It works with many third-party services, and you can construct your service to work with it as well. Additionally, you could integrate Microsoft accounts into your own service with Live Connect (http://msdn.microsoft.com/en-us/live) to provide an automatic single sign-on experience.

If the automatic authentication provided by WebAuthenticationBroker or the Microsoft account cannot work for your scenario, and you therefore must ask the user for a password, then you should be sure to use the PasswordVault class from the Windows.Security. Credentials namespace. This securely stores username/password pairs and roams them to trusted devices connected to the user's Microsoft account so the user only enters his or her username and password into your app once. Credentials stored in the PasswordVault can be seen (without the password) and managed by users in the "Credential Manager" section of the Control Panel, which gives users much more confidence and control over the whole process.

Finally, for enterprise scenarios, you can leverage CredentialPicker in the Windows.Security.Credentials.UI namespace. This presents a dialog to the user that can handle domain credentials, smart cards, and even biometrics.

Summary

Altogether, the collection of "blocks" and "boxes" covered in this chapter is a bit of an inconsistent mishmash. The distinction between TextBlock and RichTextBlock is logical, although the degree of richness already in TextBlock makes it seem odd that there even needs to be two separate controls. (Even if you were previously familiar with TextBlock, you probably didn't realize just how rich it was before reading this chapter!)

Although TextBox is essentially the editable version of TextBlock, the fact that it operates only on a string makes it a much simpler control than TextBlock in many ways. This is, of course, entirely reasonable, considering how TextBoxes are almost always used. The absence of a RichTextBox control leaves a small gap in the overall picture, although it is filled quite capably with RichEditBox, which is the richest control of them all in many ways, despite lacking a few features that RichTextBlock exposes.

Another oddity is that although the three "boxes" derive from Control, the two "blocks" derive directly from FrameworkElement. This means that despite living in the Windows.UI.Xaml.Controls namespace, TextBlock and RichTextBlock are technically not controls. (The same is true for RichTextBlockOverflow.) This doesn't mean much, because these elements end up replicating many of the properties on Control. However, they don't have some properties you might expect them to have, such as Background, BorderBrush, and BorderThickness. They also don't participate in focus (except for embedded Hyperlinks), they can't be enabled or disabled, and they can't be given a new control template.

Chapter 13

IMAGES

This chapter is quite a bit different than the other chapters in this part of the book, because it covers only one XAML element: Image. Is Image really so complex that it deserves its own chapter? Maybe not. But this chapter also covers three important Windows Runtime topics that are relevant when using an Image element:

→ Automatic support for selecting different versions of files (often image files) packaged with your app, so you can seamlessly support different scales, user themes, locales, and more.

→ Rich support for decoding, editing, and encoding images in any format (if a relevant codec is installed) that lives in the Windows.Graphics.Imaging namespace. This includes an image's pixels as well as its metadata.

→ Rendering PDF content as an image. This functionality is new to Windows 8.1, and resides in the Windows.Data.Pdf namespace.

So this chapter is not just about the Image element but all the things you can do with the underlying media. This is also the first of two chapters dedicated to non-vector-based content (images, audio, and video).

The `Image` Element

Image enables images of multiple formats to be rendered: BMP, PNG, GIF, JPEG, JPEG-XR, TIFF, and even ICO files. It has a `Source` property of type `ImageSource`, but thanks to a type converter, you can set the property to a simple string in XAML, as in this example:

```
<Image Source="Assets/Logo.png"/>
```

Source can point to an image file packaged with your app (a *resource*), a file stored in app data (see Chapter 20, "Working with Data"), or an image from the Web. The content is fetched and processed asynchronously, so a slow network connection doesn't impact your app's responsiveness. When Source is set, it results in either an `ImageOpened` event being raised on success, or an `ImageFailed` event being raised on failure. In the latter case, the Image element is left blank and the `EventArgs` object passed to any handlers contains an `Exception` object with failure details.

Image has the same `Stretch` property seen with `Viewbox` in Chapter 4, "Layout," for controlling how its content scales. Its default value is `Uniform`, so the content scales to fill Image's bounds as much as possible without cropping while still preserving its aspect ratio.

Like a `TextBlock`, Image is commonly used in a simple fashion, but a lot of power is lurking within. (It also doesn't derive from `Control`, so you can't give it a background or focus.) This section examines the following features in depth:

→ Referencing files with URIs

→ Custom stretching with nine-grid

→ Generating dynamic Images with `WriteableBitmap`

→ Generating dynamic Images with `RenderTargetBitmap`

Referencing Files with URIs

The mapping of an Image element in XAML to the equivalent C# code is not always obvious. The preceding example:

```
<Image Source="Assets/Logo.png"/>
```

is equivalent to the following C# code placed in a `Page`'s code-behind:

```
Image image = new Image();
image.Source = new BitmapImage(new Uri(this.BaseUri, "Assets/Logo.png"));
```

There are two things going on here. One is that a type converter hides the complexity involving ImageSource, the type of the Source property. An ImageSource cannot be directly instantiated, nor can its `BitmapSource` subclass, but BitmapSource has two subclasses that can be instantiated: `BitmapImage`, the one typically used, and `WriteableBitmap`, covered later in this section. ImageSource has two more direct subclasses: `RenderTargetBitmap` is covered later in this section, and `SurfaceImageSource` is covered in Chapter 26, "Integrating DirectX."

> BitmapImage, just like the Image element, has ImageOpened and ImageFailed events. However, BitmapImage also has a DownloadProgress event revealing a progress value from 0 to 100 that can easily be fed into a ProgressBar control (see Chapter 15, "Other Controls"). Once ImageOpened is raised (immediately before it gets rendered), you can check BitmapImage's PixelWidth and PixelHeight properties. You can also point BitmapImage to a new URI post-construction by settings its UriSource property.
>
> BitmapImage also defines DecodePixelWidth and DecodePixelHeight properties that, when set appropriately, can provide a huge performance benefit to apps that display many large images. These properties are meant to convey the dimensions in which the image is expected to be displayed. When specified, Images get automatically decoded to that size rather than the original size.

Second, BitmapImage must be constructed with a System.Uri. In WPF or Silverlight, you could have constructed a relative Uri, the kind seen in XAML, as follows:

```
image.Source = new BitmapImage(new Uri("Assets/Logo.png", UriKind.Relative));
```

However, this fails with an exception that explains, "The given System.Uri cannot be converted into a Windows.Foundation.Uri." BitmapImage's constructor actually requires a Windows.Foundation.Uri, the Windows Runtime class that gets automatically projected to System.Uri for .NET consumers. And Windows.Foundation.Uri doesn't allow relative paths! This is why the C# code constructs the System.Uri with a root path coming from the Page's BaseUri property.

Page's BaseUri property is set to a value such as ms-appx:/MainPage.xaml. ms-appx is the scheme for an app's resources—any files packaged with your app because they are included in your project with a Build Action of Content. Therefore, the C# code could use the absolute URI more explicitly as follows:

```
Image image = new Image();
image.Source = new BitmapImage(new Uri("ms-appx:/Assets/Logo.png"));
```

Or, more commonly, with three slashes instead of just one:

```
Image image = new Image();
image.Source = new BitmapImage(new Uri("ms-appx:///Assets/Logo.png"));
```

The absolute URI could be used in XAML as well:

```
<Image Source="ms-appx:///Assets/Logo.png"/>
```

The path in the URI matches the folder structure in your project. If you place an image.jpg file in the root of your project, its URI is ms-appx:///image.jpg.

> **(?) Why do ms-appx URIs use three slashes instead of two?**
>
> The form of the URI is *scheme://domainName/path*. The *domainName* is the app's package full name (specified in your package manifest and set to a GUID by default), but it can fortunately be omitted to imply the current app's package full name. This means that you can reference files in other packages, but this works only for *dependent packages*.

Because relative URIs in XAML always map to ms-appx (app resources), referencing a file in app data or on the Web must be done with absolute URIs. Referencing a file on the Web can be done as you would expect:

```
<Image Source="http://blog.adamnathan.net/images/logo.png"/>
```

or:

```
Image image = new Image();
image.Source = new BitmapImage(
  new Uri("http://blog.adamnathan.net/images/logo.png"));
```

Referencing a file in app data can be done with an ms-appdata scheme as follows:

```
<Image Source="ms-appdata:///location/savedFile.jpg"/>
```

or:

```
Image image = new Image();
image.Source = new BitmapImage(new Uri("ms-appdata:///location/savedFile.jpg"));
```

where *location* could be local, roaming, or temp. Chapter 20 has more information.

> **(!) Make sure resource files in your project are marked with a Build Action of Content!**
>
> Otherwise, they won't get packaged with your app. Other Build Action choices such as Embedded Resource or PRIResource do not work for this purpose.

> **(?) How can I make Image render image data from an IRandomAccessStream?**
>
> This is an important question, because the Windows Runtime uses IRandomAccessStream throughout its APIs. And the answer is simple: BitmapImage's base class (BitmapSource) exposes a SetSource method that accepts an IRandomAccessStream.
>
> The following code demonstrates this by first obtaining an IRandomAccessStream from a file chosen by the user via the Windows file picker, then by constructing an appropriate BitmapImage that uses the IRandomAccessStream, and finally assigning the BitmapImage to the Image:

```
async Task ShowUserSelectedFile()
{
  // Get a JPEG from the user
  FileOpenPicker picker = new FileOpenPicker();
  picker.FileTypeFilter.Add(".jpg");
  picker.FileTypeFilter.Add(".jpeg");
  StorageFile file = await picker.PickSingleFileAsync();
  if (file != null)
  {
    // Get the image data
    using (IRandomAccessStream ras = await file.OpenAsync(FileAccessMode.Read))
    {
      // Load the data into a BitmapImage
      BitmapImage source = new BitmapImage();
      source.SetSource(ras);

      // Assign the BitmapImage to the Image element on the page
      image.Source = source;
    }
  }
}
```

The .NET projection of IRandomAccessStream implements IDisposable, so a using block properly disposes of the stream once the Image has been updated.

This code is assumed to belong to a code-behind file for a Page with an Image named image on it, such as the following:

```
<Image Name="image"/>
```

Custom Stretching with Nine-Grid

Image has a nifty built-in *nine-grid* feature that enables you to use a single image as a flexible border by customizing how it stretches. (It's also hardware accelerated for great performance.) Without this support, you'd need to use up to nine separate images to create the same effect.

Figure 13.1 demonstrates the regular image-stretching behavior using the following Grid that contains the same image unstretched on the left versus stretched (and therefore pixelated) on the right:

```
<Page …>
  <Grid Background="{ThemeResource ApplicationPageBackgroundThemeBrush}">
    <Grid.ColumnDefinitions>
      <ColumnDefinition Width="Auto"/>
      <ColumnDefinition/>
```

```
    </Grid.ColumnDefinitions>
    <!-- The unscaled image: -->
    <Image Source="image.png" Stretch="None"/>
    <!-- The scaled image: -->
    <Image Grid.Column="1" Source="image.png" Stretch="Fill"/>
  </Grid>
</Page>
```

FIGURE 13.1   Typical Image stretching, with Stretch="None" on the left and Stretch="Fill" on the right

With nine-grid rendering, you can logically segment the source content into a nine-cell grid. When you do this, the four corners never stretch, the middle-top and middle-bottom edges stretch only horizontally, the middle-left and middle-right edges stretch only vertically, and the middle cell stretches in both directions as normal. For this behavior to make sense, the content must be designed to be stretched in this manner. The image.png file in Figure 13.1 clearly is designed this way, so the grid arrangement depicted in Figure 13.2 would prevent stretching of the four corners while stretching the four middle edges in a way that avoids visible pixelation.

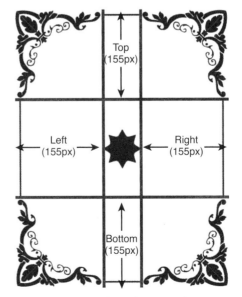

FIGURE 13.2   A logical nine-grid arrangement that avoids stretching the 155x155 pixel corners

If this behavior were represented as a nine-cell `Grid` control (containing a separate chopped-up `Image` segment in each cell), it would be equivalent to the following row and column definitions:

```
<Grid.RowDefinitions>
  <RowDefinition Height="155"/>
  <RowDefinition/>
  <RowDefinition Height="155"/>
</Grid.RowDefinitions>
<Grid.ColumnDefinitions>
  <ColumnDefinition Width="155"/>
  <ColumnDefinition/>
  <ColumnDefinition Width="155"/>
</Grid.ColumnDefinitions>
```

However, using the nine-grid support is much simpler than this. You set `Image`'s `NineGrid` property to a `Thickness` value representing the Left, Top, Right, and Bottom values depicted in Figure 13.2. Recall from Chapter 3, "Sizing, Positioning, and Transforming Elements," that `Thickness` can be specified in XAML using one, two, or four values. Because this example requires a uniform value of 155 for all four measurements, `NineGrid` can be set to the simple value of 155, as shown in this update to the original `Page`:

```
<Page …>
  <Grid Background="{ThemeResource ApplicationPageBackgroundThemeBrush}">
    <Grid.ColumnDefinitions>
      <ColumnDefinition/>
      <ColumnDefinition/>
    </Grid.ColumnDefinitions>
    <!-- The unscaled image: -->
    <Image Source="image.png" Stretch="None" />
    <!-- The scaled image with NineGrid support: -->
    <Image Grid.Column="1" Source="image.png" Stretch="Fill" NineGrid="155" />
  </Grid>
</Page>
```

The result of setting the `NineGrid` property is shown in Figure 13.3. Of course, this would typically done with a blank (or solid color) image middle to avoid any pixelation. The shape in the middle of this image is there for demonstration purposes only.

Note that `NineGrid` works only when an `Image` is stretched larger than its natural size. (If it is applied to an `Image` stretched to a smaller region, it stops rendering altogether.) Also, `NineGrid` applies only to stretching done with a `Stretch` value of `Fill`, `Uniform`, or `UniformToFill`. It has no effect when scaling an `Image` with a transform such as `ScaleTransform`.

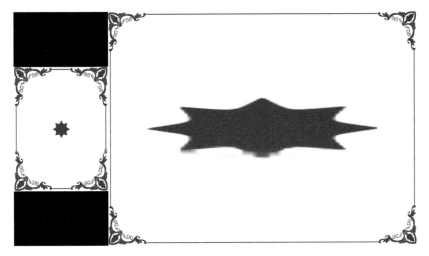

FIGURE 13.3   With `NineGrid` set, the corners and edges of the single `Image` stretch in a way that avoids the ugly pixelation seen in the middle.

Generating Dynamic **Images** with **WriteableBitmap**

`WriteableBitmap`, the other `BitmapSource` subclass, is designed for displaying dynamic pixel content. You construct an instance with a specific width and height, modify its pixels exposed via a `PixelBuffer` property, and set it as the `Source` of an `Image` element.

One common point of confusion is that `PixelBuffer` is a useless-looking Windows Runtime interface called `IBuffer`. `IBuffer` exposes only two properties: `Capacity` (the maximum number of bytes it can hold) and `Length` (the number of bytes currently in use).

C++ code can query the object for the `IBufferByteAccess` COM interface to read/write its data, but this is not an option for an app's C# code. Instead, you can use the `DataReader` and `DataWriter` classes from the `Windows.Storage.Streams` namespace, or leverage an `AsStream` extension method that wraps the object as a familiar .NET `System.IO.Stream`. (Internally, the `Stream` object leverages `IBufferByteAccess` to enable this to work.)

Therefore, suppose you have the following simple `Page` with an empty `Image`:

```
<Page …>
  <Canvas>
    <Image Name="image"/>
  </Canvas>
</Page>
```

The following code-behind creates a new 1024x768 in-memory image, fills its pixels, and uses it as the `Image`'s `Source`:

```
// Needed for AsStream extension method on IBuffer:
using System.Runtime.InteropServices.WindowsRuntime;
…
```

```
public MainPage()
{
  InitializeComponent();

  // Create a blank bitmap
  WriteableBitmap bitmap = new WriteableBitmap(1024, 768);

  // Get a .NET Stream for the bitmap's bytes
  using (Stream stream = bitmap.PixelBuffer.AsStream())
  {
    // Write each pixel (4-byte BGRA format, alpha channel ignored)
    int numPixels = bitmap.PixelWidth * bitmap.PixelHeight;
    for (int i = 0; i < numPixels; i++)
    {
      stream.WriteByte((byte)(i % 255));          // B
      stream.WriteByte(0);                        // G
      stream.WriteByte((byte)(255 - (i % 255))); // R
      stream.WriteByte(0);                        // A (ignored)
    }
  }

  // Use this as the ImageSource for an Image element
  image.Source = bitmap;
}
```

The System.Runtime.InteropServices.WindowsRuntime namespace is included so the AsStream extension method can be called. This namespace contains a number of extension methods that convert among IBuffers, arrays, and .NET Streams.

WriteableBitmap uses a pixel format known as BGRA8 (B8G8R8A8), which means that each of the four color channels is 8 bits (making each pixel 32 bits) and the order is B, G, R, then A. The loop that writes these pixel values into the Stream varies the value of the blue byte based on the pixel index, and inversely varies the value of the red byte. This results in a repeated red-blue gradient, as shown in Figure 13.4.

You can make updates to a WriteableBitmap's PixelBuffer at any time, but you must call its Invalidate method to force it to render again.

> **⚠ Beware of the performance impact of hidden managed-to-unmanaged code transitions!**
>
> Every call from managed to unmanaged code involves some overhead that doesn't exist between managed-to-managed calls and unmanaged-to-unmanaged calls. And all APIs under the Windows namespace are implemented as unmanaged code. This means that you have to be

careful to avoid being unnecessarily "chatty" with calls to Windows APIs, especially with harmless-looking property accesses.

Notice that the code that produced Figure 13.4 defines a numPixels variable to hold the value of bitmap.PixelWidth * bitmap.PixelHeight. Without this variable, every iteration of the loop would make two extra calls to unmanaged code (the property getter for PixelWidth and the property getter for PixelHeight). This difference can become quite significant for large-enough images. Even for the modest-sized 1024x768 image, this would result in over a million and a half unnecessary calls to unmanaged code!

Although the just-in-time compiler optimizes the use of an array's Length property in a loop condition (as it knows it's constant), no such optimization can be done for an arbitrary property access, regardless of whether it is implemented in managed or unmanaged code.

FIGURE 13.4   The Image element whose Source is set to a dynamically filled WriteableBitmap

Because PixelBuffer must be written to via a Stream or DataWriter, you do not get random access unless you first copy it to a byte array, do your pixel writing, and then copy it back. Another alternative would be to write a C++ component that obtains an IBufferByteAccess interface pointer, because that exposes the raw pointer. This C++ component can be called by your C# app for this purpose.

> ···
> ### WriteableBitmap and SetSource
>
> Because WriteableBitmap derives from BitmapSource, you can call SetSource to set its contents from an IRandomAccessStream, just like the previous example with BitmapImage. However, this causes it to lose all of its dynamic capabilities. Its PixelWidth, PixelHeight, and PixelBuffer properties remain unchanged, and they no longer have any relation to the content that gets rendered.

Generating Dynamic Images with RenderTargetBitmap

RenderTargetBitmap enables you to take a screenshot of any UIElement, even your entire Page! This can be especially useful when supporting the Share charm, covered in Chapter 21, "Supporting Charms." To use it, instantiate one then call its RenderAsync method with the root UIElement to capture:

```
RenderTargetBitmap rtb = new RenderTargetBitmap();
await rtb.RenderAsync(element);
```

Because RenderTargetBitmap is an ImageSource, you can use it as the source of any Image element. To extract the image data to use for other purposes, you call GetPixelsAsync to get back an IBuffer:

```
IBuffer buffer = await rtb.GetPixelsAsync();
```

From this point, you can interact with the IBuffer the same way you would with one obtained from WriteableBitmap, such as calling AsStream to get a Stream.

Multiple Files for Multiple Environments

Unlike vector graphics, you need to worry about artifacts when Images are scaled to anything other than their natural size, especially when they are scaled upward. Even if you never scale Image elements yourself, there are still cases when Windows automatically scales all content in Windows Store apps. Windows uses one of three specific scale factors to make things more manageable for apps. As with the touch-optimized pieces of the Windows shell, apps are scaled as follows:

→ **180%** (80% larger) on a screen with at least a Wide Quad High Definition (WQHD) resolution (2560x1440 pixels) and at least 240 DPI

→ **140%** (40% larger) on a screen with at least a Full HD resolution (1920x1080 pixels) and at least 174 DPI

→ **100%** (no scaling) otherwise

Scaling is also bumped up one step (100% to 140%) or (140% to 180%) if the user selects the "Change the size of apps on the displays that can support it" option in the "Display" section of the PC Settings app. This is an easy way to test one automatic scaling variation, or you can use the Visual Studio simulator to experiment with all three settings.

This automatic scaling is critical for apps to look good and be usable on traditional computer monitors as well as new high-density screens that are now commonplace on handheld devices. However, scaling images used in your app by 180% in the worst case can cause noticeable degradation of their quality.

Loading File Variations Automatically

Fortunately, Windows exposes a simple yet powerful built-in scheme for handling automatic scaling for any image file packaged in your app. You can provide three separate variations, .one for each possibly angle. If you follow one of two naming conventions, then the Image element automatically uses the correct one for the current environment.

For example, if you set an Image's Source to Assets/photo.jpg, then you can name the three variations of this file as follows to take advantage of this automatic support:

→ Assets/photo.**scale-100**.jpg

→ Assets/photo.**scale-140**.jpg

→ Assets/photo.**scale-180**.jpg

You don't even need a file matching the original name used in your C# or XAML! For conditions when the app is scaled 180%, Windows will first look for the scale-180 version. If that isn't present, it will look for the next best thing: the scale-140 version. If that isn't present, it will look for the scale-100 version. And if that isn't present, it will look for the exact photo.jpg file specified in your app (and fail if this vanilla version isn't present). These additions to the original filename are called *resource qualifiers*.

This support applies to the images referenced in the package manifest as well. This is why the files initially placed in a project's Assets folder are given names like Logo.scale-100.png despite the fact that the package manifest XML references them with their simple names such as Logo.png. Note that there's no support for scaling an app and its assets to 80%, unlike with the tile image files that you can use in your package manifest.

If you prefer to organize your three sets of assets into three separate folders, you can use the following naming pattern instead, which moves the resource qualifiers from the filename to a folder name:

→ Assets/**scale-100**/photo.jpg

→ Assets/**scale-140**/photo.jpg

→ Assets/**scale-180**/photo.jpg

This works the same way as the other naming scheme. You must choose one or the other, at least for a single file, because otherwise the MakePri tool that's invoked by Visual Studio when building your app will fail.

Just like with images referenced in your package manifest, this automatic image selection also includes support for high contrast! Therefore, if you're hardcore, you can supply *twelve* variations of every image asset by combining the three `scale` resource qualifiers with four possible `contrast` resource qualifiers:

→ `Assets/photo.`**`scale-100_contrast-standard`**`.jpg`

→ `Assets/photo.`**`scale-100_contrast-white`**`.jpg`

→ `Assets/photo.`**`scale-100_contrast-black`**`.jpg`

→ `Assets/photo.`**`scale-100_contrast-high`**`.jpg`

→ `Assets/photo.`**`scale-140_contrast-standard`**`.jpg`

→ `Assets/photo.`**`scale-140_contrast-white`**`.jpg`

→ `Assets/photo.`**`scale-140_contrast-black`**`.jpg`

→ `Assets/photo.`**`scale-140_contrast-high`**`.jpg`

→ `Assets/photo.`**`scale-180_contrast-standard`**`.jpg`

→ `Assets/photo.`**`scale-180_contrast-white`**`.jpg`

→ `Assets/photo.`**`scale-180_contrast-black`**`.jpg`

→ `Assets/photo.`**`scale-180_contrast-high`**`.jpg`

`contrast-standard`, which means normal contrast, is the default choice. Therefore, that qualifier could have been omitted, just like `scale-100` could be omitted from the first four filenames. The `contrast-high` qualifier matches any high contrast theme, whereas `contrast-white` matches the High Contrast White theme, and `contrast-black` matches the High Contrast Black, High Contrast #1, and High Contrast #2 themes. When combining these two resource qualifiers, one or both can be specified in the path rather than the filename, similar to the simpler example where only `scale` was specified.

Starting in Windows 8.1, the appropriate resource is fetched dynamically when conditions change, such as the user enabling a high contrast theme. With the new support in Windows that enables each attached monitor to have a separate scale factor, simply dragging your window from one screen to another may change its scale factor and therefore refresh its images.

Supporting all possible scale factors with your image resources increases its chance of being promoted by Microsoft in the Windows Store.

When you use `Image` elements with files that have multiple variations, you should explicitly specify their `Width` and/or `Height`. Although this goes against the typical advice of letting things size themselves, you don't want the elements to change their (pre-scaled) size when a different variation is fetched!

If you decide to forgo providing multiple sizes of your image assets, then at least consider making the files 180% of the specified size in XAML so the content only gets scaled down rather than scaled up. This can still look bad at 100% scale, however, especially for non-photographic content.

•••

Resource Qualifiers

The scale and contrast resource qualifiers are not the only ones handled automatically by Windows! There are many that can be mixed and matched to customize which image files (or other resource files packaged in your app) get loaded in a staggering number of different environments. In addition to scale and contrast, there are:

→ **language-XXX** or **lang-XXX**, where *XXX* is any BCP-47 language tag such as en-us. This represents the current preferred language for the app to use.

→ **homeregion-XXX**, where *XXX* is any BCP-47 *region* tag, which can be a two-letter region code such as US or a three-digit geographic code such as 702 for Singapore. Unlike language, this represents where the user lives. (Just because a user speaks Japanese doesn't mean he or she lives in Japan.)

→ **layoutdir-XXX**, where *XXX* is either RTL (right-to-left), LTR (left-to-right), TTBRTL (top-to-bottom, right-to-left), or TTBLTR (top-to-bottom, left-to-right). Image already reverses its content when its FlowDirection property is RightToLeft, but this enables you to do something completely custom for cultures with a different reading directionality.

→ **config-XXX**, where *XXX* is the value of the MS_CONFIGURATION_ATTRIBUTE_VALUE environment variable. This is for advanced testing purposes and not appropriate to use outside tightly controlled environments.

→ **targetsize-XXX**, where *XXX* is a number that represents both the width and height of a square image. Note that this qualifier is not automatically leveraged within apps; it is used by Windows Explorer when showing file-type-association or protocol icons. The package manifest designer has entries for four targetsize variations from 16x16 to 256x256 for what is called the "Square 30x30 Logo."

→ **altform-XXX**, which can be used for your own custom purposes if you're using Windows Runtime resources APIs directly (in the Windows.ApplicationModel.Resources.Core namespace). So it also is not relevant for Image.

These resource qualifiers always have the *name-value* form, and can be chained together with an underscore, as seen previously with scale and contrast. They can be used in the resource's filename or path, and when used in the path, each one can be delimited with a path separator rather than an underscore. The language qualifier has a special shortcut that enables just its value to be used when using the folder syntax.

For example, an app requesting photo.jpg could end up fetching it from en-US/homeregion-us/contrast-high/photo.scale-140_layoutdir-RTL.jpg.

Remember that this applies only to resource files (ms-appx URIs).

Loading File Variations Manually

If your app loads external files (such as from your own Web server), then you cannot take advantage of automatic resource qualifier support. However, you can certainly mimic it in C# by inspecting the aspects of the current environment you care about. The following code demonstrates how you might fetch different files based on the current automatic scaling and contrast mode:

```
void LoadImage(Image image, string filename)
{
  // Either "Scale100Percent", "Scale140Percent", or "Scale180Percent":
  string scale = DisplayProperties.ResolutionScale.ToString();

  // Getting the current user theme is a bit more onerous:
  AccessibilitySettings settings = new AccessibilitySettings();
  string contrast = "Standard";
  if (settings.HighContrast)
  {
    // Either "High Contrast White", "High Contrast Black",
    //        "High Contrast #1", or "High Contrast #2":
    contrast = settings.HighContrastScheme;
  }

  // Pass along this info in a way that the Web server is prepared to handle:
  image.Source = new BitmapImage(new Uri("http://pixelwinks.com/" + filename +
    "?scale=" + scale + "&contrast=" + WebUtility.UrlEncode(contrast)));
}
```

Of course, the Web server has to play along, and not only understand your custom
resource qualifier scheme, but have the appropriate files to serve!

> If you want to display thumbnail-sized images from the file system, then you should
> consider leveraging StorageFile's GetThumbnailAsync method, which automatically
> adjusts the content for the current automatic scale.

> You should strive to arrange elements on pixel boundaries divisible by 5. This ensures that
> the elements do not experience pixel shifting when automatically scaled.

Leveraging Resource Packages

Windows 8.1 supports *resource packages*, which separate your assets such that devices no
longer have to download every variation of every resource in your app. For example, a
Surface RT only needs to download the 100% scale images rather than all three scales.
And if your app provides resources for multiple languages, Windows only needs to download ones corresponding to the language(s) in use on the device.

Leveraging this support is as simple as telling the packaging wizard to generate an *app
bundle* when you select **Store, Create App Packages...** in Visual Studio. As shown in
Figure 13.5, you can select "Always" or "If Needed." The latter generates an app bundle
only if you've defined scale-specific or language-specific resources.

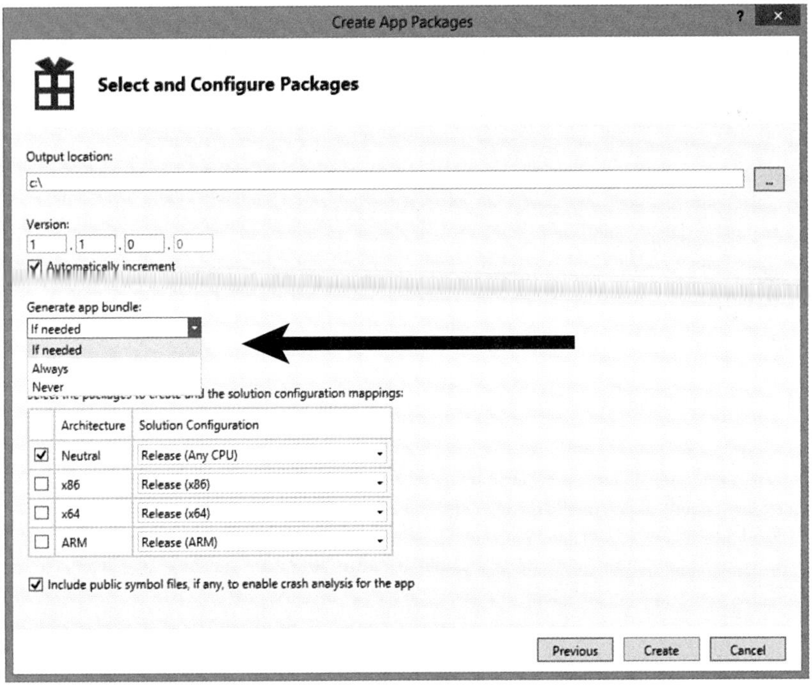

FIGURE 13.5   When you generate an app bundle, any relevant resource packages are created for you automatically.

Decoding Images

With the `BitmapDecoder` class in the `Windows.Graphics.Imaging` namespace, you get access to the decoding process that occurs automatically when displaying image content in an `Image` element. This enables you to do interesting things, such as getting the pixel data for an image file, or retrieving any metadata stored inside, such as tagged people.

To demonstrate `BitmapDecoder` throughout this section, we'll start with a method almost identical to the `ShowUserSelectedFile` example from a previous FAQ sidebar:

```
async Task DecodeUserSelectedFile()
{
  // Get a JPEG from the user
  FileOpenPicker picker = new FileOpenPicker();
  picker.FileTypeFilter.Add(".jpg");
  picker.FileTypeFilter.Add(".jpeg");
  StorageFile file = await picker.PickSingleFileAsync();
  if (file != null)
  {
    // Get the image data
```

```
    using (IRandomAccessStream ras = await file.OpenAsync(FileAccessMode.Read))
    {
        // Create the decoder
        BitmapDecoder decoder = await BitmapDecoder.CreateAsync(ras);
        // Use the decoder
        UseDecoder(decoder);
    }
  }
}
```

This code obtains an `IRandomAccessStream` from a file chosen by the user via the Windows file picker, because it is necessary in order to create a `BitmapDecoder`. After creating a `BitmapDecoder` based on this stream, it calls a `UseDecoder` method. This is a placeholder method that we'll implement a few different ways in this section, so the surrounding boilerplate code doesn't need to be repeated.

Some image formats permit multiple frames, such as an animated GIF, a multipage TIFF file, or an icon file that includes multiple sizes. `BitmapDecoder` exposes this situation with its `FrameCount` property. It also defines a `GetFrameAsync` method for retrieving a `BitmapFrame` object. `BitmapFrame` exposes much of the same functionality as `BitmapDecoder`, but specific to the chosen frame.

> **Choosing a Specific Decoder** •••
>
> An advanced overload of `BitmapDecoder.CreateAsync` enables you to pass a `Guid` that identifies the specific installed decoder you want to use. To make this easier, `BitmapDecoder` exposes a static `Guid` property for each of the built-in decoders: BMP, PNG, GIF, JPEG, JPEG-XR, TIFF, and ICO. In addition, you can enumerate all installed decoders with the static `BitmapDecoder.GetDecoderInformation-Enumerator` method.

Getting Pixel Data

`BitmapDecoder` exposes a `GetPixelDataAsync` method that ultimately gives you a raw `byte` array with the image's pixel data flattened into one dimension. However, this is done via an intermediate `PixelDataProvider` class as follows:

```
async Task UseDecoder(BitmapDecoder decoder)
{
    PixelDataProvider provider = await decoder.GetPixelDataAsync();
    byte[] pixels = provider.DetachPixelData();
    …
}
```

`DetachPixelData` can be called only once per `PixelDataProvider` instance, because it does not hold onto a copy of the bytes. (`PixelDataProvider` exists solely because of a limitation with the projection mechanism for Windows Runtime APIs: asynchronous methods cannot return arrays!)

BitmapDecoder has PixelWidth and PixelHeight properties that reveal the image's dimensions, but without knowing the pixel format and alpha mode of the image, you can't know how to interpret the returned byte array. You must check BitmapDecoder's BitmapPixelFormat and BitmapAlphaMode properties to discover this information. GetPixelDataAsync automatically converts any custom color spaces to the standard RGB color space, and automatically rotates the pixel data if orientation metadata exists and is set to a nondefault value. (Incidentally, so does the Image element.) To get the correct dimensions in the face of potential rotation, you should use BitmapDecoder's OrientedPixelWidth and OrientedPixelHeight properties instead of PixelWidth and PixelHeight.

To simplify your code, you can force the returned byte array to use a specific pixel format and alpha mode with an overload of GetPixelDataAsync. This overload also lets you apply a BitmapTransform, decide whether to respect orientation metadata, and decide whether to convert non-RGB color spaces. The following code leverages this overload to force each pixel to be four bytes long in RGBA order. It then applies a simple color inversion effect before writing these modified pixels to a WriteableBitmap in order to display it:

```
async Task UseDecoder(BitmapDecoder decoder)
{
  // Force each pixel to be 4 bytes (B, G, R, then A)
  PixelDataProvider provider = await decoder.GetPixelDataAsync(
    BitmapPixelFormat.Bgra8, BitmapAlphaMode.Straight, new BitmapTransform(),
    ExifOrientationMode.RespectExifOrientation,
    ColorManagementMode.ColorManageToSRgb);
  byte[] pixels = provider.DetachPixelData();

  // Invert the colors by subtracting each B, G, and R from 255 (byte.MaxValue)
  for (int i = 0; i < pixels.Length; i += 4)
  {
    pixels[i]     = (byte)(byte.MaxValue - pixels[i]);   // B
    pixels[i + 1] = (byte)(byte.MaxValue - pixels[i+1]); // G
    pixels[i + 2] = (byte)(byte.MaxValue - pixels[i+2]); // R
                                                         // Leave A alone
  }

  // Create a new WriteableBitmap to contain the edited pixels
  WriteableBitmap bitmap = new WriteableBitmap((int)decoder.OrientedPixelWidth,
                                               (int)decoder.OrientedPixelHeight);

  // Get a .NET Stream for the bitmap's bytes
  using (Stream stream = bitmap.PixelBuffer.AsStream())
  {
    // Write all pixels using the existing BGRA array
    await stream.WriteAsync(pixels, 0, pixels.Length);
```

```
  }

  // Assign the BitmapImage to the Image element on the page
  image.Source = bitmap;
}
```

This assumes a `Page` such as the following with an `Image` named `image`:

```
<Page …>
  <Viewbox>
    <Image Name="image"/>
  </Viewbox>
</Page>
```

The result of applying this inversion to the copy of a photo's pixels and feeding them to the `WriteableBitmap` is shown in Figure 13.6.

Original pixels   Inverted pixels

FIGURE 13.6   `BitmapDecoder`'s access to an image file's pixels enables the creation of much more interesting `WriteableBitmaps`.

`BitmapFrame` exposes the same properties discussed in this section (`BitmapAlphaMode`, `BitmapPixelFormat`, `PixelWidth`, `PixelHeight`, `OrientedPixelWidth`, and `OrientedPixelHeight`) as well as the two `GetPixelDataAsync` methods. You can therefore retrieve, interpret, and modify pixels for a specific frame in an image with the same techniques.

•••

BitmapTransform

The BitmapTransform class that can be passed to GetPixelDataAsync is a simple Windows Runtime class that has no formal relationship with the XAML-specific Transform family of classes. It is similar in spirit, however. It exposes several properties that enable you to describe how you want to transform an image's pixels. You can specify a scale factor for the width and height independently, you can specify a rotation (but only 0°, 90°, 180°, or 270°), you can specify a horizontal or vertical flip, and you can specify a rectangular region for cropping the image. BitmapTransform enables you to choose one of four standard interpolation algorithms to be used when scaling pixels: Linear, Cubic, Fant, and NearestNeighbor (the default).

If you don't want GetPixelDataAsync to do any transform, you must still pass a valid instance of BitmapTransform rather than null. This is why the code that produces Figure 13.6 constructs an instance.

The following is an update to that code that rotates the pixels 90° clockwise rather than inverting the colors:

```
async Task UseDecoder(BitmapDecoder decoder)
{
  // Force each pixel to be 4 bytes (B, G, R, then A) and rotate the content
  PixelDataProvider provider = await decoder.GetPixelDataAsync(
      BitmapPixelFormat.Bgra8, BitmapAlphaMode.Straight,
      new BitmapTransform { Rotation = BitmapRotation.Clockwise90Degrees },
      ExifOrientationMode.RespectExifOrientation,
      ColorManagementMode.ColorManageToSRgb);
  byte[] pixels = provider.DetachPixelData();

  // Create a new WriteableBitmap to contain the edited pixels,
  // with flipped width & height to account for the BitmapTransform rotation
  WriteableBitmap bitmap = new WriteableBitmap((int)decoder.OrientedPixelHeight,
                                               (int)decoder.OrientedPixelWidth);

  // Get a .NET Stream for the bitmap's bytes
  using (Stream stream = bitmap.PixelBuffer.AsStream())
  {
    // Write all pixels using the existing BGRA array
    await stream.WriteAsync(pixels, 0, pixels.Length);
  }

  // Assign the BitmapImage to the Image element on the page
  image.Source = bitmap;
}
```

Notice that the rotation does *not* affect OrientedPixelWidth and OrientedPixelHeight (only orientation metadata inside the image file does), so WriteableBitmap must be constructed with those two values reversed for the result to come out as expected.

> BitmapDecoder and BitmapFrame expose a GetThumbnailAsync method that enables you to operate on a thumbnail-sized version of the original image file. This is different from StorageFile's method of the same name, because this one fetches a thumbnail embedded in the image file—if it exists. Some image formats, such as JPEG, support thumbnails. If the current image (or frame) has no thumbnail, GetThumbnailAsync throws an exception.
>
> BitmapDecoder also exposes a GetPreviewAsync method, which is a higher-resolution thumbnail supported by JPEG-XR files. (RAW files also support this, but there is no built-in RAW decoder.)

Reading Metadata

Some image formats support embedded metadata that reveals all kinds of things about when and where a photo was taken; what camera, flash, and lens was used; people in the photo; and so on. There are three different ways to read this metadata, each one more powerful than the previous one:

→ Reading ImageProperties from a file

→ Reading common BitmapProperties from a decoder

→ Reading raw metadata with a metadata query language

Reading (and Writing) ImageProperties from a File

The first way to access basic image metadata doesn't actually require a BitmapDecoder (or even opening the file yourself). The StorageFile object returned from APIs such as the file picker exposes many collections of metadata values represented by the following classes and their properties:

→ **BasicProperties** (DateModified, ItemDate, and Size)

→ **ImageProperties** (Width, Height, CameraManufacturer, CameraModel, DateTaken, Keywords, Latitude, Longitude, Orientation, PeopleNames, Rating, and Title)

→ **DocumentProperties** (Author, Comment, Keywords, and Title)

→ **MusicProperties** (Album, AlbumArtist, Artist, Bitrate, Composers, Conductors, Duration, Genre, Producers, Publisher, Rating, Subtitle, Title, TrackNumber, Writers, and Year)

→ **VideoProperties** (Width, Height, Bitrate, Directors, Duration, Keywords, Latitude, Longitude, Orientation, Producers, Publisher, Rating, Subtitle, Title, Writers, and Year)

You can get BasicProperties with a call to GetBasicPropertiesAsync, and you can get the rest with a similar call on StorageFile's Properties property. For example, the following code retrieves the orientation and date taken for a user-selected photo from the file picker:

```
// Get a JPEG from the user
FileOpenPicker picker = new FileOpenPicker();
picker.FileTypeFilter.Add(".jpg");
picker.FileTypeFilter.Add(".jpeg");
StorageFile file = await picker.PickSingleFileAsync();

if (file != null)
{
  // Get image properties directly from the file
  ImageProperties properties = await file.Properties.GetImagePropertiesAsync();
  DateTimeOffset dateTaken = properties.DateTaken;
  PhotoOrientation orientation = properties.Orientation;
  …
}
```

Some of the properties—Width, Height, Latitude, Longitude, Orientation, and
PeopleNames— are readonly. (Latitude and Longitude are readonly because they are each
calculated from *four* separate pieces of metadata. To update these values, you need to use
an approach described later in this chapter.) For the ones that are writeable, you can
change the property values and call SavePropertiesAsync to commit the change to the
physical file:

```
// Get image properties directly from the file
ImageProperties properties = await file.Properties.GetImagePropertiesAsync();
// Overwrite DateTaken with a lie
properties.DateTaken = DateTimeOffset.Now;
// Save the change to the file
await properties.SavePropertiesAsync();
```

Note that an app needs no special capability to overwrite this metadata; the user opened
the door to such modifications by using the file picker to send this file to the app!

**(?) What's the difference between the DateTime data type and
        DateTimeOffset?**

DateTime refers to a logical point in time that is independent of any time zone, whereas
DateTimeOffset, the type of the ImageProperties.DateTaken property, is a real point in
time with an offset relative to the UTC time zone. DateTimeOffset is the most appropriate
choice for something like the date a photo was taken, because that point in time should never
be reinterpreted even if you are now in a different time zone. An Alarm Clock app, however,
should use DateTime for the alarm time. If you had set your alarm for 8:00 AM while travelling,
you probably expect it to go off at 8:00 AM no matter what time zone you happen to be in at
the time.

For most scenarios, using DateTimeOffset is preferable to DateTime. However, it was introduced into the .NET Framework years after DateTime, so the better name was already taken.

(Designers of the class rejected calling it DateTime2 or DateTimeEx). Fortunately, consumers of these data types can use them interchangeably for the most part.

It's important to note that the Windows Runtime fixed this design mistake. Its single DateTime type—Windows.Foundation.DateTime—acts like DateTimeOffset. Even better, Windows.Foundation.DateTime gets automatically projected to DateTimeOffset in .NET. (You never see Windows.Foundation.DateTime in C# code, just like you never see Windows.Foundation.Uri). This is precisely why ImageProperties.DateTaken appears to be a DateTimeOffset property.

Reading Common `BitmapProperties` from a Decoder

The second way to access image metadata is much richer than the first, and a bit more complicated. It requires a BitmapDecoder, which exposes a BitmapProperties property. (BitmapFrame exposes the same property.) The following code demonstrates how to get the same two orientation and date-taken properties for a user-selected photo by filling in a new implementation for the UseDecoder method referenced previously:

```csharp
async Task UseDecoder(BitmapDecoder decoder)
{
  try
  {
    // GetPropertiesAsync throws when codec doesn't support all passed-in values!
    BitmapPropertySet props = await decoder.BitmapProperties.GetPropertiesAsync(
      new string[] { "System.Photo.Orientation", "System.Photo.DateTaken" });
    BitmapTypedValue value;
    if (props.TryGetValue("System.Photo.Orientation", out value))
    {
      ushort orientation = (ushort)value.Value;
    }
    if (props.TryGetValue("System.Photo.DateTaken", out value))
    {
      DateTimeOffset dateTaken = (DateTimeOffset)value.Value;
    }
  }
  catch
  {
    // GetPropertiesAsync throws when codec doesn't support all passed-in values!
  }
}
```

Notice the many differences between this approach and the simpler ImageProperties approach:

→ Each piece of metadata is represented by a string name rather than a strongly typed property. The .NET projection of BitmapPropertySet implements IDictionary<string, BitmapTypedValue>, so the values are retrieved based on their keys in typical .NET fashion. The `BitmapTypedValue` representing each piece of metadata has a `Value` property of type `System.Object` and a `Type` property of type `PropertyType` (an enumeration covering every possible data type).

→ The `GetPropertiesAsync` method is hostile in the face of unsupported properties (it throws an exception), so you must guard against that. Not all formats support every piece of metadata. BMP files, for example, don't support *any* metadata!

→ The data types for the same metadata values can be a bit more "raw." It turns out that the `ushort` value returned for the photo's orientation uses the same values in the `PhotoOrientation` enumeration seen previously, so it can be cast to `PhotoOrientation` for more readable code.

Unlike the much more limited `ImageProperties`, `BitmapProperties` exposes most of the metadata stored within an image file. There's a long list of common properties you can request by name, grouped into four categories based on their namespace-like prefix:

→ **System.XXX**, where *XXX* can be `ApplicationName`, `Author`, `Comment`, `Copyright`, `DateAcquired`, `Keywords`, `Rating`, `SimpleRating`, `Subject`, or `Title`.

→ **System.Photo.XXX**, where *XXX* can be `Aperture`, `Brightness`, `CameraManufacturer`, `CameraModel`, `CameraSerialNumber`, `Contrast`, `DateTaken`, `DigitalZoom`, `EXIFVersion`, `ExposureBias`, `ExposureTime`, `Flash`, `FlashEnergy`, `FlashManufacturer`, `FlashModel`, `FNumber`, `FocalLength`, `FocalLengthInFilm`, `ISOSpeed`, `LensManufacturer`, `LensModel`, `LightSource`, `MakerNote`, `MaxAperture`, `MeteringMode`, `Orientation`, `PeopleNames`, `PhotometricInterpretation`, `ProgramMode`, `RelatedSoundFile`, `Saturation`, `Sharpness`, `ShutterSpeed`, `SubjectDistance`, `TranscodedForSync`, or `WhiteBalance`.

→ **System.Image.XXX**, where *XXX* can be `ColorSpace`, `CompressedBitsPerPixel`, `Compression`, `HorizontalResolution`, `ImageID`, `ResolutionUnit`, or `VerticalResolution`.

→ **System.GPS.XXX**, where *XXX* can be `Altitude`, `Latitude`, `Longitude`, or many more values (an astonishing 30 in total).

Note that all metadata retrieved from a `BitmapDecoder` is readonly. (The type of `BitmapDecoder`'s `BitmapProperties` property is `BitmapPropertiesView`, which doesn't expose a mechanism for saving new values.) To change metadata via `BitmapProperties`, you must use a `BitmapEncoder` instead.

Reading Raw Metadata with a Metadata Query Language
The third and final approach for reading metadata uses the same `BitmapProperties` code as the second approach, but with different strings to represent each property. Instead of using a predefined `System…` string, you can use a custom query with the Windows Imaging Component (WIC) metadata query language.

This low-level approach gives direct access to any and all metadata in the file (more than what is provided by the two other approaches). Metadata can be stored in different formats, such as Exchangeable image file format (Exif) or Extensible Metadata Platform (XMP), and in different ways within the same format (such as ASCII versus Unicode strings). Whereas `BitmapProperties` consolidates many possibilities into a consistent logical view, raw metadata queries provide no such luxury.

The following code updates the `UseDecoder` method to get the same two orientation and date-taken metadata values from the user-selected JPEG file—*if* they happen to be stored in one specific Exif format:

```
async Task UseDecoder(BitmapDecoder decoder)
{
  try
  {
    // GetPropertiesAsync throws when codec doesn't support all passed-in values!
    BitmapPropertySet props = await decoder.BitmapProperties.GetPropertiesAsync(
     new string[] { "/app1/ifd/{ushort=274}", "/app1/ifd/exif/{ushort=36867}" });
    BitmapTypedValue value;
    if (props.TryGetValue("/app1/ifd/{ushort=274}", out value))
    {
      ushort orientation = (ushort)value.Value;
    }
    if (props.TryGetValue("/app1/ifd/exif/{ushort=36867}", out value))
    {
      string dateTaken = (string)value.Value;
    }
  }
  catch
  {
    // GetPropertiesAsync throws when codec doesn't support all passed-in values!
  }
}
```

Notice that the retrieved date taken is a raw string, and not even in a format that `DateTimeOffset` can automatically parse (for example, `2013:04:01 22:43:37`).

Further examination of image metadata formats and WIC's metadata query language is beyond the scope of this book.

Encoding Images

The opposite of `BitmapDecoder` is a `BitmapEncoder` class from the same namespace. With it, you can create and modify images, and then save them to multiple formats. You can also write metadata values, if the target format supports it.

`BitmapEncoder` exposes an API that's similar to `BitmapDecoder`, or at least as similar as possible considering the different requirements of the task. `BitmapEncoder`'s `CreateAsync` method forces you to choose which encoder (and therefore which codec) to use by passing in a Guid identifying it in addition to the IRandomAccessStream. As with BitmapDecoder, BitmapEncoder exposes several public static Guid properties for the built-in BMP, GIF, JPEG, JPEG-XR, PNG, TIFF encoders. (There is no built-in ICO encoder, despite there being a built-in ICO decoder.) You can enumerate all supported encoders with the static BitmapEncoder.GetEncoderInformationEnumerator method.

To demonstrate BitmapEncoder, we'll start with an **Encode**UserSelectedFile method similar to the preceding section's DecodeUserSelectedFile method:

```
async Task EncodeUserSelectedFile()
{
  // Get a target JPEG file from the user
  FileSavePicker picker = new FileSavePicker();
  picker.FileTypeChoices.Add("JPEG file", new string[] { ".jpg", ".jpeg" });
  StorageFile file = await picker.PickSaveFileAsync();
  if (file != null)
  {
    // Get the image data
    using (IRandomAccessStream ras =
           await file.OpenAsync(FileAccessMode.ReadWrite))
    {
      // Create the JPEG encoder
      BitmapEncoder encoder =
        await BitmapEncoder.CreateAsync(BitmapEncoder.JpegEncoderId, ras);

      // Use the encoder
      await UseEncoder(encoder);

      // WARNING: This throws an exception when encoding fails:
      await encoder.FlushAsync();
    }
  }
}
```

This time, the file picker is used in its "save mode" to get a stream we can write into. Whether the user chooses an existing file to overwrite or types in a new filename, our code works the same way.

The file is opened in ReadWrite mode rather than just Read, because BitmapEncoder needs to write the encoded image into the returned stream. That stream is passed to BitmapEncoder.CreateAsync, which is used to create the built-in JPEG encoder. We'll implement UseEncoder in a moment.

 Don't forget to call FlushAsync when you are finished with a BitmapEncoder!

However, you should call it only once you're done with it. After FlushAsync is called, you must create a new BitmapEncoder instance for further encoding work.

EncodeUserSelectFile awaits the completion of the asynchronous operation returned by UseEncoder to ensure that FlushAsync isn't called too early, and that the stream isn't disposed too early. FlushAsync must be called once you're finished encoding. This is also the point where most exceptions might be raised.

Choosing Encoding Options   •••

Some encoders expose options that enable you to customize the encoded result. For example, the built-in JPEG encoder has a configurable quality setting and subsampling mode (used for image compression), the built-in PNG encoder has a configurable filter mode, and the built-in TIFF encoder has a configurable compression mode.

To pass such options to an encoder, you construct one with an overload of CreateAsync that accepts a collection of options as its third parameter. Each option is represented as a BitmapTypedValue, the same data type used for image metadata, so the easiest way to call this method is to create a BitmapPropertySet instance, fill it with appropriate values, and then pass it along. The Windows.Graphics.Imaging namespace contains enumerations for some of these options (JpegSubsamplingMode, PngFilterMode, and TiffCompressionMode).

Writing Pixel Data

BitmapEncoder exposes a SetPixelData method that is analogous to the more complex overload of BitmapDecoder's GetPixelDataAsync method. In addition to passing a flattened byte array (with pixels in row-major order), you must specify everything needed for the encoder to interpret the array: the pixel format, alpha mode, width, and height. You must also provide DPI values for both dimensions (or 0 to omit that metadata). The following implementation of UseEncoder creates a red-blue gradient image exactly like the one created with WriteableBitmap in Figure 13.4:

```
async Task UseEncoder(BitmapEncoder encoder)
{
  const int PixelWidth = 1024;
  const int PixelHeight = 728;
  const int BytesPerPixel = 4;
  const double DPI = 96.0; // Arbitrary value

  // Allocate bytes for the new image
  byte[] pixels = new byte[PixelWidth * PixelHeight * BytesPerPixel];

  // Write each pixel (4-byte BGRA format, alpha channel ignored)
  for (int i = 0; i < pixels.Length; i += BytesPerPixel)
  {
    int pixelIndex = i / 4;
    pixels[i] = (byte)(pixelIndex % 255);              // B
    pixels[i + 1] = 0;                                 // G
```

```
      pixels[i + 2] = (byte)(255 - (pixelIndex % 255)); // R
      pixels[i + 3] = 0;                                 // A (ignored)
    }

  encoder.SetPixelData(BitmapPixelFormat.Bgra8, BitmapAlphaMode.Ignore,
    PixelWidth, PixelHeight, /*horizontal*/ DPI, /*vertical*/ DPI, pixels);
}
```

SetPixelData is a synchronous method because the data is not committed until
FlushAsync is called (by the EncodeUserSelectedFile caller in this example).

Although the underlying image-generation algorithm is the same as the WriteableBitmap
example, the use of BitmapEncoder enables saving the dynamic content as a regular image
file. Figure 13.7 shows the resulting file after executing EncodeUserSelectedFile.

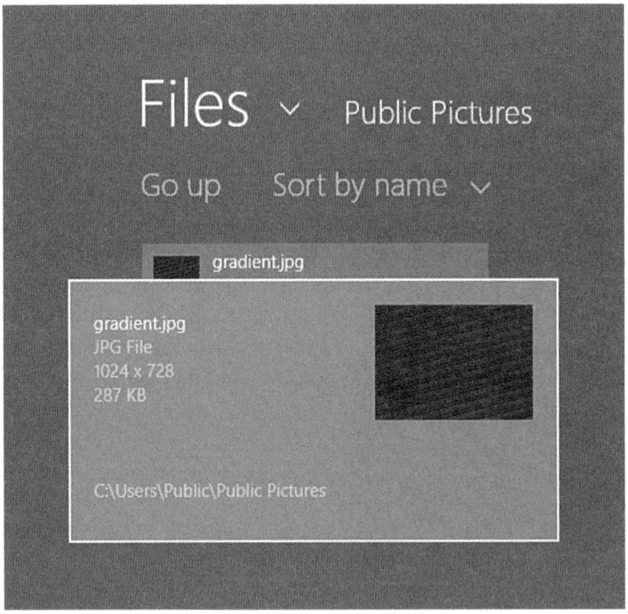

FIGURE 13.7   After the user picks a new gradient.jpg filename, the dynamic content gets
encoded and saved into the new file.

> BitmapEncoder supports writing multiple-frame images as well. SetPixelData writes the
> pixel data for the *current* frame. This is the first and only frame by default, but you can call
> BitmapEncoder's parameterless GoToNextFrameAsync method to do the following three
> things:
>
> 1. Commit the pixel data for the current frame (the same thing that FlushAsync does, but
>   leaving the encoder in a useable state)

> 2. Append a new empty frame to image being encoded
>
> 3. Set the new frame as the current frame
>
> Therefore, encoding a multiple-frame image involves a repeating pattern of `SetPixelData` then `GoToNextFrameAsync` pairs, although the final call to `SetPixelData` must be followed by a call to `FlushAsync` instead.
>
> An overload of `GoToNextFrameAsync` enables you to pass a collection of encoding options, just like what you can pass to the overload of `CreateAsync`. It turns out that the encoding options passed to `CreateAsync` apply only to the *first* frame! You must explicitly pass them to `GoToNextFrameAsync` in order to apply them to subsequent frames.

Writing Metadata

The same three approaches for reading metadata apply to writing metadata as well. The file-based `ImageProperties` approach already supports reading *and* writing most of its properties, and that was shown in the "Decoding Images" section. The two `BitmapProperties` approaches can be used with `BitmapEncoder`'s `BitmapProperties` property. This property is of type `BitmapProperties` rather than `BitmapPropertiesView`, so it enables writing properties with its `SetPropertiesAsync` method as well as reading them with its `GetPropertiesAsync` method.

The following code can be added to the end of the `UseEncoder` method to write four pieces of metadata into the red-blue gradient file:

```
BitmapPropertySet properties = new BitmapPropertySet();

// Set the same two properties used earlier in this chapter
properties.Add("System.Photo.Orientation",
  new BitmapTypedValue((ushort)PhotoOrientation.Normal, PropertyType.UInt16));
properties.Add("System.Photo.DateTaken",
  new BitmapTypedValue(DateTimeOffset.Parse("1/1/2014"), PropertyType.DateTime));

// Set two additional properties
properties.Add("System.Subject",
  new BitmapTypedValue("Lots of red, lots of blue", PropertyType.String));
properties.Add("System.Rating", new BitmapTypedValue(75, PropertyType.UInt32));

// Perform the update
await encoder.BitmapProperties.SetPropertiesAsync(properties);
```

MSDN contains documentation for each property, including its type and possible values. For example, `System.Rating` is a numeric value in which 1–12 is treated as one star, 13–37 as two stars, 38–62 as three stars, 63–87 as four stars, and any higher as five stars. (A value of zero is treated as no rating.)

After adding this code to set the four metadata values, the results can be seen in Windows Explorer, as shown in Figure 13.8. (The orientation value isn't shown; it's used to determine how Windows should display the contents.)

As with reading metadata, you can use WIC metadata query language for each property name rather than the simpler System.*XXX* values, if you have advanced scenarios that require it.

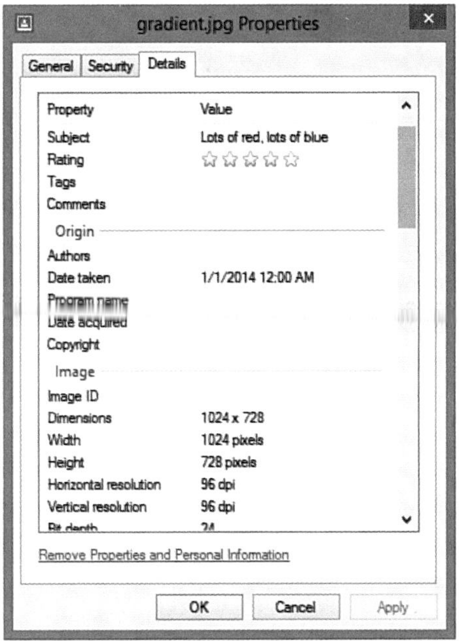

Transcoding

Transcoding refers to the conversion of data from one encoding to another. So far, the encoding examples have created a new image (the silly gradient-filled image), but you can transcode an existing image by obtaining its current data via `BitmapDecoder`, feeding it into `BitmapEncoder`, and then changing it however you see fit.

FIGURE 13.8   Viewing metadata for the image file generated by `BitmapEncoder`

You could do this by manually copying all pixel data and metadata obtained from the decoder over to the encoder, but `BitmapEncoder` has a nice shortcut for this scenario. Rather than creating a `BitmapEncoder` with its `CreateAsync` method, you can create one with its `Create`**ForTranscoding**`Async` method. You simply give it the instance of the `IRandomAccessStream` that was given to a `BitmapDecoder` and the `BitmapDecoder` instance.

Listing 13.1 contains a new version of the pixel inversion originally performed with `WriteableBitmap`. It produces the same result shown with the photo in Figure 13.6. This time, however, the code can edit the user-selected file in-place, saving the inverted result back to the source.

LISTING 13.1   Modifying a User-Selected File In-Place by Inverting Its Pixels and Changing Metadata

```
async Task InvertUserSelectedFile()
{
  // Get a JPEG from the user
  FileOpenPicker picker = new FileOpenPicker();
  picker.FileTypeFilter.Add(".jpg");
  picker.FileTypeFilter.Add(".jpeg");
  StorageFile file = await picker.PickSingleFileAsync();
  if (file != null)
  {
    // Get the image data
```

LISTING 13.1   Continued

```
using (IRandomAccessStream ras =
        await file.OpenAsync(FileAccessMode.ReadWrite))
{
  // Create the decoder
  BitmapDecoder decoder = await BitmapDecoder.CreateAsync(ras);

  // Create the encoder for transcoding
  BitmapEncoder encoder =
    await BitmapEncoder.CreateForTranscodingAsync(ras, decoder);

  // Get the current pixels, forcing each to be 4 bytes (B, G, R, then A)
  PixelDataProvider provider = await decoder.GetPixelDataAsync(
    BitmapPixelFormat.Bgra8, BitmapAlphaMode.Straight, new BitmapTransform(),
    ExifOrientationMode.RespectExifOrientation,
    ColorManagementMode.ColorManageToSRgb);
  byte[] pixels = provider.DetachPixelData();

  // Invert the colors by subtracting each channel from 255 (byte.MaxValue)
  for (int i = 0; i < pixels.Length; i += 4)
  {
    pixels[i]     = (byte)(byte.MaxValue - pixels[i]);      // B
    pixels[i + 1] = (byte)(byte.MaxValue - pixels[i + 1]); // G
    pixels[i + 2] = (byte)(byte.MaxValue - pixels[i + 2]); // R
                                                           // Leave A alone
  }

  // Use the new pixels
  encoder.SetPixelData(BitmapPixelFormat.Bgra8, BitmapAlphaMode.Straight,
    decoder.OrientedPixelWidth, decoder.OrientedPixelHeight,
    decoder.DpiX, decoder.DpiY, pixels);

  // Update a property (leaving the rest at their current values)
  BitmapPropertySet properties = new BitmapPropertySet();
  properties.Add("System.ApplicationName",
    new BitmapTypedValue("Photo Inverter", PropertyType.String));

  // Perform the update
  await encoder.BitmapProperties.SetPropertiesAsync(properties);

  // Save the updates to the original file
  // WARNING: This throws an exception when encoding fails:
  await encoder.FlushAsync();
  }
 }
}
```

This listing combines most of what we've learned about decoding *and* encoding. Notice that the stream passed to BitmapDecoder must be opened with ReadWrite access because it is the same stream passed to BitmapEncoder. You don't need to (or get to) pick the encoder when using this shortcut; it is based on the type of decoder. This means that you can't transcode an ICO file because there's no encoder to match the decoder. If you attempt to do so, CreateForTranscodingAsync throws an exception that explains, "The component cannot be found." Listing 13.1 is an end-to-end "photo inverter." Of course, with BitmapTransform, it's easy to build a photo flipper, photo rotator, photo resizer, or photo cropper. For a horizontal photo flipper, the middle part of Listing 13.1 (between the creation of the encoder and the updating of metadata) could be replaced with the following:

```
// Get the current pixels, forcing each to be 4 bytes (B, G, R, then A)
PixelDataProvider provider = await decoder.GetPixelDataAsync(
  BitmapPixelFormat.Bgra8, BitmapAlphaMode.Straight,
  new BitmapTransform { Flip = BitmapFlip.Horizontal },
  ExifOrientationMode.RespectExifOrientation,
  ColorManagementMode.ColorManageToSRgb);
byte[] pixels = provider.DetachPixelData();


// No other pixel modification necessary


// Use the new pixels
encoder.SetPixelData(BitmapPixelFormat.Bgra8, BitmapAlphaMode.Straight,
  decoder.OrientedPixelWidth, decoder.OrientedPixelHeight,
  decoder.DpiX, decoder.DpiY, pixels);
```

For a photo cropper, you could replace it with the following code instead, where chosenX, chosenY, chosenWidth, and chosenHeight are uint variables presumably set via a user interface:

```
// Get the current pixels, forcing each to be 4 bytes (B, G, R, then A)
PixelDataProvider provider = await decoder.GetPixelDataAsync(
  BitmapPixelFormat.Bgra8, BitmapAlphaMode.Straight, new BitmapTransform {
    Bounds = new BitmapBounds {
      X = chosenX, Y = chosenY, Width = chosenWidth, Height = chosenHeight
    }
  },
  ExifOrientationMode.RespectExifOrientation,
  ColorManagementMode.ColorManageToSRgb);
byte[] pixels = provider.DetachPixelData();


// No other pixel modification necessary


// Use the new pixels
encoder.SetPixelData(BitmapPixelFormat.Bgra8, BitmapAlphaMode.Straight,
  chosenWidth, chosenHeight, decoder.DpiX, decoder.DpiY, pixels);
```

Notice that the cropped width and height values need to be passed along to
`SetPixelData`, because the decoder's `(Oriented)PixelWidth` and `(Oriented)PixelHeight`
properties have no relation to the cropped `pixels` array obtained from
`GetPixelDataAsync`.

Even if you perform no transformation on the transcoded image, perhaps because you
want to edit only its metadata, there is no guarantee that the image data will be identical
after the update. Differences can happen if the original decoded image was encoded with
a different encoder with options that aren't supported by the built-in encoder.

> If the only "transcoding" you want to do is editing an image's metadata,
> `BitmapEncoder` has a separate shortcut for this. You can call its static
> `CreateForInPlacePropertyEncoding`Async method that accepts only a
> `BitmapDecoder` parameter. No stream needs to be directly passed to it, although the stream
> passed to the `BitmapDecoder` must be opened with `ReadWrite` access.
>
> `CreateForInPlacePropertyEncodingAsync` allows you to call only `GetPropertiesAsync`
> and `SetPropertiesAsync` (via its `BitmapProperties` property) and `FlushAsync` on the
> returned `BitmapEncoder` instance. Every other call will throw an exception.
>
> This shortcut exists for two reasons. One is that, if successful, it is guaranteed to preserve the orig-
> inal image data. The other is performance. When used in this way, the encoder attempts to write
> any new property values without reencoding the pixel data. Note that this type of fast metadata
> encoding doesn't work for all metadata formats, but it does for the common ones such as Exif
> and XMP. It also doesn't work if the existing metadata block in the image file doesn't contain
> enough padding to store all the new values.
>
> If the encoder returned by `CreateForInPlacePropertyEncodingAsync` is unable to perform
> fast metadata encoding, it throws an exception. Therefore, you should be prepared to handle this
> and fall back on creating the encoder with `CreateForTranscodingAsync` instead.

Rendering PDF Content as an Image

Windows 8.1 introduces APIs for loading PDF content and rendering any of its pages as
an image. For now, you can only extract the final, flattened image. So although you could
implement a magazine-style app on top of this support, you would be not be able to
make the app accessible or provide any meaningful level of interaction other than
panning and zooming. There is no way to extract the text, links, or anything else inside
PDF documents, and there is no mechanism for editing the content.

Rendering a PDF Page

Although the PDF support lacks power, its simplicity is hard to beat. Imagine that you
have a simple `Page` with an `Image` named `image` on it. The following update to the original `ShowUserSelectedFile` method from the beginning of this chapter enables the `Image`
to render the first page of a PDF file chosen by the user:

```
async Task ShowUserSelectedFile()
{
  // Get a PDF file from the user
  FileOpenPicker picker = new FileOpenPicker();
  picker.FileTypeFilter.Add(".pdf");
  StorageFile file = await picker.PickSingleFileAsync();
  if (file != null)
  {
    // Throws an exception if the document is password-protected:
    PdfDocument document = await PdfDocument.LoadFromFileAsync(file);

    // Get the first page (You can see how many exist via document.PageCount)
    using (PdfPage page = document.GetPage(0))
    {
      // Render the image to an in-memory stream then display it
      using (InMemoryRandomAccessStream ras = new InMemoryRandomAccessStream())
      {
        await page.RenderToStreamAsync(ras);

        // Load the data into a BitmapImage
        BitmapImage source = new BitmapImage();
        source.SetSource(ras);

        // Assign the BitmapImage to the Image element on the page
        image.Source = source;
      }
    }
  }
}
```

PdfDocument—from the `Windows.Data.Pdf` namespace—has static methods to either load from an `IStorageFile` (`LoadFromFileAsync`) or from an `IRandomAccessStream` (`LoadFromStreamAsync`). In case you need to open a password-protected PDF file, each has an overload with a second string password parameter. There is no way to know ahead of time whether a PDF document is password-protected, other than calling the simpler overload and catching the exception that gets thrown by not supplying the password.

From a `PdfDocument`, you can check its `PageCount` and `IsPasswordProtected` properties (although you already know whether it's password-protected if you managed to get an instance of `PdfDocument`), and call its `GetPage` method with a page index to get a `PdfPage` object representing the specific page. All the operations exposed by `PdfDocument` are fast, which is why they are all synchronous.

To render the `PdfPage` inside the `Image` element, the preceding code must call `RenderToStreamAsync` to render it to an `IRandomAccessStream`. In this case, a simple Windows Runtime in-memory stream is used. The stream can then be passed to

BitmapImage's SetSource method, and the BitmapImage can be used as the source of the Image element in the same way used earlier in this chapter. The result is shown in Figure 13.9, using a restaurant's menu downloaded from their website in PDF form.

FIGURE 13.9   PdfDocument and PdfPage makes it possible to view a PDF page inside an Image element.

PdfPage's RenderToStreamAsync method is where the bulk of the work happens. It can take a little while to render the result, which is why it's an asynchronous call. You can front-load most of the work by calling PdfPage's PreparePageAsync method, if you would like to do so before you have a stream to render into. Once a PdfPage instance has rendered once, it holds onto its resources so subsequent renderings are faster. This is important for zooming scenarios, examined in the next section. Because PdfPage holds onto many resources, it implements IDisposable so you can force it to release them without waiting for the garbage collector.

PdfPage exposes several properties:

→ **Index**—The same numeric page index passed to PdfDocument.GetPage in order to get the instance.

→ **PreferredZoom**—A float, where 1.0 means 100% zoom.

→ **Rotation**—The document's rotation, expressed as a value from the PdfPageRotation enumeration: Normal, Rotate90, Rotate180, or Rotate270.

→ **Size**—The document size expressed as a standard Windows.Foundation.Size structure.

→ **Dimensions**—An instance of `PdfPageDimensions`, with more details about the current page's size.

Although the `Size` property presents a simple description of the `PdfPage`'s size, the PDF standard has a much more complicated representation of a page's exact size. It has the concept of five different *page boxes*, each of which is exposed as a `Rect` property from `PdfPageDimensions`: `MediaBox`, `CropBox`, `BleedBox`, `TrimBox`, and `ArtBox`. It's unlikely that an app will need to act upon these values, especially considering how primitive the support is in Windows 8.1

Customizing the Page Rendering

`PdfPage`'s `RenderToStreamAsync` method has an overload than enables you to pass a `PdfPageRenderOptions` instance as a second parameter. This enables you to customize the rendering of any page in a number of ways. `PdfPageRenderOptions` exposes the following properties:

→ **BackgroundColor**—Enables you to choose a different background color rather than the default of white.

→ **BitmapEncoderId**—Enables you to use a different encoder for the rendering rather than the built-in PNG decoder. You do this by setting this property to the appropriate `Guid`.

→ **DestinationWidth** and **DestinationHeight**—Specifies the output image size so you can obtain the appropriate level of crispness. You can specify just one of these, and `RenderToStreamAsync` will preserve the aspect ratio of the page.

→ **IsIgnoringHighContrast**—This is true by default, so you can set it to false to have the PDF content leverage the current high contrast theme colors rather than the default colors.

→ **SourceRect**—Enables you to specify a subregion to render. This can help performance greatly if you don't need the whole page, as the time it takes to encode the image is proportional to its output size.

Imagine that you wrap an `Image` element in a `ScrollViewer` so the user can zoom it as well as scroll it:

```
<Page …>
  <ScrollViewer ViewChanged="ScrollViewer_ViewChanged">
    <Image Name="image"/>
  </ScrollViewer>
</Page>
```

In a handler for the `ScrollViewer`'s `ViewChanged` event, you could rerender the current `PdfPage` at a size optimized for the current zoom factor. If we change the preceding implementation of `ShowUserSelectedFile` to make the `PdfPage` a field of the class instead of a local variable, and remove the outermost using so the PdfPage doesn't get disposed right away, then the ViewChanged handler could be implemented as follows:

```
async void ScrollViewer_ViewChanged(object sender,
  ScrollViewerViewChangedEventArgs e)
{
  if (!e.IsIntermediate && this.page != null)
  {
    // Replace the current zoomed image content with
    // content optimized for the current zoom factor
    using (InMemoryRandomAccessStream ras = new InMemoryRandomAccessStream())
    {
      uint newHeight =
        (uint)((sender as ScrollViewer).ZoomFactor * this.page.Size.Height);

      await this.page.RenderToStreamAsync(ras, new PdfPageRenderOptions {
        DestinationHeight = newHeight // Let DestinationWidth be auto-calculated
      });

      // Load the data into a BitmapImage
      BitmapImage source = new BitmapImage();
      source.SetSource(ras);

      // Assign the BitmapImage to the Image element on the page
      image.Source = source;
    }
  }
}
```

Because each rerendering can be time-consuming, the IsIntermediate check to make sure we're not doing this extra work until the zooming is finished is very important. Figure 13.10 shows how a zoomed-in version of Figure 13.9 would appear with and without this handler. Rerendering the page helps the crispness of text and any vector content tremendously. Of course, it does nothing for any bitmap content inside the PDF page.

Because ViewChanged gets raised for panning as well as zooming, the code could be smarter about only rerendering when the zoom level actually changes, perhaps by a threshold. Even better, the code could determine the current viewport of the page and leverage PdfPageRenderOption's SourceRect property to only render what is visible on the screen at any time.

Although the PDF rendering support is based on the ISO 32000-1 standard, some of the more obscure features (such as interactive media) are not supported. But it's the same underlying engine used by the Windows Reader app, so it should handle most PDFs. As a final note, if you have complex PDF content and/or scenarios where a large amount of zoom is expected, you could consider using Windows 8.1 DirectX APIs to render the PDF content. The performance can be considerably better due to avoiding the cost of encoding the image, streaming it, then decoding it again.

Without the ViewChanged Handler

With the ViewChanged Handler

FIGURE 13.10   Rendering a new size of the page makes a big difference to text and vector content at high amounts of zoom.

Summary

You've seen how the simple-sounding Image element packs a lot of power with:

→ seamless fetching and rendering of content from a number of sources, local or remote

→ stretching support that includes nine-grid rendering in addition to the typical XAML stretching options

→ the ability to display dynamic in-memory images, whether crafted manually via WriteableBitmap, taken from a screenshot via RenderTargetBitmap, or produced from a PdfPage

You've also seen how sophisticated the resource qualifier support is. Although this support applies to *any* resource file, it is most commonly leveraged for image files. The flexibility of resource qualifiers along with the power of the Image element make it possible to create highly adaptive and scalable user interfaces even when you choose not to use vector graphics.

With the decoding and encoding support in the Windows Runtime, basic image transformations become trivial. You can focus your efforts on the specific pixel-based algorithms and not worry about the rest of the details. And because the Windows file picker enables apps to plug in seamless support for arbitrary storage locations, you can automatically transform photos that come from services such as Facebook without any extra work!

One thing that's relevant to the Image element that was not covered in this chapter is its built-in support for Play To, enabling users to stream its content to a device on the home network (such the Xbox One or a certified Play To television). This is covered in Chapter 21.

Chapter 14

AUDIO, VIDEO, AND SPEECH

Some of the most popular tablet apps—on any platform—are media-playing apps. Granted, this is mostly due to the popularity of the services behind them (Netflix, YouTube, Hulu, Vimeo, and so on), but audio and video is a big part of what most people do on a computer. All varieties of apps, and especially games, have the need for integrated audio and video playback in ways that are seamlessly blended with the rest of their content. Therefore, it shouldn't surprise you that Windows Store apps are given a powerful set of high-performance media features to leverage. Best of all, you don't need to be an expert in order to use these features!

In addition to traditional media, speech recognition and speech synthesis (also known as text-to-speech) are becoming popular to support in apps due to improvements in the technology and usefulness on devices. On devices without a hardware keyboard, speaking can be more convenient than typing. And for scenarios such as driving or running with your device, using your ears is a nice alternative to using your eyes. Windows 8.1 makes speech synthesis available to your apps, although there is no built-in API for speech recognition. For that, you could use Bing's service. See http://bing.com/dev for more information.

This chapter is similar to the preceding one, because the focus isn't so much on the handful of controls, but rather what you can do with a variety of media content. The audio/video support is based on Windows Media technology, which exposes many Windows Runtime APIs in the `Windows.Media` namespace. Speech synthesis is also exposed within this namespace. Most of this chapter is organized around three primary media activities—playback, capture, and transcoding—followed by a section on speech synthesis.

Windows Media supports deeper extensibility than what you can accomplish with C#, Visual Basic, or JavaScript in a Windows Store app. You can extend the set of supported formats, codecs, effects, and even content protection systems by creating and using *media extensions* (sometimes called Media Foundation components). These are COM-based C++ components that must be packaged with your app in order to be used. And unlike traditional COM components, they are always completely local to your app. If multiple apps want to use the same extension, they must each contain a copy of it. Although writing such C++ extensions is beyond the scope of this book, you can check out the informative "Media extensions sample" available in the Windows SDK at http://code.msdn.microsoft.com/Media-extensions-sample-7b466096.

Playback

Of course, the most common thing to do with audio and video is to play it. The XAML UI Framework contains one element for doing this, and it's appropriately called MediaElement.

MediaElement is a UIElement that displays a video (and plays its audio) much like Image displays image content. It plays audio-only files, too, so MediaElement is the XAML analog to HTML's audio and video tags rolled into one.

You can set MediaElement's source to a Uri that points an audio or video file, for example:

```
<MediaElement Source="Assets/video.mp4"/>
```

When you set MediaElement's Source, the content is fetched asynchronously, and then either a MediaOpened or MediaFailed event gets raised.

All the Uri options discussed in the preceding chapter for Image apply to MediaElement as well, so you can point to a file packaged with your app, a file on the Web, or a file in app data. And you can use all the same resource qualifier support in order to use different variations of the file for different environments.

> **?** **What audio/video formats are supported by MediaElement?**
>
> MediaElement can play anything that the built-in Video app can play. That means MP4 and WMV for video (H.264 and VC-1) including ASF for streaming; and MP3, AAC (also known as M4A), WMA, and WAV for audio. These are the only system-wide formats, and they are fully hardware-accelerated for great performance and reliability on the entire range of devices running Windows.
>
> There are a few options for supporting custom formats, however. See the "Playing Custom Media Formats" section later in this chapter.

> MediaElement supports *content protection*, also known as *digital rights management* or DRM. This includes PlayReady, but the support is extensible using the same media extension mechanism. To integrate with PlayReady using a prebuilt media extension, install the Microsoft PlayReady Client SDK available at http://visualstudiogallery.msdn.microsoft.com.

> MediaElement even supports stereoscopic 3D video (video you view with 3D glasses), if both the current device and current video file support it. You can check whether the device supports it with the static DisplayProperties.StereoEnabled Boolean property, and you can check whether the current video file supports it with MediaElement's IsStereo3DVideo Boolean property. This support works only with 3D metadata that is encoded in the H.264 SEI format.
>
> MediaElement won't automatically play 3D video in 3D, however, because that would annoy users who aren't currently wearing 3D glasses. When both StereoEnabled and IsStereo3DVideo are true, you can then enable the 3D playback by setting MediaElement's Stereo3DVideoRenderMode property to Stereo instead of Mono. If MediaElement is unable to detect the video's *packing mode* (whether the two images in each frame creating the 3D illusion are placed side-by-side or top-to-bottom), you can set its Stereo3DVideoPackingMode property appropriately.

If you place a MediaElement in a Grid, it will stretch to fill its cell. Its inner content stretches in a uniform fashion, so it will be letterboxed/pillarboxed if necessary. If you place it in a Canvas, it will render at its natural dimensions. In Windows 8, MediaElement was conspicuously missing a Stretch property to control the stretching of its inner content. In Windows 8.1, the Stretch property has arrived. You can use it just like the Stretch property on Image and Viewbox, although the UniformToFill option acts slightly differently. It centers the content in the dimension that doesn't fit rather than only truncating the right or bottom, which is generally what you'd want when watching a "zoomed in" video with letterboxing removed.

As with all UIElements, you can blend MediaElements with other UI. In Windows 8, you could not give a MediaElement a custom Opacity or a Projection, but these restrictions are eliminated in Windows 8.1.

The Media Content

MediaElement has a SetSource method just like BitmapSource's method seen in the preceding chapter, so you can easily initialize it with an IRandomAccessStream that comes from a variety of sources, such as a file that a user retrieves from the file picker or files that you programmatically retrieve from the user's Videos library. However, MediaElement's SetSource method also requires you to pass the relevant MIME type (as a string) in order to determine the format of the media file. For a video stream, this would be a string such as video/mp4, video/x-ms-asf, or video/x-ms-wmv. For an audio stream, this would be a string such as audio/mp3 or audio/x-ms-wma. Fortunately, every

`StorageFile` exposes its MIME type via its `ContentType` property. (This is not to be confused with its `FileType` property, which is the file extension.)

> If you're wondering whether `MediaElement` can play content with a particular MIME type, you can pass the MIME type `string` to its `CanPlayType` method. However, `CanPlayType` must be the most noncommittal API ever created; it returns either `Probably`, `Maybe`, or `NotSupported`!
>
> The reason that these are the only choices is that a MIME type alone doesn't give `MediaElement` enough information to know for sure. For the `video/mp4` example, it still doesn't know the codec or bitrate, and this can be the difference between success and failure. Therefore, the only surefire way to know whether playback is possible is to set it as a `MediaElement`'s source and see whether a `MediaOpened` event or a `MediaFailed` event is raised.

`MediaElement` exposes a number of readonly properties that enable you to discover characteristics of the opened media: `NaturalVideoWidth` and `NaturalVideoHeight`, `AspectRatioWidth` and `AspectRatioHeight` (which is redundant because you already know the dimensions), `NaturalDuration`, and `AudioStreamCount`. For video files with multiple audio streams, you can control which one plays by setting `AudioStreamIndex`. You can also get the language of any stream (as a BCP-47 language identifier) by calling `GetAudioStreamLanguage` with the appropriate index.

Using `MediaElement` to play an audio-only file can seem a little strange because you must attach the element somewhere in the current visual tree in order for it to work, despite the fact that there's nothing to visually show. Fortunately, `MediaElement` is invisible and unhittable when it plays audio, as if it has a size of zero regardless of its `Width`, `Height`, or how it is stretched by its parent. Therefore, it doesn't matter where you place it on your `Page`.

When `MediaElement` is playing audio-only content, its `IsAudioOnly` property reports `true`. Whether the audio is playing from an audio-only stream or a video stream, you can enable extra features by appropriately categorizing the type of audio. Setting `AudioCategory` to a value other than its default of `Other` enables it to be used for background audio, covered in Chapter 22, "Leveraging Contracts." Setting `AudioDeviceType` to `Console` or `Communications` instead of its default value of `Multimedia` can improve how Windows plays it, based on the user's Control Panel settings. (If you set `AudioCategory`, then `AudioDeviceType` is automatically updated to match.) For example, Windows gives preferential treatment to communications sounds, reducing the volume of other concurrent audio by default. You can also set `Balance` (a `double` whose default value is `0`) to any number from `-1` to `1`. This controls the volume ratio for stereo speakers, so `-1` means 100% on the left speaker, `0` means evenly split, and `1` means 100% on the right speaker.

Customizing Playback

Once `MediaElement`'s source is set and `MediaOpened` is raised, the media starts playing automatically. If you don't want it to, then set `AutoPlay` to `false`. When the user switches away from your app, any playing MediaElement automatically mutes. It then automatically unmutes once your app comes back to the foreground. The only way to change this behavior is with background audio support covered in Chapter 22.

Starting in Windows 8.1, you can set MediaElement's IsFullWindow property to true to make it automatically occupy the entire contents of your window. In this mode, it covers all other elements and ignores any customizations to its rendering (Opacity, RenderTransform, Projection, Margin, and so on). Think of this as a *full-screen mode*, except that it stays within the confines of your window if the user is sharing the screen with multiple windows. MediaElement's inner content still respects the Stretch property, so it is letterboxed/pillarboxed by default but you can customize this.

You can use MediaElement's Play, Stop, and Pause methods (the third one only if CanPause is true) to control playback. If CanSeek is true, you can seek to a specific position by setting its Position property to a TimeSpan value. When Position is externally set, a SeekCompleted event is raised as soon as the target location is ready for playback. Note that the CanPause and CanSeek properties are readonly; their value depends on the media being played, because not all media supports these actions.

If your app supports full-window playback (as many video-playing apps should), set IsFullWindow to true instead of manually sizing the MediaElement. If you were to do this yourself and make a small mistake, such as being off by one pixel or forgetting to hide an element that is on top of the MediaElement, the performance of your app would suffer.

You can make the media loop by setting IsLooping to true or mute it by setting IsMuted to true. You can also set Volume to any double value from 0 to 1 (the default is 0.5). When Volume is changed, a VolumeChanged event is raised.

You can speed up or slow down playback with DefaultPlaybackRate (a double set to 1.0 by default). The neat thing is that although the audio stays in sync, this setting doesn't affect its pitch! This is just like the popular "Play speed" option in Windows Media Player that is perfect for watching otherwise-slow-paced lectures. Whenever the value of DefaultPlaybackRate (or PlaybackRate) changes, the RateChanged event is raised.

The relationship between DefaultPlaybackRate and PlaybackRate is confusing. PlaybackRate is the actual rate while the content is playing, but it gets automatically set to the value of DefaultPlaybackRate whenever playback begins. Therefore, changing PlaybackRate only has an impact if it is set while content is already playing, and its impact only lasts for the current session. Normally, the best thing to do is to only set DefaultPlaybackRate and ensure you call Play *after* setting it.

If you're using MediaElement for real-time communications, you should not only set AudioCategory to Communications, but you should set RealTimePlayback to true. This raises the priority of refreshing the video content. In this mode, playback can occur only at its default 1.0 rate.

(?) **How can I get metadata associated with audio or video, such as artist or genre?**

You can use the same technique used to get ImageProperties in the preceding chapter, except you can get MusicProperties or VideoProperties instead. For example:

```
// Get an MP4 file from the user
FileOpenPicker picker = new FileOpenPicker();
picker.FileTypeFilter.Add(".mp4");
StorageFile file = await picker.PickSingleFileAsync();
if (file != null)
{
  // Get music properties from the file
  MusicProperties properties = await file.Properties.GetMusicPropertiesAsync();
  string artist = properties.Artist;
  IList<string> genres = properties.Genre;

  …
}
```

States and Events

At any time, MediaElement can be in one of the following states, revealed by its readonly CurrentState property: Closed, Opening, Buffering, Playing, Paused, or Stopped. Closed is the initial state. It transitions to Opening after the source is set, but before MediaOpened or MediaFailed is raised. During this state, any calls to Play, Pause, or Stop are queued until the media is opened. A CurrentStateChanged event is raised for every state transition. A MediaEnded event is raised once the content reaches the end and stops playback. This doesn't get raised due to programmatic Stop calls, and it never gets raised if the content is looping.

It's usually a good idea to handle Window's VisibilityChanged event so you can call Pause on any MediaElements with a CurrentState of Playing when your window leaves the screen. You could then potentially resume playback upon your window's return to the screen.

Whenever content is buffering or downloading (in the case of content from a remote server), BufferingProgressChanged and DownloadProgressChanged events are raised. In handlers for these events, you can check MediaElement's BufferingProgress and DownloadProgress properties, but be aware that these are double values with a range from 0–1 rather than the typical range of 0–100. When applicable, download requests are done in byte ranges. In such cases, a separate DownloadProgressOffset property indicates the starting position of the current range being downloaded, expressed as a percentage of the total download size. The DownloadProgress property then indicates the end point of the current range.

Markers

Some media files can have embedded *markers* at specific points in time. There are a few different types of markers, and each one can have associated text. For example, many media players recognize markers of type "caption" and automatically overlay their text at the appropriate times. Some video files use *index markers* to mark chapters or have other bookmarks that aid in user navigation, much like with a DVD. Markers also enable the host to perform custom actions in sync with specific events in the media.

MediaElement exposes these markers with its Markers property. This is a collection of TimelineMarker objects that expose three simple properties: Text (a string), Type (a string), and Time (a TimeSpan). When media content with embedded markers plays, a MarkerReached event is raised at the Time of each marker. This enables you to perform any desired action at the right time.

You can modify the Markers collection at runtime! This means that even if you're going to play a media file without any, you can programmatically add whatever markers you'd like. For example:

```
mediaElement.Markers.Add(
  new TimelineMarker {
    Text = "1", Time = TimeSpan.FromSeconds(5), Type = "custom"
  }
);
```

You can set these at any time—even while the media is playing—and the MarkerReached event will be raised for each one when appropriate, just as if the original media defined them! Note that you cannot encode and persist these changes into the media.

The Markers collection might not include all markers!

The Markers collection contains only markers from the media's header; not any encoded as a separate stream. This is because MediaOpened is raised after reading the headers and meta-data, but the full source might still be buffering and thus any separate stream markers are not available yet. Separate-stream script commands do trigger the MarkerReached event when encountered during media playback. However these markers are not accessible ahead of time using the Markers property.

Adding Effects

MediaElement enables you to add both audio and video effects with its AddVideoEffect and AddAudioEffect methods. (You can later remove them by calling RemoveAllEffects.) You pass a string ID, a Boolean that states whether the effect is optional, and extra config-uration that can be null if it doesn't apply.

The Windows Runtime currently includes just one built-in effect: video stabilization. Its ID is "Windows.Media.VideoStabilizationEffect" but you can just use the static VideoEffects.VideoStabilization string property instead. You therefore add it to a MediaElement (named mediaElement) as follows:

```
// Apply the video stabilization effect
mediaElement.AddVideoEffect(
  VideoEffects.VideoStabilization, true /*it's optional*/, null);
```

By making the effect optional, it means that playback will still occur even if there's some reason the effect can't be used.

Just like with custom formats, media extensions can be used to enable powerful custom effects. The same Windows SDK sample referenced in this chapter's introduction includes C++ source code for several video effects: grayscale, invert, fisheye, pinch, and warp. (The last three are enabled by passing custom parameters to the same PolarEffect used to implement them all.)

> **(!) Added effects apply to the next source!**
>
> You must apply any effects *before* setting MediaElement's source to the content that is meant to receive the effects.

> If you play a large background video to enhance the appearance of your app, you might want to disable the video when your app is viewed over Remote Desktop, to avoid creating significant performance problems. You can customize your app however you'd like when running under Remote Desktop by checking the static InteractiveSession.IsRemote property. This is the sole class (and member) in the Windows.System.RemoteDesktop namespace.

Using MediaElement as a Media Player

So far, everything you've read about MediaElement is great for audio and *noninteractive* video, such as a fancy extended splash screen, a looping animated background, a cutscene between levels of a game, or perhaps video-based storybook. However, most apps want to show interactive video in a player that enables the user to pause, stop, skip ahead, and so on.

With all of MediaElement's methods, properties, and events already discussed, you could certainly build your own media player user interface. But doing this well is a lot of work! Fortunately, as of Windows 8.1, MediaElement now supports an interactive media player mode. All you need to do is set its AreTransportControlsEnabled property to true, and MediaElement turns into the player shown in Figure 14.1.

In this mode, MediaElement gains a lot of functional elements: a play/pause Button, a volume Slider and mute Button, a Slider for seeking that also indicates download progress, a zoom toggle Button, a full-screen toggle Button, time-elapsed and time-remaining labels, plus the ability to jump back or forward 30 seconds by tapping on these two labels. It also shows a ProgressBar while waiting for the media to open.

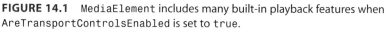

FIGURE 14.1   `MediaElement` includes many built-in playback features when `AreTransportControlsEnabled` is set to true.

All of these features are implemented with previously-discussed public APIs. The zoom `Button` add or removes any letterboxing/pillarboxing by toggling `Stretch` between `Uniform` and `UniformToFill`. If the `MediaElement` aspect ratio already matches the media aspect ratio, this `Button` does nothing. The zoom button toggles the value of `IsFullWindow`. So although its `Tooltip` says "Full Screen," it technically is a "Full Window" `Button`. This limitation is intentional. No Windows Store app, even Internet Explorer, is able to render UI over other windows when sharing the screen. (Desktop apps, such as the desktop version of Internet Explorer, can still show truly full-screen video, however, when sharing the screen with Windows Store apps.)

There is unfortunately no built-in interactive control for play speed, but you could easily add some elements for that.

> If your app is meant for prolonged video watching, then you should attempt to prevent the screen from turning off—or a screen saver from turning on—due to perceived user inactivity. Fortunately, `MediaElement` automatically does this for you while its media is playing—if `AreTransportControlsEnabled` is true.
>
> If you need to do this in other contexts, or perhaps because you've built your own user interface for interactive control of a `MediaElement`, then you can use a `DisplayRequest` object, the only class in the `Windows.System.Display` namespace. You instantiate one, call `RequestActive` when you want the prevention to begin, then call `RequestRelease` when you're ready for the screen behavior to go back to normal. Be careful, though, because all three methods (including the constructor) might throw an exception. If `RequestActive` returns without throwing an exception, then the screen is guaranteed to stay on for the life of your request. If your app gets suspended, the request is automatically reactivated when the app returns to the running state.

Setting AreTransportControlsEnabled to true works with audio-only files, too. In this case, you get all the same elements except for the zoom and full-screen Buttons. In their place, the volume Slider is placed inline on the transport controls bar.

With the simple Playlist class included in the Windows Runtime, you can integrate standard playlist files with your app. You can load a playlist file by calling LoadAsync, access and edit its collection of files (represented by a Files property that's a collection of StorageFiles), and then save it with either SaveAsync or SaveAsAsync methods. Playlist supports three file formats: M3U (.m3u), Windows Media (.wpl), and Zune (.zpl).

MediaPlayer

Microsoft provides a second control geared for advanced interactive playback called MediaPlayer. MediaPlayer derives from MediaElement, so it exposes a superset of its APIs. Everything discussed about MediaElement applies to MediaPlayer as well.

MediaPlayer is not part of any framework that ships with Windows. Rather, it is a free open-source control provided by Microsoft at http://playerframework.codeplex.com. (There are versions of the control for many other platforms as well.) This is an evolution of the same video player codebase that Microsoft used for the Beijing and Vancouver Olympics, the 2012 Super Bowl, Wimbledon, and a number of other massive live events. Because of this, it supports a number of advanced features: many forms of advertising integration, closed captioning, and adaptive streaming (via the Smooth Streaming Client SDK mentioned at the beginning of this chapter). The control isn't (yet) perfect, but you can easily tweak its source code for your needs.

Once you install the .vsix extension for Visual Studio, you can add "Microsoft Media Platform: Player Framework" to your project references. When you bring up the Reference Manager dialog in Visual Studio, you can find it under Windows, Extensions. After this, you can place the Microsoft.PlayerFramework.MediaPlayer control on your Page and set its Source to a Uri, just like with MediaElement:

```
<Page … xmlns:p="using:Microsoft.PlayerFramework">
  <Canvas Background="{ThemeResource ApplicationPageBackgroundThemeBrush}">
    <p:MediaPlayer
      Source="http://smf.blob.core.windows.net/samples/videos/bigbuck.mp4"/>
  </Canvas>
</Page>
```

This looks just like a MediaElement with AreTransportControlsEnabled set to true (because it is). With a few additional properties set as follows, MediaPlayer gains functional replay and fast-forward Buttons, a closed captions Button (functional if the video contains them), and a signal strength indicator (relevant only for adaptive streaming):

```
<p:MediaPlayer IsReplayVisible="True" IsFastForwardVisible="True"
               IsCaptionsVisible="True" IsSignalStrengthVisible="True"
   Source="http://smf.blob.core.windows.net/samples/videos/bigbuck.mp4"/>
```

The result of adding these properties is shown in Figure 14.2.

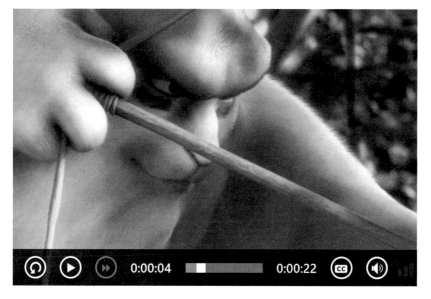

FIGURE 14.2   More `MediaPlayer` features are just a few property sets away.

`MediaPlayer` adds a *lot* of properties and events to support enabling/disabling and showing/hiding of all its extra UI elements. If you're serious about providing a first-class interactive video player with adaptive streaming support and integrated ads, then be sure to check out `MediaPlayer`.

Playing Custom Media Formats

You can support additional media formats if you have an appropriate media extension DLL packaged with your app. Microsoft is intentionally restricting the ability to install system-wide support for additional formats and codecs because that could make poorly written extensions negatively impact *every* app (as it has in the past).

The Windows SDK sample referenced in this chapter's introduction includes the C++ source code for an MPEG-1 decoder that is built and packaged with a C# app that consumes it. You can also support adaptive streaming via this mechanism by installing the Smooth Streaming Client SDK available at http://visualstudiogallery.msdn. microsoft.com and referencing it in your app. This packages the necessary prebuilt media extension DLL with your app.

However, Windows 8.1 introduces an easier way to plug custom behavior into the media pipeline without writing C++ code. This mechanism is enabled by a class called MediaStreamSource from the Windows.Media.Core namespace. To do this, you:

1. Configure an instance of MediaStreamSource with encoding information about the audio and/or video data you're going to produce.

2. Tell the MediaStreamSource how long the media will be by setting its Duration property.

3. Provide a callback with which you will deliver the audio samples by attaching a handler to its SampleRequested event.

4. Set the MediaStreamSource as the source of a MediaElement by passing it to MediaElement's Set**MediaStream**Source method instead of SetSource.

MediaStreamSource would be typically used to retrieve existing media, perhaps via a custom mechanism, and then perform custom decoding so it could be encoded to an already-supported format. However, the raw bits are entirely under your control. You could morph the content however you'd like or even generate new content on the fly. Listing 14.1 demonstrates MediaStreamSource by dynamically generating 10 seconds of random audio data for MediaElement to play. The result sounds like radio static. This listing is the code-behind for a MainPage.xaml file that is assumed to contain a MediaElement named mediaElement.

LISTING 14.1   MainPage.xaml.cs: Generating Random Audio for MediaElement to Play

```
using System;
using System.IO;
using System.Runtime.InteropServices.WindowsRuntime;
using Windows.Media.Core;
using Windows.Media.MediaProperties;
using Windows.UI.Xaml.Controls;

namespace Chapter14
{
  public sealed partial class MainPage : Page
  {
    // Details about the dynamic audio encoding
    const int SamplesPerSecond = 16000;
    const int ChannelCount = 1; // Mono
    const int BitsPerSample = 8; // Each sample is one byte

    // How frequently data needs to be requested
    // (and how much data is given to each request)
    const int RequestsPerSecond = 10;
    readonly TimeSpan RequestLength =
      TimeSpan.FromMilliseconds(1000 / RequestsPerSecond);
```

LISTING 14.1 Continued

```csharp
const int BitsPerRequest =
  (SamplesPerSecond / RequestsPerSecond) * BitsPerSample;
const int BytesPerRequest = BitsPerRequest / 8;

// Produce 10 seconds of audio
readonly TimeSpan AudioLength = TimeSpan.FromSeconds(10);

TimeSpan elapsedTime = new TimeSpan();
Random random = new Random();

public MainPage()
{
  this.InitializeComponent();

  // Capture properties about the dynamic audio
  AudioEncodingProperties audioProperties =
    AudioEncodingProperties.CreatePcm(
    SamplesPerSecond, ChannelCount, BitsPerSample);

  // Create the MediaStreamSource and provide the information it needs
  MediaStreamSource source = new MediaStreamSource(
    new AudioStreamDescriptor(audioProperties));
  source.SampleRequested += MediaStreamSource_SampleRequested;
  source.Duration = AudioLength;

  // These are only relevant for the media transport controls
  source.MusicProperties.Title = "Random Noise";
  source.MusicProperties.Album = "Disturbing Sounds";
  source.MusicProperties.Artist = "Adam Nathan";

  // Auto-play the dynamic audio
  this.mediaElement.SetMediaStreamSource(source);
}

async void MediaStreamSource_SampleRequested(MediaStreamSource sender,
  MediaStreamSourceSampleRequestedEventArgs args)
{
  if (this.elapsedTime < sender.Duration)
  {
    MediaStreamSourceSampleRequest request = args.Request;
    MediaStreamSourceSampleRequestDeferral deferral = request.GetDeferral();
```

LISTING 14.1   Continued

```
        // Generate the random audio data
        byte[] bytes = new byte[BytesPerRequest];
        this.random.NextBytes(bytes);

        // Write the data into a .NET stream
        MemoryStream stream = new MemoryStream();
        await stream.WriteAsync(bytes, 0, bytes.Length);

        // Give the data to the request
        request.Sample = MediaStreamSample.CreateFromBuffer(
                        stream.GetWindowsRuntimeBuffer(), this.elapsedTime);
        request.Sample.Duration = RequestLength;

        // Track our progress
        this.elapsedTime += RequestLength;

        deferral.Complete();
      }
    }
  }
}
```

The `MusicProperties` set for this audio only impacts the media transport controls for background audio, which are covered in Chapter 22. Because of the asynchronous call made in `MediaStreamSource_SampleRequested`, a deferral must be used. In this example, a .NET stream is used and then passed to `MediaStreamSample` as an `IBuffer` thanks to the `GetWindowsRuntimeBuffer` extension method. However, `MediaStreamSample` also has a `CreateFromStreamAsync` method that expects a Windows Runtime `IInputStream` instead.

Capture

Windows provides two distinct options for media capture. `CameraCaptureUI` makes it easy to perform basic capture by leveraging built-in Windows UI. In contrast, `CaptureElement` enables you to provide a completely custom user experience for capture, and to perform types of capture that aren't available via `CameraCaptureUI`. This section looks at both approaches.

> ⓘ **The capture features require the Microphone and/or Webcam capabilities!**
>
> This stands to reason, because audio capture is performed with a microphone, and video capture is performed with a camera. Although most Windows tablets and laptops have a built-in microphone and one or two built-in cameras, these features (and capabilities) work with external devices as well, such as a classic Webcam.

CameraCaptureUI

The `CameraCaptureUI` class enables you to launch an experience similar to the built-in Camera app (in a more limited mode and directly inside your app) in order to easily capture a photo or video. For the user, the result is like choosing the Camera app inside the Windows file picker, except it's full-screen and there's a back button on the top-left instead of a cancel button on the bottom-right.

Capturing a Photo

Assuming you have an `Image` named `image` on your `Page`:

```
<Image Name="image"/>
```

the following code-behind launches the camera UI in photo-taking mode:

```
async Task CapturePhoto()
{
  CameraCaptureUI camera = new CameraCaptureUI();
  // Get a JPEG image from the camera
  StorageFile file = await camera.CaptureFileAsync(CameraCaptureUIMode.Photo);
  if (file != null)
  {
    using (IRandomAccessStream ras = await file.OpenAsync(FileAccessMode.Read))
    {
      // Load the data into a BitmapImage
      BitmapImage source = new BitmapImage();
      source.SetSource(ras);

      // Assign the BitmapImage to the Image element on the page
      this.image.Source = source;
    }
  }
}
```

As with other code interacting with UI, the call to `CaptureFileAsync` must be made on the UI thread.

If you use `CameraCaptureUI` with only `CameraCaptureUIMode.Photo`, then you don't need the Microphone capability, just the Webcam one. The first time this code executes, the user is prompted to give his or her consent. After that, the camera UI in Figure 14.3 is shown, overlaying the app's entire window. The user can switch between available cameras, customize each camera's options (which might vary) and even use a timer. The "Video Mode" button is disabled in Figure 14.3 because `CameraCaptureUIMode.Photo` was chosen.

If a front-facing camera is used, the preview video feed is automatically mirrored horizontally. This is standard practice for video conferencing apps like Skype, although in this case the effect is jarring because as soon as you take the photo, you see the result without mirroring.

After tapping on the screen to take the photo, the user is given a choice to accept it, retake it, or crop it. The cropping UI is also shown in Figure 14.3. Once the user accepts the photo, the file is saved (in JPEG format) to the app data temporary folder. The camera UI then disappears and the StorageFile referencing the temporary file is returned to your app.

Viewing some camera options before taking the photo   Cropping the photo after taking it

FIGURE 14.3   The built-in camera UI provides a lot of options to the user.

If you forget to enable the Webcam capability in your package manifest, the call to CaptureFileAsync doesn't fail, but the resultant camera UI looks like Figure 14.4. When the user dismisses it, it returns a null file, just as when the user cancels photo-taking.

FIGURE 14.4   The built-in camera UI explains when a necessary capability is missing.

In Windows 8, calling CaptureFileAsync would throw an exception if your window is at its minimum size. In Windows 8.1, you can call CaptureFileAsync at any window size. The user interface adjusts gracefully.

Before calling CaptureFileAsync, you can set several subproperties on CameraCaptureUI's PhotoSettings property to make a number of customizations:

→ **AllowCropping**—Set this to false to remove the cropping feature.

→ **CroppedAspectRatio**—Set this to a Size to lock the aspect ratio of the cropped region. For example, perhaps you want to capture a square photo for a Facebook profile picture. When you set CroppedAspectRatio, cropping becomes mandatory for the user.

→ **CroppedSizeInPixels**—Set this to a Size to force the exact dimensions of the cropped region instead. This also makes cropping mandatory.

→ **Format**—Choose between Jpeg (the default), JpegXR, and Png.

→ **MaxResolution**—Limit the highest resolution that the user can select from a number of predefined options in the CameraCaptureUIMaxPhotoResolution enumeration. The default value is HighestAvailable.

Capturing a Video

Assuming you have a MediaElement (or MediaPlayer) named video on your Page:

```
<MediaElement Name="video"/>
```

the following code-behind launches the camera UI in video-capture mode:

```
IRandomAccessStream stream;
...
async Task CaptureVideo()
{
  CameraCaptureUI camera = new CameraCaptureUI();

  // Get an MP4 video from the camera
  StorageFile file = await camera.CaptureFileAsync(CameraCaptureUIMode.Video);
  if (file != null)
  {
    this.stream = await file.OpenAsync(FileAccessMode.Read);

    // Load the data into the MediaElement
    this.video.SetSource(stream, file.ContentType);

    // Don't dispose the stream until MediaOpened is raised!
  }
}
```

For the use of CameraCaptureUI, this is a one-word change from Photo to Video. (CameraCaptureUIMode also has a PhotoOrVideo option if you want to allow either.) This time, however, the stream is passed to the MediaElement's SetSource method along with the MIME type (video/mp4). Unlike in the Image case, the stream cannot be disposed until MediaElement's MediaOpened event is raised, so the stream is stored as a member variable that can be disposed in a MediaOpened handler:

```
void Video_MediaOpened(object sender, RoutedEventArgs e)
{
  this.stream.Dispose();
}
```

This mode, as well as the PhotoOrVideo mode, requires both Microphone and Webcam capabilities because audio gets captured as well. If you have only Webcam but not Microphone, the camera UI shows the same message as in Figure 14.4, which can be quite confusing!

Before capturing video, the user has even more options available to customize, such as which audio device to use and whether to enable any built-in effects like video stabilization. After the user captures video (with one tap to start recording and other to stop), he is presented with a trimming option rather than a cropping option.

Before calling CaptureFileAsync, you can set a few subproperties on CameraCaptureUI's VideoSettings property to make a number of customizations:

→ **AllowTrimming**—Set this to false to remove the trimming feature.

→ **MaxDurationInSeconds**—Set this to a float to limit the length of the video clip. When you do this, trimming becomes mandatory. (The user can record a much longer clip and then decide which portion to use.)

→ **Format**—Choose between Mp4 (the default) and Wmv.

→ **MaxResolution**—Limit the highest resolution that the user can select. Your choices are HighestAvailable (the default), LowDefinition, StandardDefinition, or HighDefinition.

CaptureElement

CaptureElement is basically the capture equivalent of MediaElement. MediaElement contains all the plumbing necessary for playback, and the same could be said about CaptureElement for capture. It is a UIElement with only two properties (excluding ones inherited from its FrameworkElement base class): Source and Stretch. Like MediaElement, Stretch is Uniform by default. Unlike MediaElement, but like every other element with a Stretch property, its content does not get centered when you choose UniformToFill.

CaptureElement's Source property is of type MediaCapture, a Windows Runtime class that does all the hard work. It enables you to capture videos, photos, as well as two options lacking from CameraCaptureUI: video-only recordings (with no audio) and audio-only recordings.

Showing a Preview
The first step in allowing a user to capture a photo or video is showing her a live video feed so she can frame her shot. If you define a CaptureElement named captureElement on your Page:

```
<CaptureElement Name="captureElement"/>
```

Then the following code-behind can fill it with live content from the device's default camera:

```
MediaCapture capture = new MediaCapture();
...
async Task ShowPreview()
{
  try
  {
    // Requires Microphone and Webcam capabilities!
    await this.capture.InitializeAsync();

    // Source can only be set after the MediaCapture is initialized
    this.captureElement.Source = capture;

    // Show the live content
    await this.capture.StartPreviewAsync();
  }
  catch (UnauthorizedAccessException)
  {
    // The app wasn't granted the necessary capabilities
    ...
  }
}
```

The call to InitializeAsync requires both Microphone and Webcam capabilities, otherwise it throws an UnauthorizedAccessException. If the user revokes these capabilities while your app is using a MediaCapture object (via the Settings charm), it ceases to work and raises a Failed event.

If you don't care about audio, you can avoid the need for the Microphone capability by calling an InitializeAsync overload that accepts custom settings. With this, you can set the StreamingCaptureMode to Video rather than the default value of AudioAndVideo as follows:

```
await this.capture.InitializeAsync(new MediaCaptureInitializationSettings {
  StreamingCaptureMode = StreamingCaptureMode.Video });
```

In this case, any captured video will be audio-free.

The MediaCaptureInitializationSettings instance that can be passed to the overload of InitializeAsync exposes two string properties—AudioDeviceId and VideoDeviceId—that enable you to switch audio capture to a specific microphone and video capture to a specific camera.

StartPreviewAsync starts rendering the live video feed inside the CaptureElement. You can later call StopPreviewAsync to end the feed. To mimic the video mirroring done by CameraCaptureUI, you can call MediaCapture's SetPreviewMirroring(true) method or apply a ScaleTransform to the CaptureElement with a ScaleX of -1. MediaCapture exposes a similar SetPreviewRotation method that allows only 90° increments, but again you could accomplish the same thing (and more) with a RotateTransform.

MediaCapture's Failed event is raised in a number of situations. For example, if the Camera app is sharing the screen with your app when the user triggers ShowPreview, Failed is raised because the camera is an exclusive resource that must be used only by one app at a time. The code for showing the live video feed is simple, but there are a lot of issues to be aware of, explained in the following warning sidebars.

> **⚠ The first call to InitializeAsync must be done on the UI thread!**
>
> Although CameraCaptureUI.CaptureFileAsync has the same limitation, this requirement for MediaCapture.InitializeAsync might not be as obvious because it normally doesn't show any UI. The reason for this requirement is that the *first* time the user triggers this functionality in your app, he or she is presented with a dialog asking for consent, as shown in Figure 14.5. Subsequent use does not ask for consent, although the user can allow or block access at any time via the Settings charm. This UI thread requirement is true for all the "sensitive" capabilities, because all relevant APIs prompt in the same fashion.
>
> Can Chapter 14 App use your webcam and microphone?
>
> Allow   Block
>
> **FIGURE 14.5** The consent dialog shown during the first call to MediaCapture.InitializeAsync must be triggered from the UI thread.
>
> Because of this "in your face" behavior, you should avoid automatically initializing a MediaCapture when your app is launched unless it is vital to the operation of your app.

> **⚠ Switching away from an app instantly terminates MediaCapture!**
>
> This is done automatically, which is nice because it means you don't need to worry about releasing this exclusive resource upon suspension (or if another app tries to use it while your app is still running). This does leave the MediaCapture instance in an unusable state, however. Therefore, upon your app's return to the screen (in a VisibilityChanged handler for your Window), you must recreate and reinitialize a new MediaCapture, and then set it as a new source for the CaptureElement.

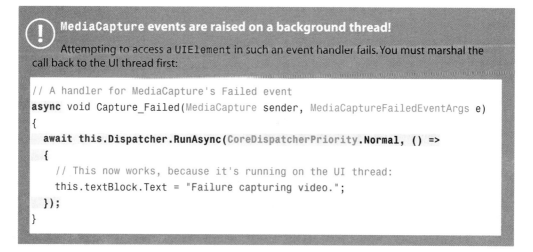

```
// A handler for MediaCapture's Failed event
async void Capture_Failed(MediaCapture sender, MediaCaptureFailedEventArgs e)
{
  await this.Dispatcher.RunAsync(CoreDispatcherPriority.Normal, () =>
  {
    // This now works, because it's running on the UI thread:
    this.textBlock.Text = "Failure capturing video.";
  });
}
```

Capturing a Photo

With a MediaCapture instance initialized as in the previous section, the live video preview optionally showing, and an Image named image on your Page, you can capture a photo as follows:

```
async Task CapturePhoto()
{
  // Capture a JPEG into a new stream
  ImageEncodingProperties properties = ImageEncodingProperties.CreateJpeg();
  using (IRandomAccessStream ras = new InMemoryRandomAccessStream())
  {
    await this.capture.CapturePhotoToStreamAsync(properties, ras);
    await ras.FlushAsync();

    // Load the data into a BitmapImage
    ras.Seek(0);
    BitmapImage source = new BitmapImage();
    source.SetSource(ras);

    // Assign the BitmapImage to the Image element on the page
    this.image.Source = source;
  }
}
```

You can construct your own custom ImageEncodingProperties instance for advanced scenarios, but for most cases you should retrieve one from its static CreateJpeg, CreateJpegXR, or CreatePng methods.

MediaCapture enables capturing a photo directly to a file instead of a stream. Its CapturePhotoToStorage-FileAsync method accepts an IStorageFile as its second parameter instead of an IRandomAccessStream.

Adjusting Camera Settings

`MediaCapture` has a `VideoDeviceController` property (of type `VideoDeviceController`) that enables you to programmatically adjust whatever settings it exposes. This can include things such as brightness, contrast, exposure, white balance, hue, and backlight compensation. For more advanced cameras, you can control focus, zoom, pan, roll, and tilt! Windows 8.1 exposes several new settings not available in Windows 8, such as ISO film speed, flash control (including red eye reduction), regions of interest, scene mode (such as backlit, candlelight, beach, or snow), a clever Photo Loop mode, and many more.

> Photo Loop is a new Windows 8.1 feature that requires hardware (and driver) support. Surface 2 supports this feature. When the user takes a photo, it is able to provide you with a sequence of photos *before* and after the photo was taken. This is like having a burst mode, with the added twist of going back in time. (This is possible because the camera is active for some period of time before the photo is actually taken.)
>
> You can check if this feature is currently supported via the `Supported` property on `VideoDeviceController`'s `LowLagPhotoSequence` property. If it is, you can call `MediaCapture`'s `PrepareLowLagPhotoSequenceCaptureAsync`, which returns a `LowLagPhotoSequenceCapture` instance. With this, you can attach a handler to its `PhotoCaptured` event that gets raised once per photo, and call `StartAsync/FinishAsync` to start and stop the capture process.

The value of many settings is represented as a `double`. The following code shows how to set brightness to 8 via a `MediaCapture` named `capture`:

```
// Try to disable automatic adjustment of the setting
if (this.capture.VideoDeviceController.Brightness.TrySetAuto(false))
{
  // Try to set it to 8
  if (this.capture.VideoDeviceController.Brightness.TrySetValue(8))
  {
    // Success!
  }
}
```

Each Windows 8 compatible property on `VideoDeviceController` is a `MediaDeviceControl` object that exposes the two `TrySetXXX` methods used in this snippet and corresponding `TryGetXXX` methods. It also has a `Capabilities` property that reveals whether the setting is supported by the current camera, whether automatic adjustment is supported, its default/minimum/maximum values, and the step size. The preceding code didn't bother checking whether `Brightness` is supported, because all the `TryXXX` methods on `VideoDeviceController` return `false` for unsupported settings.

The properties introduced in Windows 8.1, such as `IsoSpeedControl` and `SceneModeControl`, each have a custom type with less cumbersome APIs specific to each setting. Windows 8.1 also includes new properties for some of the same settings exposed in Windows 8, but this time with asynchronous APIs instead of synchronous ones. You can identify the improved properties by their `Control` suffix: `ExposureControl`, `FocusControl`, and `WhiteBalanceControl` instead of `Exposure`, `Focus`, and `WhiteBalance`.

These are all global settings, although each physical camera has its own set. For example, if the user changes his or her front-facing camera's brightness from within your app, then that change will persist and be seen the next time the front-facing camera is used in any app (including the built-in Camera app).

Although you're mostly on your own when it comes to replicating features from `CameraCaptureUI` in code based on `CaptureElement`, there is one helpful piece of built-in UI you can take advantage of. If you call the static `CameraUIOptions.Show` method with an instance of an initialized `MediaCapture`, Windows automatically displays the dialog shown in Figure 14.6 over the bottom-right corner of your app. This is the same dialog used in the Camera app and `CameraCaptureUI`, and it enables modifying the settings exposed by the relevant `VideoDeviceController`. You don't have to write any code to make this happen other than the single call to show the dialog!

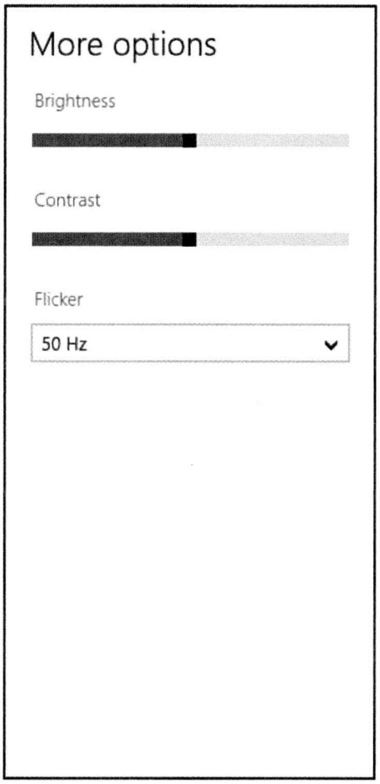

Note, however, that this is only the "More options" dialog that normally appears only after selecting "More" in the typical "Camera options" dialog seen in Figure 14.3. Therefore, if you want to enable the user to configure the resolution, audio device, or effects, you're still on your own.

`MediaCapture` exposes a separate `MediaCaptureSettings` property with readonly settings about the current camera, such as whether it supports taking a photo and recording video simultaneously, the focal length, its pitch offset, whether Windows makes a sound when a photo is taken, and even specific IDs for the camera and its microphone.

FIGURE 14.6   The dialog that appears when you call `CameraUIOptions.Show` is conveniently narrow enough to fit inside the narrowest possible window.

Capturing a Video

Capturing video with `MediaCapture` looks similar to capturing a photo, although the logic must be split into separate starting and stopping actions. The following code-behind assumes you have a `MediaElement` or `MediaPlayer` named video on your `Page`:

```
MediaCapture capture = new MediaCapture();
IRandomAccessStream ras = new InMemoryRandomAccessStream();
…
await this.capture.InitializeAsync();
…
async Task StartCapturingVideo()
{
  // Capture WMV video into the stream
  MediaEncodingProfile profile =
    MediaEncodingProfile.CreateWmv(VideoEncodingQuality.Auto);
  await this.capture.StartRecordToStreamAsync(profile, this.ras);
}

async Task StopCapturingVideo()
{
  await this.capture.StopRecordAsync();
  await this.ras.FlushAsync();

  // Load the data into the MediaElement
  this.ras.Seek(0);
  this.video.SetSource(this.ras, "video/x-ms-wmv");

  // Don't dispose this.ras until MediaOpened is raised!
}
```

Instead of an `ImageEncodingProperties` instance, `StartRecordToStreamAsync` requires a `MediaEncodingProfile` to encode the resulting video stream. You can create one from the static `CreateWmv` or `CreateMp4` methods, or you can also create a profile based on an existing media file with `CreateFromFileAsync` or `CreateFromStreamAsync`. Note that `MediaCapture` only supports one-pass constant bitrate encoding.

In addition to `MediaCapture`'s `Failed` event, which you should always handle, `MediaCapture` has a `RecordLimitation-Exceeded` event that you should handle whenever you're recording audio/video. When it is raised, it will not record any more content, so you should call `StopRecordAsync` and perform your normal logic for processing the recording.

> As with a photo, `MediaCapture` enables capturing video directly to a file instead of a stream with its `StartRecordToStorageFileAsync` method. It even supports capture (as well as preview playback) to a *custom sink*, which is another type of media extension.

Capturing Audio Only

Capturing audio with `MediaCapture` is like capturing video. You just need to create a different `MediaEncodingProfile`. Three preconfigured options are provided by the static `CreateMp3`, `CreateM4a`, and `CreateWma` methods. Capturing just audio enables us to simplify some things, however. We can stop showing the video preview. And if we initialize MediaCapture for audio-only usage, then we no longer require the Webcam capability. The following code shows this updated initialization along with the methods to start/stop capturing audio. This assumes that the MediaElement on the Page is now called audio:

```
MediaCapture capture = new MediaCapture();
IRandomAccessStream ras = new InMemoryRandomAccessStream();
…
async Task Initialize()
{
  try
  {
    // Initialize this way so we only require the Microphone capability
    await this.capture.InitializeAsync(new MediaCaptureInitializationSettings {
      StreamingCaptureMode = StreamingCaptureMode.Audio });
  }
  catch (UnauthorizedAccessException)
  {
    // Could not use the microphone!
  }
}


async Task StartCapturingAudio()
{
  // Capture MP3 audio into the stream
  MediaEncodingProfile profile =
    MediaEncodingProfile.CreateMp3(AudioEncodingQuality.Auto);
  await this.capture.StartRecordToStreamAsync(profile, this.ras);
}

async Task StopCapturingAudio()
{
  await this.capture.StopRecordAsync();
  await this.ras.FlushAsync();

  // Load the data into the MediaElement
  this.ras.Seek(0);
  this.audio.SetSource(this.ras, "audio/mp3");

  // Don't dispose this.ras until MediaOpened is raised!
}
```

Just like VideoDeviceController, MediaCapture has an AudioDeviceController property that enables you to adjust microphone settings, such as its volume and mute status.

> As with `MediaElement`, `MediaCapture` enables you to add effects. Its methods for doing this are called `AddEffectAsync` and `ClearEffectsAsync`. You apply these effects to a specific stream by passing a value from a `MediaStreamType` enumeration: Audio, Photo, VideoRecord, or VideoPreview.

Transcoding

Similar to the transcoding done with `BitmapDecoder` and `BitmapEncoder` in the preceding chapter, the Windows Media APIs enables some simple transcoding options for audio/video files. This is exposed via a single `MediaTranscoder` class. With it, you can do four basic tasks:

→ Change the encoding quality

→ Change the media format

→ Trim the media

→ Add effects

Changing the Quality

Leveraging the same `MediaEncodingProfile` class used to encode video from `MediaCapture`, you can transcode any supported media format to any other supported media format. Although you can save the output in a higher-quality encoding than the input, you obviously can't *improve* the quality. The main scenario here is reducing the size of a media file by reducing its quality.

Using `MediaTranscoder` is a two-step process. First you *prepare* it with the source media, target media, and a profile, which gives you an instance of `PrepareTranscodeResult`. If this result object tells you it can perform the transcoding (via its `CanTranscode` property), then you can call its `TranscodeAsync` method to do the work. Otherwise, you can check its `FailureReason` property to understand why `CanTranscode` is `false`.

`MediaTranscoder` supports a source and target of type `IRandomAccessStream` with its `PrepareStreamTranscodeAsync` method, so code that calls this would look similar to code from the preceding chapter. However, the following code uses a separate `Prepare`**File**`TranscodeAsync` method to directly read and write from one `StorageFile` to another. This is a nice shortcut when you're already working with two files, as with this example that uses the Windows file picker to get both the source and target files:

```
async Task ShrinkUserSelectedFile()
{
  // Get a source MP4 file from the user
  FileOpenPicker openPicker = new FileOpenPicker();
  openPicker.FileTypeFilter.Add(".mp4");
  StorageFile sourceFile = await openPicker.PickSingleFileAsync();
```

```
if (sourceFile != null)
{
  // Get a target MP4 file from the user
  FileSavePicker savePicker = new FileSavePicker();
  savePicker.FileTypeChoices.Add("MP4 file", new string[] { ".mp4" });
  StorageFile targetFile = await savePicker.PickSaveFileAsync();
  if (targetFile != null)
  {
    // Specify the output format (QVGA: 320x240)
    MediaEncodingProfile profile =
      MediaEncodingProfile.CreateMp4(VideoEncodingQuality.Qvga);

    // Transcode!
    MediaTranscoder transcoder = new MediaTranscoder();
    PrepareTranscodeResult result = await transcoder.PrepareFileTranscodeAsync(
                                          sourceFile, targetFile, profile);
    if (result.CanTranscode)
    {
      await result.TranscodeAsync();
    }
    else
    {
      // Check result.FailureReason: InvalidProfile, CodecNotFound, or Unknown
    }
  }
}
}
```

The VideoEncodingQuality options (besides Auto) are summarized in Table 14.1.

TABLE 14.1   Values in the VideoEncodingQuality Enumeration

Value	Resolution (in Pixels)	Aspect Ratio
Qvga	320x240	4:3
Ntsc	486x440	4:3
Pal	576x520	4:3
Vga	640x480	4:3
Wvga	800x480	5:3
HD720p	1280x720	16:9
HD1080p	1920x1080	16:9

As explained in Chapter 8, "Threading, Windows, and Pages," you can choose to directly retrieve a returned IAsyncOperation when calling an asynchronous method instead of awaiting, which enables you to support cancellation. In the case of the TranscodeAsync method, however, you can do something even more slick. It returns an IAsyncAction**WithProgress**<double>, which means that you can get incremental progress updates (a double value from 0 to 100) that can be fed to a ProgressBar or similar control. To apply this to the transcoding example, you can replace this block of code:

```
if (result.CanTranscode)
{
  await result.TranscodeAsync();
}
```

with this:

```
if (result.CanTranscode)
{
  this.progressBar.Visibility = Visibility.Visible;

  IAsyncActionWithProgress<double> action = result.TranscodeAsync();

  // Handler for progress updates
  action.Progress = async (self, value) =>
  {
    // Called on a different thread
    await this.Dispatcher.RunAsync(CoreDispatcherPriority.Normal, () =>
    {
      // Update a ProgressBar control on the UI thread
      this.progressBar.Value = value; // value is 0-100
    });
  };

  // Handler for completion
  action.Completed = async (self, status) =>
  {
    // Called on a different thread
    await this.Dispatcher.RunAsync(CoreDispatcherPriority.Normal, () =>
    {
      // Hide the ProgressBar because transcoding is done
      this.progressBar.Visibility = Visibility.Collapsed;
    });
  };
}
```

The biggest complication is that both the `Progress` callbacks and `Completed` callback occur on a different thread, so the Page's `Dispatcher` must be used to marshal back to the UI thread in order to update the UI. The two anonymous methods are marked `async` so they can use the `await` keyword with the calls to `RunAsync`.

Changing the Format

Changing a media file's format is done the same way as changing its quality. It comes down to your choice of `MediaEncodingProfile` (and in this example, what file extensions you force in the file picker):

```csharp
async Task ConvertUserSelectedMp4ToWmv()
{
  // Get a source MP4 file from the user
  FileOpenPicker openPicker = new FileOpenPicker();
  openPicker.FileTypeFilter.Add(".mp4");
  StorageFile sourceFile = await openPicker.PickSingleFileAsync();
  if (sourceFile != null)
  {
    // Get a target WMV file from the user
    FileSavePicker savePicker = new FileSavePicker();
    savePicker.FileTypeChoices.Add("WMV file", new string[] { ".wmv" });
    StorageFile targetFile = await savePicker.PickSaveFileAsync();
    if (targetFile != null)
    {
      // Specify the output format
      MediaEncodingProfile profile =
        MediaEncodingProfile.CreateWmv(VideoEncodingQuality.Auto);

      // Transcode!
      MediaTranscoder transcoder = new MediaTranscoder();
      PrepareTranscodeResult result = await transcoder.PrepareFileTranscodeAsync(
                                  sourceFile, targetFile, profile);
      if (result.CanTranscode)
      {
        await result.TranscodeAsync();
      }
      else
      {
        // Check result.FailureReason: InvalidProfile, CodecNotFound, or Unknown
      }
    }
  }
}
```

Trimming

To trim a file, you use TrimStartTime and TrimStopTime properties exposed by
MediaTranscoder. The following code demonstrates:

```
async Task TrimUserSelectedFile()
{
  // Get a source MP4 file from the user
  FileOpenPicker openPicker = new FileOpenPicker();
  openPicker.FileTypeFilter.Add(".mp4");
  StorageFile sourceFile = await openPicker.PickSingleFileAsync();
  if (sourceFile != null)
  {
    // Get a target MP4 file from the user
    FileSavePicker savePicker = new FileSavePicker();
    savePicker.FileTypeChoices.Add("MP4 file", new string[] { ".mp4" });
    StorageFile targetFile = await savePicker.PickSaveFileAsync();
    if (targetFile != null)
    {
      // Just use the source format
      MediaEncodingProfile profile =
        await MediaEncodingProfile.CreateFromFileAsync(sourceFile);

      MediaTranscoder transcoder = new MediaTranscoder();

      // Trim
      transcoder.TrimStartTime = TimeSpan.FromSeconds(1.5);
      transcoder.TrimStopTime = TimeSpan.FromSeconds(4);

      // Transcode!
      PrepareTranscodeResult result = await transcoder.PrepareFileTranscodeAsync(
                                        sourceFile, targetFile, profile);
      if (result.CanTranscode)
      {
        await result.TranscodeAsync();
      }
      else
      {
        // Check result.FailureReason: InvalidProfile, CodecNotFound, or Unknown
      }
    }
  }
}
```

By using a target MediaEncodingProfile that matches the source profile, the transcoding
is able to be done without reencoding the content, which avoids any potential quality

degradation. If you want to force the encoding for some reason, you can set MediaTranscoder's AlwaysReencode property to true. Along the lines of things that are strange to do, MediaTranscoder enables you to disable its hardware acceleration by setting HardwareAccelerationEnabled to false.

Adding Effects

MediaTranscoder exposes AddVideoEffect and AddAudioEffect methods just like MediaElement. (Although for some reason it has a method named ClearEffects rather than RemoveAllEffects. Both do the same thing.) It exposes simpler overloads that require only the string ID of the effect, if you want the effect to be required and you don't need to pass any settings. Therefore, you can replace the preceding example's two lines of trimming code with the following line of code to add video stabilization to the source video file instead:

```
// Apply the video stabilization effect
transcoder.AddVideoEffect(VideoEffects.VideoStabilization);
```

The ability to insert effects makes the transcoding process completely extensible for anyone who writes a media extension.

Speech Synthesis

Text-to-speech can be performed with the SpeechSynthesizer engine in the Windows.Media.SpeechSynthesis namespace. You give it text to speak, and it produces a standard Windows Runtime audio stream called SpeechSynthesisStream. This stream implements IRandomAccessStream (along with many other interfaces), so you can hand it over to a MediaElement in order to play the produced speech.

The process of turning text into speech requires a "voice." Microsoft has produced 18 voices that cover 16 different locales. You can see your installed voices in the Text to Speech section in the Windows Control Panel. On my device, I've got two voices for the United States (Microsoft David Desktop, a male, and Microsoft Zira Desktop, a female) and one for Great Britain (Microsoft Hazel Desktop, a female).

Bringing Text to Life

Getting text to be spoken is as simple as the following code-behind, assuming that a MediaElement named mediaElement is on the current Page:

```
async Task Speak()
{
  string text = "Turn left at the next intersection";

  using (SpeechSynthesizer synthesizer = new SpeechSynthesizer())
  {
    SpeechSynthesisStream stream =
      await synthesizer.SynthesizeTextToStreamAsync(text);
```

```
    // Send the audio to a MediaElement
    this.mediaElement.SetSource(stream, stream.ContentType);

    // We could dispose the stream once MediaOpened is raised
  }
}
```

The produced text uses the default voice and speed, both of which can be changed by the user in the Control Panel.

If you have multiple voices installed, you can change the voice by setting SpeechSynthesizer's Voice property to an instance of a VoiceInformation. You get VoiceInformations from the static SpeechSynthesizer.AllVoices property. Each VoiceInformation has a DisplayName, Description, Gender, and Language property, so it is natural to enable the user to choose a voice from a list in the settings for your app. (Each VoiceInformation also has an Id property, in case you need to reliably identify them in your code.) SpeechSynthesizer also reveals the user's default voice with its static DefaultVoice property.

Speech Synthesis Markup Language

If you need to customize the output of SpeechSynthesizer further, you could specify its input the form of a standard XML-based language known as Speech Synthesis Markup Language (SSML). SSML enables you to customize pronunciation, volume, pitch, *prosody* (rhythm and intonation), and more. It is a W3C Recommendation published at http://w3.org/TR/speech-synthesis.

To use SSML, you simply pass an appropriate SSML string to SpeechSynthesizer's Synthesize**Ssml**ToStreamAsync method instead of SynthesizeTextToStreamAsync. Here's an example of SSML content that demonstrates some of its features:

```
<speak version="1.0" xmlns="http://www.w3.org/2001/10/synthesis"
       xml:lang="en-US">
  3/4 is a fraction, but
  <say-as interpret-as="date_md">3/4</say-as>
  is a date.
  <break time="2000ms"/>
  Hey Zira, can you spell queue?
  <voice name="Microsoft Zira Desktop">
    <say-as interpret-as="characters">queue</say-as>
  </voice>
  Do it faster!
  <voice name="Microsoft Zira Desktop">
    <prosody rate="x-fast">
      <say-as interpret-as="characters">queue</say-as>
    </prosody>
  </voice>
</speak>
```

The ability to adjust pronunciations, such as a fraction versus a date in this example, can be vital for the context of your app. You can instruct the voice to spell out letters, perhaps for the proper pronunciation of an abbreviation, or spell out numbers so "123" is pronounced as "one two three" instead of "one hundred and twenty three." This example also demonstrates inserting pauses, switching voices midstream, and changing the speaking rate. But this only scratches the surface of what SSML can do. You should examine its specification if you'd like to understand its full feature set.

> The SSML mark element can be used to make `SpeechSynthesizer` inject markers into the audio stream. For example:
>
> ```
> <speak version="1.0" xmlns="http://www.w3.org/2001/10/synthesis"
>        xml:lang="en-US">
>   There is a marker <mark name="one"/>here.
>   There is another marker <mark name="two"/>here.
> </speak>
> ```
>
> These are the same markers described earlier, so `MediaElement` will raise the appropriate `MarkerReached` events at the appropriate times. This enables you to synchronize actions in your app with the words that are spoken.

Summary

The Windows Runtime includes a lot of options for audio/video playback, capture, transcoding, and speech synthesis. `MediaElement` (with its transport controls enabled) and `CameraCaptureUI` give you a complete user experience so you can enable many tasks just like the built-in Video and Camera apps. More importantly, with XAML elements such as `MediaElement` and `CaptureElement`, it's easy to seamlessly integrate any of this functionality into your apps that aren't trying to simply be a media player or camera.

I'm particularly struck by how few lines of code it is to perform transcoding. No more searching for buggy shareware programs the next time I want to convert an MP4 file to WMV! Combined with the power of the Windows file picker's extensibility, you can easily imagine scenarios such as trimming and applying video stabilization to a video you've stored on Facebook.

With `CaptureElement`, you can support a long list of scenarios that aren't supported by `CameraCaptureUI`: programmatically capturing photos at certain points in time, streaming the video in real-time, video-only or audio-only capture, and so on. That said, if all you need is standard photo and/or video capture for which the `CameraCaptureUI` workflow is acceptable, then by all means, use it! Users will appreciate its familiarity as well as all its standard bells and whistles.

Four topics related to audio and video are saved for later chapters: working with the user's Music and Videos library (Chapter 20, "Working with Data"), downloading large media files with the background downloader (Chapter 20), enabling users to stream content to a device on the home network with Play To (Chapter 21, "Supporting Charms"), and enabling your app's audio to continue playing in the background (Chapter 22).

On a final note, if you are looking for a way to serve your own video, whether via adaptive streaming, traditional streaming, or progressive download, you should investigate Windows Azure Media Services. It is format-, protocol-, and DRM-agnostic, and provides a number of slick features. For example, you can upload a video file to your Windows Azure portal and have it encoded to multiple bitrates for the purpose of adaptive streaming. Adaptive streaming can not only save bandwidth, but video playback performance is best when the encoded resolution matches the screen resolution.

Chapter 15

OTHER CONTROLS

J ust because the controls in this chapter mostly defy cate-
gorization, don't think that they aren't important! It's rare
to find an app that doesn't at least use a ProgressBar,
ProgressRing, or ToggleSwitch somewhere. And one
control in particular—WebView—opens the door to a
number of interesting options for constructing an app. This
chapter also covers four very important controls introduced
in Windows 8.1: SearchBox, Hub, DatePicker, and
TimePicker.

Range Controls

Range controls do not render arbitrary content like content
controls and items controls. Instead, a range control stores
and displays a numeric value that falls within a specified
range.

The core functionality of range controls comes from a
RangeBase base class. This class defines properties of type
double that store the current value and the endpoints of
the range: Value, Minimum, and Maximum. It also defines a
simple ValueChanged event.

This section examines the two major built-in range
controls—ProgressBar and Slider. A ScrollBar control
also derives from RangeBase, but you're unlikely to want to
use it directly. Instead, you would use a ScrollViewer,
which internally manages its ScrollBars.

ProgressBar

In an ideal world, you would never need to use a `ProgressBar` in your app. But when faced with long-running operations or having to wait for content to transfer over the network, showing users a `ProgressBar` helps them realize that progress is indeed being

made. Therefore, using a `ProgressBar` in the right places can dramatically improve usability. Figure 15.1 displays the default look of a `ProgressBar` with its `Value` set to 40.

FIGURE 15.1   A ProgressBar showing 40% progress

`ProgressBar` has a default `Minimum` of `0` and a default `Maximum` of `100`. It adds only three public properties to what `RangeBase` already provides:

→ **IsIndeterminate**—When this is set to `true`, `ProgressBar` shows a standard horizontal "five dancing dots" animation shown in Figure 15.2 (so the values of `Minimum`, `Maximum`, and `Value` don't matter). This is a great feature when you have no idea how long something will take. This animation is typically shown at the top of whatever region is waiting for the update.

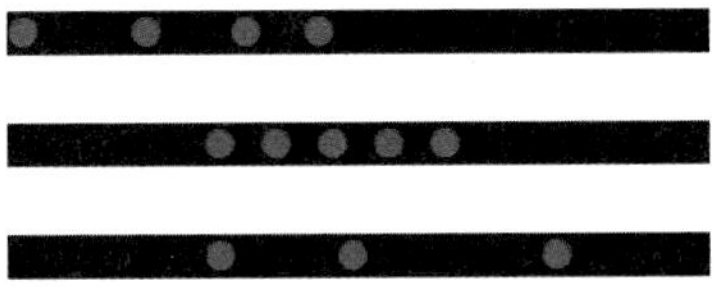

FIGURE 15.2   Three snapshots of the animation performed by an indeterminate ProgressBar

→ **ShowError**—Displays an error state when set to `true`. (Oddly, this makes the control blank instead of communicating an error clearly.)

→ **ShowPaused**—Displays a paused state when set to `true` (which is also subtle).

> **(!) Set ProgressBar's IsIndeterminate property back to false when it is not visible!**
>
> When you use a ProgressBar, it typically remains on the relevant Page but is hidden most of the time. However, even a hidden ProgressBar is still actively animating if IsIndeterminate is true, which can cause a noticeable degradation in performance! Therefore, you should always set IsIndeterminate to false when the ProgressBar is not in use.

Slider

`Slider` is a bit more complicated than `ProgressBar` because it enables users to change the current value by moving its *thumb* through the range, with any number of optional *ticks*. The default appearance of `Slider` (with no ticks) is shown in Figure 15.3. The `ToolTip` shown while dragging or hovering can be disabled by setting `IsThumbToolTipEnabled` to `false`. `Slider`, like some controls from previous chapters, exposes a `Header` property that is typically set to a simple label.

Set at 40 out of 100

A `ToolTip` shows the exact value while dragging or hovering

FIGURE 15.3   `Slider` looks like a `ProgressBar`, but it has a draggable thumb (a white square under the dark theme).

Users can also tap on the slider to make the thumb jump to the tapped location, or use the up or right arrow keys to increase the value and the down or left arrow keys to decrease the value. Each KeyDown event increments or decrements the value by the amount of the `SmallChange` property, which is 1 by default. (`Slider` also has a `LargeChange` property inherited from `RangeBase`, but it is unused.)

`Slider` has the same default range of `0` to `100`. Unlike `ProgressBar`, however, it defines an `Orientation` property (`Horizontal` by default). If you change the `Orientation` to `Vertical`, it looks just like the touch-optimized version of the Windows volume control slider. If you want the value to *decrease* when moving the thumb from left-to-right or bottom-to-top, you can set `IsDirectionReversed` to `true`.

`Slider` contains several properties for adjusting the placement and frequency of ticks. If you change `TickPlacement` from its default value of `None`, the spacing of the ticks is based on the value of `TickFrequency`. Figure 15.4 shows the other values of `TickPlacement` with a `TickFrequency` of 25 (using the default `0-100` range).

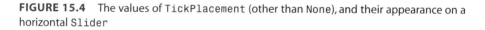

TopLeft   BottomRight   Outside   Inline

FIGURE 15.4   The values of `TickPlacement` (other than None), and their appearance on a horizontal `Slider`

The `TopLeft` and `BottomRight` values are named this way because they mean *top* and *bottom* when the `Slider` is horizontal, or *left* and *right* when the `Slider` is vertical.

By default, a `Slider`'s value changes in whole number increments. If you want to allow only coarser values, such as multiples of 5, you can set `StepFrequency` to a value other than its default of 1. (You could also set it to a smaller, fractional value if increments of 1 are too big.) And if you want the values to snap to ticks rather than steps, change the `SnapsTo` property from its default value of `StepValues` to `Ticks`.

•••

Customizing the Current Value Display

You can customize the content displayed in Slider's ToolTip by setting Slider's ThumbToolTipValueConverter to an instance of a class implementing an interface called IValueConverter (covered in Chapter 19, "Data Binding"). You must implement this yourself, but it is easy. The following simple implementation appends a " points" suffix to the number that would otherwise be displayed on its own:

```
class ToolTipValueConverter : IValueConverter
{
  public object Convert(object value, Type target, object param,
                        string language)
  {
    return value + " points";
  }

  public object ConvertBack(object value, Type target, object param,
                            string language)
  {
    throw new NotImplementedException();
  }
}
```

Although the underlying ToolTip control can contain UIElements, the customization here only allows strings. If you attempt to return a UIElement from Convert, the result of its ToString method is rendered instead.

SearchBox

In Windows 8, apps were supposed to leverage the Search charm for their own in-app search experience. In Windows 8.1, this is no longer the case. Apps are meant to be responsible for their end-to-end search experience, including providing the search box for the user to type into. Fortunately, a new SearchBox control makes this relatively easy, with all the bells and whistles you would expect.

SearchBox Basics

When you place a SearchBox in your user interface, it looks just like a TextBox with an extra button for submitting the search. Like TextBox and the other text controls, it has a PlaceholderText property. You should use this to inform the user what kind of things he or she can search for within your app. The following SearchBox is shown in Figure 15.5:

```
<SearchBox PlaceholderText="Search Chapters"/>
```

FIGURE 15.5   The SearchBox control, with and without text

SearchBox raises a QueryChanged event each time the text changes, and a QuerySubmitted event when the search button is clicked. You can retrieve the text via a QueryText property on SearchBox or on the object passed to event handlers.

When it comes to displaying search results, SearchBox doesn't help you with that. However, Visual Studio provides a template for a generic Search Results page that might meet your needs. You add it by right-clicking your project, selecting **Add, New Item...**, and then choosing **Search Results Page** from the list. Unless you change its name, this adds a Page called SearchResultsPage1.xaml to your app. You can navigate to it as follows, although the generated Page requires more code in order to be populated with real results:

```
void SearchBox_QuerySubmitted(SearchBox sender,
                              SearchBoxQuerySubmittedEventArgs args)
{
    // Pass the query text to the new page
    this.Frame.Navigate(typeof(SearchResultsPage1), args.QueryText);
}
```

> If the SearchBox is the only thing on your Page that accepts text input, you should auto-matically send the user's keystrokes from the hardware keyboard to the SearchBox even if it doesn't currently have focus. Most apps do this, and the Start screen does this with the Search pane. Fortunately, SearchBox defines a Boolean property that enables this to work simply by setting it to true: FocusOnKeyboardInput.
>
> With FocusOnKeyboardInput set to true, any normal typing causes the SearchBox to becomes focused *and* receive the keystrokes that were just typed. (This does not get triggered by tabbing, arrow keys, or even a Ctrl+V pasting gesture.) Immediately before the SearchBox gets focus, however, a PrepareForFocusOnKeyboardInput event is raised, in case you need to react to this.

Providing Suggestions

SearchBox has built-in support for four kinds of suggestions to help users find what they're looking for faster:

→ History suggestions

→ Query suggestions

→ Local content suggestions

→ Result suggestions

History Suggestions

By default, `SearchBox` remembers every query a user ever submitted within your app, even across sessions. It uses this to show matching suggestions as the user types, as shown in Figure 15.6. The user can tap a suggestion, or navigate to it with the keyboard and press Enter. When this happens, the current query is set to that suggestion, and the query is submitted.

FIGURE 15.6   The `SearchBox` control automatically provides history suggestions.

Users often search for things they have searched for in the past, so this can be very useful. However, if you want to disable this feature, set `SearchBox`'s `SearchHistoryEnabled` property to `false`.

If you have more than one `SearchBox` in your app, and they search different things, you should set each one's `SearchHistoryContext` property to a unique string. Search history is stored separately for each unique `SearchHistoryContext`, so you can control which `SearchBox`es share the same history and which don't.

 If you leave history suggestions enabled, provide a setting in your app to clear it!

Users can become very uncomfortable or annoyed by past search results that won't go away. You can clear it as follows, using a `SearchSuggestionManager` class tucked away in a `Windows.ApplicationModel.Search.Core` namespace:

```
SearchSuggestionManager manager = new SearchSuggestionManager();
manager.ClearHistory();
```

This clears it for all search contexts used by your app. There is no way to clear it for a specific context.

It turns out that you can also programmatically add history suggestions by using `SearchSuggestionManager`'s `AddToHistory` method.

You can set `SearchBox`'s `ChooseSuggestionOnEnter` property to `true` to make pressing the Enter key automatically select the topmost suggestion without having to navigate down to that result first. This works for all suggestion types. This causes the first suggestion to be highlighted while the user types, so the behavior is more obvious.

Query Suggestions

Query suggestions are meant to provide an autocomplete experience. Rather than showing you what you have typed before, they are meant to be the best guesses for what you are in the process of typing. Although SearchBox has built-in functionality for *displaying* such suggestions, you are responsible for *producing* them.

To produce query suggestions, handle SearchBox's SuggestionsRequested event and append suggestions to a passed-in collection. The following handler reports hardcoded suggestions if the user types a matching prefix (in a case-insensitive fashion):

```
// Sample static custom suggestions
static readonly string[] suggestions = { "Suggestion #1", "Suggestion #2",
  "Suggestion #3", "Suggestion #4", "Suggestion #5", "Suggestion #6" };
...
void SearchBox_SuggestionsRequested(SearchBox sender,
                              SearchBoxSuggestionsRequestedEventArgs e)
{
  if (!string.IsNullOrEmpty(e.QueryText))
  {
    foreach (string suggestion in suggestions)
    {
      if (suggestion.StartsWith(e.QueryText,
                        StringComparison.CurrentCultureIgnoreCase))
      {
        // Add the suggestion
        e.Request.SearchSuggestionCollection.AppendQuerySuggestion(suggestion);
      }
    }
  }
}
```

The result is shown in Figure 15.7. This SearchBox also has ChooseSuggestionOnEnter set to true, which automatically highlights the first suggestion.

History suggestions are still shown, when appropriate, on top of the query suggestions. The same suggestion will never appear more than once, however. For example, if the user searches for "Suggestion #2," then a later search moves that suggestion to the top of the list, as shown in Figure 15.8.

Local Content Suggestions

In some cases, such as an app that provides a browsing experience for one of the user's libraries, you might want to provide suggestions based on local files. SearchBox provides a special feature for precisely this scenario, if the local files are indexed. You can call SearchBox's SetLocalContentSuggestionSettings with an instance of a LocalContentSuggestionSettings object that specifies what files to include. The following code enables this for all libraries for which the app has the relevant capability:

```
var lcss = new LocalContentSuggestionSettings { Enabled = true };
this.searchBox.SetLocalContentSuggestionSettings(lcss);
```

FIGURE 15.7   The SearchBox control can display whatever query suggestions you provide.

FIGURE 15.8   "Suggestion #2" now comes from history, so it is placed on top and removed from the query suggestions that you provide.

Note that you must explicitly set the Enabled property to true, because it is false by default. If you don't have any of the relevant folder-access capabilities, the call to

SetLocalContentSuggestionSettings throws an exception. If you have at least one, then it silently uses whichever ones you have access to. This provides automatic query suggestions based on the relevant filenames!

If you prefer to be more explicit about which folders to include, you can specify them. For example, the following update forces the suggestions to only come from the Pictures library (and therefore requires the Pictures Library capability):

```
var lcss = new LocalContentSuggestionSettings { Enabled = true };
lcss.Locations.Add(KnownFolders.PicturesLibrary);
this.searchBox.SetLocalContentSuggestionSettings(lcss);
```

By default, all file metadata is considered in the search, but you can restrict which properties to include by adding property names to LocalContentSuggestionSettings's PropertiesToMatch collection. You can even use an Advanced Query Syntax (AQS) string to restrict the file set. For example, the following update limits the suggestions to PNG files in the Pictures library:

```
var lcss = new LocalContentSuggestionSettings { Enabled = true };
lcss.Locations.Add(KnownFolders.PicturesLibrary);
lcss.AqsFilter = "ext:=.png";
this.searchBox.SetLocalContentSuggestionSettings(lcss);
```

You can learn about AQS at http://bit.ly/R5ZyxB.

Although this feature is easy to use, the results might not always suit your needs. For one example, the suggested filenames don't include their extension, which might not be ideal for your scenario. Also, due to a limitation of the Windows indexer, files with underscores in their name do not get included.

Result Suggestions

Result suggestions are not meant to be normal search suggestions, but rather direct search *results*. For example, when you search for an installed app's name in the Windows Search pane, you get a direct link to launch that app and bypass the submission of your search query (if that's the result you wanted).

To produce result suggestions, you handle the same SuggestionsRequested event. Rather than calling AppendQuerySuggestion on the passed-in collection, you call Append**Result**Suggestion. This means that you can mix and match the two types of suggestions, but the convention is for the results to go on top. They should also be visually separated from query suggestions, which you can do by calling AppendSearchSeparator. The following handler demonstrates:

```
void SearchBox_SuggestionsRequested(SearchBox sender,
                                    SearchBoxSuggestionsRequestedEventArgs e)
{
  RandomAccessStreamReference image = RandomAccessStreamReference.CreateFromUri(
    new Uri("ms-appx:///Assets/Result.png"));
```

```
    e.Request.SearchSuggestionCollection.AppendResultSuggestion("Result",
      "You probably want this.", "tag", image, "Alt image text");
    e.Request.SearchSuggestionCollection.AppendSearchSeparator("Suggestions");
    e.Request.SearchSuggestionCollection.AppendQuerySuggestion("Suggestion #1");
    e.Request.SearchSuggestionCollection.AppendQuerySuggestion("Suggestion #2");
    e.Request.SearchSuggestionCollection.AppendQuerySuggestion("Suggestion #3");
}
```

AppendResultSuggestion enables you to produce a richer-looking item that has
an image and description in addition to the main title. Having to use the
RandomAccessStreamReference to wrap the image is an artifact of SearchBox wanting to
expose APIs that are mostly compatible with what SearchPane already exposed in
Windows 8. (See Chapter 21, "Supporting Charms," for more details.) The result of
providing these mixed suggestions is shown in Figure 15.9. Of course, because the suggestions are hard-coded for demonstration purposes, it doesn't matter what the user types in.

FIGURE 15.9   Leveraging a result suggestion and a separator in the suggestions list

When the user selects a result suggestion, SearchPane's ResultSuggestionChosen event is
raised instead of QuerySubmitted. That way, you can take an appropriate action rather
than showing search results. The result
suggestion's tag ("tag" in the preceding
code) is passed along to the
ResultSuggestionChosen event handler
so the chosen result can be identified.

> Even if you don't use result sugges-
> tions, you should consider using sepa-
> rators with appropriate labels in
> order to group different types of query
> suggestions.

Popup Controls

In addition to Flyout, MenuFlyout, and ToolTip, examined in previous chapters, several popup controls expose ways to float content over all the other content, giving a (mostly) "always on top" experience. This section looks at two dialogs, a context menu, and two custom floating regions. All but the last one are core Windows Runtime classes rather than XAML elements. Because of this, and because the one XAML element has no visuals of its own, they all look identical no matter whether the light or dark theme is used.

CoreWindowDialog

CoreWindowDialog is a title-only message box. It's what would traditionally be called a *modal dialog box* because it blocks interaction with the rest of the app until the dialog box is dismissed. Of course, this modal dialog box is more stylish and user-friendly than a desktop one, in part because it dims the rest of the app to make the situation obvious. Figure 15.10 shows what a CoreWindowDialog looks like when it is shown on top of an app (the multi-column RichTextBlock example from Chapter 12, "Text").

FIGURE 15.10   A CoreWindowDialog appears on top of the rest of the app's content.

This simple CoreWindowDialog was created and shown with the following helper method:

```
async Task ShowDialog()
{
  CoreWindowDialog dialog = new CoreWindowDialog("CoreWindowDialog Title");
  await dialog.ShowAsync();
}
```

Notice that the method to show the dialog (ShowAsync) is asynchronous. There is no synchronous version of this method, which is typical for Windows Runtime APIs. That doesn't complicate its use at all, however, thanks to the C# async and await keywords. The ShowDialog helper method is also made asynchronous with the async keyword, and this method awaits the completion of ShowAsync, which doesn't occur until the user closes the dialog. Of course, this simple method has nothing more to do after it has been closed.

The title passed to CoreWindowDialog's constructor (or later set via its Title property) gets trimmed with an ellipsis if needed; it never wraps. Note that the dialog does not have light dismiss behavior (as hinted by the dimmed area surrounding it). The user must click the Close button that gets included by default. CoreWindowDialog exposes a Showing event in case other parts of code want to react; however, it has no Closing/Hiding event.

CoreWindowDialog exposes a concept of custom *commands* that enable you to replace the default Close button with one to three buttons with custom labels. (If CoreWindowDialog were a XAML control, it would likely have an easy way to plug in a custom tree of UIElements. Because this is a UI-technology-agnostic Windows Runtime class, however, it needs a more formal approach for extensibility.)

To add custom commands to CoreWindowDialog, you add objects implementing the IUICommand interface to its Commands collection. IUICommand is a simple interface with three properties: a string label for the button, a delegate that is called when the button is clicked, and a generic ID that you can use to help identify commands by something other than their label (which may be localized). Note that IUICommand has no relation to the .NET-specific ICommand interface, but it is similar in spirit.

The Windows.UI.Popups namespace contains a UICommand class that implements IUICommand so you don't have to. It also contains convenience constructors that enable you to set some or all of its properties. The following code adds three custom commands (and therefore custom buttons) to a CoreWindowDialog, with the result shown in Figure 15.11:

```csharp
async Task ShowDialog()
{
  CoreWindowDialog dialog = new CoreWindowDialog("Do you want to save changes?");
  dialog.Commands.Add(new UICommand("Yes", OnCommand, 0));
  dialog.Commands.Add(new UICommand("No", OnCommand, 1));
  dialog.Commands.Add(new UICommand("Cancel", OnCommand, 2));
  dialog.CancelCommandIndex = 2;
  await dialog.ShowAsync();
}


void OnCommand(IUICommand command)
{
  // Handle the command here, perhaps identifying it by command.Id
}
```

FIGURE 15.11 A common question for a `CoreWindowDialog` to ask, with three custom buttons enabled by three `UICommands`

Notice that the default Close button is nowhere to be found in Figure 15.11. It appears only when the `Commands` collection is empty.

This example uses `0`, `1`, and `2` as the IDs for the `UICommands`, but you can choose anything or leave them `null` if your code has no use for them. For example, if each `UICommand` uses a separate delegate, then that is already enough to distinguish which one got invoked.

When the user clicks a button, the corresponding `UICommand`'s delegate gets invoked, and then the `CoreWindowDialog` automatically closes. `ShowAsync` returns the invoked `IUICommand` (actually, it returns an `IAsyncOperation<IUICommand>`, but the `await` keyword takes care of the `IAsyncOperation` part). Therefore, you could structure the logic without the use of any delegates:

```
async Task ShowDialog()
{
    CoreWindowDialog dialog = new CoreWindowDialog("Do you want to save changes?");
    dialog.Commands.Add(new UICommand { Label = "Yes", Id = 0 });
    dialog.Commands.Add(new UICommand { Label = "No", Id = 1 });
    dialog.Commands.Add(new UICommand { Label = "Cancel", Id = 2 });
    dialog.CancelCommandIndex = 2;
    IUICommand command = await dialog.ShowAsync();
    // Handle the command here, perhaps identifying it by command.Id
}
```

If one of your `UICommands` logically represents cancellation, as in Figure 15.11, you can set `CoreWindowDialog`'s `CancelCommandIndex` property to the zero-based index of this `UICommand`. This makes the Escape key an automatic shortcut for clicking the cancel button. `CoreWindowDialog` also exposes a `DefaultCommandIndex` property (`0` by default) that determines which one gets focus by default, as well as the special coloring.

> (!) **The `CoreWindowDialog.Commands` collection can contain no more than three items!**
>
> Adding any additional commands causes an exception to be thrown.

`CoreWindowDialog` contains special support for a *back button command* that gets rendered differently from the normal buttons. (It also doesn't count against the limit of three commands.) To enable it, you set `CoreWindowDialog`'s `BackButtonCommand` property to a delegate that gets invoked when the special back button is clicked. The back button auto-matically appears when this property is non-null, as shown in Figure 15.12.

FIGURE 15.12   When BackButtonCommand is set, a back button automatically appears.

Note that when the back button is clicked and the corresponding delegate is invoked, the dialog does *not* get automatically dismissed.

> If you're worried about the user accidentally tapping a button the instant CoreWindowDialog is shown, perhaps because the user is in the middle of a tapping-intensive action when it appears, you can change CoreWindowDialog's IsInteractionDelayed property from 0 (false) to 1 (true) to add a slight delay before it responds to input.

CoreWindowFlyout

CoreWindowFlyout is almost the same as CoreWindowDialog. Its claim to fame is its light dismiss behavior and its ability to be placed at a custom position. With light dismiss, the user can tap elsewhere (or press the Escape key) to close the CoreWindowFlyout, regardless of its content. It's like the XAML-specific Flyout, but with rigid constraints on what it can contain.

CoreWindowFlyout's API is identical to CoreWindowDialog except its constructor accepts a Point for its window-relative position and there's no CancelCommandIndex (because the user can *always* press Escape to close it). Unlike Title, there is no property to change the position after construction. There's also no settable size; it is determined by its content. Here's an example using the same options as Figure 15.12, but with the Cancel command removed:

```
async Task ShowFlyout()
{
  CoreWindowFlyout flyout = new CoreWindowFlyout(new Point(10, 10),
                                            "Do you want to save changes?");
  flyout.BackButtonCommand = OnBackButton;
  dialog.Commands.Add(new UICommand { Label = "Yes", Id = 0 });
  dialog.Commands.Add(new UICommand { Label = "No", Id = 1 });
  IUICommand command = await flyout.ShowAsync();
  …
}
```

Cancel is removed for two reasons:

1. With light dismiss, an explicit Cancel button is redundant.

2. Unlike `CoreWindowDialog`, `CoreWindowFlyout` is limited to two custom commands!

The result is shown in Figure 15.13, in context with the app content it partially covers. If the `CoreWindowFlyout` is dismissed without the user clicking a button, `ShowAsync` returns null.

FIGURE 15.13   A `CoreWindowFlyout` appears on top of the rest of the app's content at a custom position, and it does not dim anything.

> **The `CoreWindowFlyout.Commands` collection can contain no more than two items!**
>
> Although `CoreWindowDialog` supports up to three buttons, `CoreWindowFlyout` supports only up to *two*! Again, adding any additional commands causes an exception to be thrown.

The formatting of `CoreWindowFlyout` is a bit different from `CoreWindowDialog`: It doesn't dim the rest of the app but rather surrounds itself with a simple border, and its default button is rendered with the user's chosen Start screen foreground color (a tip-off that this is system-provided UI rather than XAML-based UI). Also, if its `Commands` collection is left empty, it renders a title with no buttons. (Again, no explicit Close button is needed due to its light dismiss behavior.)

> ! **You cannot show a CoreWindowFlyout while another one is currently showing!**
>
> If you attempt to do so, the call to ShowAsync throws an exception. This is true for all the classes examined in this section besides the XAML-specific Popup element, but this behavior is usually more surprising for CoreWindowFlyout (or the upcoming PopupMenu) because of its minimal screen real estate.

MessageDialog

MessageDialog is the Windows Runtime version of the classic message box. The only substantial difference between MessageDialog and CoreWindowDialog is that MessageDialog supports a second Content string in addition to the Title. The following code shows the MessageDialog in Figure 15.14:

```
async Task ShowDialog()
{
  MessageDialog dialog = new MessageDialog("MessageDialog Content",
                                           "MessageDialog Title");

  await dialog.ShowAsync();
}
```

FIGURE 15.14   MessageDialog can show text content between its title and button(s).

MessageDialog's Content property (set via its constructor in the preceding code) cannot be null. If you set it to an empty string, the result looks like a CoreWindowDialog. Unlike Title, which gets trimmed on a single line with an ellipsis, Content wraps. Furthermore, MessageDialog expands vertically, if needed, to fit additional lines from Content.

Just like with CoreWindowDialog, you can specify up to three custom buttons by using custom UICommands. The only remaining differences between MessageDialog and CoreWindowDialog are arbitrary:

→ MessageDialog has no BackButtonCommand property.

→ MessageDialog has no Showing event.

→ Instead of setting IsInteractionDelayed to 1, you accomplish the same thing with MessageDialog by setting its Options property to MessageDialogOptions.AcceptUserInputAfterDelay.

> ⓘ **The MessageDialog.Commands collection can contain no more than three items!**
>
> This is another thing that is the same between MessageDialog and CoreWindowDialog.

PopupMenu

PopupMenu is the Windows Runtime version of a context menu (and, therefore, a simpler form of MenuFlyout). In fact, it is the same control used internally by the text controls to show commands such as Copy and Select All.

Creating a PopupMenu is simple. You construct one with its default constructor and add some UICommands to it (up to six this time). When you call ShowAsync, you give it a window-relative position. The following code demonstrates this, producing the result in Figure 15.15:

```
async Task ShowMenu()
{
  PopupMenu menu = new PopupMenu();
  menu.Commands.Add(new UICommand { Label = "[spelling suggestion #1]", Id = 0});
  menu.Commands.Add(new UICommand { Label = "[spelling suggestion #2]", Id = 1});
  menu.Commands.Add(new UICommandSeparator());
  menu.Commands.Add(new UICommand { Label = "Add to dictionary", Id = 2 });
  menu.Commands.Add(new UICommand { Label = "Ignore", Id = 3 });
  IUICommand selection = await menu.ShowAsync(new Point(10, 10));
  …
}
```

Rather than using a regular UICommand, the third item is a special UICommandSeparator object that renders as an untappable line. These are commonly used to separate commands into more understandable groups.

PopupMenu doesn't dim the rest of the app's content, and it has light dismiss behavior (with ShowAsync returning null in that situation). It also auto-dismisses whenever a selection is made. Therefore, PopupMenu is like CoreWindowFlyout, but with no Title and with a different treatment for its commands (in style, layout, and number). This makes it considerably simpler, because Commands is its only property.

In addition to ShowAsync, PopupMenu has two overloads of a Show**ForSelection**Async method that enable you to pass a Rect representing an area you want the PopupMenu to appear adjacent to (but not covering). In other words, this enables the ideal placement of a context menu, where the passed-in Rect represents the selection that was right-tapped. The simpler overload centers the PopupMenu horizontally relative to the selection and places it directly above it (space permitting). The other overload enables you to specify a preferred placement (Above, Below, Left, or Right).

FIGURE 15.15   A PopupMenu appears on top of the rest of the app's content at a custom position, and it does not dim anything.

Recall from Chapter 3, "Sizing, Positioning, and Transforming Elements," that you can get a window-relative Rect for any FrameworkElement as follows:

```
GeneralTransform transform = element.TransformToVisual(null);
Rect rect = transform.TransformBounds(
  new Rect(0, 0, element.ActualWidth, element.ActualHeight));
```

> **!** **The PopupMenu.Commands collection can contain no more than six items!**
>
> This is an odd limitation, because the items could have easily become scrollable, but it is a limitation nonetheless.

Popup

A Popup is a regular UIElement that can float on top of other elements. It doesn't have any visual appearance by itself, but it can contain any System.Object as the value of its Child property, much like a content control. Besides there being no restrictions on a Popup's content, there is no restriction on the number of Popups you can show simultaneously (just as with other UIElements). This makes it the most flexible out of all the popup controls. Popups are internally leveraged by XAML controls such as Flyout, ToolTip, and AppBar for overlaying the rest of a Page's content.

Figure 15.16 demonstrates the behavior of the Popup in the following Page:

```
<Page …>
  <Grid Width="420" Height="420">
    <!-- Inner Grid with a Button-in-Popup and a separate Button -->
    <Grid Background="Red" Margin="100">
      <Popup IsOpen="True">
        <Button Content="Button in Popup in Grid" Background="Blue"/>
      </Popup>
      <Button Content="Button in Grid" Height="200" Canvas.ZIndex="100"/>
    </Grid>
    <!-- A Rectangle that overlaps the inner Grid underneath it -->
    <Rectangle Width="200" Height="200" Fill="Lime"
               HorizontalAlignment="Left" VerticalAlignment="Top"/>
  </Grid>
</Page>
```

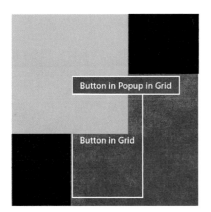

FIGURE 15.16   The Popup's content is placed in the top-left corner of its parent, but renders on top of all other elements.

There are four interesting things to note about Figure 15.16:

→ A Popup is visible only when its IsOpen property is set to true. (It is false by default.) It raises separate Opened and Closed events when the value of IsOpen changes.

→ A Popup renders in the top-left corner of its parent by default (the red Grid in this example). You can move it by giving it a Margin and/or setting its HorizontalOffset and VerticalOffset properties.

→ The layout inside a Popup is like the layout inside a Canvas; a child element is given only the exact amount of space it needs.

→ Popups have a unique power: Despite being a regular UIElement, it can render on top of all other elements on the Page. Although the sibling Button in Figure 15.16 has a larger ZIndex, and although the lime Rectangle is a sibling to the Popup's *parent* (making it the Popup's *uncle*?), it appears on top of both of them!

Only two types of things can render on top of a Popup:

→ Another Popup. This includes properly attached ToolTips and CommandBars, for example, because Popups are used as an implementation detail. Multiple Popups are rendered based only on where they are placed in the tree (with later ones on top of earlier ones); marking them with Canvas.ZIndex has no effect.

→ Windows-provided UI that can overlap your page. For example: the charms bar, app switcher, the software keyboard, notifications, and the Windows Runtime popup classes (CoreWindowDialog, CoreWindowFlyout, MessageDialog, and PopupMenu).

In contrast, the Windows Runtime popup classes are able to render on top of *any* XAML content.

> By default, a Popup opens only when IsOpen is explicitly set to true and closes only when IsOpen is explicitly set to false. However, you can set its IsLightDismissEnabled property to true to make it automatically close the next time focus changes to a different element. (Note that the Popup doesn't need to have focus in the first place. Any focus change can trigger dismissal as long as focus isn't given to the Popup.)

One interesting characteristic of Popup is that you can create and show one without ever attaching it to a parent element. Every other UIElement requires being explicitly attached in some fashion, but Popup has internal logic to attach to the root Frame if it doesn't already have a parent. The following code in a Page's constructor demonstrates this:

```
public MainPage()
{
  InitializeComponent();

  Popup popup = new Popup();
  popup.Child = new Button { … };
  popup.IsOpen = true; // Show without explicitly attaching it to anything
}
```

As a result of this code, the Button inside the Popup is rendered on top of the window's top-left corner. Note that such Frame-rooted popups do not move with the rest of the Page whenever the software keyboard automatically pushes the Page upward.

Hub

The Hub control has been introduced to make it easy for you to follow the popular hub design pattern used by Bing apps such as News, Sports, Finance, Travel, Food & Drink, and Health & Fitness. Such apps have a horizontally-scrolling landing page with many independent sections. The first section typically has a big image (called a *hero image*) as its background, and the subsequent sections are typically diverse content with links to other pages.

Hub has a Header that can be arbitrary content, although it is typically set to a simple string matching the app's name, and a collection of HubSection controls (each with its own Header) that are stacked horizontally by default. Figure 15.17 shows the following Hub in action:

```
<Page …>
  <Hub Header="Other Controls">
    <HubSection MinWidth="750">
      <HubSection.Background>
        <ImageBrush ImageSource="Assets/HeroImage.jpg" Stretch="UniformToFill"/>
      </HubSection.Background>
    </HubSection>

    <HubSection Header="Range Controls" Background="#F15A21" MinWidth="300">
      …
    </HubSection>

    <HubSection Header="SearchBox" IsHeaderInteractive="True"
                Background="#B74717" MinWidth="300">
      …
    </HubSection>

    <HubSection Header="Date and Time Controls" Background="#681A00">
      …
    </HubSection>

    <HubSection Header="ProgressRing" Background="#3E0000" MinWidth="300">
      …
    </HubSection>
  </Hub>
</Page>
```

To set the first HubSection's Background to image content, an ImageBrush is used. ImageBrush is described in Chapter 16, "Vector Graphics." This is better than placing an Image element inside the HubSection, because it wouldn't fill the entire area. As the Hub is scrolled, the Header remains stationary, as shown in Figure 15.18. Therefore, the content of each HubSection is automatically given a top margin big enough to leave room for the Header.

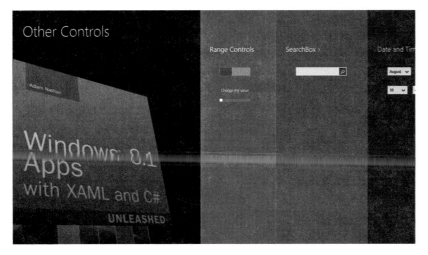

FIGURE 15.17   The Hub makes it easy to follow a popular design pattern.

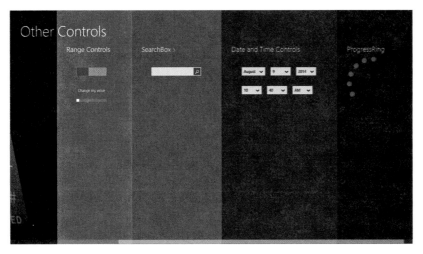

FIGURE 15.18   The Header remains stationary when scrolling to the end of the Hub.

Hub has a DefaultSectionIndex property that enables you to initialize it scrolled to a specific section. It also has a ScrollToSection method that enables you to scroll on-demand. This method expects a HubSection instance rather than an index. You can access a Hub's sections via its HubSections property, the content property set in the preceding XAML. Hub even exposes a SectionsInView property with a corresponding SectionsInViewChanged event, in case you want to change other aspects of your user interface based on what is currently in view.

Hub's Orientation property can be set to Vertical, which could be a nice way to morph your page to accommodate a narrow window or a portrait-oriented device. Be aware that it could require extra work to make your Hub look nice vertically, however! Figure 15.19 demonstrates this by adding Orientation="Vertical" to the Hub displayed in the previous two figures.

FIGURE 15.19   Hub supports a vertical orientation, but you should ensure your HubSections are the same width so it doesn't look like this.

HubSections

The content inside a HubSection is a bit special. Instead of a Content property, HubSection only has a ContentTemplate property. This means you must wrap your XAML for each HubSection inside a DataTemplate element. The following XAML shows the unabridged Hub used in the previous figures. The setting of ContentTemplate is implicit because it is HubSection's content property in the XAML sense:

```
<Page …>
  <Hub Header="Other Controls">
    <HubSection MinWidth="750">
      <HubSection.Background>
        <ImageBrush ImageSource="Assets/HeroImage.jpg" Stretch="UniformToFill"/>
```

```
      </HubSection.Background>
    </HubSection>


    <HubSection Header="Range Controls" Background="#F15A21" MinWidth="300">
      <DataTemplate>
        <StackPanel Margin="40">
          <ProgressBar Value="40" Height="32"/>
          <Slider Margin="0,40,0,0" Header="Change my value"/>
        </StackPanel>
      </DataTemplate>
    </HubSection>


    <HubSection Header="SearchBox" IsHeaderInteractive="True"
                Background="#B74717" MinWidth="300">
      <DataTemplate>
        <StackPanel Margin="40">
          <SearchBox MinWidth="200"/>
        </StackPanel>
      </DataTemplate>
    </HubSection>


    <HubSection Header="Date and Time Controls" Background="#681A00">
      <DataTemplate>
        <StackPanel Margin="40">
          <DatePicker/>
          <TimePicker Margin="0,40,0,0"/>
        </StackPanel>
      </DataTemplate>
    </HubSection>


    <HubSection Header="ProgressRing" Background="#3E0000" MinWidth="300">
      <DataTemplate>
        <Grid>
          <ProgressRing IsActive="True" Width="200" Height="200" />
        </Grid>
      </DataTemplate>
    </HubSection>
  </Hub>
</Page>
```

This extra indirection is a performance optimization; it enables the content of each
HubSection to be loaded on-demand, rather than all elements being loaded during
startup. Data templates are discussed in Chapter 19.

HubSection also has a Boolean IsHeaderInteractive property. When set to true, its
Header becomes a clickable button with a chevron glyph to indicate that it's clickable.

You can see this for the SearchBox header in the previous three figures. When such a header is clicked, a SectionHeaderClick event is raised *on the parent Hub*.

> Visual Studio includes a **Hub App** template complete with a landing page using a Hub, a group page that can be displayed when a HubSection's Header is clicked, and an item page that can be used to display details of any item, whether the navigation initiates directly from the landing page or from a group page.

Jumping to a HubSection

Hub exposes a handy SectionHeaders property that is a collection of Header objects from each HubSection. This, in combination with Hub's ScrollToSection method, makes it easy to use Hub with SemanticZoom to provide a standard way for the user to jump to any HubSection. Chapter 11, "Items Controls," shows an example of using SemanticZoom.

In this section, we leverage the same property and method to provide a much simpler shortcut mechanism. This works well if each HubSection's Header is a string rather than a UIElement. If you mark our example Hub with Name="hub", you can use the following data binding trick (see Chapter 19) to fill a ComboBox with the section names:

```
<ComboBox Header="Jump to a Section" SelectionChanged="ComboBox_SelectionChanged"
          ItemsSource="{Binding SectionHeaders, ElementName=hub}"/>
```

The SelectionChanged handler can use the ScrollToSection method to make selecting a header jump to the right section:

```
void ComboBox_SelectionChanged(object sender, SelectionChangedEventArgs e)
{
  if (this.hub != null)
  {
    ComboBox comboBox = sender as ComboBox;
    int index = comboBox.SelectedIndex;
    if (index >= 0 && index < this.hub.Sections.Count)
    {
      // Scroll the Hub to the selected section
      this.hub.ScrollToSection(this.hub.Sections[index]);
    }
  }
}
```

This ComboBox could be placed inside the first HubSection, which would be especially helpful in a small vertical view, as shown in Figure 15.20. Note that the blank entry corresponds to the first HubSection, whose Header is not set.

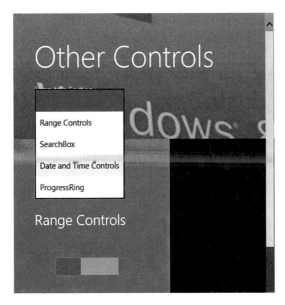

FIGURE 15.20   This `ComboBox` leverages Hub's `SectionHeaders` property to provide a shortcut to each `HubSection`.

Hub may seem like an items control, but it isn't because it doesn't contain an arbitrary collection of objects. Nor does it have selection behavior or expect each item to have the same visual template applied. Instead, it is designed to contain only `HubSections`, and each `HubSection` is responsible for its own arbitrary content.

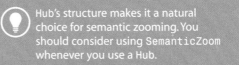

Hub's structure makes it a natural choice for semantic zooming. You should consider using `SemanticZoom` whenever you use a Hub.

Date and Time Controls

Windows 8.1 now provides two essential date and time XAML controls that were a noticeable omission from Windows 8: `DatePicker` and `TimePicker`.

DatePicker

`DatePicker`, shown in Figure 15.21, looks simplistic. It's just three `ComboBoxes` stuck together for selecting a month, date, and year. But this is definitely a control you don't want to implement yourself, as handing dates correctly for all cultures is tricky.

By default, `DatePicker` shows the current date, but you can change it by setting its `Date` property to a `DateTimeOffset`. This is also the single property whose value changes whenever the user changes the month, day, or year. Such changes raise a `DateChanged` event. You can turn `DatePicker` into just a "month picker" or "year picker" or any combination of the three date components by hiding individual `ComboBoxes` with the `DayVisible`,

MonthVisible, and YearVisible Boolean properties. You can also stack its ComboBoxes vertically if you set Orientation to Vertical.

FIGURE 15.21   The modest-looking DatePicker control packs a lot of power.

By default, the year ComboBox contains values from 100 years in the past to 100 years in the future. This is based on the current date rather than the value of the Date property, so programmatically setting Date outside that range doesn't display properly. You can change the range, however, by setting DatePicker's MinYear and MaxYear properties.

Like many controls, DatePicker has a Header, so Figure 15.21 was created as follows:

```
<DatePicker Header="Choose a date"/>
```

DatePicker uses the correct calendar for the user's current language, but Windows supports nine different calendars. You can change which one is used by setting CalendarIdentifier to a string matching one of the string properties exposed by the static Windows.Globalization.CalendarIdentifiers class (Gregorian, Hebrew, Japanese, Korean, and so on). If you're setting the value in XAML, the string you need to use matches the corresponding CalendarIdentifiers property name but has a Calendar suffix (e.g. GregorianCalendar, HebrewCalendar, and so on).

Finally, you can control the formatting of any of the date components with DayFormat, MonthFormat, and YearFormat properties. These are strings that can be set to one of many *format templates* or even more flexible *format patterns*. You can view the long list of available templates and patterns at http://bit.ly/15DIjfk, although Visual Studio 2013 includes IntelliSense that helps you pick the right values! This is shown in Figure 15.22.

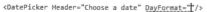

FIGURE 15.22   Choosing a format with help from IntelliSense

TimePicker

TimePicker, shown in Figure 15.23, looks like a DatePicker and follows the same pattern. It has a Time property initialized to the current time, and a corresponding TimeChanged event. It has the standard Header property, so Figure 15.23 was created as follows:

```
<TimePicker Header="Choose a time"/>
```

FIGURE 15.23   The TimePicker control looks and acts like a DatePicker.

TimePicker has only two properties for customizing the time display. One is MinuteIncrement, which can be set to an integer from 0–59. It controls how many choices appear in the minute ComboBox. By default, MinuteIncrement is 1, so the ComboBox contains every value from 00–59. For appointment scenarios, this is commonly set to 15, so the ComboBox contains only 00, 15, 30, and 45.

The other property is ClockIdentifier, a string which can be set to either 12HourClock or 24HourClock. If you're setting this in C#, you can use string properties exposed by the static Windows.Globalization.ClockIdentifiers class. The properties are called TwelveHour and TwentyFourHour. Figure 15.24 shows how the following TimePicker appears with custom values for MinuteIncrement and ClockIdentifier and with its minutes ComboBox open.

```
<TimePicker Header="Choose a time" ClockIdentifier="24HourClock"
                                   MinuteIncrement="20"/>
```

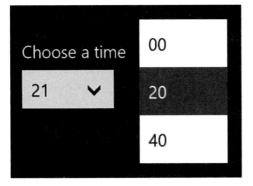

FIGURE 15.24   This TimePicker uses a 24-hour clock and limits its minutes to increments of 20.

ProgressRing

Conceptually, ProgressRing is a version of ProgressBar that is always indeterminate and has a different default style. It uses the same five dancing dots as ProgressBar with IsIndeterminate=true, but they chase each other in a circle rather than moving in a horizontal line. ProgressRing doesn't render anything by default, so to make it animate, you must set IsActive to true. (This is the analog to ProgressBar's IsIndeterminate property.)

Figure 15.25 captures a single point in the animation, which doesn't look much like a ring. When they are in motion, however, the ring is clear.

FIGURE 15.25   ProgressRing animates its five dots in a circular pattern.

Unlike ProgressBar, ProgressRing isn't a range control because its indeterminate nature has no need for a range.

You can use either ProgressRing or an indeterminate ProgressBar for the same situations. A ProgressRing is typically used for the initial *loading* of content, when there's not much on the screen to interfere with. For example, a ProgressRing is often used when simulating an extended splash screen during an application's launch. An indeterminate ProgressBar is usually preferable when *refreshing* content already on the screen, because its compact form doesn't get in the way.

> **(!) Set ProgressRing's IsActive property to false when it is not visible!**
>
> Just like with an indeterminate ProgressBar, a hidden ProgressRing is still actively animating if IsActive is true, which can cause a noticeable degradation in performance.

ToggleSwitch

Logically, ToggleSwitch is like a ToggleButton or its more well-known derived CheckBox control, just with a different default appearance that makes it look like a light switch, and with support for only two states (no indeterminate state). Figure 15.26 shows a simple ToggleSwitch with no properties set. The user can turn a ToggleSwitch on and off by tapping it or dragging the thumb.

ToggleSwitch exposes a Boolean IsOn property and raises a simple Toggled event when the value of IsOn changes.

ToggleSwitch has a standard Header property, and you can customize the "On" and "Off" labels by setting the OnContent and/or OffContent properties. For example, the following ToggleSwitch is shown in Figure 15.27:

```
<ToggleSwitch Header="Show high scores" OnContent="Yes" OffContent="No"/>
```

Off by default

On, after user interaction

FIGURE 15.26   The `ToggleSwitch` is like a light switch that can be on or off.

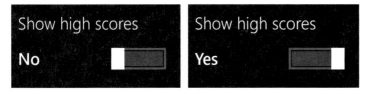

FIGURE 15.27   `ToggleSwitch` can have a custom header and custom on/off labels.

The `Header`, `OnContent`, and `OffContent` properties are all of type `System.Object`, so they each support the same content-rendering scheme as content controls. You could set them to custom `UIElements` instead of simple text. Or, you could set them to nonvisual data objects and use separate `HeaderTemplate`, `OnContentTemplate`, and `OffContentTemplate` properties to style them using the techniques of Chapter 18, "Styles, Templates, and Visual States."

`ToggleSwitches` are the preferred control to use for Boolean app settings rather than `CheckBoxes`. You can see them used throughout Windows, such as the "Airplane mode" switch in the Networks pane, or in just about every section of the PC Settings app.

WebView

The `WebView` control is what is traditionally called a *web browser control*. It hosts HTML content, either from a URL or a string containing HTML, using the same rendering engine and JavaScript engine as Internet Explorer. Figure 15.28 shows the following `Page` filled with a `WebView` whose `Source` (of type `System.Uri`) is set to `http://bing.com`:

```
<Page …>
  <WebView Name="webView" Source="http://bing.com"/>
</Page>
```

FIGURE 15.28   WebView with a URL Source (bing.com)

In addition to online content, you can point WebView to a file packaged with your app by using an ms-appx URI. And in Windows 8.1, you can now point WebView directly to an HTML file within app data by using an ms-appdata URI. See Chapter 20, "Working with Data," for more information about the various kinds of valid URIs.

Navigation

Although you can navigate the WebView by setting its Source property, it exposes four different navigation methods:

→ **Navigate**—Accepts a Uri and acts just like setting the Source property

→ **NavigateToString**—Navigates to in-memory static HTML content passed as a string

→ **NavigateWithHttpRequestMessage**—Enables you to specify the target as an HttpRequestMessage object covered in Chapter 20. This is useful for performing an HTTP POST instead of a GET, or providing custom HTTP headers.

→ **NavigateToLocalStreamUri**—A more powerful version of NavigateToString. Use this to navigate to local content that needs to reference other local files (such as images, CSS files, or scripts). You need to use a special URI with an ms-local-stream scheme, but WebView's BuildLocalStreamUri method helps you construct it. You must also pass a custom object implementing IUriToStreamResolver to resolve referenced files. With this, you can also intercept links to content that would normally be unviewable and process it to be displayed.

Figure 15.29 shows the same Page used for Figure 15.28, but with the following code in its constructor that navigates to a literal HTML string, somewhat like the RTF string example in Chapter 12:

```
public MainPage()
{
  InitializeComponent();

  this.webView.NavigateToString(
    "<span style=" font:61n0f100px;background:yellow">" +
    "This is <i>much</i> <b>simpler</b> than RTF!");
}
```

The HTML is intentionally malformed to show that the control is as resilient as Internet Explorer (because it basically *is* Internet Explorer). The reason for the WebView name rather than WebBrowser is that the control doesn't have any of the basic features that any Web browser would have, such as a URL box, a progress indicator, or Back/Stop/Refresh buttons. It also doesn't show URL tooltips when hovering over a link. You could, of course, build a nice browser that leverages WebView to do all the hard work. WebView contains a number of enhancements in Windows 8.1, and many of those additions enable you to build a better browser experience. For example, it now has the browser-like methods GoBack, GoForward, Stop, and Refresh. (It also has CanGoBack and CanGoForward properties.) It even exposes the current document title with a DocumentTitle property.

This is *much* simpler than RTF!

FIGURE 15.29   WebView navigated to a custom HTML string

When a user taps normal links (http and https) within a WebView, it navigates to the page like a Web browser. When the user taps a link with a different protocol (such as mailto, ftp, or a custom protocol registered by another app), the correct user-prompt and then app-launch behavior occurs.

Every navigation results in a NavigationCompleted whether it succeeded for failed. (The details are passed to the handler.) WebView provides three more events for various stages in the navigation: NavigationStarting, ContentLoading, and DOMContentLoaded. All four events have an equivalent event raised for any frame or iframe within HTML content: **Frame**NavigationStarting, **Frame**ContentLoading, **Frame**DOMContentLoaded, and **Frame**NavigationCompleted.

WebView also raises events for misbehaving JavaScript on the current document (LongRunningScriptDetected), for content it cannot render (UnviewableContentIdentified), and for cases when it blocks navigation with a SmartScreen alert (UnsafeContentWarningDisplaying).

> **(!) Navigating to Web pages can cause JavaScript runtime exceptions to be thrown!**
>
> Because there are some differences in the environment presented to the JavaScript engine compared to Internet Explorer (for example, there is no alert function defined by default when browsing with WebView), you can easily encounter such exceptions while debugging your app. Although this can be annoying during debugging, it doesn't impact your app (unless the failing script is important for the behavior of the Web page). Note that unchecking **JavaScript Runtime Exceptions** in Visual Studio's **Exceptions** dialog doesn't help, because the exceptions are raised in a different process than the one you're debugging.

Composing HTML with XAML

In Windows 8.1, WebView can now be seamlessly blended with other XAML elements and supports transforms and projections. This is demonstrated with the following XAML, shown in Figure 15.30:

```xml
<Page …>
  <Grid Background="{ThemeResource ApplicationPageBackgroundThemeBrush}">
    <!-- Behind the WebView -->
    <Rectangle Fill="Red" HorizontalAlignment="Stretch" Height="600"/>

    <WebView Source="http://xbox.com" Opacity=".5">
      <WebView.Projection>
        <PlaneProjection RotationY="30"/>
      </WebView.Projection>
    </WebView>

    <!-- In front of the WebView -->
    <Rectangle Fill="Blue" HorizontalAlignment="Stretch" Margin="200,0"
               Height="200"/>
  </Grid>
</Page>
```

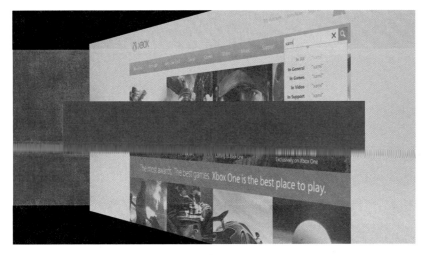

FIGURE 15.30   `WebView` can be manipulated just like other XAML elements.

In this example, the red `Rectangle` is behind the `WebView`, but still visible due to `WebView`'s `Opacity` setting, and the blue `Rectangle` is in front of it. The 3D-tilted `WebView` is still fully interactive for keyboard input, although not for pointer input. In Figure 15.30, the user has tabbed over to the search box and started typing.

With this much flexibility, `WebView` is a compelling mechanism for creating a hybrid app that blends HTML and XAML content. You could even use `WebView` to host WebGL content within your XAML app! Windows 8.1 helps this scenario even further with a new `DefaultBackgroundColor` property that lets you change `WebView`'s background color from white.

Composing JavaScript with C#

When building a hybrid app that mixes HTML and XAML, you might also find the need to execute some JavaScript code. You can easily fill a `WebView` with custom HTML, but to react to user input within the HTML content, you must write some JavaScript that can communicate back to the XAML `Page` hosting the `WebView` (or rely on triggering and intercepting navigation). You can do this by handling `WebView`'s `ScriptNotify` event, which gets raised whenever JavaScript on the current page calls `external.notify`. The following code demonstrates this:

```
public MainPage()
{
  InitializeComponent();

  webView.ScriptNotify += WebView_ScriptNotify;

  webView.NavigateToString("<script>external.notify('gotcha!')</script>");
}
```

```
void WebView_ScriptNotify(object sender, NotifyEventArgs e)
{
  // When this gets called, e.Value == "gotcha!"
}
```

If a value is passed to the JavaScript notify method, it shows up as e.Value in the C#
event handler.

You can also call a named script on WebView's current document by calling WebView's
InvokeScriptAsync method with the name of the script and a collection of arguments (all
strings). It returns any result as a string.

> ## (!) You must explicitly allow Web pages accessed via URL to raise the ScriptNotify event!
>
> The simple ScriptNotify example works as-is because the HTML content is local to the app. If
> the current page comes directly from an external website, however, Windows 8.1 introduces two
> new requirements for the ScriptNotify event to be raised:
>
> 1. **Each unique domain must be listed in your package manifest.** In the Visual Studio
>   designer, this is done on the **Content URIs** tab. You may use subdomain wildcards, but
>   the domain must be specified explicitly.
> 2. **Each URI must use the HTTPS protocol.**
>
> These two new requirements are in place to ensure app and data integrity, as ScriptNotify
> communication can be vulnerable to exploits from malicious websites. With these restrictions in
> place, you can still integrate tightly with remote Web content *that you control*, while being
> protected against malicious Web content.

Capturing Web Content

WebView's CapturePreviewToStreamAsync method enables you to take a screenshot of its
rendered HTML and retrieve it as an IRandomAccessStream. The following code uses this
on a WebView named webView then sends the content to an Image named image:

```
async Task ShowContent()
{
  using (InMemoryRandomAccessStream ras = new InMemoryRandomAccessStream())
  {
    await this.webView.CapturePreviewToStreamAsync(ras);

    WriteableBitmap bitmap = new WriteableBitmap((int)this.webView.ActualWidth,
                                                 (int)this.webView.ActualHeight);
    await bitmap.SetSourceAsync(ras);
    this.image.Source = bitmap;
  }
}
```

This is different from taking a screenshot with `RenderTargetBitmap`, because that includes any `Opacity` customizations, transforms, and projections in the screenshot:

```
async Task ShowWebView()
{
  // This approach includes transforms, projections,
  // and opacity changes on WebView itself
  RenderTargetBitmap bitmap = new RenderTargetBitmap();
  await bitmap.RenderAsync(this.webView);
  this.Source = bitmap;
}
```

`WebView` also provides a way to capture the user's *selection within* its content as a `DataPackage`, an object that can be provided to the Share charm to share with another app. See Chapter 21 for details about data packages.

Summary

You've now seen all the major built-in controls that can be used for creating a wide variety of user interfaces. Although you can radically change the *look* of these controls by using the techniques discussed in Chapter 18, the core *behavior* described in this part of the book remains the same.

The suite of built-in controls continue to be enhanced by additional toolkits that ship independently, some free and some not. For example, Telerik (http://telerik.com) sells a large suite of controls (with separate but matching implementations for XAML and HTML) that includes `Chart`, `Gauge`, `NumericBox`, and `AutoCompleteBox`. For another example, Bing provides fantastic controls for 2D and 3D maps (if you want more custom integration than what you get by launching the Maps app), language translation, Optical Character Recognition (OCR), and more. You can find them by searching the online section of Visual Studio's Extension Manager for "Bing." Their use requires credentials that you can get from the Bing Dev Center (http://bing.com/dev) and some controls require subscriptions from the Windows Azure Marketplace. For example, the first 5,000 OCR transactions are free per month, but you have to pay if you want more.

Chapter 16

In This Chapter

- → Shapes
- → Geometries
- → Brushes

VECTOR GRAPHICS

Vector graphics have been a focal point of XAML since its inception. Life becomes so much easier when your app's assets scale perfectly to any size. If you create an app that solely uses vector graphics rather than images and videos, you can avoid creating and packaging all those file variations discussed in Chapter 13, "Images," for everything except your tile and splash screen assets required by Windows. In addition, the automatic ability for vector graphics to be dynamic means you can trivially modify them for special situations or user customizations (such as changing colors).

Other than the media controls, the built-in controls all leverage vector graphics for their own visuals. And there are many ways you can leverage vector graphics for your own custom controls or artwork within your app. A number of XAML elements provide powerful options, and tools such as Blend make it easy to create sophisticated content.

This chapter focuses on the three important data types for vector graphics: Shape, Geometry, and Brush. Brushes are a vital part of all the topics in this chapter, and they have been used throughout the book for mundane tasks such as setting a control's Foreground and Background. There are several feature-rich Brushes, which is why they deserve a dedicated section.

Shapes

A Shape is a 2D vector-based drawing that can be placed anywhere that any other element can be placed. For example, Chapter 2, "Mastering XAML," shows how easy it is to embed a square in a Button by using Rectangle (which derives from Shape):

```
<Button>
  <Rectangle Height="10" Width="10" Fill="White"/>
</Button>
```

Six classes derive from Shape:

- → Rectangle
- → Ellipse
- → Line
- → Polyline
- → Polygon
- → Path

Although Shape itself can't be used in XAML, it defines many properties for controlling the appearance of its subclasses. The two most important ones are Fill and Stroke, both of type Brush. It also defines a Stretch property that acts just like Viewbox's and Image's Stretch properties, so you can customize how it reacts if it is given more space than it would naturally have. Although Shape is a UIElement and therefore supports RenderTransform, it also defines its own GeometryTransform property that enables applying the same Transform(s) to its internal geometry instead of (or in addition to) Transform(s) to the element itself. Unlike RenderTransform, GeometryTransform impacts the layout size of the element. The rest of Shape's properties are all related to customizing its Stroke, and are covered later in the "Getting Fancy with Strokes" section.

Rectangle

Rectangle doesn't define a special Size or Bounds property; it leverages the familiar XAML layout system for controlling its size and position. For example, you could set the size of a Rectangle with its Width and Height properties (among others) inherited from FrameworkElement, and set its location using Canvas.Left and Canvas.Top if it's inside a Canvas.

Rectangle, however, defines its own RadiusX and RadiusY properties of type double that enable you to give it rounded corners. Figure 16.1 shows the following Rectangles in a StackPanel with various values of RadiusX and RadiusY:

```
<StackPanel>
  <Rectangle Width="200" Height="100"
    Fill="Orange" Stroke="Black" StrokeThickness="10" Margin="4"/>
```

```
  <Rectangle Width="200" Height="100" RadiusX="10" RadiusY="30"
    Fill="Orange" Stroke="Black" StrokeThickness="10" Margin="4"/>
  <Rectangle Width="200" Height="100" RadiusX="30" RadiusY="10"
    Fill="Orange" Stroke="Black" StrokeThickness="10" Margin="4"/>
  <Rectangle Width="200" Height="100" RadiusX="100" RadiusY="50"
    Fill="Orange" Stroke="Black" StrokeThickness="10" Margin="4"/>
</StackPanel>
```

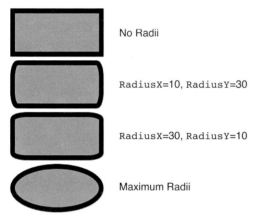

No Radii

RadiusX=10, RadiusY=30

RadiusX=30, RadiusY=10

Maximum Radii

FIGURE 16.1   Four Rectangles with different values for RadiusX and RadiusY

RadiusX can be at most half the Width of the Rectangle, and RadiusY can be at most half the Height. Setting them any higher makes no difference.

> (!) **You must explicitly set Stroke or Fill for a Shape to be seen!**
>
> Both Stroke and Fill are both set to null by default, which makes the Shape invisible (and unhittable by pointer input).

Ellipse

After discovering the flexibility of Rectangle and realizing that it can be made to look like an ellipse (or circle), you'd think that a separate Ellipse class would be redundant. And you'd be right! All Ellipse does is make it easier to get an elliptical shape. It defines no settable properties above and beyond what Shape and its base classes provide. Ellipse simply fills its rectangular region with the largest possible elliptical shape.

The following Ellipse could replace the last Rectangle in the previous XAML snippet, and Figure 16.1 would look identical:

```
<Ellipse Width="200" Height="100"
  Fill="Orange" Stroke="Black" StrokeThickness="10" Margin="4"/>
```

The only change is replacing the element name and removing the references to RadiusX and RadiusY.

Line

Line defines four double properties to represent a line segment connecting points (*x1*,*y1*) and (*x2*,*y2*). These properties are called X1, Y1, X2, and Y2. These are defined as four separate properties rather than two Point properties for ease of use in data-binding scenarios.

The values of Line's properties are not absolute coordinates. They are relative to the space given to the Line element by the layout system. For example, the following StackPanel contains three Lines, rendered in Figure 16.2:

```
<StackPanel>
  <Line X1="0" Y1="0"   X2="100" Y2="100" Stroke="Black" StrokeThickness="10"
    Margin="4"/>
  <Line X1="0" Y1="0"   X2="100" Y2="0"   Stroke="Black" StrokeThickness="10"
    Margin="4"/>
  <Line X1="0" Y1="100" X2="100" Y2="0"   Stroke="Black" StrokeThickness="10"
    Margin="4"/>
</StackPanel>
```

Notice that each Line is given the space needed by its bounding box, so the horizontal line gets only 10 pixels (for the thickness of its Stroke) plus the specified Margin. Line inherits Shape's Fill property, but it is meaningless because there is never any area to fill.

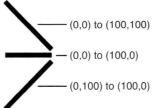

(0,0) to (100,100)

(0,0) to (100,0)

(0,100) to (100,0)

FIGURE 16.2   Three Lines in a StackPanel, demonstrating that their coordinates are relative

Polyline

Polyline represents a sequence of lines, expressed in its Points property (a collection of Point objects). The following four Polylines are rendered in Figure 16.3:

```
<StackPanel>
  <Polyline Points="0,0 100,100" Stroke="Black" StrokeThickness="10" Margin="4"/>
  <Polyline Points="0,0 100,100 200,0" Stroke="Black" StrokeThickness="10"
    Margin="4"/>
  <Polyline Points="0,0 100,100 200,0 300,100" Stroke="Black" StrokeThickness="10"
    Margin="4"/>
  <Polyline Points="0,0 100,100 200,0 300,100 100,100" Stroke="Black"
    StrokeThickness="10" Margin="4"/>
</StackPanel>
```

In XAML, Points can be specified as a simple list of alternating *x* and *y* values. The commas can help with readability but are optional. You can place commas between any two values or use no commas at all.

Figure 16.4 demonstrates that setting Polyline's Fill fills it as if a line segment connects the first Point with the last Point. Figure 16.4 was created by taking the Polylines from Figure 16.3 and marking them with Fill="Orange".

FIGURE 16.3   Four Polylines, ranging from 2 to 5 points

FIGURE 16.4   The same Polylines from Figure 16.3, but with an explicit Fill

Polygon

Just as Rectangle makes Ellipse redundant, Polyline makes Polygon redundant. The only difference between Polyline and Polygon is that Polygon automatically adds a visible line segment connecting the first Point and last Point if one doesn't already exist.

If you take each Polyline from Figure 16.4 and change each element name to Polygon, you get the result shown in Figure 16.5. Notice that the initial line segment in the first and last Polygons is noticeably longer than in Figure 16.4. This is due to Miter corners joining the initial line segment with the final line segment (which happens to share the same coordinates), which would extend infinitely if not for a StrokeMiterLimit

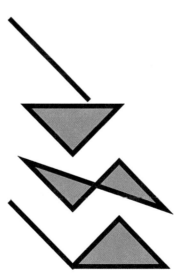

FIGURE 16.5   Polygons are just like Polylines, except that they always form a closed shape.

property limiting it to 10 pixels. The `Miter` and `StrokeMiterLimit` properties are examined in the upcoming "Getting Fancy with Strokes" section.

Path

All the preceding shapes are just special cases of a powerful shape called `Path`. `Path` adds only a single `Data` property to `Shape`, which can be set to an instance of any geometry, for example:

```
<Path StrokeThickness="10" Fill="Red">
  <Path.Data>
    <RectangleGeometry Rect="0,0,100,100"/>
  </Path.Data>
</Path>
```

`Path` made its first appearance in C# code back in Chapter 6, "Handling Input: Touch, Mouse, Pen, and Keyboard," for rendering ink strokes. This C# code revealed much more about geometries than the preceding XAML snippet, but geometries are covered in the next section. First, let's look at a number of ways to alter the appearance of any shape's strokes.

Getting Fancy with Strokes

We've already seen examples of setting the `Stroke` property on shapes, but the `Shape` class defines a number of other stroke-related properties. One simple property is `StrokeThickness` of type `double` (with a default value of 1). But that's not all:

→ **StrokeStartLineCap** and **StrokeEndLineCap**—Customize any open segment endpoints with a value from the `PenLineCap` enumeration: `Flat` (the default), `Square`, `Round`, or `Triangle`. For any endpoints that join two segments, you can customize their appearance with `StrokeLineJoin` instead.

→ **StrokeLineJoin**—Affects corners with a value from the `PenLineJoin` enumeration: `Miter` (the default), `Round`, or `Bevel`. A separate **StrokeMiterLimit** property (with a default value of `10`) can be used to limit how far a `Miter` join extends, which can otherwise be very large for small angles. For example, the angle between the two segments back in Figure 16.5 is 0°, which is why `StrokeMiterLimit` kicks in.

→ **StrokeDashArray**—Can make the stroke a nonsolid line. It can be set to a pattern of numbers that represents the widths of dashes and the spaces between them. The odd values represent the widths (relative to `StrokeThickness`) of dashes, and the even values represent the relative widths of spaces. Whatever pattern you choose is then repeated indefinitely. A separate `double` **StrokeDashOffset** property controls where the pattern begins.

→ **StrokeDashCap**—Customizes both endpoints of each dash. This works just like `StrokeStartLineCap` and `StrokeEndLineCap`, with the same default value of `Flat`.

Figure 16.6 shows each of the PenLineCap values applied to a Line's StrokeStartLineCap and StrokeEndLineCap. Figure 16.7 demonstrates each of the LineJoin values on the corners of a triangle.

 Flat

Square

Round

Triangle

Miter   Round   Bevel

FIGURE 16.6   Each type of PenLineCap on both ends of a Line

FIGURE 16.7   Each type of LineJoin applied to a triangle

Figure 16.8 shows a few different StrokeDashArray values combined with some StrokeDashCap values.

StrokeDashArray="1,1"   StrokeDashArray="2,1"   StrokeDashArray="5,1,1,1"

StrokeDashArray="1,1"   StrokeDashArray="0,1"
StrokeDashCap="Triangle"   StrokeDashCap="Triangle"

FIGURE 16.8   The effects of StrokeDashArray

The values of StrokeDashArray can be confusing when StrokeDashCap is set to anything other than its default Flat value. That's because each dash is naturally wider when given the same numeric value as a space. Giving a dash a width of 0, as done in the last triangle in Figure 16.8, is a common practice to make each dash consist solely of its starting and ending cap. This is especially confusing if you use a StrokeDashCap of Square, because you need different values to get results that look the same when using Flat. For example, marking a Shape with:

```
StrokeDashArray="0,2" StrokeDashCap="Square"
```

gives almost identical results as:

```
StrokeDashArray="1,1" StrokeDashCap="Flat"
```

which is what is used by the first triangle in Figure 16.8.

> **(!) Overuse of Shapes can lead to performance problems!**
>
> It's tempting to use Shapes as the building blocks for any 2D drawings. However, when you have Shape-based artwork, *every* Shape individually supports styles, data binding, resources, layout, input and focus, routed events, and so on. This is typically unnecessary overhead. Ask yourself whether you really need vector graphics if you find yourself using a large number of Shapes, or if you could get away with a single Image instead.

Geometries

A Geometry is not a visual element like Shape, but rather the simplest possible abstract representation of a shape or path.

Geometry has a number of subclasses:

→ **RectangleGeometry**—Has a Rect property for defining its dimensions.

→ **EllipseGeometry**—Has RadiusX and RadiusY properties, plus a Center property.

→ **LineGeometry**—Has StartPoint and EndPoint properties to define a line segment.

→ **PathGeometry**—Contains a collection of PathFigure objects in its Figures content property; a general-purpose Geometry.

→ **GeometryGroup**—Contains a collection of geometries.

These should look familiar, because they mirror the Shape classes. So what's the point of having these separate Geometry classes? You can build up and combine arbitrary geometries to form a complex shape and set it as the content of a single Path element, which has less overhead than using multiple Shapes. Furthermore, there are other scenarios for which the abstract representation of a shape comes in handy. All UIElements have a Clip property that can be set to an instance of a RectangleGeometry to describe the visual clipping. (Granted, this property could have been a simple Rect instead, but other XAML-based frameworks enable clipping by arbitrary geometries.) Also, these geometry classes are used internally by the various Shape classes. (Polyline and Polygon are simple abstractions over a PathGeometry.)

Because Geometry is not a UIElement, it does not inherit a RenderTransform property. Instead, it exposes its own Transform property. (This is the same as the GeometryTransform property exposed by Shape for its internal Geometry.)

Just as all basic Shapes can be represented as a Path, the first three geometries are just special cases of PathGeometry provided for convenience. You can express any rectangle, ellipse, or line segment in terms of a PathGeometry. So, let's dig a little more into the components of the powerful PathGeometry class.

PathFigures and PathSegments

Each PathFigure in a PathGeometry contains one or more connected PathSegments in its Segments content property. A PathSegment is a straight or curvy line segment, represented by one of seven derived classes:

→ **LineSegment**—A line segment (of course!)

→ **PolyLineSegment**—A shortcut for a connected sequence of LineSegments

→ **ArcSegment**—A segment that curves along the circumference of an imaginary ellipse

→ **BezierSegment**—A cubic Bézier curve

→ **PolyBezierSegment**—A shortcut for a connected sequence of BezierSegments

→ **QuadraticBezierSegment**—A quadratic Bézier curve

→ **PolyQuadraticBezierSegment**—A shortcut for a connected sequence of QuadraticBezierSegments

---

•••

Bézier Curves

Bézier curves (named after engineer Pierre Bézier) are commonly used in computer graphics for representing smooth curves. Bézier curves are even used by fonts to mathematically describe curves in their glyphs.

The basic idea is that in addition to two endpoints, a Bézier curve has one or more *control points* that give the line segment its curve. These control points are not visible (and not necessarily on the curve itself) but rather are used as input to a formula that dictates where each point on the curve exists. Intuitively, each control point acts like a center of gravity, so the line segment appears to be "pulled" toward these points.

Despite the scarier-sounding name, QuadraticBezierSegment is simpler than BezierSegment and computationally cheaper. A quadratic Bézier curve has only one control point, whereas a cubic Bézier curve has two. Therefore, a quadratic Bézier curve can form only a *U*-like shape (or a straight line), but a cubic Bézier curve can also take the form of an *S*-like shape.

The following `Path` contains a `PathGeometry` with two simple `LineSegments` that create the *L* shape in Figure 16.9:

```
<Path Stroke="Black" StrokeThickness="10">
  <Path.Data>
    <PathGeometry>
      <PathFigure>
        <LineSegment Point="0,100"/>
        <LineSegment Point="100,100"/>
      </PathFigure>
    </PathGeometry>
  </Path.Data>
</Path>
```

Notice that the definition for each `LineSegment` includes only a single `Point`. That's because it implicitly connects the previous point to the current one. The first `LineSegment` connects the default starting point of (0,0) to (0,100), and the second

FIGURE 16.9   A Path that contains a pair of LineSegments

`LineSegment` connects (0,100) to (100,100). (The other six `PathSegments` act the same way.) If you want to provide a custom starting point, you can set `PathFigure`'s `StartPoint` property to a `Point` other than (0,0).

You might expect that applying a `Fill` to this `Path` is meaningless, but Figure 16.10 shows that it fills the same way as a `Polyline`, pretending that a line segment exists to connect the last point back to the starting point. Figure 16.10 was created by adding the following `Fill` to the preceding XAML:

```
<Path Fill="Orange" Stroke="Black" StrokeThickness="10">
  …
</Path>
```

To turn the imaginary line segment into a real one, you can add a third `LineSegment` to the `PathFigure` explicitly, or you can set `PathFigure`'s `IsClosed` property to `true`. The result of doing either is shown in Figure 16.11.

FIGURE 16.10   The Path from Figure 16.9 with an orange Fill

The two different values of `IsClosed` produce results resembling either a `Polyline` or `Polygon`. And there's a good reason for this. Internally, `Polyline` is using a `PathGeometry` with

FIGURE 16.11   The Path from Figure 16.10, but with IsClosed="True" on the PathFigure

IsClosed=false on its PathFigures, and Polygon is using a PathGeometry with IsClosed=true on its PathFigures.

Because all PathSegments within a PathFigure must be connected, you can place multiple PathFigures in a PathGeometry if you want disjoint shapes or paths in the same Geometry. You could also overlap PathFigures to create results that would be complicated to replicate in a single PathFigure. For example, the following XAML overlaps the triangle from Figure 16.11 with a triangle that is given a different StartPoint but is otherwise identical:

```
<Path Fill="Orange" Stroke="Black" StrokeThickness="10">
  <Path.Data>
    <PathGeometry>
      <!-- Triangle #1 -->
      <PathFigure IsClosed="True">
        <LineSegment Point="0,100"/>
        <LineSegment Point="100,100"/>
      </PathFigure>
      <!-- Triangle #2 -->
      <PathFigure StartPoint="70,0" IsClosed="True">
        <LineSegment Point="0,100"/>
        <LineSegment Point="100,100"/>
      </PathFigure>
    </PathGeometry>
  </Path.Data>
</Path>
```

This dual-PathFigure Path is displayed in Figure 16.12.

FillRule

The behavior of the orange fill in Figure 16.12 might not be what you expected to see. PathGeometry enables you to

FIGURE 16.12   Overlapping triangles created by using two PathFigures

control this fill behavior with its FillRule property. Whenever you have a Geometry with intersecting points, whether via multiple overlapping PathFigures or overlapping PathSegments in a single PathFigure, there can be multiple interpretations of which area is *inside* a shape (and can, therefore, be filled) and which area is *outside* a shape. FillRule gives you two choices on how filling is done:

→ **EvenOdd**—Fills a region only if you would cross an odd number of segments to travel from that region to the area outside the entire shape. This is the default.

→ **Nonzero**—Is a more complicated algorithm that takes into consideration the direction of the segments you would have to cross to get outside the entire shape. For many shapes, it is likely to fill all enclosed areas.

The difference between EvenOdd and Nonzero is illustrated in Figure 16.13 with the same overlapping triangles from Figure 16.12.

Polyline, Polygon, and GeometryGroup also expose a FillRule property.

EvenOdd   Nonzero

FIGURE 16.13   Overlapping triangles with different values for FillRule

GeometryGroup

GeometryGroup composes one or more Geometry instances together. The Transform map's relationship to Transform, GeometryGroup derives from Geometry, so it can be used anywhere that a simpler Geometry can be used. For example, the previously shown XAML for the overlapping triangles in Figure 16.12 could be rewritten to use two geometries (each with a single PathFigure) rather than one:

```
<Path Fill="Orange" Stroke="Black" StrokeThickness="10">
  <Path.Data>
    <GeometryGroup>
      <!-- Triangle #1 -->
      <PathGeometry>
        <PathFigure IsClosed="True">
          <LineSegment Point="0,100"/>
          <LineSegment Point="100,100"/>
        </PathFigure>
      </PathGeometry>
      <!-- Triangle #2 -->
      <PathGeometry>
        <PathFigure StartPoint="70,0" IsClosed="True">
          <LineSegment Point="0,100"/>
          <LineSegment Point="100,100"/>
        </PathFigure>
      </PathGeometry>
    </GeometryGroup>
  </Path.Data>
</Path>
```

GeometryGroup, like PathGeometry, has a FillRule property that is set to EvenOdd by default. It takes precedence over any FillRule settings of its children.

This, of course, begs the question, "Why would I create a GeometryGroup when I can just as easily create a single PathGeometry with multiple PathFigures?" One minor advantage of doing this is that GeometryGroup enables you to aggregate other geometries such as RectangleGeometry and EllipseGeometry, which can be easier to use. But the major advantage of using GeometryGroup is that you can set various Geometry properties independently on each child.

For example, the following GeometryGroup composes two identical triangles but sets the Transform on one of them to rotate it 25°:

```
<Path Fill="Orange" Stroke="Black" StrokeThickness="10" StrokeLineJoin="Round">
  <Path.Data>
    <GeometryGroup>
      <!-- Triangle #1 -->
      <PathGeometry>
        <PathFigure IsClosed="True">
          <LineSegment Point="0,100"/>
          <LineSegment Point="100,100"/>
        </PathFigure>
      </PathGeometry>
      <!-- Triangle #2 -->
      <PathGeometry>
        <PathGeometry.Transform>
          <RotateTransform Angle="25"/>
        </PathGeometry.Transform>
        <PathFigure IsClosed="True">
          <LineSegment Point="0,100"/>
          <LineSegment Point="100,100"/>
        </PathFigure>
      </PathGeometry>
    </GeometryGroup>
  </Path.Data>
</Path>
```

The result of this is shown in Figure 16.14. Creating this result with a single PathGeometry and a single PathFigure would be difficult. Creating it with a single PathGeometry containing two

FIGURE 16.14   A GeometryGroup with two identical triangles, except that one is rotated

PathFigures would be easier but would still require manually doing the math to perform the rotation. With GeometryGroup, however, creating it is straightforward.

> Because Fill and all the Stroke properties are specified on a Shape rather than a Geometry, GeometryGroup doesn't enable you to combine shapes with different fills or outlines. To achieve this, you must use multiple Shape elements.

Representing Geometries as Strings

Representing each segment in a Geometry with a separate element is fine for simple shapes and paths or geometries formed dynamically in C#. For complicated artwork in XAML, however, it can get extremely verbose. Although most people use a design tool to emit XAML-based geometries rather than craft them by hand, it makes sense to keep the resultant file size as small as reasonably possible.

Therefore, XAML supports a flexible syntax for representing just about any `PathGeometry` as a string. The `PathGeometry` representing the simple triangle displayed in Figure 16.11:

```
<Path Fill="Orange" Stroke="Black" StrokeThickness="10">
  <Path.Data>
    <PathGeometry>
      <PathFigure IsClosed="True">
        <LineSegment Point="0,100"/>
        <LineSegment Point="100,100"/>
      </PathFigure>
    </PathGeometry>
  </Path.Data>
</Path>
```

can be represented with the following compact syntax:

```
<Path Fill="Orange" Stroke="Black" StrokeThickness="10"
  Data="M 0,0 L 0,100 L 100,100 Z"/>
```

Representing the overlapping triangles from Figure 16.12 requires a slightly longer string:

```
<Path Fill="Orange" Stroke="Black" StrokeThickness="10"
  Data="M 0,0 L 0,100 L 100,100 Z M 70,0 L 0,100 L 100,100 Z"/>
```

These strings contain a series of commands that control properties of `PathGeometry` and its `PathFigures`, plus commands that fill one or more `PathFigures` with `PathSegments`. The syntax is simple but powerful. Table 16.1 describes all the available commands.

TABLE 16.1   Geometry String Commands

Command	Meaning
PathGeometry and PathFigure Properties	
F *n*	Set `FillRule`, where 0 means `EvenOdd` and 1 means `Nonzero`. If you use this, it must be at the beginning of the string.
M *x,y*	Start a new `PathFigure` and set `StartPoint` to (*x,y*). This must be specified before using any other commands (excluding F). The M stands for *move*.
Z	End the `PathFigure` and set `IsClosed` to `true`. You can begin another disjoint `PathFigure` after this with an M command or use a different command to start a new `PathFigure` originating from the current point. If you don't want the `PathFigure` to be closed, you can omit the Z command entirely.

TABLE 16.1   Continued

Command	Meaning
PathSegments	
L x,y	Create a LineSegment to (x,y).
A rx,ry d $f1$ $f2$ x,y	Create an ArcSegment to (x,y), based on an ellipse with radii rx and yx, rotated d degrees. The $f1$ and $f2$ flags can be set to 0 (false) or 1 (true) to control two of ArcSegment's properties: IsLargeArc and Clockwise, respectively.
C $x1,y1$ $x2,y2$ x,y	Create a BezierSegment to (x,y), using control points $(x1,y1)$ and $(x2,y2)$. The C stands for *cubic* Bézier curve.
Q $x1,y1$ x,y	Create a QuadraticBezierSegment to (x,y), using control point $(x1,y1)$.
Additional Shortcuts	
H x	Create a LineSegment to (x,y), where y is taken from the current point. The H stands for *horizontal line*.
V y	Create a LineSegment to (x,y), where x is taken from the current point. The V stands for *vertical line*.
S $x2,y2$ x,y	Create a BezierSegment to (x,y), using control points $(x1,y1)$ and $(x2,y2)$, where $x1$ and $y1$ are automatically calculated to guarantee smoothness. (This point is either the second control point of the previous segment or the current point if the previous segment is not a BezierSegment.) The S stands for *smooth* cubic Bézier curve.
Lowercase commands	Any command can be specified in lowercase to cause its relevant parameters to be interpreted as *relative* to the current point rather than absolute coordinates. This doesn't change the meaning of the F, M, and Z commands, but they can also be specified in lowercase.

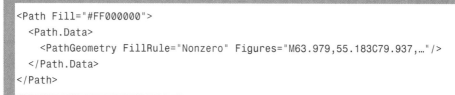

There are many places where you can find reusable SVG assets, such as thenounproject.com, which is filled with excellent icons that fit the flat style of Windows. There are not so many places where you can find reusable XAML-based graphics.

However, a number of SVG-to-XAML converters exist. A free (and open source) one I've used is part of the XamlTune project (http://xamltune.codeplex.com). It is not currently maintained, and resultant XAML needs manual adjustments for Windows Store apps, but it is still useful nonetheless.

For example, XamlTune produces Paths such as the following:

```
<Path Fill="#FF000000">
  <Path.Data>
    <PathGeometry FillRule="Nonzero" Figures="M63.979,55.183C79.937,…"/>
  </Path.Data>
</Path>
```

But the XAML parser for Windows Store apps doesn't support a type converter for setting `PathGeometry.Figures` to a geometry string. Therefore it must be converted to the following simpler `Path`:

```
<Path Fill="#FF000000" Data="M63.979,55.183C79.937,…"/>
```

Spaces and Commas in Geometry Strings

The spaces between commands and parameters are optional, and all commas are optional. But you must have at least one space or comma between parameters. Therefore, `M 0,0 L 0,100 L 100,100 Z` is equivalent to the more compact but much more confusing `M0 0L0 100L100 100Z`.

Brushes

It's usually not obvious, but XAML elements almost never interact directly with colors. Instead, most uses of color are wrapped inside objects known as `Brushes`. This is an extremely powerful indirection because many different brushes can be swapped in.

`Brush` itself exposes three properties: `Opacity`, `Transform`, and `RelativeTransform`. Unlike `Transform`, `RelativeTransform` is relative to the size of the area being covered with the `Brush`.

`Brush` has four subclasses, representing two *color brushes* and two *tile brushes*. Although this section mostly demonstrates `Brushes` on a `Path`, keep in mind that these `Brushes` can be used as the background, foreground, or outline of just about anything you can put on the screen—even the foreground for text!

Color Brushes

The two color brushes are `SolidColorBrush` and `LinearGradientBrush`. They sound straightforward, but these `Brushes` are more flexible than most people realize.

SolidColorBrush

`SolidColorBrush`, used implicitly throughout this book, fills the target area with a single color. It has a simple `Color` property of type `Windows.UI.Color`. `Color` exposes four `Byte` properties (one per channel): `A` for alpha, `R` for red, `G` for green, and `B` for blue. Because of the syntax that treats strings such as "Blue" or "#FFFFFF" as `SolidColorBrushes`, they are indistinguishable from their underlying `Color` in XAML. In fact, color strings can take one of three different forms in XAML:

→ A name, like `Red`, `Khaki`, or `DodgerBlue`, matching one of the static properties on the `Windows.UI.Colors` class.

→ The standard RGB color space (sRGB) representation #argb, where a, r, g, and b are hexadecimal values for the A, R, G, and B properties. For example, opaque Red is #FFFF0000, or more simply #FF0000 (because A is assumed to be the maximum 255 by default).

→ The enhanced RGB color space (scRGB) representation sc#a r g b, where a, r, g, and b are floating-point values. Red, green, and blue values of 0.0 represent black, whereas three values of 1.0 represent white. In this representation, opaque Red is sc#1.0 1.0 0.0 0.0, or more simply sc#1.0 0.0 0.0. Commas are also allowed between each value.

> If the hexadecimal representation for A, R, G, and B all repeat the same digit, you can leverage shortcut syntax in which you specify each digit only once. For example, you can shorten #AABBCCDD to #ABCD, or #CCDDEE (with an implicit FF alpha value) to #CDE (with an implicit F alpha value).

> It is usually more efficient to use colors with translucency coming from their alpha channels than to use UIElement's Opacity property to apply translucency to an otherwise-opaque solid color.

If you need to create a SolidColorBrush in C#, you can create one from a predefined Colors property as follows:

```
SolidColorBrush b = new SolidColorBrush(Colors.MintCream);
```

or from custom A, R, G, B values as follows:

```
SolidColorBrush b = new SolidColorBrush(Color.FromArgb(255, 173, 255, 47));
```

LinearGradientBrush

LinearGradientBrush fills an area with a gradient defined by colors at specific points along an imaginary line segment, with linear interpolation between those points. It contains a collection of GradientStop objects in its GradientStops content property, each of which contains a Color and an Offset. The offset is a double value relative to the bounding box of the area being filled, where 0 is the beginning and 1 is the end.

The following XAML applies a yellow-to-green gradient to a Canvas Background and a blue-to-red gradient to a trophy-shaped Path inside it:

```
<Canvas Width="100" Height="100">
  <Canvas.Background>
    <LinearGradientBrush>
      <GradientStop Offset="0" Color="Yellow"/>
      <GradientStop Offset="1" Color="Green"/>
```

```
      </LinearGradientBrush>
    </Canvas.Background>
    <!-- The trophy -->
    <Path Data="M63.979,55.183C79.937,53.135,92.441,…">
      <Path.Fill>
        <LinearGradientBrush>
          <GradientStop Offset="0" Color="Blue"/>
          <GradientStop Offset="1" Color="Red"/>
        </LinearGradientBrush>
      </Path.Fill>
    </Path>
  </Canvas>
```

The result is shown in Figure 16.15. The Path data is the "Trophy" symbol by Matthew R. Miller, from thenounproject.com collection. (The symbol is available as SVG, but I used XamlTune to convert it.)

The default interpolation of colors is done using the sRGB color space, but you can set LinearGradientBrush's ColorInterpolationMode property to ScRgbLinearInterpolation to use the scRGB color space instead. The result is a smoother gradient, as shown in Figure 16.16 when applied to both gradients from Figure 16.15.

FIGURE 16.15   A two simple LinearGradientBrushes applied to a square Canvas and the trophy inside

FIGURE 16.16   ColorInterpolationMode affects the appearance of both gradients.

By default, the gradient starts at the top-left corner of the area's bounding box and ends at the bottom-right corner. This is why not much blue and even less red is visible inside the trophy. The true bounding box for the trophy isn't obvious from looking at the Path in XAML, but the Visual Studio designer reveals it, as shown in Figure 16.17. The extra space is an artifact of the specified coordinates in the geometry string.

As you would expect, you can customize the gradient's starting and ending points so it doesn't always interpolate from the top-left corner to the bottom-right corner. This can be done with LinearGradientBrush's StartPoint and EndPoint properties. The values of these points are relative to the bounding box,

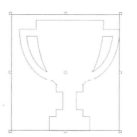

FIGURE 16.17   The trophy's bounding box extends further to the top and left, due to the coordinates chosen in its geometry.

just like the Offset in each GradientStop. Therefore, the default values for StartPoint and EndPoint are (0,0) and (1,1), respectively.

If you want to use absolute units instead of relative ones, you can set MappingMode to Absolute (rather than the default RelativeToBoundingBox). Note that this applies only to StartPoint and EndPoint; the Offset values in each GradientStop are always relative.

Figure 16.18 shows a few different settings of StartPoint and EndPoint on the two LinearGradientBrushes used in Figure 16.15 (with the default relative MappingMode and default interpolation). Notice that the relative values are not limited to a range of 0 to 1. You can specify smaller or larger numbers to make the gradient logically extend *past* the bounding box. (This applies to GradientStop Offset values as well.)

The final property for controlling LinearGradientBrush is SpreadMethod, which determines how any leftover area not covered by the gradient should be filled. This makes sense only when the LinearGradientBrush is explicitly set to *not* cover the entire bounding box. The default value (from the GradientSpreadMethod enumeration) is Pad, meaning that the remaining space should be filled with the color at the endpoint. You could alternatively set it to Repeat or Reflect. Both of these values repeat the gradient in a never-ending pattern, but Reflect reverses every other gradient to maintain a smooth transition. Figure 16.19 demonstrates each of these SpreadMethod values on the same two LinearGradientBrushes, but with the following StartPoint and EndPoint values that force the gradient to cover only the middle 10% of the bounding box:

```
<LinearGradientBrush StartPoint=".45,.45" EndPoint=".55,.55" SpreadMethod="XXX">
    ...
</LinearGradientBrush>
```

StartPoint = (0,0),
EndPoint = (0,1)

StartPoint = (0,1),
EndPoint = (0,0)

StartPoint = (0,0),
EndPoint = (1,0)

StartPoint = (0.5,0),
EndPoint = (1,0)

StartPoint = (-2,-2),
EndPoint = (2,2)

FIGURE 16.18   Various settings of StartPoint and EndPoint applied to both gradients

Pad   Repeat   Reflect

FIGURE 16.19   Different values of SpreadMethod can create vastly different effects.

And don't forget, because a Shape's Stroke, like its Fill, is a Brush rather than a simple Color, Shapes and many other elements can be outlined with complicated Brushes. Figure 16.20 shows the following version of the trophy that adds a thick rainbow-gradient stroke:

```
<Canvas Width="100" Height="100" Background="White">
  <!-- The trophy -->
  <Path StrokeThickness="4" Data="M63.979,55.183C79.937,53.135,92.441,…">
    <Path.Stroke>
      <LinearGradientBrush>
        <GradientStop Offset="0" Color="Red"/>
        <GradientStop Offset="0.2" Color="Orange"/>
        <GradientStop Offset="0.4" Color="Yellow"/>
        <GradientStop Offset="0.6" Color="Green"/>
        <GradientStop Offset="0.8" Color="Blue"/>
        <GradientStop Offset="1" Color="Purple"/>
      </LinearGradientBrush>
    </Path.Stroke>
    <Path.Fill>
      <LinearGradientBrush>
        <GradientStop Offset="0" Color="Blue"/>
        <GradientStop Offset="1" Color="Red"/>
      </LinearGradientBrush>
    </Path.Fill>
  </Path>
</Canvas>
```

FIGURE 16.20   Outlining the trophy with a LinearGradientBrush

Notice that the Stroke's LinearGradientBrush uses six GradientStops spaced equally along the gradient path, rather than just two.

> To get crisp lines inside a gradient brush, you can add two GradientStops at the same Offset with different Colors. The following LinearGradientBrush does this at Offsets 0.2 *and* 0.6 to get two distinct lines defining the DarkBlue region:

```
<LinearGradientBrush EndPoint="0,1">
  <GradientStop Offset="0" Color="Aqua"/>
  <GradientStop Offset="0.2" Color="Blue"/>
  <GradientStop Offset="0.2" Color="DarkBlue"/>
  <GradientStop Offset="0.6" Color="DarkBlue"/>
  <GradientStop Offset="0.6" Color="Blue"/>
  <GradientStop Offset="1" Color="Aqua"/>
</LinearGradientBrush>
```

Figure 16.21 shows this applied as the trophy's Fill (and with its Stroke from Figure 16.20 removed).

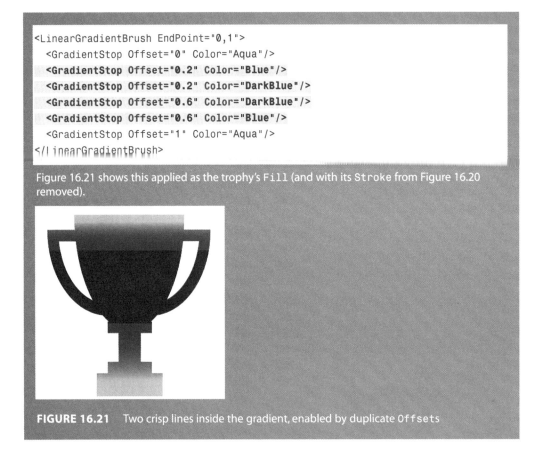

FIGURE 16.21   Two crisp lines inside the gradient, enabled by duplicate Offsets

Because all Colors have an alpha channel, you can incorporate transparency and translucency into any gradient by changing the alpha channel on any GradientStop's Color. The following LinearGradientBrush varies the alpha channel to go from a translucent red to transparent, and then back to translucent:

```
<LinearGradientBrush>
  <GradientStop Offset="0" Color="#CCFF0000"/>
  <GradientStop Offset="0.5" Color="#00FF0000"/>
  <GradientStop Offset="1" Color="#CCFF0000"/>
</LinearGradientBrush>
```

Figure 16.22 shows the result of applying this LinearGradientBrush to the trophy, on top of a photographic background so the transparency is apparent.

FIGURE 16.22   A trophy with translucency, accomplished by using colors with non-opaque alpha channels

When it comes to gradients, not all transparent colors are equal!

Notice that the second GradientStop for Figure 16.22 uses a "transparent red" color rather than simply specifying Transparent as the color. That's because Transparent is defined as white with a 0 alpha channel (#00FFFFFF). Although both colors are completely invisible, the interpolation to each color does not behave the same way. If Transparent were used for the second GradientStop for Figure 16.21, you would not only see the alpha value gradually change from 0xCC to 0, you would also see the blue and green values gradually change from 0 to 0xFF, giving the brush more of a gray look.

How can I create a radial gradient?

You can't, at least with vector graphics. WPF and Silverlight include a RadialGradientBrush class, but Windows Store apps do not currently have this feature. RadialGradientBrush was always a performance pitfall due to lack of hardware acceleration. For those rare instances where you want a radial gradient, Microsoft would prefer you use an image asset.

Tile Brushes

The two remaining brushes are *tile brushes*, because they both derive from a TileBrush base class. However, this is one of those cases where the naming doesn't make much sense because of compatibility with WPF and Silverlight. In WPF, you can specify the brush's content as infinitely repeating *tiles* and configure the tiling pattern in a number of different ways. In the XAML UI Framework for Windows Store apps, none of these options exist. Instead, the way to think about a tile brush is a brush that contains bitmap-based content. That content can never repeat (it can only stretch), so there's only ever one "tile."

That said, the two built-in tile brushes are useful even without true tiling abilities. The two types of tile brushes are ImageBrush, which enables you to fill vector graphics with image content, and WebViewBrush, which enables you to fill vector graphics with HTML content.

ImageBrush

ImageBrush's exposed API is similar to Image. It has a property of type ImageSource, although it's called ImageSource rather than just Source, and it exposes the same ImageOpened and ImageFailed events, one of which gets raised after ImageSource gets set.

Figure 16.23 shows the content of a metal.jpg file that the following XAML applies to three different elements with an ImageBrush:

```
<StackPanel Background="{ThemeResource ApplicationPageBackgroundThemeBrush}">
  <!-- The trophy, with a metal fill -->
  <Path Margin="5,0,0,0" Data="M63.979,55.183C79.937,53.135,92.441,…">
    <Path.Fill>
      <ImageBrush ImageSource="Assets/metal.jpg"/>
    </Path.Fill>
  </Path>
  <!-- A TextBlock, with a metal foreground -->
  <TextBlock HorizontalAlignment="Center" FontWeight="Bold">
    <TextBlock.Foreground>
      <ImageBrush ImageSource="Assets/metal.jpg"/>
    </TextBlock.Foreground>
    CONGRATULATIONS!
  </TextBlock>
  <!-- A Button, with a metal background -->
  <Button>
    <Button.Background>
      <ImageBrush ImageSource="Assets/metal.jpg"/>
    </Button.Background>
    Play Again
  </Button>
</StackPanel>
```

The content of metal.jpg is applied as the Fill for the familiar trophy, the Foreground for a TextBlock, and the Background for a Button. Figure 16.24 shows the result. Note that the imaging system caches images for this type of repetitive use, so you don't incur multiple copies by referencing the file multiple times.

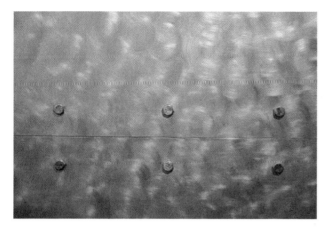

FIGURE 16.23   The metal.jpg file used in Figure 16.24

By default, the image content is stretched to fill the element's bounding box. In Figure 16.24, the horizontal image-stretching on the TextBlock and Button is obvious and perhaps undesirable. Fortunately, this behavior can be customized with three properties on the TileBrush base class. One is Stretch, which works the same way as on Image, Shape, Viewbox, and many other elements. However, TileBrush provides more customization when Stretch is set to anything other than its default value of Fill. In this case, its AlignmentX property can be set to Left, Right, or Center (the default), and its AlignmentY property can be set to Top, Bottom, or Center (the default) to control how the image gets positioned within the bounding box. Figure 16.25 demonstrates the use of a Stretch of None with two different alignments.

FIGURE 16.24   An ImageBrush in action, showing off its versatility

WebViewBrush

WebViewBrush requires a WebView instance in order to work. You can think of WebViewBrush as nothing more than an ImageBrush that is able to take a screenshot of the WebView control. The content in a WebViewBrush doesn't automatically update, nor is it interactive. (This is basically the same as retrieving a screenshot from WebView via its CapturePreviewToStreamAsync method and creating an ImageBrush from the image.)

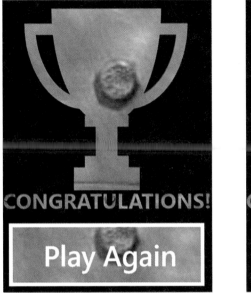

```
Stretch="None" AlignmentX="Center"        Stretch="None" AlignmentX="Left"
AlignmentY="Center"                       AlignmentY="Top"
```

FIGURE 16.25   Applying different stretching and alignment to an `ImageBrush`

To demonstrate, the following `Page` places a `WebView` side-by-side with a `WebViewBrush`-filled `Rectangle`:

```xml
<Page …>
  <Grid Background="{ThemeResource ApplicationPageBackgroundThemeBrush}">
    <Grid.ColumnDefinitions>
      <ColumnDefinition/>
      <ColumnDefinition/>
    </Grid.ColumnDefinitions>

    <!-- WebView on the left -->
    <WebView Name="webView" Margin="200,50" Source="http://xbox.com"/>

    <!-- WebViewBrush on the right -->
    <Rectangle Grid.Column="1">
      <Rectangle.Fill>
        <WebViewBrush x:Name="webViewBrush"/>
      </Rectangle.Fill>
    </Rectangle>

    <Button Grid.Column="1" Background="DarkGreen" Margin="300,15"
            VerticalAlignment="Top" Click="Button_Click">
      <Button.RenderTransform>
        <ScaleTransform ScaleX="2" ScaleY="2"/>
```

```
      </Button.RenderTransform>
      Refresh WebViewBrush
    </Button>
  </Grid>
</Page>
```

When the Button is clicked, the following handler associates the WebViewBrush with the WebView as follows:

```
void Button_Click(object sender, RoutedEventArgs e)
{
  webViewBrush.SetSource(webView);
}
```

By the way, the WebViewBrush instance is named with x:Name because it doesn't have a Name property of its own. Brushes are not FrameworkElements; they derive directly from DependencyObject.

The call to SetSource is needed to take a snapshot of the WebView contents and display it inside the WebViewBrush. Each time SetSource is called, it updates the WebViewBrush with the current content. WebViewBrush also exposes a SourceName property designed to be set in XAML to the name of the relevant WebView. WebViewBrush's parameterless Redraw method enables you to refresh the snapshot without setting the source every time. Calling Redraw at least once is necessary to see anything when SourceName is set in XAML, because that assignment is done too early for any content to be rendered in the WebViewBrush.

Figure 16.26 displays the result of the preceding XAML after the Web page has been loaded and the Button has been clicked.

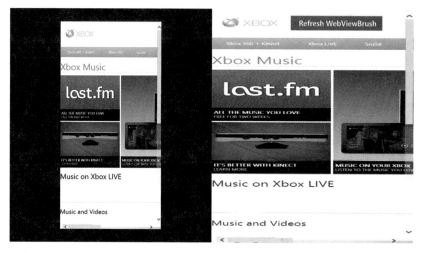

FIGURE 16.26   Applying a WebViewBrush to the Rectangle on the right with content from the WebView on the left

When I said "snapshot," I wasn't kidding! Even the scrollbars are included in the WebViewBrush's content if they are visible at the time SetSource is called! Notice also that the content matches what is rendered within the bounds of the WebView. If the size doesn't match the bounding box of the target, the content is stretched by default. (The WebView in Figure 16.26 is given a Margin solely to demonstrate this fact.) Just as with ImageBrush, you can control the stretching with the Stretch, AlignmentX, and AlignmentY properties from the TileBrush base class.

You could imagine using WebViewBrush to provide rich previews of webpages, exactly like the Internet Explorer app's links to its top app bar. Figure 16.27 shows another possible application: providing a reflection for an active WebView.

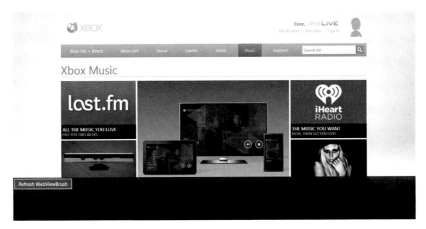

FIGURE 16.27   WebViewBrush can contribute to a simple reflection effect.

The following XAML creates this type of reflection:

```
<Page …>
  <Grid Background="Black">
    <Grid.RowDefinitions>
      <RowDefinition Height="500"/>
      <RowDefinition/>
    </Grid.RowDefinitions>

    <!-- WebView on the top -->
    <WebView Name="webView" Source="http://xbox.com"/>

    <!-- Flipped, compressed, and skewed WebViewBrush on the bottom -->
    <Rectangle Grid.Row="1">
      <Rectangle.Fill>
        <WebViewBrush x:Name="webViewBrush">
          <WebViewBrush.Transform>
            <TransformGroup>
              <!-- Flip and compress the brush before skewing it -->
```

```
              <ScaleTransform CenterY="65" ScaleX="1" ScaleY="-.2"/>
              <SkewTransform AngleX="50"/>
            </TransformGroup>
          </WebViewBrush.Transform>
        </WebViewBrush>
      </Rectangle.Fill>
    </Rectangle>

    <!-- A translucent Rectangle on top of the other one, for a fade effect -->
    <Rectangle Grid.Row="1">
      <Rectangle.Fill>
        <LinearGradientBrush StartPoint="0,0" EndPoint="0,1">
          <GradientStop Offset="-.5" Color="#0000"/>
          <GradientStop Offset=".2" Color="Black"/>
        </LinearGradientBrush>
      </Rectangle.Fill>
    </Rectangle>

    <Button Grid.Row="1" Background="DarkGreen" VerticalAlignment="Top"
            Click="Button_Click">
      Refresh WebViewBrush
    </Button>
  </Grid>
</Page>
```

This effect leverages the `Transform` property defined on all Brushes. The `WebViewBrush` reflection is flipped upside down by using a `ScaleTransform`. But rather than setting `ScaleY` to `-1`, the value of `-.2` is used to give the reflection a little bit of perspective. `TransformGroup` is used rather than `CompositeTransform` so the skewing is applied *after* the other transforms.

To make the effect more subtle, a second `Rectangle` on top of the `WebViewBrush`-filled `Rectangle` uses a `LinearGradientBrush` to fade from a "transparent black" (*not* `Transparent`, which would add a lot of gray due to the transition from white) to black.

To complete our look at `WebViewBrush`, Figure 16.28 fills the familiar trophy with one, using the following XAML:

```
<Page …>
  <Grid Background="{ThemeResource ApplicationPageBackgroundThemeBrush}">
    <Grid.ColumnDefinitions>
      <ColumnDefinition/>
      <ColumnDefinition/>
    </Grid.ColumnDefinitions>
    <WebView Name="webView" Source="http://xbox.com"/>
    <Viewbox Grid.Column="1">
      <!-- The trophy -->
      <Path Data="M63.979,55.183C79.937,53.135,92.441,…">
```

```
        <Path.Fill>
            <WebViewBrush x:Name="webViewBrush"/>
        </Path.Fill>
      </Path>
    </Viewbox>
    <Button Grid.Column="1" Background="DarkGreen" VerticalAlignment="Top"
            Click="Button_Click">
      Refresh WebViewBrush
    </Button>
  </Grid>
</Page>
```

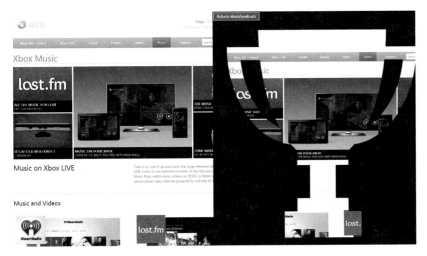

FIGURE 16.28   Filling the nonrectangular trophy with a `WebViewBrush`

Summary

The seamless support for vector graphics is just one of the many examples of the richness of XAML. As with other XAML features, a big part of the power of vector graphics comes from the tight integration with the rest of the framework. The drawing primitives used to create lines, shapes, and trophies are the same ones used to create `Buttons`, `Sliders`, and `ListViews`.

Even when you "draw" vector graphics on the screen, you're still working with a completely *retained-mode* graphics system rather than an *immediate-mode* graphics system. In an immediate-mode system (such as DirectX), you must maintain the state of all visuals. In other words, it's your responsibility to draw the correct pixels when a region of the screen is invalidated. This invalidation can be caused by user actions, such as resizing the app, or by application-specific actions that require updated visuals.

In a retained-mode system, you describe higher-level concepts such as "place a 10x10 blue square at (0,0)," and the system remembers and maintains the state for you. So, what you're really saying is, "place a 10x10 blue square at (0,0) *and keep it there.*" You don't need to worry about invalidation and repainting, the same way you don't worry about any of this when placing those `Buttons`, `Sliders`, and `ListViews` in your user interface.

Vector graphics have a lot of advantages over bitmap-based graphics, but with those advantages come inherent scalability issues. Not *visual* scalability issues, but rather *performance* scalability issues. Complex vector graphics can be expensive for the system to redraw. In scenarios where there might be a rapid succession of redrawing, as with a zooming animation, the cost of rendering can significantly impact the resulting user experience.

`UIElement` provides an interesting trick that helps in this regard, known as *cached composition*. To enable this, you set `UIElement`'s `CacheMode` property to an instance of `BitmapCache`. For example:

```
<Grid …>
  <Grid.CacheMode>
    <BitmapCache/>
  </Grid.CacheMode>
  …
</Grid>
```

This caches the visuals as a bitmap in video memory and enables hardware rendering. When the cached element (including any of its children) is updated, this feature automatically and intelligently updates only the dirty region. Updates to any parents do not invalidate the cache, nor do updates to the element's transforms or opacity! Furthermore, the system automatically leverages the live element when needed in order to preserve its interactivity.

Setting `CacheMode` is most appropriate for static content that wouldn't already be hardware accelerated, such as a complex `Path`. (Solid color rectangles, images, text, and video are already hardware accelerated.) This avoids creating a bottleneck in the rendering pipeline due to the CPU-bound work of repeated tessellation and rasterization on every frame. There is a tradeoff, however. The more you cache, the bigger the memory consumption will be on the GPU.

`BitmapCache` falls back to software rendering when hardware acceleration is not possible. However, when rendered in software, the maximum size allowed for the cached bitmap is 2048x2048 pixels.

For maximum performance, you should avoid *GPU overdraw*, which occurs when the GPU draws the same pixel multiple times for the same scene. You can detect this condition by setting the following property to `true`:

```
Application.Current.DebugSettings.IsOverdrawHeatMapEnabled = true;
```

This produces an "overdraw heat map" in which areas drawn more than once are colored in various shades of red. The darker the shade, the more times it has been drawn. If changing your code to avoid this problem is too difficult, you could consider using `CacheMode` so you only incur the cost of overdraw when the cache needs to be invalidated.

Chapter 17

ANIMATION

When most people think about animation, they think of a cartoon-like mechanism, where movement is simulated by displaying images in rapid succession. In XAML, animation has a more specific definition: varying the value of a dependency property over time. This could be related to motion, such as making an element gradually grow, shrink, rotate, skew, or move by animating properties on its RenderTransform or making it spin in 3D by animating properties on its Projection. Or it could be something like varying the value of a Color inside a Brush used as a Background or Fill.

XAML has always had strong support for integrating animations into your content. When exposed via design tools such as Blend, using the animation support can feel like you're using Adobe Flash. But because it's a core part of the platform, with APIs that are fairly simple, you can easily create a wide range of animations without the help of a tool. Indeed, this chapter demonstrates several different animation techniques with nothing more than short snippets of XAML and C#.

The animation support provided to Windows Store apps is even better than what is available to XAML-based desktop technologies. A number of standard animations are a core part of the modern Windows user experience. Some of these are automatically leveraged by your app because the built-in controls use them. For example, CommandBar and ToggleSwitch use animated transitions, and ListView and

`GridView` use animations liberally: when cross-slide selecting items, dragging and dropping items, and so on. In addition, The Windows *animation library* makes it easy to use the standard animations for your own purposes. This animation library is exposed to XAML via two features: *theme transitions* and *theme animations*.

This chapter begins by looking at the theme transitions and theme animations provided by Windows. It then looks at the XAML features for custom animations. Most of these custom animation features have been around since the inception of XAML, although there are some tweaks for Windows Store apps.

Theme Transitions

Using *theme transitions* is the best way to perform animations. They match the standard animations used by the built-in apps and Windows itself. This is a boon for developers who have no business designing animated effects. It's amazing how making a wrong choice when animating a user interface (for example, the effect is too slow, too garish, or doesn't quite match user expectations) can negatively impact an app's perceived quality.

Theme transitions bring more to the table than just consistency, however. They are guaranteed to perform well. They use animations that are all hardware-accelerated, which means they leverage the graphics processing unit (GPU) rather than solely using the central processing unit (CPU). This usually produces noticeably better results because the CPU load doesn't affect currently running transitions, and the transitions don't interfere with the "real work" being done on the CPU. Hardware-accelerated animations are also called *independent animations* because they run *independently* from the UI thread. Otherwise, they are called *dependent animations*. We'll see these terms popping up again later.

Finally, a third reason to use theme transitions is that they are incredibly easy to use. I would say they are the simplest, most magical features available to Windows Store apps. Each one is presented as an abstract concept (for example, "the transition for when an element appears on the screen," or "the transition for when an element is repositioned among other elements"). Often, all you need to do is apply one or more transitions to the desired elements. All the details, such as what events trigger them, what property values on the elements need to change, how their values change (timings, easings, and so on), are handled automatically.

Applying Theme Transitions to Elements

So how do you apply a theme transition to an element? Every `UIElement` has a `Transitions` property that can be set to a collection of `Transition` objects (the base class for all theme transitions). Using one of the theme transitions called `EntranceThemeTransition` as an example, the following XAML applies one to a `Button` on a `Page`:

```
<Page …>
  <Grid Background="{ThemeResource ApplicationPageBackgroundThemeBrush}">
    <Button Content="A Button with a Theme Transition">
```

```
        <Button.Transitions>
            <TransitionCollection>
                <EntranceThemeTransition/>
            </TransitionCollection>
        </Button.Transitions>
      </Button>
    </Grid>
</Page>
```

When this Page becomes visible for the first time (right after the splash screen dismisses for a single-Page app), the Button automatically animates to its position with a subtle fade-in and glide from a bit to the right. This is the standard Windows animation for an element "entering" the scene.

> ! **You must use an explicit TransitionCollection element when setting Transitions in XAML!**
>
> Unlike many other collection properties, Transitions is null by default. Therefore, you must wrap your list of theme transition elements in an explicit TransitionCollection element when setting it in XAML (even if it's a list of just one). If you forget to do this, you'll get a XamlParseException that explains, "Collection property '__implicit_items' is null."
>
> Similarly, in C#, you must instantiate a TransitionCollection and assign it as the property value, rather than just adding items to the default (null) property value. This adds a bit of verbosity, but the choice was made for performance reasons.

There are more places that TransitionCollections can be applied to elements:

→ Content controls have a **ContentTransitions** property that applies to its inner content. (So does ContentPresenter, an element described in the next chapter.)

→ Items controls have an **ItemContainerTransitions** property that apply to its visual children—the item containers that wrap each item, such as ComboBoxItem and ListViewItem. (So does ItemsPresenter, an element described in the next chapter.)

→ Panels have a **ChildrenTransitions** property that applies to their children.

→ ListViewBase (and therefore ListView and GridView) have a **HeaderTransitions** property that applies to the content in its Header and a **FooterTransitions** property that applies to the content in its Footer. ItemsPresenter defines these properties as well.

→ Border and Popup, which aren't content controls, have a **ChildTransitions** property that applies to the content in their Child property.

With the exception of three theme transitions that add special features when applied in bulk (called out in their upcoming sections), applying a theme transition via

ItemContainerTransitions or ChildrenTransitions is a shortcut for applying it on every child element. Note that all these properties of type TransitionCollection are null by default, so the explicit collection requirement applies to them all.

The Eight Theme Transitions

The last section discussed EntranceThemeTransition, but Windows contains eight theme transitions that can be applied to any of the Transitions or XXXTransitions properties. Let's look at them all.

EntranceThemeTransition

Timing	When an element appears for the first time
Visual Result	Glides slightly from the right with a quick fade in
Intended For	Pages or other large containers; has special staggering feature for ItemContainerTransitions and ChildrenTransitions
Properties	FromHorizontalOffset (default = 40)
	FromVerticalOffset (default = 0)
	IsStaggeringEnabled (default = true)

Instead of placing EntranceThemeTransition on a Button, the following XAML applies it to all Buttons in a StackPanel using StackPanel's ChildrenTransitions property:

```
<Page …>
  <Grid Background="{ThemeResource ApplicationPageBackgroundThemeBrush}">
    <StackPanel>
      <StackPanel.ChildrenTransitions>
        <TransitionCollection>
          <EntranceThemeTransition/>
        </TransitionCollection>
      </StackPanel.ChildrenTransitions>
      <Button Background="Red" Width="100" Height="40"/>
      <Button Background="Orange" Width="100" Height="40"/>
      <Button Background="Yellow" Width="100" Height="40"/>
      <Button Background="Green" Width="100" Height="40"/>
      <Button Background="Blue" Width="100" Height="40"/>
      <Button Background="Purple" Width="100" Height="40"/>
    </StackPanel>
  </Grid>
</Page>
```

As Figure 17.1 demonstrates, EntranceThemeTransition includes special behavior when it is applied to children in a Panel or item containers in an items control. The animation is staggered, so elements earlier in the collection animate sooner than elements items later in the collection. The order is done based on the index in the collection, which, in the case of StackPanel, matches the order on the screen.

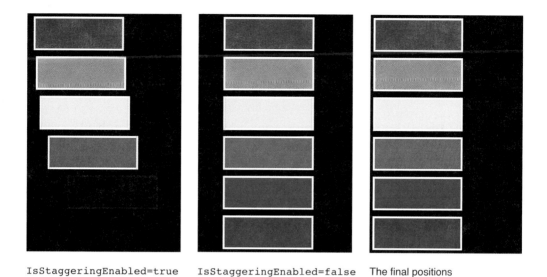

IsStaggeringEnabled=true   IsStaggeringEnabled=false   The final positions

FIGURE 17.1   The effect of `IsStaggeringEnabled` when `EntranceThemeTransition` is applied to a `ChildrenTransitions` property

You can disable this staggering feature by setting `EntranceThemeTransition`'s `IsStaggeringEnabled` property to `false`. In that case, the effect is no different than applying a default `EntranceThemeTransition` to the `StackPanel` using the `Transitions` property instead of `ChildrenTransitions`.

With the `FromHorizontalOffset` and `FromVerticalOffset` properties, you can make the animation less subtle by telling elements to travel a farther distance to get to their final locations. You can also make them come from different directions. Positive offsets make them travel from the right and/or bottom, and negative offsets make them travel from the left and/or top.

Changing an element's `Visibility` to `Collapsed` and then `Visible` again doesn't trigger the animation again; the element has already made its "entrance" onto the scene. However, if you *remove* an element from the tree (the `StackPanel`'s `Children` collection in this example) and then add it back, the animation *will* kick in.

It's worth pointing out that the timing of an `EntranceThemeTransition` is smarter than you might think. All `FrameworkElements` have a `Loaded` event that is raised when it has been added to the current element tree and is about to be rendered. However, triggering this transition based on this event isn't good enough for an app's initial UI, which might still be obscured by the splash screen. Therefore, the built-in triggering of `EntranceThemeTransition` takes the dismissal of the splash screen into account. It also waits to trigger it on elements that are initially `Collapsed`. Once such elements become visible (the *first* time), the animation begins.

PopupThemeTransition

Timing	When an element appears for the first time, and also when it is removed
Visual Result	When it appears: glides from the bottom with a quick fade in
	When it is removed: quickly fades out
Intended For	Popups (context menus and other small flyouts) that should act like `MenuFlyout`
Properties	`FromHorizontalOffset` (default = 0)
	`FromVerticalOffset` (default = 40)

For an element's first appearance, `PopupThemeTransition` is just like an `EntranceThemeTransition` that instead animates vertically by default and has no staggering feature. However, it also adds a fade-out animation for when the element is removed from the visual tree. The important difference is what this theme transition is *intended for*, which is the entrance of temporary overlays such as `Popups`. (If you use `MenuFlyout`, it already uses this transition automatically.)

This means that `Popups` must be removed from the visual tree after being dismissed and then added back before being shown again so they get animated every time. That's because `PopupThemeTransition` is triggered only upon the element's entrance and exit from the scene. Toggling its `Visibility` doesn't count. For this theme transition to work on a `Popup`, it must be applied to `Popup`'s `ChildTransitions` property.

Although `ToolTip` is rendered with a `Popup`, applying `PopupThemeTransition` to a `ToolTip` is inconsistent with standard Windows behavior. You should leave `ToolTips` with their default fade-in and fade-out effect.

ContentThemeTransition

Timing	When an element appears for the first time, and also when it is removed
Visual Result	When it appears: glides slightly from the right with a quick fade in
	When it is removed: quickly fades out
Intended For	Large controls with changing content, such as a `Frame`, and applied via `ContentTransitions` or `ChildTransitions`
Properties	`HorizontalOffset` (default = 40)
	`VerticalOffset` (default = 0)

This theme transition sounds like `PopupThemeTransition`, except the direction of the entrance-gliding matches `EntranceThemeTransition`. It basically is, which works out nicely when swapping an element's content. For example, when you apply `ContentThemeTransition` to a content control via `ContentTransitions`, the initial content will glide in like an `EntranceThemeTransition`. However, when you change the control's content, the old element fades out while the new one glides in to replace it.

Although you could produce the same visual effect with PopupThemeTransition (if you reverse the values of PopupThemeTransition to match ContentThemeTransition), you should not get hung up on the visual result. In theory, a future version of Windows could change the animation details for each theme transition. As long as you use them in a way consistent with their intent, you should be fine.

EdgeUIThemeTransition

Timing	When an element appears for the first time, and also when it is removed
Visual Result	When it appears: slides in from above
	When it is removed: slides out in the reverse direction
Intended For	An element docked to the edge of the app that acts like CommandBar and AppBar
Properties	Edge (default = Top)

Despite the name, EdgeUIThemeTransition is not automatically triggered by performing an edge gesture. It gets triggered by the typical element entrance and removal conditions that are *intended* to be performed in response to an edge gesture. EdgeUIThemeTransition provides a visual result that matches the sliding-in and sliding-out done by CommandBar and AppBar. And just like their animations, there's no fading in and out.

The Edge property represents the edge of the screen on which the gesture is supposed to happen, which determines the direction of the animation. If you choose Right, for example, the element slides from right-to-left upon entrance, and left to right upon removal.

Of course, because a properly attached CommandBar or AppBar already does the correct animations, you normally have no need to use this theme transition.

PaneThemeTransition

Timing	When an element appears for the first time, and also when it is removed
Visual Result	When it appears: slides in from the right
	When it is removed: slides out in the reverse direction
Intended For	A flyout pane that acts like SettingsFlyout
Properties	Edge (default = Right)

PaneThemeTransition is similar to EdgeUIThemeTransition but with a different default value for its Edge property and a slightly different animation speed. Again, the important difference is the intent. PaneThemeTransition is meant for large panes docked to a window edge such as SettingsFlyout (although SettingsFlyout already has these transitions). Small flyouts—ones that act like MenuFlyout—should use PopupThemeTransition instead, which fades out on exit.

Besides speed, there is one subtle visual difference between PaneThemeTransition and EdgeUIThemeTransition. With PaneThemeTransition, the animated content is clipped by the bounds of the element's resting spot. With EdgeUIThemeTransition, no clipping is done. This difference is demonstrated in Figure 17.2 with the following XAML:

```
<Page …>
  <Grid Background="{ThemeResource ApplicationPageBackgroundThemeBrush}">
    <StackPanel>
      <Button Background="Red" Width="100" Height="40">
        <Button.Transitions>
          <TransitionCollection>
            <PaneThemeTransition/>
          </TransitionCollection>
        </Button.Transitions>
      </Button>
      <Button Background="Orange" Width="100" Height="40"/>
    </StackPanel>
  </Grid>
</Page>
```

<PaneThemeTransition/>

<EdgeUIThemeTransition Edge="Right"/>

FIGURE 17.2   PaneThemeTransition clips the red Button sliding in from the right, unlike EdgeUIThemeTransition.

This difference, of course, doesn't matter for an element docked to the appropriate edge.

AddDeleteThemeTransition

Timing	When an element appears for the first time, when it is removed, and when it is repositioned by a layout change
Visual Result	When it appears: fades in and grows after a short delay
	When it is removed: fades out and shrinks after a short delay
	When it is repositioned: glides to the new position
Intended For	A collection of elements
Properties	None

AddDeleteThemeTransition's claim to fame is not what it does to the element entering or exiting, but what it does to its sibling elements when applied to the parent via

`ItemContainerTransitions` or `ChildrenTransitions`. The sibling elements glide to their new positions! This is pictured in Figure 17.3 for the following XAML:

```
<Page …>
  <Grid Background="{ThemeResource ApplicationPageBackgroundThemeBrush}">
    <StackPanel Name="stackPanel">
      <StackPanel.ChildrenTransitions>
        <TransitionCollection>
          <AddDeleteThemeTransition/>
        </TransitionCollection>
      </StackPanel.ChildrenTransitions>
      <Button Background="Red" Width="100" Height="40"/>
      <Button Background="Orange" Width="100" Height="40"/>
      <!-- The Button that will be removed: -->
      <Button Name="yellowButton" Background="Yellow" Width="100" Height="40"/>
      <Button Background="Green" Width="100" Height="40"/>
      <Button Background="Blue" Width="100" Height="40"/>
      <Button Background="Purple" Width="100" Height="40"/>
    </StackPanel>
  </Grid>
</Page>
```

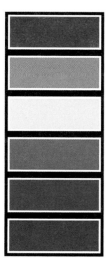

Initial positions

Shortly after the third
Button is removed

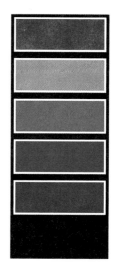

The final positions

FIGURE 17.3   The effect of `AddDeleteThemeTransition` when one of the elements in the `StackPanel` is removed

This demonstrates the condition of the yellow `Button` being removed with code such as the following:

```
this.stackPanel.Children.Remove(this.yellowButton);
```

Although the yellow Button is still visible in the middle stage of Figure 17.3, it has been removed from the collection already. There's a delay applied to the shrink-and-fade-out animation that leaves time for any sibling gliding to occur first.

There's no magic here when it comes to giving those bottom three Buttons new positions. The position change is a normal part of StackPanel's layout; if you remove an element, the remaining ones are restacked such that no "hole" is left behind. All that AddDeleteThemeTransition is doing is animating these elements to their new positions that they would instantly snap to otherwise. If these Buttons were explicitly placed in a Canvas instead, no siblings would ever move.

This fact leads to some interesting behavior. As with the other transitions, if the yellow Button's Visibility is set to Collapsed instead of being removed from the StackPanel's Children collection, it does not animate out. However, the *siblings* in the Children collection still animate to their new positions! In fact, *any* layout changes cause them to animate, even if it has nothing to do with adding/removing or showing/hiding an element. For example, if the yellow Button's Height is changed, the three Buttons below it animate to their new positions forced by that change.

If you apply AddDeleteThemeTransition directly to an arbitrary element (via its Transitions property), it will do the typical animations whenever it enters and exits the scene, and it will also animate in response to any layout changes that push it around. For example, you could apply it to the orange Button in Figure 17.3 instead of the StackPanel, and it would be the only Button that glides in response to the repositioning done when adding/removing the yellow Button.

RepositionThemeTransition

Timing	When an element is repositioned by a layout change
Visual Result	Glides to the new position
Intended For	Any element that can be moved by a layout change; has special staggering feature for ItemContainerTransitions and ChildrenTransitions
Properties	None

RepositionThemeTransition enables the generic "animate any layout changes" behavior from AddDeleteThemeTransition, but without the animations on entrance and exit, which can be undesirable due to the delayed fade-in when elements first enter. It also staggers the animations when applied to ItemContainerTransitions and ChildrenTransitions. Unlike with EntranceThemeTransition, this staggering cannot be turned off.

If you change the AddDeleteThemeTransition from Figure 17.3 to RepositionThemeTransition, the result would look *almost* the same. This time, the yellow Button would disappear instantly rather than waiting to animate out after the gliding occurs. Also, the three Buttons below it would move up in a staggered fashion, although it is barely noticeable with just three elements moving.

For that yellow `Button` in the `StackPanel` from Figure 17.3, let's add some code-behind that toggles its position in the `Children` collection every time the `Page` is tapped:

```
protected override void OnTapped(TappedRoutedEventArgs e)
{
  if (this.stackPanel.Children[0] == this.yellowButton)
  {
    // Move from index 0 to 2
    this.stackPanel.Children.Remove(this.yellowButton);
    this.stackPanel.Children.Insert(2, this.yellowButton);
  }
  else
  {
    // Move from index 2 to 0
    this.stackPanel.Children.Remove(this.yellowButton);
    this.stackPanel.Children.Insert(0, this.yellowButton);
  }
}
```

This two-step process counts as a "move" because the pair of `Remove` and `Insert` calls are made synchronously and therefore don't give the `Button` a chance to disappear before the `Insert` happens.

Figure 17.4 shows the result of invoking this code with the `AddDeleteThemeTransition` element applied. Note that this effect appears exactly the same regardless of whether `AddDeleteThemeTransition` or `ReorderThemeTransition` is applied to `StackPanel.ChildrenTransitions`, because no element visibly enters or exits.

Such animations occur only when an element moves in response to layout changes (the condition that causes `LayoutUpdated` to be raised) from code

FIGURE 17.4   The yellow `Button` is animating down to its new position while the red and orange `Button`s animate up to their new positions.

that is internal to a parent `Panel`. For example, increasing an element's `Margin` doesn't animate it, although depending on the parent `Panel` it could cause other elements to animate if the theme transition is applied to them.

The effect of `RepositionThemeTransition` (and `AddDeleteThemeTransition`) applies to external factors that trigger layout changes as well, such as the user resizing the window.

Figure 17.5 demonstrates this if we replace the previously used StackPanel with a VariableSizedWrapGrid and paste in many more copies of the six colorful Buttons.

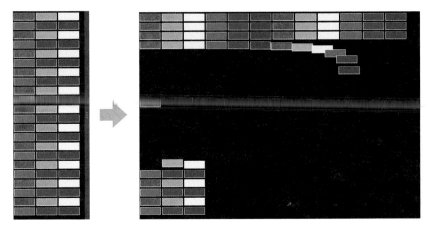

Minimum window size   Resized to be much wider

FIGURE 17.5   With RepositionThemeTransition applied to a VariableSizedWrapGrid via ChildrenTransitions, elements automatically animate to their new positions when wrapping occurs.

ReorderThemeTransition

Timing	When an element appears for the first time, when it is removed, when it is repositioned by a layout change, and when dragging-and-dropping
Visual Result	When it appears: fades in and grows
	When it is removed: fades out and shrinks
	When it is repositioned: glides to the new position
	When it is dragged: becomes translucent and sibling elements move out of the way
Intended For	A collection of elements that support drag-and-drop reordering (therefore, elements in a ListView or GridView); designed for ItemContainerTransitions
Properties	None

ReorderThemeTransition does everything that AddDeleteThemeTransition does, but it adds sophisticated effects for drag-and-drop. This is what's used by ListView and GridView to enable the automatic drag-and-drop item reordering effect already seen in Chapter 11, "Items Controls." If you apply it to the content in Figure 17.5, the result would look the same as AddDeleteThemeTransition because there's no drag-and-drop support in this case. The `Buttons` would all grow and fade in initially, and then layout changes would cause an unstaggered variation of the same repositioning animation.

> The PC Settings app exposes a setting that enables users to turn off animations. This is the "Play animations in Windows" setting under Ease of Access, Other options. Theme transitions automatically respect this setting and do nothing in this case, so your app respects the user's wishes.
>
> If you use the animation features covered by the rest of this chapter, even theme animations, it is your responsibility to respect this setting. You can check for this by creating an instance of `Windows.UI.ViewManagement.UISettings` then checking its `AnimationsEnabled` Boolean property. `UISettings` exposes other user settings such as `CaretBlinkRate`, `CursorSize`, `DoubleClickTime`, `HandPreference`, and more.

Theme Animations

Unlike theme transitions, which represent specific animations for specific actions, theme animations are specific animations for *custom* actions. Although their visual details are predetermined, you get to decide when to trigger them. There are 14 of them, but before describing them, we need to look at the *storyboard* mechanism that enables them to run.

Using a `Storyboard`

One of the theme animations is called `FadeOutThemeAnimation`, and it knows how to make any element fade out. Let's see how to apply that to a simple `Button` on a `Page`. This must be done with an object called a `Storyboard`. `Storyboards` can contain one or more animations and associate them with specific elements. Here's a `Page` with the `Button` we want to animate and the `Storyboard` that provides context to the `FadeOutThemeAnimation`:

```
<Page …>
  <Page.Resources>
    <Storyboard x:Name="storyboard" TargetName="b">
      <FadeOutThemeAnimation/>
    </Storyboard>
  </Page.Resources>
  <Canvas Background="{ThemeResource ApplicationPageBackgroundThemeBrush}">
    <Button Name="b">Animating Button</Button>
  </Canvas>
</Page>
```

Unlike with theme transitions, `UIElements` have no `Storyboards` property that can be used to attach `Storyboards`. And `Storyboard` is not a `UIElement`, so it can't be placed within the `Page` like other elements. Instead, this `Page` stores it in its `Resources` collection. The `Resources` property, defined on all `FrameworkElements`, is a dictionary that can contain arbitrary objects given either an x:Name or x:Key, as seen in Chapter 2, "Mastering XAML." Such objects are typically meant to be shared by multiple child elements, although that's not the case here. The next chapter demonstrates this kind of sharing.

With Storyboard's TargetName property assigned appropriately, we're ready to animate. All we need to do is call the Storyboard's Begin method when we want it to start:

```
void StartInitialAnimations()
{
  // start the animation
  this.storyboard.Begin();
}
```

Storyboard defines a number of methods that enable you to treat an animation like a video clip—Begin, Pause, Resume, Seek, and Stop—although normally Begin is all that gets called.

Let's say we want to call StartInitialAnimations when the Page appears, like the timing of many theme transitions. As mentioned previously, handling the Button or Page's Loaded event isn't good enough. If we start an animation too early, we run the risk of it not getting seen in its entirety if it takes the splash screen awhile to be dismissed. Therefore, the following complete code-behind for the Page leverages the host Window's Activated event for triggering the animation. It must check to trigger it only on the *first* Activated event raised, however, because it gets raised every time the Window gets or loses focus:

```
using Windows.UI.Core;
using Windows.UI.Xaml;
using Windows.UI.Xaml.Controls;

namespace Animation
{
  public sealed partial class MainPage : Page
  {
    bool firstActivation = true;

    public MainPage()
    {
      InitializeComponent();
      Window.Current.Activated += Window_Activated;
    }

    void Window_Activated(object sender, WindowActivatedEventArgs e)
    {
      // Code that only runs for the first activation:
      if (this.firstActivation)
      {
```

```
        StartInitialAnimations();
        this.firstActivation = false;
      }
    }

    void StartInitialAnimations()
    {
      // Start the animation
      this.storyboard.Begin();
    }
  }
}
```

Running this code results in the Button quickly and smoothly fading out as soon as the splash screen is dismissed. Of course, this animation-triggering logic still doesn't match the general-purpose logic within theme transitions (which waits if the element is initially Collapsed), but it's good enough for this simple example.

How can I trigger an animation without writing any C# code?

The best way to do this is to place a Storyboard inside a VisualState. VisualStates are a styling feature explained in the next chapter. There is one other way, however. It's limited and just there for compatibility with WPF and Silverlight, but it's worth knowing about nonetheless.

Although elements have no Storyboards property, they do have a property called Triggers (defined on FrameworkElement), which is sort of the same thing. It enables you to attach one or more Storyboards to an element, although they have to be wrapped in two intermediate elements. The following XAML applies the same FadeOutThemeAnimation to the same Button used previously but with no code-behind needed:

```
<Button Name="b">Animating Button
  <Button.Triggers>
    <EventTrigger RoutedEvent="FrameworkElement.Loaded">
      <EventTrigger.Actions>
        <BeginStoryboard>
          <Storyboard TargetName="b">
            <FadeOutThemeAnimation/>
          </Storyboard>
        </BeginStoryboard>
      </EventTrigger.Actions>
    </EventTrigger>
  </Button.Triggers>
</Button>
```

In this case, the Storyboard doesn't need a name because there's no code-behind referencing it, although it does still need TargetName to be set despite already being "attached" to the Button.

The BeginStoryboard element takes the place of the call to Storyboard's Begin method; it's the declarative equivalent. The EventTrigger takes the place of attaching an event handler in C#; it handles *when* to trigger the animation. But this is the part that makes it so limited. For Windows Store apps, the RoutedEvent property, which specifies the triggering event, can be set only to FrameworkElement.Loaded. (Recall from Chapter 5, "Interactivity," that the Loaded event isn't even a routed event, but that doesn't prevent it from working here!)

Of course, as we've already discussed, triggering animations based on the Loaded event isn't a good idea, at least for elements that get loaded during initialization of the first page (under the splash screen). For elements that are added dynamically, however, or for elements whose animation repeats indefinitely, this mechanism could potentially come in handy.

The 14 Theme Animations

The XAML UI Framework includes 14 theme animations. We're not going to examine each of these with the same depth as the theme transitions, but here they are:

→ **FadeOutThemeAnimation**—Animate an element's Opacity to 0.

→ **FadeInThemeAnimation**—Animate an element's Opacity back to 1. The default styles of many controls use the pair of FadeOutThemeAnimation and FadeInThemeAnimation, such as ScrollBar. This has no effect if FadeOutThemeAnimation or a similar custom animation didn't previously act upon the element.

→ **PopInThemeAnimation**—Makes the element glide in slightly from the right. (Oddly, this matches the motion of EntranceThemeTransition rather than PopupThemeTransition.) You can customize the motion with its FromHorizontalOffset and FromVerticalOffset properties, with default values of 40 and 0, respectively.

→ **PopOutThemeAnimation**—Animate an element's Opacity to 0, like when an element with PopupThemeTransition is removed.

→ **PointerDownThemeAnimation**—Creates a "pressed-in" effect by making an element shrink slightly. The default styles of ListViewItem and GridViewItem use this when they are pressed.

→ **PointerUpThemeAnimation**—Undoes the PointerDownThemeAnimation by restoring the element to its previous scale. This has no effect if PointerDownThemeAnimation or a similar custom animation didn't previously act upon the element.

→ **RepositionThemeAnimation**—This does nothing by default, but if you set its FromHorizontalOffset and FromVerticalOffset properties to values other than their default of 0, this makes the element glide into place, as with RepositionThemeAnimation. The default style of ToggleSwitch uses this to animate its "knob" between the on and off position.

→ **SwipeHintThemeAnimation**—This is the same animation that happens when the user presses and holds an item in a ListView or GridView, and it's meant to be used as a hint to the user that the cross slide selection gesture is now possible. This animation is used by the default styles of ListViewItem and GridViewItem for exactly that. This pushes the element slightly downward and then makes it quickly return to its original position. You can customize the direction and distance of the push by setting its ToHorizontalOffset and ToVerticalOffset properties to values other than their defaults of 0 and 10, respectively.

→ **SwipeBackThemeAnimation**—This is just like SwipeHintThemeAnimation and exposes the same two properties with the same default values. The only visual difference is that the initial push happens quickly and the return to its original position happens more slowly. It's the animation that happens when you deselect an item in a ListView or GridView with a cross slide gesture.

→ **DragItemThemeAnimation**—Makes the element quickly grow to its current size and then keeps it in a translucent state, just like when dragging an item in a ListView or GridView. Indeed, the default styles of ListViewItem and GridViewItem use this when dragging begins. This animation is meant to be stopped when you are done with it, rather than reversed with a different animation.

→ **DragOverThemeAnimation**—This is the animation applied to the siblings of the element being dragged for a reordering action. It makes them move out of the way. By default, this does nothing, but you can set its ToOffset property to a value other than its default of 0, and Direction property to Top (the default), Left, Bottom, or Right. For example, if Direction is Top and ToOffset is 100, the element gets pushed 100 pixels upward. The default styles for ListViewItem and GridViewItem use this, as we saw in Chapter 11.

→ **DropTargetItemThemeAnimation**—This also applies to the siblings of the element being dragged for reordering, and it is also used by the default styles of ListViewItem and GridViewItem. It makes the element quickly shrink. This animation is meant to be stopped when you are done with it, rather than reversed with a different animation.

→ **SplitOpenThemeAnimation** and **SplitCloseThemeAnimation**—These are highly specialized animations used by ComboBox when opening and closing its dropdown. The animated element gradually gets revealed from its middle with a motion that moves outward in both vertical directions. The animation requires several properties to be set and is unlikely to be directly useful unless you're writing your own ComboBox control.

(?) Why can't I get FadeInThemeAnimation to work?

Just like with PointerUpThemeAnimation and PointerDownThemeAnimation, FadeInThemeAnimation produces a visual change only if it's applied to an element that has previously been animated with FadeOutThemeAnimation or an equivalent custom animation.

These two animations change an element's opacity from 100% (for fading in) or 0% (for fading out). In the case of FadeInThemeAnimation, an element that is already opaque remains opaque.

Because these animations appear to work by altering an element's Opacity property, you might think that you could successfully apply FadeInThemeAnimation to an element whose Opacity is initially set to 0. However, this isn't the case. FadeInThemeAnimation and FadeOutThemeAnimation unfortunately operate on an element's internal member in order to change its opacity, so it doesn't cooperate with other mechanisms that touch the public Opacity property.

Tweaking Theme Animations

In addition to the already described properties that some of the theme animations expose, all animations expose a number of properties from their base class called Timeline. They also expose a simple Completed event. Every animation, even custom ones, must derive from Timeline. (The only reason this class isn't given the name Animation is that Storyboard also derives from it.)

These properties enable a variety of interesting changes, such as delaying the animation, changing its speed, making it the animation automatically play backwards once it completes, and so on. For example, the following FadeOutThemeAnimation makes an element repetitively fade out and then back in indefinitely:

```
<FadeOutThemeAnimation AutoReverse="True" RepeatBehavior="Forever"/>
```

It's the XAML equivalent of the old HTML blink tag, and just as obnoxious!

Because the point of using theme animations is to match the visual behavior of Windows and other apps, these Timeline properties are best suited for custom animations. Therefore, we'll look at them more closely later in this chapter.

> **① Don't set the Duration property of theme animations!**
>
> One of the properties inherited by all animations is Duration, but setting it on a theme animation doesn't work properly. If you want to speed up or slow down a theme animation, you can set its SpeedRatio property instead to a value other than its default of 1.

Custom Animations

In addition to the 14 theme animations, the XAML UI Framework contains seven animation classes that enable you to describe your own custom animations and apply them the same way that the theme animations are applied.

The seven custom animation classes cover four possible data types that can be animated: double, Point, Color, and object. If you want to vary the value of a double property over time (such as Width, Height, Opacity, Canvas.Left, and so on), you can use an instance of DoubleAnimation. If you instead want to vary the value of a Point property over time (such as a LinearGradientBrush's StartPoint or EndPoint property), you can use an instance of PointAnimation. DoubleAnimation is by far the most commonly used custom animation class due to large the number of useful double properties on many elements.

Using a double dependency property as an example, let's see how to animate a Button's Opacity from 0 to 1 with a DoubleAnimation to make it smoothly fade in (something that FadeInThemeAnimation is unable to accomplish without a corresponding FadeOutThemeAnimation). The following is an update to the same Page we've been using for previous examples:

```
<Page …>
  <Page.Resources>
    <Storyboard x:Name="storyboard" TargetName="b" TargetProperty="Opacity">
      <DoubleAnimation From="0" To="1"/>
    </Storyboard>
  </Page.Resources>
  <Canvas Background="{ThemeResource ApplicationPageBackgroundThemeBrush}">
    <Button Name="b" Opacity="0">Animating Button</Button>
  </Canvas>
</Page>
```

With From and To, the DoubleAnimation specifies the initial and end values for a double property—*any* double property. Unlike theme animations, custom animations are not preconfigured to work on a specific property. Therefore, the Storyboard must associate it with not only the specific Button, but its Opacity property that we want to animate.

With the same code-behind used previously that calls the Storyboard's Begin method the first time the Window's Activated event is raised, this animation successfully fades the Button in over the course of one second. The explicit Opacity="0" marked on the Button isn't needed to make the animation work, but it *is* needed to prevent a flash of it being visible immediately before the animation begins.

It's important to note that classes such as DoubleAnimation take care of smoothly changing the double value over time via *linear interpolation*. In other words, for this one-second animation, the value of Opacity is .05 when .1 seconds have elapsed (5% progress in both the value and time elapsed), .5 when .5 seconds have elapsed (50% progress in both the value and time elapsed), and so on. This is different than the interpolation used by the theme transitions and theme animations, but there are ways for custom animations to get their more "springy" behavior as well, described later.

> **! Animation classes can vary the value of a *dependency* property only!**
>
> This is one reason why the proliferation of dependency properties on elements in the XAML UI Framework is so handy.

Figuring out how to apply an animation to get the desired results can take a little practice. For example, you can't make an element fade in or out by animating its Visibility property. That's because there's no middle ground between Visible and Hidden. For another example, animating the Width of a Grid's column is not straightforward because

ColumnDefinition.Width is defined as a GridLength structure, which has no corresponding animation class built in. Instead, you could animate ColumnDefinition's MinWidth and/or MaxWidth properties, both of type double, or you could set ColumnDefinition's Width to Auto and then insert an element in that column whose Width you animate.

Independent versus Dependent Animations

Speaking of animating an element's Width, it would be natural to try to repurpose the previous DoubleAnimation to animate the Button's Width instead of its Opacity. After all, Width is a dependency property, and it's of type double. So this should work, right? Well, yes, but not by default.

Animations that operate on an element's Opacity, RenderTransform, or Projection can run on the GPU (in other words, are hardware accelerated) because the underlying visual surface being manipulated doesn't need to change. So can animations on the Canvas.Left and Canvas.Top attached properties, which is effectively the same as animating a TranslateTransform. These are examples of independent animations.

Other animations, such as directly changing an element's Width and Height, are dependent animations. For the Button example, every time its Width changes, a sequence of events occurs (for example, layout updates and changes to its inner contents that can be arbitrarily complex) that ultimately result in its visual surface needing to be re-rendered.

In previous XAML technologies, it was easy to introduce poor-performing animations if you weren't careful (and didn't know the rules about which animations are hardware accelerated). In Windows Store apps, there's one small safeguard meant to help prevent this situation: By default, *dependent animations (any animations that can't be hardware-accelerated) don't run at all*!

To make an animation work despite its lack of hardware acceleration, you must set its EnableDependentAnimation property to true. Therefore, the following update to the preceding Page successfully animates the Width of the now-always-opaque Button, performance be damned:

```
<Page …>
  <Page.Resources>
    <Storyboard x:Name="storyboard" TargetName="b" TargetProperty="Width">
      <DoubleAnimation From="0" To="500" EnableDependentAnimation="True"/>
    </Storyboard>
  </Page.Resources>
  <Canvas Background="{ThemeResource ApplicationPageBackgroundThemeBrush}">
    <Button Name="b" Width="0">Animating Button</Button>
  </Canvas>
</Page>
```

"But Adam," you might say, "I work with some careless developers who could easily let such animations creep into our codebase with EnableDependentAnimation set to true!" That is true, but at least this property gives you, the knowledgeable developer who is reading this book, a red flag to search for if your app has performance issues. Or, you can one-up your coworkers and set the static `Timeline.AllowDependentAnimations` property to `false` somewhere in your C# code. (Note the slightly different property name.) Once set, this disables *all* dependent animations in your app, regardless of their settings! (You cannot set it to `true` to achieve the reverse.) "Take that, coworkers," you might now exclaim. "They'll be left scratching their heads when their dependent animations don't work regardless of their `EnableDependentAnimation` values!"

All joking aside, dependent animations aren't *that* big of a deal if used judiciously. Sometimes you can't achieve the effect you want with an independent animation, so you might be able to enable dependent animations with a clear conscience.

> The best way to animate the size and location of an element is to attach a `ScaleTransform` and/or `TranslateTransform` and animate its properties instead. Such animations are independent animations, unlike animating `Width` and `Height`. Animating `ScaleTransform`'s `ScaleX` and `ScaleY` is generally more useful than animating `Width` and `Height` anyway because it enables you to keep the transform centered, and also change the size by a percentage rather than a fixed number of units. Animating `TranslateTransform` is also better than animating something like `Canvas.Left` and `Canvas.Top` because it works regardless of what `Panel` contains the element.

> With independent animations, you should still worry about the performance impact of GPU overdraw (drawing the same pixel multiple times). As mentioned in the preceding chapter, you can check for this by setting `DebugSettings.IsOverdrawHeatMapEnabled` to `true`.

Controlling Duration

Both `DoubleAnimations` used thus far have the default duration of one second, but you can change this by setting its `Duration` property inherited from `Timeline`:

```
<DoubleAnimation From="0" To="1" Duration="0:0:5"/>
```

This changes the duration to five seconds. The syntax for specifying the length of time in XAML is the same as what `TimeSpan.Parse` accepts: *days.hours:minutes:seconds. fraction*.

> **Be careful when specifying a `TimeSpan` or `Duration` as a string!**
>
> `TimeSpan.Parse`, which is also used automatically by a type converter for `TimeSpan` and `Duration` for the benefit of XAML, accepts shortcuts in its syntax so you don't need to specify every piece of *days.hours:minutes:seconds.fraction*. However, the behavior is not what you might expect. The string `"2"` means 2 *days*, not 2 seconds! Given that most animations are no more than a few seconds long, the typical syntax used is *hours:minutes:seconds* or *hours:minutes:seconds.fraction*. So, 2 seconds can be expressed as `"0:0:2"`, and half a second can be expressed as `"0:0:0.5"` or `"0:0:.5"`.

> ● ● ●
> ### The Difference Between Duration and TimeSpan
>
> The Duration property is of type Duration rather than TimeSpan (although there is an implicit conversion). The reason for this is that Duration has two special values that can't be expressed by TimeSpan: Duration.Automatic and Duration.Forever (or just "Automatic" and "Forever" in XAML).
>
> Automatic is the default value for every animation class's Duration property, which is equivalent to a one-second TimeSpan. Forever is nonsensical for a simple animation such as DoubleAnimation because such a Duration would make it stay at its initial value indefinitely. The class can't interpolate values between now and the end of time!

Flexibility with From and To

The following Page adds a ScaleTransform to the Button and applies two Storyboards to animate it: one triggered by PointerEntered, and one triggered by the PointerExited family of events:

```
<Page …>
  <Page.Resources>
    <!-- Two Storyboards, one for growing and one for shrinking -->
    <Storyboard x:Name="growStoryboard" TargetName="t" TargetProperty="ScaleX">
      <DoubleAnimation From="1" To="1.4"/>
    </Storyboard>
    <Storyboard x:Name="shrinkStoryboard" TargetName="t" TargetProperty="ScaleX">
      <DoubleAnimation From="1.4" To="1"/>
    </Storyboard>
  </Page.Resources>
  <Canvas Background="{ThemeResource ApplicationPageBackgroundThemeBrush}">
    <Button Content="Animating Button" Margin="50" RenderTransformOrigin=".5,.5"
            PointerEntered="Button_Entered" PointerExited="Button_Exited"
            PointerCanceled="Button_Exited" PointerCaptureLost="Button_Exited">
      <Button.RenderTransform>
        <ScaleTransform x:Name="t"/>
      </Button.RenderTransform>
    </Button>
  </Canvas>
</Page>
```

The code-behind starts the right Storyboard based on the event, and produces the result in Figure 17.6:

```
using Windows.UI.Xaml.Controls;
using Windows.UI.Xaml.Input;

namespace Chapter17
{
```

```
public sealed partial class MainPage : Page
{
  public MainPage()
  {
    InitializeComponent();
  }

  void Button_Entered(object sender, PointerRoutedEventArgs e)
  {
    this.growStoryboard.Begin();
  }

  void Button_Exited(object sender, PointerRoutedEventArgs e)
  {
    this.shrinkStoryboard.Begin();
  }
}
}
```

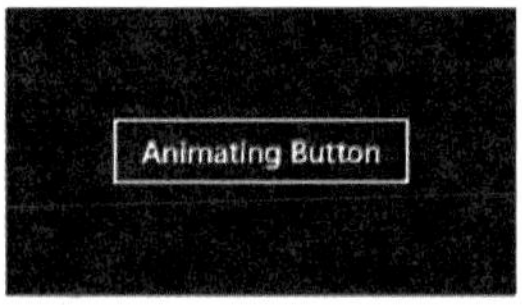

Initial appearance    While the mouse pointer hovers

FIGURE 17.6   A custom animation increases the `Button`'s horizontal scale on `PointerEntered`.

This works pretty well. However, if the pointer exits while the growStoryboard animation is still running, there's a jarring jump from the current animated scale up to 1.4 before it starts to shrink, and vice versa.

To fix this jarring "jump" effect, you can omit the From setting on both animations! When you omit From, the animation begins with the current value of the target property, whatever that might be. Therefore, the previous two animations should be updated as follows:

```
<!-- Two Storyboards, one for growing and one for shrinking -->
<Storyboard x:Name="growStoryboard" TargetName="t" TargetProperty="ScaleX">
  <DoubleAnimation To="1.4"/>
</Storyboard>
<Storyboard x:Name="shrinkStoryboard" TargetName="t" TargetProperty="ScaleX">
  <DoubleAnimation To="1"/>
</Storyboard>
```

Note that if the `ScaleTransform` named t was explicitly given a `ScaleX` of 2 rather than its default value of 1, the initial run of `growStoryboard` would *shrink* the scale rather than grow it!

In fact, the `To` setting is also optional if you've specified `From`. An animation with a `From` but no `To` means, "animate from the `From` value to the current value."

Instead of `To`, you can alternatively set a `By` property. This uses `From` + `By` for the final value, or *currentValue* + `By` if `From` is not specified. The following means "animate the current value *by .4*":

```
<DoubleAnimation By=".4"/>
```

You can also use negative values.

Note that the preceding `DoubleAnimation` is *not* the same thing as the one inside `growStoryboard`. If you were to use that instead (and leave `shrinkStoryboard` without a `From` value), then fast-enough entering and exiting of the pointer would cause the target `Button` to grow bigger and bigger! That's because `.4` would be added to the current animated value of `ScaleX` each time!

The three basic custom animation classes—`DoubleAnimation`, `ColorAnimation`, and `PointAnimation`—all expose `From`, `To`, and `By` properties.

> **(?) Why doesn't my custom animation do anything?**
>
> There are two common reasons for this. The first is related to the interpolation that must be done with a property value if you omit `From` or `To` from the animation. Unlike properties such as `Opacity` and `ScaleX` whose default value is 1, recall from Chapter 3, "Sizing, Positioning, and Transforming Elements," that the default value of properties such as `Width` and `Height` is `Double.NaN`. If you attempt to animate a property whose value is `Double.NaN` and don't specify both `From` and `To` (or `By`), the animation system has no way to interpolate values and silently fails. In this case, you need to add an explicit value somewhere. Either give the target element an explicit initial value, or add the missing `From`/`To`/`By` on the animation.
>
> Even if you do that, you are likely to run into the most common reason for an animation silently failing, and that's having a dependent animation that doesn't have `EnableDependent-Animation` set to `true`, as described previously. If that *still* doesn't work, check to see whether your coworker has snuck in a line of code somewhere in your app that sets `Timeline.AllowDependentAnimations` to `false` to globally disable them all!

Tweaking Animations with `Timeline` Properties

Now is a good time to look at the `Timeline` properties that are useful for every animation, whether it's a custom animation or a theme animation.

BeginTime

If you don't want an animation to begin immediately when you call its storyboard's Begin method (or trigger it via XAML), you can insert a delay by setting BeginTime to an instance of a TimeSpan:

```
<DoubleAnimation To="100" BeginTime="0:0:2"/>
```

This delays the animation by two seconds.

Besides being potentially useful in isolation, BeginTime can be useful for specifying a sequence of animations that start one after the other. You can even set BeginTime to a negative value:

```
<!-- Start the animation half-way through: -->
<DoubleAnimation From="50" To="100" Duration="0:0:5" BeginTime="-0:0:2.5"/>
```

This starts the animation immediately, but at 2.5 seconds into the timeline (as if the animation really started 2.5 seconds previously). Therefore, the preceding animation is equivalent to one with From set to 75, To set to 100, and Duration set to 2.5 seconds.

Note that BeginTime is of type Nullable<TimeSpan> rather than Duration because the extra expressiveness of Duration is not needed. (It would be nonsensical to set a BeginTime of Forever!)

SpeedRatio

The SpeedRatio property is a multiplier applied to Duration. It's set to 1 by default, but you can set it to any double value greater than 0:

```
<!-- Make the animation twice as fast: -->
<DoubleAnimation From="50" To="100" Duration="0:0:5" BeginTime="0:0:5"
                 SpeedRatio="2"/>
```

A value less than 1 slows down the animation, and a value greater than 1 speeds it up. SpeedRatio does not affect BeginTime; the preceding animation still has a 5-second delay, but the transition from 50 to 100 takes only 2.5 seconds rather than 5.

AutoReverse

If AutoReverse is set to true, the animation "plays backward" as soon as it completes. The reversal takes the same amount of time as the forward progress. For example, the following animation makes the value go from 50 to 100 in the first 5 seconds, and then from 100 back to 50 over the course of 5 more seconds:

```
<DoubleAnimation From="50" To="100" Duration="0:0:5" AutoReverse="True"/>
```

SpeedRatio affects the speed of *both* the forward animation and backward animation. Therefore, giving the preceding animation a SpeedRatio of 2 would make the entire animation run for 5 seconds and giving it a SpeedRatio of 0.5 would make it run for 20 seconds. Note that any delay specified via BeginTime does *not* delay the reversal; it always happens immediately after the normal part of the animation completes.

RepeatBehavior

By setting RepeatBehavior, you can accomplish one of four different behaviors:

→ Making the animation repeat itself a certain number of times, regardless of its duration

→ Making the animation repeat itself until a certain amount of time has elapsed

→ Cutting off the animation early

→ Making it repeat forever

To repeat an animation a certain number of times, you can set RepeatBehavior to a number followed by "x":

```
<!-- Perform the animation twice in a row: -->
<DoubleAnimation From="50" To="100" Duration="0:0:5" AutoReverse="True"
                 RepeatBehavior="2x"/>
```

When AutoReverse is true, the reversal is repeated as well. So, the preceding animation goes from 50 to 100 to 50 to 100 to 50 over the course of 20 seconds. If BeginTime is set to introduce a delay, that delay is *not* repeated. RepeatBehavior accepts a double, so you can repeat by a fractional amount.

To repeat the animation until a certain amount of time has elapsed, you set RepeatBehavior to a TimeSpan instead. The following animation is equivalent to the preceding one:

```
<!-- Perform the animation twice in a row: -->
<DoubleAnimation From="50" To="100" Duration="0:0:5" AutoReverse="True"
                 RepeatBehavior="0:0:20"/>
```

Twenty seconds is needed to make the animation complete two full cycles because AutoReverse is set to true. The TimeSpan-based RepeatBehavior is not scaled by SpeedRatio; if you set SpeedRatio to 2 in the preceding animation, it performs the full cycle four times rather than two.

To use RepeatBehavior as a way to cut off an animation early, you use a TimeSpan value shorter than the natural duration. The following animation makes the value go from 50 to 75 over the course of 2.5 seconds:

```
<!-- Stop the animation halfway through: -->
<DoubleAnimation From="50" To="100" Duration="0:0:5" RepeatBehavior="0:0:2.5"/>
```

Finally, you can make an animation repeat indefinitely by setting RepeatBehavior to Forever, as shown previously with the blinking FadeOutThemeAnimation example.

> ### The Total Timeline Length of an Animation
>
> With all the different adjustments that can be made to an animation by using properties such as `BeginTime`, `SpeedRatio`, `AutoReverse`, and `RepeatBehavior`, it can be hard to keep track of how long it will take an animation to finish after it is initiated. Its `Duration` value certainly isn't adequate for describing the true length of time! Instead, the following formula describes an animation's true duration:
>
> $$\text{Total Timeline Length} = \text{BeginTime} + \left(\frac{\text{Duration} * (\text{AutoReverse ? 2:1})}{\text{SpeedRatio}} * \text{RepeatBehavior} \right)$$
>
> This applies if `RepeatBehavior` is specified as multiplier (or left as its default value of 1x). If `RepeatBehavior` is specified as a `TimeSpan`, the total timeline length is simply the value of `RepeatBehavior` plus the value of `BeginTime`.

FillBehavior

By default, when an animation completes, the target property remains at the final animated value unless some other animation later changes the value. This is typically the desired behavior, but if you want the property to jump back to its pre-animated value after the animation completes, you can set `FillBehavior` to `Stop` (rather than its default value of `HoldEnd`).

Storyboards with Multiple Animations

As mentioned when `Storyboards` were introduced, they can contain one *or more* animations. Here's an update to the Button-scaling XAML that scales it in both direction simultaneously (and omits the `From` values to avoid the "jump" effect):

```
<Page …>
  <Page.Resources>
    <!-- Two Storyboards, one for growing and one for shrinking -->
    <Storyboard x:Name="growStoryboard" TargetName="t">
      <DoubleAnimation To="1.4" Storyboard.TargetProperty="ScaleX"/>
      <DoubleAnimation To="1.4" Storyboard.TargetProperty="ScaleY"/>
    </Storyboard>
    <Storyboard x:Name="shrinkStoryboard" TargetName="t">
      <DoubleAnimation To="1" Storyboard.TargetProperty="ScaleX"/>
      <DoubleAnimation To="1" Storyboard.TargetProperty="ScaleY"/>
    </Storyboard>
  </Page.Resources>
  <Canvas Background="{ThemeResource ApplicationPageBackgroundThemeBrush}">
    <Button Content="Animating Button" Margin="50" RenderTransformOrigin=".5,.5"
            PointerEntered="Button_Entered" PointerExited="Button_Exited"
            PointerCanceled="Button_Exited" PointerCaptureLost="Button_Exited">
      <Button.RenderTransform>
```

```
        <ScaleTransform x:Name="t"/>
      </Button.RenderTransform>
    </Button>
  </Canvas>
</Page>
```

The code-behind doesn't need to change, because there's still just one Storyboard to begin in Button_Entered and one to begin in Button_Exited.

Each Storyboard contains two animations, with each one targeting a different property on the same target. Both animations start simultaneously, but if you want a Storyboard to contain animations that begin at different times, you can give each animation a different BeginTime value.

What makes this possible is that Storyboard's TargetProperty (and TargetName) properties can be applied to individual animations as attached properties. If these are still specified on the Storyboard, any individual markings on animations override them.

The only limitation is that two animations in the same Storyboard can't use the same TargetProperty on the same TargetName. Multiple theme animations can be used in the same Storyboard, and you can mix and match both theme animations and custom animations. However, this can sometimes be tricky because it's not always clear which properties are animated by a theme animation.

Property Paths

Rather than showing only DoubleAnimation, the following example uses ColorAnimation to repeatedly animate the middle Color of a three-stop gradient from white to black and back again:

```
<Page …>
  <Page.Resources>
    <Storyboard x:Name="gradientStoryboard" TargetName="stop"
                TargetProperty="Color">
      <ColorAnimation From="White" To="Black" Duration="0:0:2"
                      AutoReverse="True" RepeatBehavior="Forever"
                      EnableDependentAnimation="True"/>
    </Storyboard>
  </Page.Resources>
  <Canvas Background="{ThemeResource ApplicationPageBackgroundThemeBrush}">
    <Rectangle Width="200" Height="200">
      <Rectangle.Fill>
        <LinearGradientBrush>
          <GradientStop Color="Blue" Offset="0"/>
          <GradientStop x:Name="stop" Color="White" Offset="0.5"/>
          <GradientStop Color="Blue" Offset="1"/>
        </LinearGradientBrush>
      </Rectangle.Fill>
```

```
    </Rectangle>
  </Canvas>
</Page>
```

The idea of animating a Color might sound strange, but it has a numeric representation comprised of its A, R, G, and B properties, so ColorAnimation can interpolate those values just as DoubleAnimation does for its single value. Because the animation never ends, the Storyboard can be started in the Page's constructor:

```
this.gradientStoryboard.Begin();
```

The result is shown in Figure 17.7.

Starting at white

Halfway through

Ending at black

FIGURE 17.7   A color inside a gradient can be animated with a ColorAnimation.

The syntax for TargetProperty doesn't have to be a simple property name. It can be a *property path*, which is a more complicated expression representing a chain of properties to follow starting at TargetName. Although you never need to use this syntax because you can always directly name the target, the following update to the preceding Page shows how it can be used:

```
<Page …>
  <Page.Resources>
    <Storyboard x:Name="gradientStoryboard" TargetName="r"
              TargetProperty="(Fill).GradientStops[1].Color">
      <ColorAnimation From="White" To="Black" Duration="0:0:2"
                    AutoReverse="True" RepeatBehavior="Forever"
                    EnableDependentAnimation="True"/>
    </Storyboard>
  </Page.Resources>
  <Canvas Background="{ThemeResource ApplicationPageBackgroundThemeBrush}">
    <Rectangle Name="r" Width="200" Height="200">
      <Rectangle.Fill>
        <LinearGradientBrush>
          <GradientStop Color="Blue" Offset="0"/>
          <GradientStop Color="White" Offset="0.5"/>
          <GradientStop Color="Blue" Offset="1"/>
```

```
      </LinearGradientBrush>
    </Rectangle.Fill>
  </Rectangle>
 </Canvas>
</Page>
```

The syntax for `TargetProperty` mimics what you would have to type to access the property in C#, although without casting. This `Storyboard` assumes that the `Rectangle`'s `Fill` is set to an object with a `GradientStops` property that can be indexed, assumes that it has at least two items, and assumes that the second item has a `Color` property of type `Color`. If any of these assumptions is incorrect, the animation silently fails. Of course, in this case these are all correct assumptions, so the `Rectangle` successfully animates, the same way as shown in Figure 17.7.

The "Fill" part of the property path must be placed in parentheses because it is otherwise ambiguous with a property path's support for specifying type names along with each property name, for example, `(TypeName.PropertyName).(TypeName.PropertyName)....` This support exists for attached properties, which need that extra context. Therefore, here are just a few of the valid property paths that could have been used in the preceding example, from shortest to longest:

```
(Fill).GradientStops[1].Color
Shape.Fill.GradientStops[1].Color
Rectangle.Fill.GradientStops[1].Color
(Rectangle.Fill).GradientStops[1].Color
Rectangle.Fill.LinearGradientBrush.GradientStops[1].Color
(Rectangle.Fill).(LinearGradientBrush.GradientStops)[1].Color
Rectangle.Fill.LinearGradientBrush.GradientStops[1].GradientStop.Color
(Rectangle.Fill).(LinearGradientBrush.GradientStops)[1].(GradientStop.Color)
```

Tweaking `Storyboard`s with `Timeline` Properties

A `Storyboard` is more than just a simple container that associates animations with target objects and their properties. Because `Storyboard` derives from `Timeline`, it has many of the same properties discussed previously: `Duration`, `BeginTime`, `SpeedRatio`, `AutoReverse`, `RepeatBehavior`, and `FillBehavior` (and the `Completed` event).

The following `Storyboard` fades one `TextBlock` in and out at a time, for an effect somewhat like that of a movie trailer. The `Storyboard` itself is marked with a `RepeatBehavior` to make the entire sequence of animation repeat indefinitely. Figure 17.8 shows how this is rendered at three different spots of the sequence:

```
<Page …>
  <Page.Resources>
    <Storyboard x:Name="storyboard" TargetProperty="Opacity"
                RepeatBehavior="Forever">
      <DoubleAnimation Storyboard.TargetName="title1" BeginTime="0:0:2"
```

```
            From="0" To="1" Duration="0:0:2" AutoReverse="True"/>
        <DoubleAnimation Storyboard.TargetName="title2" BeginTime="0:0:6"
          From="0" To="1" Duration="0:0:2" AutoReverse="True"/>
        <DoubleAnimation Storyboard.TargetName="title3" BeginTime="0:0:10"
          From="0" To="1" Duration="0:0:2" AutoReverse="True"/>
        <DoubleAnimation Storyboard.TargetName="title4" BeginTime="0:0:14"
          From="0" To="1" Duration="0:0:2" AutoReverse="True"/>
        <DoubleAnimation Storyboard.TargetName="title5" BeginTime="0:0:18"
          From="0" To="1" Duration="0:0:2" AutoReverse="True"/>
      </Storyboard>
  </Page.Resources>
  <Grid Background="{ThemeResource ApplicationPageBackgroundThemeBrush}">
    <TextBlock HorizontalAlignment="Center" VerticalAlignment="Center"
      Opacity="0" FontSize="50" Name="title1">In a world</TextBlock>
    <TextBlock HorizontalAlignment="Center" VerticalAlignment="Center"
      Opacity="0" FontSize="50" Name="title2">where apps need to be built
    </TextBlock>
    <TextBlock HorizontalAlignment="Center" VerticalAlignment="Center"
      Opacity="0" FontSize="50" Name="title3">one book</TextBlock>
    <TextBlock HorizontalAlignment="Center" VerticalAlignment="Center"
      Opacity="0" FontSize="50" Name="title4">will explain it all.</TextBlock>
    <TextBlock HorizontalAlignment="Center" VerticalAlignment="Center"
      Opacity="0" FontSize="50" Name="title5">
      Windows 8.1 Apps with XAML and C# Unleashed</TextBlock>
  </Grid>
</Page>
```

FIGURE 17.8   Snapshots of the movie-trailer-like title sequence

Setting the Timeline-inherited properties on Storyboard affects the entire set of child animations, although in a slightly different way than setting the same property individually on all children. For example, setting RepeatBehavior="Forever" on every child animation rather than on this Storyboard itself would wreak havoc. The first title would fade in and out as expected, but then at 6 seconds *both* title1 and title2 would fade in and out together. At 10 seconds title1, title2, and title3 would fade in and out simultaneously, and so on.

Similarly, setting SpeedRatio="2" on each DoubleAnimation would make each fade take 1 second rather than 2, but the final animation would still start 18 seconds after the animation starts. On the other hand, setting SpeedRatio="2" on the Storyboard would speed up the entire animation, including each BeginTime, by a factor of two. Therefore, the final animation would start 9 seconds after the animation starts. Setting Duration to a time shorter than the natural duration can cut off the entire sequence of animations early.

Custom Keyframe Animations

So far, all the information about custom animations applies to three basic classes: DoubleAnimation, ColorAnimation, and PointAnimation. But there are seven custom animation classes. The remaining four all enable *keyframes*, which provide specific values at specific times. You certainly can't miss this distinction from their names. They are called DoubleAnimationUsingKeyFrames, ColorAnimationUsingKeyFrames, PointAnimationUsingKeyFrames, and ObjectAnimationUsingKeyFrames.

The keyframe animation classes have the same members as their counterparts, except for the From, To, and By properties. Instead, they have a KeyFrames collection that can hold keyframe instances specific to the type being animated. There are four types of keyframes, which this section examines.

Linear Keyframes

Listing 17.1 uses DoubleAnimationUsingKeyFrames to help move a circle (Ellipse) in a zigzag pattern, as illustrated in Figure 17.9. The blue lines are there to show the path that the circle travelled to get to its final spot. Because the Image is inside a Canvas, the motion is accomplished by animating the Canvas.Left and Canvas.Top attached properties rather than using the more versatile TranslateTransform. These are still independent animations, however!

LISTING 17.1   The Zigzag Animation for Figure 17.9

```
<Page …>
  <Page.Resources>
    <Storyboard x:Name="storyboard" TargetName="circle">
      <DoubleAnimation Storyboard.TargetProperty="(Canvas.Left)"
          From="0" To="500" Duration="0:0:3"/>
      <DoubleAnimationUsingKeyFrames Storyboard.TargetProperty="(Canvas.Top)"
          Duration="0:0:3">
        <LinearDoubleKeyFrame Value="0" KeyTime="0:0:0"/>
        <LinearDoubleKeyFrame Value="200" KeyTime="0:0:1"/>
        <LinearDoubleKeyFrame Value="0" KeyTime="0:0:2"/>
        <LinearDoubleKeyFrame Value="200" KeyTime="0:0:3"/>
      </DoubleAnimationUsingKeyFrames>
    </Storyboard>
  </Page.Resources>
  <Canvas Background="{ThemeResource ApplicationPageBackgroundThemeBrush}">
```

LISTING 17.1   Continued

```
  <Ellipse Name="circle" Width="50" Height="50" Fill="Orange"/>
  </Canvas>
</Page>
```

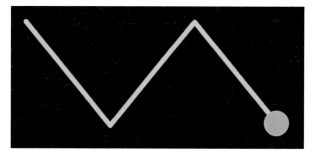

FIGURE 17.9   Zigzag motion is easy to create with a keyframe animation.

The circle's motion consists of two animations that begin in parallel when the image loads. One is a simple `DoubleAnimation` that increases its horizontal position linearly from 0 to 500. The other is the keyframe-enabled animation, which oscillates the vertical position from 0 to 200 then back to 0 then back to 200.

Each keyframe instance (`LinearDoubleKeyFrame`) in Listing 17.1 gives a specific value and a time for that value to be applied. Although the exact vertical position of the circle is specified for 0, 1, 2, and 3 seconds, the animation still needs to calculate intermediate values between these "key times." Because each keyframe is represented with an instance of `LinearDoubleKey-Frame`, the intermediate values are derived from simple linear interpolation. For example, at 0.5, 1.5, and 2.5 seconds, the calculated value is 100.

> **An attached property must be wrapped in parentheses when specified as a `TargetProperty`!**
>
> Notice that in Listing 17.1, both `Canvas.Left` and `Canvas.Top` are referenced inside parentheses when used as the value for Storyboard's `TargetProperty` property. This is a requirement for any attached properties used in a property path. Without the parentheses, the animation would look for a property on `Ellipse` called `Canvas` (expecting it to return an object with `Left` and `Top` properties) and fail because it doesn't exist.

But `DoubleAnimationUsingKeyFrames`'s `KeyFrames` property is a collection of base `DoubleKeyFrame` objects, so it can be filled with other types of keyframe objects. In addition to `LinearDoubleKeyFrame`, `DoubleKeyFrame` has three other subclasses: `SplineDoubleKeyFrame`, `DiscreteDoubleKeyFrame`, and `EasingDoubleKeyFrame`.

Spline Keyframes

All three `LinearXXXKeyFrame` classes have a corresponding `SplineXXXKeyFrame` class. It can be used just like its linear counterpart, so updating `DoubleAnimationUsingKeyFrames` from Listing 17.1 as follows produces the same result:

```
<DoubleAnimationUsingKeyFrames Storyboard.TargetProperty="(Canvas.Top)"
  Duration="0:0:3">
  <SplineDoubleKeyFrame Value="0" KeyTime="0:0:0"/>
  <SplineDoubleKeyFrame Value="200" KeyTime="0:0:1"/>
  <SplineDoubleKeyFrame Value="0" KeyTime="0:0:2"/>
  <SplineDoubleKeyFrame Value="200" KeyTime="0:0:3"/>
</DoubleAnimationUsingKeyFrames>
```

The spline keyframe classes have an additional `KeySpline` property that differentiates them from the linear classes. `KeySpline` can be set to an instance of a `KeySpline` object, which describes the desired motion as a cubic Bézier curve. `KeySpline` has two properties of type `Point` that represent the curve's control points. (The start point of the curve is always 0, and the end point is always 1.) A type converter enables you to specify a `KeySpline` in XAML as a simple list of two points. For example, the following update changes the circle's motion from the simple zigzag in Figure 17.9 to the more complicated motion in Figure 17.10:

```
<DoubleAnimationUsingKeyFrames Storyboard.TargetProperty="(Canvas.Top)"
  Duration="0:0:3">
  <SplineDoubleKeyFrame KeySpline="0,1 1,0" Value="0" KeyTime="0:0:0"/>
  <SplineDoubleKeyFrame KeySpline="0,1 1,0" Value="200" KeyTime="0:0:1"/>
  <SplineDoubleKeyFrame KeySpline="0,1 1,0" Value="0" KeyTime="0:0:2"/>
  <SplineDoubleKeyFrame KeySpline="0,1 1,0" Value="200" KeyTime="0:0:3"/>
</DoubleAnimationUsingKeyFrames>
```

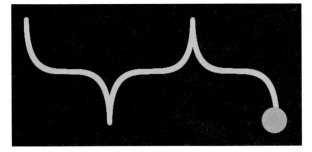

FIGURE 17.10   With `KeySpline` specified, the interpolation between keyframes is now based on cubic Bézier curves.

Finding the right value for `KeySpline` that gives the desired effect can be tricky and almost certainly requires the use of a design tool such as Blend. But several free tools can be found online that help you visualize Bézier curves based on the specified control points.

Discrete Keyframes

A *discrete keyframe* indicates that no interpolation should be done from the previous keyframe. Updating `DoubleAnimationUsingKeyFrames` from Listing 17.1 as follows produces the motion illustrated in Figure 17.11:

```
<DoubleAnimationUsingKeyFrames Storyboard.TargetProperty="(Canvas.Top)"
  Duration="0:0:3">
  <DiscreteDoubleKeyFrame Value="0" KeyTime="0:0:0"/>
  <DiscreteDoubleKeyFrame Value="200" KeyTime="0:0:1"/>
  <DiscreteDoubleKeyFrame Value="0" KeyTime="0:0:2"/>
  <DiscreteDoubleKeyFrame Value="200" KeyTime="0:0:3"/>
</DoubleAnimationUsingKeyFrames>
```

FIGURE 17.11   Discrete keyframes make the circle's vertical position jump from one key value to the next, with no interpolation.

Of course, different types of keyframes can be mixed into the same animation. The following mixture makes the circle follow the path shown in Figure 17.12:

```
<DoubleAnimationUsingKeyFrames Storyboard.TargetProperty="(Canvas.Top)"
  Duration="0:0:3">
  <DiscreteDoubleKeyFrame Value="0" KeyTime="0:0:0"/>
  <LinearDoubleKeyFrame Value="200" KeyTime="0:0:1"/>
  <DiscreteDoubleKeyFrame Value="0" KeyTime="0:0:2"/>
  <SplineDoubleKeyFrame KeySpline="0,1,1,0" Value="200" KeyTime="0:0:3"/>
</DoubleAnimationUsingKeyFrames>
```

Because the first keyframe's time is at the beginning, its type is irrelevant. That's because each frame indicates only how interpolation is done *before* that frame.

As with Spline*XXX*KeyFrame, every Linear*XXX*KeyFrame class has a corresponding Discrete*XXX*KeyFrame. But there's one discrete keyframe class that has no linear or spline counterpart: `DiscreteObjectKeyFrame`. This works with `System.Object`, so it simply changes the value of *any* property to the specified `Value` at the specified `KeyTime`. For example, the following `Storyboard` "animates" the text in a `TextBlock` from lowercase to uppercase:

```
<Storyboard x:Name="storyboard" TargetName="textBlock" TargetProperty="Text">
  <ObjectAnimationUsingKeyFrames>
    <DiscreteObjectKeyFrame Value="play" KeyTime="0:0:0"/>
    <DiscreteObjectKeyFrame Value="Play" KeyTime="0:0:1"/>
    <DiscreteObjectKeyFrame Value="PLay" KeyTime="0:0:2"/>
    <DiscreteObjectKeyFrame Value="PLAy" KeyTime="0:0:3"/>
    <DiscreteObjectKeyFrame Value="PLAY" KeyTime="0:0:4"/>
  </ObjectAnimationUsingKeyFrames>
</Storyboard>
```

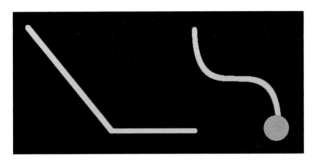

FIGURE 17.12　　Mixing three types of keyframes into a single animation

Only discrete keyframe animations can be used with `System.Object` because interpolation is impossible.

> Animations that use only `DiscreteObjectKeyFrames`—or animations with a `Duration` of 0—don't need their `EnableDependentAnimation` property set to `true` because no "real" animation (interpolation) can take place.
>
> Note that this exemption doesn't apply to an animation that uses only discrete keyframes of other types. This is a strange policy because you could represent any discrete `double` keyframe animation as a discrete `Object` keyframe animation and get the same results. But if the animation is dependent (for example, animates the circle's `Width` instead of `Canvas.Top`), the one form requires `EnableDependentAnimation` (and can be disabled with `Timeline.AllowDependentAnimations`) whereas the other is exempt!

Easing Keyframes

Every `LinearXXXKeyFrame` and `SplineXXXKeyFrame` class also has a corresponding `EasingXXXKeyFrame` class. The easing keyframe classes have an `EasingFunction` property gives a lot of flexibility in how the interpolation is done. Easing functions deserve their own separate section, and we'll examine them now.

Easing Functions

You've seen examples of the linear interpolation used with the three main custom animation classes, and the possible spline interpolation that can be used with three of the custom keyframe animation classes. All of the custom animation classes except the discrete-only `ObjectAnimationUsingKeyFrames` class enable an easing function to be plugged in to customize the interpolation. `DoubleAnimation`, `ColorAnimation`, and `PointAnimation` directly define an `EasingFunction` property, and the others can work with `EasingXXXKeyFrame` objects that define the same property.

`EasingFunction` can be set to a class deriving from `EasingFunctionBase` that controls the rate of acceleration and deceleration in arbitrarily complex ways. The XAML UI Framework ships with 11 such objects. Each of them supports three different modes with a property called `EasingMode`. It can be set to `EaseIn`, `EaseOut` (the default value), or `EaseInOut`. Here's how you can apply one of the easing function objects— `QuadraticEase`—to a basic `DoubleAnimation`:

```
<DoubleAnimation Storyboard.TargetProperty="(Canvas.Top)" From="200" To="0"
  Duration="0:0:3">
<DoubleAnimation.EasingFunction>
  <QuadraticEase/>
</DoubleAnimation.EasingFunction>
</DoubleAnimation>
```

And here is how you change `EasingMode` to something other than `EaseOut`:

```
<DoubleAnimation Storyboard.TargetProperty="(Canvas.Top)" From="200" To="0"
  Duration="0:0:3">
<DoubleAnimation.EasingFunction>
  <QuadraticEase EasingMode="EaseIn"/>
</DoubleAnimation.EasingFunction>
</DoubleAnimation>
```

`EaseIn` inverts the interpolation done with `EaseOut`, and `EaseInOut` produces the `EaseIn` behavior for the first half of the animation and the `EaseOut` behavior for the second half.

Power Easing Functions

Table 17.1 demonstrates how five of the easing functions work in all three modes by showing the path an object takes if its horizontal position animates linearly but its vertical position animates from bottom to top with each easing function and mode applied.

TABLE 17.1   Five Power Easing Functions

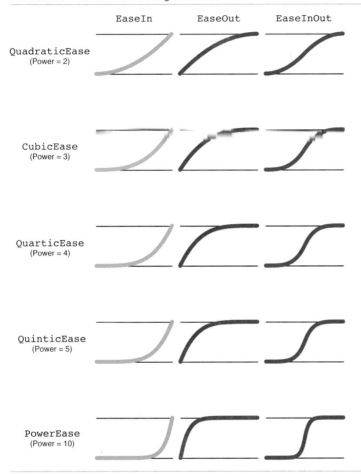

All five functions do interpolation based on a simple power function. With the default linear interpolation, when time has elapsed 50% (.5), the value has changed by 50% (.5). But with quadratic interpolation, the value has changed by 25% (.5 * .5 = .25) when time has elapsed 50%. With cubic interpolation, the value has changed by 12.5% (.5 * .5 * .5 = .125) when time has elapsed 50%, and so on. Although there are four distinct classes for powers 2 through 5, all you need is the general-purpose PowerEase class that performs the interpolation with the value of its Power property. The default value of Power is 2 (making it the same as QuadraticEase) but Table 17.1 demonstrates it with Power set to 10, just to show how the transition keeps getting sharper as Power increases. Applying PowerEase with Power set to 10 can look as follows:

```
<DoubleAnimation Storyboard.TargetProperty="(Canvas.Top)" From="200" To="0"
  Duration="0:0:3">
<DoubleAnimation.EasingFunction>
```

```
  <PowerEase Power="10"/>
</DoubleAnimation.EasingFunction>
</DoubleAnimation>
```

Other Easing Functions

Table 17.2 demonstrates the remaining six easing functions in all three modes.

TABLE 17.2   The Other Six Built-In Easing Functions

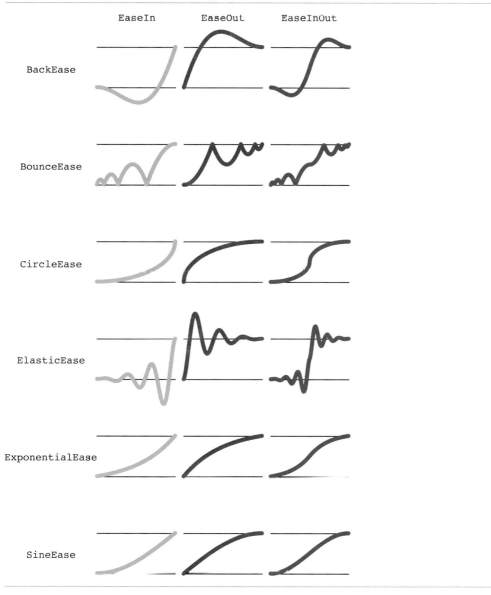

Each of these six functions has unique (and sometimes configurable) behavior:

→ **BackEase**—Moves the animated value slightly back (away from the target value) before progressing. BackEase has an Amplitude property (default=1) that controls how far back the value goes.

→ **BounceEase**—Creates what looks like a bouncing pattern (at least when used to animate position). BounceEase has two properties for controlling its behavior. Bounces (default=3) controls how many bounces occur during the animation, and Bounciness (default=2) controls how much the amplitude of each bounce changes from the previous bounce. For EaseIn, Bounciness=2 doubles the height of each bounce. For EaseOut, Bounciness=2 halves the height of each bounce. So for the more natural EaseOut case, a higher Bounciness actually makes the element appear *less* bouncy!

→ **CircleEase**—Accelerates (for EaseIn) or decelerates (for EaseOut) the value with a circular function.

→ **ElasticEase**—Creates what looks like an oscillating spring pattern (at least when used to animate position). Like BounceEase, it has two properties for controlling its behavior. Oscillations (default=3) controls how many oscillations occur during the animation, and Springiness (default=3) controls the amplitude of oscillations. The behavior of Springiness is subtle: Larger values give smaller oscillations (as if the spring is thicker and more difficult to stretch), and smaller values give larger oscillations (which, in my opinion, seems to make the motion *more* springy rather than *less*).

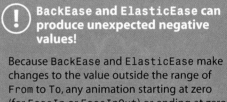

BackEase and ElasticEase can produce unexpected negative values!

Because BackEase and ElasticEase make changes to the value outside the range of From to To, any animation starting at zero (for EaseIn or EaseInOut) or ending at zero (for EaseOut or EaseInOut) will likely veer into negative territory. If such an animation is applied to a value that cannot be negative, as with an element's Width or Height, an exception will be thrown.

→ **ExponentialEase**—Interpolates the value with an exponential function, using the value of its Exponent property (default=2).

→ **SineEase**—Interpolates the value with a function based on the sine formula.

What EaseOut and EaseInOut Actually Mean

EaseIn is easy to understand because it corresponds exactly to how most people think about an animated value progressing as a function of time. To understand what the EaseOut and EaseInOut modes actually do, imagine that QuadraticEase is implemented with following method to perform its interpolation:

```
double DoQuadraticInterpolation(double normalizedTime)
{
  return normalizedTime * normalizedTime;
}
```

For EaseIn, DoQuadraticInterpolation would be called repeatedly with values starting at 0 and ending at 1. For EaseOut, DoQuadraticInterpolation would be called repeatedly with values starting at 1 and ending at 0. (The normalizedTime would be 1-normalizedTime.) The value returned by DoQuadraticInterpolation would then need to be inverted in this case; in other words 1-*returnedValue*.

For the EaseInOut case, the behavior is different between the first half of the animation (normalizedTime values from 0 up to but not including 0.5) and the second half (normalizedTime values from 0.5 to 1). For the first half, the normalizedTime value passed to DoQuadraticInterpolation would be doubled (spanning the full range of 0 to 1 in half the time), but the value returned would be halved. For the second half, the normalizedTime value passed to DoQuadraticInterpolation would be doubled *and* inverted (spanning the full range of 1 to 0 in half the time). The value returned from DoQuadraticInterpolation would then be halved and inverted, and finally .5 would be added to the value (because this is the second half of progress toward the final value). This is why every deterministic EaseInOut animation is symmetrical and hits 50% progress when 50% of the time has elapsed.

Manual Animations

Of course, even with all the fancy animation support discussed in this chapter, nothing prevents you from animating the old fashioned way. The classic way to implement animations such as the ones in this chapter is to set up a timer and a callback function that is periodically called based on the frequency of the timer. Inside the callback function, you can manually update the target property (doing a little math to determine the current value based on the elapsed time) until it reaches the final value. At that point, you can stop the timer and/or remove the event handler.

Thanks to the retained-mode graphics model, this approach doesn't take much work. The XAML UI Framework even has its own DispatcherTimer class that can be used for implementing such a scheme. You get to choose DispatcherTimer's frequency by setting its Interval property, you can attach an event handler to its Tick event, and then you can call its Start and Stop methods.

The Difference Between DispatcherTimer and ThreadPoolTimer

The key difference between DispatcherTimer and the other timer class available to C# (System.Threading.ThreadPoolTimer) is that handlers for DispatcherTimer are always invoked on the same UI thread that started it. This is convenient because you don't need to use CoreDispatcher to explicitly marshal back to the UI thread.

Although this approach might be familiar, performing animation with a timer is not recommended. The timers are not in sync with the screen's vertical refresh rate, nor are they in sync with the rendering engine, nor do they take advantage of hardware acceleration.

Instead of implementing custom timer-based animation, you could perform custom frame-based animation by attaching an event handler to the static `Rendering` event on a class called `CompositionTarget`. Rather than being raised at a customizable interval, this event is raised post-layout and pre-render *once per frame*.

Using the frame-based `Rendering` event is not only preferred over a timer-based approach, it can even preferred over the animation classes that are the focus of this chapter when dealing with hundreds of objects that require high-fidelity animations. For example, collision detection or other physics-based animations should be done using this approach. The `Rendering` event generally gives the best performance and the most customizations of all the options native to XAML apps (because you can write arbitrary code in the event handler), although there are tradeoffs. In normal conditions, frames are rendered only when part of the user interface is invalidated. But as long as any event handler is attached to `Rendering`, frames get rendered continuously. Therefore, using `Rendering` is best for short-lived animations. Furthermore, the code in your `Rendering` event handler runs on the UI thread, so you need to be careful keep your code minimal in order to have good performance.

The blue "paths" in Figures 17.9–17.12 were generated with the help of the `Rendering` event. While the `Storyboard` was running and moving the orange circle, the following handler for `CompositionTarget.Rendering` placed a smaller blue circle (dot) in the orange circle's current location on every frame:

```
void CompositionTarget_Rendering(object sender, object e)
{
  // A new small blue circle
  Ellipse dot = new Ellipse { Fill = new SolidColorBrush(Colors.Aqua),
                              Width = 10, Height = 10 };

  // Center it in the current location of the orange circle
  Canvas.SetLeft(dot, Canvas.GetLeft(this.circle) + this.circle.Width / 2);
  Canvas.SetTop(dot, Canvas.GetTop(this.circle) + this.circle.Height / 2);

  // Insert it in the beginning so it's underneath the orange circle:
  this.canvas.Children.Insert(0, dot);
}
```

This requires the `Canvas` to be given the name canvas. The orange circle (already named circle) could have been given an explicit `ZIndex` so the new blue circles could have been *added* to the `Children` collection rather than *inserted* at the beginning, but either way works. Note that for tracing the spline animation in Figures 17.10 and 17.12, the `Storyboard` needed to be slowed down considerably (with a `SpeedRatio` of .01) to produce solid lines, because the circle moved too quickly otherwise. Figure 17.13 shows what the animation from Figure 17.10 looks like when it runs at normal speed and the position is traced via the `CompositionTarget_Rendering` handler.

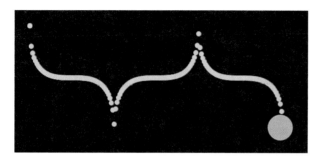

FIGURE 17.13   Tracing the animation from Figure 17.10 at its normal speed

Summary

Here is a concise way to describe the four main types of animations available to you:

→ **Theme transitions:** specific animations for specific actions

→ **Theme animations:** specific animations for custom actions

→ **Custom animations:** custom animations for custom actions

→ **Manual animations:** custom code that doesn't leverage any animation features, other than perhaps the `Rendering` event

The theme transitions are a huge timesaver when it comes to adding high-quality, high-performance, and consistent animations to your app. Try to recreate a transition with custom animations, and you'll appreciate just how much they do for you!

With all the animation choices, you can do something as simple as a subtle rollover effect or as complex as an animated cartoon. `Storyboards`, which are a necessary part of performing animations, help to orchestrate complex series of animations.

An important aspect of all these animations (except manual ones) is that they are "time resolution independent." Similar in spirit to the automatic scaling done for graphics based on DPI, transitions and animations do not speed up as hardware gets faster; they simply get smoother! The frame rate is varied based on a variety of conditions, and you as the animation developer don't need to care.

Going overboard with animation can harm the usability and performance of your app. A good way to diagnose performance problems related to rendering is to enable a special frame rate counter as follows:

```
Application.Current.DebugSettings.EnableFrameRateCounter = true;
```

Visual Studio-generated projects do this by default for debug builds with code inside `App.xaml.cs`.

Enabling the frame rate counter overlays four numbers on the top of the screen, shown in Figure 17.14.

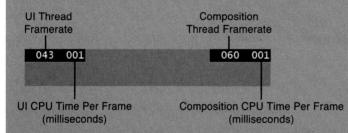

UI Thread
Framerate

Composition
Thread Framerate

UI CPU Time Per Frame
(milliseconds)

Composition CPU Time Per Frame
(milliseconds)

FIGURE 17.14   The information shown when setting `EnableFrameRateCounter` to `true`

The *composition thread* is used by independent animations. You should strive to keep this frame rate at 30 (frames per second) or higher. The UI thread is used for dependent animations. You should strive to keep this frame rate at 15 or higher.

Composition CPU time per frame isn't very actionable for developers outside of Microsoft, but it should stay below 15 milliseconds. *UI CPU time per frame* can get arbitrarily high, but if you see high values in a steady state (such as 100 milliseconds), you should try to pinpoint the code responsible for this.

You can enable the frame rate counter across all of your sideloaded apps without modifying their code. To do so, you must create and set the following registry key:

For 64-bit: HKEY_LOCAL_MACHINE\SOFTWARE\Wow6432Node\Microsoft\Xaml\ EnableFrameRateCounter = 1 (a DWORD)

For 32-bit: HKEY_LOCAL_MACHINE\SOFTWARE\Microsoft\Xaml\EnableFrameRateCounter = 1 (a DWORD)

Another new `DebugSettings` property has been added in Windows 8.1 that is useful for detecting animations that are still running unnecessarily because they are hidden under other elements. You can enable this as follows:

```
Application.Current.DebugSettings.EnableRedrawRegions = true;
```

This visually shows the areas of the screen that are being redrawn each frame. If you have a hidden animation, such as a `ProgressRing` that is still animating but completely obscured by the content that got loaded, this visualization enables you to clearly see the mistake.

`DebugSetting`'s properties, especially when used in conjunction with the Windows Performance Analyzer, are powerful tools for optimizing the performance of your animations.

Chapter 18

STYLES, TEMPLATES, AND VISUAL STATES

Arguably the most celebrated feature in XAML-based UI is the ability to give any control a radically different look without having to give up all of the built-in functionality that it provides. Even with Cascading Style Sheets (CSS), HTML lacks this much power, which is the reason most websites and HTML-based apps use images to represent buttons rather than "real buttons." Of course, it's easy to simulate a button's behavior with an image in HTML, but what if you want to give a completely different look to a SELECT element (HTML's version of ComboDox)? It's a lot of work if you want to do more than change simple properties such as its foreground and background colors.

This chapter explains the three main components of XAML control restyling support:

→ **Styles**—A simple mechanism for separating property values from user interface elements (similar to the relationship between CSS and HTML). Styles are also the foundation for applying the other mechanisms in this chapter.

→ **Templates**—Powerful objects that most people are referring to when they talk about "restyling" XAML controls.

→ **Visual States**—An important part of templates, which enable them to adjust their visuals based on the current states of the templated controls.

> **(?) Why are developers allowed to completely customize the look of XAML controls? They were designed for consistency with Windows!**
>
> The point is to enable apps to infuse their own branding into the entire user experience while not needlessly sacrificing consistency with Windows interaction model. Despite the lack of consistency (or even *because of* lack of consistency), apps with unique user experiences can do very well. XAML's philosophy is to make an application's experience limited only by the skill of its designers rather than by the underlying platform. It's hard to disagree with that stance.

Styles

A *style*, represented by the `Windows.UI.Xaml.Style` class, is a simple entity. It groups together property values that could otherwise be set individually. The intent is to then share this group of values among multiple elements. There are examples in this book in which property values are duplicated on multiple elements. Using a `Style` to avoid the duplication is a much cleaner approach.

Take, for example, the three customized `Buttons` in Figure 18.1. This look is achieved by setting seven properties. Without a `Style`, you would need to duplicate these identical assignments on all three `Buttons` as follows:

```
<Page …>
  <Grid Background="{ThemeResource ApplicationPageBackgroundThemeBrush}">
    <StackPanel Margin="20" Orientation="Horizontal">
      <Button FontSize="22" Background="Purple" Foreground="White"
        Height="60" Width="60" RenderTransformOrigin=".5,.5" Content="1">
        <Button.RenderTransform>
          <RotateTransform Angle="10"/>
        </Button.RenderTransform>
      </Button>
      <Button FontSize="22" Background="Purple" Foreground="White"
        Height="60" Width="60" RenderTransformOrigin=".5,.5" Content="2">
        <Button.RenderTransform>
          <RotateTransform Angle="10"/>
        </Button.RenderTransform>
      </Button>
      <Button FontSize="22" Background="Purple" Foreground="White"
        Height="60" Width="60" RenderTransformOrigin=".5,.5" Content="3">
        <Button.RenderTransform>
          <RotateTransform Angle="10"/>
        </Button.RenderTransform>
      </Button>
    </StackPanel>
  </Grid>
</Page>
```

FIGURE 18.1 Three `Buttons` whose look has been customized

With a `Style`, you can add a level of indirection—setting the properties in one place and pointing each `Button` to this new element:

```
<Page …>
  <Grid Background="{ThemeResource ApplicationPageBackgroundThemeBrush}">
    <StackPanel Margin="20" Orientation="Horizontal">
      <StackPanel.Resources>
        <Style x:Key="PurpleTiltStyle" TargetType="Button">
          <Setter Property="FontSize" Value="22"/>
          <Setter Property="Background" Value="Purple"/>
          <Setter Property="Foreground" Value="White"/>
          <Setter Property="Height" Value="60"/>
          <Setter Property="Width" Value="60"/>
          <Setter Property="RenderTransformOrigin" Value=".5,.5"/>
          <Setter Property="RenderTransform">
            <Setter.Value>
              <RotateTransform Angle="10"/>
            </Setter.Value>
          </Setter>
        </Style>
      </StackPanel.Resources>
      <Button Style="{StaticResource PurpleTiltStyle}" Content="1"/>
      <Button Style="{StaticResource PurpleTiltStyle}" Content="2"/>
      <Button Style="{StaticResource PurpleTiltStyle}" Content="3"/>
    </StackPanel>
  </Grid>
</Page>
```

Style definition

Applying the Style

The same `Style` instance is set as the value for each `Button`'s property called `Style`. The `Style` property is defined on `FrameworkElement`, so it can be used with non-`Controls` such as `Rectangles` and `Ellipses` as well.

`Style` uses a collection of `Setters` to set the target properties. Creating a `Setter` is a matter of specifying the name of a dependency property and a desired value for it.

The `Style` is placed in a `Resources` property on the parent `StackPanel`. All `FrameworkElements` (and `Application`) define a `Resources` property of type `ResourceDictionary` that is suited for holding `Styles`. Any element within the same scope can reference an object in a `ResourceDictionary` with `{StaticResource resourceName}` syntax. This works regardless of whether the object in the `Resources` collection is named with `x:Key` or `x:Name`, although in the latter case the generated field can be handy for code-behind.

This means that although the `Style` used in Figure 18.1 is added to `StackPanel`'s `Resources` collection, it could alternatively be added to the parent `Grid`'s `Resources` collection, the `Page`'s `Resources` collection, or even the `Application Resources` collection (in `App.xaml`).

Despite its name, there's nothing inherently visual about a `Style`. But it's typically used for setting properties that affect visuals. Indeed, `Style` enables the setting of dependency properties only, which tend to be visual in nature.

Any individual element can override aspects of its `Style` by directly setting a property to a local value. For example, the first `Button` in Figure 18.1 could do the following to retain the settings from `controlStyle` (rotation, size, and so on) yet have a red `Background` rather than a purple one:

```
<Button Style="{ThemeResource PurpleTiltStyle}" Background="Red" Content="1"/>
```

This works because of the order of precedence for dependency property values presented in Chapter 5, "Interactivity." The local value trumps anything set from a `Style`.

Style Selectors

•••

`FrameworkElement`'s `Style` property isn't the only property of type `Style` in the XAML UI Framework. For example, `ItemsControl` has an `ItemContainerStyle` property that applies to each item container such as `ListViewItem` or `ComboBoxItem`, and `GroupStyle` (described in the next chapter) has a similar `ContainerStyle` property.

These classes also have an `ItemContainerStyle`**Selector** and `GroupStyle`**Selector** property, respectively, that can be set to a custom class deriving from `StyleSelector`. This class defines a `SelectStyle` method that gets invoked whenever an item container or group is about to be rendered, enabling you to use custom logic to apply a potentially different `Style` to every item.

A more realistic example of defining and applying a `Style` would be to consolidate common visual aspects of the root panel in each `Page` within your app. You could replace the standard `Background` attribute generated by Visual Studio:

```
<Grid Background="{ThemeResource ApplicationPageBackgroundThemeBrush}">
```

with a `Style` reference like the following:

```
<Grid Style="{StaticResource LayoutRootStyle}">
```

Then, you could define the following `Style` inside the `Application.Resources` collection in `App.xaml` so all `Page`s can access it:

```
<Style x:Key="LayoutRootStyle" TargetType="Panel">
  <Setter Property="Background"
          Value="{ThemeResource ApplicationPageBackgroundThemeBrush}"/>
  <Setter Property="ChildrenTransitions">
    <Setter.Value>
      <TransitionCollection>
        <EntranceThemeTransition/>
      </TransitionCollection>
    </Setter.Value>
  </Setter>
</Style>
```

This not only applies the same `Background` as before, but it applies the staggered `EntranceThemeTransition` to the target panel's children.

Using a Base TargetType

Although the `Style` in Figure 18.1 is shared among three `Button`s, it can be shared by any kind of `Control` if you mark it with `TargetType="Control"` instead:

```
<Page …>
…
      <Style x:Key="PurpleTiltStyle" TargetType="Control">
…
      <Button Style="{StaticResource PurpleTiltStyle}" Content="1"/>
      <ToggleSwitch Style="{StaticResource PurpleTiltStyle}"/>
      <ProgressRing IsActive="True" Style="{StaticResource PurpleTiltStyle}"/>
…
</Page>
```

The result is shown in Figure 18.2. Note that `ToggleSwitch`'s default appearance enforces a minimum width, so it ignores the `Style`'s `Width` setting.

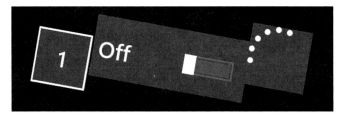

FIGURE 18.2   Heterogeneous controls given the same `Style`

Style Inheritance

The Windows SDK includes a generic.xaml file that contains, among other things, the XAML for Styles defined by the framework. You can locate it in %ProgramFiles(x86)%\ Windows Kits\8.1\Include\WinRT\Xaml\Design\generic.xaml. This file contains many good examples, including some hidden gems you might want to use or tweak for your apps.

The following Style called BaseTextBlockStyle sets several properties to make a TextBlock match the typical style of labels in Windows Store apps (and remove those pesky side bearings, explained in Chapter 12, "Text").

```
<Style x:Key="BaseTextBlockStyle" TargetType="TextBlock">
  <Setter Property="FontSize"
          Value="{ThemeResource ControlContentThemeFontSize}"/>
  <Setter Property="FontFamily"
          Value="{ThemeResource ContentControlThemeFontFamily}"/>
  <Setter Property="TextTrimming" Value="CharacterEllipsis"/>
  <Setter Property="TextWrapping" Value="Wrap"/>
  <Setter Property="Typography.StylisticSet20" Value="True"/>
  <Setter Property="Typography.DiscretionaryLigatures" Value="True"/>
  <Setter Property="Typography.CaseSensitiveForms" Value="True"/>
  <Setter Property="LineHeight" Value="20"/>
  <Setter Property="LineStackingStrategy" Value="BlockLineHeight"/>
  <Setter Property="TextLineBounds" Value="TrimToBaseline"/>
  <Setter Property="OpticalMarginAlignment" Value="TrimSideBearings"/>
</Style>
```

This Style is leveraged by more Styles in generic.xaml, because they can inherit from one another! The following two Styles add an additional property to BaseTextBlockStyle by using the BasedOn property:

```
<!-- BaseTextBlockStyle + FontWeight=SemiBold: -->
<Style x:Key="TitleTextBlockStyle" TargetType="TextBlock"
       BasedOn="{StaticResource BaseTextBlockStyle}">
  <Setter Property="FontWeight" Value="SemiBold"/>
</Style>

<!-- BaseTextBlockStyle + FontWeight=SemiLight: -->
<Style x:Key="BodyTextBlockStyle" TargetType="TextBlock"
       BasedOn="{StaticResource BaseTextBlockStyle}">
  <Setter Property="FontWeight" Value="SemiLight"/>
</Style>
```

The following Style does the same, but also overrides two of the base properties with new values:

```
<!-- BaseTextBlockStyle + FontWeight=Light,
     with different FontSize and LineHeight values: -->
<Style x:Key="HeaderTextBlockStyle" TargetType="TextBlock"
       BasedOn="{StaticResource BaseTextBlockStyle}">
  <Setter Property="FontSize" Value="56"/>
  <Setter Property="FontWeight" Value="Light"/>
  <Setter Property="LineHeight" Value="40"/>
</Style>
```

The XAML designer in Visual Studio supports IntelliSense that presents you with a list of available resources for the current target. This includes in-scope resources defined in your app as well as resources defined by the framework! It also supports the "Go To Definition" command (with the default F12 keyboard shortcut), so you can navigate from the use of a framework-defined Style directly to its definition in generic.xaml! Figure 18.3 shows this IntelliSense in action, displaying framework-defined TextBlock styles.

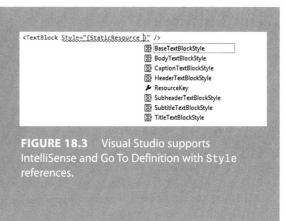

FIGURE 18.3   Visual Studio supports IntelliSense and Go To Definition with Style references.

Implicit Styles

Unlike other objects placed in a Resources collection, you can omit the x:Key *and* x:Name from a Style! If you do this, the target type of the Style (for example, typeof(Button)) is used as the key in the ResourceDictionary. This is handy, because it causes the Style to be implicitly applied to all elements of that target type within the same scope. This is typically called a *typed style* or *implicit style* as opposed to a *named style*.

The scope of a typed Style is determined by the location of the Style resource. For example, it would implicitly apply to all relevant elements in a Page if it's added to the Page's Resources collection or all relevant elements in the app if it's added to Application's Resources collection. The following could be added inside Application.Resources in App.xaml to make the Foreground of every Button red instead of the theme color (white in the dark theme):

```
<!-- Implicit style. Apply this to all Buttons. -->
<Style TargetType="Button">
  <Setter Property="Foreground" Value="Red"/>
</Style>
```

Each individual Button can still override its appearance by explicitly setting a different Style or explicitly setting individual properties. Any Button can restore its default Style by setting its Style property to null.

> (!) **TargetType must match exactly for an implicit style to be applied!**
>
> With a named style, it's okay for the target element to be a subclass of the `TargetType`, but this is not the case for implicit styles. This is done to prevent surprises. For example, maybe you've created a `Style` for all `ToggleButton`s in your application but you don't want it applied to any `CheckBox`es. (`CheckBox` is a subclass of `ToggleButton`.) For controls, this behavior is determined by its `DefaultStyleKey` property. Built-in controls always set this to `typeof(XXX)`, where *XXX* is the control, but custom controls could potentially do something different.

Theme Resources

To handle the light versus dark app themes and high contrast user theme, `ResourceDictionary` has a `ThemeDictionaries` property that can contain separate `ResourceDictionary`s, one for each possible theme. The correct one automatically gets merged into the host `ResourceDictionary` based on the current theme.

These theme dictionaries can contain any resource, such as complete `Styles`, but it's more common for them to contain specific `Brushes` referenced by a single theme-independent `Style`. The following XAML demonstrates:

```
<Page …>
  <Grid Background="{ThemeResource ApplicationPageBackgroundThemeBrush}">
    <StackPanel Margin="20" Orientation="Horizontal">
      <StackPanel.Resources>
        <ResourceDictionary>
          <ResourceDictionary.ThemeDictionaries>
            <ResourceDictionary x:Key="Default">
              <!-- Dark theme resources -->
              <SolidColorBrush x:Key="CustomBackgroundBrush" Color="Purple"/>
              <SolidColorBrush x:Key="CustomForegroundBrush" Color="White"/>
            </ResourceDictionary>
            <ResourceDictionary x:Key="Light">
              <!-- Light theme resources -->
              <SolidColorBrush x:Key="CustomBackgroundBrush" Color="Tan"/>
              <SolidColorBrush x:Key="CustomForegroundBrush" Color="Black"/>
            </ResourceDictionary>
            <ResourceDictionary x:Key="HighContrast">
              <!-- High Contrast theme resources -->
              <SolidColorBrush x:Key="CustomBackgroundBrush"
                Color="{StaticResource SystemColorButtonFaceColor}"/>
              <SolidColorBrush x:Key="CustomForegroundBrush"
                Color="{StaticResource SystemColorButtonTextColor}"/>
            </ResourceDictionary>
          </ResourceDictionary.ThemeDictionaries>
```

```
          <Style x:Key="TiltStyle" TargetType="Button">
            <Setter Property="FontSize" Value="22"/>
            <Setter Property="Background"
                    Value="{ThemeResource CustomBackgroundBrush}"/>
            <Setter Property="Foreground"
                    Value="{ThemeResource CustomForegroundBrush}"/>
            <Setter Property="Height" Value="60"/>
            <Setter Property="RenderTransformOrigin" Value=".5,.5"/>
            <Setter Property="RenderTransform">
              <Setter.Value>
                <RotateTransform Angle="10"/>
              </Setter.Value>
            </Setter>
          </Style>
        </ResourceDictionary>
      </StackPanel.Resources>
      <Button Style="{StaticResource TiltStyle}" Content="Button"/>
    </StackPanel>
  </Grid>
</Page>
```

Notice that the theme-specific resources are referenced with a markup extension called
ThemeResource instead of StaticResource. You can use StaticResource, but then the
reference is never automatically refreshed, even if the user changes the Windows theme.
To make resource references automatically update when a theme change occurs, you
should apply it with ThemeResource. This is why Visual Studio-generated Pages use
ThemeResource when applying the root Grid Background, as seen in the preceding XAML
and throughout this book. (ThemeResource works like WPF's DynamicResource, but its
refresh behavior is limited to theme changes.) ThemeResource is new to Windows 8.1. In
Windows 8, apps generally needed to be restarted to match a theme change.

In the preceding XAML, also notice that in order to set the ResourceDictionary's
ThemeDictionaries property, you must assign the Resources property to an explicit
ResourceDictionary instance rather than using the existing instance. The three valid
keys to use in the ThemeDictionaries collection are Default (or Dark), Light, and
HighContrast. The result of applying this new Style to a Button is shown in Figure 18.4
under each theme.

Dark   Light   High contrast

FIGURE 18.4   The same Button viewed under the three different themes

> Because the high contrast theme has many different variations, including user-customized
> ones, you should use only system-defined color resources in a high contrast theme dictio-
> nary, such as SystemColorButtonFaceColor and SystemColorButtonTextColor. With
> the Windows SDK installed, you can see a list of them by looking at the high contrast theme
> dictionary used by the built-in controls inside %ProgramFiles(x86)%\Windows
> Kits\8.1\Include\WinRT\Xaml\Design\generic.xaml.

More About Resource Lookup

The StaticResource and ThemeResource markup extensions accept a single parameter
representing the key or name of the item in a Resources collection. But, as described
previously, that item doesn't have to be inside the current element's collection. It could
be in any ancestor's collection, or even in the Application-level collection.

StaticResource and ThemeResource walk the element tree to find the item. They first
check the current element's Resources collection. If the item is not found, they check the
parent element, its parent, and so on, until they reach the root element. At that point,
they check the Resources collection on the Application object. (And at each level, any
theme dictionaries are merged in as appropriate.)

Because of this behavior, resources are typically stored in the root element's resource
dictionary or in the Application-level dictionary for maximum sharing potential.
Although each individual resource dictionary requires unique keys, the same key can be
used in multiple collections. The one "closest" to the element accessing the resource will
win because of the way the tree gets walked. This enables you to define one version of a
Style or other resource for the entire app, but then override it with a different one at
arbitrary spots.

ResourceDictionary exposes a MergedDictionaries property that enables you to merge
items defined in separate XAML files that each have a ResourceDictionary as its root

element. For example, Visual Studio 2012 projects for Windows 8 usually contain a StandardStyles.xaml file in a Common directory and have the following XAML inside App.xaml:

```
<Application …>
  <Application.Resources>
    <ResourceDictionary>
      <ResourceDictionary.MergedDictionaries>
        <ResourceDictionary Source="Common/StandardStyles.xaml"/>
      </ResourceDictionary.MergedDictionaries>
      <!-- More items can go here -->
    </ResourceDictionary>
  </Application.Resources>
</Application>
```

The same StandardStyles.xaml file is no longer needed in Visual Studio 2013 projects for Windows 8.1, but the MergedDictionaries mechanism is still useful for your own resources.

> If you define a lot of Styles, using the MergedDictionaries mechanism enables you to factor them into separate, more manageable files.

The CustomResource Markup Extension

You can completely customize the resource lookup process by referencing a resource with a CustomResource markup extension rather than StaticResource or ThemeResource. For this to work, you must define your own class that derives from Windows.UI.Xaml.Resources.CustomXamlResourceLoader, override its single GetResource method, and assign an instance to its static Current property.

Your GetResource method gets called by the XAML parser whenever it encounters a CustomResource markup extension, enabling you to return an arbitrary object that you obtain or create in an arbitrary fashion. Therefore, you must assign CustomXamlResourceLoader.Current before any relevant XAML parsing occurs. You must make this assignment on the UI thread, or rather on *every* UI thread if your app has more than one.

Because GetResource only gets called during relevant XAML parsing, there is no mechanism for dynamic refetching when conditions change, such as a theme change. Therefore, you can think of CustomResource as a "custom *static* resource."

Templates

Controls have many properties you can use to customize their look: Button has configurable Background and Foreground Brushes (which can even be fancy gradients or bitmap-based content), Slider's ticks can be relocated by setting the TickPlacement property, and so on. But you can do only so much with such properties.

A template, on the other hand, allows you to completely replace an element's visual tree with anything you can dream up, while keeping all of its functionality intact. And templates aren't just some add-on mechanism for third parties; the default visuals for every Control are defined in templates (and customized for light versus dark versus high contrast themes). The source code for every control is completely separated from its default visual tree representations (or "visual source code").

Templates and the desire to separate visuals from logic are also the reasons that XAML controls don't expose more simple properties for tweaking their look. For example, you might want to extend the length of the actual "switch" part of a ToggleSwitch, or change the switch color. These relatively simple changes can be accomplished only by defining a new template for ToggleSwitch, however. ToggleSwitch has no SwitchBrush or SwitchColor property because a ToggleSwitch with a custom template might not even have that graphical representation!

There are a few different kinds of templates. What has been described so far is the focus of this section: *control templates*. Control templates are represented by the ControlTemplate class that derives from the FrameworkTemplate base class. The other FrameworkTemplate-derived classes are DataTemplate (described in the next chapter) and ItemsPanelTemplate (described in Chapter 11, "Items Controls").

Introducing Control Templates

ControlTemplate can contain a custom tree of elements that defines a new appearance for any Control. You can attach it to any Control by setting it as a value for its Template property. The following XAML adds a ControlTemplate to one of two regular Buttons, producing the results shown in Figure 18.5:

```
<StackPanel Orientation="Horizontal">
  <!-- A simple Button -->
  <Button Content="Without Custom Template"/>

  <!-- A Button with a custom ControlTemplate -->
  <Button Content="With Custom Template">
    <Button.Template>
      <ControlTemplate>
        <Grid>
          <Ellipse Width="100" Height="100">
            <Ellipse.Fill>
              <LinearGradientBrush StartPoint="0,0" EndPoint="0,1">
                <GradientStop Offset="0" Color="Blue"/>
```

```
                    <GradientStop Offset="1" Color="Red"/>
                </LinearGradientBrush>
            </Ellipse.Fill>
        </Ellipse>
        <Ellipse Width="80" Height="80">
            <Ellipse.Fill>
                <LinearGradientBrush StartPoint="0,0" EndPoint="0,1">
                    <GradientStop Offset="0" Color="White"/>
                    <GradientStop Offset="1" Color="Transparent"/>
                </LinearGradientBrush>
            </Ellipse.Fill>
        </Ellipse>
      </Grid>
    </ControlTemplate>
  </Button.Template>
 </Button>
</StackPanel>
```

FIGURE 18.5   Two Buttons, one with a fancy round custom ControlTemplate

To get this look, the template's visual tree uses two circles (created with Ellipse elements) placed inside a single-cell Grid. Despite the custom look, the resultant Button still has a Click event and all the other programmatic behavior you'd expect. After all, it is still an instance of the Button class!

Of course, directly setting a control's template inline isn't common, just like directly assigning a Style object to a Style property would be strange due to the lack of sharing. You could instead define a template as a resource and then reference it when setting the Template property on multiple controls, just like what is done with Style. However, even more common is to set the Template property *inside* a Style. This is what makes Styles so powerful; they often don't just set simple properties, but Template as well.

Respecting the Target Control's Properties

There's a bit of a problem with custom template in Figure 18.5. Any Button it is applied to will look the same, no matter what the values of its properties are. Most notably, the right Button in Figure 18.5 has "With Custom Template" as its content, but it never gets displayed. If you're creating a control template that's meant to be broadly reusable, you need to do some work to respect various properties of the target control (sometimes called the *templated parent*).

Respecting `ContentControl`'s `Content` Property

The key to inserting property values from the target element inside a control template is a specialized form of data binding. Although data binding is covered in the next chapter, its use in control templates is simple. You can set a property to the markup extension value:

```
{TemplateBinding XXX}
```

where *XXX* is the name of a dependency property on the target control. (That's right, like so many features, this one works only with properties that are dependency properties.) This not only fetches the correct value, but keeps it up-to-date if the value changes.

Note that `TemplateBinding` is a shortcut for the following more complicated data-binding expression that explicitly says to fetch the property value from the templated parent:

```
{Binding RelativeSource={RelativeSource TemplatedParent}, Path=XXX}
```

The difference here is that *XXX* can be a property *path* (the same kind introduced in the preceding chapter) rather than a simple property name.

Given this, somewhere in our custom `Button` template, we could add a `TextBlock` whose `Text` gets set to the target `Button`'s `Content` as follows:

```
<TextBlock Text="{TemplateBinding Button.Content}"/>
```

`ControlTemplate`, like `Style`, has a `TargetType` property that restricts what it can be applied to. If we mark the `ControlTemplate` with `TargetType="Button"` then the setting of the `Text` property can be simplified further:

```
<TextBlock Text="{TemplateBinding Content}"/>
```

Of course, a `Button` can contain nontext `Content`, so using a `TextBlock` to display it creates an artificial limitation. To ensure that all types of `Content` get displayed properly in the template, you can use a generic `ContentControl` instead of a `TextBlock`. The following update does just that. The `ContentControl` is given a `Margin` and wrapped in a `Viewbox` so it's displayed at a reasonable size relative to the rest of the `Button`:

```
<StackPanel Orientation="Horizontal">
  <!-- A simple Button -->
  <Button Content="Without Custom Template"/>

  <!-- A Button with a custom ControlTemplate -->
  <Button Content="With Custom Template">
    <Button.Template>
      <ControlTemplate TargetType="Button">
        <Grid>
          <Ellipse Width="100" Height="100">
```

```
              <Ellipse.Fill>
                <LinearGradientBrush StartPoint="0,0" EndPoint="0,1">
                  <GradientStop Offset="0" Color="Blue"/>
                  <GradientStop Offset="1" Color="Red"/>
                </LinearGradientBrush>
              </Ellipse.Fill>
            </Ellipse>
            <Ellipse Width="80" Height="80">
              <Ellipse.Fill>
                <LinearGradientBrush StartPoint="0,0" EndPoint="0,1">
                  <GradientStop Offset="0" Color="White"/>
                  <GradientStop Offset="1" Color="Transparent"/>
                </LinearGradientBrush>
              </Ellipse.Fill>
            </Ellipse>
            <Viewbox Width="100" Height="100">
              <ContentControl Margin="20" Content="{TemplateBinding Content}"/>
            </Viewbox>
          </Grid>
        </ControlTemplate>
      </Button.Template>
    </Button>
</StackPanel>
```

Figure 18.6 shows the updated result. Figure 18.7 shows the same Button on the right if its Content is replaced with an Image. In both cases, the content is reflected in the new visuals as expected, thanks to the use of ContentControl.

FIGURE 18.6   The same two Buttons from Figure 18.5, but with an updated ControlTemplate for the Button on the right

FIGURE 18.7   If the Button with the updated custom ControlTemplate contains complex content, it still works as expected.

Rather than use a `ContentControl` inside a control template, you should use the lighter-weight `ContentPresenter` element. `ContentPresenter` displays content just like `ContentControl`, but it was designed specifically for use in control templates. `ContentPresenter` is a primitive building block, whereas `ContentControl` is a full-blown control with its own control template (that contains a `ContentPresenter`)!

For Figures 18.5 and 18.6, you can replace this:

```
<ContentControl Margin="20" Content="{TemplateBinding Content}"/>
```

with this:

```
<ContentPresenter Margin="20" Content="{TemplateBinding Content}"/>
```

and get the same result. `ContentPresenter` even has a built-in shortcut; if you omit setting its Content to {TemplateBinding Content}, it implicitly assumes that's what you want. So, you can replace the preceding line of code with the following:

```
<ContentPresenter Margin="20"/>
```

This works only when the control template is given an explicit `TargetType` of `ContentControl` or a `ContentControl`-derived class (such as `Button`).

The remaining templates in this chapter use `ContentPresenter` instead of `ContentControl`, because that's what real-world templates use. Note that `ItemsControl` has a similar companion element called `ItemsPresenter`.

Respecting Other Properties

No matter what type of control you're creating a control template for, there are undoubtedly other properties that should be honored if you want the template to be reusable: `Height` and `Width`, perhaps `Background`, `Padding`, and so on. Some properties (such as `Foreground`, `FontSize`, `FontWeight`, and so on) might automatically inherit their desired values thanks to property value inheritance in the visual tree, but other properties need explicit attention.

Listing 18.1 takes the most recent version of our custom template, morphs it to respect the `Background`, `Padding`, and `Content` properties of the target `Button`, and packages it up in a default `Style` for all `Buttons` on the `Page`. This new version of the template also implicitly respects the size of the target element by *removing* the explicit `Height` and `Width` settings and letting the layout system do its job. Listing 18.1 uses a `ContentPresenter` rather than a `ContentControl`, although both produce the same result.

LISTING 18.1   Updates to the `ControlTemplate` for `Button` That Make It More Reusable

```
<Page …>
  <Page.Resources>
    <Style TargetType="Button">
      <Setter Property="Template">
        <Setter.Value>
          <!-- The new custom template -->
```

LISTING 18.1   Continued

```xml
        <ControlTemplate TargetType="Button">
          <Grid>
            <Ellipse>
              <Ellipse.Fill>
                <LinearGradientBrush StartPoint="0,0" EndPoint="0,1">
                  <GradientStop Offset="0" Color=
                    "{Binding RelativeSource={RelativeSource TemplatedParent},
                              Path=Background.Color}"/>
                  <GradientStop Offset="1" Color="Red"/>
                </LinearGradientBrush>
              </Ellipse.Fill>
            </Ellipse>
            <Ellipse RenderTransformOrigin=".5,.5">
              <Ellipse.RenderTransform>
                <ScaleTransform ScaleX=".8" ScaleY=".8"/>
              </Ellipse.RenderTransform>
              <Ellipse.Fill>
                <LinearGradientBrush StartPoint="0,0" EndPoint="0,1">
                  <GradientStop Offset="0" Color="White"/>
                  <GradientStop Offset="1" Color="Transparent"/>
                </LinearGradientBrush>
              </Ellipse.Fill>
            </Ellipse>
            <Viewbox Width="100" Height="100">
              <ContentPresenter Margin="{TemplateBinding Padding}"/>
            </Viewbox>
          </Grid>
        </ControlTemplate>
      </Setter.Value>
    </Setter>
  </Style>
</Page.Resources>
<Grid Background="{ThemeResource ApplicationPageBackgroundThemeBrush}">
  <StackPanel Orientation="Horizontal" VerticalAlignment="Top" >
    <!-- Three buttons that use the custom template via the default style -->
    <Button Height="100" Width="100" FontSize="80"
            Padding="20" Margin="5">1</Button>
    <Button Height="150" Width="250" FontSize="90" Background="Yellow"
            Padding="20" Margin="5">2</Button>
    <Button Height="200" Width="200" FontSize="100" Background="Purple"
            Padding="20" Margin="5" Foreground="Black" FontStyle="Italic">
            3</Button>
  </StackPanel>
</Grid>
</Page>
```

The target Button's Padding is now used as the ContentPresenter's Margin. It's common to use the element's Padding in a template as the Margin of an inner element. After all, that's basically the definition of Padding!

In addition, a few nonintuitive changes have been made to the template's visual tree to accommodate an externally specified size and Background. We could have used {TemplateBinding Background} as the Fill for the outer Ellipse, giving each Button the flexibility to specify a solid color, a gradient, and so on. But perhaps the "red glow" at the bottom is a characteristic that we'd like to keep consistent wherever the template is used. In other words, we want to replace only the blue part of the gradient with the externally specified Background. However, GradientStop.Color can't be directly set to {TemplateBinding Background} because Color is of type Color, whereas Background is of type Brush! Therefore, the listing uses the more complex Binding syntax instead, which supports referencing the Color subproperty via a property path. (Note that this Binding works only when Background is set to a SolidColorBrush because other Brushes don't have a Color property!)

Both Ellipses (or the parent Grid) could have been given an explicit Height and Width matching those of the target Button by binding to its ActualHeight and ActualWidth properties. Instead, these values are omitted altogether because the root element is implicitly given the templated parent's size anyway. This means that an individual target Button now has the power to make itself look like an ellipse by specifying different values for Width and Height. If we want to preserve the perfect circular look, we can wrap the entire visual tree in a Viewbox.

The final trick used by Listing 18.1 is the ScaleTransform on the inner circle to make it 80% of the size of the outer circle. In previous versions, this transform is unnecessary because both the outer and inner circles have a hard-coded size. But with a dynamic size, ScaleTransform enables us to effectively perform a little math on the size. (If we want a fixed-size difference between the circles, a simple Margin would do the trick.)

Figure 18.8 shows the rendered result of this Page. Each Button has local values for Padding and Content that are explicitly used by the control template. The second two buttons also have explicit Background values used by the top of their gradients, whereas the first Button's gradient picks up the default Transparent Background in its gradient.

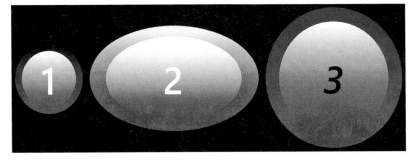

FIGURE 18.8   Buttons from Listing 18.1 that tweak the look of their custom template with local property values

The Buttons' values for Width and Height are implicitly respected by the template, and properties such as FontSize, Foreground, and FontStyle are implicitly picked up by the template's ContentPresenter thanks to property value inheritance. This is why the "3" shows up as black and italic automatically. Note that the size of the font isn't actually reflected in the rendered output because the template wraps the ContentPresenter inside a Viewbox to keep it within the bounds of the outer circle. The Margin specified on each Button is not used by the template, but it still affects the StackPanel layout as usual, giving a little bit of space between each Button.

> Although XAML controls are supposed to be lookless by nature and have an implementation independent of their actual visuals, many controls "cheat" a little and expose a TemplateSettings property with subproperties meant for the templates in their default Styles. These are calculated values that help these templates provide the desired results because they can't do the same type of calculations in XAML. These properties can also be useful for custom templates you create.

Hijacking Existing Properties for New Purposes

Sometimes, you might want to parameterize some aspect of a control template, despite there being no corresponding property on the target control. For example, the template in Listing 18.1 still has a hard-coded red Brush. If you want to keep the gradient standardized and therefore kept inside the template, what can you do to allow individual Buttons to customize both colors? There's no corresponding property already on Button to be set!

One option is to define a custom control. It wouldn't be too much work to write a new class that derives from Button and adds a single BottomColor or BottomBrush property. But that's a bit heavyweight for such a simple task. Another option would be to define several control templates that each uses a different color. But that would be reasonable only if the set of desired colors were small and known. Yet another option would be to define an appropriate attached property somewhere, perhaps on a utility class that already exists.

Instead, what many people resort to is a devious little hack known as *hijacking* a dependency property. This involves looking at the target control for any dependency properties of the desired type to see whether you can leverage them in an unintended way. For example, all Controls have three properties of type Brush: Background, Foreground, and BorderBrush. Because Background and Foreground already play important roles in Listing 18.1, neither one would be appropriate to use for the bottom color. (There would be no way to set it independently of the other two.) But BorderBrush is a different story. It's completely unused by the template in Listing 18.1, so why not use that?

There is no reason not to use it, other than the fact that it makes the usage of the template confusing and less readable. Nevertheless, here's how you could update the outer Ellipse's LinearGradientBrush inside the control template to hijack BorderBrush:

```
<LinearGradientBrush StartPoint="0,0" EndPoint="0,1">
  <GradientStop Offset="0" Color=
                "{Binding RelativeSource={RelativeSource TemplatedParent},
                          Path=Background.Color}"/>
  <GradientStop Offset="1" Color=
                "{Binding RelativeSource={RelativeSource TemplatedParent},
                          Path=BorderBrush.Color}"/>
</LinearGradientBrush>
```

If the target control doesn't have an appropriate property, you might even be able to hijack an attached property from an unrelated element! If this hack leaves a bad taste in your mouth, then by all means use an alternative approach.

Setting `Template` Inside a `Style`

It's worth emphasizing why setting the `Template` property inside a `Style` is so powerful. It has two important advantages:

→ It gives you the effect of default templates when combined with an implicit `Style`, as leveraged in Listing 18.1. Independent of this, there is no such thing as a default control template.

→ It enables you to provide default yet overridable property values that control the look of the template. In other words, it enables you to respect the templated parent's properties but still provide your own default values.

The final point is important. When Listing 18.1 changed the custom template's top gradient color from a hard-coded `Blue` to pick up the `Button`'s `Background.Color`, the default value became `Transparent`, as seen with the first `Button` in Figure 18.8. If we want the default color to still be `Blue`, but still enable individual `Button`s to change it, then we can accomplish this in the `Style` as follows:

```
<Style TargetType="Button">
  <Setter Property="Background" Value="Blue"/>
  <Setter Property="Template">
    <Setter.Value>
      <ControlTemplate TargetType="Button">
        … The same template from Listing 18.1 …
      </ControlTemplate>
    </Setter.Value>
  </Setter>
</Style>
```

The same could be done if we make the change to bind the bottom gradient color to `BorderBrush` but keep the default color as red:

```
<Setter Property="BorderBrush" Value="Red"/>
```

> **How do I make small tweaks to an existing control template rather than create a brand-new one from scratch?**
>
> There is no mechanism for tweaking existing templates (like Style's BasedOn). Instead, you must retrieve a XAML representation for any existing Style or template, modify it, and then apply it as a brand-new Style or template. In fact, even if you want to create a completely different look, the best way to become familiar with how to design robust control templates is to look at the built-in control templates used by default Styles.
>
> To obtain the "visual source code" in XAML for a built-in control template, you can do one of the following:
>
> → With the Windows SDK installed, you can look inside %ProgramFiles(x86)%\Windows Kits\8.1\Include\WinRT\Xaml\Design\generic.xaml.
>
> → Create the appropriate control in Blend or the Visual Studio XAML designer, right click and then choose Edit Template, Edit a Copy… to get a copy of its style pasted into your XAML.
>
> You can learn some neat techniques or find fascinating implementation details. For example, here is how the control template inside Button's default style represents the dotted focus rectangle that appears when giving one focus with the Tab key:
>
> ```
> <Grid>
>   ...
>   <Rectangle x:Name="FocusVisualWhite" IsHitTestVisible="False" Opacity="0"
>     StrokeDashOffset="1.5" StrokeEndLineCap="Square" StrokeDashArray="1,1"
>     Stroke="{StaticResource FocusVisualWhiteStrokeThemeBrush}"/>
>   <Rectangle x:Name="FocusVisualBlack" IsHitTestVisible="False" Opacity="0"
>     StrokeDashOffset="0.5" StrokeEndLineCap="Square" StrokeDashArray="1,1"
>     Stroke="{StaticResource FocusVisualBlackStrokeThemeBruch}"/>
> </Grid>
> ```
>
> It's simply two overlaid dotted Rectangle elements!
>
> If you look at the default control templates for ListViewItem and GridViewItem, you can see that they use a single ListViewItemPresenter and GridViewItemPresenter element, respectively. This is a Windows 8.1 performance optimization that improves ListView/GridView load time by up to 26% compared to Windows 8. Rather than using a complex tree of elements, these single items use fast drawing primitives to do everything required. They expose a few properties (like SelectionBackground and SelectionCheckMarkVisualEnabled) so you can perform basic tweaks without losing all the performance optimizations.
>
> In generic.xaml, you can also see the long list of theme-specific resources in the three theme dictionaries.

Visual States

You might have noticed that something is still missing from all versions of the custom Button template used in the preceding section. None of them have any visual reaction to being pressed, hovered over, or disabled. This might not be *that* big of a deal, depending on their usage, but imagine applying the same template to CheckBox or ToggleButton. (This can be done by changing the TargetType to ButtonBase or a more specific type.) Because the template doesn't show different visuals for the Checked versus Unchecked versus Indeterminate states, it's a pretty lousy template for these controls!

Therefore, a good control template must consider all possible visual states relevant for the target control and handle them appropriately. To do this, there are two questions we need to answer:

→ How do I find out all the visual states that need to be respected? Each control has a large number of properties, and it might not always be clear which ones are visually important.

→ How do I make a control template respond to such state changes?

It turns out that controls have a formal notion of visual states, represented by a `VisualState` class. A control can specify any number of these states, and then control templates can leverage these. Blend even provides special support for managing them when authoring a template via its "States" tool window.

Therefore, the answer to the first question is to look at the relevant template inside `%ProgramFiles(x86)%\Windows Kits\8.1\Include\WinRT\Xaml\Design\generic.xaml` (for built-in controls), or use Blend or Visual Studio to create a copy of the template, or use Blend's States tool window. The answer to the second question is the topic of the rest of this section.

Responding to Visual State Changes

The states defined by each control are grouped into mutually exclusive *state groups*. For example, `Button` has four states in a group called `CommonStates`—`Normal`, `PointerOver`, `Pressed`, and `Disabled`—and three states in a group called `FocusStates`—`Unfocused`, `Focused`, and `PointerFocused`. At any time, `Button` is in one state from every group, so it is `Normal` and `Unfocused` by default. This grouping mechanism exists to avoid a long list of states meant to cover every combination of independent properties (such as `NormalUnfocused`, `NormalFocused`, `PointerOverUnfocused`, `PointerOverFocused`, and so on).

A template for `Button` can express modifications to make to its elements when transitioning to each state. This is done by assigning a `VisualStateManager.VisualStateGroups` attached property to the root element inside the control template. This property must be set to a collection of `VisualStateGroup` objects, each with a collection of `VisualStates`. These `VisualStateGroups` and `VisualStates` must have names that match what the target control supports. Only the control author can make up new groups and states; the control *template* author can react only to what's there.

The contents of each `VisualState` describes what happens to the visuals when the control transitions to that state. Quite appropriately, the way this is done is with none other than the familiar `Storyboards` from the preceding chapter! The best way to get a grasp on how visual states work is to see an example. Listing 18.2 contains the real control template from `Button`'s default `Style`, annotated with a few comments. The core part of the template is quite simple: a `Grid` containing a `Border` containing a `ContentPresenter`, with two overlaid `Rectangles` to create the dotted focus rectangle. Most of the template manages the transitions between each of the four `CommonStates` and each of the three `FocusStates`.

LISTING 18.2   Button's Control Template from its Default Style

```
<ControlTemplate TargetType="Button">
  <Grid>
    <!-- Attached to the root element, as required: -->
    <VisualStateManager.VisualStateGroups>
      <!-- Group #1 -->
      <VisualStateGroup x:Name="CommonStates">
        <!-- Nothing to do when transitioning to Normal: -->
        <VisualState x:Name="Normal"/>
        <VisualState x:Name="PointerOver">
          <!-- Instantly change the Background and Foreground: -->
          <Storyboard>
            <ObjectAnimationUsingKeyFrames Storyboard.TargetProperty="Background"
                                           Storyboard.TargetName="Border">
              <DiscreteObjectKeyFrame KeyTime="0"
                Value="{ThemeResource ButtonPointerOverBackgroundThemeBrush}"/>
            </ObjectAnimationUsingKeyFrames>
            <ObjectAnimationUsingKeyFrames Storyboard.TargetProperty="Foreground"
                Storyboard.TargetName="ContentPresenter">
              <DiscreteObjectKeyFrame KeyTime="0"
                Value="{ThemeResource ButtonPointerOverForegroundThemeBrush}"/>
            </ObjectAnimationUsingKeyFrames>
          </Storyboard>
        </VisualState>
        <VisualState x:Name="Pressed">
          <!-- Instantly change the Background and Foreground: -->
          <Storyboard>
            <ObjectAnimationUsingKeyFrames Storyboard.TargetProperty="Background"
                                           Storyboard.TargetName="Border">
              <DiscreteObjectKeyFrame KeyTime="0"
                Value="{ThemeResource ButtonPressedBackgroundThemeBrush}"/>
            </ObjectAnimationUsingKeyFrames>
            <ObjectAnimationUsingKeyFrames Storyboard.TargetProperty="Foreground"
                Storyboard.TargetName="ContentPresenter">
              <DiscreteObjectKeyFrame KeyTime="0"
                Value="{ThemeResource ButtonPressedForegroundThemeBrush}"/>
            </ObjectAnimationUsingKeyFrames>
          </Storyboard>
        </VisualState>
        <VisualState x:Name="Disabled">
          <!-- Instantly change the Background, Border, and Foreground: -->
          <Storyboard>
            <ObjectAnimationUsingKeyFrames Storyboard.TargetProperty="Background"
                                           Storyboard.TargetName="Border">
              <DiscreteObjectKeyFrame KeyTime="0"
```

LISTING 18.2   Continued

```xml
                        Value="{ThemeResource ButtonDisabledBackgroundThemeBrush}"/>
            </ObjectAnimationUsingKeyFrames>
            <ObjectAnimationUsingKeyFrames Storyboard.TargetProperty="BorderBrush"
                                           Storyboard.TargetName="Border">
              <DiscreteObjectKeyFrame KeyTime="0"
                Value="{ThemeResource ButtonDisabledBorderThemeBrush}"/>
            </ObjectAnimationUsingKeyFrames>
            <ObjectAnimationUsingKeyFrames Storyboard.TargetProperty="Foreground"
                Storyboard.TargetName="ContentPresenter">
              <DiscreteObjectKeyFrame KeyTime="0"
                Value="{ThemeResource ButtonDisabledForegroundThemeBrush}"/>
            </ObjectAnimationUsingKeyFrames>
          </Storyboard>
        </VisualState>
      </VisualStateGroup>

      <!-- Group #2 -->
      <VisualStateGroup x:Name="FocusStates">
        <!-- Nothing to do when transitioning to Unfocused: -->
        <VisualState x:Name="Unfocused"/>
        <VisualState x:Name="Focused">
          <!-- Instantly show the two focus Rectangles: -->
          <Storyboard>
            <DoubleAnimation Duration="0" To="1"
             Storyboard.TargetProperty="Opacity"
             Storyboard.TargetName="FocusVisualWhite"/>
            <DoubleAnimation Duration="0" To="1"
             Storyboard.TargetProperty="Opacity"
             Storyboard.TargetName="FocusVisualBlack"/>
          </Storyboard>
        </VisualState>
        <!-- Nothing to do when transitioning to PointerFocused: -->
        <VisualState x:Name="PointerFocused"/>
      </VisualStateGroup>
    </VisualStateManager.VisualStateGroups>

    <!-- The actual elements in the root Grid -->
    <Border x:Name="Border" BorderBrush="{TemplateBinding BorderBrush}"
            BorderThickness="{TemplateBinding BorderThickness}"
            Background="{TemplateBinding Background}" Margin="3">
      <!-- Respect a LOT of properties in the ContentPresenter: -->
      <ContentPresenter x:Name="ContentPresenter"
        ContentTemplate="{TemplateBinding ContentTemplate}"
        ContentTransitions="{TemplateBinding ContentTransitions}"
```

LISTING 18.2   Continued

```
        Content="{TemplateBinding Content}"
        HorizontalAlignment="{TemplateBinding HorizontalContentAlignment}"
        Margin="{TemplateBinding Padding}"
        VerticalAlignment="{TemplateBinding VerticalContentAlignment}"
        AutomationProperties.AccessibilityView="Raw"/>
    </Border>
    <Rectangle x:Name="FocusVisualWhite" IsHitTestVisible="False" Opacity="0"
      StrokeDashOffset="1.5" StrokeEndLineCap="Square" StrokeDashArray="1,1"
      Stroke="{ThemeResource FocusVisualWhiteStrokeThemeBrush}"/>
    <Rectangle x:Name="FocusVisualBlack" IsHitTestVisible="False" Opacity="0"
      StrokeDashOffset="0.5" StrokeEndLineCap="Square" StrokeDashArray="1,1"
      Stroke="{ThemeResource FocusVisualBlackStrokeThemeBrush}"/>
  </Grid>
</ControlTemplate>
```

Controls such as `Button` have internal logic to transition to the named states that they define by calling a static `VisualStateManager.GoToState` method. This triggers that transition that starts any relevant `Storyboard`s in the control template.

There are two big takeaways from this listing. One is that although you can perform animated transitions from one state to another, `Button`'s default template chooses to do instantaneous transitions. It accomplishes this with single-keyframe `ObjectAnimationUsingKeyFrames` "animations" and `DoubleAnimation`s with `Duration`s of 0. These are both ways to effectively shoehorn simple property sets into the `Storyboard` model.

The other takeaway is that you don't need to bother "undoing" your animations when transitioning to a different state. The relevant `Storyboard`s are automatically stopped, which instantly removes the result of the previous animations. For example, although the transition to `Button`'s `Focused` state changes the `Opacity` of the two `Rectangle`s to 1, no animations are needed in the other two states to animate it back to 0.

Visual Transitions

Let's say you start with `Button`'s default template but morph it such that the two focus `Rectangle`s fade in gradually when the control transitions to the `Focused` state. In this case, the harsh stopping of these animations when transitioning out of `Focused` probably won't be satisfactory. However, because `Unfocused` and `PointerFocused` are left empty, the result is an instant jump to the default visual behavior. This could be solved by adding `Storyboard`s with explicit animations to the default values, but one would have to be added for every property animated by any other state in the group in order to account for all possible transitions.

Fortunately, `VisualStateGroup` has a much better solution for this. It defines a `Transitions` property that can be set to one or more `VisualTransition` objects that can automatically generate appropriate animations to smooth the transition between any state. VisualTransition has To and From string properties that can be set to the names of the source and target states. You can omit both properties to make it apply to all transitions, specify only a To to make it apply to all transitions to that state, and so on. When transitioning from one state to another, the visual state manager chooses the most specific VisualTransition that matches the transition. The order of precedence is as follows:

1. A VisualTransition with matching To and From

2. A VisualTransition with a matching To and no explicit From

3. A VisualTransition with a matching From and no explicit To

4. The default VisualTransition, with no To or From specified

If VisualStateGroup's Transitions property isn't set, the default transition between any states is a zero-duration animation.

To specify the characteristics of a VisualTransition, you can set its GeneratedDuration property to control the duration of the generated linear animation. You can also set its GeneratedEasingFunction property to get a nonlinear animation between states. For the most customization, you can even set its Storyboard property to a Storyboard with arbitrary custom animations.

> Visual transitions and VisualStateGroup's Transitions property are unrelated to the theme transitions (and corresponding Transitions properties) discussed in the preceding chapter. They share unfortunately similar names.

> **Animations generated by VisualTransitions are independent only!**
>
> This means that if you change a Color in one VisualState then apply a VisualTransition with a GeneratedDuration longer than zero, it will have no effect on the Color change. It will still happen instantaneously. The way to make this work is to give the relevant state transitions an explicit VisualTransition whose Storyboard property is set to a Storyboard containing an explicitly dependent animation. Listing 18.3 contains an example of this.

Listing 18.3 updates our custom Button template from Listing 18.1 in order to take advantage of visual states. The red part of the gradient now turns yellow when the pointer hovers over it, pressing the Button makes it shrink, disabling it turns the red or yellow to gray, and giving it focus makes it bounce continuously.

LISTING 18.3   The `ControlTemplate` for `Button` from Listing 18.1, Enhanced with Visual States

```
<Page ...>
  <Page.Resources>
    <Style TargetType="Button">
      <Setter Property="Template">
        <Setter.Value>
          <!-- The custom template -->
          <ControlTemplate TargetType="Button">
            <Grid RenderTransformOrigin=".5,.5">

              <VisualStateManager.VisualStateGroups>
                <!-- Group #1: -->
                <VisualStateGroup x:Name="CommonStates">
                  <!-- Transitions for Group #1: -->
                  <VisualStateGroup.Transitions>
                    <!-- Manually handle the transition to/from PointerOver
                         because an explicit dependent animation is needed: -->
                    <VisualTransition From="PointerOver">
                      <VisualTransition.Storyboard>
                        <Storyboard TargetName="glow" TargetProperty="Color">
                          <ColorAnimation From="Yellow" Duration="0:0:.4"
                                          EnableDependentAnimation="True"/>
                        </Storyboard>
                      </VisualTransition.Storyboard>
                    </VisualTransition>
                    <VisualTransition To="PointerOver">
                      <VisualTransition.Storyboard>
                        <Storyboard TargetName="glow" TargetProperty="Color">
                          <ColorAnimation To="Yellow" Duration="0:0:.4"
                                          EnableDependentAnimation="True"/>
                        </Storyboard>
                      </VisualTransition.Storyboard>
                    </VisualTransition>
                    <!-- Make transitions to/from Pressed instantaneous: -->
                    <VisualTransition To="Pressed" GeneratedDuration="0"/>
                    <VisualTransition From="Pressed" To="PointerOver"
                                      GeneratedDuration="0"/>
                  </VisualStateGroup.Transitions>

                  <!-- States for Group #1: -->
                  <VisualState x:Name="Normal"/>
                  <VisualState x:Name="PointerOver">
                    <!-- Still needed to make sure the yellow "sticks" after
                         the explicit transition: -->
                    <Storyboard TargetName="glow" TargetProperty="Color">
```

LISTING 18.3   Continued

```xml
            <ColorAnimation To="Yellow" Duration="0"/>
          </Storyboard>
        </VisualState>
        <VisualState x:Name="Pressed">
          <!-- "Push in" the visuals: -->
          <Storyboard TargetName="rootTransform">
            <DoubleAnimation To=".9" Storyboard.TargetProperty="ScaleX"
                             Duration="0"/>
            <DoubleAnimation Storyboard.TargetProperty="ScaleY" To=".9"
                             Duration="0"/>
          </Storyboard>
        </VisualState>
        <VisualState x:Name="Disabled">
          <!-- Just a simple change to gray: -->
          <Storyboard TargetName="glow" TargetProperty="Color">
            <ColorAnimation To="Gray" Duration="0"/>
          </Storyboard>
        </VisualState>
      </VisualStateGroup>

      <!-- Group #2 -->
      <VisualStateGroup x:Name="FocusStates">

        <!-- Transitions for Group #2: -->
        <VisualStateGroup.Transitions>
          <VisualTransition From="Focused">
            <VisualTransition.Storyboard>
              <!-- Gracefully undo the Focused animation: -->
              <Storyboard TargetName="rootTransform"
                          TargetProperty="TranslateY">
                <DoubleAnimation To="0" Duration="0:0:.4">
                  <DoubleAnimation.EasingFunction>
                    <QuadraticEase/>
                  </DoubleAnimation.EasingFunction>
                </DoubleAnimation>
              </Storyboard>
            </VisualTransition.Storyboard>
          </VisualTransition>
        </VisualStateGroup.Transitions>

        <!-- States for Group #2: -->
        <VisualState x:Name="Unfocused"/>
        <VisualState x:Name="Focused">
          <!-- A continuous animation: -->
          <Storyboard TargetName="rootTransform"
```

LISTING 18.3   Continued

```
                         TargetProperty="TranslateY">
            <DoubleAnimation To="-20" RepeatBehavior="Forever"
                            AutoReverse="True" Duration="0:0:.4">
              <DoubleAnimation.EasingFunction>
                <QuadraticEase/>
              </DoubleAnimation.EasingFunction>
            </DoubleAnimation>
          </Storyboard>
        </VisualState>
        <VisualState x:Name="PointerFocused"/>
      </VisualStateGroup>
    </VisualStateManager.VisualStateGroups>

    <!-- Used for Pressed and Focused animations: -->
    <Grid.RenderTransform>
      <CompositeTransform x:Name="rootTransform"/>
    </Grid.RenderTransform>

    <Ellipse>
      <Ellipse.Fill>
        <LinearGradientBrush StartPoint="0,0" EndPoint="0,1">
          <GradientStop Offset="0" Color=
            "{Binding RelativeSource={RelativeSource TemplatedParent},
                      Path=Background.Color}"/>
          <GradientStop x:Name="glow" Offset="1" Color="Red"/>
        </LinearGradientBrush>
      </Ellipse.Fill>
    </Ellipse>
    <Ellipse RenderTransformOrigin=".5,.5">
      <Ellipse.RenderTransform>
        <ScaleTransform ScaleX=".8" ScaleY=".8"/>
      </Ellipse.RenderTransform>
      <Ellipse.Fill>
        <LinearGradientBrush StartPoint="0,0" EndPoint="0,1">
          <GradientStop Offset="0" Color="White"/>
          <GradientStop Offset="1" Color="Transparent"/>
        </LinearGradientBrush>
      </Ellipse.Fill>
    </Ellipse>
    <Viewbox Width="100" Height="100">
      <ContentPresenter Margin="{TemplateBinding Padding}"/>
    </Viewbox>
  </Grid>
</ControlTemplate>
</Setter.Value>
```

LISTING 18.3   Continued

```
      </Setter>
    </Style>
  </Page.Resources>

  …
</Page>
```

The `Grid` is now marked with a centered `RenderTransformOrigin` and is given a `CompositeTransform` so the animations can act appropriately. The red part of the gradient is also given a name (`glow`) so animations can reference it.

To smoothly animate the glow with a dependent animation, the transitions to/from the `PointerOver` state are given explicit `Storyboards`. Note that the `PointerOver` state still needs its own `Storyboard` for "steady state" of remaining yellow while hovering, but that animation can have a `Duration` of `0` (and therefore doesn't need to be marked with `EnableDependentAnimation`).

> The easiest way to manage `VisualStates` and the transitions between them is to give the animations inside each `VisualState` a `Duration` of `0`—making the animations more like `Setters` than real animations—and specify the desired animations between states (with non-zero `Durations`) via `VisualStateGroup`'s `VisualTransitions` property. An exception to this would be states with continual animations, such as the bouncing done in the `Focused` state in Listing 18.3.

Figure 18.9 shows the effect of some of these animations on various visual states.

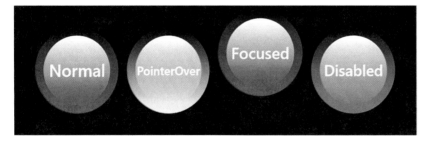

FIGURE 18.9   Four distinct visual effects from Listing 18.3

Named Elements in Templates

Outside a template, naming an element with `x:Name` generates a field for programmatic access. This is not the case when using `x:Name` inside a template, however, as with `glow` in Listing 18.3. This is because a template can be applied to multiple elements in the same scope. The main purpose of naming elements in a template is for referencing them from animations.

Summary

The combination of Styles, templates, and visual states is powerful and often confusing to someone learning about XAML. Adding to the confusion is the fact that Styles can (and often do) contain templates, and elements in templates all have their own Styles (whether marked explicitly or inherited implicitly).

These mechanisms are so powerful, in fact, that often you can restyle an existing control as an alternative to writing your own custom control. This is great news, because restyling an existing control is usually significantly easier than writing a new control, and it can perhaps be done entirely by a graphic designer rather than a programmer. Chapter 27, "Custom Controls and Components," explains how to write a custom control.

Chapter 19

DATA BINDING

No matter where data originally comes from (and the options for this are described in the next chapter), you can attach its in-memory representation to various controls by leveraging data binding. Instead of iterating through a data source and manually adding a ListViewItem to a ListView for each one, for example, it would be nice to just say, "Hey, ListView! Get your items from over here. And keep them up to date, please. Oh yeah, and format them to look like this." Data binding enables this and much more.

Introducing Binding

The key to data binding is a Binding markup extension that "glues" two properties together and keeps a channel of communication open between them. You can set up a Binding once and then have it do all the synchronization work for the remainder of the app's lifetime.

Imagine that you have a TextBlock with text that you want to automatically update as the user types in a TextBox, such as the following:

```
<StackPanel Orientation="Horizontal">
  <!-- The user should type a username here -->
  <TextBox Name="textBox"
           TextChanged="TextBox_TextChanged"/>
  <!-- This displays, "Hi, username!" -->
  <TextBlock>
    <Run>Hi, </Run>
    <Run x:Name="run"/>
    <Run>!</Run>
  </TextBlock>
</StackPanel>
```

This can be accomplished by updating the named Run's text manually whenever the TextBox's TextChanged event is raised:

```
void TextBox_TextChanged(object sender, TextChangedEventArgs e)
{
  this.run.Text = this.textBox.Text;
}
```

By using a Binding object instead, you can remove this event handler and replace it with the following one-time initialization:

```
<StackPanel Orientation="Horizontal">
  <!-- The user should type a username here -->
  <TextBox Name="textBox"/>
  <!-- This displays, "Hi, username!" -->
  <TextBlock>
    <Run>Hi, </Run>
    <Run Text="{Binding ElementName=textBox, Path=Text}"/>
    <Run>!</Run>
  </TextBlock>
</StackPanel>
```

Binding has the notion of a *source* property and a *target* property. The source property (textBox.Text, in this case) is specified in two pieces with ElementName and Path (which is a property path). The target property is the Run's Text property, because that is the property assigned to a Binding.

With this change, the Run's Text property updates automatically as the TextBox's Text property changes. Note that the Run no longer needs an x:Name because nobody needs to reference it anymore.

> The Binding markup extension supports specifying Path as a positional parameter, so you can shorten the preceding Binding as follows:
>
> ```
> <Run Text="{Binding Text, ElementName=textBox}"/>
> ```

> You can use Binding's FallbackValue property to swap in a pseudo-source value to use for data binding when a real value is unable to be retrieved. Similarly, you can use TargetNullValue to swap in a value when the source value is null. For example, this TextBlock shows the message "Nothing is selected." rather than an empty string when the source value is null:
>
> ```
> <TextBlock Text="{Binding … TargetNullValue=Nothing is selected.}" …/>
> ```
>
> Using TargetNullValue can also help in more advanced scenarios where objects do not tolerate having their properties set to null.

•••

Binding's RelativeSource

Besides ElementName, another way to specify the source object is to use Binding's RelativeSource property. The property is of type RelativeSource, which also happens to be a markup extension. Here are the two ways RelativeSource can be used:

→ To make the source element equal the target element:

```
{Binding RelativeSource={RelativeSource Self}, Path=…}
```

→ To make the source element equal the target element's templated parent (as shown in the preceding chapter):

```
{Binding RelativeSource={RelativeSource TemplatedParent}, Path=…}
```

Using RelativeSource with the mode Self is handy for binding one property of an element to another without having to give the element a name. An interesting example is the following ProgressBar, whose ToolTip is bound to its own value:

```
<ProgressBar ToolTipService.ToolTip=
  "{Binding RelativeSource={RelativeSource Self}, Path=Value}"/>
```

Using Binding in C#

The following translates the use of the Binding markup extension to C#, assuming the relevant Run is given the name run:

```
Binding binding = new Binding();
// Set source object
binding.Source = this.textBox;
// Set source property
binding.Path = new PropertyPath("Text");
// Attach to target property
this.run.SetBinding(Run.TextProperty, binding);
```

In C#, you can't set run's Text property to a Binding instance, because Text must be a string! The magic that is abstracted away by the markup extension in XAML is simply a call to run's SetBinding method (inherited from FrameworkElement) that identifies which property to associate with the binding using the relevant static DependencyProperty property. This makes it clear that for a property to be a target of data binding, it must be a dependency property.

Notice that this uses Binding's Source property to set the source object rather than ElementName. Both are valid in either context, but it's most natural to use ElementName in XAML and Source in C#.

> There are two ways to set Binding in C#. One is to call the SetBinding instance method on the relevant FrameworkElement. The other is to call the SetBinding static method on a class called BindingOperations. You pass this method the same objects you would pass to the instance method, but it has an additional first parameter that represents the target object. The benefit of the static method is that the first parameter is defined as a DependencyObject, so it enables data binding on objects that don't derive from FrameworkElement.

Binding to Plain Properties

Although the target property must be a dependency property, the source property can be any (public) property. This can be demonstrated with a slight twist to the previous example. In this case, the TextBlock next to the TextBox displays the number of characters in its text by binding to the simple Length property on the string Text property:

```
<StackPanel Orientation="Horizontal">
  <!-- The user can type anything here -->
  <TextBox Name="textBox"/>
  <!-- This displays the # of characters -->
  <TextBlock>
    <Run>Characters used: </Run>
    <Run Text="{Binding ElementName=textBox, Path=Text.Length}"/>
  </TextBlock>
</StackPanel>
```

In this case, the character count automatically stays up-to-date, but that's only because the parent Text property is a dependency property, and its value changes whenever Length changes. In general, the target is *not* notified about changes in the source when the source property is a plain property. As discussed in Chapter 5, "Interactivity," dependency properties have plumbing for change notification built in. This facility is the key to the ability to keep the target property and source property in sync.

If you want to bind to an arbitrary plain property you have defined that does not have the same kind of relationship with a dependency property, you should do one of two things if you want automatic updates:

→ Redefine it as a dependency property.

→ Make the source object implement the System.ComponentModel.INotifyPropertyChanged interface, which has a single PropertyChanged event.

Customizing the Data Flow

In the examples so far, data updates flow from the source to the target. But, in some cases, the target property can be directly changed by users, and it would be useful to support the flowing of such changes back to the source. Indeed, Binding supports this (and more) via its Mode property, which can be set to one of the following values of the BindingMode enumeration:

→ **OneWay**—The target is updated whenever the source changes.

→ **TwoWay**—A change to either the target or source updates the other.

→ **OneTime**—This works just like OneWay, except changes to the source are not reflected at the target. The target retains a snapshot of the source at the time the Binding is initiated.

TwoWay binding is appropriate for editable forms in which you might have TextBoxes that get filled with data that the user is allowed to change. In fact, whereas most dependency properties default to OneWay binding, dependency properties such as TextBox.Text default to TwoWay binding. This can be demonstrated with the following trivial XAML:

```
<StackPanel>
  <TextBox Name="textBox1" Text="{Binding ElementName=textBox2, Path=Text}"/>
  <TextBox Name="textBox2" Text="{Binding ElementName=textBox1, Path=Text}"/>
</StackPanel>
```

The text in these two TextBoxes always remains in sync. You can type/paste in the first one and watch the second one change, or vice versa.

When using TwoWay binding, you might want to control exactly when the source gets updated. For example, when a user types in a TwoWay data-bound TextBox, do you want the source to be updated with each keystroke, or only when the user is done typing? Binding enables you to control such behavior with its UpdateSourceTrigger property. This can be set to either PropertyChanged or Explicit. (There's also a Default value, but it acts no different than PropertyChanged.) These have the following meanings:

→ **PropertyChanged**—The source is updated whenever the target property value changes.

→ **Explicit**—The source is updated only when you make an explicit call to BindingExpression.UpdateSource. You can get an instance of BindingExpression by calling GetBindingExpression on any FrameworkElement.

To make a TextBox update its source only when the user is done typing, you would have to choose Explicit, then call UpdateSource in response to an appropriate event, such as the TextBox losing focus.

Sharing the Source with DataContext

It's common for many elements in the same user interface to bind to the same source object (different source *properties*, but the same source *object*). For this reason, Binding supports an implicit data source rather than explicitly marking every one with a Source, RelativeSource, or ElementName. This implicit data source is also known as a *data context*.

To designate a source object as a data context, you find a common parent element and set its `DataContext` property to the source object. (All `FrameworkElements` have this `DataContext` property of type `Object`.) When the system encounters a `Binding` without an explicit source object, it traverses up the element tree until it finds a non-`null` `DataContext`.

Therefore, you can use `DataContext` as follows to make both of the following `TextBlocks` bind to the same string:

```
<StackPanel DataContext="A DataContext string">
  <TextBlock>
    <Run># of characters: </Run>
    <!-- Bind to string's Length property -->
    <Run Text="{Binding Length}"/>
  </TextBlock>
  <TextBlock>
    <Run>The string is: </Run>
    <!-- Bind to the string itself -->
    <Run Text="{Binding}"/>
  </TextBlock>
</StackPanel>
```

The resulting `TextBlocks` display the following:

```
# of characters: 20
The string is: A DataContext string
```

This XAML takes advantage of dropping the "Path=" and specifying the path as a positional parameter in the markup extension. Note the odd-looking "empty" {Binding}. When no `Path` is specified, the binding is done to the entire source object. Chapter 12, "Text," has an example of this with `RichTextBlock`, whose `OverflowContentTarget` property needs to be set to another `UIElement`:

```
<RichTextBlock Foreground="Black" FontSize="20" FontFamily="Cambria"
               Margin="12" OverflowContentTarget="{Binding ElementName=o1}">
  …
</RichTextBlock>
```

Because `DataContext` is a simple property, it's easy to set from C#. This is the way it is usually set, rather than in XAML, because it's the most convenient for complex or dynamic objects. Often `DataContext` is set on a `Page`, and all `Bindings` within the `Page` share that source object unless `DataContext` is overridden lower in the tree (or any `Bindings` explicitly specify a source).

Binding to a Collection

One of the most common uses of data binding is to bind the items of an items control to a collection. You might try to assign a `Binding` to an items control's `Items` property, but, alas, `Items` is not a dependency property. All items controls expose a separate `Items`**Source** dependency property that exists specifically for data binding. Therefore, if you have a `Page` as follows:

```
<Page …>
  <Grid Background="{ThemeResource ApplicationPageBackgroundThemeBrush}">
    <GridView ItemsSource="{Binding}"/>
  </Grid>
</Page>
```

with the following code-behind that sets the data context to a simple array:

```
using Windows.UI.Xaml.Controls;

namespace Chapter19
{
  public sealed partial class MainPage : Page
  {
    public MainPage()
    {
      InitializeComponent();
      this.DataContext = new string[] { "one", "two", "three" };
    }
  }
}
```

then you get the three-item `GridView` pictured in Figure 19.1.

Figure 19.2 shows what happens if you change the data context to the set of files in the user's Pictures Library (which requires the Pictures Library capability):

FIGURE 19.1   A `GridView` whose data source is a simple three-element array

```
using System;
using System.Threading.Tasks;
using Windows.Storage;
using Windows.UI.Xaml.Controls;

namespace Chapter19
{
  public sealed partial class MainPage : Page
  {
    public MainPage()
    {
      InitializeComponent();
      SetDataContext();
    }
```

```
  async Task SetDataContext()
  {
    // This requires the Pictures Library capability
    StorageFolder pictures = KnownFolders.PicturesLibrary;
    this.DataContext = await pictures.GetFilesAsync();
  }
 }
}
```

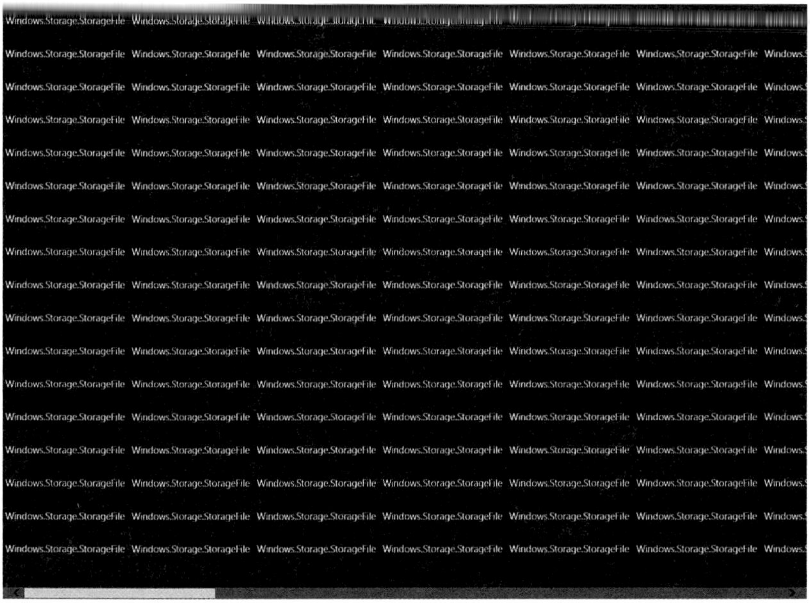

FIGURE 19.2   The GridView with an updated data source set to the collection of files in the
Pictures Library

> For the target property to automatically stay updated with changes to the source collection
> (that is, the addition and removal of elements), the source collection must implement an
> interface called INotifyCollectionChanged. Fortunately, the .NET Framework has a built-
> in class that does this for you. It's called ObservableCollection. It implements both
> INotifyCollectionChanged and INotifyPropertyChanged, so it enables all change notifica-
> tion features.

Improving the Display

Clearly, the default display of the files from the Pictures Library in Figure 19.2—a
ToString rendering—is not acceptable. One simple way to improve this is to leverage a
DisplayMemberPath property present on all items controls. This property works hand in
hand with ItemsSource. If you set it to an appropriate property path, the corresponding
property value gets rendered for each item.

Each of the `StorageFile` objects in Figure 19.2 has a `Name` property, so adding the following to the `Page`'s XAML produces the result in Figure 19.3:

```
<Page …>
  <Grid Background="{ThemeResource ApplicationPageBackgroundThemeBrush}">
    <GridView ItemsSource="{Binding}" DisplayMemberPath="Name"/>
  </Grid>
</Page>
```

FIGURE 19.3   `DisplayMemberPath` is a simple mechanism for customizing the display of items in a data-bound collection.

This is a slight improvement, but not much. One way to improve this further (not specific to data binding) is to use a data template, and another way is to use a value converter. These are the subjects of the next section.

> ⓘ **`ItemsControl`'s `Items` and `ItemsSource` properties can't be modified simultaneously!**
>
> You must decide whether you want to populate an items control manually via `Items` or with data binding via `ItemsSource`, and you must not mix these techniques. `ItemsSource` can be set only when the `Items` collection is empty, and `Items` can be modified only when `ItemsSource` is `null`. Therefore, if you want to add or remove items to/from a data-bound `GridView`, you must do this to the underlying collection (`ItemsSource`) rather than at the user interface level (`Items`). Note that regardless of which method is used to *set* items in an items control, you can always *retrieve* items via the `Items` collection.

Controlling Rendering

Data binding is simple when the source and target properties are compatible data types and the default rendering of the source is all you need to display. But often a bit of customization is required. The need for this in the previous section is obvious, because you want to display Images, not raw strings, in the GridView.

These types of customizations would be easy *without* data binding because you're writing all the code to retrieve the data on your own. But with the two mechanisms discussed in this section, you don't need to give up the benefits of data binding to get the desired results in more customized scenarios.

Using Data Templates

A *data template* is a piece of user interface that you'd like to apply to an arbitrary object when it is rendered. Many controls have properties (of type DataTemplate) for attaching a data template appropriately. For example, ContentControl and HubSection have a ContentTemplate property for controlling the rendering of its Content object, and ItemsControl has an ItemTemplate that applies to each of its items. Controls with Headers and Footers have HeaderTemplate and FooterTemplate properties to control their appearance. In addition, ComboBox has a SelectionBoxItemTemplate property and ToggleSwitch has OnContentTemplate and OffContentTemplate properties.

By setting one of these properties to an instance of a DataTemplate, you can swap in a completely new visual tree. The following update to the last section's XAML applies a DataTemplate to produce the result in Figure 19.4:

```
<Page …>
  <Grid Background="{ThemeResource ApplicationPageBackgroundThemeBrush}">
    <GridView ItemsSource="{Binding}">
      <GridView.ItemTemplate>
        <DataTemplate>
          <Grid>
            <Rectangle Fill="Blue" Width="100" Height="100"/>
            <TextBlock Text="{Binding Name}"/>
          </Grid>
        </DataTemplate>
      </GridView.ItemTemplate>
    </GridView>
  </Grid>
</Page>
```

Notice that the way to adapt the single data template to each item is to use data binding! When you apply a data template, it is implicitly given an appropriate data context. When applied as an ItemTemplate, the data context is implicitly the current item in ItemsSource. Note that Binding must be used in this case, not TemplateBinding as in control templates.

> **?** **What is the difference between a data template and a control template?**
>
> A control template, which is assigned to `Control`'s `Template` property, defines the appearance of an entire control. In contrast, a data template operates on a specific property on the control. In addition, a control template is concerned about reacting appropriately to various states (hover, focus, selection, and so on) whereas a data template is only concerned about visuals bound to data.
>
> Of course, whether a data template has any affect ultimately depends on the control template. If you look at the default control template for `ToggleSwitch`, you can see that its `HeaderTemplate`, `OnContentTemplate`, and `OffContentTemplate` data templates are applied as the `ContentTemplate` data templates for three different `ContentPresenters` in its visual tree. If the control template were replaced with a simpler one that didn't respect these properties, setting them would have no effect.

> **💡** Although data templates can be used on non-data-bound objects (such as a `GridView` with a manually constructed set of items), you'll almost always want to use data binding *inside* the template to customize the appearance of the visual tree based on the underlying object(s).

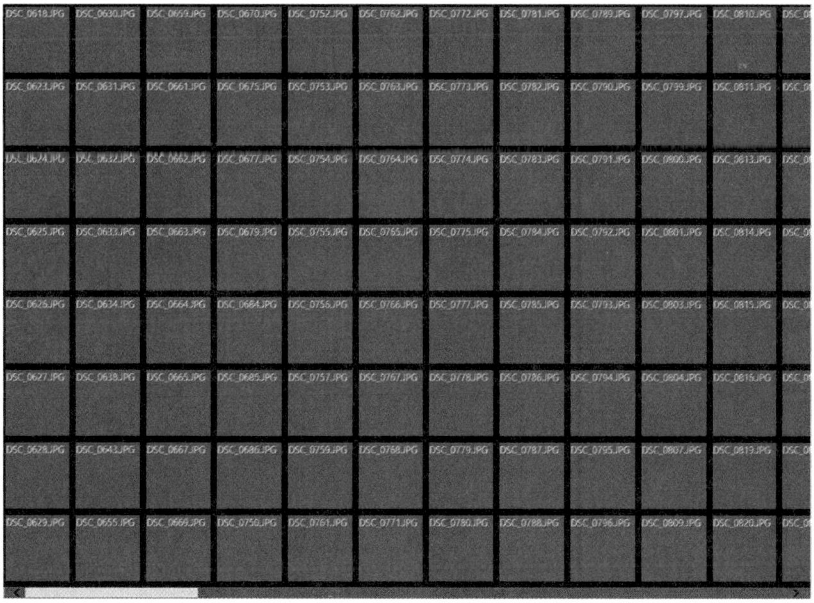

FIGURE 19.4   A simple data template makes each item in the `GridView` appear as a blue square with text.

The result of Figure 19.4 is still not satisfactory. We know that these files are images, so it makes sense to display thumbnails. However, `StorageFile` doesn't expose a suitable

Uri or ImageSource property for a thumbnail (or even the full picture, for that matter) that we could use with an Image-based data template.

Therefore, we can define a data-binding-friendly (and simpler) version of the StorageFile class as follows:

```
class Photo
{
  public ImageSource Thumbnail { get; set; }
  // More properties can be added as needed
}
```

This is commonly referred to as part of a *view model*: a representation that sits in-between the view (the GridView) and the model (the file system objects). With this class defined, we can make the data context be an ObservableCollection of Photo objects (observable so the UI receives updates) and populate that collection by changing the Page's code-behind as follows:

```
using System;
using System.Collections.ObjectModel;
using System.Threading.Tasks;
using Windows.Storage;
using Windows.Storage.FileProperties;
using Windows.UI.Xaml.Controls;
using Windows.UI.Xaml.Media.Imaging;

namespace Chapter19
{
  public sealed partial class MainPage : Page
  {
    // The new data source
    ObservableCollection<Photo> photos = new ObservableCollection<Photo>();

    public MainPage()
    {
      InitializeComponent();
      SetDataContext();
    }

    async Task SetDataContext()
    {
      // Can set this now because updates will be propagated
      this.DataContext = this.photos;

      // This requires the Pictures Library capability
      StorageFolder pictures = KnownFolders.PicturesLibrary;
```

```csharp
    foreach (StorageFile file in await pictures.GetFilesAsync())
    {
        // Retreive the thumbnail
        StorageItemThumbnail thumbnail =
            await file.GetThumbnailAsync(ThumbnailMode.PicturesView);

        if (thumbnail != null)
        {
            using (thumbnail)
            {
                // Create an ImageSource from the thumbnail stream
                BitmapImage source = new BitmapImage();
                source.SetSource(thumbnail);

                // Create a new Photo object and add it to the collection
                this.photos.Add(new Photo { Thumbnail = source });
            }
        }
    }
}
```

Finally, we must update the data template to leverage this new `Thumbnail` property on the new Photo object:

```xml
<Page …>
  <Grid Background="{ThemeResource ApplicationPageBackgroundThemeBrush}">
    <GridView ItemsSource="{Binding}">
      <GridView.ItemTemplate>
        <DataTemplate>
          <Image Width="200" Source="{Binding Thumbnail}"/>
        </DataTemplate>
      </GridView.ItemTemplate>
    </GridView>
  </Grid>
</Page>
```

With these changes, we get the result in Figure 19.5, which is finally a satisfactory representation of the user's photos from the Pictures Library. The key to making this work is the synchronous property for getting each thumbnail, rather than an asynchronous method.

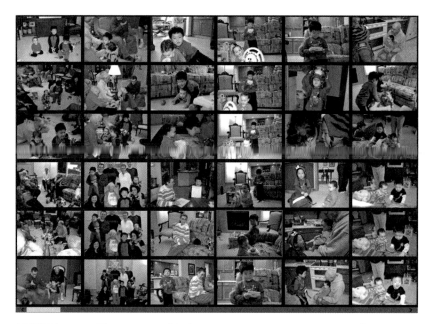

FIGURE 19.5   The `GridView` binds to an `ObservableCollection` of custom `Photo` objects that expose the thumbnail in a data-binding-friendly manner.

Template Selectors   •••

Sometimes it can be desirable to heavily customize a data template based on the input data. Although a lot can be done inside a single data template, you can use a *template selector* to select a custom template at runtime when it is time for the data to be rendered. This works much like `Style` selectors. To do this, you create a class that derives from `DataTemplateSelector` and override its virtual `SelectTemplate` method. You can then associate an instance with the appropriate element by setting that element's *XXX*`TemplateSelector` property.

Not every *XXX*`Template` property has a corresponding *XXX*`TemplateSelector` property, however. The only ones that exist in the XAML UI Framework are `ContentTemplateSelector` on `ContentControl` and `ContentPresenter`, `ItemTemplateSelector` on `ItemsControl`, and `HeaderTemplateSelector` on `GroupStyle`, a class described later in this chapter.

Using Value Converters

Whereas data templates can customize the way data is rendered, value converters can morph each piece of data before it reaches the target. They enable you to plug in custom logic without giving up the benefits of data binding.

Value converters are sometimes used to reconcile a source and target that are different data types. For example, you could change the background or foreground color of an element based on the value of some non-Brush data source, à la conditional formatting in Microsoft Excel. Or you could use it to enhance the information displayed, without the need for separate elements.

Imagine that we want to set the `Header` of the photo-filled `GridView` so it displays the number of photos. We could bind the `Header` property to the collection's `Count` property from the same implicit data context and set `HeaderTemplate` to a `DataTemplate` that improves its display:

```
<Page …>
  <Grid Background="{ThemeResource ApplicationPageBackgroundThemeBrush}">
    <GridView ItemsSource="{Binding}" Header="{Binding Count}">
      <GridView.HeaderTemplate>
        <DataTemplate>
          <TextBlock Style="{StaticResource HeaderTextBlockStyle}"
                     Text="{Binding}"/>
        </DataTemplate>
      </GridView.HeaderTemplate>
      <GridView.ItemTemplate>
        <DataTemplate>
          <Image Width="200" Source="{Binding Thumbnail}"/>
        </DataTemplate>
      </GridView.ItemTemplate>
    </GridView>
  </Grid>
</Page>
```

The `TextBlock` in the new `DataTemplate` leverages the built-in `HeaderTextBlockStyle` style. This produces the result in Figure 19.6.

FIGURE 19.6 The `GridView`'s `Header` displays the raw `Count` from the collection of photos.

This is okay, but the number could use a little context. And with a value converter, we can do better than a static " photo(s)" suffix. (I don't know about you, but when I see a user interface report something like "1 item(s)," it just looks lazy to me.) We can customize the text based on the value, so we can display "1 photo" (singular) versus "2 photos" (plural) versus a special message for zero.

A value converter is any class that implements IValueConverter, so the following class can perform the aforementioned custom logic:

```
namespace Chapter19
{
  public class RawCountToDescriptionConverter : IValueConverter
  {
    public object Convert(object value, Type targetType, object parameter,
                          string language)
    {
      // Let Parse throw an exception if the input is bad
      int num = int.Parse(value.ToString());
      if (num == 0)
      {
        return "There are no photos yet. Add some!";
      }
      else
      {
        return num.ToString("N0") + (num == 1 ? " photo" : " photos");
      }
    }

    public object ConvertBack(object value, Type targetType, object parameter,
                              string language)
    {
      return DependencyProperty.UnsetValue;
    }
  }
}
```

This interface has two simple methods—Convert, which is passed the source instance that must be converted to the target instance, and ConvertBack, which does the opposite. ConvertBack is called only when TwoWay data binding is done, so this value converter returns a standard dummy value for this case. The implementation of Convert not only customizes the message, but it provides a thousands separator with the N0 formatting. Note that this uses hard-coded English strings, whereas a production-quality converter uses localizable resources.

This converter can be applied to the Page as follows:

```
<Page … xmlns:local="using:Chapter19">
  <Page.Resources>
```

```
<!-- Create an instance of the converter that can be referenced -->
<local:RawCountToDescriptionConverter x:Key="myConverter"/>
</Page.Resources>
<Grid Background="{ThemeResource ApplicationPageBackgroundThemeBrush}">
  <GridView ItemsSource="{Binding}"
            Header="{Binding Count, Converter={StaticResource myConverter}}">
    <GridView.HeaderTemplate>
      <DataTemplate>
        <TextBlock Style="{StaticResource HeaderTextBlockStyle}"
                   Text="{Binding}"/>
      </DataTemplate>
    </GridView.HeaderTemplate>
    <GridView.ItemTemplate>
      <DataTemplate>
        <Image Width="200" Source="{Binding Thumbnail}"/>
      </DataTemplate>
    </GridView.ItemTemplate>
  </GridView>
</Grid>
</Page>
```

This produces the result in Figure 19.7. Binding has a Converter property that can be set
to any value converter, which is often defined as a resource so it can be referenced in
XAML. It also has ConverterParameter and ConverterLanguage properties that can be set
to custom values. These values get passed to the converter as the parameter and language
parameters seen previously.

FIGURE 19.7   The GridView's Header displays custom text courtesy of a value converter.

> **(?) How do I use a value converter to perform a conversion on each item when binding to a collection?**
>
> You can apply a data template to the ItemsControl's ItemTemplate property and then apply value converters to any Bindings done *inside* the data template. If you apply the value converter to the ItemsControl's Binding instead, an update to the source collection would prompt the Convert method to be called once for the entire collection (not on a per-item basis). You can implement such a converter that accepts a collection and returns a morphed collection, but that would not be an efficient approach.

Customizing the View of a Collection

Instead of binding directly to a collection, you can insert a *view* between the source and target objects that adds support for grouping and navigating items. This view is an object implementing the ICollectionView interface, and you can create one with an object known as CollectionViewSource.

Grouping

For the example of displaying a user's photos, it's natural to want to group them based on the day (or month or year) they were taken. To enable this, let's first add an appropriate property to the Photo class:

```
class Photo
{
  public ImageSource Thumbnail { get; set; }
  public DateTimeOffset DateTaken { get; set; }
  // More properties can be added as needed
}
```

Then, the following code updates the SetDataContext method shown previously with support for grouping the photos based on the day they were taken:

```
async Task SetDataContext()
{
  // This requires the Pictures Library capability
  StorageFolder pictures = KnownFolders.PicturesLibrary;

  foreach (StorageFile file in await pictures.GetFilesAsync())
  {
    // Retreive the thumbnail
    StorageItemThumbnail thumbnail =
      await file.GetThumbnailAsync(ThumbnailMode.PicturesView);
    if (thumbnail != null)
    {
      using (thumbnail)
```

```
    {
        // Create an ImageSource from the thumbnail stream
        BitmapImage source = new BitmapImage();
        source.SetSource(thumbnail);

        // Create a new Photo object and add it to the collection
        this.photos.Add(new Photo { Thumbnail = source, DateTaken =
            (await file.Properties.GetImagePropertiesAsync()).DateTaken });
    }
  }
}

// Create a view to use as the data context
CollectionViewSource viewSource = new CollectionViewSource();
viewSource.IsSourceGrouped = true;
this.DataContext = viewSource;

// Here's where the underlying collection gets associated with the view.
// Use LINQ (requires "using System.Linq") to group the photos appropriately.
viewSource.Source = from photo in this.photos
                    group photo by photo.DateTaken.Date into g
                    orderby g.Key
                    select g;
}
```

With this change alone, the GridView's items don't get grouped. For that to happen, you also need to add a GroupStyle object to the GroupStyle property defined by all items controls. GroupStyle enables you to specify a data template for each group's header, a Panel for each group's items, and more. The following update to the Page's XAML produces the result in Figure 19.8. Note that the GridView has been changed to a ListView because each group is already wrapping its items in a grid-like fashion:

```
<Page …>
  <Page.Resources>
    <local:DateConverter x:Key="myConverter"/>
  </Page.Resources>
  <Grid Background="{ThemeResource ApplicationPageBackgroundThemeBrush}">
    <ListView ItemsSource="{Binding}">
      <ListView.ItemTemplate>
        <DataTemplate>
          <Image Width="200" Source="{Binding Thumbnail}"/>
        </DataTemplate>
      </ListView.ItemTemplate>
```

```
        <!-- A style for each group -->
      <ListView.GroupStyle>
        <GroupStyle>
          <!-- The group header shows the date -->
          <GroupStyle.HeaderTemplate>
            <DataTemplate>
              <TextBlock Style="{StaticResource SubheaderTextBlockStyle}"
                Margin="5" FontWeight="Bold"
                Text="{Binding Key, Converter={StaticResource myConverter}}"/>
            </DataTemplate>
          </GroupStyle.HeaderTemplate>

          <!-- The panel for arranging the items in the group -->
          <GroupStyle.Panel>
            <ItemsPanelTemplate>
              <VariableSizedWrapGrid Orientation="Horizontal"/>
            </ItemsPanelTemplate>
          </GroupStyle.Panel>
        </GroupStyle>
      </ListView.GroupStyle>
    </ListView>
  </Grid>
</Page>
```

FIGURE 19.8   The familiar page now displays the photos in a ListView with grouping support enabled.

The data-bound text in each group header is the Key property created by the grouping done in the LINQ query. Although this has the time stripped out (thanks to grouping by photo.DateTaken.**Date**), the default display would show a time of 12:00:00 AM with each date without further customization. The Binding inside the HeaderTemplate leverages a new DateConverter value converter to customize each label, which is implemented as follows:

```
public class DateConverter : IValueConverter
{
  DateTimeFormatter formatter =
    new DateTimeFormatter("dayofweek month day year");

  public object Convert(object value, Type targetType, object parameter,
                        string language)
  {
    return this.formatter.Format((DateTime)value);
  }

  public object ConvertBack(object value, Type targetType, object parameter,
                            string language)
  {
    return DependencyProperty.UnsetValue;
  }
}
```

You can imagine supporting much fancier groupings with this mechanism, such as calculating date ranges and returning strings such as "Last Week", "Last Month", and so on.

There is quite a bit going on behind the scenes to make this work. When a CollectionViewSource is a data binding source, either explicitly or implicitly via DataContext, a separate view object is what *actually* gets used as the source. This object is exposed via CollectionViewSource's readonly View property and is the object implementing ICollectionView.

ICollectionView has a CurrentItem property. Because the Page's data context is this view object, you could make the ListView's Header show the date from the current selection as follows:

```
<ListView ItemsSource="{Binding}" Header="{Binding CurrentItem.DateTaken}">
```

Navigating

In this context, *navigating* a view refers to managing the current item—not the kind of navigation discussed in Part III, "Working with the App Model." ICollectionView not only has a CurrentItem property (and a corresponding CurrentPosition property that exposes the current item's zero-based index), but it also has a handful of methods for programmatically changing the current item: MoveCurrentToNext, MoveCurrentToPrevious, MoveCurrentToPosition, and so on.

Although a bit wordy, these navigation methods are straightforward to use. They enable not only updating the selected item in an items control without explicitly referencing it, but any additional elements that want to display information about the current item can be automatically updated as well, as long as they bind to the same source. If you paste a second, identical ListView from Figure 19.8 onto the Page (perhaps side-by-side in a two-column Grid), you'll see that selection changes made to one affect the other simultaneously!

High Performance Rendering with `ListView` and `GridView`

The preceding chapter mentioned that Windows 8.1 significantly improves the load time of ListViews and GridViews containing a lot of items by simplifying the default control templates used by their item containers. Windows 8.1 also adds two features to significantly improve the *perceived* performance of ListView/GridView scrolling. One is trivial to take advantage of, but one requires work on your end. These are not technically related to data binding, but data binding is usually involved when you're dealing with displaying large collections of objects.

The first feature is called *scrolling placeholders*. By setting the ShowsScrollingPlaceholders property (defined by ListViewBase) to true, the control will show placeholders whenever the user is scrolling faster than your items can be rendered. Each placeholder is a grey rectangle with a size matching your items. This looks much better than the flash of blankness that would otherwise occur, as illustrated in Figure 19.9. Just like the flash of blankness, the placeholders are temporary. They are replaced with the real elements once rendering catches up.

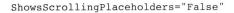 

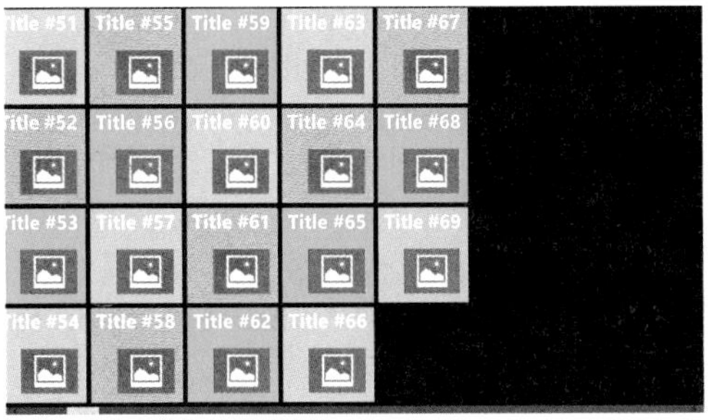

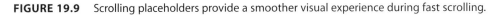

ShowsScrollingPlaceholders="False" 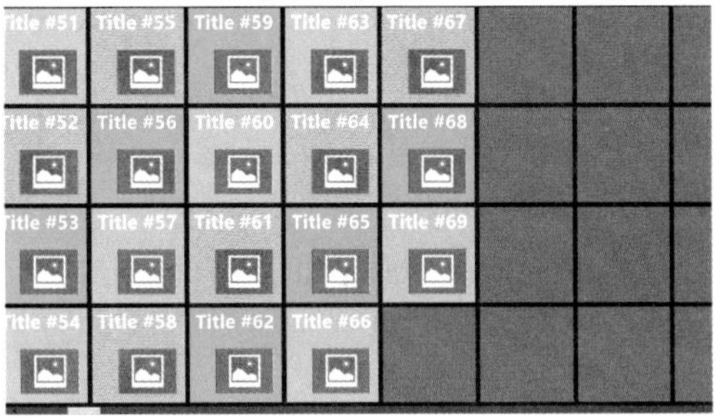   ShowsScrollingPlaceholders="True"

FIGURE 19.9   Scrolling placeholders provide a smoother visual experience during fast scrolling.

The second feature is *incremental item rendering*, which can be thought of as more powerful placeholders. When all of your newly-onscreen items can't be rendered in time, this feature gives you a mechanism to partially render items. The idea is that you prioritize the individual elements that make up each item, so partial rendering can be done in a way that makes sense for your content.

For example, imagine that your items contain a solid background color, a title, and an image, as in Figure 19.9. You might rank the background as most important (similar to a placeholder but a better color), followed by the title, followed by the image. Without incremental item rendering, when new items become visible, each one is fully rendered one-by one until time runs out and the screen contents need to be displayed to the user. Instead, with this feature, each new item's background can be rendered first. Once all have been rendered, then each new item's title gets rendered. Finally, once all titles are ready, each new item's image gets rendered. Therefore, if time runs out in the middle of this process, the user is likely left with all new items at least partially rendered rather than some completely rendered and some not at all. This is illustrated in Figure 19.10. In this example, when time runs out, all new backgrounds have been rendered, but only six new title (and therefore zero new images) have been rendered.

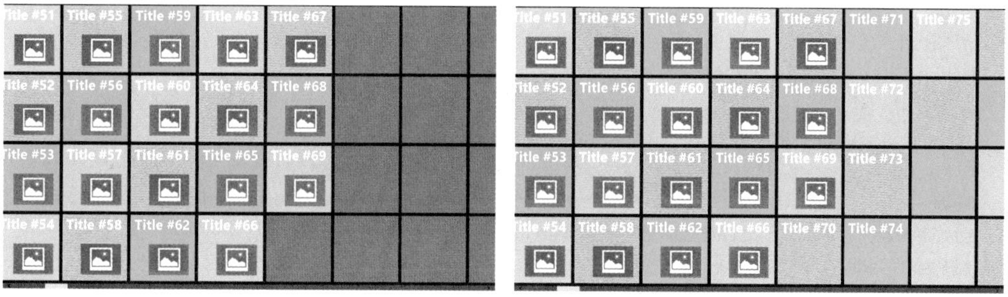

Without incremental rendering   With incremental rendering

FIGURE 19.10   Partial item rendering looks much better than standard placeholders.

So how do you enable this feature? By handling `ListViewBase`'s `ContainerContentChanging` event, which is called for every item as it comes into view. In a `ContainerContentChanging` handler, you do your highest priority rendering then provide a callback for the next phase of rendering. From that callback, you can provide yet another callback for the phase after that. And so on. Your callbacks get called at the appropriate times for each item.

The following code demonstrates this approach, assuming each item in a `GridView` has a data template consisting of a `Grid` with a `TextBlock` named `title` and an `Image` named `image`, as in Figures 19.9 and 19.10:

```
// A handler for GridView's ContainerContentChanging event
void GridView_ContainerContentChanging(ListViewBase sender,
                                ContainerContentChangingEventArgs args)
{
  // We're handling the rendering
  args.Handled = true;

  // This is Phase 0
  Debug.Assert(args.Phase == 0);
```

```
  // Hide everything (except the background)
  Grid root = args.ItemContainer.ContentTemplateRoot as Grid;
  (root.FindName("title") as TextBlock).Opacity = 0;
  (root.FindName("image") as Image).Opacity = 1;

  // Manually set the background brush
  root.Background = (args.Item as MyDataItem).Background;

  // Schedule the next phase
  args.RegisterUpdateCallback(RenderPhase1);
}


void RenderPhase1(ListViewBase sender, ContainerContentChangingEventArgs args)
{
  // This is Phase 1
  Debug.Assert(args.Phase == 1);

  // Manually set the title, then show it
  Grid root = args.ItemContainer.ContentTemplateRoot as Grid;
  TextBlock title = root.FindName("title") as TextBlock;
  title.Text = (args.Item as MyDataItem).Title;
  title.Opacity = 1;

  // Schedule the next phase
  args.RegisterUpdateCallback(RenderPhase2);
}


void RenderPhase2(ListViewBase sender, ContainerContentChangingEventArgs args)
{
  // This is Phase 2
  Debug.Assert(args.Phase == 2);

  // Manually set the image, then show it
  Grid root = args.ItemContainer.ContentTemplateRoot as Grid;
  Image image = root.FindName("image") as Image;
  image.Source = (args.Item as MyDataItem).Image;
  image.Opacity = 1;

  // This item is now done
}
```

There are a few things to note about this approach:

→ For the best performance, always set args.Handled to true in the handler for
ContainerContentChanging to avoid having the framework set each item's content
as if you weren't doing incremental rendering.

→ For the best performance, you should minimize the rendering you do in phase 0 (the handler for `ContainerContentChanging`).

→ The `GridView` or `ListView` should have `ShowsScrollingPlaceholders` set to `false` because you're already providing (better) placeholders.

→ Phase 0 of this process should always explicitly make the relevant elements invisible. That's because the content containers get recycled. Failure to do so would show elements with content from a different item that went offscreen.

→ You should always show/hide elements by setting their `Opacity`. This avoids expensive layout invalidations, and the change can be handled by the composition thread rather than the UI thread.

→ You can access the relevant data item with `args.Item`. This code assumes that the `GridView` is filled with `MyDataItem` objects, a view model that conveniently exposes the three properties we need for our visuals.

→ Notice that the three properties of the data object (`Background`, `Title`, and `Image`) are applied manually to the instantiation of the data template. This whole approach is actually an *anti-data-binding* one! To exploit the incremental nature and prevent a bunch of work from happening up-front, the data template is the following "empty" one with no `Binding`s at all:

```
<GridView ContainerContentChanging="GridView_ContainerContentChanging" …>
  <GridView.ItemTemplate>
    <DataTemplate>
      <!-- Set the background, text, and image incrementally in code-behind -->
      <Grid Width="210" Height="210">
        <TextBlock Name="title" FontSize="44" FontWeight="Bold"
                   Margin="12,0,0,0" />
        <Image Name="image" Width="130" VerticalAlignment="Bottom"
               HorizontalAlignment="Right" Margin="20"/>
      </Grid>
    </DataTemplate>
  </GridView.ItemTemplate>
  …
</GridView>
```

Although the relevant data template should not use data binding in this scenario, the `GridView` or `ListView` can certainly use data binding for its data items.

Summary

Data binding is a powerful feature, although its use is also optional. After all, it's not hard to write code that ties two objects together. (The new incremental rendering feature for `ListView` and `GridView` even requires it for its item template!) But writing such code can be tedious, error prone, and a maintenance hassle, especially when managing multiple data sources that might need to be synchronized as items are added, removed, and changed. Such code also tends to tightly couple business logic with the user interface, which makes apps more brittle.

There's more to data binding than cutting down on the amount of code you need to write, however. Much of the appeal of data binding comes from the fact that the majority of it can be done declaratively. This has some important implications. Design tools such as Visual Studio and Blend can (and do) surface data-binding functionality, so nonprogrammers can add sophisticated functionality to a user interface. This support also enables designers to specify easily removable dummy data for testing data-bound user interfaces.

Chapter 20

WORKING WITH DATA

The preceding chapter discusses binding to in-memory data. Excluding hardcoded data in your source code, from where might such data come? Windows Store apps have three primary options:

→ App Data

→ User Data

→ Networking

The distinction of app data versus user data is designed to give users control over who has access to their files and give them confidence that they are reasonably protected from malicious people. At the same time, the functionality is designed to be useful and flexible enough for developers like you to implement your ideas without feeling overly constrained.

This chapter, the first of this part of the book that solely covers Windows Runtime features that aren't specific to XAML apps, examines these three choices. But first, it summarizes the Windows Runtime representation of files and folders, which are the primary objects for working with persisted data.

An Overview of Files and Folders

The core representation of storage objects in the Windows Runtime is the IStorageItem interface. It supports rename and delete operations, and getting/setting basic properties.

Windows 8.1 introduces two new methods to storage items, placed on a new IStorageItem2 interface: IsEqual, which reports if two IStorageItems are the same, and GetParentAsync, which returns the parent folder if you can access it. GetParentAsync is useful if all you have is a file but you want to save a separate file alongside it in the same folder.

Two classes implement IStorageItem (and IStorageItem2): StorageFile and StorageFolder. On top of StorageItem, StorageFile supports move and copy operations, getting extended properties and thumbnails, and being opened as a stream. StorageFolder supports the creation of files and folders within it, queries for filtering and enumerating its contents, getting its files or folders by name, and getting thumbnails. In Windows 8.1, you can try to get a folder's item by name via a new TryGetItemAsync method. Unlike GetItemAsync, which existed in Windows 8, TryGetItemAsync simply returns null upon failure rather than throwing an exception.

> You can read, write, and append content to a StorageFile with handy APIs exposed by the static Windows.Storage.FileIO class. These methods work directly on the file; no streams are involved. There are methods for working with strings, collections of strings (one per line), byte arrays, or buffers represented by IBuffer.

Files and folders can come from anywhere. Whether they come from the local PC, SkyDrive (Microsoft's cloud storage service that might have a new name by the time you read this), a network share, or from another app (which could be fetching the content from a Web service), they are still represented as StorageFiles and StorageFolders.

One of the most interesting enhancements to the Windows 8.1 file system is even deeper integration with SkyDrive. Windows now has the concept of a file from SkyDrive being "available offline" or "online only." In the latter case, the local file is just a placeholder file that serves as a proxy to the real file on SkyDrive. The placeholder file contains metadata and thumbnails for pictures, so the real file can feel like it's really there for both users and developers alike. For example, the Windows file picker shows the placeholder files to users, but at 40% opacity and with an "online only" label. And if an app tries to perform an operation that requires the real file to be downloaded, such as opening it or editing its metadata, Windows will automatically fetch it if network conditions permit. Note that you can successfully rename or delete a placeholder file, even when offline, and the change will be propagated later.

You can check whether it's safe to treat a file as a local file with StorageFile's IsAvailable Boolean property. This is true if the file is either local, cached locally, or *can be* downloaded. This means that there are only two conditions that cause it IsAvailable to be false:

→ The file is a network file or SkyDrive placeholder file and there is currently no network connection

→ The file is a network file or SkyDrive placeholder file, the user is on a metered network, and his or her settings instruct Windows to not perform the download when on such a network

Of course, even if IsAvailable reports true, the network conditions could change and still cause later file operations to fail due to an unsuccessful download.

Because files seen by your app may not be available or must be fetched over a slow network connection, you should follow these guidelines:

→ Check the IsAvailable property and treat unavailable files differently, such as showing them at 40% opacity and disabling relevant editing features.

→ Whenever opening a file, show an indeterminate ProgressBar or ProgressRing and allow users to cancel the operation. It may take a while, and you want your users to understand what is happening and be able to change their minds.

→ Use thumbnails whenever possible. At least some size is always available locally, and can prevent a costly download.

Thumbnails can be good enough even for full-screen viewing, as the resolutions of most photos are eclipsing resolutions of most screens! StorageFile and StorageFolder have always exposed a GetThumbnailAsync method, but in Windows 8.1 they also support a GetScaledImageAsThumbnailAsync method. This new method is the best choice, as it can return thumbnails for any size up to 1600 pixels in the longest dimension, and it works with SkyDrive placeholder files.

How can I save files to arbitrary spots on the local file system?

You can't automatically, and good riddance to that ability! Other than your app's own isolated location, or a few special locations such as the user's libraries (which require capabilities), the only way this can happen is by the user explicitly picking the location or filename(s). In all these cases, you save *user data* instead of app data.

If you're interested in working with APIs exposed by SkyDrive independently from the Windows 8.1 integration, visit the Live Connect Developer Center at http://go.microsoft.com/fwlink/?LinkId=203291 for more information.

App Data

App data refers to any persistent data that an app reads and writes "privately." An app's settings or a game's high scores are an example of this type of data. App data normally does not get directly exposed to users, and one app cannot view such data from another app. Most importantly, when an app is uninstalled, all of its app data automatically gets deleted as well.

There are two types of app data: *app settings* and *app files*. Access to both of these mechanisms is available via the Windows.Storage.ApplicationData class.

> **(!) Don't use app data for storing usernames and passwords!**
> Instead, use PasswordVault for a similar but secure experience that gives the user more
> control. Or even better, use WebAuthenticationBroker if you can. Both of these are explained
> in the "PasswordBox" section of Chapter 12, "Text."

App Settings

App settings are small, primitive values that are easy to store and retrieve. Using them
looks much like using session state with SuspensionManager. However, these are typically
used for settings that persist regardless of how the app exited. Furthermore, you have two
options: *local settings* and *roaming settings*.

Local Settings

The following code shows how to do the three basic actions of reading/writing/deleting a
local setting:

```
ApplicationDataContainer settings = ApplicationData.Current.LocalSettings;

// (1) Store a setting
settings.Values["CurrentIndex"] = 5;

// (2) Retrieve a setting
object value = settings.Values["CurrentIndex"];
if (value != null)
{
  // The setting exists
  int currentIndex = (int)value;
}

// (3) Delete a setting (this silently returns if the setting doesn't exist)
settings.Values.Remove("CurrentIndex");
```

Although this code checks for a null value to determine whether the specific setting
exists, another approach is to call the settings.Values.ContainsKey method.

> **(!) Only a few primitive data types can be used as a value for an app setting!**
> App settings always have a string key and a value that's either a bool, byte, int, uint,
> long, ulong, float, double, or string. (You can combine multiple primitive values into an
> ApplicationDataCompositeValue instance, however, as described in the "Roaming Settings"
> section.) There is no built-in support for binary data. For this, you should use an app file instead.

`ApplicationDataContainer`, the type of the `LocalSettings` property, enables you to create and name subcontainers for organizing your settings into different buckets or "folders." This is managed with its `CreateContainer` and `DeleteContainer` methods. You can nest them, but only up to 32 levels deep.

> ## Using too many settings can slow your app's launch!
>
> App settings are simpler to use than app files, but you have less control over them. All settings are automatically read from disk when your app is launched. With app files, on the other hand, you control when each file is opened and read.

Roaming Settings

Traditionally, to roam a user's settings to any device, you set up a Web service, deal with user accounts, security, synchronization, and so on. Or find a service that can do this for you in a satisfactory way. For most apps, it's not worth the hassle or cost.

However, Windows Store apps can roam settings simply by changing the word `Local` to `Roaming` in the preceding code, as follows:

```
ApplicationDataContainer settings = ApplicationData.Current.RoamingSettings;
```

That's it! If the user has a Microsoft account linked to the logged-in account and allows roaming, then Windows automatically replicates settings to Microsoft's cloud when they are updated, and it synchronizes the data to wherever the user logs in (if the same app is installed on the device). In the case of a conflict, the last writer wins.

If the user isn't leveraging a Microsoft account or doesn't allow roaming, then roaming settings don't act any differently from local settings. Local settings and roaming settings are two completely independent containers that are both stored locally; the only difference is the synchronization policy associated with the roaming ones. An app can use both types of settings for separate reasons. If your session state is small enough, you can enable "roaming session state" with `RoamingSettings` and not even bother with `SuspensionManager`.

If an app is used on multiple devices by the same user simultaneously, an update to the roaming settings in one place eventually causes `ApplicationData`'s `DataChanged` event to be raised in the other instance(s). By attaching a handler to this event, you can choose to refresh your app with the synchronized update. This is also the place to perform your own conflict resolution logic, if the default last-writer-wins policy is too simplistic for your needs. You might consider raising the `DataChanged` event yourself whenever you locally modify app settings, just to consolidate your logic that handles setting changes in one spot.

Independent settings aren't guaranteed to roam at the same time, so if you have several settings that need to roam as an atomic unit, you can use a special class called `ApplicationDataCompositeValue` to combine separate settings together. For example:

```
ApplicationDataCompositeValue value = new ApplicationDataCompositeValue();
// Add two values that should stay in sync:
value["StartIndex"] = 5;
value["EndIndex"] = 15;
// Add the composite value to the settings container:
settings.Values["IndexRange"] = value;
```

Roaming works only if the total amount of data remains small!

Each app receives a quota for roaming data, which is 100 kilobytes at the time of this writing. This applies to the combination of roaming settings *and* roaming files. If you exceed this limit, roaming will silently stop happening until the size of the data goes back under the threshold.

You can programmatically discover your app's quota by checking `ApplicationData`'s `RoamingStorageQuota` property, which returns the number of kilobytes. However, it's unfortunately up to you to figure out the total number of bytes currently being used!

Roaming typically occurs within 15-30 minutes after the data has changed, so you can't expect it to happen quickly. However, if you name one of your roaming settings `"HighPriority"` and if it is under 8KB in size, Windows will attempt to roam it within a minute instead! You can only do this with one setting, although that setting can be a `ApplicationDataCompositeValue`. For example, you could store a video URL and playback position in this manner so users can get a nice experience when quickly switching devices.

Of course, you can never rely on roaming happening quickly or at all. If the network connection has high latency, Windows will delay roaming. Delays also happen if changes are made while the user is offline, or if the user disables roaming on a particular network to avoid charges.

App Files

App files are regular files on the local file system, but in a private location specific to your app. Therefore, as with app settings, you can interact with app files without needing any capabilities. You can create any number of files and subfolders without worrying about quotas (except for roaming files), although there is still the limitation of supporting subfolders up to only 32 levels deep.

This section examines the three types of app files: *local files*, *roaming files*, and *temporary files*. It also includes files packaged with your app ("packaged files" or "resources") for completeness. Although such files are not part of the app data mechanism, shipping read-only data files with your app can be a great option to keep in mind.

Packaged Files

Although you can't programmatically add to or edit the files packaged with your app, you can retrieve one as follows:

```
StorageFolder folder = Package.Current.InstalledLocation;
StorageFile file = await folder.GetFileAsync("Assets\\Logo.png");
```

This file location corresponds to the URI ms-appx:///Assets/Logo.png. This works for any files marked with a Build Action of Content in your project.

Local Files

The following code demonstrates creating a local file called MyFile.txt in a MyFolder subfolder and writing "data" into it using one of the handy FileIO helpers:

```
StorageFolder folder = ApplicationData.Current.LocalFolder;
StorageFile file = await folder.CreateFileAsync("MyFolder\\MyFile.txt",
  CreationCollisionOption.ReplaceExisting);
if (file != null)
{
  await FileIO.WriteTextAsync(file, "data");
}
```

The file gets saved as **%USERPROFILE%\AppData\Local\Packages**_**PackageFamilyName**_**** **LocalState**\MyFolder\MyFile.txt. You can never access it via this full path in your code. You can, however, access it with the URI ms-appdata:///**local**/MyFolder/MyFile.txt. For example, you can make an Image element display content from a local file as follows:

```
<Image Source="ms-appdata:///local/image.png"/>
```

> The CreationCollisionOption enumeration value that can be passed to StorageFolder's CreateFileAsync method enables several different behaviors for what to do when the file already exists: replacing it, failing, opening it, or even automatically choosing a new filename (by appending a number) for the new file.

> You can get Windows to automatically index local data from your app for fast searches. To do this, simply create a top-level local folder called Indexed and place everything there! (Further subfolders are okay.) Both the file contents and file metadata get indexed. Windows 8.1 also introduces a ContentIndexer class in the Windows.Storage.Search namespace that enables you to add content to the index programmatically.

Roaming Files

As with local settings versus roaming settings, you can switch from local files to roaming files by changing a single Local to a Roaming:

```
StorageFolder folder = ApplicationData.Current.RoamingFolder;
StorageFile file = await folder.CreateFileAsync("MyFolder\\MyFile.txt",
  CreationCollisionOption.ReplaceExisting);
if (file != null)
{
  await FileIO.WriteTextAsync(file, "data");
}
```

The file gets saved locally as %USERPROFILE%\AppData\Local\Packages\
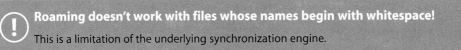 Package(unityName\RoamingState\MyFolder\MyFile.txt, and has all the same synchronization behavior discussed previously for roaming settings. You can access it with the URI ms-appdata:///**roaming**/MyFolder/MyFile.txt. For the image example, that looks as follows:

```
<Image Source="ms-appdata:///roaming/image.png"/>
```

Remember to handle ApplicationData's DataChanged event to refresh your app in response to external changes to a file, because this applies equally to roaming settings and files. Note that any changes made locally to a file don't get roamed until your code closes the file.

> **(!)   Roaming doesn't work with files whose names begin with whitespace!**
> This is a limitation of the underlying synchronization engine.

> **(💡)**   You can version app data by calling the ApplicationData.SetVersionAsync method with a custom version number and a callback that you handle to migrate your data from one version to another. This encompasses all of your app settings and app files, enabling you to gracefully manage breaking changes to your schema. You can check the version of the stored data with the ApplicationData.Version property. For roaming settings and files, Microsoft maintains multiple versions of a user's data for a given app until the user has upgraded the app on all relevant devices. You can even use a background task triggered by a ServicingComplete complete trigger to migrate your app data when a new version of your app is installed, rather than waiting to do it the next time your app is launched.

Temporary Files

This should be no surprise at this point, but working with temporary files is just a matter of changing the folder:

```
StorageFolder folder = ApplicationData.Current.TemporaryFolder;
StorageFile file = await folder.CreateFileAsync("MyFolder\\MyFile.txt",
  CreationCollisionOption.ReplaceExisting);
```

```
if (file != null)
{
  await FileIO.WriteTextAsync(file, "data");
}
```

This file is saved as %USERPROFILE%\AppData\Local\Packages*PackageFamilyName*\
TempState\MyFolder\MyFile.txt, and you can access it with the URI ms-appdata:///
temp/MyFolder/MyFile.txt.

Placing files in the temporary folder is just like placing them in the local folder. The only difference is the intent of the files, and that Windows provides a mechanism for helping users automatically delete temporary files. You should assume that temporary files only exist for the current app session.

> Several libraries exist that build useful abstractions on top of app files. For example, if you're interested in using a local database within your app, check out SQLite (http://www.sqlite.org) and the sqlite-net project (http://github.com/praeclarum/sqlite-net) that exposes the functionality to .NET languages. Even better, you can install SQLite as a Visual Studio extension. Under Tools, Extensions and Updates, Online, you can search for "SQLite." After installing it, you can add it to any project via Add Reference, Windows, Extensions, SQLite.

User Data

User data refers to files that are visible to the user and likely to be managed outside of your app. For example, a painting app would likely enable the user to save a creation as a regular image file. (Before the user saves it, however, it is likely to be stored as an app file so the work-in-progress doesn't get lost.) User files could be on the local PC, a network share, on SkyDrive, or hosted by an arbitrary Web service. User files do *not* get deleted when an app is uninstalled.

An app cannot create/change/delete user files without permission from the user. Fortunately, such permission does not come in the form of an annoying "Do you trust this app to open this file?" prompt, but it is an implicit part of normal user actions. Here are the ways you app can be granted access to certain user files:

→ The user hands your app a file from the Windows file picker.

→ The user hands your app an entire folder from the Windows folder picker.

→ Your app requires a relevant capability, and the user has decided to install your app with this knowledge.

→ Your app has declared its ability to open files of a certain type, and the user has decided to use your app to open such a file.

This section looks at the first three situations. The fourth one is explained in Chapter 22, "Leveraging Contracts."

File Picker

The file picker has two modes, exposed as two different classes in the Windows.Storage.Pickers namespace: FileOpenPicker and FileSavePicker. You see the FileOpenPicker used in Chapter 13, "Images," as follows:

```
// Get a JPEG from the user
FileOpenPicker picker = new FileOpenPicker();
picker.FileTypeFilter.Add(".jpg");
picker.FileTypeFilter.Add(".jpeg");
StorageFile file = await picker.PickSingleFileAsync();
```

By selecting the file, the user has given your app permission to work with it. And this file can come from anywhere, even arbitrary Web services, thanks to the file picker's extensibility.

In addition to PickSingleFileAsync, you can call PickMultipleFilesAsync, which returns a collection of StorageFiles. With this one bulk action, your app gets permission to work with all the returned files.

You can customize the text on the "Open" button by setting CommitButtonText to a custom string, customize the view by setting ViewMode to List or Thumbnail, and change SuggestedStartLocation to one of many values in the PickerLocationId enumeration: Desktop, Downloads, DocumentsLibrary, PicturesLibrary, HomeGroup, and so on.

In Chapter 13, you also see the FileSavePicker used as follows:

```
// Get a target JPEG file from the user
FileSavePicker picker = new FileSavePicker();
picker.FileTypeChoices.Add("JPEG file", new string[] { ".jpg", ".jpeg" });
StorageFile file = await picker.PickSaveFileAsync();
```

This enables the user to name a new file for you to use for saving the content. You don't have to know or care what the filename is; you can simply call one of the WriteXXX methods on FileIO with the StorageFile instance returned to you.

FileSavePicker has the same CommitButtonText property, which you can set if you want to change the "Save" button's text, and the same SuggestedStartLocation property. In addition, you can set

If you're worried about missing a valid file extension from your list of file type filters given to FileOpenPicker, you can always specify a filter of "*".

SuggestedFileName or SuggestedSaveFile to pre-fill the text box shown to the user. Or you can set DefaultFileExtension if you don't want to suggest a specific filename.

Folder Picker

The folder picker is a powerful component, perhaps more so than most users realize. If a user selects an existing folder, or uses it to name a new folder, he or she is giving your app read/write access to the entire folder, including subfolders! Note that only appropriate folders are exposed via the folder picker, so the user can never select the Program Files or Windows folders, for example.

The folder picker is exposed as a `FolderPicker` class, also in the `Windows.Storage.Pickers` namespace.

The `FolderPicker` works similarly to the other two classes:

```
// Get an entire folder from the user
FolderPicker picker = new FolderPicker();
picker.FileTypeFilter.Add("*");
StorageFolder folder = await picker.PickSingleFolderAsync();
```

`FolderPicker` supports the same `SuggestedStartLocation` and `ViewMode` properties supported by `FileOpenPicker`. You may only ask for one folder at a time. There is no `PickMultipleFoldersAsync` method.

> **FolderPicker.PickSingleFolderAsync throws an exception if you don't specify a FileTypeFilter!**
>
> This is a little silly and misleading because it has no bearing on what folder the user may select, nor does it restrict the file types you have permission to read/write within the selected folder. (You can still access all files within the selected folder and its subfolders.) It only impacts the files that happen to be shown to the user while navigating folders, so the idea is that you should add filters for the file types that are relevant for your app. Of course, as shown in the `PickSingleFolderAsync` example, you can specify a filter of * if you want all files to be shown.

> Once an app grants you permission to files and/or folders, you likely want to continue being able to access them in the future. By default, however, you lose access once your app has been terminated.
>
> To keep your access across restarts of your app, you can add any `IStorageItem` to a static `StorageApplicationPermissions.FutureAccessList` property in the `Windows.Storage.AccessCache` namespace. You can add it with a string token of your choosing with its `AddOrReplace` method, then later attempt to retrieve it by passing that same token to `GetItemAsync` (or the more specific `GetFileAsync`/`GetFolderAsync` methods). For example:

```
StorageFolder folder = null;

// First try to get access to the folder from the access cache
if (StorageApplicationPermissions.FutureAccessList.ContainsItem("MyToken"))
{
    folder = await StorageApplicationPermissions.FutureAccessList.GetFolderAsync(
            "MyToken");
```

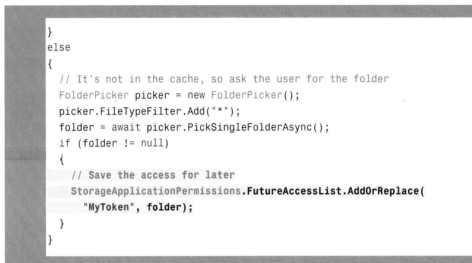

```
}
else
{
  // It's not in the cache, so ask the user for the folder
  FolderPicker picker = new FolderPicker();
  picker.FileTypeFilter.Add("*");
  folder = await picker.PickSingleFolderAsync();
  if (folder != null)
  {
    // Save the access for later
    StorageApplicationPermissions.FutureAccessList.AddOrReplace(
      "MyToken", folder);
  }
}
```

You don't need to worry about doing this for files and folders from app data, as your app never loses access to those.

Windows.Storage.AccessCache.StorageApplicationPermissions has a second handy use. It exposes a second property—MostRecentlyUsedList—that gives you a list of the most recent IStorageItems used by your app. (These are all files and folders for which you have previously been granted permission.) With this, you could provide your users with a handy most recently used (MRU) list inside your own user interface.

Libraries and Other Special Folders

With the right capability granted to your app, you can access the user's Music, Pictures, or Videos libraries without any prompt or file picker. (The Documents Library capability is more restrictive, because it works only for file type associations registered by the app, discussed in Chapter 22.) The same is true for a few more special folders: the HomeGroup folder, the removable devices folder, and the DLNA devices folder.

Accessing Known Folders

Accessing any of the special folders is trivial, thanks to a static KnownFolders class that exposes several StorageFolder properties. As with the different types of app files, all you need to do is start off with the right StorageFolder. For example:

```
// This requires the Music Library capability:
StorageFolder music = KnownFolders.MusicLibrary;
// This requires the Pictures Library capability:
StorageFolder pictures = KnownFolders.PicturesLibrary;
// This requires the Videos Library capability:
StorageFolder videos = KnownFolders.VideosLibrary;
```

KnownFolders also exposes properties for two special library subfolders: the Playlists folder in the Music Library and the Camera Roll folder in the Pictures Library. With the appropriate capabilities, you can access them as follows:

```
// This requires the Music Library capability:
StorageFolder playlists = KnownFolders.Playlists;
// This requires the Pictures Library capability:
StorageFolder photos = KnownFolders.CameraRoll;
```

After you have the StorageFolder, you can use all the regular file APIs to enumerate, read, write, create, and delete files. Recall that with each StorageFile, you can get relevant metadata. This can be retrieved with calls to methods such as GetMusicPropertiesAsync, GetImagePropertiesAsync, and GetVideoPropertiesAsync. This makes it easy to provide a nice browser-style experience for each collection of specific file types.

> StorageFolder exposes a GetFoldersAsync method that enables you to specify a CommonFolderQuery enumeration value (as well as an overload that enables you to retrieve the files in chunks) for grouping the results by common media properties. For example, you can specify GroupByAlbum, GroupByArtist, GroupByGenre, GroupByRating, or many more. This is valid only for library folders or subfolders, and the HomeGroup folder.

The other folders exposed by KnownFolders are DocumentsLibrary, HomeGroup, MediaServerDevices (DLNA devices), and RemovableDevices.

Managing Libraries

Windows 8.1 provides more power for interacting with the user's libraries via a StorageLibrary class. It enables you to trigger requests to add/remove additional folders to any of the four libraries: Documents, Music, Pictures, and Videos. This makes it easy for your app to work with files from anywhere, such as SkyDrive or an external drive, as long as the user feels it is appropriate to add such folders to one of his or her libraries.

You request the addition of a folder as follows, using the Pictures Library as an example:

```
// This requires the Pictures Library capability:
StorageLibrary library =
  await StorageLibrary.GetLibraryAsync(KnownLibraryId.Pictures);
StorageFolder folder = await library.RequestAddFolderAsync();
```

The call to RequestAddFolderAsync presents the user with the folder picker, although its main button now says "Add this folder to Pictures." Because the folders associated with a library are managed by the user, such changes are visible to all apps with the appropriate capabilities. Once the user adds a SkyDrive folder to her Pictures Library, all apps with the Pictures Library capability have access to it.

You can similarly prompt the user to remove a folder from a library by passing a StorageFolder to RequestRemoveFolderAsync. This presents the user with the simple dialog shown in Figure 20.1, then returns true if the folder has been removed.

FIGURE 20.1   `RequestRemoveFolderAsync` asks the user if she wants to remove a folder named "Graphics" from the Pictures Library.

You can be notified of any change to the folders in a library, whether it happened within the current app or elsewhere, by handling `StorageFolder`'s `DefinitionChanged` event. You can also get the whole collection of folders with its `Folders` property, and its default save location with its `SaveFolder` property.

Networking

If the data you need to access isn't app data or user data, then you must need to directly fetch it over the network. Windows Store apps have the following options for networking:

→ Performing direct HTTP Requests

→ Performing background download/upload

→ Using sockets (or WebSockets)

→ Working with syndicated feeds (RSS or Atom)

HTTP Requests

In Windows 8, C# apps could use the `System.Net.Http.HttpClient` class to send and receive HTTP requests: GET, POST, PUT, DELETE, or others. In Windows 8.1, the Windows Runtime has introduced a new class—**Windows.Web**`.Http.HttpClient`—that is now the preferred choice. It is modeled after the .NET-specific `HttpClient` in `System.Net.Http`, but it adds a lot of new capabilities. (And, being a Windows Runtime API, it can be used naturally from any language.) Three interesting new benefits for C# developers are:

→ Its cache, cookies, and credentials are shared with `Image`, `MediaElement`, and `WebView` (within your app)

→ Cookies now persist across runs of your app

→ It gives you a lot of control over caching

→ You can leverage HTTP prefetching to make Windows update your cache when your app isn't even running

`HttpClient` works with `HttpRequestMessages` and `HttpResponseMessages`. It exposes `GetAsync`, `PostAsync`, `PutAsync`, and `DeleteAsync` methods, all of which construct an appropriate `HttpRequestMessage` on your behalf then asynchronously return an

HttpResponseMessage. It also exposes a general-purpose SendRequestAsync method that you call with an instance of HttpRequestMessage that you can create. This enables you to craft other types of requests, such as HEAD or TRACE.

Making an HTTP GET Request

You often don't need to interact with the HttpRequestMessage and HttpResponseMessage objects in your code. HttpClient provides simpler methods for performing an HTTP GET when all you care about it the content within the response: GetStringAsync returns the result as a string, GetBufferAsync returns the result as an IBuffer, and GetInputStreamAsync returns the result as an IInputStream. For example, the following simple code uses HttpClient to perform a search via the Bing API:

```
using Windows.Web.Http;
...
HttpClient client = new HttpClient();

// Perform an HTTP GET and get the response content as a string
string content = await client.GetStringAsync(new Uri(
  "http://api.bing.net/xml.aspx?Appid=<AppID>&query=httpclient&sources=web"));
```

HttpClient's methods throw exceptions on failure, which of course can happen due to a number of issues with the network or the server.

Some Web servers require a User-Agent header with each request, so you could add one that matches Internet Explorer 10 as follows:

```
using Windows.Web.Http;
...
HttpClient client = new HttpClient();

// Make the client look like Internet Explorer 10
client.DefaultRequestHeaders.UserAgent.ParseAdd(
  "Mozilla/5.0 (compatible; MSIE 10.0; Windows NT 6.2; WOW64; Trident/6.0)");

// Perform an HTTP GET and get the response content as a string
string content = await client.GetStringAsync(new Uri(
  "http://api.bing.net/xml.aspx?Appid=<AppID>&query=httpclient&sources=web"));
```

This leverages a strongly-typed UserAgent property rather than identifying it via a string. Leveraging strongly-typed headers, especially on the returned response, can save you from writing a lot of error-prone code.

Depending on your request, you can get different results by mimicking different browsers. The Bing API requires an AppID belonging to a registered developer, which should replace the "<AppId>" in the URL passed to GetStringAsync. You can get one at the Bing Developer Center (http://www.bing.com/developers). Here's the XML returned by ReadAsStringAsync if you leave the AppID as the bogus string:

```xml
<?xml version="1.0" encoding="UTF-8"?>
<?pageview_candidate ?>
<SearchResponse Version="2.2"
  xmlns="http://schemas.microsoft.com/LiveSearch/2008/04/XML/element">
 <Query>
   <SearchTerms>httpclient</SearchTerms>
 </Query>
 <Errors>
   <Error>
     <Code>1001</Code>
     <Message>Parameter has invalid value.</Message>
     <Parameter>SearchRequest.AppId</Parameter>
     <Value>&lt;AppID&gt;</Value>
     <HelpUrl>http://msdn.microsoft.com/en-us/library/dd251042.aspx</HelpUrl>
   </Error>
 </Errors>
</SearchResponse>
```

The returned XML is not pretty-printed, however.

> As seen with MediaTranscoder in Chapter 14, "Audio, Video, and Speech," the asynchronous methods on HttpClient leverage IAsyncActionWithProgress, rather than just IAsyncAction. This means that, by retrieving the direct returned object instead of using await, you can receive progress information about each request while you wait for it to complete. HttpClient provides detailed status information through the HttpProgress structure passed the callback: the current stage of the connection (such as ResolvingName or NegotiatingSsl), bytes sent, bytes received, total bytes to send, total bytes to receive (if known), and how many retries there have been.

HTTP Filters

HttpClient supports working with a pipeline of filters that get to see and potentially modify each outgoing request and incoming response. Each filter implements IHttpFilter, which defines a method that accepts an HttpRequestMessage and must return an HttpResponseMessage. Therefore, to be chained together into a pipeline, each filter must cooperate. A filter typically can be given an "inner filter" that it delegates to between its own incoming request and outgoing response logic.

Filters are a great mechanism for integrating complex behavior while keeping your app's main code simple. You could plug in filters that do authorization, custom retry logic, logging, custom caching, and so on. And when your code makes an HTTP GET request, it can still use the simple GetStringAsync method because the custom configuration is handled elsewhere.

By default, a single filter called HttpBaseProtocolFilter is used. It performs the actual network communication, and exposes many properties for tweaking its behavior. It is designed to be the final filter in the pipeline, and therefore does not support delegating to an inner filter. See Chapter 27, "Custom Controls and Components," for an example of a custom filter that can be chained to an `HttpBaseProtocolFilter`.

Although `HttpBaseProtocolFilter` is used implicitly in the preceding code snippets, you must use it explicitly to customize any of its properties. You do this by constructing an instance and passing it to `HttpClient`'s overloaded constructor that requires an `IHttpFilter`. For example:

```
HttpBaseProtocolFilter baseFilter = new HttpBaseProtocolFilter();
baseFilter.MaxConnectionsPerServer = 10;


HttpClient client = new HttpClient(baseFilter);
```

As with the simpler code snippets, `HttpBaseProtocolFilter` is both the first and last filter in the pipeline used by `HttpClient`. By specifying it explicitly this time, we are able to change the maximum number of concurrent connections per server from the default of 6 (on a broadband connection if an administrator hasn't changed the setting) to 10.

Manipulating Cookies

All interaction with cookies is done via an `HttpCookieManager` object that exposes `GetCookies`, `SetCookie`, and `DeleteCookie` methods. You get to an instance of `HttpCookieManager` via the `CookieManager` property on `HttpBaseProtocolFilter`—*not* on `HttpClient`. The following code demonstrates:

```
HttpBaseProtocolFilter baseFilter = new HttpBaseProtocolFilter();
foreach (HttpCookie cookie in baseFilter.CookieManager.GetCookies(
                              new Uri("http://www.msn.com")))
{
  // Examine Domain, Expires, Name, Path, Value, Secure, and HttpOnly
}
```

If the app has previously fetched content from msn.com either by using `HttpClient`, `Image`, `MediaElement`, or `WebView`, this code should retrieve several cookies. Notice that no `HttpClient` is even necessary if all you're doing is cookie management.

Controlling Caching

`HttpBaseProtocolFilter` has a `CacheControl` property that exposes two of its own properties for independently controlling reading from the cache and writing from the cache. `ReadBehavior` can be set to one of the following values from the `HttpCacheReadBehavior` enumeration:

→ **Default**—Act just like a normal Web browser, following the standard cache algorithm.

→ **MostRecent**—Use the cache if possible, but send a request to the server with an If-Modified-Since header to check if there's a newer version of the content. This gives you the freshest data possible, but results in more network activity.

→ **OnlyFromCache**—Be in an offline mode, and never make a network request.

WriteBehavior can be set to one of the following values from the
HttpCacheWriteBehavior enumeration:

→ **Default**—Act just like a normal web browser, and cache the content if the server
says it is cacheable.

→ **NoCache**—Never cache the content. This is useful for requests that you know will
never be made again, because caching the result could evict useful content from
the cache.

Whenever you get an HttpResponseMessage, such as from a call to HttpClient.GetAsync,
you can check where the content actually came from with its Source property. It is one of
the following values from the HttpResponseMessageSource enumeration: Cache, Network,
or None. You'll never see None from a normal request, although it's the default value for
Source if you construct a new HttpResponseMessage on your own.

HTTP Prefetching

With the HTTP prefetching feature, you can give Windows a list of Uris. Windows
may periodically fetch the content and update your cache used by HttpClient, Image,
MediaElement, and WebView without your app ever running! The team that works on this
feature affectionately calls it the "fresh apps" feature.

The frequency of prefetching and whether it is done at all for your app is based on a
number of conditions. There are required system conditions (such as available battery,
CPU, and a non-metered network), required user behavior (how frequently and when is
your app used), and evidence of prior benefit (Windows prioritizes the apps in which
prefetching seems to make a big difference). Therefore, there's no guarantee that prefetching will happen for your app, but it can be a huge benefit for the heaviest users of your
app. For example, someone who opens the News app daily should benefit from fast app
launches with recent news cached and ready to be displayed without relying on the
network.

To tell Windows about your URLs to prefetch, simply add Uris to the static
ContentPrefetcher.ContentUris list from the Windows.Networking.BackgroundTransfer
namespace. Alternatively, you could set ContentPrefetcher.IndirectContentUri to a
single Uri that specifies the list in the following XML format:

```xml
<?xml version="1.0" encoding="UTF-8"?>
<prefetchUris>
  <uri>URI1</uri>
  <uri>URI2</uri>

  …
</prefetchUris>
```

This enables you to manage the list from a Web service, which is especially helpful for
Uris that are going to change regularly.

Background Transfer

If you download a large file that could take a significant amount of time, you should use the BackgroundDownloader class instead of HttpClient. BackgroundDownloader, from the Windows.Networking.BackgroundTransfer namespace, helps your app behave appropriately in the face of suspension or changing network conditions.

You can instantiate a BackgroundDownloader then call its CreateDownload method, which accepts a source Uri and a destination StorageFile. This returns a DownloadOperation object that enables starting, pausing, resuming, and progress reporting. If your app (and therefore a download) is terminated, you can enumerate pending downloads the next time your app runs with the static BackgroundDownloader.GetCurrentDownloadsAsync method and resume them. A similar Background**Uploader** class exists, with a CreateUpload method that returns a BackgroundUploader object.

The following code demonstrates a simple use of BackgroundDownloader:

```
IRandomAccessStreamWithContentType stream;

async Task DownloadAndPlayMedia(Uri uri)
{
  // Create a local temp file to use as the download destination
  StorageFolder folder = ApplicationData.Current.TemporaryFolder;
  StorageFile file = await folder.CreateFileAsync("temp.mp4",
    CreationCollisionOption.GenerateUniqueName);

  if (file != null)
  {
    // Download from uri to file
    BackgroundDownloader downloader = new BackgroundDownloader();
    DownloadOperation operation = downloader.CreateDownload(uri, file);

    // New in Windows 8.1:
    operation.Priority = BackgroundTransferPriority.High;

    // You could use the returned IAsyncOperationWithProgress to show progress
    await operation.StartAsync();
    // The download is now finished

    this.stream = await operation.ResultFile.OpenReadAsync();
    this.mediaElement.SetSource(stream, stream.ContentType);
    // Dispose the stream after the MediaOpened event!
  }
}
```

As with HttpClient, you can get progress callbacks from the StartAsync method. Windows 8.1 enables you raise the priority of a download, which can move it toward the front of the queue when there are multiple pending downloads.

In order to save battery power, Windows throttles background downloads when the current device isn't plugged in. This might not always be the best choice, however. The increased time for downloads can be frustrating for users, and sometimes they might prefer the download to occur at full speed. Therefore, Windows 8.1 introduces a new API that enables you to put the user in control of this decision: BackgroundDownloader. RequestUnconstrainedDownloadAsync.

You can call this static method (on the UI thread) with a collection of DownloadOperations, as done in the following code with the single DownloadOperation:

```
IRandomAccessStreamWithContentType stream;

async Task DownloadAndPlayMedia(Uri uri)
{
  // Create a local temp file to use as the download destination
  StorageFolder folder = ApplicationData.Current.TemporaryFolder;
  StorageFile file = await folder.CreateFileAsync("temp.mp4",
    CreationCollisionOption.GenerateUniqueName);

  if (file != null)
  {
    // Download from uri to file
    BackgroundDownloader downloader = new BackgroundDownloader();
    DownloadOperation operation = downloader.CreateDownload(uri, file);

    // New in Windows 8.1:
    operation.Priority = BackgroundTransferPriority.High;

    // Request unconstrained download for just this one download
    UnconstrainedTransferRequestResult result = await
      BackgroundDownloader.RequestUnconstrainedDownloadsAsync(
        new DownloadOperation[] { operation } );

    if (result.IsUnconstrained)
    {
      // Hooray! It won't take as long.
    }

    // You could use the returned IAsyncOperationWithProgress to show progress
    await operation.StartAsync();
    // The download is now finished

    this.stream = await operation.ResultFile.OpenReadAsync();
    this.mediaElement.SetSource(stream, stream.ContentType);
    // Dispose the stream after the MediaOpened event!
  }
}
```

If the device is plugged in when the call to RequestUnconstrainedDownloadsAsync is made, it does nothing and the returned object's IsUnconstrained property returns true because it's already the case that the download will occur unrestrained. If the device is running on battery power, however, the user is shown the dialog in Figure 20.2. In this case, IsUnconstrained reports the result of the user's choice, which automatically impacts the download without you having to do anything else. Considering the wording of the dialog, you might consider waiting to initiate the download (or pausing an existing one) rather than continuing it as a constrained download.

FIGURE 20.2   RequestUnconstrainedDownloadsAsync prompts the user if the device is running on battery power.

This feature exists for uploads, too. You can call BackgroundUploader.Request-UnconstrainedUploadsAsync with a collection of UploadOperations.

Sockets

The Windows.Networking.Sockets namespace contains classes that enable you to send and receive data via TCP sockets (reliable bidirectional streams), UDP sockets (unreliable datagrams), or WebSockets (both styles, but over HTTP):

→ DatagramSocket is a UDP socket.

→ StreamSocket is a TCP socket.

→ MessageWebSocket is basically a UDP-like WebSocket.

→ StreamWebSocket is basically a TCP-like WebSocket.

Syndication

The Windows.Web.Syndication namespace contains functionality for accessing RSS and Atom feeds. The RSS support covers standards 0.91 to 2.0, and the Atom support covers standards 0.3 to 1.0.

The following complete code-behind is for an RSS Reader page that shows the latest items from Engadget's RSS feed:

```
using System;
using System.Threading.Tasks;
using Windows.UI.Xaml.Controls;
using Windows.Web.Syndication;
```

```
namespace RssReader
{
  public sealed partial class MainPage : Page
  {
    public MainPage()
    {
      InitializeComponent();
      FillContentAsync();
    }

    async Task FillContentAsync()
    {
      SyndicationClient client = new SyndicationClient();
      try
      {
        SyndicationFeed feed = await client.RetrieveFeedAsync(
          new Uri("http://engadget.com/rss.xml"));

        this.DataContext = feed;
      }
      catch
      {
        // Handle any errors, such as a 404 from an unavailable site
        …
      }
    }

    void ListView_SelectionChanged(object sender, SelectionChangedEventArgs e)
    {
      if (e.AddedItems.Count == 0)
        return;

      // Show the selected item's content in the WebView because it is HTML
      this.webView.NavigateToString(
        (e.AddedItems[0] as SyndicationItem).Summary.Text);
    }
  }
}
```

The SyndicationFeed object returned by RetrieveFeedAsync exposes information about the feed itself (such as a title) and a collection of SyndicationItem objects that reveals all the information about each entry in the feed. Rather than extract such info in C#, this code sets the returned feed as the Page's data context so the XAML can data bind to it. Here is the corresponding XAML:

```
<Page …>
  <Grid Background="{ThemeResource ApplicationPageBackgroundThemeBrush}">
    <Grid.ColumnDefinitions>
      <ColumnDefinition/>
      <ColumnDefinition/>
    </Grid.ColumnDefinitions>

    <!-- A ListView on the left shows the title of each item -->
    <ListView Header="{Binding Title.Text}" ItemsSource="{Binding Items}"
              SelectionChanged="ListView_SelectionChanged">

      <!-- Display the feed title in a larger-than-default TextBlock -->
      <ListView.HeaderTemplate>
        <DataTemplate>
          <TextBlock Style="{StaticResource HeaderTextStyle}" Text="{Binding}"/>
        </DataTemplate>
      </ListView.HeaderTemplate>

      <!-- Display only the title for each item in a subheader style -->
      <ListView.ItemTemplate>
        <DataTemplate>
          <TextBlock Style="{StaticResource SubheaderTextStyle}" Margin="10"
                     Text="{Binding Title.Text}"/>
        </DataTemplate>
      </ListView.ItemTemplate>
    </ListView>

    <!-- A WebView on the right renders the selected item's content -->
    <WebView Name="webView" Grid.Column="1"/>
  </Grid>
</Page>
```

This Page has a ListView on the left and a WebView on the right. The ListView's Header is bound to the feed title (Title.Text on the SyndicationFeed object) and its ItemsSource is bound to the feed's Items collection. Each item's title is shown by binding to Title.Text. When a selection is made, ListView_SelectionChanged is invoked to make the WebView render the content from the selected item. (This is done because the content in each item is HTML.) The result is shown in Figure 20.3. It's not perfect, as it would be better to call WebUtility.HtmlDecode on each item's Title.Text before displaying it to avoid text like "AT&T" being shown as "AT&T."

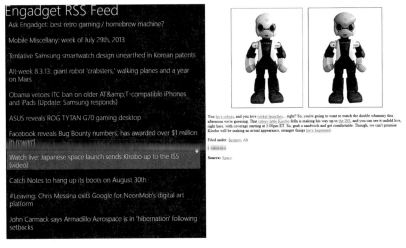

FIGURE 20.3   A simple RSS reader is easy to create with `SyndicationClient` to fetch and parse the feed and `WebView` to display the HTML content.

> You can perform Atom feed *publication* with the `AtomPubClient` class in the `Windows.Web.AtomPub` namespace.

> Feed items often contain custom elements or attributes. To retrieve these, you can access the XML representation via `SyndicationFeed`'s and `SyndicationItem`'s `GetXmlDocument` method or `ElementExtensions` property.

Connection Info

Through the static `NetworkInformation` class, you can discover details about all current network connections. You can also be notified of any changes via its `NetworkStatusChanged` property. For example, `NetworkInformation`'s `GetConnectionProfiles` method returns a collection of `ConnectionProfiles`, which have methods that expose the cost of the connection (including whether the user is roaming or over the data limit) and how much of the connection is used. You can use information like this to warn a user who is about to download a large file through your app while on a costly network. However, for some scenarios in which you already have `StorageFile`(s), checking `IsAvailable` is much simpler than manually examining the current connection info.

> The Visual Studio 2013 simulator supports the simulation of metered network connections or going offline. (Although the latter is pretty easy to make happen without the simulator's help!)

Summary

The options for working with data are powerful yet straightforward, and they became even easier to use in Windows 8.1. They balance the needs of app developers with the important need for users to be able to trust what their apps are doing.

To me, what is most striking about the features in this chapter is how easy Microsoft made it to index your app's data and to roam it. With automatic roaming, it's trivial to keep a consistent experience across devices. You don't need to directly interact with a Web service or understand anything about Microsoft accounts in order to take advantage of it.

Chapter 21

SUPPORTING CHARMS

The charms bar, shown in Figure 21.1, provides a consistent mechanism for users to accomplish a few tasks with any apps that support them. Each "charm," except for Start, brings up a corresponding pane on the edge of the screen. In Windows 8, the charms apply to the app currently occupying the screen (or most of the screen). In Windows 8.1, the charms now apply to whichever app's window is currently has focus, even if it is at its minimum size at the opposite edge of the screen.

All the panes presented by the charms can be exploited by apps to varying degrees. This chapter explains how you can take advantage of each one.

The Search Charm

The behavior of the pane shown by the Search charm has changed significantly from Windows 8 to Windows 8.1. In Windows 8, its job is to enable searching Windows and searching within apps (for the apps that support it). The default scope of the search depends on which app occupies most of the screen, and changing the scope is often awkward. You can search the Web on the Search pane in Windows 8, but only by choosing to search within in app like Internet Explorer or Bing.

In Windows 8.1, the Search pane's job is to enable searching Windows *and the Web—not* within apps. (It also now searches "everywhere" by default— files, settings, installed app names, and the Web— so users normally don't have to worry about changing the scope of the search.) This means that apps must take responsibility for their own in-app searching. As you saw in Chapter 15, "Other Controls," the new SearchBox control fortunately makes this easy. In fact, interacting with SearchBox is almost identical to how you would interact with the Search pane in Windows 8 to integrate your in-app search.

Why did Microsoft make this change? There are several reasons:

→ Showing search directly on your app's surface makes it more discoverable, and usually faster to access.

→ The Search pane is now able to act consistently. Users know what to expect when they invoke the Search charm, no matter what app(s) are on the screen. In this way, it acts like the Search hardware button on Windows Phones.

FIGURE 21.1   The charms bar with its five charms

→ In-app searching can be handled much better when the app has more control over the process. For example, the app can provide search filtering options *before* the user starts searching rather than the Windows 8 model of filtering after the search.

In short, this change is designed to make both system-provided searching and in-app searching better for users. And it means that app integration with the Search pane only exists for compatibility with Windows 8. This section looks at what it means to integrate with the Search pane the "Windows 8 way" when your app runs on Windows 8.1.

The Windows 8 Search Contract

To integrate with the Search pane, you must support the Search contract. In Visual Studio 2012, you can do this by right-clicking your project, select **Add**, **New Item...**, and then choose **Search Contract** from the list. This option has been removed from Visual Studio 2013, as it is designed for Windows 8.1 apps which aren't expected to use the Search contract. If it's not convenient for you to use Visual Studio 2012 and later migrate your app to Visual Studio 2013, then you can leverage the code that comes with this book's download and add it to your app.

When you add a Search contract in Visual Studio 2012, it adds a search results page to your app similar to the one examined in the "SearchBox" section of Chapter 15. (It was designed for Windows 8, however, so you should eventually replace it with a new search results page from the Add New Item dialog in Visual Studio 2013.) It also adds "Search" to the list of supported declarations to your package manifest, which registers the app as a search provider. Code such as the following is automatically added to App.xaml.cs, which makes your app display the search results page whenever it is activated via the Search pane:

```
/// <summary>
/// Invoked when the application is activated to display search results.
/// </summary>
/// <param name="args">Details about the activation request.</param>
protected override void OnSearchActivated(SearchActivatedEventArgs args)
{
  Chapter21.SearchResultsPage1.Activate(args.QueryText,
                                        args.PreviousExecutionState);
}
```

If you run your app with these changes and then invoke the Search charm, you see the result in Figure 21.2. Your app is automatically added to the list of search scopes, although on Windows 8.1 it is not selected by default, nor does your app appear in the list if it is not currently on the screen.

If you select your app as the search scope and then search for something, your app is activated and your search results page is shown thanks to the code inside OnSearchActivated. At this point, you just need to flesh out the functionality of the search results page, just as we did in Chapter 15 when integrating it with SearchBox.

FIGURE 21.2   Once you support the Search contract, your app appears in the Search pane while it is on-screen.

Customizing the Search Pane

The Search pane is represented by a SearchPane class in the Windows.ApplicationModel.Search namespace. To ease the migration of

Windows 8 apps to Windows 8.1, SearchBox was designed to be practically a drop-in replacement for SearchPane. These two classes support most of the same features and expose practically identical APIs. So interacting with SearchPane should look very familiar.

SearchPane exposes many of the same useful properties and events, such as PlaceholderText, QueryText, QueryChanged, and QuerySubmitted. Just as with SearchBox, your app can provide query suggestions that are shown as the user types. To do this, you must retrieve an instance of the SearchPane class as follows ꜰꜰꜰ ꜰꜰꜰꜰꜰꜰꜰ ꜰꜰ ꜰꜰꜰꜰꜰꜰꜰꜰꜰꜰꜰꜰꜰꜰꜰꜰꜰꜰꜰ ꜰꜰꜰꜰꜰ꞉

```
SearchPane searchPane = SearchPane.GetForCurrentView();
searchPane.SuggestionsRequested += OnSuggestionsRequested;
```

This is best done in App.xaml.cs from OnWindowCreated so you won't miss the event even if the app wasn't originally activated via the Search charm.

The following implementation of the OnSuggestionsRequested handler matches the handler from Chapter 15 for SearchBox's same event, reporting hardcoded suggestions if the user types a matching string (in a case-insensitive fashion):

```
// Sample static custom suggestions
static readonly string[] suggestions = { "Suggestion #1",
  "Suggestion #2", "Suggestion #3", "Suggestion #4", "Suggestion #5" };

void OnSuggestionsRequested(SearchPane sender,
                      SearchPaneSuggestionsRequestedEventArgs e)
{
  if (!string.IsNullOrEmpty(e.QueryText))
  {
    foreach (string suggestion in suggestions)
    {
      if (suggestion.StartsWith(e.QueryText,
                          StringComparison.CurrentCultureIgnoreCase))
      {
        // Add the suggestion to the Search pane
        e.Request.SearchSuggestionCollection.AppendQuerySuggestion(suggestion);
      }
    }
  }
}
```

The result is shown in Figure 21.3.

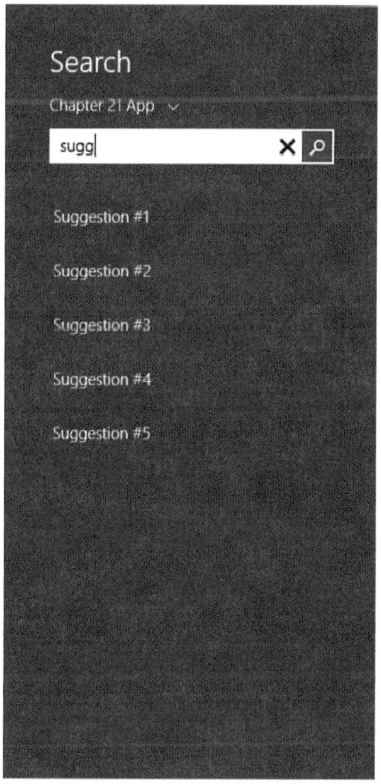

FIGURE 21.3   App-provided query suggestions can appear in the Search pane.

The Search pane automatically remembers the user's previous searches and provides them as history suggestions at a higher priority than query suggestions. You can turn this off by setting SearchPane's SearchHistoryEnabled property to `false`. Again, this is just like with SearchBox.

> **(!) Unlike SearchBox, the Search pane only shows up to five suggestions from your app!**
>
> Therefore, code that produces them might as well exit early after five have been added to the collection.

In addition to AppendQuerySuggestion, SearchSuggestionCollection exposes AppendSearchSeparator and AppendResultSuggestion methods. The following code uses all three methods to produce the result in Figure 21.4, just like in Chapter 15 with SearchBox. Note that the search separator counts against the limit of five items:

```
void OnSuggestionsRequested(SearchPane sender,
                        SearchPaneSuggestionsRequestedEventArgs e)
{
```

```
if (!string.IsNullOrEmpty(e.QueryText))
{
  RandomAccessStreamReference image = RandomAccessStreamReference.CreateFromUri(
    new Uri("ms-appx:///Assets/Result.png"));

  e.Request.SearchSuggestionCollection.AppendResultSuggestion("Result",
    "You probably want this.", "tag", image, "Alt image text");
  e.Request.SearchSuggestionCollection.AppendSearchSeparator("Suggestions");
  e.Request.SearchSuggestionCollection.AppendQuerySuggestion("Suggestion #1");
  e.Request.SearchSuggestionCollection.AppendQuerySuggestion("Suggestion #2");
  e.Request.SearchSuggestionCollection.AppendQuerySuggestion("Suggestion #3");
}
}
```

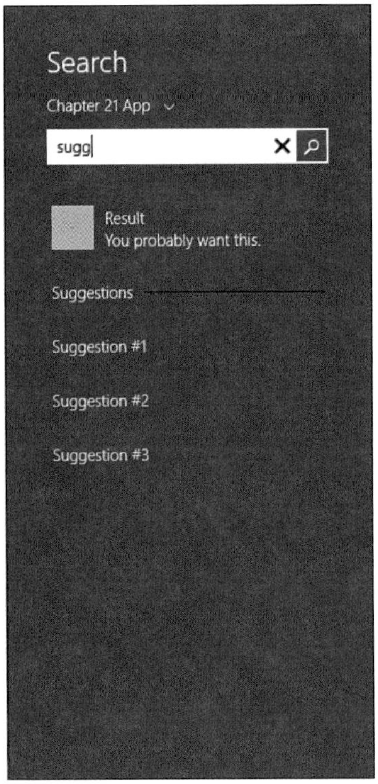

FIGURE 21.4   Leveraging a separator and a result suggestion in the suggestions list

The result suggestion's tag ("tag" in this example) is not displayed, but is passed along to the ResultSuggestionChosen event handler.

Programmatically Showing the Search Pane

If your app is searchable and the current page has no use for text input, you should automatically send the user's keystrokes from the hardware keyboard to the Search pane. Like SearchBox's FocusOnKeyboardInput property, SearchPane has a simple **Show**OnKeyboardInput Boolean property. When you set this to true, any key press automatically shows the Search pane if it's not already visible, gives focus to its search box, and populates it with the relevant text.

If your app requires text input for other reasons, you can still provide a search button of some sort that manually shows the Search pane by calling SearchPane's Show method. There's even an overload for populating the Search pane's search box with an initial query string.

When an app programmatically shows the Search pane via either of these mechanisms, the search scope is automatically set to that app. In Windows 8.1, this is the only time that this occurs, and it is done for compatibility with apps designed for Windows 8 that leverage the Search pane in this manner.

> If you want to enable in-app searching, you should use the SearchBox control, never programmatically show the Search pane, and not even bother with the Search contract. However, if you're working on an existing Windows 8 app and inserting a SearchBox control into your user interface is too big of a change for you to consider, then you should at least add a custom search button that programmatically shows the Search pane. (This does require you to support the Search contract.) Because it defaults the Search to be within your app, it provides a reasonable Windows 8-style search experience for your app in spite of all the changes that have been made to the Search pane in Windows 8.1.

The Share Charm

The Share charm is a richer version of the Windows clipboard, enabling one app to send another anything that they both claim to support: plain text, rich text, images, specific document types, or completely custom binary data. It also enables an app to automatically decide what information is currently worth sharing, unlike the explicit selection and copying done with clipboard operations. With this sharing scheme, an app can play the part of the sender (source), receiver (target), or both, for any number of formats.

Being a Share Source

If your app contains data that is potentially worth sharing (above and beyond text that can be copied and pasted via normal gestures), it should be a share source. Most apps fall into this category. For example, games should enable the user to share a high score, news apps should enable the user to share an article, drawing apps should enable the user to share each creation, and so on.

In Windows 8.1, the user can invoke the Share charm on any app and share a screenshot or a link to the app in the Windows Store (without any work done by the app). Still, it might be useful for you to share a screenshot of just a portion of your window. With `RenderTargetBitmap` in Windows 8.1, you can easily do this by rendering an appropriate `UIElement` then supporting the share source mechanism.

You can be a share source without doing anything special to support the contract in the package manifest. You must provide a *data package* to the *data package manager* when requested. This involves handling a `DataRequested` event as follows:

```
DataTransferManager dtm = DataTransferManager.GetForCurrentView();
dtm.DataRequested += OnDataRequested;
```

This event gets raised whenever the user invokes the Share charm.

The following implementation of `OnDataRequested` stuffs the data package (`e.Request.Data`, which is of type `DataPackage`) with data:

```
void OnDataRequested(DataTransferManager sender, DataRequestedEventArgs e)
{
  // These are shown in the Share pane, and may also be used by the target
  e.Request.Data.Properties.Title = "DataPackage Title";
  e.Request.Data.Properties.Description = "Description for the Share pane";

  // Data in various formats
  e.Request.Data.SetText("Text to share");
  e.Request.Data.SetHtmlFormat(
    HtmlFormatHelper.CreateHtmlFormat("<b>Richer</b> content to share"));
  e.Request.Data.SetWebLink(new Uri("http://bing.com"));
}
```

How the data gets used ultimately depends on the share target. However, the two properties being set—Title and Description—are shown in the Share pane that gets displayed when the user invokes the Share charm. The main data can be specified in many formats—plain text, HTML, a link to a website or app, RTF, IStorageItem (the interface implemented by StorageFile and StorageFolder), image, or custom—and it makes sense to provide the same data in as many formats as possible to maximize the number of share targets your app works with. This sample implementation of OnDataRequested provides data in three formats, although for demonstration purposes it doesn't use equivalent data for all three. If you need to perform asynchronous actions, you can call e.Request.GetDeferral beforehand and then call Complete on the returned DataRequestDeferral object when all the work is done.

DataPackage's SetWebLink method (used in the preceding code) and SetApplicationLink method (used to share a link that can be handled by an app) are new to Windows 8.1. In Windows 8, there is only a SetUri method that is now deprecated. Now, URIs with an http or https scheme should be passed to SetWebLink, and schemes that would be handled by apps should be passed to SetApplicationLink. This split was done so that an app is able to pass *both* types of links when the content exists in both forms. (For example, an article on Wikipedia's website versus the same article within Wikipedia's app.) The share target can potentially provide an experience that leverages both types of links.

In the share APIs, as with SearchPane, images are not represented directly as streams, but rather as RandomAccessStream**Reference** objects that wrap streams. You can construct one with one of its three static methods: CreateFromStream, CreateFromFile, or CreateFromUri.

(!) **Always use HtmlFormatHelper.CreateHtmlFormat when passing an HTML string to SetHtmlFormat!**

Target apps won't be able to process an arbitrary HTML fragment because they expect a specific format returned by CreateHtmlFormat. For example, here is the string returned by CreateHtmlFormat for the simple input of "Richer content to share":

```
Version:1.0
StartHTML:00000097
EndHTML:00000216
StartFragment:00000153
EndFragment:00000183
<!DOCTYPE><HTML><HEAD></HEAD><BODY><!--StartFragment --><b>Richer</b> content
to share<!--EndFragment --></BODY></HTML>
```

With this handler for DataRequested in place, Figure 21.5 demonstrates the appearance of the Share pane after the user invokes the Share charm.

The user can choose to share either your data package, the automatic screenshot of your window, or the Windows Store app link (if your app is already in the Windows Store) by tapping the down arrow next to your data package title.

Figure 21.6 demonstrates how three different share targets handle the data being shared. The Mail app uses the title for the email message subject and the Web link for the message body. It ignores the text and HTML, although if no Web link is shared, it would use the HTML for the body instead. If there were no HTML or if the HTML is invalid, it would use the plain text. The People app acts the same way (when posting to Facebook) although it doesn't do anything with the title. And Rowi, a Twitter app, displays the plain text *and* the Web link!

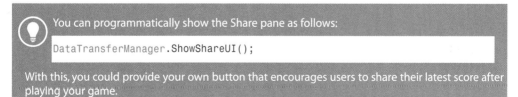

You can programmatically show the Share pane as follows:

```
DataTransferManager.ShowShareUI();
```

With this, you could provide your own button that encourages users to share their latest score after playing your game.

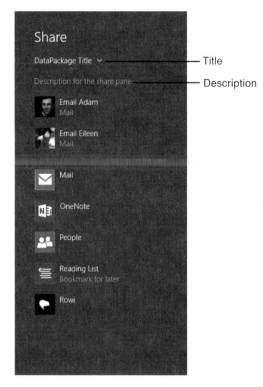

Title

Description

FIGURE 21.5   The Share pane shows the title and description set by the handler of the `DataRequested` event.

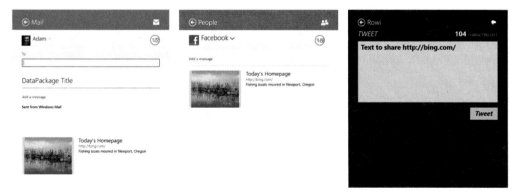

FIGURE 21.6   Three share targets handle the same data package in slightly different ways.

In addition to the built-in formats, you can share data in a custom format using `DataPackage`'s generic `SetData` or `SetDataProvider` methods. (The former accepts the data as a generic `object`, whereas the latter accepts a delegate that provides the data when invoked by the target.) The first parameter of both of these methods is a string ID identifying the format. In fact, the various methods such as SetText, SetHtml, and so forth, are shortcuts for calling SetData with the appropriate ID. The IDs for the six built-in formats are represented by properties on the static StandardDataFormats class: ApplicationLink, Bitmap, Html, Rtf, StorageItems, Text, Uri (which is deprecated), and WebLink.

As for your own custom formats, they are good only if other apps are built to receive such data. Therefore, you should stick to standard IDs (and therefore standard representations) that are widely used. Conventions are bound to emerge over time for representations of people, places, movies, and so on, perhaps based on schemas such as what is shared at http://schema.org.

> DataPackage has a property called Properties (of type DataPackagePropertySet) that enables you to send a bunch of extra property values to the share target. For example, if you're sharing an image, you should set the Thumbnail property to a small thumbnail so the share target can potentially show it while waiting for the operation to complete.
>
> If you're sharing an app link, you should set the PackageFamilyName property of the app that can handle it. The share target can leverage this information in the future if that app has been uninstalled (or the data has roamed to a device without it installed). When the share target calls LaunchUriAsync with the app link it received, it can specify the PackageFamilyName within LauncherOptions so the fallback prompt that launches the Windows Store can navigate to the specific app that is needed.

Being a Share Target

Apps that are appropriate share targets are more rare than apps that are appropriate share sources. However, any app involved with publishing, storing, or transforming data—even something silly such as adding speech bubbles to photos—can be a good share target.

Being a share target is more involved than being a share source. To be able to receive content, an app must declare itself as a share target in the package manifest for specific formats and/or file types.

The easiest way to support the Share Target contract is to right-click on your project in Visual Studio, select **Add, New Item...**, then choose **Share Target Contract** from the list. Unless you change its name, this adds a Page called ShareTargetPage1.xaml to your app. It also adds "Share Target" to the list of supported declarations to your package manifest, as shown in Figure 21.7. You must specify which formats you want to support here, and/or list extensions for file types you want to support.

The generated Page is used to fill in the Share pane once the user selects your app as the share target. In this situation, your app gets activated specifically for the sharing action, so this is enabled by the following code that gets automatically added to App.xaml.cs:

```
/// <summary>
/// Invoked when the app is activated as the target of a sharing operation.
/// </summary>
/// <param name="args">Details about the activation request.</param>
protected override void OnShareTargetActivated(
  ShareTargetActivatedEventArgs args)
{
  var shareTargetPage = new Chapter21.ShareTargetPage1();
  shareTargetPage.Activate(args);
}
```

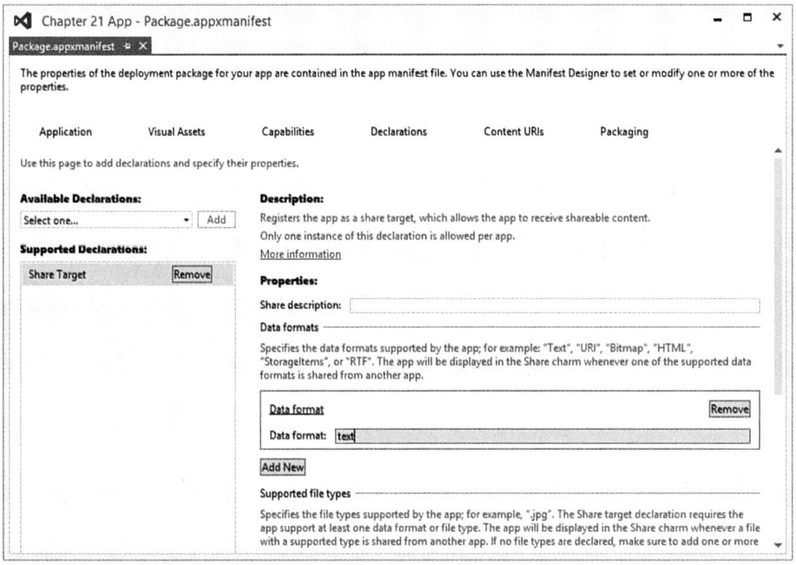

FIGURE 21.7   The auto-generated Share Target contract, edited to claim support for receiving text

If you run your app at least once (to get it deployed) after following these steps, and then invoke the Share charm from a *different* app (such as the share source shown earlier), you see the result in Figures 21.8 and 21.9. Your app is automatically added to the list of available targets as long as the data to share is in a format your app claims to handle.

In Figure 21.9, the top part of the Share pane is provided by Windows, but it is based on your app's display name, icon ("30x30") logo, and background color in your package manifest.

ShareTargetPage1 is a simple page that doesn't do much. It displays some information from the data package, has a TextBox for hypothetically adding a comment to the shared data, and a "Share" Button that doesn't do anything other than report that it completes the action so the pane automatically dismisses.

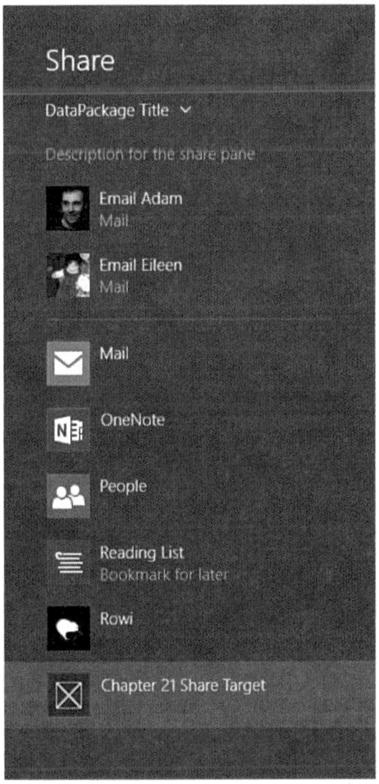

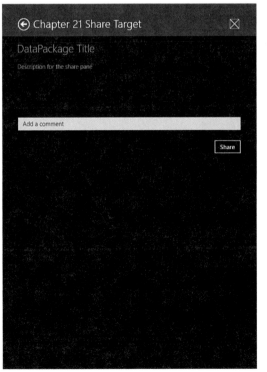

FIGURE 21.8   The Share pane lists your app if it supports the Share Target contract for any of the available data formats.

FIGURE 21.9   When your app is selected, the auto-generated `ShareTargetPage1` is hosted inside the Share pane.

The data package is exposed to the target app via the `ShareTargetActivatedEventArgs` instance initially passed to `OnShareTargetActivated`. It has a `ShareOperation` property (of type `ShareOperation`) with a `Data` property that reveals the available formats and provides methods (`GetTextAsync`, `GetHtmlFormatAsync`, and so on) for retrieving the data. When you start processing the data, you should call `ShareOperation`'s `ReportStarted` method, and when you're done, you should call its `ReportCompleted` method. The latter is what makes the Share pane automatically dismiss. Although if the user dismisses the pane while you're still doing work, Windows will still give you 10 more seconds to complete your task. If completing your task involves a background task, you should call

Windows 8.1 introduces a `DismissUI` method on `ShareOperation` that you can call to hide the Share pane (and still get 10 more seconds to complete your task). This is exactly like the user dismissing the pane by tapping elsewhere. However, many users are reluctant to do so because they think that dismissing the pane cancels the operation. By dismissing it for them, it makes the operation appear to finish quickly and removes user doubt about whether to wait.

When getting HTML-formatted data via `GetHtmlFormatAsync`, be sure to pass it to `HtmlFormatHelper.GetStaticFragment` in order to get a plain HTML fragment!

This is because the share source is (or should be) passing a specially formatted string that was returned from `HtmlFormatHelper.CreateHtmlFormat`.

Notice that the list of share targets in Figure 21.8 contains links to specific actions that can be performed by the Mail app. These are called *quick links*, and any app can provide them. To do this, you can create a `QuickLink` object (which has properties such as `Id`, `Title`, and `Thumbnail`) and pass it to an overload of `ShareOperation.ReportCompleted` when you complete a share operation as the share target. This, of course, means that you can provide a quick link to Windows only if the user has previously shared something for your app. The idea is that the `QuickLink` you provide is supposed to represent the action just performed, because if the user did it once, then she is likely to want to do it again.

If you are later invoked via a quick link, the `ShareOperation` object given to you has its `QuickLinkId` property properly filled out so you can take the appropriate action. If your quick link doesn't make sense to persist after it is invoked, you can call `ShareOperation.RemoveThisQuickLink` to prevent it from appearing in the list in the future.

The Devices Charm

The Devices pane shown by invoking the Devices charm contains three to four pages: Play, Print, Project, and Tap and Send if the PC supports it. You can think of each of the first three much like the Share pane. The current app is the *source* that has content to send to a *target* device. Each page enables the user to choose a target device appropriate for whatever content is available to send.

Only Windows-certified devices such as printers, screens, speakers, and receivers can be exposed via this mechanism as target devices. However, with a little work, any app can be a *source* for registered devices. An app can supporting printing to work with the Print page, and it can support Play To streaming to work with the Play page. Although all apps automatically support being projected to secondary screens via the Project page, you can actually customize your projection behavior a bit. This section looks at all three of these scenarios.

Printing

Supporting printing in your app is straightforward. With a little interaction with a `PrintManager` class and the use of a XAML-specific `PrintDocument` class that knows how to print any `UIElement`, you can integrate with the built-in print—and print preview—

functionality accessible through the Devices charm. Note that you must opt into this support. The Windows team chose not to enable every app to be automatically printable, because the results are likely to not be great without explicit support from the app.

> Windows 8.1 enables apps to support 3D printing, but this is exposed as unmanaged APIs directly available only to Windows Store apps that use C++.

Listing 21.1 demonstrates the code needed to supply the print manager with a simple two-page document that can be previewed and printed. Although the content supplied to the print manager should often match what's on-screen, or be a print-friendly reformatting of the content on-screen, this listing actually provides arbitrary XAML content that has nothing to do with the current (blank) page. This is done for demonstration purposes, just to emphasize the flexibility you have with printing.

LISTING 21.1   `MainPage.xaml.cs`: Supporting Print and Print Preview

```
using System;
using Windows.Graphics.Printing;
using Windows.UI;
using Windows.UI.Core;
using Windows.UI.Xaml.Controls;
using Windows.UI.Xaml.Media;
using Windows.UI.Xaml.Printing;
```

LISTING 21.1   Continued

```csharp
namespace Chapter21
{
  public sealed partial class MainPage : Page
  {
    // Supports printing pages, where each page is a UIElement
    PrintDocument doc = new PrintDocument();

    public MainPage()
    {
      InitializeComponent();

      // Attach handlers to relevant events
      doc.GetPreviewPage += OnGetPreviewPage;
      doc.AddPages += OnAddPages;

      PrintManager printManager = PrintManager.GetForCurrentView();
      printManager.PrintTaskRequested += OnPrintTaskRequested;
    }

    // Prepare the print preview pages
    void OnGetPreviewPage(object sender, GetPreviewPageEventArgs e)
    {
      this.doc.SetPreviewPageCount(2, PreviewPageCountType.Final);
      if (e.PageNumber == 1)
      {
        this.doc.SetPreviewPage(1, new Viewbox { Child = new Button {
          Content = "PAGE 1!", Background = new SolidColorBrush(Colors.Red) } });
      }
      else
      {
        this.doc.SetPreviewPage(2, new Viewbox { Child = new Button {
          Content = "PAGE 2!", Background = new SolidColorBrush(Colors.Red) } });
      }
    }

    // Prepare the real pages
    void OnAddPages(object sender, AddPagesEventArgs e)
    {
      this.doc.AddPage(new Viewbox { Child = new Button {
        Content = "PAGE 1!", Background = new SolidColorBrush(Colors.Red) } });
      this.doc.AddPage(new Viewbox { Child = new Button {
        Content = "PAGE 2!", Background = new SolidColorBrush(Colors.Red) } });
      this.doc.AddPagesComplete();
    }
```

LISTING 21.1   Continued

```
// Prepare and perform the printing
void OnPrintTaskRequested(PrintManager sender,
                          PrintTaskRequestedEventArgs args)
{
  // This is invoked when the Print section of the Devices pane opens
  PrintTask task = args.Request.CreatePrintTask("Document Title",
    async (taskArgs) =>
    {
      // This is invoked on a background thread when the Print
      // button is clicked
      var deferral = taskArgs.GetDeferral();
      await this.Dispatcher.RunAsync(CoreDispatcherPriority.Normal, () =>
      {
        // This must run on the UI thread
        taskArgs.SetSource(doc.DocumentSource);
        deferral.Complete();
      });
    });
  }
}
}
```

Although PrintDocument exposes methods for adding preview pages and "real" pages, this must be called inside relevant events: GetPreviewPage and AddPages. Similarly, initializing the *print task* must be done from a PrintTaskRequested event on the PrintManager object. All of this is set up inside MainPage's constructor. Be careful where you attach (and/or detach) handlers to these events in a multi-Page app to make sure the right thing happens regardless of which Page is currently on the screen.

For print preview, you can tell the print manager how many pages exist with a call to PrintDocument's SetPreviewPageCount method, but only once OnGetPreviewPage is already being called requesting a preview of the first page. This implementation creates two preview pages, with each one containing a simple Button in a Viewbox (so it scales to uniformly fill the space on the page). This XAML content happens to be identical to the XAML content used for the real pages, but this doesn't have to be the case. For example, you can choose to do something different because it's significantly faster than producing the real page.

> **(!) Treat a print preview as required, not optional!**
>
> The Printing pane shows a print preview regardless. If you don't provide one, it shows a ProgressRing indefinitely, and that makes your app appear to be broken.

The handler for the AddPages event is similar to the handler for the GetPreviewPage event, except all pages should be added at once, followed by a call to AddPagesComplete.

The handler for PrintTaskRequested is more complicated. This event is raised as soon as the Print section of the Devices pane is accessed by the user, although typically all that is done by a handler at that point is call CreatePrintTask. The rest of the logic is in a delegate passed to CreatePrintTask that gets invoked when the user clicks the Print button (after selecting a printer and changing any options).

The job of the delegate is to hand the *document source* to the print manager. This is exposed via the DocumentSource property on PrintDocument, which is a UI-technology-agnostic Windows Runtime object, unlike the XAML-specific PrintDocument. The document source is given to the print manager by a call to SetSource on the argument passed to the delegate. To complicate matters, however, this delegate gets invoked on a background thread, but accessing the DocumentSource property must be done on the UI thread. Therefore, this code uses the typical Dispatcher trick to marshal back to the UI thread, but it must use a deferral so the caller of the delegate knows to wait until the marshaled code completes.

The handling of PrintManager's PrintTaskRequested method and the call to CreatePrintTask is what populates that Printers section of the Devices pane, as seen in Figure 21.10. Once a printer is selected, Figure 21.11 shows the print preview rendering the content created inside OnGetPreviewPage. After the Print button is clicked and printing completes, the user gets a notification about the new file as shown in Figure 21.12 if the Microsoft XPS Document Writer is selected as the printer (because it prints to a file). If the user taps the notification and opens the document in the Windows Reader app, he or she can see the two-page document as shown in Figure 21.13.

FIGURE 21.10   Handling PrintTaskRequested and calling CreatePrintTask makes Windows show target printers for your app.

There are a number of additional events you can handle in order to customize the experience further. For example, PrintDocument exposes a Paginate event that enables you to update your content in response to user settings changes that affect pagination (such as page size or orientation), PrintTask exposes a Completed event so you can see whether the printing finished successfully, and so on.

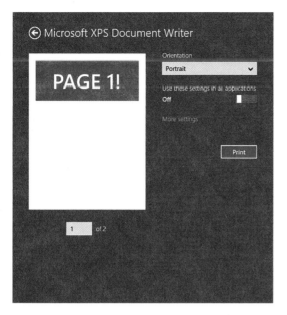

FIGURE 21.11   The print preview experience shows the rendered XAML passed to PrintDocument's SetPreviewPage method.

FIGURE 21.12   The notification that appears once printing to a file completes

FIGURE 21.13   The final document, as seen in the Reader app

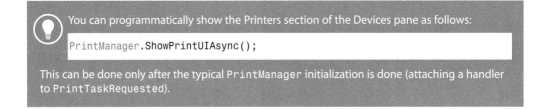

You can programmatically show the Printers section of the Devices pane as follows:

```
PrintManager.ShowPrintUIAsync();
```

This can be done only after the typical `PrintManager` initialization is done (attaching a handler to `PrintTaskRequested`).

You can also customize the printing options in three basic ways: changing default options, configuring which options are displayed, and adding your own custom options.

Changing Default Options

Once you create a `PrintTask` inside the handler for `PrintTaskRequested`, you can override its default options via its `Options` property of type `PrintTaskOptions`. For example, the following addition changes the default page orientation to landscape instead of portrait:

```
void OnPrintTaskRequested(PrintManager sender, PrintTaskRequestedEventArgs args)
{
  // This is invoked when the Print section of the Devices pane opens
  PrintTask task = args.Request.CreatePrintTask("Document Title",
    async (taskArgs) =>
    {
      …
    });

  task.Options.Orientation = PrintOrientation.Landscape;
}
```

Configuring Displayed Options

If you pass the `PrintTaskOptions` object to `PrintTaskOptionDetails.GetFromPrint-TaskOptions`, you get back a `PrintTaskOptionDetails` instance that can be used to completely customize which options are displayed inside the printing pane. You can add, remove, and reorder them. The following change clears the default list of options and adds four specific ones:

```
void OnPrintTaskRequested(PrintManager sender, PrintTaskRequestedEventArgs args)
{
  // This is invoked when the Print section of the Devices pane opens
  PrintTask task = args.Request.CreatePrintTask("Document Title",
    async (taskArgs) =>
    {
      …
    });
```

```
  PrintTaskOptionDetails details =
    PrintTaskOptionDetails.GetFromPrintTaskOptions(task.Options);
  details.DisplayedOptions.Clear();
  details.DisplayedOptions.Add(StandardPrintTaskOptions.Copies);
  details.DisplaycdOptions.Add(StandardPrintTaskOptions.PrintQuality);
  details.DisplayedOptions.Add(StandardPrintTaskOptions.HolePunch);
  details.DisplayedOptions.Add(StandardPrintTaskOptions.MediaSize);
}
```

Note that not all printers support all options, and unsupported ones are ignored. For example, out of these four chosen options, the Microsoft XPS Document Writer displays only the MediaSize one.

Adding Custom Options

PrintTaskOptionDetails supports exposing custom options that make sense only to your app. For example, the Calendar app could support printing modes of Day, Work week, Week, or Month, independently of the current display on the screen.

The following code adds two custom options. One can be set to freeform text, whereas the other must be set to a value from a predefined list:

```
void OnPrintTaskRequested(PrintManager sender, PrintTaskRequestedEventArgs args)
{
  // This is invoked when the Print section of the Devices pane opens
  PrintTask task = args.Request.CreatePrintTask("Document Title",
    async (taskArgs) =>
    {
      …
    });

  PrintTaskOptionDetails details =
    PrintTaskOptionDetails.GetFromPrintTaskOptions(task.Options);
  details.DisplayedOptions.Clear();
  details.DisplayedOptions.Add(StandardPrintTaskOptions.MediaSize);

  // A custom text option
  PrintCustomTextOptionDetails option1 = details.CreateTextOption(
    "CustomId1", "Header");
  details.DisplayedOptions.Add("CustomId1");

  // A custom list option
  PrintCustomItemListOptionDetails option2 = details.CreateItemListOption(
    "CustomId2", "Contents");
  option2.AddItem("customItemId1", "As Seen on Screen");
  option2.AddItem("customItemId2", "Summary View");
  option2.AddItem("customItemId3", "Full Details");
```

```
    option2.AddItem("customItemId4", "Multiple Columns");
    details.DisplayedOptions.Add("CustomId2");

    // Handle options changes
    details.OptionChanged += OnOptionChanged;
}
```

The IDs you choose are used to understand the user's selection when the `OptionChanged` event is raised with a specific ID and value. You should act upon your custom settings in the handler for OptionChanged (whose implementation is not shown in this example). The result of adding these two custom options is shown in Figure 21.14.

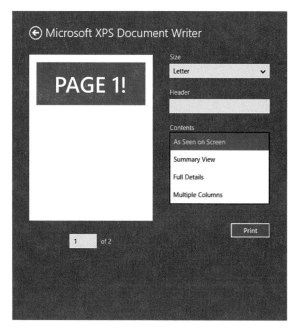

FIGURE 21.14   Two custom options are shown when printing from the Devices pane.

Supporting the "Play To" Feature

With the Play To feature, you can stream images, audio, and video from your app to an Xbox One or any compatible device, such as certain TVs and audio receivers. The device must be on the same local, private network with sharing enabled (typically done when first connecting to a private network). On a public network or one without sharing enabled, you can manually add the target device from the Devices section of the PC Settings app. When an app supports Play To and compatible devices are available, they appear on the Play section of the Devices pane.

To support this in your app, you work with a *Play To manager* in much the same way you interact with the print manager. When the user reveals the Play section on the Devices pane, PlayToManager's SourceRequested event is raised, so you must attach a handler as follows:

```
PlayToManager playToManager = PlayToManager.GetForCurrentView();
playToManager.SourceRequested += OnSourceRequested;
```

The job of the handler is to hand a *Play To source* to the Play To manager. Much like PrintDocument's DocumentSource property that exposes a document source, two UIElements in the XAML UI Framework expose a PlayToSource property (of type PlayToSource): Image and MediaElement. (MediaPlayer does, too, as it derives from MediaElement).

Therefore, you can send an audio/video file from a MediaElement named mediaElement to the Play To device as follows:

```
void OnSourceRequested(PlayToManager sender, PlayToSourceRequestedEventArgs args)
{
  // This is invoked on a background thread when
 // the Play section of the Devices pane opens
  var deferral = args.SourceRequest.GetDeferral();
  var handler = this.Dispatcher.RunAsync(CoreDispatcherPriority.Normal, () =>
  {
    // This must run on the UI thread
    args.SourceRequest.SetSource(mediaElement.PlayToSource);
    deferral.Complete();
  });
}
```

This is the same pattern as printing, including the marshaling from a background thread to the UI thread in order to access MediaElement's PlayToSource property. Doing this with an Image looks identical; replace mediaElement with an appropriate Image variable.

That's all there is to it! Finding a compatible device is the hard part; writing the code is the easy part. Documentation sometimes mentions a "Play To contract," but nothing needs to be done with the package manifest.

You can programmatically show the Play To user interface as follows:

```
PrintManager.ShowPlayToUI();
```

A few more features exist for customizing the experience a bit more. For example, you can stream a whole playlist (or a slideshow of images) by chaining multiple PlayToSources together. This is done with PlayToSource's Next property, which can be set to another PlayToSource. Through PlayToSource's Connection property, you can discover the current state of the Play To connection (Connected, Rendering, or Disconnected). You can also attach handlers to events for state changes, errors, or when the next PlayToSource is transferred for the playlist/slideshow scenario. This enables you to customize what you show in your app in response to what is happening on the other device.

> Don't have an Xbox One or a fancy TV that supports Play To? It's okay, because you can still test Play To as long as you have a second computer on the same local network (with the same sharing requirements described earlier). Here's what you must do on the second computer:
>
> 1. Launch Windows Media Player.
> 2. In the Library view, open the Stream menu, and then check the **Allow remote control of my Player...** option. Leave Windows Media Player open.
> 3. In the Devices and Printers control panel, click **Add a device**. Your Windows Media Player instance should appear as a **Digital media player**. Add it.
>
> On the first computer, you should now be able to select this as a Play To target.

Customizing Projection

When an app uses multiple windows, and more than one screen is available on the current PC, it can project one window on one screen while keeping another window on the other. This is useful for any apps that want to support the notion of a public view versus a private view, such as a PowerPoint-style app in which one screen shows the presentation and the other screen shows speaker notes. The projection APIs can be found on the static `ProjectionManager` class in the `Windows.UI.ViewManagement` namespace.

First, your app can check if a second screen is available with `ProjectionManager`'s Boolean `ProjectionDisplayAvailable` property and be notified of any status changes with its `ProjectionDisplayAvailableChanged` event. To project a window onto a second display, call `StartProjectingAsync` with two window IDs. Recall that a window ID is the int returned by `ApplicationView.GetForCurrentView().Id`. The first ID is for the window to be projected, and the second one is for the window that is meant to stay on the original screen. If there are more than two screens, or if the user wants to share one or more screens with other apps, the user needs to manage the windows and get them to the desired spots. In order for `StartProjectingAsync` to succeed, one of the two windows must have focus.

Although the user can drag windows from one screen to the other, you do have the ability to programmatically swap the two windows no matter where they currently reside. Just call `SwapDisplaysForViewsAsync` with the same two window IDs passed to `StartProjectingAsync`. To stop projecting and automatically close the projected window, call `StopProjectingAsync` with the same two IDs. See Chapter 8, "Threading, Windows, and Pages," for more details about working with multiple windows.

The Settings Charm

Any app can integrate with the Settings pane shown by the Settings charm. The pane enables you to add custom links to its list. The goal, much like with the other charms, is to make it easy for all apps to expose a consistent mechanism for exposing settings so users know how to find them.

Showing Links

Documentation sometimes refers to a "Settings contract" for integrating with the Settings pane, but you don't need do anything special in your package manifest. You simply need to handle SettingPane's CommandsRequested event as follows:

```
SettingsPane.GetForCurrentView().CommandsRequested += OnCommandsRequested;
```

Then you can add links from within the event handler as follows:

```
void OnCommandsRequested(SettingsPane sender,
                         SettingsPaneCommandsRequestedEventArgs e)
{
  e.Request.ApplicationCommands.Add(new SettingsCommand(1, "#1", OnCommand));
  e.Request.ApplicationCommands.Add(new SettingsCommand(2, "#2", OnCommand));
  e.Request.ApplicationCommands.Add(new SettingsCommand(3, "#3", OnCommand));
  e.Request.ApplicationCommands.Add(new SettingsCommand(4, "#4", OnCommand));
  e.Request.ApplicationCommands.Add(new SettingsCommand(5, "#5", OnCommand));
  e.Request.ApplicationCommands.Add(new SettingsCommand(6, "#6", OnCommand));
  e.Request.ApplicationCommands.Add(new SettingsCommand(7, "#7", OnCommand));
  e.Request.ApplicationCommands.Add(new SettingsCommand(8, "#8", OnCommand));
  // Adding any more throws an exception!
}
```

You can add up to eight links. Each one has an ID (of type object), a string label, and a callback that is invoked when the link is clicked. Figure 21.15 shows the resultant Settings pane.

You can programmatically show the Settings pane as follows:

```
SettingsPane.Show();
```

You can provide a separate callback for each command, or you can use the same one (as done in the preceding code) and distinguish which command was invoked via its ID. For example:

```
void OnCommand(IUICommand command)
{
  int id = (int)command.Id;
  switch (id)
  {
    case 1:
```

```
    ...
  }
}
```

Handling Links with SettingsPane

When one of the links is clicked, you can do whatever you'd like, but the convention is to show a new piece of UI that mimics the Settings pane. Unlike when your app is a share target, you cannot inject custom UI into the pane itself. When one of the links is clicked, the Settings pane closes.

In Windows 8, you needed to craft your own user interface that mimics the Settings pane, but in Windows 8.1, you can use the new SettingsFlyout content control. SettingsFlyout can be confusing to use, because it is not meant to be statically placed in the element tree on any of your pages. The easiest way to work with one is to add a new **User Control** to your project from Visual Studio's Add New Item dialog, and then replace the contents of the XAML and C# files so you're left with a class that derives from SettingsFlyout. Listings 21.2 and 21.3 show what this can look like for an added file named CustomSettingsFlyout.xaml and its code-behind file named CustomSettingsFlyout.xaml.cs.

FIGURE 21.15   The maximum eight app-specific links are added to the Settings pane, along with the ever-present Permissions link.

LISTING 21.2   CustomSettingsFlyout.xaml: The User Interface for a Custom Settings Pane

```xml
<SettingsFlyout x:Class="Chapter21.CustomSettingsFlyout"
  xmlns="http://schemas.microsoft.com/winfx/2006/xaml/presentation"
  xmlns:x="http://schemas.microsoft.com/winfx/2006/xaml"
  Title="Custom Settings" IconSource="Assets/SmallLogo.png"
  Background="Green" RequestedTheme="Dark">
    <StackPanel>
        <!-- Example settings -->
        <ToggleSwitch Header="One"/>
```

LISTING 21.2   Continued

```
        <ToggleSwitch Header="Two"/>
        <ToggleSwitch Header="Three"/>
    </StackPanel>
</SettingsFlyout>
```

LISTING 21.3   CustomSettingsFlyout.xaml.cs: The Code-Behind File for a Custom
Settings Pane

```
using Windows.UI.Xaml.Controls;

namespace Chapter21
{
  public sealed partial class CustomSettingsFlyout : SettingsFlyout
  {
    public CustomSettingsFlyout()
    {
      InitializeComponent();
    }

    Change settings in response to ToggleSwitch events…
  }
}
```

With this in place, you can instantiate one and call its Show method inherited from
SettingsFlyout in response to a link being clicked on the Settings pane. For example:

```
void OnCommand(IUICommand command)
{
  int id = (int)command.Id;
  switch (id)
  {
    case 1:
    CustomSettingsFlyout flyout = new CustomSettingsFlyout();
    flyout.Show();
      break;
    …
  }
}
```

When Show is called, the custom flyout slides in from the edge, just like the Settings pane.
The transition is almost as natural as transitioning from the Devices pane to one of its
subpages, despite the fact that the user interface is completely controlled by your app.
The resultant CustomSettingsFlyout is shown in Figure 21.16.

This flyout has light dismiss behavior, just like panes from the charms bar. If the user clicks the back button, the flyout dismisses and the Settings pane reappears. (Internally, the control calls SettingsPane.Show on your behalf.) If, for some reason, you don't want the Settings pane to reappear when the back button is clicked, you should show it with a call to SettingsFlyout's Show**Independent** method instead of Show. In this case, clicking the back button simply dismisses the flyout. You can, however, handle SettingsFlyout's BackClick event in order to do something custom.s

In Listing 21.2, the control's Title and IconSource are set in order to populate the header at the top of Figure 21.16. You can't make the background of the flyout match the user-chosen background color of the Settings pane, so you should make it fit in with the style of your app. SettingsFlyout's default Background is white, so its default value of RequestedTheme is Light. Listing 21.2

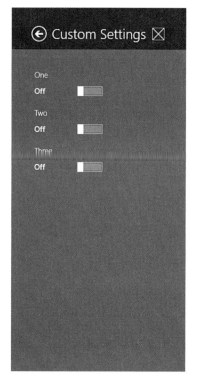

FIGURE 21.16   The custom SettingsFlyout acts like another page of the Settings pane.

changes Background to green, so it must change RequestedTheme accordingly. You can also change the header brushes with SettingsFlyout's HeaderForeground and HeaderBackground properties. It's common to make these match your app's tile colors specified in your package manifest.

Settings you expose in a SettingsFlyout should be simple, concise, and get applied instantly. In other words, there should not be any OK or Apply Button for committing the changes. In Figure 21.16, toggling the ToggleSwitches should be enough.

You should also avoid using SettingsFlyout or any large side panes for any purposes other than handling links from the Settings pane. Design guidelines state that you should use smaller flyouts that hover close to the action that trigger their appearance.

Summary

Integrating with Windows charms is a great way to differentiate your apps from others, increase your chances of Microsoft promoting your app, and help users spread the word about your app. Even more to the point, as users become accustomed to using these charms to share, print, stream, and adjust settings, they will be frustrated by apps that do not follow these conventions. Sometimes it might still make sense to have your own button or link for some of these concepts, but you can just programmatically show the relevant pane when your own user interface element is invoked.

As a user of Windows, you should be aware of the following handy keyboard shortcuts related to the charms and their panes:

Windows+C: Show the charms bar

Windows+Q: Show the Search pane in its default mode

Windows+W: Show the Search pane defaulted to searching settings

Windows+F: Show the Search pane defaulted to searching files

Windows+H: Show the Share pane

Windows+K: Show the Devices pane

Windows+P: Show the Project page on the Devices pane

Windows+I: Show the Settings pane

Chapter 22

LEVERAGING CONTRACTS

Contracts enable your app to cooperate with another app, or Windows itself, to complete a well-defined task. These enable very compelling scenarios with very few lines of code. Because your app can delegate the completion of some sophisticated end-to-end features, it frees up your development time to work on your unique functionality. And the contract-based scenarios often get better automatically as the user installs more apps. For example, Windows 8.1 includes a new Reading List app that enables users to bookmark content for later reading. Any Windows 8 or Windows 8.1 app that already supported the generic sharing of links now automatically gains an "add a bookmark to Reading List" feature without doing a thing.

The preceding chapter showed examples of two contracts: the Share contract and the Search contract. Every contract has a *source* that initiates the task and a *target* that completes it. For the Share contract, the source is the active app when the Share charm is invoked and the target is the app that receives the content. For the Search contract, the source is Windows itself (the Search pane) and the target is the active app that receives the search query.

Conceptually, this is straightforward. But technically, what distinguishes a contract from any other API provided by Windows? For example, why isn't the functionality for adding links to the Settings pane, covered in the preceding chapter, considered part of a "Settings contract?" The answer is that a contract is only involved whenever the target must be activated in a special manner by Windows.

When a share operation occurs, the target app cannot be launched normally. It must be told that it has been activated specifically to be a share target so it can act accordingly. This requires a contract. On the other hand, because interaction with the Settings pane only occurs when your app is already running, there is no need for activation at all. When the user clicks a link, Windows can just return focus and data back to your app (via a regular callback given to the `SettingsCommand`).

For this reason, contracts are often referred to as *activation contracts*. The only way that an app can be the target for a given contract is by informing Windows that it can be activated in the corresponding special manner. You do this by declaring this fact in your package manifest, as exposed on the Declarations tab of Visual Studio's package manifest designer. If you add a declaration for "Search" and "Share Target" (with a supported data format of "Text") in this designer and then view the raw `Package.appxmanifest` file, you can see the simple XML representation for each contract for which you support being a target:

```
<Extensions>
  <Extension Category="windows.search" />
  <Extension Category="windows.shareTarget">
    <ShareTarget>
      <DataFormat>Text</DataFormat>
    </ShareTarget>
  </Extension>
</Extensions>
```

Because the source doesn't need special activation to participate in a contract, the source doesn't need to declare anything. As with the share source example in the preceding chapter, participating in the contract indeed involves no more than calling regular Windows Runtime APIs. (The Share Target contract could really just be called the Share contract, which is what people usually call it anyway.)

As another example, when you use the file picker, your app is actually acting as the source for either the File Open Picker contract or File Save Picker contract. The target is usually Windows itself, but it can also be other apps that appear in the picker user interface due to declaring themselves as targets for the relevant picker contract.

It's also worth noting that, unlike capabilities, contract activations declared by your app are *not* listed in the Windows Store as potentially unwanted features. There's nothing about being a contract target that is inherently dangerous for the user. Supporting certain contracts does require relevant capabilities, but many don't require any.

This chapter covers several interesting contracts from the perspective of the target app requiring special activation. The names of most of the sections correspond directly to items in the Available Declarations drop-down on the package manifest designer's Declarations tab. Some of the sections also discuss how to be the source.

Account Picture Provider

Any app—even one with no capabilities—has the power to change the current user's account picture. This is exposed via a few simple methods on the `Windows.System.UserProfile.UserInformation` class. Fortunately, if an app attempts to do this, the user is prompted to consent to the change.

Of course, just because an app *can* change the user's account picture doesn't mean it should. If this makes sense for your app, perhaps because it's an image-effects app, you should declare it as a target for the Account Picture Provider contract in its package manifest. When you add Account Picture Provider to the declarations list and deploy your app, Windows places a link to your app inside the relevant part of the PC Settings app, as shown in Figure 22.1.

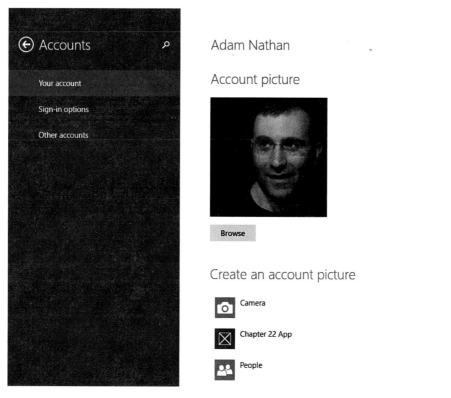

FIGURE 22.1   Your app is added to the "Create an account picture" list when you add the Account Picture Provider declaration to your package manifest.

When the user invokes your app through this link, it is a *protocol* activation. You can detect this condition as follows by overriding the `OnActivated` method in `App.xaml.cs`:

```
protected override void OnActivated(IActivatedEventArgs args)
{
  // Note: If Window.Current.Content isn't null, this is an existing
  //       window from a running or suspended instance of the app.
  //       You might need to handle this case differently.

  if (args.Kind == ActivationKind.Protocol)
  {
    ProtocolActivatedEventArgs protocolArgs = (ProtocolActivatedEventArgs)args;
    if (protocolArgs.Uri.Scheme == "ms-accountpictureprovider")
    {
      // The user just picked this app via the "Create an account picture" link.
      // Initialize the app appropriately for setting it.
      SetAccountPicture();
    }
  }
}
```

There is no specific On*XXX*Activated method for this type of activation, which is why the generic OnActivated must be used. There are multiple reasons for an app to receive an activation of type Protocol, so the ProtocolActivatedEventArgs.Uri must be checked to determine what happened. The actual URI (ms-accountpictureprovider:///) doesn't point to anything; it is used to distinguish the action that provoked the activation.

Once you have checked for a URI scheme of ms-accountpictureprovider and therefore determined that your app has been activated to handle the creation of an account picture, you can show a relevant user interface. Keep in mind that, as the first comment in the code points out, activations are not necessarily handled by a freshly-launched instance of your app. An existing instance of your app will be the one activated if it is already running or suspended. In this case, you might just update your existing window content rather than replacing it.

When it comes time to hand a picture back to Windows, you must use the aforementioned UserInformation class. It contains several methods for getting information about the current user (GetDisplayName, GetAccountPicture, GetFirstName, GetLastName, and so on). It even defines an AccountPictureChanged event, just in case you use the picture within your user interface and need to refresh it. Most importantly for this topic, it also defines four methods for setting the account picture:

→ **SetAccountPictureAsync**—Sets the picture to a passed-in StorageFile.

→ **SetAccountPictureFromStreamAsync**—Sets the picture to a passed-in RandomAccessStream instead.

→ **SetAccountPicturesAsync**—Simultaneously sets a small picture, large picture, and even a video from three passed-in StorageFiles. (You can set a subset of these, but you must at least include a large picture or video.)

→ **SetAccountPicturesFromStreamAsync**—Simultaneously sets the three versions with passed-in RandomAccessStreams instead.

The following code implements the SetAccountPicture method called from the preceding implementation of OnActivated. For demonstration purposes, it doesn't bother creating and showing a Page. It simply uses the file picker to prompt the user for an existing JPEG file, and then attempts to set the returned file as the new account picture:

```
async Task SetAccountPicture()
{
  // Get a JPEG from the user
  FileOpenPicker picker = new FileOpenPicker();
  picker.FileTypeFilter.Add(".jpg");
  picker.FileTypeFilter.Add(".jpeg");
  picker.SuggestedStartLocation = PickerLocationId.PicturesLibrary;
  StorageFile file = await picker.PickSingleFileAsync();
  if (file != null)
  {
    SetAccountPictureResult result =
      await UserInformation.SetAccountPictureAsync(file);
    if (result == SetAccountPictureResult.Success)
    {
      // Congratulations! This is your new account picture.
    }
  }
}
```

There are a number of ways the operation can fail, indicated by the returned SetAccountPictureResult enumeration, such as a file that is too large. The feature to change the account picture could be disabled altogether, which causes the call to return SetAccountPictureResult.ChangeDisabled.

When your app is activated in this fashion, it remains on the screen until the user closes your app or moves it off the screen. There is unfortunately no supported way to dismiss your app when it is done with this task.

AutoPlay Content and AutoPlay Device

An app that declares itself as a target for the AutoPlay Content contract can be listed as a choice for the user to launch when he or she inserts new content, such as a CD, DVD, or Blu-ray disc. This situation can even be triggered when content is shared between two PCs via a tap-and-send gesture (leveraging Near Field Communication). If you add AutoPlay Content to the declarations list in your package manifest, you'll notice that you must explicitly define at least one *launch action*. Each launch action consists of three pieces of data:

→ **Content event**—The name of a predefined AutoPlay event that you want to handle. A list of these is available at http://bit.ly/StSRHf.

→ **Action display name**—The text that is displayed to the user inside the AutoPlay UI.

→ **verb**—An ID that that your code can use if you need to distinguish between multiple launch actions for the same event.

There are a number of specific AutoPlay events, such as ShowPicturesOnArrival, PlayMusicFilesOnArrival, PlayVideoFilesOnArrival, HandleDVDBurningOnArrival. There's also a fallback event if all else fails: UnknownContentOnArrival. Figure 22.2 shows what happens if you add the following launch action to your package manifest and then insert a disc with no recognizable media:

→ Content event: **UnknownContentOnArrival**

→ Action display name: **Browse the files with this app, please!**

→ verb: **browse**

The initial AutoPlay notification

The AutoPlay user interface that appears when the notification is tapped

FIGURE 22.2   Your app is added to the AutoPlay user interface when you add the AutoPlay Content declaration to your package manifest with an appropriate launch action.

Adding launch actions for certain events requires you to add the Removable Storage capability to your app. But don't worry; Visual Studio refuses to build your project and prompts you to add the capability if it is missing.

When your app is activated via this mechanism, it is a *file* activation. That means that you must override the OnFileActivated method in App.xaml.cs; the generic OnActivated method is not called. For this example, you can do this as follows:

```
protected override void OnFileActivated(FileActivatedEventArgs args)
{
  // Note: If Window.Current.Content isn't null, this is an existing
  //       window from a running or suspended instance of the app.
  //       You might need to handle this case differently.

  if (args.Verb == "browse") // Our only specified verb
  {
    foreach (IStorageItem item in args.Files)
    {
      // args.Files is a collection of relevant StorageFiles and StorageFolders
      …
    }
  }
}
```

If you add two launch actions for the same event, as shown in Figure 22.3, then you get two links in the relevant AutoPlay user interface, as shown in Figure 22.4.

The AutoPlay Device contract works the same way as AutoPlay Content—it's just meant for the subset of AutoPlay events that correspond to attaching a device, such as a digital camera. These events have names such as WPD\ImageSource, WPD\AudioSource, and WPD\VideoSource. (WPD stands for Windows Portable Devices.)

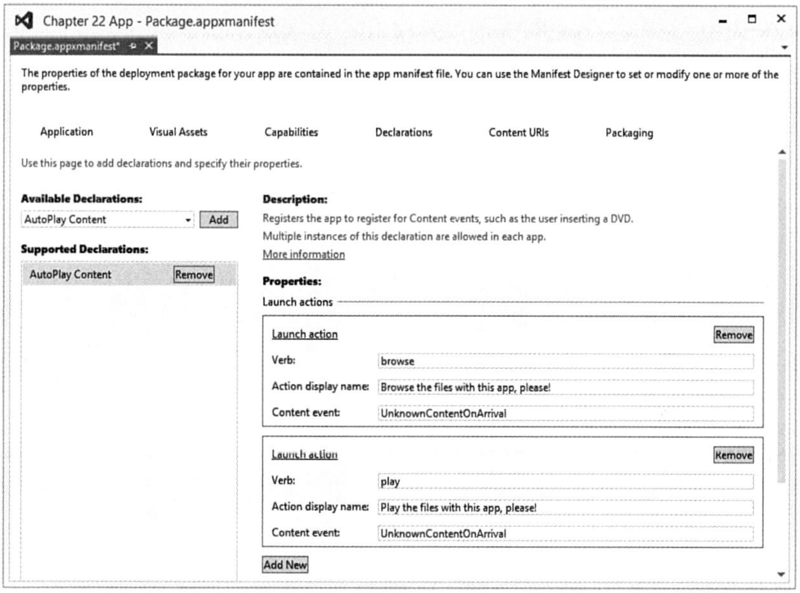

FIGURE 22.3   Defining two launch actions for the same event: a "browse" action and a "play" action

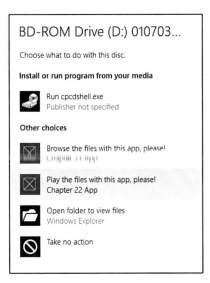

FIGURE 22.4   Having two launch actions for the same event means two links in the AutoPlay user interface.

File Type Associations

You can add any number of File Type Associations declarations to your package manifest, one per file type. With each one, you have a few pieces of information to fill out:

→ **Display name**—Text used to describe the type of file in Control Panel.

→ **Logo**—An image used for file icons in the Windows desktop. If you don't specify one, your app's square 30x30 logo is used.

→ **Info tip**—Text used for the icon's tooltip in the Windows desktop.

→ **Name**—An all-lowercase ID used by Windows that should never change, even if you update the display name in a future version of your app.

→ **Edit flags**—You can decide whether downloaded files of this type are safe to automatically open. The choices are "Open is safe" or "Always unsafe."

→ **Supported file types**—You can specify one or more file extensions for the same logical file type, such as having both .jpg and .jpeg for a JPEG file. With each file type, you must specify the content type (a MIME type) and the file type (the extension, beginning with a period).

If you add a File Type Associations declaration to your package manifest with the following values, deploy your app, and then create a new file.adam file, you'll see the result shown in Figure 22.5 inside File Explorer:

FIGURE 22.5   Viewing a custom file in File Explorer on the Windows desktop

→ Name: **adam**

→ Info tip: **An Adam File**

→ Supported file types: Content type=**application/adam**; File type=**.adam**

Even if the app's 30x30 icon weren't white-on-transparent, it's still not a great choice for a file icon because it doesn't get scaled. Therefore, whether you use your default 30x30 logo or you explicitly specify a different image file (and include it in your project), you should also leverage resource qualifier support to supply multiple sizes: 16x16, 32x32, 48x48, and 256x256. This is done with the `targetsize` resource qualifier. If you specify a logo of `Assets/logo.png` in your package manifest, then you should include the following files in your project:

→ `Assets/logo.`**`targetsize-16`**`.jpg`

→ `Assets/logo.`**`targetsize-32`**`.jpg`

→ `Assets/logo.`**`targetsize-48`**`.jpg`

→ `Assets/logo.`**`targetsize-256`**`.jpg`

Recall that the package manifest designer encourages you to include these extra four variations for the square 30x30 icon. This is the main reason why.

If the file is double-clicked in File Explorer, or a `.adam` file is used in an app's call to `Launcher.LaunchFileAsync`, your app gets a file activation, just like in the AutoPlay example. This time, however, the verb is "open." The following code handles this:

```
protected override void OnFileActivated(FileActivatedEventArgs args)
{
  // Note: If Window.Current.Content isn't null, this is an existing
  //       window from a running or suspended instance of the app.
  //       You might need to handle this case differently.

  if (args.Verb == "open")
  {
    foreach (IStorageItem file in args.Files)
    {
      // args.Files contains each StorageFile being opened
      ...
    }
  }
}
```

If you add a file extension already being handled by other apps (such as `.jpg`), then the user gets a notification the next time he or she attempts to open a file of that type, shown in Figure 22.6. Your app is also added to the list of choices, also shown in Figure 22.6.

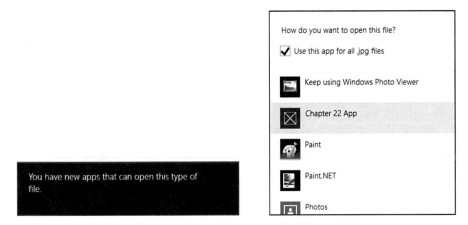

The initial notification   The **Choose Default Program...** dialog

FIGURE 22.6   Windows handles multiple apps wanting to handle the same file type gracefully.

> In Windows 8.1, `FileActivatedEventArgs` now has a `NeighboringFilesQuery` prop-
> erty that enables you to access other files of the same type within the same folder. With
> this, you can provide an experience in which the user can navigate back and forward
> among files. For example, with this feature, the Photos app can allow users to flip back and forth
> among neighboring photos even when it was activated to show just one specific photo.

Protocol

With the Protocol contract, you can handle URI protocols such as `mailto` for email, `tel`
for a phone call, or completely custom ones. This is basically the URL equivalent to File
Type Associations. With each one you add to your package manifest, you can specify the
following information:

→ **Display name**—Text used to describe the protocol.

→ **Logo**—An image used for icons in the Windows desktop, just like with the File Type
  Associations setting. If you don't specify one, your app's square 30x30 logo is used.

→ **Name**—The URI scheme without any colons or slashes, such as `mailto`.

If you add a Protocol declaration with `Name` set to `adam` (and the other values blank)
and deploy your app, you can then type a URL like `adam://blah` in Internet Explorer
and you'll get a prompt like the one shown in Figure 22.7 before launching your
app. The same is true for an app uses a URL with an `adam` scheme in a call to
`Launcher.LaunchUriAsync`.

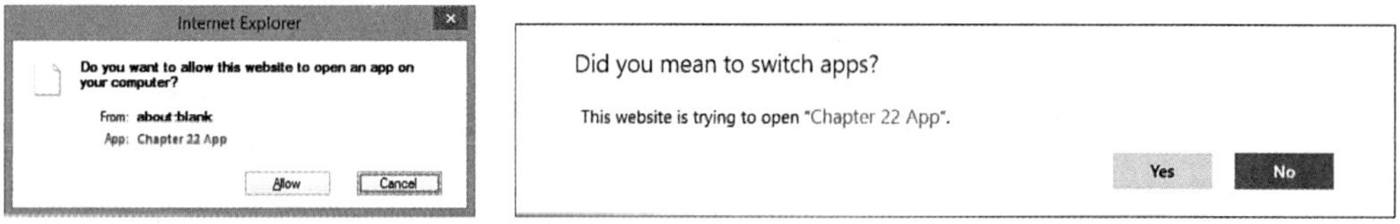

From desktop Internet Explorer   From the Internet Explorer app

FIGURE 22.7   Getting prompted before launching an app for a custom URI scheme

When invoked in this way, your app gets a protocol activation, just like with the Account Picture Provider contract. This time, however, the Uri reveals the exact URL being invoked:

```
protected override void OnActivated(IActivatedEventArgs args)
{
  // Note: If Window.Current.Content isn't null, this is an existing
  //       window from a running or suspended instance of the app.
  //       You might need to handle this case differently.

  if (args.Kind == ActivationKind.Protocol)
  {
    ProtocolActivatedEventArgs protocolArgs = (ProtocolActivatedEventArgs)args;
    // Act upon protocolArgs.Uri
    …
  }
}
```

If you want Windows to consider your app as a Web browser, you can declare that you handle the http (and https) protocol.

File Open Picker

Arbitrary apps can be listed within the Windows file picker as a place from which files can be chosen. They do this by declaring themselves as a target for the File Open Picker contract. This section examines what it means to be a File Open Picker target. Code throughout this book has already demonstrated what it means to be a File Open Picker *source*. (You simply use the FileOpenPicker class to show the file picker and retrieve the result.)

If you add File Open Picker to the list of declarations in your package manifest and deploy your app, your app then appears as a choice in the file picker whenever it is invoked for opening a file, as shown in Figure 22.8. In the package manifest designer, you can specify whether your app should only appear for certain file types, or if it can handle any file type.

FIGURE 22.8   Your app is added to the file picker's list of apps in its open mode when you add the File Open Picker declaration to your package manifest.

When your app is selected, it is activated with a file open picker activation, which has its own unique method to override in App.xaml.cs:

```
protected override void OnFileOpenPickerActivated(
  FileOpenPickerActivatedEventArgs args)
{
  // The user just picked this app in the file picker's open mode,
  // so create a new page for this and pass along the args
  MyCustomFileOpenPickerPage page = new MyCustomFileOpenPickerPage();
  page.Initialize(args);

  // This is a brand new window, so you must set its content and activate it
  Window.Current.Content = page;
  Window.Current.Activate();
}
```

The Page you display is hosted inside the file picker, occupying the yellow area shown in Figure 22.9. Windows customizes the text and background colors in the standard header and footer to match the tile colors chosen by your app in its package manifest.

FIGURE 22.9   Your app presents custom content in a new window hosted by the file picker.

Like the previous activations in this chapter, OnFileOpenPickerActivated is handled by an existing instance of your app if it is running or suspended. However, unlike the other activations, this always occurs in a brand new window (with its own UI thread). Therefore, although args.PreviousExecutionState is Running or Suspended in this situation, Window.Current.Content is always null. You must initialize Content and call Window.Current.Activate to dismiss the splash screen that appears when this hosted window is first displayed.

This behavior is the same for all contract activations for which the target app is hosted within Windows-provided UI, such as the Share contract and all the picker contracts. (The same was true in Windows 8, so apps were able to have multiple windows in this context.)

Visual Studio contains a template for handling the File Open Picker contract. If you select **File Open Picker Contract** from the **Add New Item** dialog, Visual Studio will add the File Open Picker declaration to your package manifest, add a Page to your project to handle the request (called FileOpenPickerPage1 by default), and generate an implementation of OnFileOpenPickerActivated similar to the one shown previously. Similar to the Visual

Studio-generated search results Page, the new Page contains presents a standard user interface designed to work with a data source that you can plug in.

Your page that gets displayed within the file picker needs to know whether the file picker was invoked for single selection (PickSingleFileAsync) or multiple selections (PickMultipleFilesAsync). It also needs to know what types of files to show in order to match the specified file filters. Of course, it must also communicate any file selections and return the actual files back to Windows. Your page does this with a FileOpenPickerUI property on the passed-in FileOpenPickerActivatedEventArgs object. This property, whose type is also called FileOpenPickerUI, contains the following properties:

→ **AllowedFileTypes**—Reveals the current file filters as a collection of strings.

→ **SelectionMode**—Either Single or Multiple, based on how the file picker was invoked

→ **Title**—Can be set to a string that gets displayed next to your app name in the file picker header. You can use this to help explain where the files are logically coming from.

→ **SettingsIdentifier**—A string provided by Windows that is like a session ID. You can optionally use this in a later invocation to restore your own context.

FileOpenPickerUI contains the following methods:

→ **CanAddFile**—You pass an IStorageFile, and it tells you whether the file can be added to the user's selection. For example, if the picker is in single selection mode and a file is already selected, CanAddFile would return false for a second file.

→ **AddFile**—You pass a string ID that uniquely identifies the file, and the actual IStorageFile to add to the current selection.

→ **RemoveFile**—You pass the appropriate string ID to remove a file from the current selection.

→ **ContainsFile**—You pass a string ID to find out whether the current selection includes a file with that ID.

Finally, it also contains the following events:

→ **FileRemoved**—Reveals when the user has removed a file from the current selection using the Windows-provided user interface in the footer of the file picker. You need to know when this happens in order to keep your user interface in-sync.

→ **Closing**—Raised when the file picker is about to be closed by the user.

(?) Can my app integrate with the folder picker?

No, unlike the other pickers covered in this chapter, the folder picker is not extensible. Besides the current PC, it only supports SkyDrive, network locations, and a HomeGroup if applicable.

File Save Picker

Integrating your app into the file picker's save mode parallels integrating it into its open mode. It is a distinct contract, however, enabling you to support one or the other if you don't want to support both. Although it's hard to imagine an app that integrates saving without integrating opening, it's natural for some apps to only support opening because their source of files is readonly.

If you add File Save Picker to the list of declarations in your package manifest and deploy your app, your app then appears as a choice in the file picker whenever it is invoked for saving a file, just like Figure 22.8 shows for opening a file. Again, in the package manifest designer, you can specify whether your app should only appear for certain file types, or if it can handle any file type.

When your app is selected, it is activated with a file save picker activation, which has its own unique method to override in App.xaml.cs:

```
protected override void OnFileSavePickerActivated(
  FileSavePickerActivatedEventArgs args)
{
  // The user just picked this app in the file picker's save mode,
  // so create a new page for this and pass along the args
  MyCustomFileSavePickerPage page = new MyCustomFileSavePickerPage();
  page.Initialize(args);

  // This is a brand new window, so you must set its content and activate it
  Window.Current.Content = page;
  Window.Current.Activate();
}
```

The Page you display is hosted inside the file picker, and it is a fresh window even if your app is already running or suspended. Note that Visual Studio does *not* contain a template for the File Save Picker contract. Fortunately, the implementation of your custom Page is likely to be almost identical to the implementation of your Page for file opening, at least where it handles any folder and file browsing of your custom data store.

To enable your Page to communicate with the file picker, the passed-in FileSavePickerActivatedEventArgs object has a FileSavePickerUI property of type FileSavePickerUI. It has the same AllowedFileTypes, Title and SettingsIdentifier properties as FileOpenPickerUI, but it also has a FileName property that reveals the full filename chosen by the user within the footer of the file picker. A FileNameChanged event is raised whenever the user changes the filename, including changing the extension from the picker's drop-down.

The only method exposed by FileSavePickerUI is TrySetFileName, which you can use to attempt to change the user-selected filename, presumably in response to the user navigating to different folders within your hosted user interface. FileSavePickerUI doesn't have a Closing event, but rather a TargetFileRequested event that is raised when the user clicks the save button. You must handle this in order to save the user's data. In the `TargetFileRequestedEventArgs` object passed to handlers, its `Request` property exposes a `TargetFile` property. This is an `IStorageFile` that contains the user's data to save. The `Request` property also exposes a typical `GetDeferral` method so you can use the deferral pattern as you save the data asynchronously..

Contact Picker

Windows provides a contact picker .that enables the user to provide an app with information about his or her contacts. It's much lesser known than the file picker, but it follows the same usage and extensibility pattern. It has a corresponding Contact Picker contract, as target apps can integrate with the picker. Because this book hasn't previously shown an example of consuming the contact picker, this section looks at the contract from both perspectives: the source and the target.

Being a Contact Picker Source

Initiating the contact picker user interface looks just like initiating the file picker. You can use a `ContactPicker` class from the `Windows.ApplicationModel.Contacts` namespace as follows:

```
// Get a contact from the user
ContactPicker picker = new ContactPicker();
Contact contact = await picker.PickContactAsync();
```

The resultant picker is shown in Figure 22.10. This enables the user to pick a contact to provide to your app. You don't get to access the entire contacts database yourself. (There's not even a capability for such a thing.) You can, however, ask the user to pick several contacts by calling `PickContact`**s**`Async` instead.

The returned `Contact` object exposes a lot of information: a thumbnail photo, a display name plus separate first/middle/last names and prefix/suffix (and other names relevant for Japanese), email addresses, physical addresses, phone numbers, job information, significant others, important dates, connected service accounts, and more! If you require only a subset of the information (as is usually the case), then you should set `ContactPicker`'s `DesiredFieldsWithContactFieldType` property to restrict the information that is obtained. This is a collection of `ContactFieldType` enumeration values. The following addition grabs only the email address(es) of the chosen contact:

```
ContactPicker picker = new ContactPicker();
picker.DesiredFieldsWithContactFieldType.Add(ContactFieldType.Email);
Contact contact = await picker.PickContactAsync();
```

`ContactPicker` also exposes a `CommitButtonText` property for customizing the label on its OK button, and a `SelectionMode` property that provides a hint to the UI that you're interested only in certain fields. This can potentially affect the display, depending on the Contact Picker contract target.

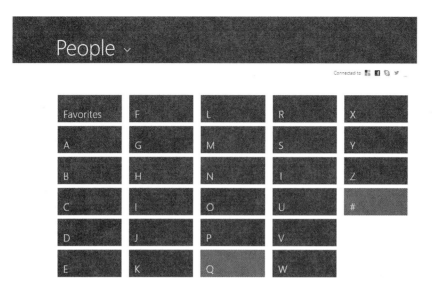

FIGURE 22.10   The Contact Picker enables you to ask the user for information about one or more contacts.

Being a Contact Picker Target

By default, the contact picker uses the People app as the target. The People app is the user's interface into the Windows contact database, allowing adding/removing/editing contacts as well as importing them from a number of different accounts such as Facebook, Twitter, LinkedIn, and Google. Still, the contact picker enables other apps to plug in and provide their own notion of contacts independently from the People app. That's why an app would want to be a Contact Picker contract target.

If you add Contract Picker to the list of declarations in your package manifest and deploy your app, your app then appears as a choice in the contact picker's top drop-down. When your app is selected, it is activated with a contact picker activation. There is no unique method for this activation, but you can detect this condition as follows by overriding the OnActivated method in App.xaml.cs:

```csharp
protected override void OnActivated(IActivatedEventArgs args)
{
  if (args.Kind == ActivationKind.ContactPicker)
  {
    // The user just picked this app in the contact picker,
    // so create a new page for this and pass along the args
    MyCustomContactPickerPage page = new MyCustomContactPickerPage();
    page.Initialize((ContactPickerActivatedEventArgs)args);
```

```
    // This is a brand new window, so you must set its content and activate it
    Window.Current.Content = page;
    Window.Current.Activate();
  }
}
```

The Page you display is hosted inside the contact picker, and it is a fresh window even if your app is already running or suspended. To enable your Page to communicate with the contact picker, the passed-in ContactPickerActivatedEventArgs object has a ContactPickerUI property of type ContactPickerUI.

ContactPickerUI exposes AddContact, ContainsContact, and RemoveContact methods. AddContact accepts a Contact object (the same object given to the source that requested the contact picker). Its string Id property must be set to a unique identifier. That same string is what you can pass to ContainsContact and RemoveContact. Because the user might remove contacts from the picker's footer that is outside of your control, ContactPickerUI raises a ContactRemoved event so you can keep your selection in-sync.

ContactPickerUI also exposes the same SelectionMode and DesiredFieldsWithContactFieldType properties that may have been set on ContactPicker, so you can optionally customize your Page based on these choices. For example, the People app adjusts its display to show the most important desired field. Note that the value of SelectionMode is either Contacts (the source wants the entire contact) or Fields (the source wants only specified fields). There is no property that reveals whether you have been invoked for single selection or multiple selection. The only way you can find out is by the second AddContact call failing.

The New Contact Contract

Windows 8.1 introduces a Contact contract to enable deeper integration with contacts that is much more useful than the contact picker. It enables you to show a *contact card*, a lightweight flyout that Windows can render on top of your app. This can greatly enhance any piece of contact information displayed by your app. The displayed card not only shows rich information about the contact (if available), but it provides actions to interact with the contact, such as sending an email or initiating a Skype call. For example, the Mail app leverages the contact card whenever you tap an email address.

This means that the valuable information inside the Windows contact database (which is usually valuable due to imported data from Facebook, LinkedIn, and other services) is no longer confined to the People app. Yet users are protected from apps harvesting information about their contacts and spamming them. The source app that displays the contact card never gets any information about the contact other than what it already has! (The flyout provided by Windows is isolated from the app.) The target app that might be used to communicate with the contact only gets information for that specific person. As the previous section explained, there's not even a capability that enables a third-party app to access all contacts in bulk.

Again, because this functionality hasn't been covered previously in this book, this section examines both the source and target aspects of this contract.

Being a Contact Source

To show a contact card, you need to provide Windows with as much information you have about the contact and tell Windows where to show the card. You do this by calling the static `ContactManager.ShowContactCard` method from the `Windows.ApplicationModel.Contacts` namespace. It accepts a `Contact` instance, which you should create and fill with as much relevant information as you can, and a `Rect` representing the position of the element that already shows the contact in your app's user interface. Windows places the contact card flyout adjacent to this region, but it also does its best not to cover it up.

For example, if you are displaying an email address in an element named `element` and want to show the contact card when it is tapped, you can use code such as the following in a `Tapped` handler to display the contact card:

```
// Build up a partial contact object with whatever information you know
Contact contact = new Contact();
contact.Emails.Add(new ContactEmail { Address = "…" });

// Get the window-relative coordinates of the relevant element
Rect selectionRect = this.element.TransformToVisual(null).TransformBounds(
  new Rect(0, 0, this.element.ActualWidth, this.element.ActualHeight));

// Show the contact card
ContactManager.ShowContactCard(contact, selectionRect);
```

`ContactManager` has an overload of `ShowContactCard` that accepts a value from the same `Placement` enumeration seen with the popup controls in Chapter 15, "Other Controls." You can set this to values such as `Above`, `Below`, `Left`, and `Right`.

`ContactManager` attempts to match your new `Contact` object with an existing contact from the Windows contact database. To do this, it requires that your `Contact` either has its `Id` property set or at least one email address or phone number. Because a correct ID should uniquely identify a contact, Windows first looks for a contact with a matching ID. If there's no match or no ID specified, it looks for the best match based on the email addresses and/or phone numbers.

When a match is found, the contact displayed is solely based on information from the database. (At that point, your data is ignored.) This is shown in Figure 22.11. If no match can be found, however, the contact card shows the information you specify along with a link that enables the user to add this new contact to the database.

The colors used at the top of the contact card match your app's tile colors from your package manifest. Once you have displayed the contact card, there is nothing more for your app to do. The user can initiate an action by tapping a link on the card, and these are automatically handled by other apps that are targets for the Contact contract.

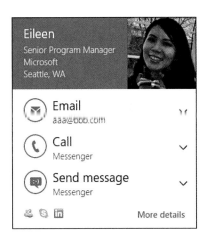

Eileen
Senior Program Manager
Microsoft
Seattle, WA

Email
aaa@bbb.com

Call
Messenger

Send message
Messenger

More details

FIGURE 22.11 The contact card shows detailed information about the contact with links to perform relevant actions.

> If you want to populate your Contact object with more information to help get a match, but getting the extra information could be time-consuming, you can call ShowDelayLoadedContactCard instead of ShowContactCard. This shows the card instantly but enables you to populate the remaining information at a later point in time. You use it as follows:

```
// Show the contact card with an initial Contact object
using (ContactCardDelayedDataLoader loader =
        ContactManager.ShowDelayLoadedContactCard(contact, selectionRect))
{
  // Update the Contact object, perhaps involving a network request
  contact = await UpdateContactWithMoreInfo(contact);
  if (contact != null)
  {
    // Refresh the contact card with the additional data
    loader.SetData(contact);
  }
}
```

Being a Contact Target

Apps that want to be listed in the contact card must specify actions that they can handle. In Windows 8.1, these actions can be emailing, calling, video calling, sending a message, mapping an address, and posting to a social network. It turns out that you can be included for two of these actions by supporting the Protocol contract. If your app is a target for the Protocol contract for the `mailto` scheme, it is automatically included in the list of apps on the contact card that can send mail. And if your app is a target for the Protocol contract for the `tel` scheme, it is automatically included in the list of apps that can make a phone call. For all the other actions, you must declare yourself as a target for the Contact contract.

Visual Studio's package manifest designer doesn't yet support the Contact contract. Therefore, you must select "View Code" for `Package.appxmanifest` to manually edit the XML. The following snippet demonstrates declaring the Contact contract for three types of actions:

```xml
<Extensions>
  <!-- Declare the Contact contract -->
  <m2:Extension Category="windows.contact">
    <m2:Contact>
      <m2:ContactLaunchActions>
        <!-- map -->
        <m2:LaunchAction Verb="map"/>

        <!-- call -->
        <m2:LaunchAction Verb="call">
          <m2:ServiceId>telephone</m2:ServiceId>
        </m2:LaunchAction>

        <!-- message -->
        <m2:LaunchAction Verb="message">
          <m2:ServiceId>skype.com</m2:ServiceId>
        </m2:LaunchAction>
      </m2:ContactLaunchActions>
    </m2:Contact>
  </m2:Extension>
</Extensions>
```

The Contact contract and related elements use the 2013 XML namespace identified by an m2 prefix because these are all new elements in Windows 8.1. This XML namespace is defined at the top of the package manifest file (not shown here). The supported `Verb` values for `LaunchAction` are `call`, `videoCall`, `message`, `map`, and `post`. Even though you can handle emailing and calling via the Protocol contract, you can also do so via the Contact contract.

When your app is selected, you can detect contact activation as follows by overriding the `OnActivated` method in `App.xaml.cs`:

```csharp
protected override void OnActivated(IActivatedEventArgs args)
{
  // Note: If Window.Current.Content isn't null, this is an existing
  //       window from a running or suspended instance of the app.
```

```
//      You might need to handle this case differently.

if (args.Kind == ActivationKind.Contact)
{
  IContactActivatedEventArgs contactArgs = (IContactActivatedEventArgs)args;
  // Act upon contactArgs.Verb

  …
}
}
```

When this happens, your app is launched alongside the source app. Recall from Chapter 7, "App Lifecycle," that the target app can specify its desired size in the package manifest on a per-contract basis. If you're editing the raw XML, you could add an attribute such as `m2:DesiredView="useMinimum"` to the `m2:Contact` element, for example. If your app is already running or suspended, your existing window gets activated.

Although you can discover which contact action you are expected to fulfill by checking the `Verb` property on the `IContactActivatedEventArgs`, you need to fetch more information to complete the task, such as the relevant address, phone number, or user ID. You do this by casting the `IContactActivatedEventArgs` object to the relevant class, based on its `Verb`:

- → **ContactCallActivatedEventArgs**—for the `call` verb
- → **ContactVideoCallActivatedEventArgs**—for the `videoCall` verb
- → **ContactMapActivatedEventArgs**—for the `map` verb
- → **ContactMessageActivatedEventArgs**—for the `message` verb
- → **ContactPostActivatedEventArgs**—for the `post` verb

All of these expose the entire relevant `Contact` object via a `Contact` property. With this, you can not only act open the relevant piece of information, but you can also customize your user interface with the contact's name, photo, and so on. Four of these classes also expose `ServiceId` and `ServiceUserId` properties, which could be needed for completing the action. The one that doesn't is `ContactMapActivatedEventArgs`, although it exposes a separate `Address` property that reveals the specific address that should be mapped.

Just because you are a target for the Contact contract, it doesn't mean that your app will get prominent placement on the contact card. The card limits itself to the top three types of actions, giving priority to email, call, and message in that order. If multiple apps handle the same action, a drop-down is used to select the app. Windows remembers the user's most recent choice and uses that as the default selection.

The New Appointments Provider Contract

The new Appointments Provider contract in Windows 8.1 provides apps with an easy way to schedule appointments. It follows the same pattern as the Contact contract. The source app can show a Windows-provided flyout for adding, removing, or replacing an appointment. It can also launch the user's calendar initialized to a specific timeframe to help him or her decide when to schedule the appointment. As with the Contact contract, information in the user's calendar is kept isolated from the source app. The app only knows about appointments that it helped create.

The reason this is a contract is that any app can choose to be an appointments provider, not just the built-in Calendar app. By declaring itself as a target for the Appointments Provider contract, any app could potentially be activated for completing these calendar-based scenarios.

Being an Appointments Provider Source

The source app can launch the calendar with a call to the static `AppoinmentManager.ShowTimeFrameAsync` method from the `Windows.ApplicationModel.Appointments` namespace. For example:

```
// Show the calendar for today
await AppointmentManager.ShowTimeFrameAsync(
        DateTimeOffset.Now, TimeSpan.FromDays(1));


// Show the calendar for this week
await AppointmentManager.ShowTimeFrameAsync(
        DateTimeOffset.Now, TimeSpan.FromDays(7));
```

The only requirement is that the source app must be visible at the time of this call.

To show the appointment flyout, you call `AppointmentManager.ShowAddApointmentAsync`, which looks a lot like `ContactManager.ShowContactCard`. It expects an `Appointment` object describing the appointment and a `Rect` representing the piece of UI in your app that the user interacted with to trigger this action. There's also an overload for controlling the placement of the flyout with a value from the `Placement` enumeration. This method returns a string ID that you use when calling `ShowRemoveAppointmentAsync` or `ShowReplaceAppointmentAsync`. None of these methods update the appointment directly; they all show a flyout that enables the user to control and confirm each action.

The `Appointment` object exposes 13 properties representing the important information that modern appointment providers support plus a little more: `Subject`, `StartTime`, `Duration`, `Invitees`, `Location`, `Details`, `Reminder`, `Organizer`, `Recurrence`, `AllDay`, `Sensitivity`, `BusyStatus`, and `Uri`..

Being an Appointments Provider Target

The Appointment Provider target must declare the `windows.appointmentProvider` contract in XML and specify one or more of the following verbs: `addAppointment`, `removeAppointment`, `replaceAppointment`, and `showTimeFrame`. As with the Contact contract, the Visual Studio package manifest designer does not yet support this.

When your app is selected as the appointments provider for one of the four tasks, you handle an appointments provider activation as follows by overriding the OnActivated method in App.xaml.cs:.

```
protected override void OnActivated(IActivatedEventArgs args)
{
  // Note: If Window.Current.Content isn't null, this is an existing
  //       window from a running or suspended instance of the app.
  //       You might need to handle this case differently.

  if (args.Kind == ActivationKind.AppointmentsProvider)
  {
    IAppointmentsProviderActivatedEventArgs appointmentsProviderArgs =
      (IAppointmentsProviderActivatedEventArgs)args;
    // Act upon appointmentsProviderArgs.Verb

    …
  }
}
```

When the verb is showTimeFrame, your app is shown alongside the source app, and your window is reused if your app is running or suspended. For the other verbs, you get a new window that is hosted in the small flyout.

Once you check the Verb property on the IAppointmentsProviderActivatedEventArgs, you can cast it to the relevant class:

→ **AppointmentsProviderAddAppointmentActivatedEventArgs**—for the addAppointment verb

→ **AppointmentsProviderRemoveAppointmentActivatedEventArgs**—for the removeAppointment verb

→ **AppointmentsProviderReplaceAppointmentActivatedEventArgs**—for the replaceAppointment verb

→ **AppointmentsProviderShowTimeFrameActivatedEventArgs**—for the showTimeFrame verb

Each of these expose properties specific to the task at hand. The first three provide ReportCompleted, ReportCanceled, and ReportError methods via a subproperty. You should call one of these three methods once you're done scheduling, updating, or removing an appointment.

Background Tasks

Background tasks enable an app to run custom code in response to certain system events or at timed intervals, even if it isn't running. If you want to play audio in the background, a lot of support exists specifically for this. Therefore, we first look at background audio and then look at every other kind of background task.

Background Audio

As explained in Chapter 14, "Audio, Video, and Speech," if you switch away from your app while it plays an audio file, the audio instantly fades out. When you switch back, it fades back in. If you want the audio to continue being audible while your app is offscreen, you need to do three simple things:

1. Set the AudioCategory appropriately on the MediaElement playing the audio.

2. Add an appropriate Background Tasks declaration to your package manifest.

3. Write some code to keep the MediaElement in sync with a class called SystemMediaTransportControls.

Setting the AudioCategory

MediaElement's AudioCategory property can be set to influence how Windows treats the audio. To enable audio to play in the background, you must set AudioCategory to either BackgroundCapableMedia or Communications. (Communications is higher-priority, but it is appropriate only for real-time chat apps.) The following code does this for a user-selected MP3 file that gets automatically played by setting it as the source for a MediaElement named mediaElement:

```
IRandomAccessStream stream;

async Task PlayUserSelectedMusic()
{
  // Get an MP3 file from the user
  FileOpenPicker picker = new FileOpenPicker();
  picker.FileTypeFilter.Add(".mp3");
  picker.SuggestedStartLocation = PickerLocationId.MusicLibrary;
  StorageFile file = await picker.PickSingleFileAsync();
  if (file != null)
  {
    this.stream = await file.OpenAsync(FileAccessMode.Read);
    this.mediaElement.SetSource(this.stream, "audio/mp3");
    this.mediaElement.AudioCategory = AudioCategory.BackgroundCapableMedia;
  }
}

void MediaElement_MediaOpened(object sender, RoutedEventArgs e)
{
  this.stream.Dispose();
}
```

Adding the Background Tasks Declaration

When you add a Background Tasks declaration to your package manifest, you must fill out two pieces of information: the supported task type(s) and the entry point. For the supported task type(s), select the Audio option. For the entry point, you can put a dummy value when the background task is background audio. Although Visual Studio enforces that you must put *something* for this (or the HTML-specific start page option), the actual value is unused in this case.

Working with `SystemMediaTransportControls`

The final thing you must do to enable background audio is add support for the *media transport controls*. This is the user interface that enables the user to interact with the audio regardless of whether the source window is on the screen. The Windows volume control ꞏꞏꞏꞏꞏ ꞏꞏꞏꞏꞏꞏꞏ ꞏꞏꞏꞏꞏꞏ ꞏꞏꞏꞏꞏꞏꞏ ꞏꞏꞏꞏ ꞏꞏꞏꞏꞏꞏꞏꞏ ꞏꞏꞏꞏꞏ ꞏꞏꞏꞏꞏ ꞏꞏ the user summons it by changing the current volume.

To support the media transport controls, you get an instance of `Windows.Media.SystemMediaTransportControls`, enable the specific buttons you are interested in, and hook up two events to keep the state of the media transport controls in sync with the state of the `MediaElement` playing the audio. This can be done as follows, within a `Page` containing a `MediaElement` named `mediaElement`:

```
SystemMediaTransportControls mediaControls =
  SystemMediaTransportControls.GetForCurrentView();

// Enable the system-wide Play, Pause, and Stop buttons
mediaControls.IsPlayEnabled = true;
mediaControls.IsPauseEnabled = true;
mediaControls.IsStopEnabled = true;

// Update the MediaElement state whenever the system-wide state changes
this.mediaElement.CurrentStateChanged += MediaElement_CurrentStateChanged;

// Update the system-wide state whenever the MediaElement state changes
mediaControls.ButtonPressed += SystemMediaTransportControls_ButtonPressed;
```

Notice that the `SystemMediaTransportControls` instance is per-window, so you can have a separate session for each window if your app uses more than one. The media transport controls support many potential buttons. In addition to play, pause, and stop, there's rewind, fast forward, previous, next, channel down, channel up, and record.

The two event handlers referenced in the preceding code can be implemented as follows:

```
// Update the media transport controls to match the new MediaElement state
void MediaElement_CurrentStateChanged(object sender, RoutedEventArgs e)
{
  SystemMediaTransportControls mediaControls =
    SystemMediaTransportControls.GetForCurrentView();

  switch (this.mediaElement.CurrentState)
  {
```

```
    case MediaElementState.Playing:
      mediaControls.PlaybackStatus = MediaPlaybackStatus.Playing;
      break;
    case MediaElementState.Paused:
      mediaControls.PlaybackStatus - MediaPlaybackStatus.Paused;
      break;
    case MediaElementState.Stopped:
      mediaControls.PlaybackStatus = MediaPlaybackStatus.Stopped;
      break;
    case MediaElementState.Closed:
      mediaControls.PlaybackStatus = MediaPlaybackStatus.Closed;
      break;
    default:
      // Nothing to do for this state
      break;
  }
}

// Update the MediaElement to match the new media transport controls state
async void SystemMediaTransportControls_ButtonPressed(
  SystemMediaTransportControls sender,
  SystemMediaTransportControlsButtonPressedEventArgs args)
{
  // This is invoked on a background thread
  await this.Dispatcher.RunAsync(CoreDispatcherPriority.Normal, () =>
  {
    switch (args.Button)
    {
      // We only need to worry about the buttons we explicitly enabled
      case SystemMediaTransportControlsButton.Play:
        this.mediaElement.Play();
        break;
      case SystemMediaTransportControlsButton.Pause:
        this.mediaElement.Pause();
        break;
      case SystemMediaTransportControlsButton.Stop:
        this.mediaElement.Stop();
        break;
      default:
        // Unexpected button
        break;
    }
  });
}
```

Although not required, you should also use the `DisplayUpdater` property on
SystemMediaTransportControls to improve its display:

```
SystemMediaTransportControls mediaControls =
  SystemMediaTransportControls.GetForCurrentView();

// Provide a thumbnail
mediaControls.DisplayUpdater.Thumbnail =
  RandomAccessStreamReference.CreateFromUri(
    new Uri("ms-appx:///Assets/AlbumArt.png"));

// This must be set before setting the music-specific properties
mediaControls.DisplayUpdater.Type = MediaPlaybackType.Music;

// Now we can set the music-specific properties
mediaControls.DisplayUpdater.MusicProperties.Title = "The Title";
mediaControls.DisplayUpdater.MusicProperties.Artist = "The Artist";

// Commit the update
mediaControls.DisplayUpdater.Update();
```

Of course, you can often get the real track and artist names from file metadata.

With all these steps taken, background audio not only works, but the volume control gets
the additional media transport controls while the audio is playing. This is shown in
Figure 22.12.

The volume control with no background audio   The volume control with added media transport controls
when background audio is active

FIGURE 22.12   When background audio is working, media transport controls are automatically
shown alongside the volume control.

One neat thing about supporting `SystemMediaTransportControls` is that it makes your
app automatically work with hardware media buttons on remote controls, keyboards, or
any other relevant peripherals.

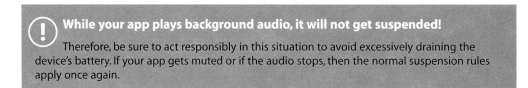

(!) **While your app plays background audio, it will not get suspended!**

Therefore, be sure to act responsibly in this situation to avoid excessively draining the
device's battery. If your app gets muted or if the audio stops, then the normal suspension rules
apply once again.

Custom Background Tasks

For any type of background task other than playing audio, you have more work to do. You must create a class that implements an interface called IBackgroundTask, register the task, choose a trigger, and potentially more.

Implementing IBackgroundTask

IBackgroundTask is a simple interface with a single Run method. The following dummy implementation does nothing other than show how to report progress and support cancellation, which are two features that can be leveraged by your app when it runs in the foreground:

```
public sealed class CustomBackgroundTask : IBackgroundTask
{
  bool isCanceled;

  public void Run(IBackgroundTaskInstance taskInstance)
  {
    // Support cancellation
    taskInstance.Canceled += (sender, reason) => this.isCanceled = true;

    for (uint progress = 0; progress <= 100; progress++)
    {
      if (this.isCanceled)
        break;

      // Send progress information
      taskInstance.Progress = progress;
    }
  }
}
```

To perform asynchronous work, you must follow the typical deferral pattern initiated by calling GetDeferral on the passed-in IBackgroundTaskInstance. Note that your background task is hosted specially and runs in a different process than the rest of your app. Its execution is independent of whatever your app is doing at the time.

Registering the Task

As with background audio, you must add two pieces of information to the package manifest: the supported task type(s) and the entry point. For the supported task type(s), select the relevant type, such as "System event" or "Timer." (These choices are discussed in a moment.) For the entry point, put the namespace-qualified type name of your class that implements IBackgroundTask, such as Chapter22.CustomBackgroundTask.

You must also write some registration code that you typically run every time your app runs. The following helper method does this work for any task whose information is passed in:

```
static BackgroundTaskRegistration RegisterBackgroundTask(string name,
  string entryPoint, IBackgroundTrigger trigger,
  IBackgroundCondition[] conditions)
{
  // If it's already registered, be sure to return the existing task
  // to avoid registering the same task multiple times
  foreach (BackgroundTaskRegistration task in
           BackgroundTaskRegistration.AllTasks.Values)
  {
    if (task.Name == name)
      return task;
  }

  // Register and return a new task
  BackgroundTaskBuilder builder = new BackgroundTaskBuilder {
    Name = name, TaskEntryPoint = entryPoint };

  // Specify what triggers the task
  builder.SetTrigger(trigger);

  // Add any conditions
  if (conditions != null)
  {
    foreach (IBackgroundCondition condition in conditions)
    {
      builder.AddCondition(condition);
    }
  }

  return builder.Register();
}
```

The code must first check whether the task has been registered to avoid registering it multiple times. If it is registered, it returns the previously registered instance. If this is the first time, it constructs a custom background task with a BackgroundTaskBuilder. In addition to a name and an entry point (the same namespace-qualified task class name), the task must be given a trigger that determines when it runs. It can also be given any number of conditions that further restrict when it runs. Triggers and conditions are discussed in a moment.

> **! Don't register your background task multiple times!**
>
> A background task can be registered multiple times, which is why it's important to guard against that. It can negatively impact the performance of your task, or even its correctness.

> If your background task is a one-time activity or has a limited timeframe in which it is useful, you can unregister it with BackgroundTaskBuilder's Unregister method when the time is right.

Windows doesn't do anything with the progress reported by a background task or whatever results it produces, but your app can. The BackgroundTaskRegistration object (returned by our RegisterBackgroundTask helper) exposes two events: Progress and Completed. Your app's initialization code might do something like the following:

```
BackgroundTaskRegistration task = RegisterBackgroundTask("My Task",
  "Chapter22.CustomBackgroundTask", trigger, null);
task.Progress += OnProgress;
task.Completed += OnCompleted;
```

If your app happens to be running in the foreground while your background task reports progress and/or completes, these events get raised instantly. If either of these conditions happens while your app is suspended, then the events are raised when your app resumes.

No data gets passed directly from the background task to the foreground app, but you can write both sides such that they agree upon a place to look for any necessary data. For example, you can use local app settings or app files.

Triggers

Every background task must be given a single trigger that determines what causes it to run. There are nine kinds of triggers: TimeTrigger, MaintenanceTrigger, SystemTrigger, PushNotificationTrigger, LocationTrigger, DeviceUseTrigger, DeviceServicing-Trigger, and the limited-use NetworkOperatorHotspotAuthenticationTrigger and NetworkOperatorNotificationTrigger.

TimeTrigger and MaintenanceTrigger both enable a background task to run at a regular interval. In their constructors, you specify the interval in terms of the number of minutes and a Boolean that determines whether the task should be executed only once (when true) or if it should continuously be invoked until the task is unregistered (when false). For example:

```
MaintenanceTrigger trigger =
  new MaintenanceTrigger(freshnessTime: 30, oneShot: false);
BackgroundTaskRegistration task = RegisterBackgroundTask("My Task",
  "Chapter22.CustomBackgroundTask", trigger, null);
```

Regardless of which you use, you must choose "Timer" as the task type in your package manifest.

So what's the difference between TimeTrigger and MaintenanceTrigger? MaintenanceTrigger causes the task to be invoked only while the PC is on AC power, whereas TimeTrigger runs the task regardless. To help conserve battery power, Windows doesn't allow just any app to use a TimeTrigger, however. It has to be an app that the user has added to the lock screen. That's because presumably the user cares about frequent updates for such apps. Note that for either type of trigger, Windows doesn't invoke the task *exactly* on the requested interval. It claims to do so only within 15 minutes of the scheduled interval.

SystemTrigger covers a number of different events, and you choose the specific one with a value from the SystemTriggerType enumeration. For example:

```
SystemTrigger trigger = new SystemTrigger(
  triggerType: SystemTriggerType.NetworkStateChange, oneShot: false);
BackgroundTaskRegistration task = RegisterBackgroundTask("My Task",
 "Chapter22.CustomBackgroundTask", trigger, null);
```

Some trigger types require the app to be added to the lock screen, whereas others don't. Here's the full list:

→ **TimeZoneChange**

→ **SmsReceived**

→ **LockScreenApplicationAdded** and **LockScreenApplicationRemoved**

→ **InternetAvailable** and **NetworkStateChange**. The latter includes changes in network cost as well as connectivity.

→ **OnlineIdConnectedStateChange**, for when the user's Microsoft account changes.

→ **ServicingComplete**, for when an app has been updated.

→ **UserPresent** and **UserAway** (lock screen app only).

→ **NetworkStateChange**, for when there is either a change in connectivity or in cost.

→ **BackgroundWorkCostChange**, for when the cost of background work changes (such as switching to battery power).

→ **ControlChannelReset** (lock screen app only).

→ **SessionConnected** (lock screen app only).

Be sure to select "System event" for the task type in your package manifest when you use a SystemTrigger.

Conditions

To help preserve battery life, you can further restrict when your background task runs by applying any number of extra conditions. Each condition is an instance of SystemCondition constructed with a SystemConditionType enumeration value that describes it. For example:

```
IBackgroundCondition[] conditions = new IBackgroundCondition[] {
  new SystemCondition(SystemConditionType.InternetAvailable),
  new SystemCondition(SystemConditionType.UserPresent);
};
BackgroundTaskRegistration task = RegisterBackgroundTask("My Task",
 "Chapter22.CustomBackgroundTask", trigger, conditions);
```

The values of SystemConditionType are:

→ **UserPresent** and **UserNotPresent**

→ **InternetAvailable** and **InternetNotAvailable**

→ **SessionConnected** and **SessionDisconnected**

→ **FreeNetworkAvailable**

→ **BackgroundCostWorkNotHigh**

For example, specifying a condition of FreeNetworkAvailable means the task will run only if a non-metered network connection is being used.

Summary

Contracts enable an app to do some powerful things that you might not expect. Some of this power, such as file type associations, is even able to impact the desktop experience.

Although you can do a lot with background tasks, there are some other options for keeping your app looking up-to-date, such as using live tiles or scheduled notifications. These are explained in the final chapter of this part of the book.

A few more contracts exist that aren't examined by this chapter:

→ **Camera Settings**—Enables an app to add custom options (such as special effects) to the Camera app. Meant for developers who make cameras (independent hardware vendors or original equipment manufacturers).

→ **Print Task Settings**—Enables an app to replace the default print settings with a custom user interface (and code that communicates directly with the printer).

→ **Cached File Updater**—Enables an app to perform custom actions whenever specific files are accessed. For example, the app can be activated immediately before a file is read and/or immediately after a file is modified. The idea is to use this with local files that are a cached version of data that exists elsewhere. The target app can therefore refresh the cached version and propagate updates to the source version on-demand.

→ **Certificates**—Enables an app to install digital certificates. The main reason for this is to authenticate a user to Web services over SSL.

Chapter 23

READING FROM SENSORS

This chapter shows how to interact with the large number of sensors that are standard on Windows tablets. Of course, you must not assume that any of these sensors are available to your app given that Windows runs on so many different form factors, including traditional desktop PCs. Not only that, but sensors that reveal sensitive data—the ones that provide location and proximity data—can be disabled for your app at any time via the Permissions link on the Settings pane.

All of the sensor APIs covered in this chapter can be found in the Windows.Devices.Sensors namespace, except for Location (Windows.Devices.Geolocation) and Proximity (Windows.Networking.Proximity).

Accelerometer

Several times a second, the accelerometer reports the direction and magnitude of the total force applied to the device. This force is expressed with three values—X, Y, and Z—where X is horizontal, Y is vertical, and Z is perpendicular to the screen, as shown in Figure 23.1.

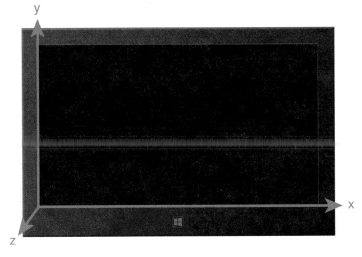

FIGURE 23.1   The three accelerometer dimensions, relative to the screen

The magnitude of each value is a multiplier of *g* (the gravitational force on the surface of Earth). Each value is restricted to a range from -2 to 2. If the device rests flat on a table with the screen up, the values reported for X and Y are roughly zero, and the value of Z is roughly -1 (1 *g* into the screen toward the ground). That's because the only force applied to the device in this situation is gravity. By shifting the device's angle and orientation and keeping it roughly still, the values of X, Y, and Z reveal which way is down in the real world thanks to the ever-present force of gravity. When you abruptly move or shake the device, the X, Y, and Z values are able to reveal this activity as well.

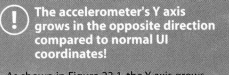

> **The accelerometer's Y axis grows in the opposite direction compared to normal UI coordinates!**
>
> As shown in Figure 23.1, the Y axis grows upward rather than downward.

To get the accelerometer data, you call the static `Accelerometer.GetDefault` method and attach a handler to its `ReadingChanged` event. You can also get the current reading on demand by calling its `GetCurrentReading` method. Both of these techniques provide you with an `AccelerometerReading` class with four simple properties: `AccelerationX`, `AccelerationY`, `AccelerationZ` (all doubles), and `Timestamp` (a `DateTimeOffset`). The physical accelerometer is always running, but data is reported to your app only while you have a `ReadingChanged` event handler attached.

> Regardless of how you contort your device, the X, Y, and Z axes used for the accelerometer data remain fixed to it. For example, the Y axis always points toward the top edge of the screen.

> ⚠ **Be sure to handle the case when `Accelerometer.GetDefault` returns `null`!**
>
> This is what happens when the current PC has no accelerometer. And as with all the sensors, your app could run on PCs without one.

> 💡 To get the best performance and battery life, it's good to detach your `ReadingChanged` handler when you don't need the data. You can also adjust `Accelerometer`'s `ReportInterval` property by setting it to a larger number of milliseconds than its default refresh rate (revealed by its `MinimumReportInterval` property).

Tossing Motion

The following handler for `Accelerometer`'s `ReadingChanged` event contains a simple algorithm for detecting a tossing motion, such as pretending to flip a coin in the air (except in this case, the coin is the PC):

```csharp
// Process data coming from the accelerometer
void OnReadingChanged(Accelerometer sender,
                      AccelerometerReadingChangedEventArgs e)
{
  // We want the threshold to be negative, so
  // forward motion is up and out of the screen
  double threshold = -1;

  // Only pay attention to large-enough magnitudes in the Z dimension
  if (Math.Abs(e.Reading.AccelerationZ) < Math.Abs(threshold))
    return;

  // See if the force is in the same direction as the threshold
  // (forward throwing motion)
  if (e.Reading.AccelerationZ * threshold > 0)
  {
    // Forward acceleration
    this.acceleratingQuicklyForwardTime = e.Reading.Timestamp;
  }
  else if (e.Reading.Timestamp - this.acceleratingQuicklyForwardTime
          < TimeSpan.FromSeconds(.2))
  {
    // This is large backward force shortly after the forward force.
    // Time to invoke the tossing action!

    this.acceleratingQuicklyForwardTime = DateTimeOffset.MinValue;
```

```
    // We're on a different thread, so transition to the UI thread
    await this.Dispatcher.RunAsync(CoreDispatcherPriority.Normal, () =>
    {
        // A toss happened! React appropriately.
        …
    });
  }
}
```

Only two properties of `AccelerometerReading` are examined by the code: `AccelerationZ` and `Timestamp`. The algorithm is as follows: If the app detects a strong forward force followed quickly by a strong backward force, it considers it a toss.

Notice that the threshold is negative, which seems to contradict the description of the Z axis in Figure 23.1. That's because when you hold a device flat and accelerate it upward, it "feels heavier" in the opposite direction, causing the value of `e.Reading.AccelerationZ` to *decrease*. You experience the same sensation when going up in a fast-moving elevator. The same behavior applies to either direction in any dimension. This is the difference between measuring g-forces (what accelerometers do) versus actually measuring acceleration.

> ⚠ **The accelerometer's ReadingChanged event is raised on a background thread!**
>
> This is great for processing the data without creating a bottleneck on the UI thread, but it does mean that you must explicitly transition to the UI thread before performing any work that requires it. This is true for other sensor events covered in this chapter as well.

> 💡 Because of hardware variations between different devices, apps that use the accelerometer should often enable the user to adjust or otherwise calibrate the interpretation of the raw data.

Shake Detection

A common use of the accelerometer is to detect when the user shakes the device. This is not trivial to detect from the raw data, however, especially if you want the recognition of the gesture to feel the same as shake detection done by other apps. (In the past, I've implemented this logic by detecting if at least two out of the three acceleration values are sufficiently different from previously-recorded values. Of course, "sufficiently different" can be hard to judge.) Fortunately, `Accelerometer` has a built-in `Shaken` event that tells you when a standard shake has occurred. `AccelerometerShakenEventArgs` exposes nothing other than a `Timestamp` property.

Gyrometer

Whereas an accelerometer detects linear motion, a gyrometer reports *angular* motion. You can get this data with a Gyrometer class that looks almost identical to Accelerometer. You get an instance by calling Gyrometer.GetDefault, you can attach a handler to its ReadingChanged event (or call its GetCurrentReading method for data on demand), and you can adjust its ReportInterval. The only difference—other than the lack of a Shaken event—is that GyrometerReading's properties are **AngularVelocity**X, **AngularVelocity**Y, **AngularVelocity**Z, and Timestamp.

Inclinometer

The inclinometer is a bit harder to understand, and you probably don't need to use it unless you write a flight simulator. It measures *pitch*, *roll*, and *yaw*, which maps to an airplane's elevator, aileron, and rudder inputs, respectively.

The members exposed by the Inclinometer class look like the members exposed by Gyrometer. You get an instance by calling Inclinometer.GetDefault, you can attach a handler to its ReadingChanged event (or call its GetCurrentReading method), and you can adjust its ReportInterval. InclinometerReading's properties are PitchDegrees, RollDegrees, YawDegrees, and Timestamp.

Compass

The compass sensor follows the same pattern as the others. The Compass class has identical members to Inclinometer and Gyrometer, except the readings returned are of type CompassReading. CompassReading exposes three properties:

→ **HeadingMagneticNorth**—A double representing the magnetic-north heading in degrees.

→ **HeadingTrueNorth**—A nullable double representing the true-north heading in degrees. This can't always be determined, so the property is null in such cases.

→ **Timestamp**—The date and time that the measurement was taken; a DateTimeOffset, like all the other Timestamp properties.

Light Sensor

With the ambient light sensor, you can automatically dim, brighten, or otherwise adjust your app's content based on the surrounding lighting conditions. (If you do this, please make it optional, otherwise you will annoy users like me!)

The light sensor once again follows the same pattern as the others. The class is called LightSensor and the readings returned are of type LightSensorReading. This has two properties: IlluminanceInLux and Timestamp. IlluminanceInLux measures the amount of light in lux units.

Orientation

Chapter 4, "Layout," describes how you can detect orientation changes with the static `DisplayProperties.OrientationChanged` event. This enables you to detect landscape, landscape-flipped, portrait, and portrait-flipped orientations. There are two orientation-related sensor APIs, however, that expose richer data: `SimpleOrientationSensor` and `OrientationSensor`.

SimpleOrientationSensor

`SimpleOrientationSensor` is much simpler to use than `OrientationSensor`, and its APIs are a bit simpler than the other sensors, too. Besides its `GetDefault` method, it exposes only a `GetCurrentOrientation` method and an `OrientationChanged` event. The device's current orientation is reported via a member of the `SimpleOrientation` enumeration:

→ **NotRotated** (the same as *landscape*: horizontal and upright, like a laptop screen)

→ **Rotated180DegreesCounterclockwise** (the same as *landscape-flipped*: horizontal and upright, but upside down)

→ **Rotated270DegreesCounterclockwise** (the same as *portrait*: vertical and upright, with the hardware Start button on the left)

→ **Rotated90DegreesCounterclockwise** (the same as *portrait-flipped*: vertical and upright, with the hardware Start button on the right)

→ **Faceup** (lying flat on a horizontal surface, screen up)

→ **Facedown** (lying flat on a horizontal surface, screen down)

The detection of `Faceup` and `Facedown` is the added benefit of using `SimpleOrientationSensor` compared to `DisplayProperties` from Chapter 4.

OrientationSensor

The full `OrientationSensor` class is like a combination of the accelerometer, gyrometer, and compass. It reveals a 3x3 *rotation matrix* and a *quaternion*. This class has the same surface area as most of the other sensor classes: `GetDefault` and `GetCurrentReading` methods, a `ReadingChanged` event, and `ReportInterval` plus `MinimumReportInterval` properties. The `OrientationSensorReading` class, which reveals the orientation data, exposes two properties besides `Timestamp`: `RotationMatrix` and `Quaternion`.

Location

With the `Geolocator` class—and the Location capability—you can retrieve the PC's geographic location. This information can come from GPS hardware, or from an algorithm that estimates location (perhaps using Wi-Fi triangulation or the current IP address) if no GPS hardware exists. In addition, a set of classes in a new

Windows.Devices.Geolocation.**Geofencing** namespace make it easy to track when the device crosses a geographic boundary.

Getting the Current Location

To get the current location, you create an instance of Geolocator and call GetGeopositionAsync:

```
Geolocator locator = new Geolocator();
try
{
  Geoposition position = await locator.GetGeopositionAsync();

  …
}
catch (UnauthorizedAccessException)
{
  // Location is not enabled for this app
}
```

Because GetGeopositionAsync prompts the user with a "Can [*app name*] use your location?" prompt the first time your app calls it, this call must be made on the UI thread. If the user chooses "Block" or later disables the Location capability for your app via the Settings pane, GetGeopositionAsync throws an UnauthorizedAccessException.

The data may be cached for performance reasons, so an overload of GetGeopositionAsync enables you to specify your tolerance for how old the data may be. You can also specify how long you're willing to wait to get data. Both of these are expressed as TimeSpans:

```
Geolocator locator = new Geolocator();
TimeSpan maximumAge = TimeSpan.FromSeconds(5);
TimeSpan timeout = TimeSpan.FromSeconds(3);
Geoposition position = await locator.GetGeopositionAsync(maximumAge, timeout);
```

If the data cannot be returned within the timeout specified, GetGeopositionAsync throws an exception.

If you require high accuracy at the expense of battery life, you can change Geolocator's DesiredAccuracy property from Default to High. When set to High, Geolocator always attempts to get its data from the GPS, if it exists. For Default, Geolocator only uses the GPS if it cannot get the data via other means (such as Wi-Fi triangulation).

However, it can be hard to know which value to choose. Therefore, Windows 8.1 introduces a DesiredAccuracyInMeters property that you can set instead. You specify your desired accuracy in terms of meters, and it will automatically set DesiredAccuracy accordingly. It turns out that requesting accuracy within less than 100 meters requires a DesiredAccuracy of High, otherwise Default is fine.

Getting the user's location once might be acceptable for some scenarios, but most location-based apps want to track the user's location as he or she moves. You can do this by handling Geolocator's PositionChanged event. Handlers are given a PositionChangedEventArgs object with a Position property of type Geoposition, the same object returned by GetGeopositionAsync. You can control how frequently updates are provided by changing Geolocator's ReportInterval and/or MovementThreshold properties.

Geolocator also exposes a LocationStatus property with a corresponding StatusChanged event. This property tells you whether the location provider is still initializing, ready, disabled, and so on.

Understanding the Current Location

The returned Geoposition object is not a simple latitude/longitude pair, but rather the starting point for accessing a rich set of objects. Geoposition contains two properties: Coordinate and CivicAddress.

CivicAddress attempts to map the precise location to an address. It exposes the following properties, all strings except for the last one:

→ **City**

→ **State** (which could also be the province, if applicable)

→ **PostalCode**

→ **Country** (the two-letter ISO-3166 country code)

→ **Timestamp**

If some of these can't be determined, they are left as empty strings. When running this on an older PC, the only piece of information you might get is the Country.

In Windows 8, Geoposition's Coordinate property is where you would find Latitude, Longitude, Altitude, and several other properties. However, in Windows 8.1, these three properties have been deprecated. Instead, you should use a new version of them buried inside a new Geopoint object. This revamping of the APIs was done to support geofencing, although the result is an API that is so nested, it can be hard to keep the abstractions straight. Figure 23.2 summarizes the main objects involved in understanding the current location.

Geoposition's Coordinate property is of type Geocoordinate, Geocoordinate's Point property is of type Geopoint, and Geopoint's Position property is of type BasicGeoposition. The bottom line is that instead of writing the following to get the current longitude:

```
Geoposition position = await locator.GetGeopositionAsync();
double longitude = position.Coordinate.Longitude; // Deprecated
```

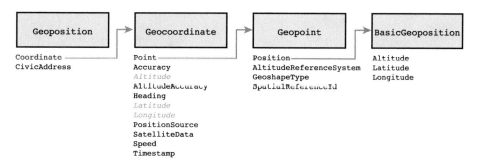

FIGURE 23.2   The four most important geolocation data types and their properties. Italicized properties are deprecated in Windows 8.1.

You should write the following:

```
Geoposition position = await locator.GetGeopositionAsync();
double longitude = position.Coordinate.Point.Position.Longitude;
```

Coordinate, of type Geocoordinate, exposes the following properties:

→ **Point**—Contains the actual coordinate data (buried one level deeper).

→ **PositionSource**—Reveals the technique used to produce this data: Satellite (i.e. GPS), WiFi, Cellular, IPAddress, or Unknown.

→ **Accuracy**—The accuracy of the latitude and longitude information, specified in meters.

→ **AltitudeAccuracy**—The accuracy of the altitude, specified in meters.

→ **SatelliteData**—When PositionSource is Satellite, this contains more information about the coordinate's precision via three subproperties: HorizontalDilutionOfPrecision, VerticalDilutionOfPrecision, and PositionDilutionOfPrecision.

→ **Speed**—A nullable double specified in meters per second, if the user is moving.

→ **Heading**—A nullable double that reveals the direction of any motion, specified in degrees relative to true north.

→ **Timestamp**—The date and time that the measurement was taken.

→ **Latitude**, **Longitude**, and **Altitude**—Now deprecated.

The Point, PositionSource, and SatelliteData properties are new to Windows 8.1.

> It may be tempting to adjust your app based on the value of Geocoordinate's PositionSource, but it's usually better to make adjustments based on the value of Accuracy instead. Each source has the full range of accuracy, so you shouldn't assume that a non-Satellite PositionSource means that accuracy is low.

Geocoordinate's Point property, of type Geopoint, exposes the following properties:

→ **Position**—A BasicGeoposition structure that finally contains the real data: Latitude, Longitude, and Altitude, all specified as doubles.

→ **GeoshapeType**—A value from the GeoshapeType enumeration. Always set to GeoshapeType.Geopoint.

→ **AltitudeReferenceSystem**—Describes how the altitude has been calculated, using a value from an AltitudeReferenceSystem enumeration.

→ **SpatialReferenceId**—An ID for the geographic point according to the European Petroleum Survey Group (EPSG) standard.

The AltitudeReferenceSystem enumeration has the following values:

→ **Geoid**—The altitude is expressed as distance above sea level.

→ **Terrain**—The altitude is expressed as distance above ground level.

→ **Surface**—The altitude is expressed as distance above surface structures such as trees and buildings.

→ **Ellipsoid**—The altitude is based on an ellipsoid that approximates the shape of the earth.

→ **Unspecified**—The default value when code manually constructs a Geopoint.

Implementing Geofencing

Geofencing refers to constructing a virtual perimeter (fence) around a geographic region. Software in many different types of devices perform geofencing in order to alert someone when the device enters or leaves a perimeter. Such alerts can be used to prevent theft, protect children, notify a spouse when you leave work, tempt you with a discount for a nearby store, produce location-based reminders ("The next time I'm at my brother's house, remind me to get my skis that he borrowed."), and so on.

A constantly-running Windows Store app could manually perform geofencing in Windows 8 with the location APIs already discussed, but Windows 8.1 includes system support for this. Windows not only manages geofences on behalf of all apps (which is more efficient), but your app doesn't necessarily need to be running when the perimeter is entered/exited thanks to new background task support. Plus, the new geofencing APIs make supporting geofences easy!

To create a geofence, you construct a `Geofence` object with a string ID of your choosing and a circle that defines its area. To activate it, you add it to `GeofenceMonitor`'s `Geofences` collection. To be notified when it gets triggered, you handle `GeofenceMonitor`'s `GeofenceStateChanged` event.

In Windows 8.1, only circular regions are supported. The circle is represented by a `Geocircle` object, which looks just like `Geopoint` except its `GeoshapeType` is always set to `GeoshapeType.Geocircle`, its `BasicPosition` property is called `Center` instead of `Position`, and it has an additional `Radius` property. (Both `Geocircle` and `Geopoint` implement the same `IGeoshape` interface.) `Radius` is a `double` that is specified in meters, unless you set `AltitudeReferenceSystem` to `Ellipsoid`.

`Geofence` has a few other options that you can set only by calling one of its overloaded constructors. These options are then exposed by the following readonly properties (in addition to `Id` and `Geoshape`):

→ **MonitoredStates**—Which conditions trigger the geofence. Can be one or more of the following `MonitoredGeofenceStates` enumeration values bitwise-ORed together: `Entered`, `Exited`, and `Removed`. If this isn't specified in an overloaded constructor, its value is `Entered | Exited`.

→ **SingleUse**—`true` if the geofence should be removed after it triggers once, `false` otherwise. The default is `false`.

→ **DwellTime**—When the perimeter is crossed, how long the device must stay on the new side before the geofence is triggered. The default is 10 seconds.

→ **StartTime**—When you want the monitoring to begin. By default, the monitoring starts as soon as the `Geofence` is added to `GeofenceMonitor`'s collection.

→ **Duration**—How long you want the monitoring to last. By default, it lasts forever (or until you manually remove the `Geofence` from `GeofenceMonitor`'s collection).

Listing 23.1 demonstrates creating a geofence, activating it, and responding to it being triggered.

LISTING 23.1   `MainPage.xaml.cs`: Creating and Monitoring a Geofence

```
using System;
using System.Threading.Tasks;
using Windows.Devices.Geolocation;
using Windows.Devices.Geolocation.Geofencing;
using Windows.UI.Popups;
using Windows.UI.Xaml.Controls;

namespace Chapter23
{
  public sealed partial class MainPage : Page
  {
```

LISTING 23.1   Continued

```csharp
public MainPage()
{
  InitializeComponent();

  // Get notified when a geofence is triggered
  GeofenceMonitor.Current.GeofenceStateChanged += OnGeofenceTriggered;

  CreateGeofence();
}

async Task CreateGeofence()
{
  try
  {
    // Ensure that location is enabled, and get a starting point
    Geolocator locator = new Geolocator();
    Geoposition position = await locator.GetGeopositionAsync();

    // Define a 5-meter radius around the current location
    Geocircle circle = new Geocircle(position.Coordinate.Point.Position, 5);

    // Create a corresponding geofence that monitors any exit and enter
    // with the default 10-second dwell time
    Geofence fence = new Geofence("myFence", circle);

    try
    {
      // Add the geofence to the system-managed list for this app.
      // This addition persists across app restarts.
      GeofenceMonitor.Current.Geofences.Add(fence);
    }
    catch
    {
      ShowError("A geofence with the same ID is already in the list.");
    }

  }
  catch (UnauthorizedAccessException)
  {
    ShowError("Location is not enabled for this app.");
  }
}
```

LISTING 23.1   Continued

```
// This handler is called on a background thread
void OnGeofenceTriggered(GeofenceMonitor sender, object args)
{
    foreach (GeofenceStateChangeReport report in sender.ReadReports())
    {
        switch (report.NewState)
        {
        case GeofenceState.Entered:
            // The fence has been entered!
            break;
        case GeofenceState.Exited:
            // The fence has been left!
            break;
        case GeofenceState.Removed:
            // We didn't ask to be notified for this condition
            break;
        }
    }
}

async Task ShowError(string message)
{
    MessageDialog dialog = new MessageDialog(message);
    await dialog.ShowAsync();
}
    }
}
```

In this example, GetGeopositionAsync is called because the current location is used as the center of the fence. It also ensures that the location capability is still enabled for this app, and triggers the required user consent prompt the first time the app runs (or whenever the capability is re-enabled).

GeofenceMonitor's Geofences collection persists across runs of the app. If you try to add a Geofence with an ID that matches an existing item in the collection, the call to Add throws an exception. The collection has a Contains method that would ordinarily enable you to easily check before calling Add, but this unfortunately checks based on reference equality, which produces a false negative in most cases.

In the handler for the GeofenceStateChanged event, you call GeofenceMonitor's ReadReports method to get a collection of state change reports. The report exposes four properties: Geofence (the affected Geofence object), Geoposition (the position at the time of the state change), NewState (either Entered, Exited, or Removed), and RemovalReason (either Expired or Used). Unless the Geofence is configured to report removals, an event is

not raised for NewStates of Removed.
When it is raised, the RemovalReason is
Expired when the Geofence's Duration
has ended, or Used if it's a single-use
Geofence that has just been triggered.
Removed does not get reported in
response to manual removals from
GeofenceMonitor's collection.

GeofenceMonitor has a
LastKnownGeopostion property, which

> ⊘ **Background geofencing only works for lock screen apps!**
>
> You can create a Location background task (one triggered by a LocationTrigger) in order to receive geofence triggers when your app isn't running. However, like some of the other trigger types, the user must add your app to his or her lock screen in order for the notifications to be delivered.

could be null, and a Status property (with a corresponding StatusChanged event) that
reports NotInitialized, Initializing, Ready, NoData, Disabled, or NotAvailable.

Proximity

Many Windows tablets have a Near Field Communication (NFC) chip, which can communicate with another NFC chip up to about 4cm away. Because of this close range, the two
devices are meant to be tapped together to trigger a custom action on one or both
devices. This gesture is often referred to as *tap and send*.

NFC is mostly associated with making payments from a smartphone by tapping a special
reader, but there are several "proximity" scenarios enabled by NFC. You can tap two NFC-
enabled devices together to send/receive a simple message. You can tap the devices
together as a simple way to bootstrap a normal WiFi or Bluetooth network connection
between two instances of your app. (Even better, your app doesn't need to be running or
installed on the second device! If your app isn't running, the second user is invited to

launch it. If your app isn't installed, the
second user is offered a link to it in the
Windows Store!) You can even tap a
little card or sticker with an unpowered
NFC chip inside to receive a message
from it. These are sometimes called *NFC
tags*. To use the proximity APIs discussed
in this section, your app must have the
Proximity capability.

> 💡 By supporting the Share charm, you can support proximity-based sharing without doing any extra work—and without requiring the Proximity capability. The user can select "someone nearby" on the Share pane and let Windows automatically use proximity as the mechanism for sharing without your app knowing what happened.

Sending and Receiving Messages

To receive a message from an NFC tag or device when it is tapped on your local device,
you attach a callback to ProximityDevice:

```
// Receive an NFC message
ProximityDevice device = ProximityDevice.GetDefault();
long id = device.SubscribeForMessage("WindowsUri", OnMessageReceived);
```

In the rare case you don't want to use the default proximity device, you can enumerate
available devices and select one by its string ID via other static ProximityDevice methods.

The first parameter to SubscribeForMessage describes the type of message you want to handle. The list of possible types is documented at http://bit.ly/S6hHGz, although you can append a period and a subtype to some to create your own custom types. The preceding code snippet is subscribing for URI messages. The returned ID can be passed to ProximityDevice.StopSubscribingForMessage, although calling this is optional.

The callback looks as follows:

```
void OnMessageReceived(ProximityDevice sender, ProximityMessage message)
{
  string uriString = message.DataAsString;
  // Use the URI

  …
 }
```

You can either get the message as a string via ProximityMessage's DataAsString property, or as an IBuffer via its Data property. You can copy an IBuffer to a byte array with the ToArray extension method defined in the System.Runtime.InteropServices. WindowsRuntime extension method.

To send a message, you can call one of the publishing methods on ProximityDevice:

```
// Send an NFC message
ProximityDevice device = ProximityDevice.GetDefault();
long id = device.PublishUriMessage(new Uri("http://pixelwinks.com"));
```

Once you do this, any later tap-and-send gestures send the message. Alternatively, you can call PublishMessage with a string message and string message type, or PublishBinaryMessage with an IBuffer message and a string message type.

Finding and Communicating with a Peer Device

To connect to a nearby peer device and initiate a network connection, you can use the following code:

```
ProximityDevice device = ProximityDevice.GetDefault();
// Handle tap from peer:
PeerFinder.TriggeredConnectionStateChanged += OnConnectionStateChanged;
PeerFinder.Start(); // Call Stop when done
```

Windows chooses the best available option for the connection, although you can exclude specific options by setting static PeerFinder properties such as AllowBluetooth and AllowWiFiDirect to false.

The event handler can look as follows:

```
void OnConnectionStateChanged(object sender,
                        TriggeredConnectionStateChangedEventArgs args)
{
```

```
switch (args.State)
{
  case TriggeredConnectState.Connecting:
    // This instance of the app is the "server" or "host"
    this.isClient = false;
    break;
  case TriggeredConnectState.Listening:
    // This instance of the app is the "client"
    this.isClient = true;
    break;
  case TriggeredConnectState.Completed:
    // The connection is complete, so start communicating
    StreamSocket socket = args.Socket;
    if (this.isClient)
    {
      socket.InputStream.AsStreamForRead().ReadAsync(…);
      …
    }
    else
    {
      socket.OutputStream.AsStreamForWrite().WriteAsync(…);
      …
    }
    break;
  case TriggeredConnectState.Failed:
    …
    break;
  case TriggeredConnectState.Canceled:
    …
    break;
  case TriggeredConnectState.PeerFound:
    // Could show an optional message
    …
    break;
}
}
```

This handler gets called more than once in both instances of the app. The one chosen as the "server" gets called first with TriggeredConnectState.Connecting, and the one chosen as the "client" gets called first with TriggeredConnectState.Listening. When subsequently called with TriggeredConnectState.Completed, both sides can communicate with each other via a socket. This code uses the AsStreamForRead and AsStreamForWrite extension methods to communicate by reading from/writing to a standard .NET stream.

Summary

Despite there being a long list of sensors to take advantage of, they are all simple to use. The trick is not how to get the raw data, but rather how to devise suitable algorithms that operate on the data! Unlike in Windows Phone, almost none of these sensors require a capability. Only the sensors revealing sensitive data—location and proximity—do.

Chapter 24

CONTROLLING DEVICES

Windows 8.1 introduces a lot of new support for interacting with devices. In fact, everything in this chapter is
new to Windows 8.1. The support falls into two categories.
Documentation sometimes refers to these as *device scenario
APIs* versus *device protocol APIs*.

Device scenario APIs are built-in support for well-known
devices. Some of the APIs may require capabilities, but they
are ordinary Windows Runtime APIs tailored to specific
scenarios. This includes support for fingerprint readers,
image scanners, printers (covered in Chapter 21,
"Supporting Charms"), barcode scanners, magnetic stripe
readers, physical smart cards, and virtual smart cards based
on a TPM chip. (The smart card support is not covered in
this chapter, but you can find the relevant APIs in the
Windows.Devices.SmartCards namespace.)

Device protocol APIs, on the other hand, enable you to
communicate with custom devices that Windows does not
already support. This is done by enabling you to use one of
many industry standard protocols: Bluetooth, Bluetooth
Smart, USB, HID, or Wi-Fi Direct.

This chapter first examines the use of four well-known
devices. After that, it looks at all five protocols for communicating with custom devices.

Fingerprint Readers

Windows 8.1 supports fingerprint authentication for sign
in, buying content from the Windows Store, and more.

Once a user configures this feature for recognizing his or her fingerprint, Windows Store apps can leverage the same authentication mechanism for custom purposes. It is exposed in a UserConsentVerifier class in the Windows.Security.Credentials.UI namespace.

UserConsentVerifier has two static methods:

→ **CheckAvailabilityAsync**—Checks whether the PC has a fingerprint reader, and if it is configured, enabled, and ready to be used.

→ **RequestVerificationAsync**—Asks the user for his or her fingerprint, along with a message you pass as a string parameter.

If fingerprint authentication can be done, CheckAvailability returns UserConsentVerifierAvailability.Available. Otherwise, it returns DeviceNotPresent, DeviceBusy, DisabledByPolicy, or NotConfiguredForUser. If you call RequestVerificationAsync when a device is not available, you get back one of those same four error conditions, although defined as fields of a separate UserConsentVerificationResult enumeration. Its other values are Verified (meaning the authentication succeeded), RetriesExhausted (meaning the authentication was attempted but failed), or Canceled.

So what can you do with fingerprint authentication? You could use it as a convenient alternative for password-protecting sensitive data owned by your app. Or, if you need to connect to a password-protected Web service, you can use it to provide fast sign-ins. The first time you need to connect, you can ask the user for a username and password, and then store them securely with PasswordVault. Subsequent times, you could use fingerprint authentication to determine whether it's okay to fetch the stored credentials from PasswordVault.

> Fingerprint authentication can be a convenient alternative to using passwords, especially with handheld devices on which typing can be cumbersome, and the risk of someone looking over your shoulder is higher. Modern fingerprint readers have a number of anti-spoofing features, including protection against the use of a fake (or severed!) finger. Still, the use of fingerprint authentication is controversial, as evidenced by reactions to its inclusion in the iPhone 5s.

Image Scanners

Classes in the Windows.Devices.Scanners namespace enable apps to initiate scans from a flatbed scanner or one with a document feeder. This support is built on top of Windows Image Acquisition 2.0, which was introduced in the Windows Vista timeframe, so it should work with any scanner with a Windows logo.

In this section, we look at the following tasks:

→ Getting an instance of ImageScanner

→ Performing a scan

→ Configuring scan sources

→ Showing a preview

Getting an Instance of `ImageScanner`

Unlike the sensors and other devices, there is no API for retrieving a default image scanner. Instead, you must create one from a specific device ID using the static `ImageScanner.FromIdAsync` method. If a scanner is connected, you can get its ID with APIs from the `Windows.Devices.Enumeration` namespace. For example, you can enumerate available scanners as follows:

```
foreach (DeviceInformation deviceInfo in await
        DeviceInformation.FindAllAsync(DeviceClass.ImageScanner))
{
  // Examine each matching device
}
```

You can also use `DeviceWatcher`, which raises events as devices are added, removed, and updated.

The `DeviceInformation` instances you get from these mechanisms expose the string `Id` property you need.

Performing a Scan

Once you have an instance of `ImageScanner`, you can perform a scan by calling `ScanFilesToFolderAsync`. You give it a `StorageFolder`, and it will create one or more files inside that folder with auto-generated filenames. You must also specify a *scan source*, which is the location of the physical document(s) on the scanner: Feeder, Flatbed, or AutoConfigured. You first check whether the scanner supports a specific scan source by calling `IsScanSourceSupported`. The following code demonstrates this:

```
async Task Scan(string deviceId, StorageFolder folder)
{
  // Get the scanner object
  ImageScanner scanner = await ImageScanner.FromIdAsync(deviceId);

  if (scanner != null &&
      scanner.IsScanSourceSupported(ImageScannerScanSource.Flatbed))
  {
    // Scan from its flatbed
    ImageScannerScanResult result = await scanner.ScanFilesToFolderAsync(
      ImageScannerScanSource.Flatbed, folder);

    foreach (StorageFile file in result.ScannedFiles)
    {
      // This is a new file with scanned content
    }
  }
}
```

The asynchronously-returned result contains the collection of StorageFiles that got saved to the input StorageFolder. Whether you get more than one file depends on the scan source and the target image format. You can only scan multiple pages simultaneously when using the Feeder scan source, because that's how scanners are designed. In this case, for most image formats, you get one image file per page. However, for multi-page image formats like PDF, TIFF, or XPS, you get a single multipage file. Customizing the output format is discussed in the next section.

When initiating a scan, your app's relevant window must visible and have focus. However, scanning continues and successfully completes even if your app gets minimized during the process.

> The benefit of choosing a specific scan source of Flatbed or Feeder is that you can customize some of the scanning settings, as described in the "Configuring Scan Sources" section.
>
> If you don't require a specific scan source or customizing settings, you should just use ImageScanner's DefaultScanSource property whenever you need to pass an ImageScannerScanSource value. This is set to AutoConfigured if the current scanner is capable of auto configuration, otherwise Flatbed if it is supported, otherwise Feeder.

> ScanFilesToFolderAsync doesn't just return an IAsyncOperation<ImageScannerScanResult>, but rather an IAsyncOperation**WithProgress**<ImageScannerScanResult,**uint**> that enables you to retrieve and report progress during the typically-slow scanning operation. Unfortunately, this is only useful for multipage scans, as the uint value reported is the number of pages scanned so far.

Configuring Scan Sources

ImageScanner exposes three properties for configuring each of the possible scan sources independently:

→ **AutoConfiguration**—Enables you to choose the output file format with its Format property. Applies only when the AutoConfigured scan source is used.

→ **FlatbedConfiguration**—Exposes six more options in addition to Format: AutoCroppingMode, Brightness, ColorMode, Contrast, DesiredResolution, and SelectedScanRegion. Applies only when the Flatbed scan source is used.

→ **FeederConfiguration**—Exposes all the options that FlatbedConfiguration exposes plus six more: AutoDetectPageSize, Duplex, MaxNumberOfPages, PageOrientation, PageSize, and ScanAhead. Applies only when the Feeder scan source is used.

For each scan source that is not supported by the current scanner, the corresponding configuration property is null.

Some of the properties have an associated Is*XXX*Supported method or Can*XXX* property that enables you to check the scanner's support for a certain feature before attempting to use it. For example, the following code attempts to configure the feeder to scan its pages to a PDF file:

```
if (scanner.FeederConfiguration.IsFormatSupported(ImageScannerFormat.Pdf))
{
  scanner.FeederConfiguration.Format = ImageScannerFormat.Pdf;
}
```

The available options for ImageScannerFormat are DeviceIndependentBitmap, Png, Jpeg, Pdf, Tiff, Xps, and OpenXps.

Many properties also have corresponding readonly properties that expose default values or the supported range of values. For example, there is DefaultFormat, DefaultBrightness/MinBrightness/MaxBrightness, DefaultContrast/MinContrast/MaxContrast, and so on.

Showing a Preview

Most scanning software provides the ability to quickly scan a low-resolution preview. This is especially helpful for enabling the user to crop the region to scan. You can support cropping with FlatbedConfiguration or FeederConfiguration's SelectedScanRegion property, and you can support previews with ImageScanner's ScanPreviewToStreamAsync method. You can use it as follows:

```
async Task ShowPreview(string deviceId, Image targetImage)
{
  // Get the scanner object
  ImageScanner scanner = await ImageScanner.FromIdAsync(deviceId);

  if (scanner != null &&
      scanner.IsScanSourceSupported(ImageScannerScanSource.Flatbed) &&
      scanner.IsPreviewSupported(ImageScannerScanSource.Flatbed))
  {
    using (InMemoryRandomAccessStream ras = new InMemoryRandomAccessStream())
    {
      // Get a preview from its flatbed
      ImageScannerPreviewResult result = await scanner.ScanPreviewToStreamAsync(
        ImageScannerScanSource.Flatbed, ras);

      if (result.Succeeded)
      {
        // Display the preview
        BitmapImage source = new BitmapImage();
```

```
        source.SetSource(ras);
        image.Source = source;
      }
    }
  }
}
```

You should first check that the current scanner and scan source support previewing with the `IsPreviewSupported` method. The asynchronously-returned result not only has a `Supported` property, but a `Format` property in case you plan on doing more with the data written to the stream than send it along to an `Image` element.

Barcode Scanners

The `Windows.Devices.PointOfService` namespace supports two types of *point of service* devices (sometimes called *point of sale* devices): barcode scanners and magnetic stripe readers. The APIs are based on the Unified Point of Service 2.0 international standard, so if you have used another point of service technology for desktop apps, such as POS for .NET, they should feel very familiar to you. This section looks at barcode scanners, and the next section looks at magnetic stripe readers.

> **(!) The APIs in `Windows.Devices.PointOfService` require a pointOfService capability!**
>
> This capability is not exposed by Visual Studio's package manifest designer. You must select "View Code" then add the XML element manually as follows:
>
> ```
> <Capabilities>
>   <Capability Name="internetClient" />
>   <DeviceCapability Name="pointOfService"/>
> </Capabilities>
> ```
>
> Notice that device capabilities use a different XML element than other capabilities. If you fail to add this, `BarcodeScanner.GetDefaultAsync` always returns `null`.

Using a barcode scanner involves four steps:

1. Getting an instance
2. Claiming the device
3. Enabling the device
4. Retrieving the data

Getting an Instance of **BarcodeScanner**

Unlike with ImageScanner, you can get an instance of BarcodeScanner simply by calling its static parameterless GetDefaultAsync method. In most cases, this is likely to be good enough, as it would be rare for more than one to be connected to the same PC.

Still, you could alternatively call its static FromIdAsync method to retrieve one by its device ID, which you could get as follows:

```
foreach (DeviceInformation deviceInfo in await
         DeviceInformation.FindAllAsync(BarcodeScanner.GetDeviceSelector()))
{
  // Examine each matching device
}
```

Or you could use DeviceWatcher to be notified if any barcode scanners are added or removed.

Claiming the Device

Point of service devices must be *claimed* for exclusive access by an app before being accessible. This is done to handle the case when more than one active app wants to use the same device. To claim a barcode scanner, simply call ClaimScannerAsync, which returns an instance of a **Claimed**BarcodeScanner:

```
BarcodeScanner scanner = await BarcodeScanner.GetDefaultAsync();
if (scanner != null)
{
  ClaimedBarcodeScanner claimedScanner = await scanner.ClaimScannerAsync();
  if (claimedScanner != null)
  {
    // We got it!
  }
}
```

If the device cannot be claimed, ClaimScannerAsync returns null.

Unlike other shared resources, like a camera, apps have a little more control over the claiming process. By default, an app keeps its claim until one of the following things happens:

→ The app calls Dispose on the ClaimedBarcodeScanner instance to explicitly release its claim

→ The app is suspended or closed

→ Another app claims the same device

This means that, by default, claiming the device for exclusive access doesn't really provide exclusive access! Anyone else who claims it automatically gets it! However, an app can

optionally refuse to give up its claim by handling ClaimedBarcodeScanner's
ReleaseDeviceRequested event. This is raised when someone else tries to claim it. By
calling RetainDevice inside a handler for this event, you can keep your claim:

```
void ClaimedScanner_ReleaseDeviceRequested(object sender,
                                           ClaimedBarcodeScanner e)
{
  // Transition back to the UI thread so we can call RetainDevice
  await this.Dispatcher.RunAsync(CoreDispatcherPriority.Normal,
    () => e.RetainDevice()));
}
```

Like most non-UI events in the Windows Runtime, ClaimedBarcodeScanner's events are
raised on a background thread. RetainDevice must be called on the UI thread, however.
Notice how the handler awaits the completion of the asynchronous object returned by
RunAsync. This ensures that the handler doesn't return until RetainDevice is called, which
is essential for this call to work as intended.

To play along nicely with other apps, you should only call RetainDevice if you're in the
middle of a transaction. Even if you always try to keep your claim, your app will still lose
it upon suspension (or exit). This means that you must reclaim the device upon resuming.

Enabling the Device

Once you get an instance of ClaimedBarcodeScanner, you should attach handlers to
its relevant events. The main event is DataReceived, but you can also handle
TriggerPressed, TriggerReleased, ErrorOccurred, and ImagePreviewReceived (in
addition to ReleaseDeviceRequested).

Once you do this, you can enable it by setting its IsEnabled property to true. If you want
to automatically disable it after you receive data, you can set IsDisabledOnDataReceived
to true. Otherwise, you can just manage the value of IsEnabled yourself.

Retrieving the Data

You cannot ask the barcode scanner for data. Once it is enabled, you must wait for the
DataReceived event to deliver you data, which is triggered by the user.

DataReceived handlers are passed a BarcodeScannerDataReceivedEventArgs instance,
which has a single Report property of type BarcodeScannerReport. This exposes three
properties:

→ **ScanData**—The complete, raw data

→ **ScanDataLabel**—The primary data decoded into a form suitable to display

→ **ScanDataType**—The type of the decoded label

Many different types of barcodes exist, and barcode scanners work with more than just
traditional, vertical-striped symbols. With ScanDataType, you can figure out which type of

symbols are being scanned. ScanDataType is a uint, but you can compare it against static uint properties defined by the BarcodeSymbologies class. For example, it has properties for Qr (QR codes), UpcCoupon, UsPostNet, ChinaPost, SwedenPost, and many, many more.

Both ScanData and ScanDataLabel are of type IBuffer, so you can use Windows.Storage.Streams.DataReader to extract data from it. Although processing ScanData requires knowledge of the data format, ScanDataLabel contains string data. Therefore, you can retrieve it as follows:

```
void ClaimedScanner_DataReceived(ClaimedBarcodeScanner sender,
                                 BarcodeScannerDataReceivedEventArgs args)
{
  // Remember, this is running on a background thread
  string label = DataReader.FromBuffer(args.Report.ScanDataLabel).ToString();
}
```

> (!) **ScanDataLabel is always null by default!**
>
> You must opt into the label-decoding feature if you want to retrieve it. To do this, you must set ClaimedBarcodeScanner's IsDecodeDataEnabled property to true before the DataReceived event is raised.

Magnetic Stripe Readers

Because a magnetic stripe reader is another point of service device, its APIs follow the same pattern as the barcode scanner APIs:

→ You must declare a pointOfService device capability.

→ You get an instance of MagneticStripeReader using one of the same approaches: calling its GetDefaultAsync method or FromIdAsync in conjunction with an API from the Windows.Devices.Enumeration namespace to get the device ID.

→ It has the same claiming model, so you must call ClaimReaderAsync to get an instance of **Claimed**MagneticStripeReader then potentially handle its ReleaseDeviceRequested event to call RetainDevice.

→ You must handle events to retrieve data, and then enable the ClaimedMagneticStripeReader by setting IsEnabled to true. It has the same IsDisabledOnDataReceived and IsDecodeDataEnabled properties.

Therefore, this section focuses on the differences between the magnetic stripe reader APIs and the barcode scanner APIs discussed in the preceding section.

Three Types of Magnetic Stripe Cards

Although there are many different types of barcodes, the APIs are the same. The differences are only revealed via the ScanDataType property retrieved inside the DataReceived event.

In contrast, MagneticStripeReader supports three kinds of cards, and this distinction is visible throughout the API. The three types are:

→ Bank cards (e.g. credit cards)

→ American Association of Motor Vehicle Administrators (AAMVA) cards, which are drivers licenses in certain states that have a magnetic stripe

→ Vendor-specific cards, which could be anything: a hotel room key, a grocery store loyalty card, a gym card, and so on

MagneticStripeReader exposes several properties that reveal its capabilities. There's a Capabilities property that reveals things like SupportedEncryptionAlgorithms and IsStatisticsReportingSupported. There's a DeviceAuthenticationProtocol property that is either set to ChallengeResponse or None. And there's a SupportedCardTypes property that returns an array of uints. These values can be compared against static uint properties on the MagneticStripeReaderCardTypes class: Bank, Aamva, ExtendedBase (vendor-specific), or Unknown.

Retrieving the Data

On the ClaimedMagneticStripeReader class, there is no general-purpose DataReceived event. You must instead choose the one(s) you support by handling either BankCardDataReceived, AamvaCardDataReceived, or VendorSpecificDataReceived.

Each type of event handler is passed a distinct *XXX*EventArgs object. However, they all expose a Report object of type MagneticStripeReaderReport. This exposes the main data, as well as authentication data, additional security information, and a dictionary of string properties, if applicable. Unlike with a barcode reader, the data from a magnetic stripe comes in the form of four tracks. These are exposed as Track1, Track2, Track3, and Track4 properties of type MagneticStripeReaderTrackData. This type exposes three IBuffer properties: Data, DiscretionaryData, and EncryptedData.

For vendor-specific cards, you only get the data back in this raw form. (MagneticStripeReaderVendorSpecificCardDataReceivedEventArgs only has the single Report property.) You must parse the data you need based on the format of the cards you support.

For bank cards and AAMVA cards, the data is already parsed for you and placed in convenient properties. That's because the data format is standardized. MagneticStripeReader-**Bank**CardDataReceivedEventArgs exposes additional AccountNumber, Title, FirstName, MiddleInitial, Surname, Suffix, ExpirationDate and ServiceCode properties. MagneticStripeReader**Aamva**CardDataReceivedEventArgs exposes 18 additional properties that cover everything from LicenseNumber, Height, Weight, and HairColor to Endorsements and Restrictions. And yet, both objects still expose the Report property in case you need to process the raw track data.

With the new *assigned access* feature, you can easily put a Windows 8.1 PC into a dedicated kiosk mode. You set up a user account that can only run one app of your choosing. When that user signs in, the app is automatically launched. Closing the app is disabled, switching to another app (or the desktop) is disabled, and invoking the charms bar is disabled. This is great for using a PC in a point of service environment.

Custom Bluetooth Devices

In this section, we look at the first of two Bluetooth protocols supported: Bluetooth RFCOMM. This is a serial port emulation protocol that gives you control over "classic" Bluetooth. Its APIs can be found in the `Windows.Devices.Bluetooth.Rfcomm` namespace. The next section examines the newer Bluetooth Smart protocol.

Declaring the Right Device Capability

To use a custom device, regardless of protocol, you must specify an appropriate device capability in your package manifest. The one exception to this is Wi-Fi Direct, covered at the end of this chapter. Specifying the capability must be done directly in the XML as follows, due to lack of support in Visual Studio's package manifest designer:

```
<Capabilities>
  <m2:DeviceCapability Name="protocol">
    <m2:Device Id="device">
      <m2:Function Type="functionType"/>
    </m2:Device>
  </m2:DeviceCapability>
  ...
</Capabilities>
```

Unlike the `DeviceCapability` element used with `pointOfService`, this one must be prefixed with the `m2` prefix that corresponds to the Windows 8.1 XML namespace. That's because the Windows 8 `DeviceCapability` element does not support child elements.

This `DeviceCapability` specifies three things: the protocol you want to use, the device, and its function type:

→ *protocol* must be set to `bluetooth.rfcomm` for Bluetooth (RFCOMM)

→ *device* can be set to any to work with any device, or it can be set to a specific device. This can be specified as model:*manufacturerName*;*modelName* or as a combination of a vendor ID (VID) and product ID (PID) as follows: vidpid:*vendorID* *productID* bluetooth. Both *vendorID* and *productID* are hexadecimal values.

→ *functionType* can be set to a friendly name for certain well-known services (with the syntax name:*friendlyName*) or the ID for a custom service (with the syntax serviceId:*ID*).

Therefore, for the Bluetooth (and Bluetooth Smart) protocol, *functionType* represents a service. USB and HID devices use this value for other purposes, as you'll see later in this chapter.

You can specify multiple m2:Device elements for the same DeviceCapability, and each m2:Device may contain multiple m2:Function elements. The following service friendly names are supported:

→ serialPort

▌ ⸱⸱⸱⸱ ⸱⸱⸱⸱⸱⸱⸱⸱ ⸱⸱ ⸱⸱⸱⸱

→ obexFileTransfer

→ phoneBookAccessPce

→ phoneBookAccessPse

→ genericFileTransfer

The following DeviceCapability enables the app, with user consent, to use the Serial Port Profile (SPP) service on any Bluetooth RFCOMM device:

```
<m2:DeviceCapability Name="bluetooth.rfcomm">
  <m2:Device Id="any">
    <m2:Function Type="name:serialPort"/>
  </m2:Device>
</m2:DeviceCapability>
```

Connecting to the Device

Fortunately, you don't have to implement device discovery and pairing. That is handled by Windows with its standard user interface. You just need to create an instance of an RfcommDeviceService via its static FromIdAsync and the device ID. As with the device scenario APIs, you can get the appropriate device ID with the help of classes from the Windows.Devices.Enumeration namespace:

```
async Task<RfcommDeviceService> GetSerialPortProfileServiceAsync()
{
  foreach (DeviceInformation deviceInfo in await
          DeviceInformation.FindAllAsync(RfcommDeviceService.GetDeviceSelector(
                                         RfcommServiceId.SerialPort)))
  {
    // Return the first one (null if user doesn't consent)
    // Be sure to call FromIdAsync on the UI thread!
    return await RfcommDeviceService.FromIdAsync(deviceInfo.Id);
  }

  return null;
}
```

`RfcommDeviceService.GetDeviceSelector` returns an appropriate query string based on information you provide. In this example, it's leveraging one of a handful of `RfcommServiceId` properties for well-known services. (`SerialPort` refers to the Serial Port Profile service.) `RfcommServiceId` also has `FromUuid` and `FromShortId` methods that you can use with a custom service ID.

Because Windows doesn't know what the custom device is doing, it assumes the worst and treats it like a device with sensitive personal information. That means that this device capability acts like the Location capability, and prompts the user the first time the app tries to access the device. (The user can also revoke access at any time from the Settings charm.) This capability check is triggered by the call to `FromIdAsync`, so this method must be called from the UI thread. `FromIdAsync` returns `null` if the device capability is missing from the package manifest, if the user disallows access, or if another app is currently using the device. This behavior applies to all the protocols covered in the remainder of this chapter.

> Whenever a call to a `FromIdAsync` method returns `null`, you can retrieve information about why you failed to get the device. To do this, call the static `Windows.Devices.Enumeration.DeviceAccessInformation.CreateFromId` method with the same device ID. This returns a `DeviceAccessInformation` object with a `CurrentStatus` property that reports either `DeniedBySystem`, `DeniedByUser`, `Allowed`, or `Unspecified`. Furthermore, you can attach a handler to its `AccessChanged` event to be notified about any changes in the device's availability.

Communicating with the Device

You communicate with a Bluetooth RFCOMM service using a standard `StreamSocket`. `RfcommDeviceService` provides `ConnectionHostName` and `ConnectionServiceName` properties that you can use to connect, and then you can use `DataWriter` and/or `DataReader` to work with the socket's `OutputStream` and `InputStream`:

```
RfcommDeviceService service = await GetSerialPortProfileServiceAsync();
if (service != null)
{
  StreamSocket socket = new StreamSocket();
  await socket.ConnectAsync(service.ConnectionHostName,
         service.ConnectionServiceName,
         SocketProtectionLevel.BluetoothEncryptionAllowNullAuthentication);

  DataWriter writer = new DataWriter(socket.OutputStream);
  DataReader reader = new DataReader(socket.InputStream);
  …
}
```

The `SocketProtectionLevel` enumeration provides two Bluetooth-specific options. The one used in this example is `BluetoothEncryptionAllowNullAuthentication`, which uses SSL if it can, but permits no encryption if necessary. The other one is `BluetoothEncryptionWithAuthentication`, which requires SSL.

When you're done with the socket, you should call `Dispose`. (You should also call `DataWriter`'s and `DataReader`'s `DetachStream` methods, if you use these classes.) Your app automatically loses its connection upon suspension, so it's best if you explicitly perform this disposal in response to your app's `Suspending` event.

> This section discussed the typical client usage of a remote service via `RfcommDeviceService`. However, the `Windows.Devices.Bluetooth.Rfcomm` name-space also contains an `RfcommServiceProvider` class that enables you to create and host RFCOMM services on the local PC. This includes support for the Service Discovery Protocol (SDP), which enables you to publish metadata about your service.

Custom Bluetooth Smart Devices

Bluetooth Smart refers to the Bluetooth Low Energy (Bluetooth LE) protocol, which is designed to use much less power than classic Bluetooth. This protocol is used by a wide range of portable devices, such as blood pressure monitors, blood glucose monitors, and heart rate monitors. Bluetooth Smart is not backwards-compatible with Bluetooth, although there are some devices that implement both protocols.

Bluetooth devices conform to one or more *profiles* defined by the Bluetooth Special Interest Group, and all current Bluetooth Smart profiles are based on what is called the Generic Attribute Profile (GATT). GATT defines how data is sent and received, which is in the form of small pieces of data known as *attributes*. Therefore, you can find the APIs for communicating with a Bluetooth Smart device in the `Windows.Devices.Bluetooth.GenericAttributeProfile` namespace.

Declaring the Right Device Capability

You declare a device capability for a Bluetooth Smart device the same way as shown in the previous section. In this case, however, the protocol (the `Name` value for the `m2:DeviceCapability` element) must be set to `bluetooth.genericAttributeProfile`. A different set of friendly service names are supported for well-known GATT services:

→ `battery`

→ `bloodPressure`

→ `cyclingSpeedAndCadence`

→ `genericAccess`

→ `genericAttribute`

→ glucose

→ healthThermometer

→ heartRate

→ runningSpeedAndCadence

These names are used with the m2:Function element, so here's an example of declaring a capability for using any Bluetooth Smart blood pressure device:

```
<m2:DeviceCapability Name="bluetooth.genericAttributeProfile">
  <m2:Device Id="any">
    <m2:Function Type="name:bloodPressure"/>
  </m2:Device>
</m2:DeviceCapability>
```

Connecting to the Device

Connecting to a Bluetooth Smart device also looks the same as connecting to a Bluetooth RFCOMM device:

```
async Task<GattDeviceService> GetBloodPressureServiceAsync()
{
  foreach (DeviceInformation deviceInfo in await
    DeviceInformation.FindAllAsync(GattDeviceService.GetDeviceSelectorFromUuid(
                              GattServiceUuids.BloodPressure)))
  {
    // Return the first one (null if user doesn't consent)
    // Be sure to call FromIdAsync on the UI thread!
    return await GattDeviceService.FromIdAsync(deviceInfo.Id);
  }

  return null;
}
```

One difference is that GattDeviceService forces you to specify a service ID when getting a device selector, either via GetDeviceSelectorFromUuid or GetDeviceSelectorFromShortId. However, GattServiceUuids exposes a static Guid property for each of the nine common services. The preceding code leverages this to connect to a blood pressure device.

A single device can support multiple services. You can enumerate all the supported services by calling the GattDeviceService instance's GetIncludedServices methods.

Communicating with the Device

You don't write and read data directly to/from a service. Instead, you do this with one of a service's *characteristics*. A characteristic represents a single logical data value. For example, a blood pressure service may expose BloodPressureMeasurement, BloodPressureFeature, IntermediateCuffPressure, and BodySensorLocation characteristics. Each characteristic is identified by a Guid, and 21 well-known characteristics are represented as static Guid properties on the GattCharacteristicUuids class.

A service might not only support multiple characteristics, but it may have more than one instance of each characteristic! Therefore, to get a characteristic, you must call GattDeviceService's GetCharacteristics (plural) method with the Guid for the desired characteristic. This returns a collection of GattCharacteristic objects that you can use for reading and writing the data:

```
GattDeviceService service = await GetBloodPressureServiceAsync();
if (service != null)
{
  foreach (GattCharacteristic characteristic in service.GetCharacteristics(
          GattCharacteristicUuids.BloodPressureMeasurement))
  {
    // In this case, we expect only one characteristic to be returned
    GattReadResult result = await characteristic.ReadValueAsync();
    if (result.Status == GattCommunicationStatus.Success)
    {
      DataReader reader = DataReader.FromBuffer(result.Value);

      …
    }
  }
}
```

GattCharacteristic has ReadValueAsync and WriteValueAsync methods. Both of these work with IBuffers, so you can use DataReader and DataWriter to work with them. The value returned by ReadValueAsync might be cached by Windows, but you can force the value to come directly from the device by calling a ReadValueAsync overload and passing BluetoothCacheMode.Uncached.

GattCharacteristic has a ValueChanged property, but notifications or indications must be enabled for this to be raised. (An indication is the same as a notification, except it requires a confirmation response from the client back to the device.) If the device supports this, you can enable it by calling WriteClientCharacteristicConfiguration-DescriptorAsync with either the Notify or Indicate value from the GattClientCharacteristicConfigurationDescriptorValue enumeration.

As with the socket you use with Bluetooth RFCOMM, you should call Dispose on GattDeviceService upon suspension. You lose the connection when suspended anyway, so your logic is cleaner when you treat this condition the same as when you are really done with the device.

 You can find detailed GATT specifications, including the values and data formats for each characteristic, at http://developer.bluetooth.org.

Custom USB Devices

The `Windows.Devices.Usb` namespace contains functionality for interacting with custom USB devices. *Custom* is the key word here; you cannot use this to communicate with devices that are already well-known to Windows.

> (!) **Only certain USB device classes can be used with `Windows.Devices.Usb` APIs!**
>
> There are nine supported device classes, and WinUSB must be the device driver for them. Because this support is meant for custom USB devices, it cannot be used with devices that are already supported by Windows, such as keyboards and mice. See http://msdn.microsoft.com/en-us/library/windows/apps/dn303351.aspx for more details.

Declaring the Right Device Capability

Declaring a device capability for a USB device is similar to declaring one for a Bluetooth device, except the `m2:Function Type` value is used to specify the device class:

```
<Capabilities>
  <m2:DeviceCapability Name="usb">
    <m2:Device Id="device">
      <m2:Function Type="deviceClass"/>
    </m2:Device>
  </m2:DeviceCapability>
  …
</Capabilities>
```

The *device* specification supports the `vidpid` format shown earlier, or it can be set to any. However, any is only supported for device classes that are narrow enough. (For example, it doesn't make sense for an app to claim that it can communicate with any vendor-specific device.)

The *deviceClass* value supports three formats:

→ `name:friendlyName`

→ `winUsbId:WinUSBInterfaceClass`

→ `classId:class subclass protocol`

Nine `name` values are supported, such as `personalHealthcare`, `activeSync`, or the catch-all `vendorSpecific`. `winUsbId` must be set to a UUID representing the WinUSB interface class. The three values for `classId` are space-delimited hexadecimal numbers, although either of the last two can be set to a * wildcard.

> If you don't know the vendor ID, product ID, and/or device class for the device you are trying to use, you can get this information from Device Manager on the Windows desktop. A device's **Hardware Ids** (under **Properties, Details**) reveals the vendor ID and product ID, and its **Compatible Ids** reveals its class, subclass, and protocol.

Connecting to the Device

Connecting to a USB device follows the same, familiar pattern as the other types of devices:

```
async Task<UsbDevice> GetUsbDevice(uint vendorId, uint productId)
{
  foreach (DeviceInformation deviceInfo in await
    DeviceInformation.FindAllAsync(UsbDevice.GetDeviceSelector(
                                 vendorId, productId)))
  {
    // Return the first one (null if user doesn't consent)
    // Be sure to call FromIdAsync on the UI thread!
    return await UsbDevice.FromIdAsync(deviceInfo.Id);
  }

  return null;
}
```

UsbDevice's version of GetDeviceSelector has three overloads: one that lets you specify a vendor ID and product ID, one that lets you specify a Guid representing the WinUSB interface class, and one that lets you specify all three.

Communicating with the Device

USB defines four types of transfers:

→ **Control**—Typically used for commands or status updates

→ **Bulk**—For sending a large amount of data efficiently

→ **Interrupt**—Notifications, although delivered by the host polling

→ **Isochronous**—For streaming data, such as audio/video

You can perform the first three types of USB transfers; isochronous transfers are not supported.

Control Transfers

You send control transfers with UsbDevice's SendControlInTransferAsync and SendControlOutTransferAsync methods. The IN transfer method is for reading, and the OUT transfer method is for writing. These require a UsbSetupPacket and optionally an

IBuffer containing transfer data. You can construct a UsbSetupPacket with its parameter-less constructor and then set its five properties, or you can construct it from an IBuffer containing a standard USB eight-byte setup packet. Either way, constructing the packet requires knowledge of the specific hardware connected to the USB port.

Bulk Transfers

To send a bulk transfer to a device that supports it, you must first get the appropriate communication channel known as a *pipe*. UsbDevice's DefaultInterface property, of type UsbInterface, exposes two collections: BulkInPipes and BulkOutPipes. Bulk IN pipes are for reading, and bulk OUT pipes are for writing. Each UsbBulkInPipe object returned by BulkInPipes exposes an InputStream property of type IInputStream, and each UsbBulkOutPipe returned by BulkOutPipes exposes an OutputStream property of type OutputStream. Therefore, you can use these streams with DataReader and DataWriter just like you would use streams throughout other Windows Runtime APIs:

```
DataReader reader = new DataReader(bulkInPipe.InputStream);
DataWriter writer = new DataWriter(bulkOutPipe.OutputStream);

try
{
  // Bulk read a string
  uint numBytes = await reader.LoadAsync(
                        bulkInPipe.EndpointDescriptor.MaxPacketSize);
  string data = reader.ReadBuffer(numBytes).ToString();

  // Bulk write a string
  writer.WriteString(data);
  numBytes = await writer.StoreAsync();
}
catch
{
  …
}
```

Interrupt Transfers

To send an interrupt transfer, you get the appropriate interrupt pipe. Similar to the bulk pipes, UsbInterface exposes InterruptInPipes and InterruptOutPipes collections. Interacting with an interrupt OUT pipe looks just like interacting with a bulk OUT pipe.

Interacting with an interrupt IN pipe is different, because the sending of the data is initiated by the USB device. UsbInterruptInPipe performs the underlying polling on your behalf, providing you with a nicer event-driven API. When you get a UsbInterruptInPipe object from InterruptInPipes, you attach a handler to its DataReceived event. This begins the automatic IN transfers. When data is available, handlers are delivered the interrupt data in the form of an IBuffer

Other Concerns

If the device supports multiple interfaces, then UsbDevice's DefaultInterface property returns the default or first one. There's a separate UsbInterfaces collection that exposes them all, but it's not exposed directly on UsbDevice. Rather, it's exposed by UsbDevice's Configuration property of type UsbConfiguration.

As with the other device APIs, you should call Dispose on a UsbDevice upon suspension. Because I/O may complete after a device is closed, there can sometimes be a small delay before the same device can be reopened.

> Windows automatically puts USB devices in a low power state when they are idle, so you don't need to worry about this kind of power management.

Custom HID Devices

The Human Interface Device (HID) protocol started as a standard for keyboards, mice, and joysticks, but it is used by a much wider range of devices, including barcode scanners and magnetic stripe readers. In addition, HID was defined over USB, but it is now used over other transports, including Bluetooth and Inter-Integrated Circuit (I²C). The APIs for communicating with HID devices can be found in the Windows.Devices. HumanInterfaceDevice namespace.

Declaring the Right Device Capability

When you declare a device capability for a HID device, you use humaninterfacedevice as the protocol name, and the m2:Function Type value is used to specify the *usage*:

```
<Capabilities>
  <m2:DeviceCapability Name="humaninterfacedevice">
    <m2:Device Id="device">
      <m2:Function Type="usage:usagePage usageId"/>
    </m2:Device>
  </m2:DeviceCapability>
  …
</Capabilities>
```

The *device* specification supports the vidpid format shown earlier, or it can be set to any. The *usagePage* and *usageId* values are hexadecimal numbers that identify the intended usage of the device. (There can be more than one m2:Function element if more than one usage applies.) A usage page represents a broad category of usages, such as game controls or LEDs. The usage ID can be set to a * wildcard.

> You can determine a HID device's usage page(s) and usage ID(s) with the HClient sample desktop app available at http://code.msdn.microsoft.com/windowshardware/HClient-HID-Sample-4ec99697. This also shows the device's vendor ID and product ID.

> **① Only certain usage pages are supported with Windows.Devices.HumanInterfaceDevice APIs!**
>
> As with the custom USB device support, you cannot use the HID APIs to communicate with devices used by Windows or exposed in other ways. This includes keyboards, mice, digitizers, barcode scanners, magnetic stripe readers, and more.

Connecting to the Device

At this point in the chapter, you should be intimately familiar with the typical pattern for getting an instance of a HID device:

```
async Task<HidDevice> GetHidDevice(ushort usagePage, ushort usageId)
{
  foreach (DeviceInformation deviceInfo in await
    DeviceInformation.FindAllAsync(HidDevice.GetDeviceSelector(
                                      usagePage, usageId)))
  {
    // Return the first one (null if user doesn't consent)
    // Be sure to call FromIdAsync on the UI thread!
    return await HidDevice.FromIdAsync(deviceInfo.Id, FileAccessMode.ReadWrite);
  }

  return null;
}
```

HidDevice's GetDeviceSelector method requires a usage page and usage ID, and there's an overload that requires a vendor ID and product ID in addition to those two pieces of data.

One new twist is the second parameter to HidDevice's FromIdAsync method. With this, you can open a device for read access only, or for read/write access. When an app opens a device for read access, the device can be shared with other apps that only require read access. Read/write access, on the other hand, requires exclusivity.

It should also come as no surprise that you should call Dispose on HidDevice when your app is suspended, as with all the other types of devices.

Communicating with the Device

Communicating with a HID device is done with up to three kinds of reports: input reports, output reports, and feature reports.

Input Reports

Input reports contain data from the device. You can attach a handler to HidDevice's InputReportReceived event to receive these reports. Each report is delivered as a HidInputReport object that exposes, among other things, the raw Data as an IBuffer and a numeric Id. At any time, independent of this event, you can call HidDevice's GetInputReportAsync method with no parameters to retrieve the device's default input report. You can also call an overload with a report ID to get a specific one.

Output Reports

Output reports are used to send data to the device. You create one with HidDevice's CreateOutputReport method, which returns a HidOutputReport. You need to set its Data property to an IBuffer with the report data, which you presumably create with a DataWriter. Once your output report is ready, you call HidDevice's ̶S̶e̶n̶d̶O̶u̶t̶p̶u̶t̶R̶e̶p̶o̶r̶t̶A̶s̶y̶n̶c̶ ̶m̶e̶t̶h̶o̶d̶.

Feature Reports

Feature reports, which are used for configuration and settings, are bi-directional. Similar to input reports, you can retrieve one at any time by calling HidDevice's GetFeatureReportAsync method, with or without a report ID. And similar to output reports, you can create one with CreateFeatureReport, set its Data property to a new IBuffer, then send it to the device via SendFeatureReportAsync.

Controls

Rather than parsing the data in a report yourself, you can leverage automatic parsing done by Windows. This is exposed in a *controls* abstraction. On/off data values are represented as HidBooleanControl objects, and scalar data values are represented as HidNumericControl objects.

All three types of report objects expose GetBooleanControl and GetNumericControl methods. You pass these methods the relevant usage page and usage ID, and they return either the HidBooleanControl or HidNumericControl instance. HidBooleanControl exposes a simple IsActive Boolean property (among others), and HidNumericControl exposes a simple Value property of type long (among others).

The three report objects also expose GetBooleanControlByDescription and GetNumericControlByDescription methods, which are given a special description object to identify the control. These description objects can be retrieved by methods on HidDevice that reveal all possible controls its supports: GetBooleanControlDescriptions and GetNumericControlDescriptions.

Input reports have additional shortcuts. HidInputReport has an ActivatedBooleanControls property that reveals all Boolean controls that are currently on, as well as a TransitionedBooleanControls property that reveals all Boolean controls that recently changed from on to off or vice versa.

Custom Wi-Fi Direct Devices

Wi-Fi Direct connects the current PC *directly* to another endpoint over Wi-Fi in a peer-to-peer fashion. Windows already leverages Wi-Fi Direct for printing, for wireless displays via Miracast, and for the Play To feature via DLNA. With APIs in the Windows.Devices. WiFiDirect namespace, however, you can use Wi-Fi Direct for custom purposes.

Wireless devices must be paired with the current PC. Fortunately, as with Bluetooth devices, Windows handles locating devices and pairing them so your app doesn't need to worry about that step.

Working with Wi-Fi Direct is much easier than working with the previous protocols. For example, the only capability you need to declare is Proximity! No device capabilities are needed.

To connect with an already-paired Wi-Fi Direct device, you can follow the same pattern we've seen many times:

```
async Task<WiFiDirectDevice> GetWiFiDirectDevice()
{
  foreach (DeviceInformation deviceInfo in await
    DeviceInformation.FindAllAsync(WiFiDirectDevice.GetDeviceSelector()))
  {
    // Return the first one (null if user doesn't consent)
    // Be sure to call FromIdAsync on the UI thread!
    return await WiFiDirectDevice.FromIdAsync(deviceInfo.Id);
  }

  return null;
}
```

The asynchronously-returned WiFiDirectDevice has a ConnectionStatus property whose valid values are Connected or Disconnected, and a corresponding ConnectionStatusChanged event. You should handle this event so you get notified if the connection gets disconnected.

To communicate with the device, you a standard StreamSocket. WiFiDirectDevice's GetConnectionEndpointPairs method returns a list of Windows.Networking.EndpointPair objects with the information you need to connect. EndpointPair is a simple class with four properties: LocalHostName, LocalServiceName, RemoteHostName, and RemoteServiceName. The following code demonstrates connecting a socket on TCP port 2001:

```
WiFiDirectDevice device = await GetWiFiDirectDevice();

// Just use the first endpoint pair
EndpointPair pair = null;
foreach (EndpointPair p in device.GetConnectionEndpointPairs())
{
  pair = p;
  break;
}

if (pair != null)
{
```

```
// Connect to port 2001
pair.RemoteServiceName = "2001";
StreamSocket socket = new StreamSocket();
await socket.ConnectAsync(pair);

DataWriter writer = new DataWriter(socket.OutputStream);
DataReader reader = new DataReader(socket.InputStream);
…
}
```

In addition to calling `Dispose` on the `StreamSocket` when you're done (or when the `ConnectionStatusChanged` event tells you you've been disconnected), you should also call `Dispose` on the `WiFiDirectDevice`. If desired, you can use multiple `StreamSockets` with the same `WiFiDirectDevice`.

Summary

The functionality covered in this chapter is a testament to the design of the Windows Runtime. Despite being a wide variety of devices and protocols, you can apply the same basic coding patterns to each one.

Although the list of well-known devices is relatively short, the ability to interact with custom devices opens the door to an enormous and ever-growing list of devices: game controllers, heart rate monitors, robots, programmable toys, and much, much more. Although this chapter outlines how to work with each protocol, you still need to know the details of a specific device's protocol in order to work with it.

The Windows 8.1 protocol support is not just good news for app developers, but for hardware developers, too. As long as they do the following, then anyone can write apps using their devices:

→ Use one of the standard protocols in this chapter

→ Use Microsoft drivers

→ Publish their protocol

For every custom device out there, there's also the opportunity to simplify its consumption by providing your own "scenario API" on top of the protocol-based code that uses it. This can be done by exposing such code as a Windows Runtime Component, as described in Chapter 27, "Custom Controls and Components."

Chapter 25

THINKING OUTSIDE THE APP: LIVE TILES, NOTIFICATIONS, AND THE LOCK SCREEN

Windows Store apps have opportunities to impact the user's experience even when they are not running. You might be surprised how easy they are to leverage! Live tiles enable you to have a rich presence on the Start screen, toast notifications enable you to alert the user and make your app a click away (even while the user is working on the Windows desktop), and the lock screen provides some extensibility points that make it possible to give the user important status updates. And with Windows Azure Mobile Services, using push notifications to drive these mechanisms is easier than ever before.

Live Tiles

Chapter 1, "Hello, *Real* World!" shows how to customize your tile in a few basic ways and optionally support different tile sizes. All of the choices are static, however. In this section, you can see how to turn your tile into a dynamic *live tile*, which can update in a number of rich ways at any point in time. You can even support *secondary tiles* hat provide users with even more information right on the Start screen, and can also serve as helpful shortcuts into specific areas in your app.

Tile Templates

Your live tile cannot contain arbitrary XAML (or HTML). Its appearance is tightly controlled by an XML template. With such a template, you choose one of several prede-fined layouts and, depending on the choice, you can specify a few lines of text and a few images. Although this means your customization possibilities are limited, it also means that it's easy to give your app a live tile with a standard look-and-feel, including animations.

For example, Listing 25.1 contains a method that can be invoked at any time to update an app's tile with brand-new content. The call to `CreateTileUpdaterForApplication` returns a `TileUpdater` instance that exposes a variety of interesting behaviors. For now, this listing just calls its `Update` method to perform the update.

LISTING 25.1   Updating an App's Tile with Content for Three Tile Sizes

```
void UpdateTile()
{
  // This is the tile template
  string xmlString = @"
<tile>
  <visual version='2'>
    <!-- Medium tile -->
    <binding template='TileSquare150x150Block'
             fallback='TileSquareBlock'>
      <text id='1'>25</text>
      <text id='2'>Live Tile</text>
    </binding>
    <!-- Wide tile -->
    <binding template='TileWide310x150BlockAndText01'
             fallback='TileWideBlockAndText01'>
      <text id='1'>Wide</text>
      <text id='5'>25</text>
      <text id='6'>Live Tile</text>
    </binding>
    <!-- Large tile -->
    <binding template='TileSquare310x310BlockAndText01'>
      <text id='1'>Large</text>
      <text id='8'>25</text>
      <text id='9'>Live Tile</text>
    </binding>
  </visual>
</tile>";

  // Load the content into an XML document
  XmlDocument document = new XmlDocument();
  document.LoadXml(xmlString);
```

LISTING 25.1   Continued

```
  // Create a tile notification and send it
  TileNotification notification = new TileNotification(document);
  TileUpdateManager.CreateTileUpdaterForApplication().Update(notification);
}
```

This XML actually contains three tile updates, one per `binding` element. The first one updates the medium tile with a template called `TileSquare150x150Block`, the second one updates the wide tile with a template called `TileWide310x150BlockAndText01`, and the last one updates the large tile with a template called `TileSquare310x310BlockAndText01`. You *could* choose to update only one tile size, but updating every size you support simultaneously is a best practice, as it prevents the user from seeing inconsistent content when resizing your tile. Small tiles do not support such updates, so you have at most three sizes to worry about.

The `version` attribute on the `visual` element is used to distinguish between Windows 8.1 XML (`version="2"`) and Windows 8 XML (`version="1"`, which is the default value). Windows 8.1 XML uses new tile template names and supports several new attributes. In fact, because the template names changed in Windows 8.1, you can specify the old Windows 8 name with the `fallback` attribute. In this example, `TileSquareBlock` is the old name for the `TileSquare150x150Block` template. Specifying a `fallback` for each `binding` (except for the large tile template, which has no Windows 8 equivalent) enables the same tile update to work on both Windows 8 and Windows 8.1 PCs. The only gotcha is that your large tile template, if you have one, must be listed last. That's because Windows 8 doesn't understand such content, and stops processing the XML once it encounters it.

Figure 25.1 shows how an app's tile changes after the call to `UpdateTile` is made in Listing 25.1. This assumes the app supports every tile size in its package manifest, has a **Short name** specified, and has the **Show name** option checked for every size. It also assumes the package manifest lists yellow as the tile's background color, which is used as the background color for any tile updates. (No yellow was seen before the tile update because none of the default tile logo images have any transparency.) The icon shown in the resultant live tile is not just a shrunken version of the same logo image; it is the square 30x30 logo specified in the package manifest. The text in this, and other, examples is dark gray because "Dark" is chosen as the foreground text color in the package manifest so it shows up nicely on the yellow background.

The small tile doesn't change in Figure 25.1 because that size doesn't support any dynamic content other than a badge (covered later in the "Badges" section). The chosen medium tile template expects two pieces of text. The one with an `id` of 1 appears on the top in a large font, and the one with an `id` of 2 appears underneath in a small font. The chosen wide and large tile templates expect many more pieces of text, but Listing 25.1 only sets three of them for demonstration purposes.

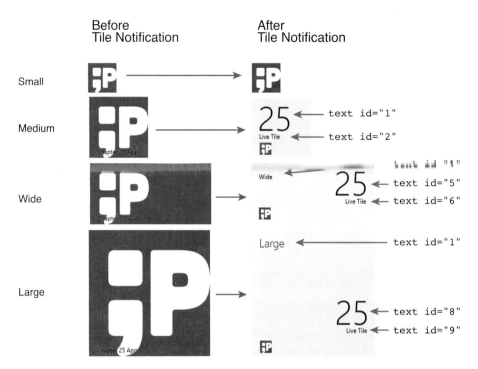

FIGURE 25.1   Transitioning from a static tile to a live tile, shown at each possible tile size

After the call to `UpdateTile` is made, the visual update to the tile animates in the next time the user views the tile. This type of update to a tile is called a *local notification*. There are other ways to update your tile, and these ways are covered in the upcoming "Options for Updating Tiles" section. For now, we look at all the different types of templates, categorized into medium, wide, and large. The template names are horrible, but if you mentally replace each occurrence of "TileSquare150x150" with "Medium," "TileWide310x150" with "Wide," and "TileSquare310x310" with "Large," then they are much more understandable.

> You can provide multiple `text` elements with the same `id` simultaneously with the text translated into different languages, and Windows uses the appropriate one. Simply set each element's `lang` attribute to an appropriate BCP 47 language code.

Medium Tile Templates

We can subdivide the medium tile templates into static ones that don't move after their initial entrance animation, and "peek" ones that periodically animate between two different regions.

Static Medium Templates   Figure 25.2 displays all the static medium templates. The ones with text expect 1–5 text elements with ids of 1, 2, 3, 4, and 5, respectively. The tiles in the figure indicate which id belongs to each piece of text. The one with an image also expects an `image` element with an `id` of 1. When used with a right-to-left language, the alignment of text is flipped accordingly.

TileSquare150x150Block (TileSquareBlock)

one
two
three
four

TileSquare150x150Text01 (TileSquareText01)

one
two: Up to three
lines of wrapped
text

TileSquare150x150Text02 (TileSquareText02)

one
two
three
four

TileSquare150x150Text03 (TileSquareText03)

one: A single line
of text that can
wrap for up to
four lines

TileSquare150x150Text04 (TileSquareText04)

TileSquare150x150Image (TileSquareImage)

FIGURE 25.2   Each of the static medium live tile templates, with the Windows 8 fallback name in parentheses

Notice that Figure 25.2 shows no more than four lines of text in each template. In order to fit one additional line of text, you must mark the `binding` element in your tile template with `branding="none"` to remove the 30x30 logo in the bottom corner. This also enables the wrapped line of text in `TileSquare150x150Text04` to occupy five lines.

> If you don't want your app's small logo to appear in the corner of your live tile, you can mark the `binding` element in your tile template with `branding="name"` to show its name instead, or `branding="none"` to show nothing (and fit more dynamic text). The default value for `branding` is `logo`. You can also set `branding` on the parent `visual` element to provide a new default value for all bindings inside.

The following template is used to create the image-based tile in Figure 25.2:

```
<tile>
  <visual version="2">
    <!-- Only update the medium tile, for demonstration purposes -->
    <binding template="TileSquare150x150Image" fallback="TileSquareImage">
      <image id="1" src="Assets/tileImage.jpg" alt="A description"/>
    </binding>
  </visual>
</tile>
```

In this case, the implicit ms-appx URI requires that the image is packaged along with the app in an Assets folder. The URI can alternatively fetch an image from the Web (http or https) *if* the app has the "Internet (Client)" capability. It can also fetch an image from local app data using an ms-appdata:///local/ URI. And, of course, it can use an explicit ms-appx URI, such as ms-appx:///Assets/tileImage.jpg.

The alt text is not used in a tooltip for the image, but it is used by assistive technologies such as screen readers.

On an image element that uses an http(s) URI, you can set addImageQuery="true" to make Windows automatically append a query string that specifies three resource qualifiers (in a slightly different syntax than what was introduced in Chapter 13, "Images"). For example, http://pixelwinks.com/tileImage.jpg can become http://pixelwinks.com/tileImage.jpg**?ms-scale=100&ms-contrast=standard&ms-lang=en-US**. This enables a Web server to serve different variations of an image based on characteristics of the current device. You can also set addImageQuery to true on a binding element to affect all its images, or on a visual to affect all its bindings.

Another handy image-related attribute is baseUri. You can set this on any binding or on the visual element to have its value automatically prepended to any relative URIs used by child image elements.

> **Tile images can be at most 1024x1024 pixels!**
> They also must be no more than 200 KB, and must be a PNG, JPEG, or GIF.

Peek Medium Templates   The other type of medium tile templates—peek templates—are not square. They expect 1–5 pieces of text (with ids from 1–5), depending on the chosen template and the branding setting, and one image (with an id of 1). The image is placed above the text, and the tile periodically slides between the image filling the square region and the text-based area filling the square region. These templates are visualized in Figure 25.3, as if you could see the whole surface simultaneously. Note that any branding (if shown) remains stationary, so it appears over the image when the image is shown.

TileSquare150x150PeekImageAndText01
(TileSquarePeekImageAndText01)

TileSquare150x150PeekImageAndText02
(TileSquarePeekImageAndText02)

TileSquare150x150PeekImageAndText03
(TileSquarePeekImageAndText03)

TileSquare150x150PeekImageAndText04
(TileSquarePeekImageAndText04)

FIGURE 25.3   Each of the "peek" medium live tile templates, with the Windows 8 fallback name in parentheses

The TileSquare150x150PeekImageAndText04 template is used by the People app's medium tile. As with the static templates, setting branding to none enables you to fit one more line of text.

> If using XML strings inside your code leaves a bad taste in your mouth, there are two other options. One is to use the `TileUpdateManager.GetTemplateContent` method, which requires a value of the `TileTemplateType` enumeration that lists all possible templates. This returns an `XmlDocument`, which you can modify before constructing a `TileNotification` with it. The other option is to use the `NotificationsExtensions` project that is included in the Windows SDK sample at `http://bit.ly/I8Bpga`. This includes a `TileContentFactory` class that exposes a static method for creating each type of template, such as `CreateTileSquarePeekImageAndText04`. This returns an object with simple properties to set, and a `CreateNotification` method that returns the necessary `TileNotification` instance.

Wide Tile Templates

To take advantage of the extra space, many more templates exist for wide live tiles. These can be divided into three categories: text-only templates, templates that use images, and "peek" templates.

Static Text-Only Wide Templates   Figure 25.4 shows all the text-only templates. They indicate which `id` belongs to each piece of text; from 1 all the way to 8 (or 10 if the `binding` is marked with `branding="none"`). `TileWideBlockAndText01` is used by the Calendar app, and `TileWideText01` is used by the Finance app.

Recall that for an app to support a wide tile, it needs only to provide a wide logo in its package manifest.

Static Image-Based Wide Templates   Figure 25.5 shows the image-based templates for wide live tiles.

`TileWide310x150ImageAndText01` is a popular template and used by Bing apps, such as News and Sports. `TileWide310x150ImageCollection` is recognizable as the template used by the People app. It supports five different images, with `ids` from 1–5, where 1 gets the large display. Note that the regions are not *quite* square, but the uniform scaling and centered cropping does a good job of displaying the images in a reasonable fashion.

Peek Wide Templates   Figure 25.6 illustrates all the peek templates for wide live tiles, which animate between the upper rectangular region and the lower one. These consist of six basic templates with a single image on top, two extra templates with a single image on top, and the original six wide templates with an image collection on top instead. It's unclear why the single-image variety gets two extra templates: `TileWide310x150PeekImageAndText01` and `TileWide310x150PeekImageAndText02`. To make matters more confusing, `TileWide310x150PeekImageAndText01` looks no different than `TileWide310x150PeekImage04`!

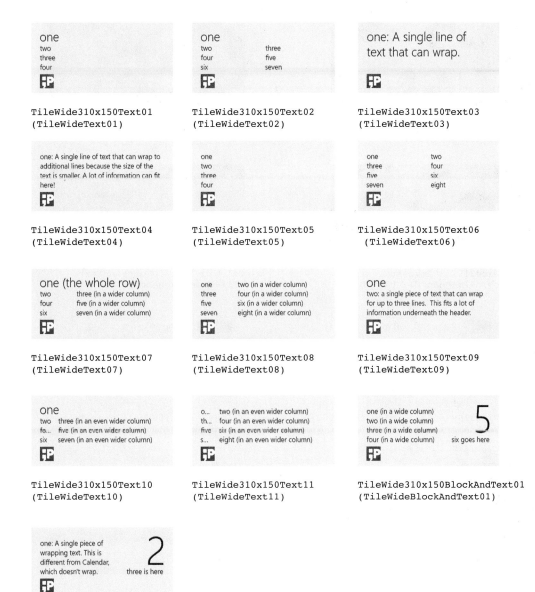

TileWide310x150Text01
(TileWideText01)

TileWide310x150Text02
(TileWideText02)

TileWide310x150Text03
(TileWideText03)

TileWide310x150Text04
(TileWideText04)

TileWide310x150Text05
(TileWideText05)

TileWide310x150Text06
(TileWideText06)

TileWide310x150Text07
(TileWideText07)

TileWide310x150Text08
(TileWideText08)

TileWide310x150Text09
(TileWideText09)

TileWide310x150Text10
(TileWideText10)

TileWide310x150Text11
(TileWideText11)

TileWide310x150BlockAndText01
(TileWideBlockAndText01)

TileWide310x150BlockAndText02
(TileWideBlockAndText02)

FIGURE 25.4   Each of the text-only wide live tile templates, with the Windows 8 fallback name in parentheses

TileWide310x150Image
(TileWideImage)

TileWide310x150ImageCollection
(TileWideImageCollection)

 one: A single piece of
wrapping text.

TileWide310x150ImageAndText01
(TileWideImageAndText01)

one
two

TileWide310x150ImageAndText02
(TileWideImageAndText02)

 one: A single
piece of text
that wraps.

TileWide310x150SmallImageAndText01
(TileWideSmallImageAndText01)

one
two
three
four

TileWide310x150SmallImageAndText02
(TileWideSmallImageAndText02)

 one: A single piece of text
that wraps. This holds a lot
of information because the
size of the text is smaller.

TileWide310x150SmallImageAndText03
(TileWideSmallImageAndText03)

one
two: A single piece of text
(smaller than the header)
that wraps.

TileWide310x150SmallImageAndText04
(TileWideSmallImageAndText04)

one
two: A single piece of text
(smaller than the header) that
wraps.

TileWide310x150SmallImageAndText05
(TileWideSmallImageAndText05)

FIGURE 25.5 Each of the static wide live tile templates that use images, with the Windows 8 fall-back name in parentheses

TileWide310x150PeekImage01
(TileWidePeekImage01)

TileWide310x150PeekImage02
(TileWidePeekImage02)

TileWide310x150PeekImage03
(TileWidePeekImage03)

TileWide310x150PeekImage04
(TileWidePeekImage04)

TileWide310x150PeekImage05
(TileWidePeekImage05)

TileWide310x150PeekImage06
(TileWidePeekImage06)

TileWide310x150PeekImageAndText01
(TileWidePeekImageAndText01)

TileWide310x150PeekImageAndText02
(TileWidePeekImageAndText02)

TileWide310x150PeekImageCollection01
(TileWidePeekImageCollection01)

TileWide310x150PeekImageCollection02
(TileWidePeekImageCollection02)

TileWide310x150PeekImageCollection03
(TileWidePeekImageCollection03)

TileWide310x150PeekImageCollection04
(TileWidePeekImageCollection04)

TileWide310x150PeekImageCollection05
(TileWidePeekImageCollection05)

TileWide310x150PeekImageCollection06
(TileWidePeekImageCollection06)

FIGURE 25.6   Each of the "peek" wide live tile templates, with the Windows 8 fallback name in parentheses

Large Tile Templates

Large tile templates, new to Windows 8.1, can be divided into two categories: text-only templates and templates that use images. There are no "peek" templates for large tiles, as they are already large enough to show a lot of content at once.

Text-Only Large Templates   Figure 25.7 shows all the text-only templates. They indicate which id belongs to each piece of text; from 1 all the way to 22. In these examples, the content of each text element is repeated to demonstrate which text wraps and which text gets truncated when too long.

TileSquare310x310BlockAndText01   TileSquare310x310Text01   TileSquare310x310Text02

TileSquare310x310Text03   TileSquare310x310Text04   TileSquare310x310Text05

TileSquare310x310Text06   TileSquare310x310Text07   TileSquare310x310Text08

TileSquare310x310TextList01   TileSquare310x310TextList02   TileSquare310x310TextList03

FIGURE 25.7   Each of the text-only large live tile templates

These templates have no `fallback` names because Windows 8 does not have large tiles. Also, for large tiles, setting `branding` to `none` does *not* enable additional text to be shown. The area at the bottom is simply left blank.

Recall that for an app to support a large tile, it needs only to provide a large logo in its package manifest.

Image-Based Large Templates   Figure 25.8 shows the image-based templates for large live tiles, using a photo that is a little more suitable for dark text placed on top (plus more pleasant to view than a photo of me making a goofy face).

FIGURE 25.8   Each of the large live tile templates that use images

Most of the templates use a single image with an id of 1, although some support up to three or five. The first template, TileSquare310x310BlockAndText02, is used by the Weather app's large tile.

Remember to update all your supported tile sizes at the same time, use the `fallback` attribute to specify Windows 8 names for the medium and wide templates, and place the large tile template last so the update for the other sizes works on Windows 8 devices.

A Windows 8.1 app can still use the Windows 8 XML schema (without `version="2"`) and Windows 8 template names without any `fallback`. This works for both Windows 8 and Windows 8.1 devices, except such XML is unable to update the large tile.

You can set a `contentId` attribute on `binding` to an arbitrary string that serves as a unique identifier for your tile content. This can be useful for telling Windows to ignore a `binding` in your XML that you may have already sent previously. For example, if you use the `TileSquare310x310SmallImagesAndTextList01` large template to display three new social network posts, you might send that same large tile content with three distinct updates for the medium and wide tiles: one for the first post, one for the second, and one for the third. If the large `binding` is given the same `contentId` in all three updates, Windows knows to ignore the second and third copy of the large tile content.

Options for Updating Tiles

You have four options for updating a live tile:

→ Local

→ Scheduled

→ Pull

→ Push

The first two must be initiated when your app (or a background task used by your app) is running. The last two can be initiated no matter what state your app is in.

Regardless of which approach(es) you use to update a live tile, you can set an expiration date with `TileNotification`'s `ExpirationTime` property (a nullable `DateTimeOffset`). The different types of notifications have different default expiration times. When live tile content expires, the tile reverts back to its original state.

Instead of only showing the most recent update, you can change the behavior of your live tile to automatically cycle among the five most recent updates. The Photos app does this to provide a slideshow experience, and the People and Sports apps do this to maximize the amount of interesting content shown.

To enable this, call `TileUpdater`'s `EnableNotificationQueue` method and pass `true`. The tile continues to behave in this fashion, regardless of whether your app is running, until or unless you eventually call EnableNotificationQueue again with a value of false. Unfortunately, there is no way to know which of the five pieces of content is showing when the user taps your tile.

By default, EnableNotificationQueue enables/disables the notification queue for all three relevant tile sizes. If you want to limit it to a specific tile size, you can instead call EnableNotificationQueueForSquare150x150 to enable/disable it for your medium tile only, EnableNotificationQueueForWide310x150 to enable/disable it for your wide tile only, or EnableNotificationQueueForSquare310x310 to enable/disable it for your large tile only.

If you want to update any of the queued tile contents in-place, then you should assign TileNotification's (or ScheduledTileNotification's) Tag property to an arbitrary string of your choosing. If you perform a new tile update with a tag that matches an existing one in the queue, the existing one gets replaced. This is great for displaying changing values such as stock prices without worrying about stale information being displayed to the user along with the newer information.

Local Updates

This is what has already been shown: calling TileUpdater's Update method at any time. By default, local updates never expire.

Scheduled Updates

To schedule an update for a specific date and time, you call TileUpdater's AddToSchedule method rather than Update. AddToSchedule requires a **Scheduled**TileNotification object, which is like TileNotification but must be constructed with a DateTimeOffset representing the delivery time (along with the XmlDocument defining the content). When the delivery time arrives, Windows updates the tile regardless of whether your app is running. To cancel a pending update, you can call TileUpdater's RemoveFromSchedule method.

By default, scheduled updates expire three days after they are delivered, because the assumption is that the information won't be interesting for long. As always, you can override this by setting ExpirationTime appropriately.

Pull Updates

Although you could trigger updates to your tile on a regular interval by performing local updates from a background task, Windows provides a much easier option for periodic updates. By calling TileUpdater's StartPeriodicUpdate method, you can specify a URI that points to a place to fetch tile XML along with a recurrence. Windows updates the tile according to this schedule, regardless of whether your app is running. With an overload of StartPeriodicUpdate, you can also specify a starting time other than the default of "right now."

The URI presumably points to a website under your control. Because the URI is specified in your code, you are able to customize it in order to serve custom tile content based on the user's identity or preferences. The recurrence for this method is specified with one of the following values from a PeriodicUpdateRecurrence enumeration: HalfHour, Hour, SixHours, TwelveHours, or Daily. If you want a higher frequency, then you need to use push notifications instead.

Both overloads of `StartPeriodicUpdate` have a corresponding `StartPeriodicUpdate`**Batch** method that accepts a collection of URIs—up to five. All five are invoked each time Windows performs the update. This option makes sense when you use the notification queue to cycle between five pieces of content. You can stop the periodic updates by calling `TileUpdater`'s parameterless `StopPeriodicUpdate` method.

> Windows 8.1 provides a slick new option for performing pull updates. Instead of writing code that calls `StartPeriodicUpdate`, you can simply specify a URL and recurrence in your package manifest. This appears on the **Application** tab under **Tile Update**. The choices for recurrence are the same ones you can specify in code, from every 30 minutes up to one a day. The URL can have `{language}` and `{region}` placeholders that get dynamically replaced with values corresponding to the current user.
>
> The idea behind this is not just to make it simpler, but to enable the first tile update to occur before your app is ever launched! The first fetch occurs as soon as your app is installed.
>
> With this mechanism, you might never need to write corresponding code unless you want to leverage the batch URI mechanism, make the URI more dynamic than what the limited place-holders allow, or stop the updates. As soon as you call one of `TileUpdater`'s periodic methods, the manifest information for tile updates is ignored.

Push Notifications

Push notifications, which go through Windows Push Notification Services, can trigger live tile updates, badge updates, toast notifications, and even arbitrary background tasks via `PushNotificationTrigger`. See the "Setting Up Push Notifications" section for more information.

Badges

Tiles, whether "live" or not and regardless of size, support a numeric or graphical *badge* that overlays status on the bottom-right corner (or bottom-left corner when a right-to-left language is in use). For example, a numeric badge is used by the Mail app to show the number of new messages. Graphical badges can be used for some limited additional scenarios, such as showing the user's online status in a chat app. Badges are the only form of dynamic content supported by the small tile size.

Applying a badge looks much like updating a tile, but even simpler. The following `UpdateBadge` method places a badge with the number two on the app's tile, with differences from the previous `UpdateTile` method highlighted:

```
void UpdateBadge()
{
  // This is the badge template
  string xmlString = @"<badge value='2'/>";
```

```
// Load the content into an XML document
XmlDocument document = new XmlDocument();
document.LoadXml(xmlString);

// Create a badge notification and send it
BadgeNotification notification = new BadgeNotification(document);
BadgeUpdateManager.CreateBadgeUpdaterForApplication().Update(notification);
}
```

This produces the result shown in Figure 25.9. You can specify a version on the badge element, but its schema has not changed between Windows 8 and Windows 8.1.

FIGURE 25.9   A numeric "2" badge applied to a tile

The number must be greater than or equal to one. Trying to display a badge with a value of zero, for example, makes the badge disappear altogether. Oddly, any number greater than 99 is forced to be displayed as "99⁺," regardless of tile size, as shown in Figure 25.10.

Graphical badges cannot be an arbitrary picture; you have eleven icons available. To choose one, set badge's value attribute to one of the strings in Figure 25.11 rather than a number. (You can also set the value to none to make the badge disappear, just like setting it to 0.)

FIGURE 25.10   Badge numbers don't go higher than 99.

available   unavailable   away   busy   error

attention   alert   playing   paused   activity   newmessage

FIGURE 25.11   All possible values for graphical badges

> (!) **The first four graphical badges in Figure 25.11 do not respect the package manifest's foreground text setting!**
>
> Although all the other images have a "light mode" and a "dark mode" to correspond to the two foreground text choices, the four status circles always render with a white border. This makes them not very suitable for light tiles, such as the yellow ones used throughout this section.

Badges have many of the bells and whistles that live tiles have. You can set an ExpirationTime on BadgeNotification, and you can use BadgeUpdater's StartPeriodicUpdate/StopPeriodicUpdate methods for the same type of pull updates. Note that there is no package manifest mechanism for updating a badge, however. You can use push notifications as well.

You also have the same two options for interacting with badges without manipulating XML strings, although the XML is so simple in this case that these other mechanisms don't add much value.

Secondary Tiles

As mentioned in Chapter 7, "App Lifecycle," an app can have any number of additional tiles known as *secondary tiles*. These are meant to jump to a specific part or mode of the app. For example, the Finance app enables the user to pin individual stocks to the Start screen. The user gets one secondary tile per stock, and clicking one brings up a page populated with data specific to that stock. By default, secondary tiles are roamed to the user's other devices.

An app cannot spam the Start screen with arbitrary secondary tiles; each tile must be added with user consent. You do this with the SecondaryTile class in the Windows.UI.StartScreen namespace. After you construct one, you can set a number of properties (or use an overloaded constructor that sets the same values). Most important are the TileId and Arguments properties, because this information gets passed to OnLaunched via LaunchActivatedEventArgs so your app can identify whether a secondary tile (and which secondary tile) was just clicked. You can set these however you like.

To control the appearance of the secondary tile, you can set several subproperties on SecondaryTile's VisualElements property of type SecondaryTileVisualElements: DisplayName, ForegroundText (a poorly-named property that can be set to Dark or Light), BackgroundColor, XXXLogo, and ShowNameOnYYYLogo, where XXX covers five different sizes (small, medium, wide, large, and 30x30) and YYY covers the three relevant sizes (medium, wide, and large). All the ShowName properties are false by default.

After you construct and configure a SecondaryTile instance, you can call its RequestCreateAsync method to prompt the user to pin the tile. For example, the following code presents the user interface shown in Figure 25.12:.

```
SecondaryTile tile = new SecondaryTile();

// Set some required properties
tile.TileId = "1";
tile.DisplayName = "Display Name";
tile.Arguments = "args";
tile.VisualElements.Square150x150Logo = new Uri("ms-appx:///Assets/Logo.png");

// Show the "Pin to Start" user interface
await tile.RequestCreateAsync();
```

All four properties set in this code are required. (Even `Arguments` must be set to a non-null and nonempty `string`, regardless of whether you have any use for this value.) If not set, the values of properties such as `BackgroundColor` and `ForegroundText` are inherited from the app's primary tile.

The built-in flyout comes complete with a preview, the ability to assign a new display name to the tile, and the ability to choose a tile size with arrows on either side of the preview. Although the

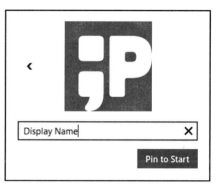

FIGURE 25.12   Presenting the built-in Pin to Start user interface is easy.

display name only appears on the tile if the corresponding `ShowName` property is set to `true`, it is still used to name the item in the Start screen's Apps list.

Windows 8.1 includes a new `PhoneticName` property on `SecondaryTile` that you can use to override what Windows guesses to be the phonetic spelling of your `DisplayName` for languages such as Japanese. This can be important for proper sort order within the Apps list. However, if the user changes the display name in the flyout, your `PhoneticName` is ignored.

Secondary tiles support all the same sizes as your primary tile, although Windows only offers it as a choice to the user if you provide a logo that is the correct size or larger. (Windows will scale one of your logo images down, but it will not scale it up.) Therefore, in this example with only a medium logo supplied, the user can only choose between a medium and small tile.

If you want to place the flyout in a specific location, you can call an overload of `RequestCreateAsync` that accepts a `Point`, or one of two overloads of `RequestCreateForSelectionAsync` that position it relative to a `Rect` that is supposed to represent the element that triggered the request..

`SecondaryTile` exposes Request**Delete**Async and Request**Delete**ForSelectionAsync methods that prompt the user to unpin a tile with the user interface shown in

Figure 25.13. You must call this on an instance of SecondaryTile that has a matching TileId. Providing this feature in your app is optional, of course, because users are able to unpin tiles directly from the Start screen.

SecondaryTile also enables enumerating all the secondary tiles you create with its static FindAllAsync method, or checking for the existence of one with its static Exists method that must be passed a tile ID. You can also update a secondary tile's properties by constructing an instance with the right ID and calling its UpdateAsync method.

FIGURE 25.13   Presenting the built-in "Unpin from Start" user interface is also easy.

Secondary tiles can be live tiles and support badges, just like primary tiles. You follow the same procedures described previously, but call TileUpdateManager's CreateTileUpdaterFor**SecondaryTile** method instead of CreateTileUpdaterForApplication, and BadgeUpdateManager's CreateBadgeUpdaterFor**SecondaryTile** method instead of CreateBadgeUpdaterForApplication. Both of these methods must be passed a tile ID.

> You can provide up to three alternate images for each secondary tile size (although not for the 30x30 logo), enabling the user to choose among them. To do this, attach a handler to SecondaryTile's VisualElementsRequested event, which gets raised immediately after you call RequestCreateAsync. With the VisualElementsRequestedEventArgs instance passed to the handler, you can add up to three instances of SecondaryTileVisualElements to its Request.AlternateVisualElements property.

Toast Notifications

Toast notifications, affectionately called this because they "pop up" like toast in a toaster, are the little messages in rectangles that appear in the upper-right corner of the screen (or upper-left when a right-to-left language is used). Creating and showing a toast notification has many parallels to creating and updating live tiles.

> **If your app uses toast notifications, don't forget to set "Toast capable" to "Yes" in the package manifest!**
>
> This can be found on the Application tab in Visual Studio. If you do not set this to **Yes**, attempting to show a toast notification silently fails.

Toast Templates

As with live tiles and badges, toast notifications are defined by simple XML templates. For example, the following method can be invoked at any time to trigger a toast notification, with differences from live tiles and badges highlighted:

```
void SendToast()
{
  // create a string with the toast template xml
  string xmlString = @"
<toast>
  <visual>
    <binding template='ToastText01'>
      <text id='1'>Alert!</text>
    </binding>
  </visual>
</toast>";

  // Load the content into an XML document
  XmlDocument document = new XmlDocument();
  document.LoadXml(xmlString);

  // Create a toast notification and send it
  ToastNotification notification = new ToastNotification(document);
  ToastNotificationManager.CreateToastNotifier().Show(notification);
}
```

This produces the result in Figure 25.14. It automatically picks up the colors and small icon from the package manifest. You can specify a version on the visual element, but its schema in the context of toast notifications has not changed between Windows 8 and Windows 8.1.

The fallback attribute is also supported on visual, but it is not needed because the template names haven't changed either.

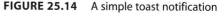

FIGURE 25.14   A simple toast notification

Here, the chosen template is called ToastText01. It expects a single piece of text that can wrap. Figure 25.15 demonstrates all eight available templates. Four are text-only, and the other four are the same as the first four with an added image.

In these templates, the text elements have ids from 1–3 and the image element, if present, has an id of 1. The same rules about image size and formats that apply to live tiles apply to toast notifications as well. As with live tiles, text elements support the lang attribute, and image elements support the addImageQuery attribute. In addition, the two options for avoiding XML manipulation are available for toast notifications: ToastNotificationManager.GetTemplateContent and the NotificationsExtensions project in the Windows SDK.

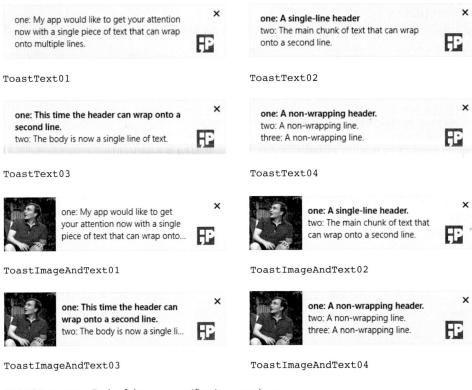

FIGURE 25.15   Each of the toast notification templates

By default, a toast notification stays on the screen for seven seconds unless the user interacts with it. However, by setting the `toast` element's `duration` attribute to `long`, you can make it remain on the screen for *twenty-five seconds*! For example:

```
<toast duration="long">
  <visual>
    …
  </visual>
  <audio …/>
</toast>
```

This is meant for situations in which a person is waiting for you to respond, such as in a chat session. The exact length of time is configurable by the user, under the Ease of Access section of the PC Settings app.

> You can customize the audio that gets played by a toast notification by including an audio element as a child of the toast element in the XML template. For example:

```
<toast>
  <visual>
    <binding template="ToastText01">
      <text id="1">Alert!</text>
    </binding>
  </visual>
  <audio src="ms-winsoundevent:Notification.Mail"/>
</toast>
```

> You have only eight sounds to choose from (in addition to the default ms-winsoundevent:Notification.Default sound):
>
> → ms-winsoundevent:Notification.IM
> → ms-winsoundevent:Notification.Mail
> → ms-winsoundevent:Notification.Reminder
> → ms-winsoundevent:Notification.SMS
> → ms-winsoundevent:Notification.Looping.Alarm
> → ms-winsoundevent:Notification.Looping.Alarm2
> → ms-winsoundevent:Notification.Looping.Call
> → ms-winsoundevent:Notification.Looping.Call2
>
> The sounds with "Looping" in the name support looping *if* the toast element's duration is set to long *and* audio's loop attribute is set to true. You can also mute the sound altogether by setting audio's silent attribute to true. If the user has disabled system sounds, then no audio is played for any toast notifications.

Responding to a Clicked Toast Notification

One important issue that hasn't yet been addressed is how you can respond to a user clicking on a toast notification. Doing so switches to your app if it's already running, or launches it otherwise. Either way, it looks like a regular launch activation.

However, you can customize how you react to a toast being clicked by setting the toast element's launch attribute to a custom string. This string gets passed to your app's OnLaunched method as LaunchActivatedEventArgs.Arguments, just like with a secondary tile. With this, you can act in a custom manner for the specific toast that is clicked

Alarm and Incoming Call Notifications

In Windows 8.1, an app can be designated as the *alarm app* in the **PC & devices** section of the PC Settings app. This gives it the ability to send special alarm toast notifications that have higher accuracy and optional buttons for snoozing and dismissing the alarm.

For your app to be eligible to be chosen as the alarm app, it must be marked as toast capable and able to update the lock screen. This is done on the Application tab of the package manifest designer. The lock screen setting requires you to declare a background task in your package manifest, but you can declare one with a dummy entry point name without actually implementing one. You must also declare your alarm support by adding the following XML element to the Extensions node in the package manifest XML, as the Visual Studio designer doesn't expose it:

```
<m2:Extension Category="windows.alarm"/>
```

If your app has been chosen as the alarm app, you can send an alarm toast by including a commands element in your toast XML as follows:

```
<toast duration="long">
  <visual>
    …
  </visual>
  <audio …/>
  <commands scenario="alarm">
      <command id="snooze" arguments="…"/>
      <command id="dismiss" arguments="…"/>
  </commands>
</toast>
```

You can include just one of the two commands if you don't want both buttons. The optional arguments are used to tell your app which button (if any) was clicked when your app gets the launch activation. The alarm app's toast notifications are treated with a higher-than-normal priority, within an accuracy of one second from the scheduled time. If your app is not currently the alarm app, the commands element is ignored, and your toast notification looks and acts just like a normal one.

You can prompt the user to make your app the alarm app by calling AlarmApplicationManager.RequestAccessAsync. This presents a standard dialog that gives the user the choice. RequestAccessAsync returns a value from the AlarmAccessStatus enumeration: AllowedWithWakeupCapability (which means the toasts can appear during the user-specified *quiet hours*), AllowedWithoutWakeupCapability, Denied, or Unspecified. You can also check this status at any time with AlarmApplicationManager.GetAccessStatus.

Windows supports one more type of special toast notification for incoming calls. Designated apps can send an incoming call toast notification with the following XML:

```
<toast duration="long">
  <visual>
    …
  </visual>
  <audio …/>
  <commands scenario="incomingCall">
      <command id="voice" arguments="…"/>
```

```
        <command id="video" arguments="…"/>
        <command id="decline" arguments="…"/>
    </commands>
</toast>
```

As with alarm toast notifications, you can choose which of the three possible buttons to add to your notification: a voice call button, a video call button, and a decline button.

Options for Showing Toast Notifications

Although toast notifications don't have the same kind of pull option that live tiles have, there are three ways to show one:

➜ Local

➜ Scheduled

➜ Push

This section examines local and scheduled notifications, as push notifications are discussed in the next section.

Just like `TileNotification`, `ToastNotification` defines an `ExpirationTime` property, although it's not meaningful due to the short-lived nature of notifications.

Local

This is the approach that has already been shown. In addition to calling `ToastNotifier`'s `Show` method, you can call its `Hide` method to hide the toast early, presumably due to some user action inside your app. However, local toast notifications are not the most common kind because toast notifications are generally meant to be shown when your app is *not* already running.

For locally shown toast notifications, you have another option besides logic in `OnLaunched` for responding to a click. You can attach event handlers to some events on the `ToastNotification` object: `Activated`, `Dismissed`, and `Failed`. Although the terminology is confusing, the `Activated` event is raised if the user clicks the notification. In a `Dismissed` event handler, you can determine why it was dismissed with a value from the `ToastDismissalReason` passed through `ToastDismissedEventArgs`. `ApplicationHidden` means the app called `ToastNotifier.Hide`, `TimedOut` means the seven (or twenty-five) seconds elapsed with no interaction, and `UserCanceled` means that the user clicked the little X button on the notification.

Scheduled

To schedule a notification for a specific date and time, you call `ToastNotifier`'s `AddToSchedule` method instead of `Show`. `AddToSchedule` requires a **Scheduled**`Toast` `Notification` object that must be constructed with a `DateTimeOffset` representing the delivery time (along with the `XmlDocument` defining the content). If you want to cancel a pending notification, you can call `ToastNotifier`'s `RemoveFromSchedule` method.

`ScheduledToastNotification` provides a slick additional feature. Via an overloaded constructor, you can specify a *snooze interval* (a nullable `TimeSpan` that must be between

60 seconds and 60 minutes) and maximum snooze count (a uint from 1–5). This enables you to easily support alarm-style functionality, even if your app has not been designated as the system-wide alarm app.

Setting Up Push Notifications

The idea of a push notification is that a Web service can, at an arbitrary time, push data to a Windows device. A Web service cannot do this directly, however. It must communicate with Windows Push Notification Services to do the push on its behalf.

Therefore, to participate in push notifications, a Web service must know:

1. How to communicate with Windows Push Notification Services

2. The specific user, device, and tile (in the case of secondary tiles) that should receive the notification

Both of these details are represented by a special URI known as a *channel URI*. An app retrieves a channel URI by calling PushNotificationChannelManager's CreatePushNotificationChannelForApplicationAsync method (or CreatePushNotificationChannelForSecondaryTileAsync for a secondary tile). This URI, which is provided by the Windows Store, uniquely identifies the current user and device (and tile). At the same time, it points to the Windows Push Notification Services endpoint that must be used to trigger a push notification. It looks like the following:

```
https://datacenterId.notify.windows.com/?token=[long string]
```

An app must send the channel URI to its Web service, which can store it in order to perform push notification at later times. It does this by performing an HTTP POST to the channel URI with an appropriate payload. However, channel URIs expire after 30 days. Therefore, an app should retrieve a fresh channel URI every time it launches and update its Web service with this information. Some apps might even consider doing this in a background task with a MaintenanceTrigger (and a condition of InternetAvailable), in case there's a risk of users not running the app once every 30 days.

There are four kinds of push notifications: tile, badge, toast, and raw. In the first three cases, the HTTP POST payload given to the channel URI is the appropriate XML shown throughout this chapter. For the raw case, the data can be arbitrary, as long as it is no more than 5 KB in size. Windows itself does nothing with a raw push notification, but the app receiving it can perform custom actions based on the data.

If an app is running when a relevant push notification arrives, PushNotification-Channel's PushNotificationReceived event is raised. (You get an instance of PushNotificationChannel by calling one of PushNotificationChannelManager's CreatePushNotificationChannelXXX methods, which you should already be calling to ensure your service has a fresh channel URI.) This is true for all four types of push notifications. This means that even on a tile, badge, or toast notification, an app can perform custom actions. If it wants to cancel the system's handling of the tile/badge/toast notification, it can set the passed-in PushNotificationReceivedEventArgs instance's Cancel property to `true`. Setting this has no effect on raw notifications because the system does nothing with it other than deliver it to the app.

If the app is not running but has a background task registered with a `PushNotificationTrigger`, the background task is invoked when the push notification arrives. If the app is not running and doesn't have such a background task, it will miss the notification. Any tile, badge, or toast notifications would still work, but the app would not be able to respond in a custom fashion. More importantly, any raw notifications would be completely lost. Therefore, it doesn't make sense to enable raw push notifications for an app unless it has a corresponding background task.

Setting up your app and a Web service to manage all the push notification details can be a lot of work. Fortunately, Windows Azure Mobile Services now makes supporting push notifications easy, and a wizard in Visual Studio 2013 makes it even easier.

Using the Push Notification Wizard

To begin, right-click on your project in Visual Studio then select **Add, Push Notification....** This brings up a wizard that explains everything it is going to do. You must sign in with your developer account, then select an app name that you've already reserved in the Windows Store. If you haven't reserved the relevant one yet, you can do so directly in the wizard.

With the app selected, you must now import your subscriptions from Windows Azure. If you don't already have a Windows Azure account, now is the time to create one at http://windowsazure.com. Windows Azure provides a pay-as-you-go option with no up-front costs, as well as a free trial. Once you have an account, you can click the wizard's **Import subscriptions...** link, then click **Download subscription file**. This opens your Web browser to a page that downloads a .publishsettings file. You can then point the wizard's **File location** box to the downloaded copy and click **Import**.

> **① Delete your .publishsettings file after you've used it!**
>
> This file contains credentials that enable you to manage your subscriptions and services. You don't want it getting into the wrong hands!

Once the wizard can see your subscription(s), you must select one of your existing Windows Azure mobile services or create a new one. When you create a new one, you must choose a name, a geographic region for the datacenter, then details about a database that will be created for your service. This is shown in Figure 25.16 for a new service named **chapter25**. The URL created for this service is http://chapter25.azure-mobile.net.

After selecting the newly-added service then clicking **Next** followed by **Finish**, you are done! The wizard configures your service for push notifications, adds a reference to your project for a Windows Azure Mobile Services Client SDK (called MobileServicesManaged-Client), and adds code to both your service and your app.

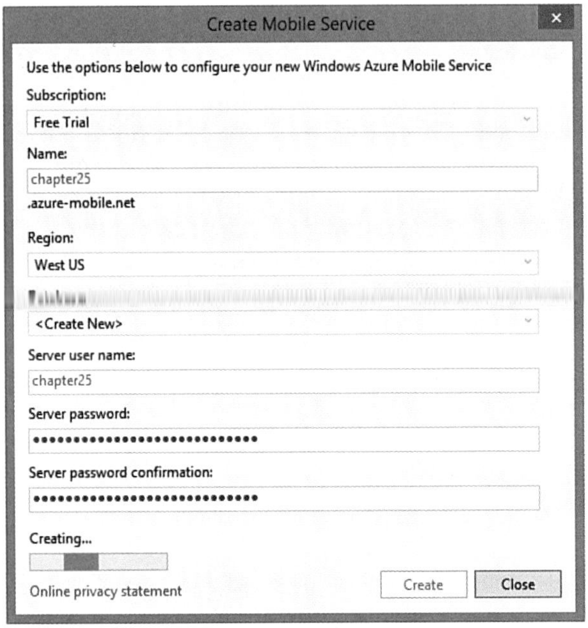

FIGURE 25.16   Creating a Windows Azure mobile service from Visual Studio

Server-Side Code

Your service is given a table called "channels" for storing the current channel URI for each unique client. It is also given four scripts for acting on this table, written in JavaScript: `delete.js`, `insert.js`, `read.js`, and `update.js`. You can see them in your portal at http://windowsazure.com, or in Visual Studio's Server Explorer tool window, shown in Figure 25.17.

FIGURE 25.17   The Server Explorer is automatically configured to show each of your Windows Azure mobile services.

The `insert.js` script, shown in Listing 25.2, inserts or updates a record in the channels table, using the passed-in `installationId` as the key. The most interesting thing, however, is that it contains some sample code for sending a push toast notification using the passed-in `channelUri`. This is done just so you can see it working when running your app, but you will want to move this logic out of this script.

LISTING 25.2 `insert.js`: The Auto-Generated Insert Script, with Demo Code for Sending a Push Toast Notification

```javascript
// See documentation at http://go.microsoft.com/fwlink/?LinkId=296704&clcid=0x409
function insert(item, user, request) {

  // The following call is for illustration purpose only
  // The call and function body should be moved to a script in your app
  // where you want to send a notification
  sendNotifications(item.channelUri);

  // The following code manages channels and should be retained in this script
  var ct = tables.getTable("channels");
  ct.where({ installationId: item.installationId }).read({
    success: function (results) {
      if (results.length > 0) {
        // we already have a record for this user/installation id - if the
        // channel is different, update it otherwise just respond
        var existingItem = results[0];
        if (existingItem.channelUri !== item.channelUri) {
          existingItem.channelUri = item.channelUri;
          ct.update(existingItem, {
            success: function () {
              request.respond(200, existingItem);
            }
          });
        }
        else {
          // no change necessary, just respond
          request.respond(200, existingItem);
        }
      }
      else {
        // no matching installation, insert the record
        request.execute();
      }
    }
  })

  // The following code should be moved to appropriate
  // script in your app where notification is sent
  function sendNotifications(uri) {
    console.log("Uri: ", uri);
    push.wns.sendToastText01(uri, {
      text1: "Sample toast from sample insert"
    }, {
```

LISTING 25.2   Continued

```
    success: function (pushResponse) {
      console.log("Sent push:", pushResponse);
    }
  });
  }
}
```

To demonstrate triggering a push notification outside of the insert.js script, we'll create a custom API in our service. To do this, go to your Windows Azure portal at http://windowsazure.com, navigate to your mobile service, click the **API** link along the top, then click the **CREATE A CUSTOM API** link. In the resultant dialog, shown in Figure 25.18, you give it a name, such as testPush, change **GET PERMISSION** to **Everyone**, then click the checkmark button. This produces the following sample implementation, which handles both HTTP POST and GET requests:

```
exports.post = function(request, response) {
  // Use "request.service" to access features of your mobile service, e.g.:
  //   var tables = request.service.tables;
  //   var push = request.service.push;
  response.send(statusCodes.OK, { message : 'Hello World!' });
};


exports.get = function(request, response) {
  response.send(statusCodes.OK, { message : 'Hello World!' });
};
```

The URL generated for this API is http://chapter25.azure-mobile.net/api/testPush. Visiting the page in a Web browser produces a testPush.json file with {"message":"Hello World!"} as its content. You can change the script to the following, leveraging the sample code from insert.js:

```
exports.get = function (request, response) {
  sendNotifications(request.query.channelUri);
  response.send(statusCodes.OK);

  function sendNotifications(uri) {
    console.log("Uri: ", uri);
    request.service.push.wns.sendToastText01(uri, {
      text1: "Sample toast from sample insert"
    }, {
      success: function (pushResponse) {
        console.log("Sent push:", pushResponse);
      }
    });
  }
};
```

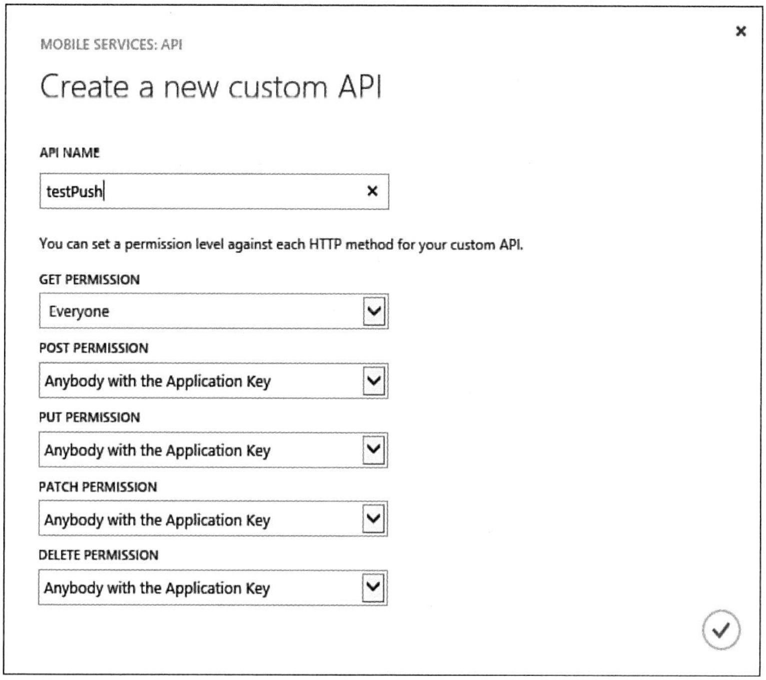

FIGURE 25.18   The dialog for creating a new custom API in your Windows Azure mobile service.

This expects `channelUri` to be passed as a query string parameter. The calls to `console.log` send text to your service's log, which you can access in your portal.

Notice that server-side scripts have rich APIs available, such as the `wns` object that defines a separate easy-to-use function for each available tile and toast template. In this example, the toast notification is sent using the `ToastText01` template. In addition to `sendTileXXX` and `sendToastXXX`, `wns` provides `sendBadge` and `sendRaw` functions. These functions enable you to set additional HTTP headers to customize the response, such as the `X-WNS-Expires` header that specifies an expiration time. The parent `push` object not only has the `wns` member for sending Windows push notifications, but it has members for sending Windows Phone, Apple, and Google push notifications as well.

That's all we need to do on the server-side, so now we're ready to look at the client-side code.

> Each HTTP method on each custom API can be assigned one of the following permission levels: Everyone, Anybody with the Application Key, Only Authenticated Users, or Only Administrators. Windows Azure provides built-in authentication provided by Microsoft Accounts, Facebook logins, Twitter logins, or Google logins. You configure this in your portal, set the appropriate permissions on the appropriate APIs, and can prompt for login in your client app as follows:

```
App.serviceNameClient.LoginAsync(MobileServiceAuthenticationProvider.Facebook);
```

This method uses the WebAuthenticationBroker to manage credentials, so the result is a seamless end-to-end experience. (serviceNameClient is a field that gets automatically added to your App class by the push notification wizard in Visual Studio.)

You can leverage a custom API in your Windows Azure mobile service to act as the URL driving pull notifications for your tiles and/or badges.

Client-Side Code

After completing the push notification wizard, the following field is placed inside your App class in App.xaml.cs:

```
// http://go.microsoft.com/fwlink/?LinkId=290986&clcid=0x409
public static MobileServiceClient chapter25Client = new MobileServiceClient(
  "https://chapter25.azure-mobile.net/",
  "…");
```

This configures the object that communicates with your service with the service's URL and its application key. The awkwardly-lowercase chapter25Client name comes from the service's name of chapter25.

In addition, the following code is inserted at the end of App's OnLaunched method:

```
// http://go.microsoft.com/fwlink/?LinkId=290986&clcid=0x409
Chapter25.chapter25Push.UploadChannel();
```

This renews the user's channel URI every time your app is launched to prevent the URI from expiring. It does this by inserting it into the service's channels table, which invokes the server-side insert.js script. The code for this chapter25Push class can be found in a separate push.register.cs file, shown in Listing 25.3.

LISTING 25.3   push.register.cs: Sending the Current Channel URI to the Service's insert.js Script

```
using Newtonsoft.Json.Linq;
using System;
using Windows.Networking.PushNotifications;
using Windows.Security.Cryptography;
using Windows.System.Profile;
```

LISTING 25.3   Continued

```
namespace Chapter25
{
  internal class chapter25Push
  {
    public async static void UploadChannel()
    {
      var channel = await PushNotificationChannelManager.
        CreatePushNotificationChannelForApplicationAsync();

      var token = HardwareIdentification.GetPackageSpecificToken(null);
      string installationId = CryptographicBuffer.EncodeToBase64String(token.Id);

      var ch = new JObject();
      ch.Add("channelUri", channel.Uri);
      ch.Add("installationId", installationId);

      try
      {
        await App.chapter25Client.GetTable("channels").InsertAsync(ch);
      }
      catch (Exception exception)
      {
        HandleInsertChannelException(exception);
      }
    }

    static void HandleInsertChannelException(Exception exception)
    {
    }
  }
}
```

In `UploadChannel`, you can see the call to `CreatePushNotificationChannelFor-ApplicationAsync` that retrieves the current channel URI for the current user and app. The returned object is a `PushNotificationChannel` class with `Uri` and `ExpirationTime` properties. For the `installationId` that is used as the key to the service's channels table, this code uses the App Specific Hardware ID (ASHWID) introduced in Chapter 9, "The Many Ways to Earn Money." In the rare case that a significant hardware change changes the ASHWID, the service will simply get a stale entry in the table.

If you run the app without any modifications to the client or server code, you should see a toast notification appear due to the sample code inside the service's `insert.js` script. To trigger a push notification using the custom API we added in the "Server-Side Code" section, we could add code such as the following:

```
async void Button_Click(object sender, RoutedEventArgs e)
{
  HttpClient client = new HttpClient();
  try
  {
    await client.GetStringAsync(new Uri(
      "http://chapter25.azure-mobile.net/api/testPush?channelUri=" +
      WebUtility.UrlEncode(App.PushNotificationChannel.Uri)));
  }
  catch
  {
    // The request failed
  }
}
```

This requires adding a PushNotificationChannel member to our App class in
App.xaml.cs:

```
public static PushNotificationChannel PushNotificationChannel;
```

which we could set from the end of OnLaunched:

```
PushNotificationChannel = await Chapter25.chapter25Push.UploadChannel();
```

if we return it from UploadChannel:

```
public async static Task<PushNotificationChannel> UploadChannel()
{
  ...
  return channel;
}
```

The Lock Screen

Using the same techniques already demonstrated for live tiles, an app can easily display
status information on the user's lock screen. The lock screen has two regions you can
update, with the user's permission. One is a badge that works much like the badge on a
tile, and one is a larger region that can contain text, much like the text on a live tile. The
user is able to select up to seven apps that show badges on the lock screen, and only one
that shows custom text. This is controlled in the **PC & devices** section of the PC Settings
app, shown in Figure 25.19.

To enable your app to be selectable as a lock screen app, you must set "Lock screen notifications" to "Badge" in your package manifest, and you must assign a 24x24 badge logo.
This logo is not only used for badges on the lock screen, but they are shown in the PC
Settings user interface in Figure 25.19. By convention, they should be white-on-transparent, although the app in this chapter uses a red and white icon so it stands out.

Lock screen apps

Choose apps to run in the background and show quick status and notifications, even when your screen is locked

Choose an app to display detailed status

Choose an app to show alarms

FIGURE 25.19   Choosing which apps can update the lock screen

To enable your app to be selectable as the one-and-only lock screen app that shows detailed status, you must change "Lock screen notifications" in your package manifest from "Badge" to "Badge and Tile Text."

The amazing thing about the two lock screen regions is that if your app already supports badges and a wide live tile, you don't need to do anything else! If the user designates your app as a lock screen app, then any badge update—numeric or graphical—gets echoed on the lock screen. If the user designates your app as the lock screen app that can display detailed status, then updating your wide live tile automatically updates the detailed region on the lock screen. This is pictured in Figure 25.20.

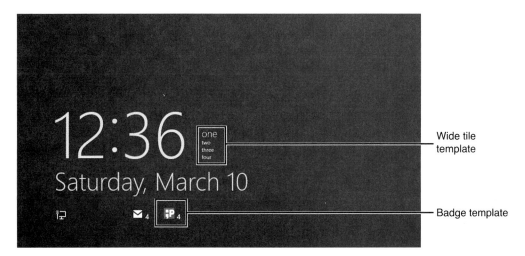

FIGURE 25.20   The lock screen simply reflects existing wide tile and badge content.

There are a few limitations to note. The text area works only with a wide tile template; medium and large tile templates are ignored. Furthermore, if the template contains images, these are ignored (but accompanying text is still shown). This lock screen region also doesn't perform periodic rotation of notifications or any animations. It simply shows the most recent text. Also, for some reason, the numeric badge doesn't show 99⁺ for numbers greater than 99. It shows 99 instead.

Rather than passively hoping that the user adds your app to the lock screen, you can prompt the user to add your app by calling `BackgroundExecutionManager.RequestAccessAsync`. This presents a standard dialog that gives the user the choice to allow or deny the action. An app is allowed to make this request only once. After that, calls to `RequestAccessAsync` are ignored (unless the reason the user decided against allowing it is that all seven spots on the lock screen were already filled).

Secondary tiles can also be added to the lock screen separately from the app. To make it eligible to become a lock screen badge, you must set `SecondaryTile`'s `LockScreenBadgeLogo` property to an appropriate `Uri`. To make it eligible to become the provider of the lock screen's detailed status, you must set `SecondaryTile`'s `LockScreenDisplayBadgeAndTileText` property to `true`.

As mentioned in Chapter 22, "Leveraging Contracts," lock screen apps have additional triggers available to them for running background tasks. Not only that, but their background tasks are given more CPU cycles to do their work and a higher allowance of network data usage.

Summary

With live tiles, badges, toast notifications, and lock screen features, your apps can integrate nicely with Windows without any special capabilities required. All these mechanisms still keep the user in control. A user can "turn off" a live tile, decide what size it should be, or even completely unpin a tile from the Start screen. A user can also disable toast notifications (completely or app-by-app) and notification sounds from within the PC Settings app. And a user can decide which apps, if any, get one of the coveted spots on the lock screen.

Chapter 26

INTEGRATING DIRECTX

XAML is highly productive for building rich user interfaces. It handles so many details for you when it comes to
rendering, input, accessibility, localization, and more. Still,
there are graphics-intensive apps, such as games or photo
effects apps, where it can make more sense to use DirectX.
DirectX is the lowest-level graphics API available on
Windows, and therefore offers the potential for the
highest performance.

As the introduction to this book mentioned, the power
provided by DirectX has a cost: enormous complexity.
Fortunately, Windows Store XAML apps provide great
DirectX integration, so you can easily mix and match the
technologies. Although a game may use DirectX for its
main content, it can (and should) use XAML for its app
bars, flyouts, menus, and things that don't necessarily
require consistently hitting 60 frames per second rendering.

In Windows 8.1, the XAML UI Framework provides the best
and highest-performance DirectX integration that any UI
platform has ever seen. It even performs better than WPF's
DirectX integration for desktop apps. A lot of work was
done for Windows 8.1 to integrate XAML's compositor with
DirectX's DirectComposition technology. This same work is
what enables WebView to integrate HTML content seamlessly with XAML. So with XAML as the foundation, you
could even mix HTML/WebGL content with DirectX
content thanks to WebView and the features described in
this chapter.

Although a tutorial on DirectX is outside the scope of this book, this chapter examines the two options for integrating arbitrary DirectX content into a XAML app. For the DirectX pieces, it uses code based on the Windows SDK samples. Although only snippets are shown here, you can get the full source code in the download accompanying this book.

Note that DirectX is a COM-based API, *not* a Windows Runtime API. This means that it is only directly callable from C++. Therefore, a XAML app that leverages DirectX integration typically has a C++/DirectX project referenced by a C#/XAML project.

> Although C# can't *directly* consume DirectX APIs, there are some compelling options for consuming it indirectly. SharpDX (http://sharpdx.org) is an open-source project with automatically-generated DirectX .NET APIs that come from DirectX header files. ANX (http://anxframework.codeplex.com is another open-source project that is written on top of SharpDX. It is a higher-level graphics, input, and sound framework that aims to be compatible with Microsoft's XNA Framework that is no longer actively developed. (ANX is XNA backwards.)

Integrating as an Image Source

The first mechanism for integrating DirectX content into a XAML app requires a special subclass of ImageSource called SurfaceImageSource. With C++, you can create a class that derives from SurfaceImageSource and fills it with DirectX content. This object can then be used as the Source for any Image element or the ImageSource for any ImageBrush.

From a C# perspective, SurfaceImageSource doesn't appear to expose any APIs beyond what it has inherited. That's because they are hidden behind a COM interface called ISurfaceImageSourceNative. This interface is implemented by SurfaceImageSource, but it must be retrieved by the C++ derived class. This is done with a call to COM's standard QueryInterface method on the IUnknown interface implemented by all COM objects. For example:

```
// Query for the ISurfaceImageSourceNative interface
ComPtr<ISurfaceImageSourceNative> sisNative;
ThrowIfFailed(
  reinterpret_cast<IUnknown*>(this)->QueryInterface(IID_PPV_ARGS(&sisNative))
);
```

ISurfaceImageSourceNative exposes three methods: SetDevice, BeginDraw, and EndDraw. The SurfaceImageSource subclass must call SetDevice during its initialization to associate the current Direct3D device:

```
// Associate the DXGI device with the SurfaceImageSource
ThrowIfFailed(sisNative->SetDevice(dxgiDevice.Get()));
```

When it is ready to render content, it must call BeginDraw to retrieve a DirectX surface to draw upon, along with the coordinates for the top left corner. (To avoid extra allocations, the surface may be larger than necessary.) When it is done drawing, it must call EndDraw. This automatically updates all consumers of the SurfaceImageSource. Both SetDevice and EndDraw must be called on the UI thread.

Using Direct2D Content

The first `SurfaceImageSource` example uses Direct2D, DirectX's 2D drawing API. The C++ code is based on the Windows SDK sample from `http://code.msdn.microsoft.com/windowsapps/XAML-SurfaceImageSource-58f7e4d5`. Although its implementation is not shown here, the following is its C++/CX API that is callable from C#:

```
namespace DirectXSamples
{
  public ref class SampleD2DImageSource sealed : SurfaceImageSource
  {
  public:
    SampleD2DImageSource(int pixelWidth, int pixelHeight, bool isOpaque);
    void BeginDraw();
    void BeginDraw(Rect updateRect);
    void Clear(Color color);
    void EndDraw();
    void FillSolidRect(Color color, Rect rect);
    void SetDpi(float dpi);

  private protected:
    void OnSuspending(Object^ sender, SuspendingEventArgs^ e);
    void CreateDeviceResources();

    // Direct3D device
    ComPtr<ID3D11Device> m_d3dDevice;

    // Direct2D objects
    ComPtr<ID2D1Device> m_d2dDevice;
    ComPtr<ID2D1DeviceContext> m_d2dContext;

    int m_width;
    int m_height;
  };
}
```

`SampleD2DImageSource`'s constructor matches a constructor on the `SurfaceImageSource` base class. It must be given a size up front. The `isOpaque` parameter enables a performance optimization. If the content is not going to leverage translucency, then passing `true` improves performance.

This class exposes `BeginDraw` and `EndDraw` methods that trigger the `BeginDraw` and `EndDraw` calls on the base class (via `ISurfaceImageSourceNative`). Between calling `BeginDraw` and `EndDraw`, its consumer can fill its background with any color via the `Clear` method, and draw a rectangle on the surface with its `FillSolidRect` method. The implementation of `Clear` and `FillSolidRect` just use the Direct2D device context; no communication with `ISurfaceImageSourceNative` is needed.

Now we'll look at a regular C# XAML app whose project is in the same solution as the C++ project. It references the C++ project so it can use SampleD2DImageSource. This app has the following MainPage.xaml content:

```
<Page x:Class="Chapter26.MainPage"
  xmlns="http://schemas.microsoft.com/winfx/2006/xaml/presentation"
  xmlns:x="http://schemas.microsoft.com/winfx/2006/xaml">
  <Grid Background="{ThemeResource ApplicationPageBackgroundThemeBrush}">
    <StackPanel Orientation="Horizontal">
      <Image Name="image" Width="400" Height="400" />
      <TextBlock Name="textBlock" FontWeight="Black" FontSize="200">
        DIRECT2D
      </TextBlock>
    </StackPanel>
  </Grid>
</Page>
```

The code-behind file creates the SampleD2DImageSource. It applies it directly to the Image and to the TextBlock's Foreground via an ImageBrush:

```
using System;
using Windows.Foundation;
using Windows.UI;
using Windows.UI.Xaml.Controls;
using Windows.UI.Xaml.Media;
using DirectXSamples; // namespace used by C++ component

namespace Chapter26
{
  public sealed partial class MainPage : Page
  {
    SampleD2DImageSource imageSource;
    Random random = new Random();

    public MainPage()
    {
      InitializeComponent();

      this.imageSource = new SampleD2DImageSource((int)this.image.Width,
                                        (int)this.image.Height, true);

      // Apply to the Image
      this.image.Source = this.imageSource;

      // Apply to the TextBlock as an ImageBrush
      this.textBlock.Foreground = new ImageBrush() {
```

```
      ImageSource = this.imageSource, Stretch = Stretch.UniformToFill };

    CompositionTarget.Rendering += CompositionTarget_Rendering;
  }


  // Update the ImageSource on each frame (not needed for static content)
  void CompositionTarget_Rendering(object sender, object args)
  {
    this.imageSource.BeginDraw();
    this.imageSource.Clear(Colors.Orange);

    // Draw 100 random squares
    const int SIZE = 20;
    byte[] rgb = new byte[3];
    for (int i = 0; i < 100; i++)
    {
      Rect bounds = new Rect(this.random.Next((int)this.image.Width - SIZE),
                             this.random.Next((int)this.image.Height - SIZE),
                             SIZE, SIZE);
      this.random.NextBytes(rgb);
      this.imageSource.FillSolidRect(
        new Color() { A = 255, R = rgb[0], G = rgb[1], B = rgb[2] }, bounds);
    }


    this.imageSource.EndDraw();
  }
 }
}
```

This code uses CompositionTarget's Rendering event to redraw the contents of the image source shared by both elements on every frame. It draws 100 random squares on top of an orange background, resulting in a fast, flashy animation. Figure 26.1 shows one frame.

Note that you do *not* need to keep redrawing the contents if they do not change. The visuals are retained by the XAML elements. Despite being filled with DirectX content, the elements still support transforms, projections, and translucency, as always.

> If you need to draw to multiple SurfaceImageSources at the same time, you can improve performance by doing the drawing in batch. To do this, query for the ISurfaceImageSourceNative**WithD2D** interface instead of ISurfaceImageSourceNative. Its BeginDraw method works differently. Rather than getting back a pointer to a surface, you get back a pointer to the device context. You can perform all your drawing with each SurfaceImageSource instance, and it gets automatically batched up and flushed all at once.

In addition, ISurfaceImageSourceNativeWithD2D exposes SuspendDraw and ResumeDraw methods. This can be helpful when drawing to multiple SurfaceImageSources, because you may have only one unsuspended/unterminated BeginDraw in your app at any time. Note that BeginDraw, SuspendDraw, and ResumeDraw can be called from any thread.

FIGURE 26.1   The SampleD2DImageSource fills the Image and the TextBlock simultaneously.

Using Direct3D Content

The Windows SDK sample contains another C++ subclass of SurfaceImageSource that uses Direct3D to render a spinning 3D cube. It exposes the following API:

```
namespace DirectXSamples
{
  public ref class SampleD3DImageSource sealed : SurfaceImageSource
  {
  public:
    SampleD3DImageSource(int pixelWidth, int pixelHeight, bool isOpaque);
    void BeginDraw();
    void Clear(Color color);
    void RenderNextAnimationFrame();
    void EndDraw();

  private protected:
    void OnSuspending(Object^ sender, SuspendingEventArgs^ e);
    void CreateDeviceResources();

    // Direct3D objects
    ComPtr<ID3D11Device> m_d3dDevice;
```

```
    ComPtr<ID3D11DeviceContext> m_d3dContext;
    ComPtr<ID3D11RenderTargetView> m_renderTargetView;
    ComPtr<ID3D11DepthStencilView> m_depthStencilView;
    ComPtr<ID3D11VertexShader> m_vertexShader;
    ComPtr<ID3D11PixelShader> m_pixelShader;
    ComPtr<ID3D11InputLayout> m_inputLayout;
    ComPtr<ID3D11Buffer> m_vertexBuffer;
    ComPtr<ID3D11Buffer> m_indexBuffer;
    ComPtr<ID3D11Buffer> m_constantBuffer;

    ModelViewProjectionConstantBuffer m_constantBufferData;
    uint32 m_indexCount;
    int m_width;
    int m_height;
    float m_frameCount;
  };
}
```

Although its implementation is much different than the preceding class that uses Direct2D, the interaction with ISurfaceImageSourceNative is the same. RenderNextAnimationFrame is similar to the other example's FillSolidRect method in that it draws using the Direct3D device context without any communication with the ISurfaceImageSourceNative interface.

The C# app that consumes SampleD3DImageSource uses the same XAML as before, just with different text:

```
<Page x:Class="Chapter26.MainPage"
  xmlns="http://schemas.microsoft.com/winfx/2006/xaml/presentation"
  xmlns:x="http://schemas.microsoft.com/winfx/2006/xaml">
  <Grid Background="{ThemeResource ApplicationPageBackgroundThemeBrush}">
    <StackPanel Orientation="Horizontal">
      <Image x:Name="image" Width="400" Height="400" />
      <TextBlock x:Name="textBlock" FontWeight="Black" FontSize="200">
        DIRECT3D
      </TextBlock>
    </StackPanel>
  </Grid>
</Page>
```

And here is the corresponding code-behind:

```
using System;
using Windows.Foundation;
using Windows.UI;
using Windows.UI.Xaml.Controls;
using Windows.UI.Xaml.Media;
```

```
using DirectXSamples; // namespace used by C++ component

namespace Chapter26
{
  public sealed partial class MainPage : Page
  {
    SampleD3DImageSource imageSource;

    public MainPage()
    {
      InitializeComponent();

      this.imageSource = new SampleD3DImageSource((int)this.image.Width,
                                     (int)this.image.Height, true);

      // Apply to the Image
      this.image.Source = this.imageSource;

      // Apply to the TextBlock as an ImageBrush
      this.textBlock.Foreground = new ImageBrush() {
        ImageSource = this.imageSource, Stretch = Stretch.UniformToFill };

      CompositionTarget.Rendering += CompositionTarget_Rendering;
    }

    // Update the ImageSource on each frame
    void CompositionTarget_Rendering(object sender, object args)
    {
      this.imageSource.BeginDraw();
      this.imageSource.Clear(Colors.Orange);
      this.imageSource.RenderNextAnimationFrame();
      this.imageSource.EndDraw();
    }
  }
}
```

Figure 26.2 displays a snapshot of the animated content.

Some pixelation is noticeable within the ImageBrush because the SurfaceImageSource is initialized to 400x400 pixels to match the size of the Image, but it gets scaled up over twice that size to fill the TextBlock.

FIGURE 26.2   The `SampleD3DImageSource` fills the `Image` and the `TextBlock`.

> If you need to render a very large surface (more than the size of the screen), you should derive your image source class from **Virtual**`SurfaceImageSource`. This is a subclass of `SurfaceImageSource` with support for virtualization of the surface into individual tiles. Rather than querying for the `ISurfaceImageSourceNative` interface, you query for `IVirtual`SurfaceImageSourceNative` instead. This adds a number of methods, such as `RegisterForUpdatesNeeded`. You must implement an `IVirtualSurfaceImageSource-CallbackNative` interface and pass it to this method. You will be called back whenever tiles need to be rendered, and for that, you use the familiar `BeginDraw` and `EndDraw` methods. `VirtualSurfaceImageSource` automatically caches tiles for you, which has huge performance benefits from avoiding redrawing, but you can call `Invalidate` to clear the cache for a specific tile if needed.

Integrating the Swap Chain

With the image source approach, it is possible to achieve 60 frame-per-second animations, but it greatly depends on the hardware and what else is currently happening on the UI thread. The image source approach is really designed for periodic updates to the content rather than continuous animations.

For continuous animations, the preferred approach involves integrating the DirectX *swap chain*. A swap chain is a series of frame-buffers used to perform rendering offscreen. When an app performs double buffering, it is using a swap chain with two framebuffers.

> Use `SwapChainPanel` to get the lowest possible latency for rendering frequently updated DirectX content. Unlike `(Virtual)SurfaceImageSource`, the updates are not bound to the UI thread.

To integrate the swap chain into XAML content, you use a `SwapChainPanel` element. The approach is similar to the use of `SurfaceImageSource`: You write a C++ subclass of `SwapChainPanel`, and the C# XAML app can instantiate and use the object. However, `SwapChainPanel` is a `Panel` rather than an `ImageSource`, so you can directly place it in your user interface just like any other `UIElement`.

As with `SurfaceImageSource`, there's nothing for the C++ subclass to override from the base class. Instead, it must query for the `ISwapChainPanelNative` COM interface implemented by the base class:

```
// Query for the ISurfaceImageSourceNative interface
ComPtr<ISwapChainPanelNative> panelNative)
ThrowIfFailed(
  reinterpret_cast<IUnknown*>(this)->QueryInterface(IID_PPV_ARGS(&panelNative))
);
```

`ISwapChainPanelNative` exposes a single method: `SetSwapChain`. This associates the DirectX code's swap chain (an `IDXGISwapChain` interface) with the panel:

```
// Associate the swap chain with the SwapChainPanel
ThrowIfFailed(
  panelNative->SetSwapChain(m_swapChain.Get())
);
```

Although `SetSwapChain` must be called on the UI thread, you can render and present to that swap chain on a background thread.

This is the only integration needed. The rest of the C++ code performs its normal DirectX rendering in a render loop completely under its control (and presumably on a background thread).

This book's source code demonstrates a `SwapChainPanel` subclass called `D3DPanel` based on the Windows SDK sample at http://code.msdn.microsoft.com/windowsapps/XAML-SwapChainPanel-00cb688b. It uses a C# app that consumes it as follows:

```
<Page … xmlns:dx="using:DirectXSamples">
  <Grid>
    <TextBlock FontWeight="Black" FontSize="200">Behind</TextBlock>
    <dx:D3DPanel Name="dxPanel" Height="400" Width="400">
      <dx:D3DPanel.RenderTransform>
        <CompositeTransform SkewY="15"/>
      </dx:D3DPanel.RenderTransform>
    </dx:D3DPanel>
  </Grid>
</Page>
```

The `D3DPanel` implementation in C++ performs the same 3D cube rotation seen previously. The result is shown in Figure 26.3.

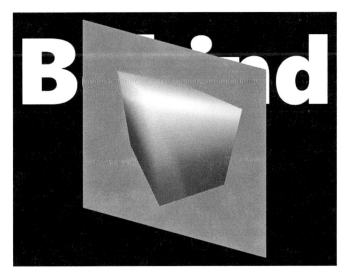

FIGURE 26.3   A SwapChainPanel element blends seamlessly with other UI elements, as with SurfaceImageSource, but it provides better animation performance.

This particular subclass exposes methods for stopping and starting its render loop, so the Page's code-behind starts and stops it accordingly:

```
protected override void OnNavigatedTo(NavigationEventArgs e)
{
  this.dxPanel.StartRenderLoop();
}

protected override void OnNavigatedFrom(NavigationEventArgs e)
{
  this.dxPanel.StopRenderLoop();
}
```

SwapChainPanel exposes a CompositionScaleChanged event that is raised whenever its rendered size changes. The C++ subclass can handle this event to resize its swap chain to match, thereby avoiding scaling artifacts. SwapChainPanel's CompositionScaleX and CompositionScaleY properties can be used to calculate the true render target size.

SwapChainPanel actually derives from Grid rather than Panel directly, so it inherits its layout for any supplied children. The following XAML demonstrates, with the result shown in Figure 26.4:

```
<Page … xmlns:dx="using:DirectXSamples">
  <Grid>
    <TextBlock FontWeight="Black" FontSize="200">Behind</TextBlock>
    <dx:D3DPanel Name="dxPanel" Height="400" Width="400" Opacity=".5">
      <dx:D3DPanel.RenderTransform>
        <CompositeTransform SkewY="15"/>
```

```
    </dx:D3DPanel.RenderTransform>
    <dx:D3DPanel.RowDefinitions>
      <RowDefinition/>
      <RowDefinition/>
    </dx:D3DPanel.RowDefinitions>
    <dx:D3DPanel.ColumnDefinitions>
      <ColumnDefinition/>
      <ColumnDefinition/>
    </dx:D3DPanel.ColumnDefinitions>
    <Button HorizontalAlignment="Stretch" VerticalAlignment="Stretch"
        Background="Red">one</Button>
    <Button HorizontalAlignment="Stretch" VerticalAlignment="Stretch"
        Background="Green" Grid.Column="1">two</Button>
    <Button HorizontalAlignment="Stretch" VerticalAlignment="Stretch"
        Background="Blue" Grid.Row="1" Grid.ColumnSpan="2">three</Button>
  </dx:D3DPanel>
  </Grid>
</Page>
```

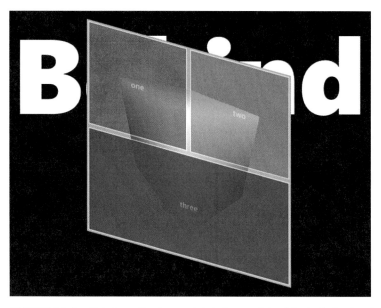

FIGURE 26.4   This SwapChainPanel is being exploited for its behaviors inherited from Grid.

> ## ! SwapChainPanel doesn't support custom Projection values!
>
> Although SwapChainPanel acts like any other UIElement in most regards, including its support for transforms, it does not support having a 3D projection applied to it. Furthermore, as demonstrated by Figure 26.4, its support for custom Opacity values depends on its implementation. This D3DPanel sets its swap chain's alpha mode to DXGI_ALPHA_MODE_UNSPECIFIED, which ignores the alpha channel as a performance optimization. This causes the Opacity setting of .5 to apply only to D3DPanel's child Buttons rather than to D3DPanel's own rendering. If you set its Opacity to 0, however, it will still be completely hidden.

...

SwapChainBackgroundPanel

An element called SwapChain**Background**Panel serves the same role as SwapChainPanel, but it has more limitations. It must occupy the entire screen, can only render content underneath all XAML content, and it does not support transforms or custom opacity. It exists solely because it was the only option for swap chain integration in Windows 8. With Windows 8.1's more flexible SwapChainPanel, there's no need to use SwapChainBackgroundPanel.

Independent Input

SwapChainPanel (and SwapChainBackgroundPanel) support a feature known as *independent input*. Independent input refers to the ability to process pointer input on a background thread. (The term is used just like the *independent animations* term.) When you combine background input processing with SwapChainPanel's background rendering capabilities, you can produce a high-performance, low-latency, graphics-intensive *interactive* user experience.

The Pointer input events on UIElement are always raised on the UI thread. This is usually fine when you respond to the input with discrete updates, but responding with continuous updates (such as dragging and dropping elements) can suffer when there is already a lot of activity on the UI thread. With independent input, you can avoid this problem.

To begin, you call SwapChainPanel's CreateCoreIndependentSource method *on the background thread that should receive the events*. This is demonstrated with the following C# code:

```
CoreIndependentInputSource coreInput;
…
void ProcessInput(DirectXPanels.D3DPanel panel)
{
  WorkItemHandler handler = new WorkItemHandler((target) =>
  {
    // Raise pointer events for all three types of input
    this.coreInput = panel.CreateCoreIndependentInputSource(
```

```
      CoreInputDeviceTypes.Touch | CoreInputDeviceTypes.Mouse |
      CoreInputDeviceTypes.Pen);

   // These events are raised on the current (background) thread
   this.coreInput.PointerPressed += OnPointerPressed;
   this.coreInput.PointerMoved += OnPointerMoved;
   this.coreInput.PointerReleased += OnPointerReleased;

   // Start processing input events
   this.coreInput.Dispatcher.ProcessEvents(
     CoreProcessEventsOption.ProcessUntilQuit);

   // Another thread can call this.coreInput.Dispatcher.StopProcessEvents(),
   // and this thread will exit
 });

 // Run this on a high-priority background thread
 IAsyncAction action = ThreadPool.RunAsync(handler, WorkItemPriority.High,
                                   WorkItemOptions.TimeSliced);
}
```

When you create an instance of CoreIndependentInputSource, you get to decide which types of input you wish to process (Touch, Mouse, and/or Pen). CoreIndependentInput-Source exposes familiar Pointer events that match the events from UIElement, as well as several properties and methods such as SetPointerCapture and ReleasePointerCapture. Therefore, the code you write can be familiar, even though you're on a background thread.

You should always give input processing a high priority, as done with the WorkItemPriority.High parameter in the preceding code. Note that the CoreIndependentInputSource only works for input being received by the SwapChainPanel associated with it.

Summary

XAML apps have two options for integrating DirectX content. SurfaceImageSource (and VirtualSurfaceImageSource) is designed for mostly-static content, or at least content that doesn't need to refresh at 60 frames per second. SwapChainPanel (and SwapChainBackgroundPanel) is designed for content that requires smooth, continuous animation.

With SwapChainPanel's option for independent input, you can perform the whole cycle from input through output on a background thread for maximum responsiveness. Internally, ScrollViewer uses independent input to provide the best possible performance for zooming and panning. Therefore, if all you require is standard zooming and panning of DirectX content, placing a `SurfaceImageSource`-backed `Image` in a `ScrollViewer` gives you a great result. If you want to support custom input gestures with the same responsiveness, however, then you should switch to a `SwapChainPanel` and handle the independent input on your own.

Mixing XAML with DirectX has proven to be a very popular option. Most games in the Windows Store are XAML apps hosting DirectX content, as are Fresh Paint, OneNote, Reader, and Maps.

Chapter 27

CUSTOM CONTROLS AND COMPONENTS

Part IV, "Understanding Controls," claims that no modern presentation framework would be complete without a standard set of controls that enable you to quickly assemble standard user interfaces. I think it's also safe to say that no modern presentation framework would be complete without the ability to create your own reusable controls. You might want to create a control because your own applications have custom needs, or because there's money to be made by selling unique controls to other software developers! This chapter describes the two mechanisms for creating a custom control: creating a *user control* (the easier option) and creating a *templated control* (the harder option). It also describes how to create non-visual components that can be consumed by any Windows Store app, even HTML/JavaScript apps or C++/DirectX apps.

The role that custom controls play in XAML is quite different than in traditional UI technologies. In other technologies, custom controls are often created simply to get a nonstandard look. But the XAML UI Framework has many options for achieving nonstandard-looking controls without creating brand-new controls. You can completely restyle built-in controls, demonstrated in Chapter 18, "Styles, Templates, and Visual States." Or you can sometimes simply embed complex content inside built-in controls to get the look you want. In other technologies, a Button containing animated vector graphics might necessitate a custom control, but not in XAML!

The decision to create a new control should be based on the APIs you want to expose rather than the look you want to achieve. If no existing control has a *programmatic* interface that naturally represents your concept, go ahead and create a custom control. The biggest mistake people make with custom controls is creating one from scratch when an existing control can suffice!

Creating a User Control

In this section, we'll create a simple user control called NumericUpDown, which provides a numeric display with associated increment and decrement buttons that enable the user to change its value.

First, we add a new user control to a Visual Studio solution by selecting **User Control** from the **Add New Item** dialog. If you do this and name it NumericUpDown, you get NumericUpDown.xaml and its NumericUpDown.xaml.cs code-behind file added to your project. This defines a NumericUpDown class that derives from UserControl, a simple control with a Content property of type UIElement. (Note that Content does not support generic objects, so UserControl is not a content control.)

Creating the User Interface

Listing 27.1 replaces the auto-generated NumericUpDown.xaml contents with content that is appropriate for our user control.

LISTING 27.1   NumericUpDown.xaml: The User Interface for NumericUpDown

```
<UserControl x:Class="Chapter27.NumericUpDown" xmlns:local="using:Chapter27"
  xmlns="http://schemas.microsoft.com/winfx/2006/xaml/presentation"
  xmlns:x="http://schemas.microsoft.com/winfx/2006/xaml"
  xmlns:d="http://schemas.microsoft.com/expression/blend/2008"
  xmlns:mc="http://schemas.openxmlformats.org/markup-compatibility/2006"
  mc:Ignorable="d" d:DesignHeight="300" d:DesignWidth="400">
  <Grid Margin="4">
    <Grid.RowDefinitions>
      <RowDefinition/>
      <RowDefinition/>
    </Grid.RowDefinitions>
    <Grid.ColumnDefinitions>
      <ColumnDefinition/>
      <ColumnDefinition Width="Auto"/>
    </Grid.ColumnDefinitions>
    <TextBlock Name="numberText" Grid.RowSpan="2" FontWeight="Bold"
      HorizontalAlignment="Center" VerticalAlignment="Center" FontSize="50"
      Padding="12">0</TextBlock>
    <Button Grid.Column="1" FontWeight="Bold" FontSize="30"
      HorizontalAlignment="Stretch" Click="Increment_Click">+</Button>
```

LISTING 27.1 Continued

```
    <Button Grid.Row="1" Grid.Column="1" FontWeight="Bold" FontSize="30"
      HorizontalAlignment="Stretch" Click="Decrement_Click">-</Button>
  </Grid>
</UserControl>
```

This uses a `TextBlock` named `numberText` to display the number and two `Button`s, one with a plus sign and one with a minus sign. Each `Button` has a `Click` handler that needs to be implemented in the code-behind file. The `DesignWidth` and `DesignHeight` attributes on the root element provide a reasonable design-time preview in Visual Studio.

Creating the Behavior

Listing 27.2 contains the entire code-behind file for Listing 27.1. This gives `NumericUpDown` the appropriate behavior when each `Button` is clicked and exposes the number as a read/write `Number` property.

LISTING 27.2 `NumericUpDown.xaml.cs`: The Logic for `NumericUpDown`

```
using Windows.UI.Xaml;
using Windows.UI.Xaml.Controls;

namespace Chapter27
{
  public sealed partial class NumericUpDown : UserControl
  {
    int number;

    public NumericUpDown()
    {
      InitializeComponent();
    }

    public int Number
    {
      get { return this.number; }
      set { this.number = value; this.numberText.Text = number.ToString(); }
    }

    void Increment_Click(object sender, RoutedEventArgs e)
    {
      this.number++;
      this.numberText.Text = number.ToString();
    }
```

LISTING 27.2   Continued

```
  void Decrement_Click(object sender, RoutedEventArgs e)
  {
    this.number--;
    this.numberText.Text = number.ToString();
  }
 }
}
```

That's all there is to it! Sure, this control could instead define Number as a dependency property and use data binding to keep the TextBlock in sync, but it's not necessary. Simplicity is usually the name of the game when it comes to user controls. If you don't care about broadly sharing your user control or maximizing the integration with subsystems such as styling/animation/data binding, you can often expose plain .NET methods, properties, and events and have a control that's "good enough."

Consuming the User Control

Consuming a user control is straightforward. You must simply reference the appropriate namespace for the element, which, in this case, is Chapter27. Figure 27.1 shows three instances of the control on the following Page:

```
<Page x:Class="Chapter27.MainPage" xmlns:local="using:Chapter27"
  xmlns="http://schemas.microsoft.com/winfx/2006/xaml/presentation"
  xmlns:x="http://schemas.microsoft.com/winfx/2006/xaml">
  <Grid Background="{ThemeResource ApplicationPageBackgroundThemeBrush}">
    <StackPanel HorizontalAlignment="Left">
      <local:NumericUpDown/>
      <local:NumericUpDown Number="5"/>
      <local:NumericUpDown Number="10"/>
    </StackPanel>
  </Grid>
</Page>
```

With this simple control, setting various visual properties generally doesn't do anything. For example, setting Background or BorderBrush has no effect unless you change the control to respect these properties. Even setting Template to a custom control template doesn't work. Setting Foreground and the various FontXXX properties do impact the control's TextBlock thanks to property

FIGURE 27.1   NumericUpDown enables interactive incrementing and decrementing of a number.

value inheritance, although setting
FontSize does nothing due to the local
FontSize setting already on the
TextBlock.

There are still ways for consumers to
customize the appearance

> If you want to prevent an application's implicit styles from impacting elements inside your control, your best bet is to give them an explicit Style value (which can be null to get the default look).

NumericUpDown instances, however. For example, if some parent scope (such as the Page or Application) places an implicit style for Button in its Resources resource dictionary, the style gets automatically applied to the Buttons inside each relevant NumericUpDown control.

Creating a More Complex Control

The beauty of the user control model lies in having the class definition spread across a XAML file and a C# code-behind file. This provides a familiar development experience, just like creating a Page. We can leverage this model for a more sophisticated control, even one that doesn't derive from UserControl. In this section, we're going to create such a control called PlayingCard, which represents a playing card to be used in card games. We'll iterate until it starts to look much more like a templated control than a user control.

Some might argue whether a control that doesn't derive from UserControl should still be called a "user control." To me, the term refers to the structure of having XAML plus code-behind rather than the base class of the control.

> User controls don't have to derive from the UserControl class. You can often find a more appropriate base class that can save you a lot of work by inheriting its members and visual states.

The tendency for designing a simple user control is to start with the user interface and then later add behavior, as we did with NumericUpDown. For a control that includes better support for things like restyling, it usually makes more sense to start with the behavior. That's because a good custom control has a pluggable user interface. Therefore, this section looks at how to implement PlayingCard's behavior before worrying about its visuals.

Creating the Behavior

The PlayingCard control should have a notion of a *face*, which can be set to one of 52 possible values. It should be clickable. It could also have a notion of being *selected*, for which each click toggles its state between selected and unselected. (This behavior could be provided by an items control containing each PlayingCard, but for the purposes of this example we'll make it a built-in part of the control.)

Before implementing the control, it helps to think about the similarities between the control and any of the built-in controls. That way, you can choose a better base class than just UserControl and leverage as much built-in support as possible.

For PlayingCard, the notion of a face is sort of like the Foreground property that all controls have. But Foreground is a Brush, and I want to enable setting the control's face to a simple string such as "H2" for two of hearts or "SQ" for queen of spades. We could hijack some control's existing property of type string (for example, TextBlock.Text), as described in Chapter 18, but such a hack would be a poor experience for consumers of the control. Therefore, it feels logical to implement a distinct Face property.

The notion of being clickable is what defines a Button, so it seems obvious that Button should be the base class we choose. But what about the notion of being *selected*? ToggleButton already provides that in the form of an IsChecked property, as well as the notion of being clickable! So ToggleButton sounds like an ideal base class.

With the Click, Checked, and Unchecked events and the IsChecked property inherited from ToggleButton, all PlayingCard needs to do is implement a Face property.

To begin, you can add a new **User Control** from the **Add New Item** dialog, just as before, but this time name it PlayingCard. Listing 27.3 updates the automatically-generated PlayingCard.xaml.cs file by changing its base class to ToggleButton and adding a simple Face property.

LISTING 27.3   PlayingCard.xaml.cs: The Logic for PlayingCard

```
using Windows.UI.Xaml.Controls;
using Windows.UI.Xaml.Controls.Primitives;

namespace Chapter27
{
  public partial class PlayingCard : ToggleButton
  {
    string face;

    public PlayingCard()
    {
      InitializeComponent();
    }

    public string Face
    {
      get { return face; }
      set {
        face = value;

        // Find a control template resource with a key matching the face name
        ControlTemplate template = (ControlTemplate)this.Resources[face];
```

LISTING 27.3   Continued

```
        // Apply the control template to an inner content control
        this.contentControl.Template = template;
      }
    }
  }
}
```

The consumer can set Face to a string such as "HA", "H2", "H3", and so on. This implementation expects to be able to find a resource of type ControlTemplate with a matching key that can be applied to an inner ContentControl. We must therefore provide these resources and the inner control in the XAML file. Note that an invalid Face string results in an exception being thrown (due to not having a matching resource), which is reasonable behavior.

Creating the User Interface

The auto-generated PlayingCard.xaml file must now change to use the ToggleButton base class, contain the appropriate resources, and have an inner ContentControl named contentControl. Listing 27.4 shows what this looks like.

LISTING 27.4   PlayingCard.xaml: The User Interface for PlayingCard

```
<ToggleButton x:Class="Chapter27.PlayingCard" xmlns:local="using:Chapter27"
  xmlns="http://schemas.microsoft.com/winfx/2006/xaml/presentation"
  xmlns:x="http://schemas.microsoft.com/winfx/2006/xaml">
  <ToggleButton.Resources>
    <ControlTemplate x:Key="HA">
      <Grid>
        <Path Fill="White" Stroke="Black" Data="…"/>
        <Path Fill="Red" Data="…"/>
        …
      </Grid>
    </ControlTemplate>
    <ControlTemplate x:Key="H2">
      …
    </ControlTemplate>
    …The remaining 50 resources are here…
  </ToggleButton.Resources>
  <ToggleButton.Style>
    <Style TargetType="local:PlayingCard">
      <Setter Property="Template">
        <Setter.Value>
          <ControlTemplate TargetType="local:PlayingCard">
            <ContentPresenter RenderTransformOrigin=".5,.5">
              <VisualStateManager.VisualStateGroups>
```

LISTING 27.4   Continued

```xml
<VisualStateGroup x:Name="CommonStates">
  <VisualState x:Name="Normal"/>
  <VisualState x:Name="PointerOver" />
  <VisualState x:Name="Pressed">
    <Storyboard>
      <DoubleAnimation Duration="0" To=".9"
        Storyboard.TargetProperty="ScaleX"
        Storyboard.TargetName="rootTransform"/>
      <DoubleAnimation Duration="0" To=".9"
        Storyboard.TargetProperty="ScaleY"
        Storyboard.TargetName="rootTransform"/>
    </Storyboard>
  </VisualState>
  <VisualState x:Name="Disabled" />
  <VisualState x:Name="Checked">
    <Storyboard>
      <DoubleAnimation Duration="0" To="-400"
        Storyboard.TargetProperty="TranslateY"
        Storyboard.TargetName="rootTransform"/>
    </Storyboard>
  </VisualState>
  <VisualState x:Name="CheckedPointerOver">
    <Storyboard>
      <DoubleAnimation Duration="0" To="-400"
        Storyboard.TargetProperty="TranslateY"
        Storyboard.TargetName="rootTransform"/>
    </Storyboard>
  </VisualState>
  <VisualState x:Name="CheckedPressed">
    <Storyboard>
      <DoubleAnimation Duration="0" To="-400"
        Storyboard.TargetProperty="TranslateY"
        Storyboard.TargetName="rootTransform"/>
      <DoubleAnimation Duration="0" To=".9"
        Storyboard.TargetProperty="ScaleX"
        Storyboard.TargetName="rootTransform"/>
      <DoubleAnimation Duration="0" To=".9"
        Storyboard.TargetProperty="ScaleY"
        Storyboard.TargetName="rootTransform"/>
    </Storyboard>
  </VisualState>
  <VisualState x:Name="CheckedDisabled">
    <Storyboard>
      <DoubleAnimation Duration="0" To="-400"
```

LISTING 27.4   Continued

```
                        Storyboard.TargetProperty="TranslateY"
                        Storyboard.TargetName="rootTransform"/>
                    </Storyboard>
                  </VisualState>
                  <VisualState x:Name="Indeterminate"/>
                  <VisualState x:Name="IndeterminatePointerOver" />
                  <VisualState x:Name="IndeterminatePressed" />
                  <VisualState x:Name="IndeterminateDisabled" />
                </VisualStateGroup>
                <VisualStateGroup x:Name="FocusStates">
                  <VisualState x:Name="Focused"/>
                  <VisualState x:Name="Unfocused"/>
                  <VisualState x:Name="PointerFocused"/>
                </VisualStateGroup>
              </VisualStateManager.VisualStateGroups>
              <ContentPresenter.RenderTransform>
                <CompositeTransform x:Name="rootTransform" />
              </ContentPresenter.RenderTransform>
            </ContentPresenter>
          </ControlTemplate>
        </Setter.Value>
      </Setter>
    </Style>
  </ToggleButton.Style>
  <Viewbox>
    <ContentControl Name="contentControl" />
  </Viewbox>
</ToggleButton>
```

The largest part of this listing is omitted (but available in this book's source code): 52 Grids, each with vector graphics that draw one of the 52 playing card faces. (I created these in Adobe Illustrator and then exported them to XAML using the exporter from http://mikeswanson.com/xamlexport.) Because you can't successfully reference UIElements placed directly in a resource dictionary, each one is instead wrapped in a ControlTemplate. This is why PlayingCard uses an inner ContentControl and applies the relevant visuals to it via the control template mechanism, rather than attempting to directly set its Content to the appropriate Grid.

We want the control to visually react to state changes such as being pressed or being checked. Therefore, it is given a Style with a control template of its own. This Style was copied from ToggleButton's default style in %ProgramFiles(x86)%\Windows Kits\ 8.1\Include\WinRT\Xaml\Design\generic.xaml, and then drastically simplified. Visually, it is just a ContentPresenter with a CompositeTransform and a RenderTransformOrigin that centers any transforms applied. The visual states in Listing 27.4 make the control shrink to 90% of its size when pressed, and push upward when it is checked. For simplicity, many of the states are left empty, but it would be nice to provide updated visuals for when the control has focus or is disabled.

Consuming the Control

Figure 27.2 shows instances of PlayingCard in action, using the following content of MainPage.xaml:

```
<Page x:Class="Chapter27.MainPage" xmlns:local="using:Chapter27"
      xmlns="http://schemas.microsoft.com/winfx/2006/xaml/presentation"
      xmlns:x="http://schemas.microsoft.com/winfx/2006/xaml">
  <Grid Background="{ThemeResource ApplicationPageBackgroundThemeBrush}">
    <Viewbox>
      <StackPanel Orientation="Horizontal">
        <local:PlayingCard Face="HA"/>
        <local:PlayingCard Face="D2"/>
        <local:PlayingCard Face="C3"/>
        <local:PlayingCard Face="S4"/>
      </StackPanel>
    </Viewbox>
  </Grid>
</Page>
```

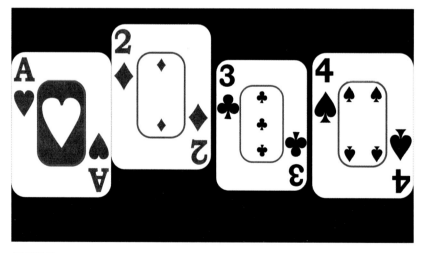

FIGURE 27.2   Four PlayingCard instances, after the two of diamonds is clicked (making it checked) and while the three of clubs is being pressed

Like NumericUpDown, PlayingCard ignores several visual properties like Background and BorderBrush. It has another oddity, though. If a consumer of the control sets its Content property (PlayingCard is a content control, after all), this Content replaces all of its visuals. As seen in Listing 27.4, Content is initialized to the Viewbox containing the important ContentControl that takes on the appearance of each face, but nothing prevents Content from being reassigned.

We can make it so setting Content doesn't wipe out a PlayingCard's appearance. The next section does this, although its main goal is to further separate PlayingCard's implementation from its visuals.

Making the Control "Lookless"

As with NumericUpDown, the PlayingCard implementation from Listing 27.3 makes assumptions about its visuals. It doesn't have to be this way. It would be nice to remove the code that retrieves the ControlTemplate resource and applies it to a ContentControl named contentControl, and somehow make this happen with the Style applied to PlayingCard. This would leave us with the following simple property:

```
public string Face
{
  get { return face; }
  set { face = value; }
}
```

Even better, let's go ahead and turn Face into a dependency property so it can participate in data binding, styling, and animation. Listing 27.5 updates Listing 27.3 with these changes, giving the final implementation of the PlayingCard user control.

LISTING 27.5   PlayingCard.xaml.cs: The Final Logic for PlayingCard

```
using Windows.UI.Xaml;
using Windows.UI.Xaml.Controls.Primitives;

namespace Chapter27
{
  public partial class PlayingCard : ToggleButton
  {
    public static readonly DependencyProperty FaceProperty =
      DependencyProperty.Register("Face", typeof(string), typeof(PlayingCard),
      new PropertyMetadata("HA"));

    public PlayingCard()
    {
      InitializeComponent();
    }

    public string Face
    {
      get { return (string)GetValue(FaceProperty); }
```

LISTING 27.5   Continued

```
    set { SetValue(FaceProperty, value); }
    }
  }
}
```

It almost seems too simple, but this is all the logic you need (with a corresponding XAML update that we'll do next). The code captures the essence of `PlayingCard`: The only way it's unique from `ToggleButton` is that it has a string `Face` property. There is just a difference in default visuals. When a control's implementation is completely separate from its visuals, it is sometimes called *lookless*. Ideally all custom controls would strive to be this way.

> ⓘ **Avoid implementing logic in a dependency property's property wrapper other than calling `GetValue` and `SetValue`!**
>
> If you deviate from the standard implementation, you'll introduce semantics that apply only when the property is directly set from procedural code. To react to calls to `SetValue`, regardless of the source, you should register for a dependency property changed notification and place your logic in the callback method instead. Or you can find another mechanism to respond to property value changes with the help of data binding.

Listing 27.6 updates the XAML from Listing 27.4 to enable the new code-behind.

LISTING 27.6   `PlayingCard.xaml`: The Final User Interface for `PlayingCard`

```
<ToggleButton x:Class="Chapter27.PlayingCard" xmlns:local="using:Chapter27"
  xmlns="http://schemas.microsoft.com/winfx/2006/xaml/presentation"
  xmlns:x="http://schemas.microsoft.com/winfx/2006/xaml">
  <ToggleButton.Resources>
    …The 52 ControlTemplate resources go here…
  </ToggleButton.Resources>
  <ToggleButton.Style>
    <Style TargetType="local:PlayingCard">
      <Setter Property="Template">
        <Setter.Value>
          <ControlTemplate TargetType="local:PlayingCard">
            <ContentPresenter RenderTransformOrigin=".5,.5">
              <ContentPresenter.Resources>
                <local:PlayingCardToTemplateConverter x:Key="myConverter"/>
              </ContentPresenter.Resources>
              <VisualStateManager.VisualStateGroups>
                …
              </VisualStateManager.VisualStateGroups>
```

LISTING 27.6   Continued

```
            <ContentPresenter.RenderTransform>
              <CompositeTransform x:Name="rootTransform" />
            </ContentPresenter.RenderTransform>
            <Viewbox>
              <ContentControl Template="{Binding
                  RelativeSource={RelativeSource TemplatedParent},
                  Converter={StaticResource myConverter}}"/>
            </Viewbox>
          </ContentPresenter>
        </ControlTemplate>
      </Setter.Value>
    </Setter>
  </Style>
</ToggleButton.Style>
<!-- There is no longer any direct content -->
</ToggleButton>
```

The idea is to move the ToggleButton's content (the Viewbox containing the ContentControl) into its control template. Instead of naming the ContentControl and updating its Template property from code-behind, this listing binds Template to the resource with a key matching Face. Ideally, this would be done with an assignment like the following:

```
<ContentControl Template="{StaticResource {Binding Face,
                RelativeSource={RelativeSource TemplatedParent}}}"/>
```

However, StaticResource's parameter (named ResourceKey) cannot be set to a Binding. It is not a dependency property. Therefore, this listing uses a custom value converter that can produce the appropriate ControlTemplate resource given a PlayingCard instance as input. (Notice that the Binding uses the entire templated parent—the PlayingCard—as the data source.) This converter, named PlayingCardToTemplateConverter, is shown in Listing 27.7.

LISTING 27.7   PlayingCardToTemplateConverter.cs: The Value Converter Used by Listing 27.6

```
using System;
using Windows.UI.Xaml;
using Windows.UI.Xaml.Data;

namespace Chapter27
{
  class PlayingCardToTemplateConverter : IValueConverter
  {
    public object Convert(object value, Type targetType,
                          object parameter, string language)
```

LISTING 27.7   Continued

```
  {
    PlayingCard playingCard = value as PlayingCard;
    return playingCard.Resources[playingCard.Face];
  }

  public object ConvertBack(object value, Type targetType,
                            object parameter, string language)
  {
    return DependencyProperty.UnsetValue;
  }
  }
}
```

The reason this converter wants the entire PlayingCard instance to be passed in is to access two of its properties: Resources and Face.

With the new PlayingCard implementation spanning Listings 27.5–27.7, the control can be consumed the same way as before. This might not seem like an improved implementation, as the C# code that performs the resource lookup has simply been moved from PlayingCard.xaml.cs to PlayingCardToTemplateConverter.cs rather than eliminated. It is an improvement, however, because the use of this second class is entirely contained to the default Style. Because the control itself no longer has this resource-lookup dependency, PlayingCard can be restyled with maximum flexibility. Because it no longer requires 52 ControlTemplates for its faces, you could even plug in a Style with a ControlTemplate for PlayingCard that represents each card as a simple TextBlock.

One side effect of moving the Viewbox into PlayingCard's default control template is that setting Content on an instance no longer wipes out its visual content. The value of Content is simply ignored by the default style, despite PlayingCard being a content control. But given that a built-in control like AppBarButton also ignores its Content property, this is nothing to be ashamed of!

One thing that is still not ideal about this implementation is that each instance's Resources collection contains the 52 control templates, even if the instance is restyled to not use them. It also means that a consumer of the control can tamper with the Resources collection, for better or worse. An instance can assign a new resource with a key of "D2", for example, to override the appearance of just that face. If that resource isn't a ControlTemplate, the internal Binding fails.

We can change this and make this control act more like a typical XAML control by moving the 52 resources out of PlayingCard's own Resources collection and into the Resources collection on the ContentControl used inside PlayingCard's default style. But we'll save this enhancement for the "Creating a Templated Control" section.

Defining Visual States

The long list of visual states used by PlayingCard, shown back in Listing 27.4, helps to highlight the value of having ToggleButton as a base class. The FocusStates group is provided by Control, some of the states in CommonStates are provided by ButtonBase, and the rest (involving being checked, unchecked, or indeterminate) are provided by ToggleButton.

Thanks to the richness of PlayingCard's base classes, defining additional states is not necessary. Still, it's worth looking at how this might be done. For example, it might be nice to define the notion of a PlayingCard being flipped on its back rather than always showing its face. That way, a graphic designer could easily plug in a beautiful design for a card back without worrying about what events or properties might cause the card to be flipped over.

For this scenario, it makes sense to have two states—Front and Back—and assign them to a new state group called FlipStates. (Every new state group should include one state that acts as the default state.) You should document the existence of these states by marking the PlayingCard class with two TemplateVisualState custom attributes:

```
[TemplateVisualState(Name="Front", GroupName="FlipStates")]
[TemplateVisualState(Name="Back", GroupName="FlipStates")]
public class PlayingCard : ToggleButton
{
  …
}
```

> **(!) Controls should not add any states to state groups already defined by a base class!**
>
> New states should be added to new state group(s). Because each state group works independently, new transitions among states in a new state group cannot interfere with base class logic. If you add new states to an existing state group, there's no guarantee that the base class logic to transition among states will continue operate correctly.

> **(!) Every state must have a unique name, even across different state groups!**
>
> Despite any partitioning into multiple state groups, a control must not have two states with the same name. This limitation can be surprising until you've implemented state transitions and realize that VisualStateManager's GoToState method doesn't have the concept of state groups. State groups are really just a documentation tool for understanding the behavior of a control's states and the possible transitions.
>
> This limitation is why state names tend to be very specific. For example, the default visual states for SemanticZoom include ZoomInView (from the SemanticZoomStates group) and ZoomOutButtonVisible (from the ZoomOutButtonStates group). They could not both simply be called Default.

Once you have chosen and documented your states, the only other thing to do is transition to the appropriate states at the appropriate times by calling VisualStateManager's static GoToState method. This is usually done from a helper method such as the following:

```
internal void ChangeState(bool useTransitions)
{
  // Assume that IsShowingFace is the property that determines the state:
  if (this.IsShowingFace)
    VisualStateManager.GoToState(this, "Front", useTransitions);
  else
    VisualStateManager.GoToState(this, "Back", useTransitions);
}
```

Controls typically call such a method in the following situations:

→ Inside OnApplyTemplate (with useTransitions=false)

→ When the control first loads (with useTransitions=false)

→ Inside appropriate event handlers (for this example, it should be called inside a PropertyChanged handler for the IsShowingFace property)

There is no harm in calling GoToState when the destination state is the same as the current state. (When this is done, the call does nothing.) Therefore, helper methods such as ChangeState typically set the current state for *every* state group without worrying about which property just changed.

> **(!)   When a control loads, it must explicitly transition to the default state in every state group!**
>
> If a control does not explicitly transition to the default state(s), it introduces a subtle bug for consumers of the control. Before the initial transition for any state group, the control is not yet in *any* of those states. That means that the first transition to a non-default state will not invoke any transition from the default state that consumers may have defined.
>
> When you perform this initial transition, you should pass false for VisualStateManager.GoToState's useTransitions parameter to make it happen instantaneously.

GoToState returns false if it is unable to transition to a state. This happens if a template has been applied that simply doesn't include a corresponding VisualState definition. Controls should be resilient to this condition, and normally they are by simply ignoring the return value from GoToState. ToggleButton, however, attempts to transition to the Unchecked state if an Indeterminate state doesn't exist. (Note that this condition does not affect the value of IsChecked; the ToggleButton is still logically indeterminate even if visually it looks unchecked.)

Creating a Templated Control

Templated controls are constructed the same way as the built-in controls in the XAML UI Framework. Being lookless is the main trait that typically distinguishes a templated control from a user control. We pushed the PlayingCard user control so far down the lookless path that creating a templated control version of it doesn't look much different. In this section, we'll create a templated control version of PlayingCard for comparison.

You can add a new templated control to your solution by selecting **Templated Control** from Visual Studio's **Add New Item** dialog. If you do this and name it PlayingCard, you get a PlayingCard.cs file added to your project. This C# file completely defines the PlayingCard class; there's no PlayingCard.xaml file sharing its definition! Instead, a generic.xaml file gets added under a Themes folder. This file contains a resource dictionary meant to contain your control's default style, also called its *theme style*. This structure forces you to write code that doesn't depend on specific elements, unlike with a code-behind file.

Creating the Behavior

Listing 27.8 replaces the auto-generated PlayingCard.cs with an implementation that looks almost identical to the final user control implementation from Listing 27.5.

LISTING 27.8   PlayingCard.cs: The Implementation for a PlayingCard Templated Control

```csharp
using Windows.UI.Xaml;
using Windows.UI.Xaml.Controls.Primitives;

namespace Chapter27
{
  public class PlayingCard : ToggleButton
  {
    public static readonly DependencyProperty FaceProperty =
      DependencyProperty.Register("Face", typeof(string), typeof(PlayingCard),
      new PropertyMetadata("HA"));

    public PlayingCard()
    {
      this.DefaultStyleKey = typeof(PlayingCard);
    }

    public string Face
    {
      get { return (string)GetValue(FaceProperty); }
      set { SetValue(FaceProperty, value); }
    }
  }
}
```

The only difference between this listing and Listing 27.5 is that the class is no longer identified a *partial* class, and that InitializeComponent is replaced with an assignment of a DefaultStyleKey property. This assignment is what makes implicit styles work. The ToggleButton base class assigns its DefaultStyleKey to typeof(ToggleButton). If PlayingCard didn't assign it to typeof(PlayingCard), then the default implicit style (or any implicit ToggleButton style used by a consuming app) would end up providing the default visuals for PlayingCard. This is not what we want. Instead, we want to be able to define our own default style.

Creating the User Interface

This default style for PlayingCard must be put in generic.xaml's resource dictionary. Listing 27.9 does this. The resulting generic.xaml looks a lot like the final PlayingCard.xaml from Listing 27.6, although there are a handful of differences.

LISTING 27.9   PlayingCard.cs: The Implementation for a PlayingCard Templated Control

```
<ResourceDictionary xmlns:local="using:Chapter27"
  xmlns="http://schemas.microsoft.com/winfx/2006/xaml/presentation"
  xmlns:x="http://schemas.microsoft.com/winfx/2006/xaml">
  <Style TargetType="local:PlayingCard">
    <Setter Property="Template">
      <Setter.Value>
        <ControlTemplate TargetType="local:PlayingCard">
          <ContentPresenter RenderTransformOrigin=".5,.5">
            <ContentPresenter.Resources>
              <local:KeyToResourceConverter x:Key="myConverter"/>
              <ResourceDictionary x:Key="dictionary">
                …The 52 ControlTemplate resources go here…
              </ResourceDictionary>
            </ContentPresenter.Resources>
            <VisualStateManager.VisualStateGroups>

              …

            </VisualStateManager.VisualStateGroups>
            <ContentPresenter.RenderTransform>
              <CompositeTransform x:Name="rootTransform" />
            </ContentPresenter.RenderTransform>
            <Viewbox>
              <ContentControl Template="{Binding Face,
                RelativeSource={RelativeSource TemplatedParent},
                Converter={StaticResource myConverter},
                ConverterParameter={StaticResource dictionary}}">
              </ContentControl>
            </Viewbox>
          </ContentPresenter>
        </ControlTemplate>
```

LISTING 27.9   Continued

```
      </Setter.Value>
    </Setter>
  </Style>
</ResourceDictionary>
```

Basically, only one change was made to the `Style`, compared to the one used with the user control, and that change triggered the rest of the changes. As promised earlier, the set of 52 resources was moved from the `Resources` collection on the `PlayingCard` itself to the `Resources` collection on the `ContentControl` used by the default control template. It is also added as a single `ResourceDictionary` resource (with 52 of its own resources) rather than as 52 direct resources. This is a more natural spot for them, and frees up `PlayingCard`'s own `Resources` collection to be used by consumers for their own needs.

Because the 52 resources are no longer on the same `PlayingCard` object that contains the `Face` property, the `PlayingCardToTemplateConverter` used previously will not work here. Instead, the `Binding` in this listing binds directly to the `Face` property, and uses the `ConverterParameter` mechanism to pass along the resource dictionary separately. Because the value converter needed to handle this no longer has any dependency on the `PlayingCard` class, it is given a more general-purpose name that represents its behavior: `KeyToResourceConverter`. This new general-purpose value converter is shown in Listing 27.10. It simply performs the lookup based on the passed-in key and resource dictionary.

LISTING 27.10   `KeyToResourceConverter.cs`: The Value Converter Used by Listing 27.9

```csharp
using System;
using Windows.UI.Xaml;
using Windows.UI.Xaml.Data;

namespace Chapter27
{
  class KeyToResourceConverter : IValueConverter
  {
    public object Convert(object value, Type targetType,
                          object parameter, string language)
    {
      return (parameter as ResourceDictionary)[value];
    }

    public object ConvertBack(object value, Type targetType,
                              object parameter, string language)
    {
      return DependencyProperty.UnsetValue;
    }
  }
}
```

That completes the templated control version of `PlayingCard`. It is consumed the same way as the user control version of `PlayingCard`.

• • •

Other Approaches for Designing `PlayingCard`

You could also rewrite `PlayingCard` as a simple data object rather than a custom control—perhaps even as a simple string. In this case, you would use a data template to give it the appropriate visuals. This could work especially well if you are leveraging an items control to host the objects and provide the desired selection behavior.

A sophisticated control might want to determine whether it is running in *design mode* (for example, being displayed in the Visual Studio or Blend designer) and behave slightly differently. The static `Windows.ApplicationModel.DesignMode` class exposes a Boolean `DesignModeEnabled` property that gives you this information. Design tools change the default value when appropriate.

Handling Interactivity

The `PlayingCard` control has minimal interactivity that could be handled in the control template with visual states. But controls with more interactivity need to use other techniques. For example, imagine that you want to change `NumericUpDown` from the beginning of this chapter from a user control to a templated control. This implies that you'll move its user interface (repeated in the following XAML) into a control template in `generic.xaml`:

```
<Grid Margin="4">
  <Grid.RowDefinitions>
    <RowDefinition/>
    <RowDefinition/>
  </Grid.RowDefinitions>
  <Grid.ColumnDefinitions>
    <ColumnDefinition/>
    <ColumnDefinition Width="Auto"/>
  </Grid.ColumnDefinitions>
  <TextBlock Name="numberText" Grid.RowSpan="2" FontWeight="Bold"
    HorizontalAlignment="Center" VerticalAlignment="Center" FontSize="50"
    Padding="12">0</TextBlock>
  <Button Grid.Column="1" FontWeight="Bold" FontSize="30"
    HorizontalAlignment="Stretch" Click="Increment_Click">+</Button>
  <Button Grid.Row="1" Grid.Column="1" FontWeight="Bold" FontSize="30"
    HorizontalAlignment="Stretch" Click="Decrement_Click">-</Button>
</Grid>
```

But how should you attach the clicking of each `Button` to the event handlers? You can't set the `Click` event the same way inside the control template without a corresponding code-behind file.

You could handle this kind of interactivity using commands instead of events (see Chapter 5, "Interactivity"), or you could follow a pattern known as defining *control parts*. A control part is a loose contract between a control and its template. A control can retrieve an element in its template with a given name and then do whatever it desires with that element.

After you decide on elements to designate as control parts, you should name them. You can optionally document each part's existence by marking your class with `TemplatePartAttribute` (one for each part). This looks as follows for a version of `NumericUpDown` that expects an increment and decrement `Button` in its control template:

```
[TemplatePart(Name="incrementButton", Type=typeof(Button))]
[TemplatePart(Name="decrementButton", Type=typeof(Button))]
public class NumericUpDown : Control
{
  ...
}
```

`TemplatePartAttribute` doesn't impact any runtime behavior, but it serves as documentation that design tools can leverage.

To process your specially designated control parts, you should override the `OnApplyTemplate` method inherited from `FrameworkElement`. This method is called any time a template is applied, so it gives you the opportunity to handle dynamic template changes gracefully. To retrieve the instances of any elements inside your control template, you can call `GetTemplateChild`, also inherited from `FrameworkElement`. The following implementation retrieves the designated `Button`s and attaches the necessary logic to their `Click` events:

```
public override void OnApplyTemplate()
{
  base.OnApplyTemplate();

  // Retrieve the Buttons from the current template
  Button incrementButton = base.GetTemplateChild("incrementButton") as Button;
  Button decrementButton = base.GetTemplateChild("decrementButton") as Button;

  // Hook up the event handlers
  if (incrementButton != null)
    incrementButton.Click += Increment_Click;
  if (decrementButton != null)
    decrementButton.Click += Decrement_Click;
}
```

Note that this implementation gracefully handles templates that omit `incrementButton` and/or `decrementButton`, causing the `Button` variable(s) to be `null`. This is the recommended approach, making your control handle any control template with varying degrees of functionality. After all, it's reasonable to imagine someone wanting to restyle `NumericUpDown` such that it doesn't use `Buttons`. If you want to go against recommendations and be stricter, you could always throw an exception in `OnApplyTemplate` if the template doesn't contain the parts you require. But such a control likely won't work well inside graphic design tools such as Blend.

Supporting UI Automation

For a custom control to be truly first class, it should support UI Automation. The pattern for doing this is to create a companion class that derives from `FrameworkElementAutomation-Peer`, named `ControlNameAutomationPeer`, that describes the control to the automation system. You should then override `OnCreateAutomationPeer` (inherited from `UIElement`) in the custom control, making it return an instance of the companion class:

```
protected override AutomationPeer OnCreateAutomationPeer()
{
  return new NumericUpDownAutomationPeer(this);
}
```

Whenever an event occurs that should be communicated to the automation system, you can retrieve the companion class and raise an automation-specific event as follows:

```
NumericUpDownAutomationPeer peer =
  FrameworkElementAutomationPeer.FromElement(myControl)
  as NumericUpDownAutomationPeer;
if (peer != null)
  peer.RaiseAutomationEvent(AutomationEvents.LiveRegionChanged);
```

Creating a Windows Runtime Component

A Windows Runtime component is a reusable class library that can be consumed by any Windows Store app written in any language. You can write the component in C#, Visual Basic, or C++ (although not in JavaScript), and consume it in JavaScript, C#, Visual Basic, or C++. Just like the APIs exposed by Windows itself, it provides standard metadata that gets projected appropriately into the target language, so the consuming app doesn't need to know what language the component was written in.

Visual Studio provides Windows Runtime component project templates for C#, Visual Basic, and C++. For the broadest use, it's best to write a Windows Runtime Component in C++, so JavaScript and C++ consumers don't need to load .NET solely for the use of your component. However, writing one in C# is a perfectly valid thing to do.

To create a new C# Windows Runtime component, choose **Windows Runtime Component** from the **New Project** dialog. This creates a simple-looking project that looks like a Class Library project. You get an empty class defined in Class1.cs, like the following, along with a standard AssemblyInfo.cs file:

```
using System;
using System.Collections.Generic;
using System.Linq;
using System.Text;
using System.Threading.Tasks;

namespace Chapter27
{
  public sealed class Class1
  {
  }
}
```

What makes a Windows Runtime Component project special is the build output. Instead of an .exe or .dll file, you get a .winmd file. (This is controlled by a setting in the project's properties. The output type is set to **Windows Runtime Component** instead of **Class Library** or **Windows Store App**.) When you build your project, it first gets compiled by the C# compiler, and then a tool known as the Windows Runtime Metadata Export Tool (winmdexp.exe) produces the .winmd file. This file can then be referenced by any Windows Store project.

Listing 27.11 updates the blank class and turns it into an HTTP filter component that performs custom logging. As explained in Chapter 20, "Working with Data," you can plug custom behavior into the pipeline of filters used by Windows.Web.Http.HttpClient by implementing IHttpFilter and accepting an inner filter that you can delegate to.

LISTING 27.11   An HttpLoggingFilter Windows Runtime Component

```
using System;
using System.Threading.Tasks;
using Windows.Foundation;
using Windows.Web.Http;
using Windows.Web.Http.Filters;

namespace Chapter27
{
  public sealed class HttpLoggingFilter : IHttpFilter
  {
    IHttpFilter innerFilter;

    public HttpLoggingFilter(IHttpFilter innerFilter)
    {
```

LISTING 27.11   Continued

```
    if (innerFilter == null)
    {
      throw new ArgumentNullException("innerFilter");
    }
    this.innerFilter = innerFilter;
  }

  public IAsyncOperationWithProgress<HttpResponseMessage, HttpProgress>
    SendRequestAsync(HttpRequestMessage request)
  {
    // Log the request before passing it along to the inner filter
    Log(request);
    return innerFilter.SendRequestAsync(request);
  }

  async Task Log(HttpRequestMessage request)
  {
    ...
  }

  public void Dispose()
  {
    // IHttpFilter derives from IDisposable, but we have nothing to dispose
  }
  }
}
```

Although writing a Windows Runtime component in C# feels like writing any C# class library, there are some additional limitations imposed on your public APIs. Most of these limitations come from the fact that they must conform to the lowest common denominator metadata representation that is supported by all relevant programming languages. The Windows Runtime Metadata Export Tool reports such violations in the Visual Studio Error List, so they are easy to understand and fix.

One of the biggest limitations is that you cannot publicly expose .NET-specific data types (such as a Tuple) unless it is a primitive or something that gets projected to a Windows Runtime data type. For example, you cannot expose a List<int> return type, but it's fine to use IList<int>, IReadOnlyList<int>, or IEnumerable<int>, because these get projected to Windows Runtime interfaces (IVector<int>, IVectorView<int>, and IIterable<int>, respectively). You cannot return a Task from a publicly exposed method, either. Instead, you must return one of the Windows Runtime equivalents: IAsyncAction, IAsyncActionWithProgress<P>, IAsyncOperation<T>, or IAsyncOperationWith-Progress<T, P>. *Inside* your method, you can use a Task. You just must call an extension method such as AsAsyncOperation in order to return it.

Here are a few examples of additional limitations:

→ Publicly-exposed arrays must be one-dimensional.

→ Public classes must be sealed and non-generic.

→ Public members cannot use `ref` parameters. (Using `out` is fine.)

→ A class cannot publicly expose fields, and a struct can *only* publicly expose fields.

→ Public classes cannot expose overloaded operators.

→ Each public constructor on a public class must differ in its number of parameters. Constructors distinguished only by the types of their parameters are not allowed.

→ Publicly exposed overloaded methods cannot have the same number of parameters unless one is marked with `DefaultOverloadAttribute`.

→ Public types must be in a namespace whose root matches your project name (the name of your produced `.winmd` file). (And you cannot use the `Windows` namespace!)

The custom C++ classes used in Chapter 26, "Integrating DirectX," are Windows Runtime Components so they can be consumed by the C# code in that chapter. This is why those classes are defined to be sealed.

Summary

Creating a user control, or any control that uses a XAML file with a C# code-behind file, is a straightforward way to encapsulate some elements that you want to use multiple times. Creating a Windows Runtime component is also straightforward, once you're used to the extra limitations enforced on your public surface area.

Creating a templated control, however, involves many unorthodox concepts for people who aren't familiar with styles, templates, resources, and data binding. If such a developer doesn't care about restyling and theming, the extra complication doesn't add much value! That's why the XAML UI Framework has a bifurcated view of custom controls versus user controls.

Of course, even these two approaches are not the only options for reusable UI elements. For example, you could create a custom lower-level element that derives directly from `FrameworkElement`. A common non-`Control` to derive from is `Panel`, for creating custom layout schemes. That's the topic of the next (and final) chapter.

Should I write a user control or a templated control?

You should create a user control if its reuse will be limited and you don't care about exposing rich styling and theming support. You should create a templated control if you want it to be a robust first-class control (like the built-in controls). A user control tends to contain a logical tree defining its look and tends to have logic that directly interacts with these child elements. A templated control, on the other hand, tends to get its look from a visual tree defined in a separate control template and generally has logic that works even if a consumer changes its visual tree completely.

This distinction is mostly imposed by the default development experience provided by Visual Studio, however. Visual Studio pushes you in a certain direction, based on the type of control you add to a project. As you have now seen, when you add a user control, you get a XAML file with a corresponding code-behind file, so you can easily build your user control much as you would build a Page. But when you add a templated control to a project, you get a normal .cs code file plus a theme style with a simple control template injected into the project's generic dictionary (themes\generic.xaml).

If you want to distribute your component or control to others, you have three options:

→ Just copy the relevant files

→ Create an extension SDK

→ Create a package using NuGet, an open-source package manager

Copying the files can be sufficient if you have a single .winmd file with potentially a few more files (such as a .pri file for resources). See http://msdn.microsoft.com/library/jj161096.aspx for a comparison of the extension SDK versus NuGet options.

Chapter 28

LAYOUT WITH CUSTOM PANELS

Chapter 4, "Layout," examines the variety of panels included in the XAML UI Framework. If none of the built-in panels do exactly what you want, you have the option of writing your own panel. Of course, with all the flexibility of the built-in panels, the layout properties on child elements (discussed in Chapter 3, "Sizing, Positioning, and Transforming Elements"), plus the ability to embed panels within other panels to create arbitrarily complex layout, it's unlikely that you're going to need a custom panel. Actually, you never *need* a custom panel: with enough C# code, you can achieve any layout with just a Canvas. It's just a matter of how easy and automatic you want to be able to repetitively apply certain types of layout.

Although writing a custom panel can often be avoided by combining more primitive panels, creating a new panel can be useful when you want to repetitively arrange elements in a unique way. Encapsulating the custom logic in a panel can make the arrangement of a user interface less error prone and help to enforce consistency. Panels that are made for very limited scenarios can also perform better than the super-flexible built-in panels, especially if you replace multiple nestings of generic panels with a single, limited one.

To understand the steps involved in creating a custom panel, we'll first create two panels in this chapter that replicate the functionality of existing panels. After that, we'll create a simple but unique panel. The good news is that there is no special mechanism for creating a custom panel; you use exactly the same approach used by the built-in panels. But this also means we should take a closer look at how panels and their children communicate, which was glossed over in Chapters 3 and 4.

Communication Between Parents and Children

Chapters 3 and 4 explain that parent panels and their children work together to determine their final sizes and positions. To strike a reasonable balance between the needs of the parent and its children, layout is a recursive two-pass process. The first pass is called *measure*, and the second pass is called *arrange*.

The Measure Step

In the measure step, parents ask their children how big they want to be, given the amount of space available. Panels (and children, when appropriate) do this by overriding the MeasureOverride method from FrameworkElement. Here's an example:

```
protected override Size MeasureOverride(Size availableSize)
{
  …
  // Ask each child how big it would like to be, given a certain amount space
  foreach (UIElement child in this.Children)
  {
    child.Measure(new Size(…));
    // The child's answer is now in child.DesiredSize
    …
  }
  …
  // Tell my parent how big I would like to be given the passed-in availableSize
  return new Size(…);
}
```

All children can be accessed via the panel's Children collection (a UIElementCollection), and asking each child for its desired size is done by simply calling its Measure method (inherited from UIElement). Measure doesn't return a value, but after the call, the child's DesiredSize property contains its answer. As the parent, you can decide if you want to alter your behavior based on the desired sizes of any of your children.

> **① In MeasureOverride, panels must always call Measure on each child!**
>
> You might want to implement a panel that doesn't have any use for checking its children's DesiredSize values simply because it doesn't care how big its children want to be. Still, all panels *must* ask their children anyway (by calling Measure) because some elements don't work correctly if their Measure method never gets called. This is somewhat like asking your spouse "How was your day?" when you really don't care about the answer but want to avoid the repercussions. (Or so I'm told.)

The preceding snippet of C# code, like all `MeasureOverride` implementations, uses two important `Size` values, discussed in the following sections.

The `Size` Passed to Each Child's `Measure` Method

This value should represent the amount of space you're planning to give the child. It could be all the space given to the parent (captured in `MeasureOverride`'s `availableSize` parameter), some fraction of your space, or some absolute value, depending on your desires.

In addition, you can use `Double.PositiveInfinity` for either or both of `Size`'s dimensions to find out how large the child wants to be in an ideal situation. In other words, the following line of code means, "How big do you want to be given all the space in the world?"

```
child.Measure(new Size(Double.PositiveInfinity, Double.PositiveInfinity));
```

The layout system automatically handles the child layout properties discussed in Chapter 3, such as `Margin`, so the size ultimately passed to the child's implementation of `MeasureOverride` is the size you passed to `Measure` minus any margins. This also means that the `availableSize` parameter passed to your own `MeasureOverride` implementation represents whatever *your* parent allocated for you minus your own margins.

The `Size` Returned by `MeasureOverride`

The `Size` you return represents how big you want to be (answering your parent's request, just as your children have already answered it for you). You could return a fixed size, but that would ignore the requests from your children. More likely, you'd pick a value that enables you to "size to content," being big enough to fit all your children in their ideal sizes but no bigger.

> ⚠ **You can't simply return `availableSize` from `MeasureOverride`!**
>
> Whether because of its simplicity or because of your own greediness, it's tempting to use the passed-in `availableSize` parameter as the return value for `MeasureOverride`. This basically means, "Give me all the space you've got."
>
> However, whereas a `Size` with `Double.PositiveInfinity` in both dimensions is a legal value for `availableSize`, it is not a valid value for `DesiredSize`. Even when given unlimited space, you must choose a concrete size. If you ever end up returning an infinite size, `UIElement`'s `Measure` implementation throws an `InvalidOperationException`.

If you have only one child, sizing to your content is as simple as returning that child's `DesiredSize` as your own desired size. For multiple children, you would need to combine the widths and heights of your children according to how you plan to arrange them.

The Arrange Step

After measurement has been completed all the way through the element tree, it's time for the physical arranging of elements. In the arrange step, parents *tell* their children where they are getting placed and how much space they are given (which might be a different Size than the one given earlier). Panels (and children, when appropriate) do this by over-riding the ArrangeOverride method from FrameworkElement. Here's an example:

```
protected override Size ArrangeOverride(Size finalSize)
{
  …
  // Tell each child how much space it is getting
  foreach (UIElement child in this.Children)
  {
    child.Arrange(new Rect(…));
    // The child's size is now in child.ActualHeight & child.ActualWidth

    …
  }
  …
  // Set my own actual size (ActualHeight & ActualWidth)
  return new Size(…);
}
```

You tell each child its location and size by passing a Rect to its Arrange method (inherited from UIElement). For example, you can give each child its desired size simply by passing the value of its DesiredSize property to Arrange. You can be certain that this size is set appropriately because all measuring is done before any arranging begins.

Unlike with Measure, you cannot pass an infinite size to Arrange (and the finalSize passed to you will never be infinite). The child can choose to occupy a different amount of space than what you've specified, such as a subset of the space. Parents can determine what actions (if any) they want to take if this happens. The actual size chosen by each child can be obtained from its ActualHeight and ActualWidth properties after the call to Arrange.

As with your children, the size you return from ArrangeOverride becomes the value of your RenderSize and ActualHeight/ActualWidth properties. The size must not be infinite, but unlike with MeasureOverride, it's valid to simply return the passed-in Size if you want to take up all the available space because finalSize can never be infinite.

As with the measure step, in the arrange step, properties such as Margin are handled auto-matically, so the information getting passed to children (and the finalSize passed to you) has any margins subtracted. In addition, alignment is automatically handled by the arrange step. When a child is given exactly the amount of space it needs (for example, passing its DesiredSize to its Arrange method), alignment appears to have no effect because there's no extra space for the element to align within. But when you give a child more space than it occupies, the results of its HorizontalAlignment and/or VerticalAlignment settings are seen.

> **⚠ Don't do anything in MeasureOverride or ArrangeOverride that invalidates layout!**
>
> You can validly do some exotic things in MeasureOverride or ArrangeOverride, such as apply additional transforms to children. However, be sure that you don't invoke any code that invalidates layout; otherwise, you could wind up in an infinite loop!
>
> Any method or property invalidates layout if it calls UIElement.InvalidateMeasure or UIElement.InvalidateArrange. These are public methods, however, so it can be difficult to know what code calls them.
>
> If you feel that you must execute some code that invalidates layout, and you have a plan for avoiding a never-ending cycle, you can factor that logic into a separate method then use CoreDispatcher.RunAsync to schedule its execution after the current layout pass completes.

Creating a `SimpleCanvas`

Before creating some unique panels, let's see how to replicate the behavior of existing panels. The first one we'll create is a simplified version of Canvas called SimpleCanvas. SimpleCanvas behaves exactly like Canvas, except that it only respects Left and Top attached properties on its children rather than Left, Top, and ZIndex.

Implementing SimpleCanvas (or any other custom panel) consists of the following four steps:

1. Create a class that derives from Panel.

2. Define any properties that would be useful for customizing layout, potentially including attached properties for the children.

3. Override MeasureOverride and measure each child.

4. Override ArrangeOverride and arrange each child.

Listing 28.1 contains the entire implementation of SimpleCanvas.

LISTING 28.1   `SimpleCanvas.cs`: The Implementation of `SimpleCanvas`

```
using System;
using Windows.Foundation;
using Windows.UI.Xaml;
using Windows.UI.Xaml.Controls;

namespace CustomPanels
{
  public class SimpleCanvas : Panel
  {
    public static readonly DependencyProperty LeftProperty =
      DependencyProperty.RegisterAttached("Left", typeof(double),
        typeof(SimpleCanvas), new PropertyMetadata(0.0, OnPropertyChanged));
```

LISTING 28.1   Continued

```csharp
public static readonly DependencyProperty TopProperty =
  DependencyProperty.RegisterAttached("Top", typeof(double),
  typeof(SimpleCanvas), new PropertyMetadata(0.0, OnPropertyChanged));

static void OnPropertyChanged(DependencyObject d,
                             DependencyPropertyChangedEventArgs e)
{
  FrameworkElement element = d as FrameworkElement;
  if (element != null)
  {
    SimpleCanvas canvas = element.Parent as SimpleCanvas;
    if (canvas != null)
    {
      // We don't need to remeasure, but we need to rearrange
      canvas.InvalidateArrange();
    }
  }
}

public static double GetLeft(UIElement element)
{
  if (element == null) { throw new ArgumentNullException("element"); }
  return (double)element.GetValue(LeftProperty);
}

public static void SetLeft(UIElement element, double length)
{
  if (element == null) { throw new ArgumentNullException("element"); }
  element.SetValue(LeftProperty, length);
}

public static double GetTop(UIElement element)
{
  if (element == null) { throw new ArgumentNullException("element"); }
  return (double)element.GetValue(TopProperty);
}

public static void SetTop(UIElement element, double length)
{
  if (element == null) { throw new ArgumentNullException("element"); }
  element.SetValue(TopProperty, length);
}
```

LISTING 28.1   Continued

```
    protected override Size MeasureOverride(Size availableSize)
    {
      foreach (UIElement child in this.Children)
      {
        // Give each child all the space it wants
        if (child != null)
          child.Measure(new Size(Double.PositiveInfinity,
                              Double.PositiveInfinity));
      }

      // The SimpleCanvas itself needs no space
      return new Size(0, 0);
    }

    protected override Size ArrangeOverride(Size finalSize)
    {
      foreach (UIElement child in this.Children)
      {
        if (child != null)
        {
          // Respect any Left and Top attached properties,
          // otherwise the child is placed at (0,0)
          double x = GetLeft(child);
          double y = GetTop(child);

          // Place at the chosen (x,y) location with the child's DesiredSize
          child.Arrange(new Rect(new Point(x, y), child.DesiredSize));
        }
      }

      // Whatever size you gave me is fine
      return finalSize;
    }
  }
}
```

Listing 28.1 begins by defining the Left and Top attached properties, which each consist of the DependencyProperty field with the pair of static Get/Set methods. The PropertyMetadata instance provides the default value and an (optional) property change callback. As with Canvas's Left and Top attached properties, their default value is 0.0. The static Get/Set methods are a standard implementation of the two attached properties.

The property change callback, OnPropertyChanged, is needed to act appropriately in case a child's SimpleCanvas.Left or SimpleCanvas.Top attached property is ever updated in code that doesn't already trigger a new layout pass. Without this, updating a child's position in response to a Button Click handler, for example, wouldn't cause the child to actually move until something else invalidates layout, like a window resize.

Because the property change callback must be a static method, it retrieves the relevant instance of the SimpleCanvas by asking the child for its parent. It also guards against an element using one of the SimpleCanvas attached properties despite not being a child of a SimpleCanvas. A change to a child's Left or Top has no bearing on the measure step in this panel, so OnPropertyChanged doesn't need to call InvalidateMeasure. Instead, it calls InvalidateArrange to force the arrange step to rerun.

The implementation of MeasureOverride couldn't be simpler, which makes sense considering the desired behavior of SimpleCanvas. It just tells each child to take all the space it wants, and then it tells its own parent that it doesn't require any space for itself (because its children do not get clipped to its bounds unless ClipToBounds is set to true, thanks to behavior inherited from FrameworkElement).

ArrangeOverride is where the interesting work is done. Each child is placed according to its Left and Top attached properties, both of which are 0.0 unless it was given explicit values.

You can see that the panel doesn't need to care about any of the children's layout properties (Height, MinHeight, MaxHeight, Width, MinWidth, MaxWidth, Margin, Padding, HorizontalAlignment, VerticalAlignment, and so on). In addition, tabbing between child elements is handled automatically. The tab order is defined by the order in which children are added to the parent.

The project included with this book's source code consumes SimpleCanvas as follows:

```
<Page x:Class="CustomPanels.MainPage"
      xmlns="http://schemas.microsoft.com/winfx/2006/xaml/presentation"
      xmlns:x="http://schemas.microsoft.com/winfx/2006/xaml"
      xmlns:local="using:CustomPanels">
  <local:SimpleCanvas>
    <Button Content="1" Background="Red"/>
    <Button local:SimpleCanvas.Left="40" local:SimpleCanvas.Top="40"
            Content="2" Background="Orange"/>
    <Button local:SimpleCanvas.Left="80" local:SimpleCanvas.Top="80"
            Content="3" Background="Yellow"/>
    <Button local:SimpleCanvas.Left="120" local:SimpleCanvas.Top="120"
            Content="4" Background="Lime"/>
  </local:SimpleCanvas>
</Page>
```

The XAML for the Page maps the CustomPanels .NET namespace to a local prefix, so SimpleCanvas and its attached properties can be used with the local: prefix.

Note that the SimpleCanvas implementation could attempt to reuse Canvas's existing Left and Top attached properties instead of defining its own. This wouldn't fully work, however, because it wouldn't be able to call InvalidateArrange in response to any Canvas.Left and Canvas.Top changes.

Creating a `SimpleStackPanel`

Let's look at replicating one more existing panel, but one that does a bit more work while measuring and arranging. We'll create a SimpleStackPanel that acts just like StackPanel. The only major difference between SimpleStackPanel and StackPanel is that our version is missing some performance optimizations. Listing 28.2 contains the entire implementation.

LISTING 28.2   SimpleStackPanel.cs: The Implementation of SimpleStackPanel

```csharp
using System;
using Windows.Foundation;
using Windows.UI.Xaml;
using Windows.UI.Xaml.Controls;

namespace CustomPanels
{
  public class SimpleStackPanel : Panel
  {
    // The direction of stacking
    public static readonly DependencyProperty OrientationProperty =
      DependencyProperty.Register("Orientation", typeof(Orientation),
      typeof(SimpleStackPanel),
      new PropertyMetadata(Orientation.Vertical, OnOrientationChanged));

    static void OnOrientationChanged(DependencyObject d,
                                    DependencyPropertyChangedEventArgs e)
    {
      FrameworkElement element = d as FrameworkElement;
      if (element != null)
      {
        SimpleStackPanel stackPanel = element.Parent as SimpleStackPanel;
        if (stackPanel != null)
        {
          // We need to remeasure (and rearrange)
          stackPanel.InvalidateMeasure();
        }
      }
    }

    public Orientation Orientation
    {
      get { return (Orientation)GetValue(OrientationProperty); }
```

LISTING 28.2   Continued

```csharp
    set { SetValue(OrientationProperty, value); }
  }

  protected override Size MeasureOverride(Size availableSize)
  {
    Size desiredSize = new Size();

    // Let children grow indefinitely in the direction of stacking
    // overwriting what was passed in
    if (Orientation == Orientation.Vertical)
      availableSize.Height = Double.PositiveInfinity;
    else
      availableSize.Width = Double.PositiveInfinity;

    foreach (UIElement child in this.Children)
    {
      if (child != null)
      {
        // Ask the first child for its desired size, given unlimited space in
        // the direction of stacking and all our available space (whatever was
        // passed in) in the other direction
        child.Measure(availableSize);

        // Our desired size is the sum of child sizes in the direction of
        // stacking, and the size of the largest child in the other direction
        if (Orientation == Orientation.Vertical)
        {
          desiredSize.Width = Math.Max(desiredSize.Width,
                                       child.DesiredSize.Width);
          desiredSize.Height += child.DesiredSize.Height;
        }
        else
        {
          desiredSize.Height = Math.Max(desiredSize.Height,
                                        child.DesiredSize.Height);
          desiredSize.Width += child.DesiredSize.Width;
        }
      }
    }

    return desiredSize;
  }
```

LISTING 28.2   Continued

```
protected override Size ArrangeOverride(Size finalSize)
{
  double offset = 0;

  foreach (UIElement child in this.Children)
  {
    if (child != null)
    {
      if (Orientation == Orientation.Vertical)
      {
        // The offset moves the child down the stack.
        // Give the child all our width, but as much height as it desires.
        child.Arrange(new Rect(0, offset, finalSize.Width,
                                          child.DesiredSize.Height));

        // Update the offset for the next child
        offset += child.DesiredSize.Height;
      }
      else
      {
        // The offset moves the child down the stack.
        // Give the child all our height, but as much width as it desires.
        child.Arrange(new Rect(offset, 0, child.DesiredSize.Width,
                                          finalSize.Height));

        // Update the offset for the next child
        offset += child.DesiredSize.Width;
      }
    }
  }

  // Fill all the space given
  return finalSize;
}
```

Similar to Listing 28.1, this listing begins with the definition of a dependency property—Orientation. Its default value is Vertical. A change in Orientation can impact the size of its children, so its property change callback calls InvalidateMeasure instead of InvalidateArrange. Because Orientation is a regular dependency property rather than an attached one, this class defines a simple .NET property wrapper rather than the pair of Get/Set methods.

In MeasureOverride, each child is given the panel's available size in the non-stacking direction (which may or may not be infinite) but is given infinite size in the stacking direction. As each child's desired size is revealed, SimpleStackPanel keeps track of the results and updates its own desired size accordingly. In the stacking dimension, its desired length is the sum of all its children's desired lengths. In the non-stacking dimension, its length is the length of its longest child.

In ArrangeOverride, an offset ("stack pointer," if you will) keeps track of the position to place the next child as the stack grows. Each child is given the entire panel's length in the stacking direction and its desired length in the non-stacking direction. Finally, SimpleStackPanel consumes all the space given to it by returning the input finalSize. With that, SimpleStackPanel behaves just like the real StackPanel.

Creating a UniformGrid

UniformGrid is similar to a panel with the same name that is included in WPF but is not a part of the XAML UI Framework for Windows Store apps. It is like a Grid where all rows and columns are of size * and can't be changed, and each child is automatically placed in a new cell in row-major order. It automatically chooses how many rows and columns exist, but it keeps a square shape. For example, 2–4 elements are placed in a 2x2 arrangement, 5–9 elements are placed in a 3x3 arrangement, 10–16 elements are placed in a 4x4 arrangement, and so on. It defines no dependency properties. (The WPF version of UniformGrid defines two double dependency properties—Rows and Columns—that enable the user to choose the number of rows and columns, and an int FirstColumn property that enables the user to place leading blank cells in the first row. These are omitted here for simplicity.)

Figure 28.1 demonstrates UniformGrid when used with the following four Ellipses:

```
<Page x:Class="CustomPanels.MainPage"
    xmlns="http://schemas.microsoft.com/winfx/2006/xaml/presentation"
    xmlns:x="http://schemas.microsoft.com/winfx/2006/xaml"
    xmlns:local="using:CustomPanels">
  <local:UniformGrid>
    <Ellipse Fill="Red"/>
    <Ellipse Fill="Orange"/>
    <Ellipse Fill="Yellow"/>
    <Ellipse Fill="Lime"/>
  </local:UniformGrid>
</Page>
```

Figure 28.2 shows how the layout changes when one more Ellipse is added:

```
<Page x:Class="CustomPanels.MainPage"
    xmlns="http://schemas.microsoft.com/winfx/2006/xaml/presentation"
    xmlns:x="http://schemas.microsoft.com/winfx/2006/xaml"
    xmlns:local="using:CustomPanels">
```

```
<local:UniformGrid>
  <Ellipse Fill="Red"/>
  <Ellipse Fill="Orange"/>
  <Ellipse Fill="Yellow"/>
  <Ellipse Fill="Lime"/>
  <Ellipse Fill="Aqua"/>
</local:UniformGrid>
</Page>
```

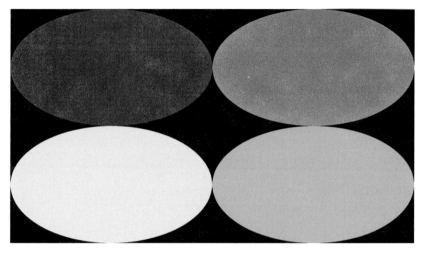

FIGURE 28.1   Four Ellipses in a UniformGrid are automatically arranged 2x2.

FIGURE 28.2   Five Ellipses shift the layout to 3x3.

Listing 28.3 contains the entire implementation of `UniformGrid`.

LISTING 28.3   `UniformGrid.cs`: The Implementation of `UniformGrid`

```
using System;
using Windows.Foundation;
using Windows.UI.Xaml;
using Windows.UI.Xaml.Controls;

namespace CustomPanels
{
  public class UniformGrid : Panel
  {
    int _numRowsAndCols;

    protected override Size MeasureOverride(Size availableSize)
    {
      Size maxChildSize = new Size();

      foreach (UIElement child in this.Children)
      {
        if (child != null)
        {
          // See how big each child wants to be given all our available space
          child.Measure(availableSize);

          // Keep track of the maximum child width and maximum child height
          if (child.DesiredSize.Width > maxChildSize.Width)
          {
            maxChildSize.Width = child.DesiredSize.Width;
          }
          if (child.DesiredSize.Height > maxChildSize.Height)
          {
            maxChildSize.Height = child.DesiredSize.Height;
          }
        }
      }

      // Determine how many rows and columns we need based on the # of children
      _numRowsAndCols = (int)Math.Ceiling(Math.Sqrt(this.Children.Count));

      // Our desired size is the same in each dimension
      Size desiredSize = new Size();
      desiredSize.Width = maxChildSize.Width * _numRowsAndCols;
      desiredSize.Height = maxChildSize.Height * _numRowsAndCols;
```

LISTING 28.3   Continued

```
      return desiredSize;
    }


    protected override Size ArrangeOverride(Size finalSize)
    {
      double leftOffset = 0;
      double topOffset = 0;
      int childIndex = 0;

      // Give each child the same-sized cell by splitting our final size
      Size finalChildSize = new Size(finalSize.Width / _numRowsAndCols,
                                    finalSize.Height / _numRowsAndCols);

      foreach (UIElement child in this.Children)
      {
        if (child != null)
        {
          // Place the child at (leftOffset, topOffset)
          child.Arrange(new Rect(new Point(leftOffset, topOffset),
                        finalChildSize));

          // Update the offsets for the next child
          childIndex++;
          if (childIndex % _numRowsAndCols == 0)
          {
            // The next child begins the next row
            leftOffset = 0;
            topOffset += finalChildSize.Height;
          }
          else
          {
            // Move to the next column
            leftOffset += finalChildSize.Width;
          }
        }
      }

      // Fill all the space given
      return finalSize;
    }
  }
}
```

MeasureOverride has two jobs to do (in addition to the requisite calling of each child's MeasureOverride method): obtaining the largest desired width and height from all of its children, and setting the _numRowsAndCols member to the square root of the number of children. The maximum desired child size is used to calculate this panel's own desired size, as it attempts to give its children all the space they want. Note that the maximum width and height can come from two separate children, which might be necessary in order to accommodate everyone while simultaneously giving them all the same dimensions.

In ArrangeOverride, the finalSize dictated by the panel's parent is subdivided appropriately, leveraging the value of _numRowsAndCols set during the measure step. Each child is then placed at an appropriate offset to produce the grid effect.

Figure 28.3 demonstrates the following use of UniformGrid:

```
<Page x:Class="CustomPanels.MainPage"
      xmlns="http://schemas.microsoft.com/winfx/2006/xaml/presentation"
      xmlns:x="http://schemas.microsoft.com/winfx/2006/xaml"
      xmlns:local="using:CustomPanels">
  <local:UniformGrid x:Name="uniformGrid">
    <local:UniformGrid.ChildrenTransitions>
      <TransitionCollection>
        <RepositionThemeTransition/>
      </TransitionCollection>
    </local:UniformGrid.ChildrenTransitions>
    <Button Click="Button_Click" HorizontalAlignment="Center">
      Add more children
    </Button>
  </local:UniformGrid>
</Page>
```

This uses code-behind to dynamically add children to the panel:

```
void Button_Click(object sender, RoutedEventArgs e)
{
  this.uniformGrid.Children.Add(
    new Ellipse { Fill = new SolidColorBrush(Colors.Pink) }
  );
}
```

Notice that applying HorizontalAlignment to the Button works as expected inside our custom panel. This changes the default left alignment, although the default VerticalAlignment is already Center, so it doesn't need to be explicitly set in order to center the Button in its cell.

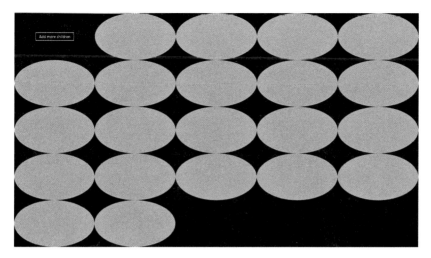

FIGURE 28.3   Clicking the Button 21 times updates the UniformGrid from 1x1 to 5x5.

Also notice that RepositionThemeTransition is applied to the children of the
UniformGrid. This means that—without any work done by the panel itself—the children
automatically animate to their new positions every time the Button is clicked! This is
shown in Figure 28.4, which demonstrates starting with Figure 28.3 then clicking the
Button four more times to trigger an increase in rows and columns. The children also
animate to their new sizes when the app's window is resized, as this triggers another
layout pass.

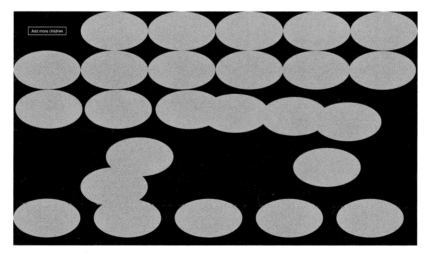

FIGURE 28.4   The animated transition from 25 children in a 5x5 layout to 26 children in a 6x6
layout, thanks to RepositionThemeTransition.

Summary

This chapter digs into the mechanism that child elements and parent panels use, and how they compromise to give great results in a wide variety of situations. Implementing your own custom panels is considered an advanced topic only because it's rare that you would need to do so. As you've seen, custom panels are pretty easy to write. Because of the measure/arrange protocol and all the work automatically handled by the rest of the system, existing controls can be placed inside brand-new custom panels, and they still behave very reasonably.

As with creating a custom control, you should spend a little time determining the appropriate base class for a custom panel. The choices for panels are more straightforward, however. Most of the time, as with the panels in this chapter, it makes sense to simply derive from Panel. If you plan on supporting user interface virtualization, you should derive from VirtualizingPanel, the base class of VirtualizingStackPanel.

INDEX

Symbols & Numerics

A

B

M

S

V

W

UNLEASHED

Unleashed takes you beyond the basics, providing an exhaustive, technically sophisticated reference for professionals who need to exploit a technology to its fullest potential. It's the best resource for practical advice from the experts, and the most in-depth coverage of the latest technologies.

informit.com/unleashed

C# 5.0 Unleashed
ISBN-13: 9780672336904

OTHER UNLEASHED TITLES

Windows Phone 8 Unleashed
ISBN-13: 9780672336898

ASP.NET Dynamic Data Unleashed
ISBN-13: 9780672335655

Microsoft System Center 2012 Unleashed
ISBN-13: 9780672336126

System Center 2012 Configuration Manager (SCCM) Unleashed
ISBN-13: 9780672334375

Windows Server 2012 Unleashed
ISBN-13: 9780672336225

Microsoft Exchange Server 2013 Unleashed
ISBN-13: 9780672336119

Microsoft Visual Studio 2012 Unleashed
ISBN-13: 9780672336256

System Center 2012 Operations Manager Unleashed
ISBN-13: 9780672335914

Microsoft Dynamics CRM 2011 Unleashed
ISBN-13: 9780672335389

Microsoft Lync Server 2013 Unleashed
ISBN-13: 9780672336157

Visual Basic 2012 Unleashed
ISBN-13: 9780672336317

HTML5 Unleashed
ISBN-13: 9780672336270

Microsoft Visual Studio LightSwitch Unleashed
ISBN-13: 9780672335532

WPF 4.5 Unleashed
ISBN-13: 9780672336973

Windows 8.1 Apps with HTML5 and JavaScript Unleashed
ISBN-13: 9780672337116

informit.com/sams

Your purchase of **Windows® 8.1 Apps with XAML and C# Unleashed** includes access to a free online edition for 45 days through the **Safari Books Online** subscription service. Nearly every Sams book is available online through **Safari Books Online**, along with thousands of books and videos from publishers such as Addison-Wesley Professional, Cisco Press, Exam Cram, IBM Press, O'Reilly Media, Prentice Hall, Que, and VMware Press.

Safari Books Online is a digital library providing searchable, on-demand access to thousands of technology, digital media, and professional development books and videos from leading publishers. With one monthly or yearly subscription price, you get unlimited access to learning tools and information on topics including mobile app and software development, tips and tricks on using your favorite gadgets, networking, project management, graphic design, and much more.